Management for Professionals

More information about this series at https://link.springer.com/bookseries/10101

Timothy Adesanya Ibidapo

From Industry 4.0 to Quality 4.0

An Innovative TQM Guide for Sustainable Digital Age Businesses

Springer

Timothy Adesanya Ibidapo
Grand Prairie, TX, USA

ISSN 2192-8096 ISSN 2192-810X (electronic)
Management for Professionals
ISBN 978-3-031-04191-4 ISBN 978-3-031-04192-1 (eBook)
https://doi.org/10.1007/978-3-031-04192-1

This Springer imprint is published by the registered company Springer Nature Switzerland AG
The registered company address is: Gewerbestrasse 11, 6330 Cham, Switzerland

To:

All those whose qualitative and invaluable love keeps me going:

My wife, Mojisola Bimbo$_{(\text{'Yemi})}$, a model of patience, love, and peace;

My loving daughters Olufemi Kugel, Olubunmi Adebowale, Toluwani Adefoyinsola$_{(\text{mom})}$,

Tiwatope Adekanyinsola$_{(\text{grandma})}$, and Titobioluwa Adefayosola;

My son, Tiwaloluwa Adedamola$_{(\text{dad})}$;

My grandsons, Dariusz Kugel and Fabian Kugel;

My most loving and affectionate great-grandson, Milan Olumide Kugel;

and my beloved ones of blessed memory:

Mother/Grandmother, Lydia Adegbemisola Aladewolu, ('Yemi, motherly than any other);

My brothers, Frederick Ayodele Sule, Samuel Adebayo Ogundeji, Benjamin Olusola Awogbayila, Dr. Reverend Olorunleke O. Banjoko, and Prof. Vincent O.S. Olunloyo; and

Dr. Manisha Raja of Parkland Health and all other frontline healthcare workers across the globe for their commitment to adaptive and innovative selfless patient care during the COVID-19 pandemic era and beyond

Preface

Managing change is the most universal phenomenon of quality most commonly exhibited in the lives and activities of human beings – individually and collectively. Hence, the assumption that we are naturally endowed with the qualitative ability to manage change, though some people may be better at it than others. The brain is the powerhouse for man's change management capabilities. We are born in change management, grow up with, and in it, and struggle with it at old age until the 360° circle of life is completed. Hence, every living being lives managing change(s), a strong quality management skill. This is the reason why people commonly refer to the constancy or permanency of change.

The changes portended in *digital transformation*, which is generally termed the *fourth (4.0) industrial revolution*, lead to the dawn of a new era, generally envisaged to transform the industrial landscape vis-à-vis the way quality management tools are deployed and practiced. It is an era in which both the environment and people's values are daily becoming increasingly complex and diverse. The potentials for digital transformation to create new values – businesses, people, and society – have therefore been the major driving force for its pursuit.

The new era and the changes that come with it are primarily precipitated by the rapid evolution of information and communications technology (ICT), which is later co-polymerized with globalization and the "*swiftly*" evolving digital technologies, such as robotics, artificial intelligence (AI), industrial Internet of Things (IIoT), Internet of Things (IoT), 5G, blockchain, big data, and so on.

The initial postulation and recognition of the potential ability of digital transformation to create value across most activities of man have most recently spurred governments and organizations across the globe to make digital transformation the cornerstone of their developmental policies. Viewing digital transformation from this perspective has so far earned the digital transformation, popularly referred to as the fourth industrial revolution, many appellations among the people of the world, some of which are listed hereunder:

- "Industrie 4.0" (Germany)
- "Industry 4.0" (Europe)
- "Industrial Internet of Things" (US) – (also referred to as Industry 4.0)
- "Society 5.0" (Japan)
- "Made in China 2025" (China)

- "Smart Nation" (Singapore)
- "Smart Cities" (Asia)
- "SmartFactory"
- "Super Smart Society"

These appellations, no doubt, elucidate the fact that we are in the era of digitalizing not just industrial production processes but also other businesses and social infrastructures.

While the second decade of the twenty-first century gave birth to *disruptive* industrial revolutionary changes, the people of the world have not been spared from other challenges and uncertainties of global magnitude – terrorism, depletion of the world's natural resources, global warming and other environmental changes, the novel coronavirus COVID-19 pandemic, and the daily increasing economic disparity among the people and nations of the global community.

Innovative TQM Guide to Sustain Digital Age Businesses is an innovative book which offers quality in totality, both in contents and in context, to make available to readers the **A–Z** of quality as a body of knowledge (BoK), from its genealogy to its anatomy.

It thus provides quality and quality management researchers, practitioners, organizations, professionals, and other entities a critically relevant knowledge base, thus serving as a very critical resources platform, useful in the currently evolving digital age practices, to define and evolve future quality management practices – *Quality 4.0.* Successfully transforming, blending, or applying traditional quality management practices to Industry 4.0's digital technologies can be facilitated and achieved on the basis of the full understanding of existing quality management practices, tools, techniques, and principles as holistically presented in *Innovative TQM Guide to Sustain Digital Age Businesses*, thereby serving as the bridge of quality knowledge linking the past with the future of quality – *Quality 4.0* – to create increased operational efficiency, improved business performance, and business models.

The smart and innovative construct of this digital age quality management book is an exhortation of transformational quality in a digital industrial manufacturing era, in which traditional quality management tools and practices are relied upon as a critical and solid fundamental rooting for grafting Industry 4.0 technologies unto Industry 4.0 initiatives, to extrapolate *Quality 4.0* professional practices of the future. Quality 4.0 therefore requires that traditional quality management principles/philosophy, techniques, tools, and practices, as presented in this book, be leveraged with digital technologies to evolve the most effective total quality management (TQM) methodologies for suring that operational processes are innovatively optimized to consistently achieve product/service excellence.

The intense literature review provided in Chaps. 21 and 22 of *Innovative TQM Guide to Sustain Digital Age Businesses* identified some critical essential global research and survey findings that will likely culminate in the successful application of Industry 4.0 technologies for implementing Quality 4.0 initiatives at organizational levels:

- Extrapolating organizational ***Quality 4.0 culture*** beyond traditional quality practices to embrace Quality 4.0 initiatives to motivate all employees to willingly take ownership and accountability of quality – training and upskilling in the use and application of 4.0 technologies, confidence building, effective communication, leadership clear vision and objective, developing innovative and quality thinking abilities, and so on.
- ***Targeted training*** to fill missing gaps for quality professionals relevant to Quality 4.0, hence the general need to assess and define a digital talent strategy relative to 4.0 technologies and their application. Training, upskilling, and/or recruiting qualified and capable hands is key to the successful implementation of Quality 4.0 due to the critical fact of Quality 4.0 not being merely about technologies but more about the people engaged in their usage and application as well as their processes.
- Transformational/transactional ***knowledge-oriented innovative leadership*** with clarity of vision and strategy and an ability to communicate and collaborate at all levels.
- Provision of ***adequate resources***, especially ***human capital*** capable of handling relevant 4.0 technologies and their outputs, especially in the generation, collection, and analysis of data to achieve product quality and reliability, and in the effective monitoring of performance.
- Glaring and open demonstration of ***top management support and collaboration*** toward the implementation of Quality 4.0.
- ***Quality metrics***, though not known to be a serious problem in traditional quality management practices because quality professionals are used to it, may however constitute some challenges to digital age quality.

While we may not be able to predict the exact picture of Quality 4.0 practices, there is the certainty that it will emanate from the structural knowledge base of traditional quality management principles, philosophy, techniques, tools, and practices which are fully embodied in *Innovative TQM Guide to Sustain Digital Age Businesses.*

Grand Prairie, TX, USA Timothy Adesanya Ibidapo

Proem

Using Traditional Quality Knowledge Base to Define Quality 4.0 Practices

Most organizations and businesses all over the world have kept faith in the culture of quality to achieve and sustain competitive advantage. Hence, implementing quality management practices has today become an integral part of virtually every operational process. However, facing new production paradigms, such as *Industry 4.0*, poses a new challenge as to how quality management processes could adapt in the new era of digital technologies.

Innovative TQM Guide to Sustain Digital Age Businesses thus provides a reliable broad-based, A–Z quality knowledge linking traditional quality management principles, tools, and practices with the fourth industrial revolution, *Industry 4.0*, and applicable 4.0 base technologies, to extrapolate digital age quality management practices, Quality 4.0, in line with the usual trend of quality evolving with each stage of industrial manufacturing evolutions witnessed by man.

The ongoing transformational changes of quality, which began generally with quality leadership transformation, from the age of the *quality gurus* of the twentieth century to the digital era of newly evolving quality leadership of the twenty-first century, hold the key essential for global sustainability.

This book is therefore written not just to create a quality knowledge reservoir for quality professionals, practitioners, researchers, students, academics, equipment manufacturers, business executives, management consultants, various leadership cadres, and other interested parties, but as a key contributory platform for aiding and strengthening the overall integration and evolution of digital age quality management principles, tools, techniques, and practices of the future.

With its tentacles and influence properly balanced between academics and industry, quality and its most comprehensive phenomena – total quality management (TQM), quality control, Lean, and Six Sigma, among others – have united to grow quality to maturity as an independent body of knowledge (BoK), vast and diverse in application and use than most of its contemporaries in social and management sciences. This book is structured to project all ramifications of quality as a body of knowledge useful in all ramifications of life, hence human sustainability.

The organization and contents of this book practically demonstrate the maturity of the "*science of quality*" or "*quality management sciences*," its tools and practices, to be able to evolve, in the most transformational way and manner, into becoming a stand-alone "*discipline*," or "*body of knowledge*" (BoK) with strong potentials to thrive and flourish at all academic-degree levels of studies and research in the twenty-first century. This book presents all aspects and branches of quality as guidelines for identifying and drawing fully fledged academic syllabi in the area of total quality management (TQM).

With the experience and proof of quality being massively deployed to rescue humanity, whether in preventative measures or in the manufacture and distribution of vaccines to fight and conquer the deadly claws of the COVID-19 pandemic, the global community is, more than ever, aware and convinced of the global capabilities and universal application of quality and its tools. Quality has, since the advent of the novel coronavirus, become a household name and perhaps even a way of healthy living to preserve humanity in its entirety. Whether it is social distancing or mask wearing, quality has, in one way or the other, become a way of life for the global community than it has ever been. Quality has, consciously or subconsciously, gradually become our universal culture – mindset, quality thinking, quality practice, and especially in its general application to various aspects of the human life and environment.

Innovative TQM Guide to Sustain Digital Age Businesses is thus the most updated and complete quality book to facilitate organizations, institutions, professional organizational members, and individuals in imbibing the quality culture – mindset, thinking, activities, and ways of life.

This section of the book thus stands out to most distinctively portray the perspicuity of *Innovative TQM Guide to Sustain Digital Age Businesses*, while at the same time, gradually guiding your way to effectively and qualitatively generate the natural momentum of digital age reader comprehensibility, with no atom of boredom. This definitely distinguishes this book from most of the other ordinary compendia of quality books. Relax therefore, and read the first two chapters; after which you can read any of the chapters, from 3 to 22, based on your intuition or interest. *Innovative TQM Guide to Sustain Digital Age Businesses* offers you the opportunity of a complete quality knowledge base, from its genealogy to its anatomy.

Quality in the digital age, Quality 4.0, is going to encompass both the traditional quality practices and its adapted components to suit Industry 4.0 initiatives in an environment of 4.0 technologies. Quality in its present context involves the management of processes, to deliver excellent outcomes or products/services, which represent the values of customers/recipients or the marketplace, in a *culturally* balanced environment of sustainable *relationships*. Culture and relationships are quite critical to quality, hence the need for its consideration in redefining quality in the most appropriate way.

My experience in the manufacturing industry showed generally that the ability of an organization to innovate is deeply rooted in that organization's own culture. Organizational culture is also responsible for providing the avenue and fertile soil for using innovation to improve the quality of its products/services or outcomes of its processes. In most cases therefore, organizational culture helps in facilitating and achieving certain goals, and contributes largely to innovation and any type of change management that may become necessary. Hence, businesses must, in one way or the other, and especially at difficult times, use innovation, through the collective responsibilities of their human capital, to meet expectations, else they may have to reorganize for this to take place. This is the reason why the author believes in redefining quality in terms of its relationship to culture and relationships.

A good-quality product, that is, that which meets customer/marketplace SNEaRs (*specifications*, *needs*, *expectations*, and *requirements*) and represents customer values, will likely attract good and sustainable relationships among organizations (or suppliers), the supply chain, customers, and stakeholders. Examples of relationships in quality management are those within the

- organization/supply chain,
- organization/customer,
- organization/investors/stakeholders,
- organization/marketplace, and
- organization/community/global market community.

Similarly, a quality product/service cannot be achieved without consideration for the need to balance product application/use with end-user or marketplace culture or their cultural influence on the product.

There have however been reported grave incidences of extreme negative repercussions of "quality products" despite their reflection of the existing definition of quality as "the characteristics of a product or service that bear on its ability to satisfy stated or implied needs." For example, the air quality issue involving Volkswagen's reported use of "*defeat device*" in the U.S. and the incidences of the Max 737 air crashes are classical examples here that may motivate redefining quality. In these two cases, commitment to regulatory SNEaRs may have been silently avoided, or perhaps deceitfully achieved too.

These two incidences coupled with the high-profile organizational failures such as the globally reported cases of Enron, Lehman Brothers, and FIFA, and other abuses of authority globally experienced in the last few decades have made it highly essential to redefine quality with equal emphasis on all ***three*** recipients of products and services – customer/end-users/marketplace, regulatory bodies, and the community/environment impacted by the product/service:

- ***Primary (1°) customers*** – direct and indirect recipients of products/services, end-users, and the marketplace.
- *Regulatory bodies or government* **(secondary, 2° customers)** – they are direct or indirect recipients of products, though with a different objective, that is, to ensure that products/services are fit for use by end-users and without adverse effects and/or impacts on the community and environment of use and application.

- *The community/environment (or the public) in which the product/service is made/ rendered and that of its end-use, both of which may be impacted by the product/ service* ***(tertiary, 3º customer)*** – for example, product packaging that may have adverse effects on the community and environment, or pollutants resulting from the production processes and activities which may impact the people and their surrounding environment. The passengers of a plane are a further example.

The impact of the novel coronavirus on the people of China and the entirety of the global community has most convincingly demonstrated the global nature and relevance of quality. It is for this and other reasons that quality has to be more appropriately defined, beyond mere slogan of "*fitness for use*," or "*a product or service free of deficiencies*," or "*conformance to requirements.*" This is however to categorically say that quality is more than and surpasses "compliance with customer SNEaRs."

In a globalized economic setting, consideration for cultural balance is highly important, while sustainability should be a constant reminder in an era of disruptive changes and digital transformational issues.

It is for these and other reasons that the author, after all considerations, decides to redefine quality in *Innovative TQM Guide to Sustain Digital Age Businesses* with considerations for sustainability and cultural balance as explained in Chap. 19.

Quality may therefore be defined as follows, building on one of the existing definitions of quality by the American Society for Quality (ASQ) which states that quality is

> *The characteristics of a product or service that bear on its ability to satisfy stated or implied needs.*

In order to complement the existing definition of ***quality*** and make it all embracing, the author views quality as:

1. *The measure/perception of the level/degree to which the inherent characteristics of a product/service bear on its ability to fulfill/meet customer and regulatory SNEaRs in a culturally balanced environment of sustainable relationships without any adverse effects whatsoever on any stakeholder or other relevant entities*; or,
2. *the level/extent to which the values of the outcomes of inputs and efforts, that is, products/services, are acknowledged to have met or not, stated and/ or implied customer, regulatory, and stakeholder values, in a culturally balanced environment of sustainable relationships without any adverse effects whatsoever on any stakeholder or other relevant entities.*

(*Note*: SNEaRs is the abbreviation for *specifications*, *needs*, *expectations*, and *requirements*.)

This innovative book is a complete book of the quality "*body of knowledge*" (BoK) written to present quality in all ramifications of its context, from the genealogy to the anatomy of quality. It therefore covers the ***A–Z*** of the subject matters of quality and quality management principles/philosophy, tools, and techniques, and hence is very handy for quality professionals, practitioners, and students. It provides insights, guidance, and tools to innovatively capture and share knowledge about effectively managing organizational and business operational processes and activities/changes, just as it provides the highlights for organizational performance improvement options.

It covers an array of appropriate quality management methodologies, philosophies, standards, tools, and techniques for organizations, businesses, and other entities that value quality as an integral part of human life, work, products/services, and the environment as well as those interested in quality as a professional and/or career pathway.

This book therefore provides, in terms of the depth and width of its coverage, fundamental quality management foundational guides and insights, suitable for all types of businesses – small, medium, and large organizations, to innovatively engage their employees to consistently achieve improved performance across the value chain for business sustainability.

Written in the simplest and easiest-to-understand language and format, *Innovative TQM Guide to Sustain Digital Age Businesses* innovatively facilitates an all-time understanding of quality and its management principles/philosophy, tools, and techniques, in order to proliferate quality practices, thereby making it very easy to cultivate a quality culture and sustain the *quality mindset*, while at the same time growing the *quality thinking* among the people of the world.

This book thus understandingly and greatly enhances the interests of all those that speak English across the globe, particularly those whose first language is not English. This is especially so because it is very easy to read, and focuses more on quality and quality management body of knowledge, uses, and application rather than just being theoretical.

Hence, *Innovative TQM Guide to Sustain Digital Age Businesses* is written as a handy book of professional companionship for chief executives and business owners, who may want to get familiar with and understand quality management standards, principles, and practices for effective leadership; every quality professional and practitioners wanting to continuously enhance their quality practices from day to day; organizations and businesses interested in the use of international and national standards, either for certification purposes or for the general enhancements of their quality management systems standards; those who are coming in contact with quality for the first time, either as students of quality or in newer situations and circumstances, at work, or career change opportunities; students of other professional leanings wanting to embrace the quality mindset/culture and quality management principles in their career paths; postgraduate students and researchers, as well as those who may be interested in the concept of quality to enhance the quality of their lives and living patterns.

Innovative TQM Guide to Sustain Digital Age Businesses is written with a strong commitment and objective of propagating quality as a stand-alone "body of knowledge" worthy of being globally seen, viewed, and acknowledged as an academic "*discipline*," where it actually belongs (Chap. 19). This innovative book provides guides for businesses to understand how to integrate their human capital, processes, and technologies to create greater efficiencies and profit.

Apart from introducing organizations and their leadership to Industry 4.0, Quality 4.0, and 4.0 base technologies and the clamor for organizational digital transformation, it provides some basic understandings of the "SmartFactory" concept and the digital industrial manufacturing setting and ecosystem.

Research Vacuum in Quality

Similarly, this book brings to the fore the academic vacuum created by the nature and way quality has evolved outside the academia, over the century, to identify the immense research opportunities inherent therein. An example here is the immense knowledge vacuum existing in the area of Quality 4.0 initiatives, which development or implementation portends the "*SmartFactory*."

This, coupled with the author's exploits of the literature, exposes the immense research potentials of quality, quality management principles/philosophy, tools, and techniques. Another critical research vacuum frequently referred to in the literature is the need for advancing into the scientific and/or mathematical basis for justifying and supporting quality terms, concepts, and definitions (Chaps. 4, 9, 10, and 17). Similarly, the area of continuous improvement (CI) deserves, on its own, the general need for critical analysis to establish the theoretical basis for conducting research in this expansive field of knowledge.

Although the International Organization for Standardization (ISO) is deeply and continuously engaged in developing new and updated quality management systems and other international standards for its members, the sky is the limit here for researchers that are keen and interested in standards development, commercially and otherwise.

Research opportunities and exploits are heavily laden and waiting to be tapped in the area of establishing and developing various integrated or stand-alone industry- and application-specific quality management systems (QMS) and/or standards, as emphasized with the example of London et al.'s "GAP" [17] and in Chap. 4 of this book.

A–Z of Quality: Chaps. 1, 2, 3, 4, 5, 6, 7, 8, 9, 10, 11, 12, 13, 14, 15, 16, 17, 18, 19, 20, 21, and 22

While the first chapter of this book provides the *genealogy of quality*, its definition, and the needs for creating the culture of quality, Chap. 2 offers a general overview about its universality, growing the quality culture, and the ways to apply quality, quality management principles/philosophy, tools, and techniques in businesses to gain competitive edge through innovation and employee engagement.

The first two chapters (Chaps. 1 and 2) therefore jointly serve the interests of

- those entering into quality and quality management for the first time, either as students, or taking up quality as a career path, or field of interest, or changing to jobs at quality-conscious organizations;
- those who are already engaged in other professional fields and governance, but keen to have and build a fundamental knowledge base of quality;
- busy top organizational management team members who are keen to have and build a fundamental knowledge base, of quality and its tools, within a short time frame, for effective organizational management, or simply interested in getting acquainted with quality and quality concepts and terms;
- those interested in acquiring the quality mindset in building the *quality culture* within the shortest time – businesses, organizations, management consultancy, equipment and machine manufacturers, and so on;
- those embarking on the implementation of an international quality management systems (QMS) standard, such as ISO 9001 QMS and ISO 14001 Environmental Management System (EMS), or other quality systems for the first time; and
- those who most importantly seek to understand the origin, vocabulary, and trends in the industrial manufacturing digital transformational age – Industry 4.0, Quality 4.0, 4.0 technologies, digitization, digitalization, and so on.

The author uses the first two chapters (Chaps. 1 and 2) to explore the true value of understanding the fears (of the unknown) and anxieties that employees, or quality team members, go through, when jumping headfirst into new roles, positions, career paths, and organizational roles.

In addition, this book covers virtually all themes, from the genealogy to the anatomy of quality. In providing the A–Z of quality, *Innovative TQM Guide to Sustain Digital Age Businesses* successfully established the needed evidence-based facts for recognizing quality as a field of study, or discipline, worthy of a stand-alone recognition, as a body of knowledge (BoK), spread across 17 chapters (Chaps. 2, 3, 4, 5, 6, 7, 8, 9, 10, 11, 12, 13, 14, 15, 16, 17, and 18). It begins with an overview of international quality (management) standards, with special emphasis on industry-specific and application-specific series of standards (Chap. 3) as examples for researchers to emulate.

An example is ISO 56000 and ISO 56002, *innovation management*, which has been designed by the ISO to specifically integrate with ISO 9001, putting a high-level structure to use, in order that an integrated system can be developed to uniquely drive both quality and innovation (Chaps. 2 and 3).

The author deliberately used the ISO 56000 series as an example of application-specific standards so as to bring out the benefits of its application, that is, giving the customers, business partners, academia, and other stakeholders the confidence that an organization can, on a consistent basis, deliver innovation.

The author tapped on the immediate global experience of managing the COVID-19 pandemic-induced changes, to provide the perspectives for consideration in designing a quality team, division, or organization for strongly innovative thinking. The COVID-19 pandemic experience thus taught us all that an organization's ability and capacity to innovatively achieve effective *change management* is key for organizational *sustainability* (Chap. 4). Emphasis here is on the need for ensuring business sustainability, with reliance on an organizational continuity plan. Examples of standards to help organizations include, among others:

ISO 22301:2019 *– Security and resilience – Business continuity management systems – Requirements*

This standard is established in the words of the ISO, specifying the requirements "to implement, maintain and improve a management system to protect against, reduce the likelihood of the occurrence of, prepare for, respond to and recover from disruptions when they arise."

Here, the role of leadership understanding and establishing the strategic, operational, and tactical perspectives – business model, potential competition, and the desired structure – of an organization, no doubt, help to create an organizational *culture of innovation.*

This standard helps to understand the role of organizational leadership as well as the impact of a product/service on the three cadres of customers – primary (1°), secondary (2°) and tertiary (3°), and the consequences of organizations neglecting their social corporate responsibility (CSR). This is emphasized in terms of the global leadership handling of the novel coronavirus and its aftermath, the COVID-19 pandemic.

The inability of the global community to ***cage*** the novel coronavirus ***in-place,*** like it was done for the Ebola virus in 2014, is seen and viewed as being probably due to relevant organizations paying poor attention, or not paying attention at all, to issues of corporate social and environmental responsibility (CSER, or CSR/CER) – that is, the tertiary (3°) customer SNEaRs – and perhaps noncompliance with any existing regulatory (2° customer), national, and/or international guidelines and/or regulatory requirements.

One of the key essences of quality should therefore, most understandably, include, among others, the responsibility of organizations to comply with regulatory (2° customer) and interested entities' (3° customer) SNEaRs, even when not expressly or clearly stated. The criticality of recognizing (or not) organizational CSR/CER is highly embedded in the consequences of not being compliant, or nonconforming. The role of the CSR/CER thus greatly enhances quality and its universal application to life and most human activities, from education to research to business processes and activities.

The A–Z of quality is capped with the literature review of Industry 4.0 and Quality 4.0, respectively, in Chaps. 21 and 22 to keep readers updated with the current situation of the fourth industrial revolution and the challenges that come with it in terms of quality management.

Quality of Covid-19-Induced Change Management

The universality of the relevance of quality in our socio-cultural world has never been as critical as it is today. This has been adequately brought to the awareness of the global community since the disruptive insurgency of the novel coronavirus against humanity in December 2019/January 2020, a century after its senior counterpart, the Spanish flu, struck planet earth, like lightning. Quality was just beginning its genealogical journey then; hence, its role may have gone unrecognized in dealing with the Spanish flu.

The origin of the novel coronavirus has been officially marred in denials and controversies, thus slowing down the ability for a swift quality response and the deployment of adaptive capacity. It is obvious however that the worsened and rapid spread of COVID-19 pandemic may have been accelerated by the general lack of transparency and mis-leadership (i.e., poor quality leadership), coupled with the overall poor display of corporate social responsibility (CSR) and corporate environmental responsibility (CER), or the lack thereof, on the part of both relevant organizations and governments. This is perhaps partly understandable because of the novel nature of the coronavirus, the causal virus of the pandemic.

The extremely poor quality of the initial responses, and perhaps immediate responses thereafter, to the COVID-19 pandemic, from both its suspected location of origin and overseas, actually aggravated the deadly impacts of the novel coronavirus, across the nations of the world and among their people. The poor quality of the initial responses therefore greatly impacted the resultant consequences on the global population, leading to the deterioration of the quality of people's lives. This happened as if the people of the world and their leadership were completely ignorant of the way the largest Ebola epidemic in West Africa was "*caged in-place*" by the U.S. administration of President Barack Obama in 2014, in alliance with the U.N. and other international partners.

The razzle-dazzle political theatrics of the COVID-19 pandemic-era U.S. government actually diminished and dwarfed the usual quality of the U.S. government leadership responses, as well as the global political leadership expectations, for which the U.S. government has always been known prior to the 2016–2020 era of governance.

At the end of the day, the U.S. lost 0.1815% of her total population of 331,449,281 million (U.S. Census Bureau [21]), or 601,626 people, as at June 2021 (about 18 months after the outbreak of the COVID-19 pandemic).

Caging COVID-19 pandemic "*in-place*" like the West African Ebola epidemic, that is, not allowing it to spread outside its point of origin, by nipping it in the bud, especially in an era of global transportation, which provides people with the "ability to traverse the globe in about 2 days" Curtin [5], would have been the best quality management approach.

Failure to cage the coronavirus "*in-place*" was a kiss of death for the people of the world. Bang! Bang!! Bang!!! And it cost the U.S. a loss of over 601,626 lives, or about 15.6111% of the globally recorded deaths of 3,853,843 lives, as at June 19, 2021 [13]. Most of the victims of the COVID-19 pandemic died an unusually "dehumanized, dishonorable," low "*quality of death and burial*" entirely different from centuries-long traditional practices that we used to know. This is because, as it happened in most cases, family members never got the chance to hug or bid farewell, to their loved ones, who died alone and isolated, in hospital wards, for the fear of spreading the COVID-19 pandemic.

Prioritizing political arrogance over the embrace of quality, quality management principles, tools, and techniques, to swiftly "*cage the coronavirus in-place*," has not only cost the entirety of the global community about four million lives but an additional "estimated $26 trillion worth of economic damage," according to Curtin [5].

Of course, the impact on the global economy is predictable as we shall continue to experience price increases of most products and services for some time after the peak of the COVID-19 pandemic, which may not completely disappear from planet earth. The COVID-19 pandemic has not only changed the world, by forcing or creating new norms for the people to live with, for the rest of their lives, but has demonstrably amplified the universality of quality being integral to man's existential potentials, by boldly crystalizing quality and quality management tools as the clearest options to uphold humanity and its future life, especially at times of existentially disruptive changes like we witnessed with the COVID-19 pandemic.

This is particularly so "because pandemic outbreaks are both predictable (they will occur) and unpredictable (we don't know where or when)," according to Curtin [5]. Global health agencies, governments, and other relevant organizations around the globe therefore need to adaptively embrace quality principles/philosophy, tools, and techniques in all ramifications of man's life, in preparation for appropriate and timely responses to looming catastrophes and disasters, especially now that modern developments, such as those listed below, have put the world at higher risks of more pandemics [5]:

- **Globalized transportation systems** – the advantage of quickly traversing the globe in about two days crystallizes the risk of swiftly spreading a deadly virus, or other diseases, across the globe.
- **Social media** – fake news, falsehoods, misinformation, and conspiracy theories spread at "lightning speeds," taking advantage of the world's advanced internet and communications technological systems (ICTs) to negatively influence other people. For example, the expansion of the anti-vaccination movement across the globe, to the dismay of some innocent citizens of the world who would have had the opportunity of the herd immunity.
- **Overpopulation of urban centers** –viruses and diseases spread more rapidly in urban centers of the world due to overpopulation.
- **Human encroachment on wildlife** – rampant occurrence of zoonotic diseases such as the Ebola virus through human encroachment on wildlife.
- **Climate change** – the global climate change, such as global warming, is daily facilitating the growing reach of vectors such as mosquitoes into other regions of the world. It is, however, unfortunate for the human race that some political misleaders of the world decide to give flimsy political excuses and baseless conspiracy theories to wave this reality into obscurity.
- **Vaccine resistance** – prevention of human communities from the opportunity of reaching herd immunity, due to the baseless resistance of some groups of people from being vaccinated.

In highlighting the above identified risks, this book specifically draws attention to the clear fact that by adapting quality measures, risks could generally be mitigated. Such applicable quality management concepts and/or tools include, among others, innovation, adaptive space, commitment to CSR, quality mindset and culture, and so on. The way we do a lot of things is changing daily, hence the general need to pay attention to risks and risk mitigation. This thus, in turn, raises the question of the need for quality to be considered an essential part of most of the human activities and life sustainability.

To guide organizations to remain compliant and manage risks in the most appropriate ways, the ISO has established relevant ISO standards for different specificities.

Change Management: Risk Management Standards

While clearly identifying the purpose of quality *risk management* (RM), as embedded in the need to accurately appraise organizational objectives, achievement paths, and continuous improvement; prevention of undesirable outcomes; value retention/addition; and overall sustainability, this book also identifies relevantly applicable international standards for risk prevention and handling, bio-risk inclusive (Chaps. 3, 4, and 8):

ISO/IEC 31010:2019 – *Risk management – Risk assessment techniques*
ISO 31000:2018 – *Risk management – Guidelines, provides principles, framework, and a process for managing risk*
ISO 9001:2015 – Some clauses (Clause 6.1.) of this standard provide guidelines for effective risk management procedures
ISO 35001:2019 – *Bio-risk management for laboratories and other related organizations*

This document, ISO 35001:2019, "a process to identify, assess, control, and monitor risks associated with hazardous biological materials."

Building on the global COVID-19 pandemic experiences across the globe, from North America to China and Australia, the author brought out the post-COVID-19 pandemic ensuing new norms in organizational quality *change management* – planned and unplanned – for sustainability with reference to the supply chain, today and tomorrow (Chaps. 4 and 15).

This book also provides guidelines about resistance to change, managing the risks of change, and creating adaptive capacity. It similarly highlights using the ISO 9001:2015 QMS international standard to enhance the requirements for handling changes in organizational quality management systems, processes, and other activities.

Improvement Guide

Twenty-three universal business improvement guidelines (UBIG) for change management, named for the purpose of quick reference, 23-UBIG helps generally to facilitate any change management process for any organization irrespective of size, nature of business, as well as products/services (Chap. 15). *Innovative TQM Guide to Sustain Digital Age Businesses* is particularly handy for top organizational management team members, who, in most cases, have little or no time at all to delve too deeply and too often into the literature in search of quality knowledge.

This book opens up the need to redefine quality to reflect the cultural affiliation of quality and its purpose of maintaining relationships – customer/supply chain, organization/stakeholders, employees/management, employee/employee, organization/regulatory bodies, and so on. When viewed from this perspective of its growing importance, and relevance to mankind, quality is about relationships too.

The role of quality as a critical change management tool can therefore not be overemphasized. Both organizations and individuals are daily faced with challenges of a consistently changing world. And as if to complicate the dynamism of change, for both the manufacturing industry and the people in this century, the COVID-19 pandemic-induced changes, fortunately or unfortunately, coincided with the already planned technology-driven changes thrown upon the industrial manufacturing sector all over the world since 2011, by the fourth industrial revolution, generally code-named *Industry 4.0* in Europe, its birthplace, and "*Internet of Things*" (IoT) in North America.

In Disruptive Times

Change management thus remains a critical quality management tool for people, businesses, and organizations. Hence, quality is the first point of call in change management for overcoming the usually disruptive changes immediately impacting on organizations and businesses, to achieve organizational sustainability.

There are no doubts whatsoever that the first two years or so of the third decade of the twenty-first century saw us through one of the most dreadful and stressful disruptive cultural and socio-economic changes of the modern world. It was a change in the magnitude of a *cultural* and *economic shock* to the people of the world, perhaps last experienced over a hundred years ago, with the Spanish flu in 1918. And as truly asserted by Whitacre [23], "changing times make us *learn, grow* and *adapt* more than we ever could imagine or anticipate."

It is partly in fulfillment of this natural human instinct to *learn*, *adapt*, and *grow* that *Innovative TQM Guide to Sustain Digital Age Businesses* is written, to provide a concise learning experience of the innovative application and role of total quality management (TQM) principles, tools, and techniques (Chaps. 11 and 16), and to accentuate the need for the effective management of Industry 4.0 vis-à-vis Quality 4.0 initiatives (Chaps. 19 and 21) as well as the COVID-19 pandemic-induced disruptive changes of 2020/21. It was an era of COVID-19 pandemic's global tsunami of unimaginable damage and disruption to humanity, its social life, and economic sustainability.

The COVID-19 pandemic experience is emphasized throughout this book and shared with readers to enhance the understanding of the impacts of changes, with up-to-date change management theories and principles as well as improvement concepts (Chap. 17) and guides (Chap. 15).

Innovative TQM Guide to Sustain Digital Age Businesses also provides insights, guidance, and fundamental emphasis on the science, procedures, principles, tools, techniques, history, and evolution of quality to the level of Quality 4.0, in order to enhance organizational/business processes and individual potentials to *learn*, *grow*, and *adapt* to disruptive changes to build adaptive capacity.

The future of quality, though not exactly predictable, is therefore highly dependent on learning how to be *adaptive* to disruptive changes of, for example, the current digital transformation era, and to *grow* organizational performances and improvement measures, through innovation and employee engagement.

Industry 4.0 – The Birth of the "SmartFactory"

The concept of Industry 4.0, which can be said to be open to interpretation, has assumed various definitions in the literature. Hence, Industry 4.0 is used to describe

> *[t]he organization of production processes based on technology and devices autonomously communicating with each other along the value chain in virtual computer models: a model of the smart factory of the future where computer-driven systems monitor physical processes, create a virtual copy of the physical world and make decentralized decisions based on self-organization mechanisms.* (Smit et al. [20])

Similarly, Rick et al. [19] defined the smart factory as

> *[a] flexible system that can self-optimize performance across a broader network, self-adapt to and learn from new conditions in real or near-real time, and autonomously run entire production processes.*

Hermann et al. [12], from their own consideration, defined Industry 4.0 as

> *[a] collective term for technologies and concepts of value chain organization. Within the modular structured SmartFactories of Industry 4.0, CPS monitor physical processes, create a virtual copy of the physical world and make decentralized decisions. Over the IoT, CPS communicate and cooperate with each other and humans in real time. Via the IoS, both internal and cross-organizational services are offered and utilized by participants of the value chain.*

(where CPS stands for Cyber-Physical Systems, IoT Internet of Things, and IoS Internet of Services)

It is in this way that Industry 4.0 is conceptualized to disruptively transform the traditional industrial manufacturing model, giving birth to the "SmartFactory" model. This digital transformation or digitalization process in industrial manufacturing thus comes with "disruptive changes," enormous changes.

In the SmartFactory concept therefore, the digital transformational, or Industry 4.0 implementational/developmental steps, can assumably be "simplified" as shown below to ensure a full understanding of this concept:

- ***Individual organizational asset*** – equipment, machinery, tools, inventory, personnel or entity is first and foremost ***digitized***.
- Then they (digitized assets) are ***linked*** or ***connected together*** using appropriate devices and technologies to improve the performance of a series of dependent assets in processes, such as in the production line or manufacturing cell. This is done for each process phase of an industrial manufacturing factory.
- Taking advantage of the Internet of Things (IoT) and the Industrial Internet of Things (IIoT) to ***connect and interconnect*** the assets of individual organizations and their processes of a factory within themselves and also with other relevant factories' assets (digitalization) elsewhere can help in optimizing overall plant and organizational performances.
- ***Interconnecting*** digitally transformed factories together with a network of other similar factories, and with the entire supply chain and product development cycle across different sites in real time, leads generally to the maximization of factory network performance [19].
- This digital transformation is highly punctuated with massive ***data*** generation, collection, and analytics in an ***agile*** and ***flexible*** ecosystem or environment.

Although the conceptualization of Industry 4.0 harped most importantly on industrial manufacturing processes, the digitalization of other arms of the economy is not totally foreclosed.

In what may have been seen as a global technological prophesy by Friedrich-Ebert-Stiftung and reported by Buhr [4], and Smit et al. [20] then, the generally assumed intent of Industry 4.0 is perhaps revealed in the global statement that ***"anything that can be digitized will be digitized."*** This idea thus crystalizes the digital transformational ideology of cross-fertilizing Industry 4.0 initiatives across industries, businesses, organizational activities, city management processes, and any other possible arenas of human endeavor. The extent of the current digitization and digitalization outcomes of the economy and human environment can however not be predicted. "Time will however tell."

The "SmartFactory" concept, or digitalization, or digital transformation, may from literature findings be brought to realization using "the combination of several major innovations in digital technology," which, according to Geissbauer et al. [11], include, among others, the following:

- Advanced robotics and artificial intelligence;
- sophisticated sensors;
- cloud computing;
- the Internet of Things (IoT);

- data capture and analytics;
- digital fabrication (including 3D printing);
- software-as-a-service and other new marketing models;
- smartphones and other mobile devices;
- platforms that use algorithms to direct motor vehicles (including navigation tools, ride-sharing apps, and autonomous vehicles); and
- the embedding of all these elements in an interoperable global value chain, shared by many companies from many countries.

These authors further reinforced the critical role of connectivity and integration of these technologies, which are often looked at separately, in their affirmation that "[w]hen robotics, 3D printing, data analytics, Internet of Things, and digital fabrication are joined together, they integrate the physical and virtual worlds."

"SmartFactory" is used here as a representative outcome of the complex technological networks of machinery and devices "that have engendered industrial society become hyperaware systems of highly flexible technology, responding rapidly not just to human commands but to their own perceptions and self-direction" [11].

In brief summary therefore, Industry 4.0 has to do with connectivity and integration of systems to generate, gather, and analyze data in an ecosystem of digitalized operations.

Digital Transformational Changes and Quality

The current transformational age of quality is, among other things, being propelled today by multi-dimensional momenta, generated in the developed economies of the world, traversing the globe from Europe and North America to Japan, Asia, and China.

Digital transformation has thus become a universal symbolism of the dictates of advanced technological development across the globe – big data, data analytics, robotics, artificial intelligence (AI), blockchain, machine learning (ML), Internet of Things (IoT), and Industrial Internet of Things (IIoT).

It is, in fact, gradually turning into the nucleus of a global industrial manufacturing policy, except for the dead silence of the deteriorating economically retrogressive countries from the continent of Africa. It is unfortunate however that a once promising economy like Nigeria is retrogressively sinking its resources in re-tracing her medieval cattle-grazing routes of the *n*th century, rather than moving with the world in this critical digitally transitioning era.

Although Industry 4.0 (in Europe) is multilingual – "Industrial Internet" in North America, "Society 5.0" in Japan [10], and "Made in China (MIC) 2025" [6] and "Smart Cities" in Asia – the objective of these initiatives is quite similar, in as much as quality is concerned, though *Quality 4.0* initiatives will effectively emerge as immediate follow-ups of Industry 4.0 initiatives.

Perhaps most unfortunate here is the absence a relevant language for Industry 4.0 (or simply cyber-connected manufacturing) in the continent of Africa, where

Nigeria, one of its hopes for industrial development, is busy focusing attention on "Nigeria 1700 – back-tracking the cattle-grazing routes," which were perhaps not documented, instead of matching forward with the rest of the world with Industry 4.0 initiatives, thereby playing the catching-up game.

Innovative TQM Guide to Sustain Digital Age Businesses provides, on a general basis, the fundamental quality body of knowledge (BoK) and literature informational findings, which organizations, businesses, and quality practitioners and professionals can easily tap into, to *adaptively and innovatively* drive the ensuing paradigm shifts in quality, and to *grow* business performance through the delivery of "*excellence*" in awareness of the challenges of Quality 4.0 changes, and the need to appropriately manage those changes as they evolve.

Building the adaptive capacity to effectively cope with both the COVID-19 pandemic-induced changes and those technologically inherent in Industry 4.0/ Quality 4.0 initiatives, such as artificial intelligence, large-scale additive manufacturing or 3D printing, the Internet of Things (IoT), the Industrial Internet of Things (IIoT), data, data analytics, and the ways in which they can interact, is not just a necessity but an opportunity to adapt to the world's new industrial reality of high interconnectivity in the manufacturing setting, including machine-to-machine (M2M) and person-to-machine, and vice versa.

The resultant impact here is obviously synonymous with that of a cultural change, that is, a transformation in the way organizations conduct their day-to-day manufacturing activities, or businesses. This shall undoubtedly affect both the workforce (creating new skills gaps) and leadership capabilities (Chap. 10), as well as factors such as product innovation, production/manufacturing efficiency, compliance with stated and unstated regulatory (2° customer) requirements (Chaps. 19 and 20), supply chain performance (Chap. 13), and quality itself.

Industry 4.0/Quality 4.0 Connectivity

Quality 4.0 can, in terms of its relationship to *Industry 4.0*, be seen as a concept of strong affiliation with the fourth industrial manufacturing revolution, in terms of the digitalization of TQM and quality management activities/processes. This thus brings out the concept of *Quality 4.0,* being viewed in its simplest form, as the alignment of total quality management practices with the emerging Industry 4.0 initiatives, whose pivotal factors are as listed below.

Hence, the main task lies mainly in the ability of organizations and businesses to effectively adopt Industry 4.0 initiatives and integrate them appropriately into their quality management systems, or vice versa.

The pivotal factors of Quality 4.0 viewed from the perspective of *Industry 4.0* initiatives involve but are not limited to the following areas of application:

- Error-free process control
- Cyber security, data security, privacy issues

- Analytics – data generation, sharing, analysis, and their appropriate and error-free application to achieve customer SNEaRs, deduce predictive and preventive maintenance needs, prevent wastes and scraps generation, and so on
- Collaboration – machine/machine and human/machine
- Interconnectivity
- Quality management systems
- Conformity/compliance
- App development
- Software development
- Culture of quality
- Leadership
- Competency

The connectivity of Quality 4.0 with Industry 4.0 is glaring and obvious, hence its definition with relativity to Industry 4.0 initiatives. This is highly reflected in the proposed definition of Quality 4.0 by Forero and Sisodia [9] as shown below:

> *Quality 4.0 refers to the digitalization of Total Quality Management and its impact on quality technology, processes and people. It builds upon traditional quality tools and considers also connectedness, intelligence and automation for improving performance and making timely data-driven decisions in an end-to-end scenario involving all stakeholders and providing visibility and transparency.*

Promises of Quality

When the quality of an organization's entire processes and activities is sustained by a foundational culture of continuous improvement, employee engagement and creativity, innovation and excellence, the customer/marketplace and other beneficiaries of the output always get some level of confidence and assurance that the things they are getting now, and perhaps in the future, are not just sustainable but embodiments of their individual values cross-balanced with culture and sustainable relationships. Quality is value, and value is oftentimes interactive with culture, hence the need for balancing value with culture in a sustainable relationship. This is the basis for redefining quality in this book.

Being Prepared

The aftermath of the COVID-19 disruptive environment actually "brought nurses' exceptionalism to the forefront of many nations' collective conscience – not just in the *qualities* of compassion, dedication, and self-sacrifice, but the ability to be *leaders, innovators,* and *decision makers* during the defining healthcare crisis of our lifetime," according to Osborne [18].

Engaged healthcare employees embraced the adaptive space in their effective *emergent change management* approaches to at least minimize COVID-19 cases and deaths. This accomplishment represents the urgent need of the time and age we now find ourselves in, as confirmed in the report of Edmund [7], "The COVID-19 era has demonstrated the need to be able to respond more swiftly and effectively to unexpected disruption," that is, being adaptive. Being able to cultivate *adaptive capacity* in times of disruption now becomes an integral part of any organizational QMS. Businesses must hence "*be prepared for change*."

While government officials all over the world, including China, reeled in confusion, nurses and other healthcare professionals across the globe relied most importantly on, and stuck to, *quality* – its principles, tools, and techniques, to *manage the emergent change* by pivoting and focusing on ways to minimize the impacts of the pandemic on human lives until defeated.

The author is a beneficiary of the telemedicine and its excellent adaptive capabilities of the Dallas Parkland Health healthcare management teams.

Global Cultural and Economic Shocks

People's lives were spun round 360° by the COVID-19 pandemic, upending the world around us – the way people work and move around, social gathering, schooling, and the way we shop, just to name a few. It was simply an era of "*cultural and business shocks*." A key area of perhaps the most impactful disruption has been the workplace. Organizational vis-à-vis industrial production activities were not spared either, as the supply chain was shaken beyond reasons claimed to have been attributable to the impacts of Lean manufacturing, or just-in-time (JIT).

For example, one of the immediate manufacturing impacts of the COVID-19 pandemic was the scarcity of paper products, such as paper towels and toilet paper, and other items like laptop computers. While some (42%) of the respondents of a research survey pointed accusing fingers to Lean manufacturing and just-in-time (JIT), which I do not in any way agree with, the majority (49%) of the respondents disagreed. Instead, it was "conceded that some of the causes for the shortage that occurred during the pandemic are attributable to *management* … Poorly constructed supply systems can be brittle even when their designers call them Lean. Evidence shows, however, that true Lean thinking and practice help prevent supply problems than causing them" [16].

Integrating the *adaptive space* into the quality management system, to enable organizational swift reaction to any disruptive challenge, or environment, thus becomes highly imperative, especially when we realize the critical fact that "[i]t would be extremely rare for a manufacturer to deliberately build up sufficient inventory to address a once-in-a-lifetime event such as a pandemic" [14], and the fact too, that, change is inevitable.

The reported chip shortage in the early parts of 2021 in the automotive industry has caused automakers, including General Motors, Toyota, and Ford, to suspend production and extended downtime [2].

Apart from individual and organizational disruptive changes, there are other changes associated with the COVID-19 pandemic. For example, a Harvey Nash/ KPMG CIO survey [15] reportedly revealed that "[o]rganizations spent the equivalent of about $15 billion extra a week this year, on technology to enable safe and secure remote working during COVID-19."

The urgent need to avoid the risk of concentrating the supply chain mostly in the hands of China-based manufacturing organizations is a lesson learnt from our experiences from the COVID-19 pandemic. Hence, the need for organizations to diversify their sources of supply, perhaps bringing them nearest home as much as possible. Another key change emanating from the COVID-19 pandemic is the renewed interest in automation and robotics in order to overcome people's movement restrictions. It must however be mentioned here that this development tallies with the initiatives of Industry 4.0.

All in all, "'Quality's Impact on the Global Pandemic Response' highlights how quality principles and best practices are foundational for industries integral to each stage of the responses to COVID-19 pandemic, including vaccine development, distribution, and administration" [1].

Quality in Double Transition

The aftermath of the COVID-19 pandemic is a matter which involves some permanent changes for manufacturers and employees, most of whom had already planned to initiate the planned *Industry 4.0* initiatives, thus creating a double momentum for quality management dynamism. Manufacturers have not been hesitant to affirm that "their operations will be altered permanently because of COVID-19" [22]. Some of the highlighted changes include, among others:

- Cutting of labor/employees
- Increased investment in technology, R&D, and innovation
- Use of data/analytics platform to adapt to the pandemic
- Mergers and acquisitions as a response to the economic circumstances caused by the COVID-19 pandemic
- Short-term economic instability with a downward trend

Similarly, a survey by the Association for Advancing Automation [3] revealed that about 26% of manufacturers have established the end-to-end artificial intelligence (AI) solution, 40% still rely on manual processes for visual inspection, while 60% of the respondents claimed that data scarcity is a primary hindrance for manufacturers' difficulty in applying AI.

A survey report from Essentium Inc., a provider of 3D printing or large-scale additive manufacturing (AM), claimed that AM "has evolved from the prototyping phase" and that manufacturers are already deploying it into actual manufacturing, to save costs and, at the same time, build supply chains that are capable of withstanding the worst type of unforeseen events like the pandemic [8].

There are increased tendencies for an upsurge in job opportunities in various fields, including but not limited to engineering; design; IT; electrical systems engineers; developers for Java, Android, iOS, and other platforms; controls engineers; infotainment software engineers; programmers; support technicians; and so on. Similarly, there is going to be a general need for updating much-needed skills in the field of quality (Chaps. 19, 20, and 21).

The sudden increase in goods, particularly in the earlier to the second half of 2021, may likely have been ignited by organizations trying to make up for their losses during the COVID-19 severe periods of 2020.

Digital Transformation

The dynamism of quality and its roles in business successes are, as experienced in the twentieth century, always at the dictates of changes in the business world. The degree to which quality practices such as TQM and quality professionals at the helm of quality management practices have differentiating effects and impacts on business performance has long been established, both in practice and in the literature.

This is the reason why the current changes in organizational and business activities must be appropriately responded to by quality practitioners and professionals as they emerge from

- the aftermath of the COVID-19 pandemic – impacts and changes, and
- digital transitioning activities emanating from digital transformation and other Industry 4.0 initiatives

It is therefore highly imperative to identify the quality management skills, knowledge, and competences necessary for supporting and upholding organizational business improvement activities and sustainability during and into the new phases of transitional manufacturing operational changes.

The global environment is in transition, changing at an amazingly fast pace, as if to challenge the adaptive competences of quality professionals and practitioners, now and in the future. Quality and quality professionals therefore urgently need to be constantly developing qualified and skilled hands or professionals, as well as newer quality management tools as may be deemed necessary, for keeping up with the dynamism of business and industrial manufacturing organizational digital changes.

Quality as an Academic Discipline

For the future, quality should be seen as a management strategy for organizational and business sustainability, with full executive management involvement, and employee engagement and involvement to imbibe and plant the quality-thinking mentality and mindset. These are two key essentials of organizational sustainability factors, which benefits are maximized when the quality mindset and cross-organizational quality culture are instilled and applied conscientiously throughout the organization.

With quality seen and viewed from the perspective of a stand-alone discipline, or body of knowledge (BoK), universities and other higher institutions around the globe, especially in the continents of Africa and South America, may need to embrace quality as a strong discipline of prime choice, from the undergraduate level to postgraduate studies – the time is now.

Quest for the Scientific Basis for Continual/ Continuous Improvement

Business survival is today most importantly dictated by the relationship that exists between suppliers and customers/consumers or the marketplace. This relationship is, in turn, promoted and sustained by *quality* vis-à-vis the value of the product or service which binds or bonds them together, as the object of their interactive interplay. The healthiness of this relationship, as dictated by its quality and/or values, keeps organizations going, hence the need to ensure that products/services exhibit those characteristics that bear on their ability to meet the SNEaRs of all categories of customers – primary (1°), secondary (2°), and tertiary (3°). The dynamism of customer values (including cultural considerations) directly dictates the dynamics of quality itself.

It follows from here therefore that the upward movement or assumed changes in customer values is directly proportional or equivalent to the expected product/service improvement, in order to keep up with the changes in customer SNEaRs and, most importantly too, to remain competitively strong in order to be able to sustain the customer/supplier relationships, otherwise that relationship may crash or disappear. The ensuing momentum thus drives business or organizational improvement dynamics. Hence, the need and desire to meet the changing customer and/or market SNEaRs have increasingly taken the driver's seat of the management vehicles of most organizations, enterprises, and businesses. These relationships could, if considered from a scientific point of view, generate critical research and/or discussion.

Business Need for Driving Along the Quality Alley

Competition in the business world generally requires, particularly in the present globalized economic age and time, that, as business drivers, management teams of various organizations and businesses must constantly drive along the quality route to outpace each other, if survival and sustainability are the ultimate target.

The current globalization of the world market economy has therefore driven the global market competition to unprecedented heights. Most organizations, in attempts to meet customer and market SNEaRs, have turned their focus and attention on the use and application of quality management standards, TQM, and other continuous improvement tools, strategies, and concepts. Obvious examples here are the ISO 9000 series of quality management systems (QMS) international standards, Lean, Six Sigma, and so on. They are critical tools to sharpen business and organizational market competitiveness through the continual improvement of your products, services, work environment, product/service values, and ultimately your bottom line, while reducing your production costs.

This, in turn, enables businesses or organizations to function efficiently, in the production of goods and services, for their customers vis-à-vis consumers, whose desires and economic appetite for quality goods are getting increasingly insatiable. It is for these and other reasons that the fourth industrial revolution, *Industry 4.0*, was initiated in the second decade of the twenty-first century.

Role of Generic International Standards

The ISO 9000 series of international quality management systems (QMS) standards is one of the most widely used generic standards. ISO 9000 is not only international in its acceptance, scope, and application, but has assumed, through its certification/registration requirements, a status much different from those of the other quality concepts, and that of the ordinary individual national standards that we all used to know.

The generic nature of the ISO 9000 series of QMS international standards has contributed largely to their broad-based application and usage. Hence, the aim of ISO 9000 is not to force uniformity on the approaches of different organizations to quality management, but to make available to them ingenious and innovative guidelines and tools, suitable for achieving the continual improvement of the performance of any business or enterprise.

The implementation and certification to the requirements of these standards increases and provides organizations/firms in any part of the globe with more opportunities and competitive advantages for marketing vis-à-vis exporting their products and services generally to the international community, but particularly to the European Economic Area (EEA).

ISO 9000 requirements state what organizations have to do but not how to do them. Going through this book introduces and focuses your attention basically on the development of quality, its business/economic importance/relevance, developing the right attitude for quality, and the steps to take to achieve and maintain quality management systems, concepts, and programs. In addition, this book also highlights the advantages of the standards (Chaps. 3 and 14) and the need for certification by organizations and enterprises/firms interested in taking advantage of the various benefits of the QMS standards to improve their systems and aid their survival in a globally competitive market (Chaps. 3 and 14).

In addition, this book provides simplified information based on decades of international industrial and academic experiences, to enable even those hearing the word "quality" for the first time to be able to appreciate and make quick "*in-road*" into the full understanding and appreciation of various quality management principles/philosophies, tools, and techniques, in a short time, irrespective of their background.

The targeted audience is, on the basis of the universality of quality, a limitless one, stretching from academics, research, business management to quality practitioners and professionals. It therefore encompasses those in the manufacturing sector – small, medium, and large scale – design and engineering, education, curbing of bribery and corruption, construction, consultancy, logistics and the supply chain, government/governance and public services, election management, international trade, sales and marketing, hotels and tourism, hospitals and other healthcare systems, legal practice, and all other services or product providers in other disciplines and areas of human endeavor.

This book therefore provides guides and the knowledge base to motivate readers, businesses, and organizations whose intention it is to use well-thought-out tools to create value, efficiency, customer satisfaction, adaptive capacity, leadership, and people engagement, within and outside the organization or business.

The major attributes of quality and its management tools are, on a general basis, for the purposes of achieving organizational or business quality results, continual improvement, and sustainability. It is for this purpose too that businesses are set up – quality results keep businesses alive and healthy. This is the reason too why ISO 10014:2021 and ISO 18091:2019 are being introduced to you now:

ISO 10014:2021 *– Quality management systems – Managing an organization for quality results – Guidance for realizing financial and economic benefits*
ISO 18091:2019 *– Quality management systems – Guidelines for the application of ISO 9001 in local government*

Fourth Industrial Revolution: Literature Review

In order to aid and deepen your understanding of quality, some common terms and expressions of quality and its management tools are listed at the end of each chapter, and at the end of the book itself.

A literature review of the concepts of *Industry 4.0* and *Quality 4.0* initiatives is, respectively, provided in Chaps. 21 and 22 not just to share their findings with you but also to answer the many questions that may have been lingering in your minds about the fourth industrial revolution, and perhaps the onset of global economic revolution.

The wave of the emerging potentials of digital transformation speculates on its massive innovative capabilities to virtually transform every facet of our day-to-day life – from business models to fully automated driverless automobiles to wearable devices for monitoring health conditions.

References

1. ASQ Whitepaper. (2021, April). Links between quality and the COVID-19 response. *Quality Progress*, p. 9. https://tinyurl.com/5d35llmr
2. ASQ. (2021, June). Automotive – Chip shortage causes automakers to hit pause. *Quality Progress*, p. 11.
3. Association for Advancing Automation. (2021, January). Manual inspection. *Quality Progress*, p. 10. https://www.tinyurl.com/ai-visual-inspect
4. Buhr. (2015). *Social innovation policy for Industry 4.0*. The Friedrich-Ebert-Stiftung.
5. Curtin, L. (2021). Pandemics and "one health." *American Nurse Journal, 16*(6), 48.
6. Cyrill, M. (2018). What is made in China 2025 and why has it made the world so nervous? *China Briefing*, December 2018.

7. Edmund, M. (2021, January). Laying into Lean – Pushing back on critics that blame Lean manufacturing, just-in-time inventory for COVID-19 shortages. *Quality Progress*, pp. 8–9.
8. Essentium Inc. (2021, January). Manufacturing – 3D printing ramping up. *Quality Progress*, p. 11. https://www.tinyurl.com/3d-survey-manufacturers
9. Forero, D. V., & Sisodia, R. (2020). *Quality 4.0 – How to handle quality in Industry 4.0 revolution*. Department of Technology Management and Economic, Chalmers University of Technology, Gothenburg, Sweden, January 2020. https://www.researchgate.net/publication/338936455_Quality_40_How_to_Handle_Quality_in_the_Industry_40_Revolution
10. Fukuyama, M. (2018). Society 5.0: Aiming for a new human-centered society. *Japan Spotlight*, July/August 2018, pp. 47–50. https://www.jef.or.jp/journal
11. Geissbauer, R., Vedso, J., & Schrauf, S. (2016). A strategist's guide to Industry 4.0. *Manufacturing*, May 9, 2016. Summer 2016, Issue 83. https://www.strategy-business.com
12. Hermann, M., Pentek, T., & Otto, B. (2015), Design Principles for Industrie 4.0 scenarios, 3928–3937. https://doi.org/10.1109/HICSS.2016.488
13. John Hopkins University & Medicine Coronavirus Center. https://www.coronavirus.jhu.edu. Retrieved on June 19, 2021.
14. Jusko, J. (2020). COVID-19 puts Lean in the crosshairs of controversy. *Industry Week*, October 19, 2020. https://www.industryweek.com/operations/continuous-improvement/article/21145065/covid19-plus-lean-in-the-crossairs-of-controversy
15. KPMG. (2020, December). COVID-19 sparks more tech investment, cyberattacks. *Quality Progress*, p. 8. https://tinyurl.com/covid-kpmg-it-survey
16. Lean Enterprise Institute. (2020). *Lean Enterprise Institute responds to the Wall Street Journal's Mischaracterization of Just-in-Time*, August 31, 2020. https://www.lean.org/common/display/?o=5342
17. London, C., Comeros, R. C., & Nguyen, A. (2020). Mind the GAP – A new adaptable QMS offers a common standard for all disciplines. *Quality Progress*, pp. 30–37.
18. Osborne, G. P. (2021). From the publisher. *American Nurses Journal*, 6(6), 4.
19. Rick, B., Mussomeli, A., Laaper, S., Hartigan, M., & Sniderman, B. (2017). The smart factory: Responsive, adaptive, connected manufacturing. A Deloitte series on Industry 4.0, digital manufacturing enterprises, and digital supply networks. *Deloitte University Press*. https://www2.deloitte.cm. Retrieved August 23, 2021.
20. Smit, J., Kreutzer, S., Moeller, C., & Carlberg, M. (2016). European Parliament – Directorate General for Internal Policies. Policy Department A: Economic and Scientific Policy. *Industry 4.0*. https://www.europarl.europa.eu/studies. Retrieved on August 24, 2021.
21. U.S. Census Bureau. (2021). US population rises to 331,449,281, Census Bureau says. *U.S. News, Associated Press*, April 26, 2021. https://www.usnews.com
22. West Monroe Partners. (2021, January). Survey: Manufacturers plan for permanent changes. *Quality Progress*, p. 10. https://www.tinyurl/west-monroe-covid-survey .
23. Whitacre, T. (2021, January). Surviving the Storm – Test your competencies in challenging times. *Quality Progress*, pp. 6–7.

Acknowledgments

The author would like to thank Olufemi Banjoko, a consultant industrial engineer; Opeoluwa Banjoko, a consultant architect; and Dariusz Kugel, a consultant graphic designer, for their suggestions and other contributions, especially in the design of the 4.0 tripartite logo.

Contents

Key Abbreviations

23-UBIG	23 universal business improvement guidelines
5S	*seiri* (sort/organize), *seton* (straighten/neatness, *seiso* (shine/clean), *seiketsu* (standardize), and *shitsuke* (sustain/discipline)
5W2H	**w**hat? **w**hy? **w**here? **w**hen? **w**ho? (5 "W" words); **h**ow and **h**ow much? (2 "H" words)
AI	Artificial intelligence
ANCC	American Nurses Credentialling Center
ANOVA	Analysis of variance
ANSI	American National Standards Institute
APQC	American Productivity and Quality Center
ASD	Aviation, space, and defense
ASQ	American Society of Quality
ASQC	American Society for Quality Control
ASQE	Is a derivative of the American Society for Quality (ASQE) as a symbol to inspire excellence. ASQE is a registered trademark of the ASQ. ASQE was founded in January 2020 as a trade association whose mission is to set the standard for quality-driven offerings and insights worldwide, inspiring the organizations it serves to achieve excellence.
ASTM	American Society for Testing and Materials
AZD	Achieving zero defect
BEM	Business excellence management
BoK	Body of knowledge
CAA	Clean Air Act
CCSR	Citizens' collective social responsibility
CE	Conformitè Europëenne (or European conformity). This mark which represents a manufacturer's declaration that its goods or products conforms with EU New Approach Directives is the European Union conformity mark for regulating the goods sold within its borders.
CER	Corporate environmental responsibility
CFM	Continuous flow manufacturing
CI	Continuous improvement

CIE	International Commission on Illumination
CMI	Continuous measurable improvement
CoQ	Cost of quality (term was used by Philip Crosby for cost of poor quality)
CPI	Continuous process improvement
CSER	Corporate social and environmental responsibility
CSR	Corporate social responsibility
C-TPAT	Customs-trade partnership against terrorism
CTQ	Critical to quality
DfD	Design for disassembly
DfE	Design for environment
DFKI	Deutsches Forschungszentrum fuer Kuenstliche Intelligenz, meaning German Center for Artificial Intelligence
DIS	Draft International Standard
DMADV	**D**efine, **m**easure, **a**nalyze, **d**esign, and **v**erify. This is a quality strategy for designing products and processes. It is an integral part of Six Sigma quality initiative.
DMAIC	**D**efine, **m**easure, **a**nalyze, **i**mprove, and **c**ontrol. This is a data-driven quality strategy for improving processes which is an integral part of Six Sigma.
DNA	Deoxyribonucleic acid
EFQM	European Foundation for Quality Management
EMS	Environmental management systems
EPA	Environmental Protection Agency
ERM	Enterprise risk management
FAA	Federal Aviation Administration
FDA	Food and Drug Administration
FIFO	First in first out
FMEA	Failure mode effects and analysis
FPI	Financial performance indicator
FSMS	Food safety management system
GAP	Good affiliate practices (an adaptable healthcare QMS developed by a group of pharmaceutical companies)
GATT	General agreement on tariffs and trade. This agreement which is directed toward reducing trade barriers was signed in 1947 by a collection of countries.
GMP	Good manufacturing practice
GRC	Governance, risk, and compliance
HACCP	Hazard analysis and critical control point
IATF	International Automotive Task Force
IEC	International Electro-technical Commission
IEEE	Institute of Electrical and Electronics Engineers
IIoT	Industrial Internet of Things
ILCT	Interlaboratory comparison testing
IoT	Internet of Things

ISO	International Organization for Standardization
JIT	Just-in-time
KPI	Key performance indicator
LCA	Life cycle assessment
LCL	Lower control limit
MBNQA	Malcolm Baldrige National Quality Award
MIPS	Minimum inventory production system
ML	Machine learning
MMS	Measurement management system
NCBI	National Center for Biotechnology Information
NIH	National Institutes of Health
NIS	Nigeria Industrial Standards
OEM	Original equipment manufacturer
OHSAS	Occupational health safety and standards
OMCL	Official Medicines Control Laboratories
OSHA	Occupational Safety and Health Administration
PAIAM	Plan, analyze, integrate, action, and monitor
PDCA/PDSA	Plan-do-check-act/plan-do-study-act (aka the Deming wheel or Shewhart cycle)
PET	Polyethylene terephthalate
PHHS	Parkland Health & Hospital System
PPE	Personal protective equipment
ppm	Parts per million
PPM	Process performance
PT	Proficiency testing
QA	Quality assurance
QC	Quality control
QFD	Quality function deployment
QM	Quality management
QMS	Quality management system
ROI	Return on investment
SCS	Supply chain sustainability
SIPOC	Suppliers, inputs, process, outputs, and customers
SNEaRs	Specifications, needs, expectations, and requirements
SON	Standards Organization of Nigeria
SONCAP	Standards Organization of Nigeria Conformity Assessment Program
SOP	Standard operating procedure
SPC	Statistical process control
SQC	Statistical quality control
TCS	Total customer satisfaction
TEI	Total employee improvement
TGE	Target for excellence
TPM	Total preventive maintenance
TPS	Toyota production system
TQC	Total quality control

TQE	Total quality environment
TQM	Total quality management
TRIZ	*Teoriya Resheniya Izobreatatelskikh Zadatch* is the Russian translation for theory of inventive problem-solving (TIPS)
UCL	Upper control limit
USP	US Pharmacopeia
USP-NF	US Pharmacopeia-National Formulary
VOC	Voice of the customer
W IIFM	What's in it for me?
WEF	World Economic Forum
WIP	Work-in-progress
ZIPS	Zero inventory production system
ZUD	Zero unplanned downtime

Introduction to Quality

1

Historical Background of Quality

The quality concept is generally naturally manifested in the human body systems. The concept of quality management as manifested in some of the cultures of the Yoruba people in Nigeria and some other parts of the West African subregion dates as far back as the early twelfth century. Here farmers organized themselves in unified and organized workforce movement termed the "owe" (pronounced "or-wea" as in "or" and in "weather"). Membership of the team is not fixed and could generally be more than five depending on the amount of work to be done and the level of trust they have for each other. A similar quality culture existed much earlier among the industrious people of Owo Kingdom in Nigeria where it is known as "*ebeshe*" since the tenth century.

These organized workforces were used for the construction of mud houses and the construction of communal roads, bush clearing, land cultivation, planting, harvesting of farm/agricultural produce (e.g., cocoa, kola nuts, and corn), etc. Each participant within the team ensured that the job carried out by him was done to the satisfaction of the host (or in this case the assumed "*customer*") of the "*owe*" who benefited solely from the teamwork. Since the "*owe*" is in most cases rotated around the members of the team, the work done by the team is to the benefit of virtually every participant who in turn can be seen as a potential customer. The rotation of the "*owe*" serves both as a motivational factor and it made the fulfillment of the requirements, needs, and expectations of the service recipient an obvious issue. Hence, the quality of work done by every participant was more or less guaranteed to a certain extent or level.

The "*owe*" of the Yoruba people of Nigeria, which was based on good team spirit, highlights participant integrity, confidence, trust, and the quality as well as the quantity of the output. The "*owe*" can, in fact, be compared with the guilds *(unions)* which began quality movement in medieval Europe in the thirteenth century though at different levels of operation.

T. A. Ibidapo, *From Industry 4.0 to Quality 4.0*, Management for Professionals,
https://doi.org/10.1007/978-3-031-04192-1_1

The motivating factors in the "*owe*" activities are the quality and quantity of work, the teamwork or organizational culture of the Yoruba people, and the resultant positive effect of the teamwork on the value and competitiveness of the agricultural produce resulting from the exercise which simply put here is the *output*.

Yoruba farmers selected their farmlands also on the basis of quality of the land (as fertilizers were not available then for improving land quality) just as the seeds for planting were selected strictly on the basis of quality to achieve good yields of crops and other agricultural produce during the harvest. These cultural practices actually culminated into what is known today in modern quality terms as "*doing it right the first time*." Quality in agricultural practices therefore begins with excellent seedlings.

In a similar vein, the production of textile yarns then in Nigeria and some other parts of the West African subregion was itself an embodiment of quality management from the time of the harvest of the plant known in Yoruba as "*elu*," the *Indigofera* or *Lonchocarpus cyanescens* species, to the dye extraction process itself. For example, in Owo, Nigeria, the quality of the dyestuff ("*aro*") extracted for the dyeing of cotton yarns (mainly light blue to dark blue coloration) then was usually assured through close monitoring from the plant stage (i.e., maturity of the virgin leaves) to ensure that only the virgin leaves are used so as to optimize the extraction process for achieving maximum amounts of dyes from the leaves and branches which were crushed and dried before the extraction process took place.

Lydia Adegbemisola Aladewolu, my grandmother, a renowned textile technologist—spinning, weaving, finishing, indigo dye production, and dyeing—often added special wood ashes to improve dye absorption, and the dye affinity for the substrate (yarns), mainly 100% cotton grown in her farms and spun by her into fibers that were also dyed by her.

The extraction bath was for the purpose of obtaining optimum dye fastness maintained at a certain level or degree of sourness or in modern terms the pH of the dye vat. To control this, the dye extraction baths which were usually carried out in massive clay pots were measured for the degree of sourness (through tasting with the tip of the tongue), on a daily basis as from the 8th to the 10th day of the bath being put in place. The dyeing of yarns was also programmed to take place in the driest months of the year, usually from October/November to April/May and at times during the August drought to ensure that the yarns get dried on a daily basis throughout the 2–3 weeks dyeing periods. The Nigerian textile dyers and weavers then had only three colors : white (i.e., yarns that were not dyed at all), light blue (i.e., lightly dyed), and dark blue (i.e., heavily dyed) at their disposal. To get yarns in these three colors, my grandmother who was a textile weaver, dyer, and merchant used to dye the yarns for varied periods of time ranging from a few times to long periods of time (up to 2 years).

Hereby, it was total quality management (TQM) at play by the highly industrious Yoruba women who were the main textile dyeing professionals involved in the production and trading of dyed textiles (mostly cotton yarns) in the then medieval Oyo Kingdom and in various parts of the South Western zone of the present Nigeria. This is probably a proof too that the South Western states of Nigeria are homes bases for quality application.

The quality movement in Europe, on the other hand, had its origin as far back as the thirteenth century when craftsmen began grouping or organizing themselves into unions known as guilds. The factory system which emphasized product inspection did not, however, come into the limelight until the middle of the 1750s in Great Britain. This later developed into or gave birth to the industrial revolution in the early 1800s. It was however, not until the dawn of the industrial revolution, and the rise in mass production in the early twentieth century, that manufacturers began to focus attention on the need to control the quality of their products. It was therefore the industrial revolution that initially led to the establishment of a quality concept nearest to what is today known to us, as quality management.

Here drastic changes were made in the way work was done. As against the previous mode whereby goods were produced from start to finish by the same person or set of people, mass production brought huge teams of people together to work on identified production stages so that one person would not necessarily complete a product from start to finish. Despite this, there were still variations in the quality of the output *(i.e., product variation)*.

This thus made it necessary to establish quality units/departments strictly to oversee and manage product quality through product inspection and rectification of errors. Ford (USA) however soon recognized that product quality is still irregular. In order to combat this problem, a bold step was taken by Ford emphasizing the *standardization of design and components* so as to ensure the standardization of industrial production outputs.

The application of statistical control to quality emerged more or less, at a later time from the World War production methods. From here quality developed further as a vehicle for controlling *process variation* as a route for achieving better product/service quality or better performance.

On a general basis, the science of quality management system, as we know it today developed as the outgrowth of the works done, by various organizations, the military and some devoted individuals or quality practitioners (gurus). These individuals or quality gurus worked tirelessly to ensure that the application of quality grew beyond the industrial or manufacturing world to other spheres of human endeavor. Today, we are talking of quality in the hospitality industries, pharmaceutical industries, insurance organizations, healthcare services providers, transportation, educational, financial, and other sectors of the economy. Today quality is applicable to all spheres of human endeavor.

Evolution of Quality

When viewed from the general perspective, quality can be said to have broadly evolved over the years through various developmental phases, one of which may be said to begin from, the *recognition of product variation, standardization of design and components, product inspection, statistical control and statistical quality control* (SQC), *quality control* to *total quality management* (TQM) before arriving at the present quality techniques that are more or less embedded in the principles of *quality management system* (QMS). It is worth mentioning here too, that the present globally acknowledged generic quality management system (QMS) principles is a far diversion from the then individual National Standards practice which emphasized individual national standards, on a product-by-product basis.

In general terms, therefore, quality can be said to have emerged from product-specific standards which were in most cases of national character, to what we globally know today as *generic standards* that are applicable and acceptable beyond national boundaries, that is, *globally*. The era of national standards saw various countries setting their own norms or standards product by product, based on different criteria. Popular were the Deutscher Industrial Norm (DIN) which actually set the pace for my early introduction to quality control in the chemical, mechanical, polymer, automobile, and textile industries just to name a few.

In depicting the historical development of quality, Weckenmann et al. [26], identified its advancement from the stage of quality inspection to total quality management (TQM) in the following order:

(i) Quality inspection—Detection and separation of deficient product.
(ii) Quality control—Identification and elimination of causes of faulty products.
(iii) Quality assurance—Ensuring preventive quality of materials immaterial products.
(iv) Quality management—Ensuring the preventive quality of processes.
(v) Total quality management—Ensuring the quality of the organization.

It must however, be mentioned here that the quality journey through these phases has generally led in one way or the other, to the development of various quality and process development concepts, systems, or programs, some of which are today of wide application, in assuring product quality and product performance improvement in various industries and enterprises including the military.

Today, the journey of quality, which began from quality control, has transmuted to the application of software in production process to achieve today's total quality management systems.

Quality by Product Inspection

Although the concept of quality has been in existence for many years, its meaning has often changed and evolved through various developmental phases over a period of time too. In the early twentieth century, it was *quality control* of finished products. Here, finished products were inspected for their degree of conformity to specifications which were then assumed to be those that would please the-then buyers or relevant to the levels acceptable in the market.

Then finished products were inspected and sorted out firstly into two classes of whether they were acceptable or not before they were further classified into the various order/level of their acceptability. While first-choice products were reserved for the primary customers or markets, second- and third-choice products were sold then at prices lower than those of the first choice to willing buyers or to members of staff at specially reduced prices or at times given free to staff.

Statistical Quality Control (SQC)

This is the application of statistical techniques to control product quality. Toward the middle of the last century, that is, in the 1940s, attention was focused more on statistical sampling techniques in the evaluation of quality. Hereby production processes were monitored with the aid of control charts also known as *quality control charts* or *run charts/tests.*

Statistical process control emphasizes the fact that random variations will always occur in a process; hence, there is the need to focus attention more toward distribution control rather than individual dimensions. Some of the common uses and application of the control chart include but are not limited to the following:

- Determination of process capability
- Process monitoring
- Achieving statistical control of a process
- Distinguishing variations in a process over a period of time

Statistical quality control (SQC) is often used interchangeably with statistical process control (SPC) which is the application of statistical techniques in evaluating the output of a process during production. This helps in controlling a process in terms of ensuring that it achieves the intent of its design.

Since quality control is concerned with the quality of conformance of the product of a process to the intent of its design, statistical process control is used to evaluate the acceptability of the product. In order to achieve this, samples of products/outputs from processes are taken periodically and comparison made with predetermined standard. Satisfactory product samples signal satisfactory quality products vis-à-vis process. Unsatisfactory sample results indicate, on the other hand, poor quality product; hence, there is the immediate need to stop the process and take corrective measures until samples compare favorably with the predetermined standard.

Modern quality management in terms of total quality management (TQM) began in the United States of America (USA) which had to respond to the then quality revolution which evolved in Japan after the Second World War. Many industries in the USA lost their market shares to foreign competitors. For example, the products of Japanese manufacturers such as Toyota and Honda in the automobile industry and Toshiba and Sony in the consumer goods market gained market advantages over those of other organizations then because of their emphasis on quality.

Total Quality Management (TQM)

It was not until the 1960s that the then *quality gurus* shifted attention toward viewing quality from a broader perspective by extending the concept of quality to encompass or include organizational-wide activities including those of its management and operational processes.

Total quality management emanated from the integration of total quality theories and management theories, with consideration for customer focus, continuous improvement and teamwork in terms of principles, practices, and techniques [9]. Slack and Lewis [25] view TQM as a philosophy for organizing quality improvement by giving considerations to the SNEaRs of both internal and external customers, across the entirety of the organization, examining the cost of quality (CoQ), being proactive and developing systems to support performance improvement.

Total quality management therefore translates into a management approach which enables an organization to achieve long-term goals [20] and sustainable development of society [19]. Such goals include among others, the embrace of customer satisfaction and achieving more competitive business activities. In further elaborating the dimensions of TQM, Oliveira et al. [17] identified the following critical organizational scopes of activities:

- Leadership management
- Employee relationships
- Reporting and data quality
- Training and skill development of employees
- Supplier quality management
- Product and service design
- Process management

Viewing TQM from a holistic perspective therefore, led to its definition by Bergman and Klefsjö [5] as:

> A constant endeavor to fulfil, and preferably exceed, customer needs and expectations at the lowest costs, by continuous improvement work, to which all involved are committed, focusing on the processes in the organization.

Both quality assurance and quality control are thus inherent parts of TQM. Quality control focuses on inspection and the use of techniques such as statistical sampling and statistical process control to achieve organizational product/services quality requirements (Bergman and Klefsjö [5]; Sader et al. [23] an ISO [11]) by ensuring that unwanted or unexpected changes or variations are prevented in order to achieve product stability and consistency [22]. Quality assurance, on the other hand, generally provides the confidence that organizational product/services quality requirements are fulfilled.

To further expatiate on TQM-related factors that may be necessary or needed to develop an organizational culture built on continuous improvement and consistent management commitment, Bergman and Klesjö [5] identified the following major aspects:

- Leadership commitment
- Customer focus
- Making decisions on the basis of facts
- Continuous/continual improvement
- Process approach
- People involvement

The ISO has in its fifth iteration—*ISO 9001:1987; ISO 9001:1994; ISO 9001:2000; ISO 9001:2008; ISO 9001:2015*—of its popular ISO 9000 series of quality management systems (QMS) standards, ISO 9001:2015, similarly introduced TQM-related seven quality management principles, as critical to the implementation of the requirements of the ISO 9001:2015 [10]. They are quite similar to the suggestions of Bergman and Klefsjö [5]—*customer focus, leadership, engagement of people, process approach, improvement, evidence-based decision-making, and relationship management.*

TQM principles were therefore developed for all processes in an organization or company including both the management functions and service sectors of the economy. This new way of viewing quality easily gained acceptance worldwide particularly since it was appreciated then that the quality of the product is affected by all organizational-wide functions and decisions. The general definition and perception restricting quality to the reactive product inspection and separation of bad ones from the good ones then had to make way for a more strategic and proactive concept.

Viewing the concept of quality from the totality of organizational-wide activities, therefore, spurred companies to pursue market survival activities based on the TQM concept by introducing various changes in their quality programs. Some organizations hired quality experts and carried out training programs for their employees.

As time went by, organizations began to realize the relevance, importance, and advantages of quality to their products/services and market performance with the appreciation of the fact that if they have to be competitive, there has to be improvement in the quality of their products or services on a continuous basis. This is a recognition too, of the fact that good quality products are likely going to get more market attention than poorer ones. Hence, there are likely going to be more sales and an improvement in the overall performance of the business.

The 1970s therefore witnessed an era of quality-based competition. Soon, the customer emerged as the first focus of quality so that the definition of quality began to shift in its emphasis to include such terms as "*meeting or exceeding customer specifications, needs, expectations and requirements,*" *(SNEaRs)*. With the concept of meeting customer specifications, needs, expectations, and requirements as the target or first priority of quality, activities surrounding quality now began to focus attention on building quality into organizational product realization processes right from the design stage through the raw materials procurement stages to the product realization stages and specified post-sales period to even include some post-sales activities.

The inclusion of product post-sales performance in organizational quality considerations actually heightened competition as more responsibilities are put into the hands of manufacturers or product makers to the advantage of end users through product guarantee/warranty to beat competition and attract customer interests in the product concerned.

While the old concept of quality control of finished products can be termed as *reactive* since they were designed and fashioned to put corrective actions in place after the product would have been made, the new concept is *proactive* with quality designed into the various product realization phases or processes across organizational-wide activities including the design stage, management activities, sales (including post-sales) delivery, organizational resources—human (employees) and materials, supplies and suppliers' activities, environment, and society in which an organization operates and responsibilities to the society at large. Other stake holders are similarly not of less importance here.

One of the hottest issues of the greatest concern to man today is the adequate disposal of postconsumer materials (including packaging). This is also a quality issue which must be considered at the design stage if the status of the quality of our environment has to be maintained to reduce environmental pollution effects and impacts on life.

The idea of TQM practice emphasizes not only the statistical process control (SPC) inputs but the consideration of other approaches which cut across the entire organizational processes. History has it today that a part of the credit of modern TQM practices which uplifted the competitive edge of Japanese products after the Second World War and beyond goes among others to quality gurus such as W. Edwards Deming, Joseph M. Juran, Phillip B. Crosby, G. Taguchi, and K. Ishikawa just to mention a few. They were among the leading pioneers in quality through the improvement of all organizational processes with the involvement of the people involved in such processes.

There is no way we can make reference to the evolution of quality from quality control to its present concept which today has embedded in it, such terms as "*continual/continuous improvement*" without mentioning the military and military industries, Ford Motors of the USA, General Motors, Toyota Production Systems, Volkswagen (VW), and the generally known quality culture of Germany and her various arms of industries ranging from textiles, automotive, chemicals to those of machinery and car production just to mention a few.

It was common in the early parts to the middle of the twentieth century to talk of the quality of manufactured products. However, the latter part of the same century witnessed tremendous improvements in the quality of products and services as well as in the development of new quality management systems (QMS) and improvement concepts based on contributions and/or foundation works of Deming, Juran, Crosby, Feigenbaum, Shewart, Ishikaya (father of quality circles), and others too many to be included here. We are today actually building on some of their foundation works to further improve and develop quality management systems, standards, or concepts that transverse national borders and cut across the various areas and aspects of production and service provision the world over.

Today, quality in its entirety has evolved beyond manufacturing systems to include heathcare, education, transportation (air, road, and railways), consultancy, hotel and catering services and pharmaceutical industries; engineering, architecture, and other services in all sectors of the global economy and every aspect of life—private and public, tangible and intangible. The developments that have so far been experienced in quality management evolved over the years because of the dynamism of change and that of people's thinking; people who took the bull by the horn, to change the status quo by positively inciting people to think differently from the usual way/practice. Various contributors to the foundation work of quality came up with many ideas, concepts, programs, and strategies which include but are not limited to the following:

- Total quality management
- Continuous improvement, or continual improvement
- Statistical quality control
- Total quality control
- Root cause analysis
- Do it right first time

The recognition of the importance of TQM in the field of quality far transcends its application in product/services provision to encompass education and research. However, research works within this domain is reportedly claimed to be still at its early stages [2] thus emphasizing the need for further research especially, in this area so as to be able to gain a clearer theoretical base of TQM [6, 8].

From my experience in small, medium, and large-scale manufacturing enterprises, it is evident that the adequate use and deployment of the four critical elements of TQM which comprises of customer focus, continuous improvement, strategic based, and total employee involvement in taking responsibilities for their individual activities generally lead to improved organizational performance in both the manufacturing and services sectors of the economy. This conclusion supports research findings by various researchers.

For example, Li et al. [15] confirmed that continuous improvement is recognized as the most useful aspect to enhance competitiveness, efficiency, quality, and performance in both manufacturing and service industries, while Abusa and Gibson [1] showed in their research works that continuous improvement was significantly correlated with customer satisfaction while describing top management commitment as the most crucial factor for TQM to succeed. This thus makes it a key critical financial performance predictor. Pambreni et al. [18] in their more expansive studies established the fact too that "total employee involvement had a positive and significant effect on organization performance."

Quality Footprints

Quality gurus are people who have made tremendous contributions to the growth and development of the science of quality and its management methodologies over the years. People who gained prominence by working tirelessly to create and/or change the techniques, perceptions, and general views about quality are today referred to as "*quality gurus.*" It is apparent and obvious from the history of the development of quality and quality management that they will forever be remembered for their respective roles as major contributors and innovators.

You may wonder why the author decides to mention the quality gurus in this book when there are sufficient references to them and their works on quality. Mentioning the names of some quality gurus and some of their achievements in this book generally serve here to motivate young or potential experts in the field of quality and quality management just as I have been motivated by their efforts and achievements.

Though most writers trace the origin of the quality movement to W. Edward Deming, Joseph M. Juran, and Philip B. Crosby, the contributions of Frederick W. Taylor, the father of scientific management, in 1911 and those of others have been of great importance in the development of quality to its present level of importance.

Some of the publications of the quality gurus generally serve as the fundamental academic references and building blocks of the global quality library and development. Most prominent in this long list of quality achievers and thinkers who have changed the global market economy, include but are not limited to the following:

- W. Edwards Deming
- Philip B. Crosby
- Armand V. Feigenbaum
- Kaoru Ishikawa
- Joseph M. Juran
- Walter A. Shewhart

W. Edwards Deming

Deming was a great believer in quality. His devotion to quality was outstanding particularly during and after the Second World War. Deming along with Walter Shewhart pioneered statistical quality control (SQC). Deming who taught statistical methods in Japan is credited with a lot of accomplishments in global quality management most particularly in the post-Second World War era. Some of his landmark achievements in quality include but are not limited to the following:

- 14 Points eliminating the Seven Deadly Diseases and help organizations to survive and flourish in the long term.
- The Deming Cycle, Plan-Do-Study-Act (PDSA), a variation of the Shewhart cycle, Plan-Do-Check-Act.

- The red bead experiment which showed that the only way to improve a product or service is for management to improve the system.

The indelible quality footprints left for us by Deming was explicitly described by him in his own words (ASQ) [4]:

- "Quality is everybody's responsibility."
- "There is no substitute for knowledge."
- "It is not enough to do your best. You must know what to do and then do your best."
- "If you can't describe what you are doing as a process, you don't know what you're doing."
- "It is not necessary to change. Survival is not mandatory."
- "Defects are not free. Somebody makes them and he is paid for making them."
- "He who runs his company on visible figures alone will soon have neither company nor visible figures to work with."
- "The job of management is not supervision but leadership."

These are actually motivational expressions that will continue to be relevant to quality management for ever, Moen and Norman [16].

Philip B. Crosby
Philip Crosby is one of the foremost contributors to the development of quality management. Some of his achievements are briefly summed up as follows:

- The *zero defects* concept as a standard of excellence by which it is required for people to perform to the requirement that has been agreed to, and *do it right every time*.
- Cost of quality.
- Fourteen (14) Steps of Quality Improvement including the *zero defects* concept.
- *Crosby* developed the concept of "*zero defects,*" and the phrase "*do it right the first time*" and promoted "*prevention.*"
- Four absolutes of quality management
- His definition of quality and non-quality, "Quality is conformance to requirements; non-quality is nonconformance."

The contributions of Crosby to permanently change the quality world could also be found in some of his quotes [14] which still serve today as part of his quality footprints:

- "Quality is free. It's not a gift but it's free. What costs money are the '*unquality*' things—all the actions that involve not doing jobs right the first time."
- "Good things only happen when planned; bad things happen on their own."
- "Why spend all this time finding, fixing and fighting when you could have prevented the problem in the first place?"

- "It isn't what you find; it's what you do about what you find."
- Quality management is needed because nothing is simple anymore, if indeed it ever was."
- "The customer deserves to receive exactly what we have promised to produce-a clean room, a hot cup of coffee, a nonporous casing, a trip to the moon on gossamer wings."
- "You as a manager have an obligation to demand continual improvement from your operation, whether you are in the accounting business or a machine shop. You have an obligation to provide thoughtful and imaginative leadership. What you put out is what you get back" [7]

Armand V. Feigenbaum

Feigenbaum, who through his coinage of the term *total quality control* (TQC), could be said to be the architect of today's modern quality management, *total quality management* (TQM). As one of the world's first true quality professionals, Feigenbaum indelibly inscribed his footprints in the world of quality and quality management. Some of these quality footprints are visibly expressed in Feigenbaum's own words as indicated in the following:

- "An important feature of a good quality program is that it controls quality at the source."
- "Total quality control is an effective system for integrating the quality development, quality maintenance, and quality improvement efforts of the various groups in an organization so as to enable production and service at the most economical levels which allow for full customer satisfaction."
- "[Quality is] the total composite product and service characteristic of marketing, engineering, manufacturing and maintenance through which the product and service in use will meet the expectations of the customer."

Joseph M. Juran

Juran was one of the earliest to effectively identify and rightly point out the need for the enhancement of the *human side of quality* in *managing for quality*. Some of the key contributions of Juran to quality management include but are not limited to the following:

- The Juran Trilogy which emphasizes the roles of planning, control, and improvement in quality management.
- Quality planning roadmap for product and process development.
- The application of the Pareto principle, or the 80–20 rule to quality. In this, he stressed that 80% of problems come from 20% of causes.
- Quality is fitness for use.

Kaoru Ishikawa

Ishikawa was best known for starting the Japanese *Quality Circle* and the *Cause-and-Effect diagram*, a quality tool also known as the *Fishbone diagram* or *Ishikawa diagram* (named after him). He was a quality pioneer in Japan where he worked with some other quality gurus to promote quality practices that helped in the growth and development of industries in Japan. Ishikawa contributed to the recognition of the fact too that, *customers are the only reasons for the existence of a business.*

- Cause-and-Effect diagram/Fishbone diagram/Ishikawa diagram
- Quality Circle Movement

Water A. Shewhart

Shewhart was known as the father of statistical quality control. He became prominent particularly in the area of quality improvement through his work in the following:

- Development of the control chart
- Use and application of statistical quality control for quality improvement and in the explanation of process variability
- Problem-solving concepts, that is, the Shewhart straight line process and Shewhart cyclical concept, which were the evolutionary basis for the Deming Plan-Do-Study-Act (PDSA) and the Plan-Do-Check (PDCA), commonly referred to today as the Shewhart Cycle [7]

The contributions of the quality gurus and other individuals, organizations, and the military in quality development is enormous and have jointly given today's world open ticket for future growth and development of quality. They are all appreciated even though we cannot mention their names in just one book.

Definition of Quality

Quality has actually assumed various definitional dimensions as it evolved and grew from one stage/phase to another. Quality has been defined at one stage or the other and by one author or the other variously and vividly as follows:

- Compliance with specified requirements
- Reduction of variation
- Fitness for use
- Value added
- Conformance to requirements
- Conformance to specifications
- Meeting customer requirements
- Customer satisfaction

- Degree to which a set of inherent characteristics fulfill requirements (ISO 9000:2015) [11]
- Degree of excellence
- Meeting determined standard
- Excellent
- Delighting customers

Customer Focus

Viewing the various definitions of quality gives us the opportunity to identify the fact that the focus of quality is on the customer and should be on the customer. This is very obvious as the terms "requirements" and "specifications" that your goods have to "conform to" or "comply with" as referred to in the various definitions are those of the products and/or services of your customer. The focus of quality is therefore directly on the final customer of your production process. This is like beginning a journey with the focus of your mind and attention on the destination despite the fact that you may have some other critical issues to view in the intermediate stages. As a result of this, every manufacturer, services provider, and any other business enterprise owner need to realize the fact that customers are the final judges of their activities through their impression off your process output. The customers' decision may go three ways when they are not satisfied:

- Inform you directly, as a product/service provider, of their dissatisfaction
- Make it known simply by withdrawing their patronage
- Tell others about their dissatisfaction

The withdrawal of patronage has further consequences and impact on your business as every unsatisfied customer may likely inform potential buyers or customers. The ultimate impact here is summed up as follows:

- Loss of sales
- Reduction in market share
- Probable loss of business

Misconception of the Term "Quality"

The term "*quality*" is more often than not erroneously emphasized as being only applicable to manufactured products. This is a common perception generally by various consumers all over the world but particularly people in the West African subregion where, due to its high level of poverty and low level of manufacturing or industrial activities, quality was until recently more an issue of rhetoric than a tool for measuring product and service acceptability by respective customers.

The commencement of the use of the term "*quality*" actually had its origin from its use and application in manufacturing. This is probably the reason why in most cases and in most parts of the West African subregion quality is today still misconstrued by most people as being only applicable or referring to the manufacturing industry and the products emanating from it.

In the manufacturing environment, quality has been found, over the years, to have aided the improvement of products and services, product and process reliability as well as leading to increased productivity and product performance.

It is also true too that the effective application of a suitable quality management system (QMS) or quality concept in manufacturing and other processes often results in improved productivity, measurable in terms of some appropriate key performance indicators (KPIs). Examples of the basis of some KPIs are as follows:

- Number of defective products in relationship to number of products manufactured
- Percentage production wastages both in terms of either acceptable products or total materials (input) consumed
- Efficiency (e.g., process, labor, materials, and machine)
- Down time including breakdown time (unplanned)
- Productivity (e.g., machine-, labor-, energy-, materials-, and capital productivity)
- Product sales both in terms of number and value
- Product cost—cost-effective production
- Material efficiency—level of material wastages and other wastages emanating from the quality and suitability of materials used for production or inventory
- Number, quantity, and frequency of product recalls per unit time
- Level of product noncompliance with statutory regulations over a period of time
- Profit/loss
- Management reaction time to production, sales customer matters/issues
- Customer feedback preferably in a measurable form/pattern

The effective implementation of specific or suitable quality management systems (QMS) or concepts in the manufacturing and services industries has today assumed more relevant position in the current globalization of the world market economy than it has ever been. In order for an organization to be on top of competition both in terms of value and product performance, the present and future levels of competitiveness in the global market place calls more and more for improved dynamism in the following:

- Developing new routes for business performance and improvement
- The methods and ways of designing products and services
- Production techniques
- Marketing and selling mechanism
- Delivering products and services which meet and surpass customer specifications, needs, and requirements as well as environmental requirements (i.e.,

stated, generally implied, in line with market demands, and obligatory/statutory guidelines)
- Moving with technological advancements/developments
- Branding and re-branding
- Benchmarking
- Differentiating your products/services (and even your organization) from the others through innovation

An important route for achieving this is the proper implementation, application, and maintenance of a suitable quality management and/or improvement concept/system or integrated quality management systems. The use of an integrated management system (IMS) may even be what is needed or appropriate for your own type of business situation. In order to have a good understanding of the science of quality, some of the terms commonly used are listed and defined in various parts of this book and at the end.

Need to Redefine Quality

The growing needs of quality or the spreading application of quality is by its own right calling for or necessitating a redefinition of quality (Chap. 19). Viewing quality from the point of view of its evolution in the twentieth century and its application then reveals so much about the extent of how much quality has grown in the universality of its use and application. Hence, quality is more universal today than in the era of our "*quality gurus*" and it is going to be more and more universal from year to year.

Growing from industrial production application to the current global use and application of quality in virtually all aspects of human endeavor—business, services, healthcare, governance, environment, human living standard, aerospace, transportation, education, etc., makes quality a key part of human existential essentials, needs and requirements.

The application and use of quality management principles, tools, and techniques, not just in suppressing the pains of the COVID-19 pandemic but also in the production of vaccines to eradicate the coronavirus, is definitely the greatest pointer to the fact that quality is universal in protecting both our planet and the human beings living in it. Quality is universal; hence, there is the need to redefine quality from the daily emerging perspectives of its use and application. Quality does not discriminate; it respects the culture and relationship of the recipients and beneficiaries of the valued outcome of its efforts.

As we move deeper into the first half of the twenty-first century, quality shall most assuredly grow to be a global culture not just of organizational sustainability but also that of human existential sustainability. This is particularly so in our present world in which the intertwining of nature, wildlife, and humans accelerates the risks of disruptive disease spread across the globe to threaten the quality of human life.

Quality has neither religion nor political affiliation, hence, its accessibility to all peoples of the global community as a strong binding force, once its potentials are realized by all the people of the world, irrespective of race and nationality.

It is very interesting to take note that the dynamism of quality shall continuously be redefined by envisaged business changes that we may experience in the twenty-first century. These envisaged changes may be defined from the perspectives of the following developmental features:

- Business *sustainability* in the face of predictable/unpredictable, foreseen, and unforeseen environment and circumstances.
- *Technological* advances as they may be emerging now and how they will emerge in the future—5th- to nth-generation cellular wireless technology, advancements in artificial intelligence (AI) use and application, machine learning, information technology, social media, etc. Impact of *Industry 4.0 initiatives* on quality as they evolve in industrial manufacturing sector.
- *Globalization* of the world economy.
- Changing *customer and market culture* and organizational ability to exhibit the needed flexibility and adaptability.
- The impact of *changing demographics* creating the general need for diversity in quality professionalism and skills acquisition.
- Growing need for supply chain reevaluation and restructuring as and whenever needed.

Quality management dynamism is going to be at the dictates of the changes in the business environment and their interrelationships. This shall, in turn, require the attention of quality professionals to fill the resulting loopholes in quality management skills.

It follows therefore that the concept of quality is not just becoming more and more universal in use and application but a globally available *value* phenomenon of extreme values to individuals and entities to the extent that any organization that fails to embrace quality at all operational levels, does so at its own peril. Well, it depends on whether survival is compulsory or not. Quality is the way for value creation and sustainability of relationships.

Approach to Quality

Systems Approach

The systems approach for finding solutions to quality problems has most recently gained more and more prominence. It is for this reason that the author finds it necessary to discuss it here. You will observe too that the word "system" is frequently used in the quality world too.

A system can generally be defined as "*a set or group of interdependent processes/activities and/or functions that work together to achieve a common goal.*" A good example of a system is the production system whereby various equipment/machinery, processes, and functions are put together by people to transform appropriate combination of resources (input) into products (output).

Systems common to the productive sectors of the economy include but are not limited to the following:

- Economic system
- Personnel/Human Resources system
- Quality management system (e.g., ISO 9000 QMS)
- Environmental management system (e.g., ISO 14000 EMS)
- Risk management system
- Health and safety management system (OHSAS 18000 HSMS)
- Production system
- Central nervous system
- Management information system

Management System

The management system can simply be defined as "*a set of coordinated interrelated or interacting activities/elements that is put in place to direct and control an organization.*" It should, among others, lead to the establishment of organizational policy and objectives and its achievement.

The management system of an organization generally includes different management systems such as the following:

- Quality management system (customer/clientele need to feel certain that they will get what they ordered as and when they need it).
- Financial management system.
- Environmental management system (society at large and authorities expect businesses to care for the environment).
- Engineering management system.
- Project management system.
- Risk management system (the expectations here are that businesses should generally be managed in such a way as to protect shareholder interests by ensuring that efforts are made to identify all possible and potential risks and/or risk areas and appropriate measures or machineries put in place to completely avert them or at least to reduce the negative impact on affected businesses to the barest minimum. It is the failure to recognize the relevance and importance of risk management or the absence of risk management systems in the Nigerian Banking sector of her economy coupled with the global meltdown that almost led to the collapse of some Nigerian banks toward the end of the last decade).
- Safety management system (it is expected that businesses shall maintain a safe working environment where workers and all others transacting businesses with an organization are protected against any danger/risk).

Production System

The production system is, according to Kolarik [13], "an integrated collection of people and processes that together transforms resources into products." The individual or component parts around which the production system hovers are based as follows:

- Resources, (i.e., people and materials)
- Processes, (i.e., machinery/equipment and technology)
- Products, (i.e., output)

The process can therefore be generally seen as the vehicle for the transformation of resources, that is, *inputs* into value-added products/services (i.e., outputs). The production system is generally driven by the need to meet market or customer (internal and external) demands, needs, requirements (stated, generally implied or regulatory) and expectations while getting some returns on whatever investments that may have been made. Hence, products are at the end of the day assessed by customers on the basis of the following:

- Their ability to perform the functions and/or purposes for which they were meant
- Their durability
- The values/benefits derivable from them.

Similarly, Kolarik [13] defines *value* as "*the ratio of worth to cost*"

$$\text{Value} = \text{Worth} / \text{Cost}$$

Worth is associated here with customer benefits while cost is associated with customer burdens.

Artzt [3] expresses customer value as

$$\text{Value} = \text{Performance} / \text{Cost} = \text{Quality} + \text{Speed} + \text{Flexibility} / \text{Cost}$$

Using the general perception, one can easily say that the production system transforms a set of resources into a set of products and by-products by adding value to them. This is referred to as *value-added* which is the term used in industry to describe the difference between the cost of inputs and the value (or price) of outputs.

The inputs may include among others the following:

- Knowledge/intellectual
- Skill
- Machines/equipment
- Information
- Tools
- Energy
- Supplies
- Experience

- Facilities—clinics/hospitals, buildings, offices, etc.
- Materials
- Vehicles
- Water
- Land

Transformation of inputs into outputs can be achieved through processes, examples of which are, drilling, mixing, farming, packing, canning, punching, consulting, teaching, transporting, extrusion, molding (injection- and blow-molding), and painting.

Outputs could be tangible or intangible. Tangible outputs are goods (e.g., computers, houses, vehicles, food products, and textbooks), while intangible ones are in the form of services (e.g., vehicle repairs, entertainment, legal services, banking, communication, consultancy, and counseling).

Value System

Value is one of the most commonly used expressions or concepts among consumers who are always desirous of getting "*value for money.*" In order to get desired value for money, every consumer tends to weigh and calculate the total worth of a product to him against the price he is expected to pay for it in the market before purchasing. Determining the worth of a product/service requires a consideration of many individual factors and their individual components. Some of such factors include but are not limited to the following:

- Product reliability.
- Product availability.
- Product durability.
- Competitive product prices.
- The ability of product to adequately and conveniently meet customer needs, requirements, and specifications.
- Potential of product to meet performance requirements.
- Offering customers the option of choice in terms of product variety.
- Readily available and easily accessible post-sales customer support services.
- Compliance of product use and/or application with statutory/regulatory guidelines.
- Provision of necessary guidelines/information and their clarity for the use of consumers in the safe handling of product and its packaging.
- Ease of disposal of product after its consumption.
- Reputation and integrity of product and its manufacturer/maker coupled with the degree of product (or brand) acceptance in the market. For example, a loyal customer would place more value and priority to purchase a product to which he has loyalty than the one to which he has none.

- Product service system, that is, downstream after-sales, or sales follow-up, is a necessary quality management process representing a core part of an organization's key quality approach to doing business. This is particularly at the forefront of quality, in an era of global embrace of e-commerce and online market platform.

The dynamism of the buying patterns thus require that any noticeable changes should increasingly integrate quality with customer value. This is the reason why, according to Sampaio and Saraiva [24], organizations committed to quality must have to "build their quality programs, throughout the customer value chain, by integrating and connecting all key quality work process," a principle claimed here to be applicable to quality in both the public sector, and society at large, particularly viewed at the local, state, regional, and even international levels.

Most of the factors listed above generally help the customer to decide the level of product acceptability and to define the level of customer satisfaction for a particular product or service. Both of these are in turn used jointly to determine or estimate how much that product is worth. Hence, it can generally be said that the value that a customer attaches to a product is most times generally a reflection of considerations given to the above-specified factors since virtually every customer calculates product value at one stage or the other before any purchases so as to be able to determine items of acceptable values. Despite the complex nature of the customer value system, the key factors at play here may be grouped generally into three categories as indicated in the following:

- Quality of product/service
- Price of product/service
- Market reputation/integrity of product/service (i.e., brand) and/or that of the manufacturer

Since most of your customers or consumers of your products would always want to have "*value for money*" in all their transactions with you vis-à-vis your products, it is very important for you to pay particular attention to the continual use and application of the "value" concept and its full implications as a very useful competitive tool to improve the market performance of each of your product lines especially since value is not only relative but product and market specific.

Competitiveness

Competitiveness can generally be described as the "*degree of effectiveness with which an organization meets the needs of customers relative to its contemporaries or other organizations that offer similar goods and services.*". Competition is a healthy development particularly for the consumers who actually derive some benefits from it. Consumers or customers generally weigh the values they attach with goods and services before they decide to purchase a particular product or service.

Competition can be viewed or assessed from various perspectives which include but are not limited to the following:

- Product/service quality
- The way customers are handled or treated
- Delivery time/timeliness/response time
- Yield
- The ease with which customers are rewarded, for example, in terms of warranty and insurance claims as examples here.
- Precision
- Safety and ease of product use and/or application
- Product price/cost/value
- Product packaging
- Specific features—design, ease of use, perception of long product life, guarantee/warranty, risk of use, etc.
- Clear communication to the consumers/users in the clearest and most unambiguous language
- After-sales services and accessibility to manufacturer representative regarding user or consumer complaints
- Post-usage disposal (including packaging) with reference to impact on the environment and respect to statutory/regulatory guidelines or requirements
- Maintainability
- Adaptability
- Durability
- Reliability
- Listening to the voice of the customer (VOC)

A key factor that effectively aids the competitiveness of any organization is the ability of the concerned organization to identify and determine the needs, requirements, and the expectations of its customer(s). This is very important just as it is a key customer satisfaction factor needed to keep your customers; hence, every organization must strive to achieve and even exceed or surpass the needs, requirements, and expectations of its customers.

Quality Control (QC) to Quality Assurance (QA)

Quality as we know it today evolved initially from product inspection which gave birth to quality control. With the aid of product inspection, poor quality or defective products are removed after production and classified into various "*degrees of goodness or categories of how bad they are.*" Those with less defects and can be reworked are selected and reworked before being sold to customers. Those that cannot be reworked are selected and separated into various classes or categories (e.g., grades 2, 3, 4, ……. *n*, or simply 2nd, 3rd, 4th…. *n*th grades) before they are sold at reduced prices and at times given to employees or in the worse scenario scrapped and/or recycled.

The quality control concept and the processes associated with it which dominated most parts of the last century were emphasized mainly for finished products. The implication here is that the total cost of all the inputs such as raw materials, direct and indirect labor, administrative costs, energy, special tooling, finishing, processing, machinery and equipment maintenance, and transportation of those defective or substandard products which are, as a result of the defects, sold at reduced prices or given away or scrapped or recycled may be wholly or partially irrecoverable thereby negatively affecting the targeted business profits and at the same time hinder an organization's ability to effectively compete in the global market place which is getting more and more competitive day in day out.

On the other hand, quality control does not actually assure the product buyer/end-user/consumer the quality of the product. Instead, the responsibility for the monitoring of the product quality when in use or in service is more or less wholly or completely transferred to the end-users such that the "buyer beware" (caveat emptor) warning had to be used directly or indirectly to caution end-users in some cases.

Product quality was somehow revolutionized toward the end of the last century by emphasizing quality assurance (QA) of all the inputs (tangible and intangible) and processing activities from design, development, supplies, production, manufacturing, installation/assembly, documentation to servicing, inventory, maintenance, and even after sales services.

It follows therefore from here that the quality assurance concept focuses attention generally on every stage of the work (i.e., process approach) and all the processes for realizing the product. These include but are not limited to the following:

- The conceptual or pre-design stage.
- Design stage.
- Regulation of resources—human, raw materials, and all other inputs.
- Control of assembly/processing/manufacturing processes.
- Regulation, measuring, and monitoring of production and manufacturing parameters and equipment; maintenance of components and machinery.
- Regulation and regular calibration of all monitoring and measurement equipment/devices.
- Measurement and monitoring of in-process products as they evolve from one production stage to the other. The earlier a bad subproduct is withdrawn from the production process or cycle, the less the total input into a product that would be rejected at the end of the day on the grounds of quality failure. It is therefore better to identify any bad subproduct exactly at the processing stage in which the cause of failure was inflicted. Hence, it is highly imperative that production *errors/faults* must be discovered and discarded at the point of commitment to assure and ensure that no other value is further added to it.
- The control of all other services linked with production. For example, the supplier activities must be controlled not just in terms of quality and quantity but

also in terms of delivery time, regular payment to suppliers, adequate and effective communication, etc.
- Marketing and sales activities.
- After sales services (including product/service warranty/guarantee) and the implementation of customer feedback.
- Provision of guidelines for the disposal and/or handling of product packaging materials and in some cases the products themselves after usage.
- Strict compliance with regulatory and environmental requirements and guidelines applicable to products and services both during and after usage.

It follows from here that in contrary to the QC concept of the old time in which end-users still bear some responsibilities for some quality checks for products purchased by them, quality assurance measures have brought more quality services to the doorsteps of product purchasers or end-users by entrenching quality control measures at the various processing levels and stages of production. It may therefore be said that QC is a key element of QA.

First of all, QA ensures that the product is made to meet the requirements, needs, and specifications of the customer/end-users. This has led to the goods and/or services providers or suppliers accepting responsibilities for certain factory/production defects and/or malfunctions discovered in use/service. Hence, products carry today more warranty/guarantee than it has ever been.

Recalls of defective products from the market are also ways of ensuring customer satisfaction and delight though at a cost higher than cases of defect detection before the products get to the market (see cost of quality). The recall of thousands of cars of various models by some vehicle manufacturing companies and the huge costs incurred by the company in the USA in 2009 is still fresh in our minds.

It has therefore become very clear to both suppliers and customers today that in order to achieve products and services of value that are fit for the purposes for which they are meant in all ramifications (i.e., performance and physical), every input and process involved in product development and production as well as those involved in the provision of various other services mus be "*done right the first time.*" This is not just one of the most important routes for assuring product and service quality but should be seen simply as the universal basics of assuring the quality of products and services.

Principles of Quality Assurance

The term Quality Assurance is described by the International Organization for Standardization, ISO in ISO 9000:2015 as "*part of quality management focused on providing confidence that quality requirements will be fulfilled*" [10, 11] generally encompasses the following principles:

- Getting and considering information from customer about product/service requirements and specifications.

- Getting and following regulatory requirements that are applicable, related to, or associated with product/service, its usage, application, and at times its disposal (after use).
- Planning of product/service design and manufacturing/processing with consideration for customer requirements, specifications, and needs as well as regulatory/statutory guidelines.
- Controlling, ensuring, and regulating the quality of all the inputs and resources which serve as input into a system (including materials and human capital).
- Designing and/or selecting the most suitable, appropriate, and most valuable production methodology/principles/processes.
- Monitoring and regulating production process parameters.
- Measuring and controlling production processes to ensure process optimization devoid of wastages.
- Analysis of data to assess process effectiveness and identify areas for continual improvement.
- Using key performance indicators (KPIs) to provide needed feedback about the performance of the system (including departmental and organizational) and to assess its improvement status on a regular basis.
- Documenting the processes, monitoring, and operating parameters.
- Keeping the record of major and critical activities for a planned and suitably determined period of time for use in the improvement of the quality management systems.
- Checking/reviewing of the processes, products/services, and other output to plan and achieve the continual improvement of the system.
- Using results of product and process checks/reviews and experience as key inputs into the improvement cycle.
- Using technological development as a basis for updating and improving machinery/equipment and processes in the improvement cycle.

The principles of QA can generally be said to have aided the focus of attention on customer needs, requirements, expectations, and specifications thereby deviating from the concept of product inspection which used to be the core activity for controlling product quality. It is in view of the recognition of the need to satisfy and delight the customer that various quality management systems (QMSs), quality concepts and programs which focus attention on the customer were developed and introduced for use to assure the quality of products and services.

Quality assurance/quality control may therefore be viewed as actions that are generally performed to ensure the quality of a product/service or process. Both quality assurance and quality control thus form fundamental parts of *quality management* which may be defined according to the ISO as the, "*coordinated activities to direct and control an organization with regard to quality.*"

Some of these quality management systems, quality concepts and programs, and their application to improve and develop industry/enterprises/businesses in order to improve their performance are the major focus of this book which provides guide for product performance improvement.

Commercial Birth of Quality

The original approach to quality prior to and including quality activities in the twentieth century completely relegated humanity and the quality of life to the back seat as quality interests were viewed strictly from the purview of the commercial activities of men and country, and the value system emanating from their output. Quality was then mainly about industry and the industrial value systems to boost national economies.

Consumed by global wars of international political and economic supremacy, there was no reference at all then, as to quality in the way people live, and should live from day to day. This situation continued through a major part of the twentieth century. Although the activities of war, especially those pertaining to the fallen heroes of war, irrespective of nationality, should have evoked our senses of the quality of life, it did not. It is therefore clearly evident that quality was born mainly out of the commercial and economic interests of man rather than that of man himself. This, however, negates the Godly emergence of quality in the Garden of Eden, when "the tree of the knowledge of good and evil" was qualitatively rendered noncompliant with man's originally planned quality of life.

References

1. Abusa, F. M., & Gibson, P. (2011). TQM implementation in developing countries: A case study of the Libyan industrial sector. *Benchmarking: An International Journal, 20*(5), 693–711.
2. Aquilani, B., Silvestri, C., Ruggieri, A., & Gatti, C. (2017). A systematic literature review on total quality management critical success factors and the identification of new avenues of research. *The TQM Journal, 29*(1), 184–218. https://doi.org/10.1108/TQM-01-2016-0003
3. Artzt, E. L. (1992). CEO of Procter and Gamble, Quality Forum VIII, October.
4. ASQ. Quality Glossary. www.asq.org
5. Bergman, B., & Klefsjö, B. (2010). *Quality from customer needs to customer satisfaction* (3rd ed.). Student literature.
6. Carnerud, D., & Backstrom, I. (2021). Four decades of research on quality, summarizing, trendspotting and looking ahead. *Journal of Total Quality Management and Business Excellence, 32*, 1023–1045. https://doi.org/10.1080/14783363.2019.1655397
7. Crosby, P. B. (2005). Crosby's 14 steps to improvement. *Quality Progress*, pp. 60–64.
8. Dahlgaard-Park, S. M., Reyes, L., & Chen, C.-K. (2018). The evolution and convergence of total quality management and management theories. *Journal of Total Quality Management and Business Excellence, 29*(9–10), 1108–1128, 20th QMOD.
9. Dean, J. W., Jr., & Bowen, D. E. (1994). Management theory and total quality: Improving research and practice through theory development. *Academy of Management Review, 19*(3), 392–418.
10. International Organization for Standardization, ISO (2015), ISO 9001:2015, Quality management systems – Requirements.
11. International Organization for Standardization, ISO, (2015), ISO 9000:2015, Quality management systems – Fundamentals and vocabulary.
12. International Standards Organization. (2005). *ISO 9000:2005, Quality management systems – Fundamentals and vocabulary*. ISO.
13. Kolarik, W. J. (1999). *Creating quality, process design for results*. McGraw-Hill.
14. Krzykowski, B., & Adrian, N., & Edmund, M. (2010). Guru guide. *Quality Progress*, pp. 14–21.

15. Li, J., Papadopolous, C. T., & Zang, L. (2016). Continuous improvement in manufacturing and service systems. *International Journal of Production Research, 54*, 6281–6284.
16. Moen, R. D., & Norman, C. L. (2010, November). Circling back. *Quality Progress*, pp. 22–28.
17. Oliveira, G. S., Correa, J. E., Balestrassi, P. P., Martins, R. A., & Turrioni, J. B. (2017). Investigation of TQM implementation: Empirical investigation in Brazilian ISO 9001-Registered SMEs. *Total Quality Management and Business Excellence, (30)*2, 1–19.
18. Pambreni, Y., Khatibi, A., Azam, F. S. M., & Tham, J. (2019). The influence of total quality management toward organization performance. *Management Science Letters, 9*, 1397–1406.
19. Petrovic, N., Ivin, D., Joksimovic, D., Sajifert, D., & Mjedenjak, M. (2018). The role of implementation of the concept – Total quality management in organizations. In *VIII International conference on industrial engineering and environmental protection*, Zrenjanin, Serbia.
20. Petrovic, N., Terek, E., Sajifert, D., & Rajkovic, J. (2020). The role of engineering and TQM in improving the quality of business in organizations, *Acta Technica Corviniensis, Bulletin of Engineering*, Tome XIII, 2020, Fascicule1, January-March.
21. Radziwill, N. (2018). Designing a quality 4.0 strategy and selecting high-impact initiatives. In *ASQ quality 4.0 summit, disruption, innovation and change*. ASQ.
22. Radziwill, N. (2018, October). Let's get digital: The many ways the fourth industrial revolution is reshaping the way we think about quality. *Quality Progress*, pp. 24–29.
23. Sader, S., Husti, I., & Daroczi, M. (2019). Industry 4.0 as a key enabler toward successful implementation of total quality management practices. *Periodica Politechnica Social and Management Sciences, 27*(2), 131–140.
24. Sampaio, P., & Saraiva, P. (2016). Quality. In *From past perfect to future conditional, quality in the 21st century* (p. 20). Springer Nature.
25. Slack, N., & Lewis, M. (2017). *Operations strategy* (5th ed.). Pearson Education Ltd.
26. Weckenmann, A., Akkasoglu, G., & Werner, T. (2015). Quality management – History and trends. *The TQM Journal, 27*(3), 281–293. https://doi.org/10.1108/TQM-11-2013-0125

Quality Overview

2

Natural Phenomenon in Quality

Nature itself appreciates the general need for the "*homo sapiens*" to appreciate the quality of his/her immediate environment in order to be able to define its survival criteria. This is generally reflected and demonstrated in the abilities of the Homo sapiens to see (*eye*), smell (*nose*), feel (*nerves*), hear (*ears*), and think (*brain*). These senses which are present in virtually all animals serve as natural tools for assessing the quality of the environment in which they live in and carry out their day-to-day activities and their subsequent reaction with the sole objective of determining the quality, that is, risk or suitability of a particular environment for their continued stay, existence, and survival.

Smell, for example, can be used to remind us of when to take out the baggage for disposal, change baby diapers, and for the perception and recognition of the things that we taste.

Our sense of smell has been a major quality tool for the detection of danger, for example, gas leakages in the kitchen and exposure to car exhaust fumes in the garage or burnt food in the kitchen. Nature therefore can actually be seen as an embodiment and pioneer of environmental quality management and assessment which preceded the evolution of the term "*quality*" as it is known to us today.

The *E-nose* (electronic nose) which is a modern mimic of the natural nose is, according to some works of the author and some other scientists, getting more and more prominent as a modern tool in defining the quality of some agricultural produce such as cassava, tomatoes, mango, and cocoa [1, 2].

Journey to Quality

The evolution of quality which began with product inspection about two centuries ago has so far been punctuated mainly with quality control, quality assurance, and quality management systems (QMS) to ensure and achieve what is lately known as

T. A. Ibidapo, *From Industry 4.0 to Quality 4.0*, Management for Professionals,
https://doi.org/10.1007/978-3-031-04192-1_2

customer satisfaction on a continual improvement basis. Hence, quality may be seen as an endless journey full of drive to achieve the never-ending desires of customers to get more and more and ever renewed value of the products and services that are put at their disposal or made available for their consumption.

Despite the evolutionary changes in quality and the way it has been managed, there seem to have been no changes per se in the basic objectives of quality which is to achieve as *effectively* and *efficiently* as possible only those products and services that are needed, wanted (i.e., those that meet customer *requirements* and *specifications*), and are of *value* to the customer/consumers. It is therefore critical here to ensure, on a general basis, that variations and defects are avoided in all inputs and outputs just as it should be in all processing stages. Hence, key production processes, if not all, need to be put under the strictest possible control and monitoring measures. To achieve this, attention has to be generally focused on the following:

- Ways to prevent defects, wastes, and process variability through effective planning using the most suitable and adequate resources (human and materials alike) at the barest minimum costs following the "*do it right first time*" and "*quality from source*" slogans of quality management.
- The identification and elimination of sources of defects/wastes and variations in production processes or in the way services are provided or achieved so as to enhance product/service values as seen from the customer and/or consumer perspectives.
- Ways for achieving effective and efficient process control and the measurement and quantification of defects/wastes and process variability with the intention and motive of putting in place preventive and/or corrective measures with the ultimate objectives of achieving as much as is possible "*zero defects.*"
- Adding values to products and services through effective communication with the customer and listening to and keeping in constant touch with the voice of the customer (VOC), acting on customer and/or consumer feedback, ensuring prompt and timely deliveries on the basis of the terms agreed with the customer.
- Achieving regular management reviews of your quality management system based on customer feedback, internal and external audit reports, corrective and preventive actions, technological developments/advancement in terms of machinery, equipment, and techniques, current competitive market demands and ways to bridge any competitive gaps through benchmarking, the introduction of innovations and innovative ideas, and the introduction of any other improvement measures.

The endless journey to quality has, along the way, in the last century attracted the attention of many quality gurus and followers, some of whom have walked and worked tirelessly and assiduously along the way to create quality systems and concepts for the improvement of the quality of the human society and its entire environment.

The globalization of the world market economy has in the most recent times led to situations whereby quality has completely taken the driver's seat of the developmental vehicle of virtually all businesses including large and small organizations/businesses, companies, and enterprises in their drive to achieve and adequately manage their production operations in a bid to promote their products and services in a global market economy that is not only shrinking due to effective communication (e.g., through the internet and information technology (IT) such as the global system telecommunications (GSM)), but also becoming more and more competitive and customer focused.

Hence, we are all working as quality professionals to continuously improve our organizations using adequate and specialized knowledge, tools, techniques, skills, and management systems so as to be able to sustain an organization's ability to gain more and more competitive advantage in the global marketplace. Here improvement in product and service quality may be achieved by focusing attention primarily on the following:

- Reduction of costs.
- Prevention, reduction, or elimination of all types of defects/wastes (e.g., resources—human and materials).
- Elimination/minimization of process and product variability.
- Innovation or the use of innovative ideas.

Quality Culture

Necessity for Organizational Culture

Culture has been confirmed, as "an important aspect of any institution and yet, it is difficult to find a single, unified definition of culture" [3]. Schein [4] has given the definition of organizational culture as "the pattern of basic assumptions that a given group has invented, discovered, or developed in learning to cope with its problems of external adaption and internal integration, and that have worked well enough to be considered valid and, therefore, to be taught to new members as the correct way to perceive, think, and feel in relation to those problems."

The general trend is for organizations to begin with individuals coming together with the desire to achieve common goals, followed by the establishment of artifacts (i.e., roles and rules), and then the creation of norms and values among members [5]. These thus represent the three levels of organizational culture—artifacts, espoused beliefs and values, and the basic underlying assumptions, which is an invisible dimension of the organization not easily expressed in concrete ways [3]. Organizational culture, therefore, sets the foundation or basis for the strategy of an organization, guiding its internal technical routines, managerial processes, and employee behavior [6]. A strong culture is plainly shown through common values and norms (positive culture), with a high degree of consensus among the members of an organization (cohesive culture).

Bou-Llusar (2018) and Luria [7] gave the psychological explanation for employees' behaviors toward quality and the importance of leadership in managing those behaviors. The role and actions of transformational leadership quickly surfaced here, as a very important aspect of managing such behaviors to achieve a strong quality culture. Mishra and Delgado [8] have said it all that, "A strong quality culture (that is, the quality aspect of a strong organizational culture) is built by transformational leaders who provide the mechanism for employee participation and consultation, thus encouraging a highly engaged workforce." This is obviously indicative of the fact that leadership success can be directly or indirectly achieved through employee engagement. Hence, organizational leaders need to exhibit and display actions capable of raising the needs and motivations of his or her followers, in promoting dramatic changes in individuals, groups, and organizations [9, 10].

The need for organizations to create the quality culture is reinforced in the research findings of Kujala and Ullrank (2004) [11] about quality management which "should be studied as a cultural phenomenon with a coherent set of underlying assumptions that form an ideal quality culture."

Hospital performance have been largely reported to be affected by organizational culture [12]. Likewise, the argument of Belohlav et al. [13] in their publication that a hospital that has the ability to adopt core cultural values exhibits an important factor for improving the overall level of safety performance in that hospital.

It follows therefore that organizational culture is a strong backbone structure, for organizational quality and performance achievement, as it rightly constitutes the concrete and nucleus aspects of organizations. That is the outcome of creating or running organizations with members exhibiting very high level of consensus rooted in strong organizational culture.

Sustaining the Quality Culture

It is one thing to establish a quality culture, and it is another to be able to maintain and sustain it. My fears generally about organizations implementing one quality management concept/system or the other especially in the underdeveloped or developing parts of the world (where the maintenance culture is extremely poor) is actually not that of achieving or successfully implementing stipulated or needed requirements but the sustainability of the system after implementation, that is, accepting it as a culture, on which further improvement shall be based. The fear of the author here is, justifiably or unjustifiably, hinged on the fact that most organizations, small and large, often see quality and its quality assurance team as a financial burden necessary only when it pleases the top echelon of management. This usually happens when business results are great and/or when there is a change in leadership or leadership perception. The leadership then wrongly sees the success of the business as being somehow independent of the quality assurance department and its activities which the organization can overlook and no more requires. To such organizational leadership the first area to look out for cost cuts in any restructuring exercise or during the downturn or meltdown in the economy is most often than not usually the quality assurance department.

At times too, when your quality management team is very efficient and effective in maintaining and sustaining your QMS so that there are no issues of bad products, customer complaints, recalls, returned products, wastages, etc., the QA department and its staff may be seen as being no more of relevance to or of good use to the organization to the extent that the department would be drastically rationalized, pruned down, or maintained at the barest minimum level of staffing. It is therefore very unfortunate too, that quality jobs tend generally to be more often than not the first to be axed during tough economic times.

All in all, there is the need for management to react with caution and always give adequate consideration in maintaining, retaining, and supporting its quality management team at all times. Management must therefore be careful to ensure that quality management measures are maintained and quality management staff given the needed support and opportunity to independently and effectively carry out its responsibilities.

It must, therefore, dawn on organizational management leadership that it is only through the complete and absolute reliance and commitment to quality that an organization can most readily come out of any economic meltdown/downturn or recession. This reality must be well understood by organizational leadership since it is a complete reliance on quality that can truly and readily contribute to an organization getting out of the woods or other economic downturn. This is because there are lots of big organizations that are today in existence mainly because they have embraced and successfully walked and traveled the path of quality.

It is therefore the opinion of the author that the quality unit/department should be seen as the stronghold of any organization at all times including periods of economic depression/financial downturn or even to ensure steady economic growth. The sustainability of an organization's QMS is hence a critical issue which must be handled with the utmost care and attention of top management in order to sustain its journey toward economic growth and survival.

This is even more so in the weak economies of the world and those that are heavily reliant or dependent on imported goods where due to one reason or the other sufficient attention is not paid to the quality of goods/products and services. Even when attention is paid to quality, it is usually difficult to control (partly or wholly) product quality from product source because of their reliance on imported products/raw materials which are produced outside their (importers) domains or from different parts of the world where they have no control. In most cases too, such countries also find it difficult to regulate the same through bilateral trade agreements because their economic weaknesses also translate directly or indirectly into their weakness in any economic negotiation.

Another factor that works against the sustainability of quality in the poorer countries of the world is the issue of corruption which could lead to quality being compromised especially in transactions and businesses involving government. Here the value of merit is thrown to the dogs, quality suspended, and product or service patronage influenced by "*what is in it for the respective decision makers*" or "*assumed customers.*" This singular act has drastically affected the quality of public services—be it the quality of education, roads, hospitals, transportation, and other public services—in a country like Nigeria which has over the years earned billions of dollars from crude oil sales but has nothing to show for it, especially in terms of the quality of life of her citizens. The bulk of the oil wealth has ended up in the hands of a pocket of greedy hawks that claimed to be in government or public service to serve the people but instead, robbed them and their future generations of their rightful belongings/heritage.

Quality and Business Growth

For your business or enterprise (no matter how small) to function efficiently and to continue to achieve, maintain, and sustain optimum growth, it is very important and critical for you to embark on and maintain some types of continuous improvement initiatives and some types of organizational standards through the application or implementation of a suitable and adequate quality management philosophy. An appropriate quality management initiative wholeheartedly and genuinely implemented by the A to Z of your business or organizational team can help you to achieve what would normally be seen as business common sense, that is:

- Continual improvement of your products and services and work environment
- Consistently improve your bottom line vis-à-vis financial performance
- Reduction in product/process defects and any other type of wastes

How an organization achieves this is usually the task. For example, most private businesses that sprang up in Nigeria and the West African subregion in the early 1980s failed on the one hand, as a result of the general lack of, or poor-quality management considerations, and on the other hand, due to political instability and the poor quality of government policies. Examples of such quality management considerations include but are not limited to the following factors:

- Failure to identify enterprise risks and averting them or managing them effectively
- Failure to separate the individual from the business
- Lack of qualified and competent manpower
- The general lack of effective planning even before the setting up of such industries
- The general lack of reliable statistical data for economic planning
- Poor quality of regulatory guidelines and implementation
- Bribery and corruption which may hinder the objectivity or objective assessment of quality assessments and considerations

Quality management is a structure or framework used for improving products/services and processes.

Essence of Quality Management

Quality management is all about an organization carrying out all its activities in a planned, controlled, and systematic pattern with the optimization of its resources (human and materials) such that wastages are as much as possible avoided (lean production); competitive products which are reproducible and consistent in their abilities to meet customer needs, specifications, and requirements are achieved first time under strict compliance with organizational production standard operating procedures and statutory/regulatory guidelines to the advantage of the organization's overall performance (financial inclusive). This is with the background of continually improving the management system from time to time and the use of a feedback system from the customer/market confirming product satisfaction or not. To achieve its ultimate goal, top management has the responsibility to provide both the physical and psychological needs and backup.

From the explanation given above, it is obvious that most quality management systems/concepts/programs are generally designed to partly or wholly achieve the following goals/objectives:

- Planned production
- Controlled processes
- Systematic approach to QMS implementation
- Resources (human and materials) optimization
- Avoiding resources wastages, "*muda*"
- Making competitive products
- Reproducibility
- Consistent products
- Products which meet customer needs, specifications, and requirements
- Producing the "right products" the first time, to avoid rework, or materials wastages
- Production or operation strictly under organizational procedural guidelines and compliance with statutory/regulatory guidelines
- Ensuring achieving products of intended quality characteristics first time
- Continual improvement of QMS
- Use of customer feedback to assess product performance and identify needed corrective action and areas of needed improvement
- Top management support of the implementation of QMS
- Improved overall product vis-à-vis organizational performance

Most of the quality management systems/concepts/programs tend to serve as the driving force and momentum for achieving the common quality goals of meeting customer needs, requirements, and specifications in different specified ways and manner.

Output of Quality Management

Effective and efficient quality management activities have the capability to result to the consistent production of excellent product quality. And we all know that exceptional product quality contributes largely to enhance product values particularly in terms of concrete business benefits as listed as follows:

- Lower costs
- Increased customer satisfaction
- Sustainable product improvement
- Sustainable profitability vis-à-vis business performance

The success of future businesses will not only demand exceptional product (output) quality but service differentiation through innovation to enable them tackle new, tougher, and emerging market challenges.

Innovation and Quality Management

Innovation is a key quality management term that is most often than not usually confused with the term *improvement*. This is clearly the case in situations when, for example, new functionalities and features are added to a product one after the other such that there would be uncertainties as to when the product that is being improved becomes a new version of its own self, that is, an innovation.

Innovation simply implies the streamlining of product development, manufacturing, and sales/marketing processes through creativity, use of new ideas, and inventiveness. It is defined by the ISO in its international standard, ISO 9004:2009 [14], as implying "*the development of something new (for example, new products and processes)*."

Innovation can therefore be viewed and seen as a process which uses information and data as input to achieve new solutions whereas *improvement* uses the same to achieve improved solutions to existing systems/problems. This is adequately captured by Scriabina [15] who considered innovation as a next step after improvement when she confirmed that "*improvement is a practical use of information and data to develop better solutions*" while according to her "*innovation takes a step further in using information and data to produce new solutions.*"

A more applicable definition of innovation in terms of quality management is, however, provided by Lee, S.M. (2015), [16, 17] in their definition of innovation as, "the ongoing process of exploring for new ideas and approaches that can be applied differently than before to create new or greater value." This definition is a far departure from the previous often complex definition of innovation by most people. At times, innovation was according to Reid [18], often contrasted with continual improvement in its portrayal as an "activity limited to R & D and other specialists, and was viewed as technology-dependent and sporadic."

While the Oslo Manual 2018: Guidelines for collecting, reporting, and using data on innovation defines four types of innovation: *organization, process, product*, and *marketing*; the ISO and its technical committee for innovation management, ISO/TC279 cooperated with the Oslo Manual in agreeing that an "entity" is an innovation when it is "new or improved and realizes or redistributes value."

The role and contribution of novel and innovative ideas to help improve an organization's ability to adapt in times of uncertainties and/or disruptive environments, as well as providing opportunities for improved earnings through better ways of working, is a portrayal of how importantly *innovation* has grown to become in organizational success, resilience, and sustainability. Hence, there is the general need for harnessing and managing innovation, especially to create a culture of innovation and "Building an Innovative Management System" [19].

This increasing role of innovation in organizational quality platform thus justifies the focus of attention of the ISO on the need for the publication of new generic international standards:

ISO 56000:2020—Innovation management—Fundamentals and vocabulary (ISO).
ISO 56002:2019—Innovation management—Innovation management system—Guidance [20]. This standard can easily be integrated with ISO 9001 using the high-level structure to develop an integrated system capable of driving both quality and innovation.

Apart from providing the vocabulary, fundamental concepts, and the principles of innovation management, and the systems for its implementation, ISO 56000 addresses some interests of various organizations and other interested parties. From ISO's detailed information, some of such interested areas include among others the following needs for:

- Implementing an innovation management system (IMS) or in need of performing innovation management assessment.
- Improving organizational ability to effectively manage innovation activities.
- Users, customers, and other interested parties, such as, suppliers, partners, investors, funding entities, universities and public services groups who are desirous of the need to establish confidence in the capability of an organization to innovate.
- All interested parties wishing to improve their communication skills for the purpose of understanding the vocabulary used in innovation management.
- Those who are professionally or otherwise involved in training in, assessment of, or consultancy about innovation management and innovation management systems.
- People involved in the development of innovation management and related standards.

The key clauses of ISO 56002 are context, leadership, planning, support, operation, performance management, and improvement. The benefit of ISO 56000 [21] is laden in the fact that it gives customers, business partners, academia, investors, and other stakeholders the confidence that an organization can deliver innovation on a consistent basis. This standard is thus identified as one which has the ability to be of very good use to those involved in innovation, auditing, and management.

Today, innovation should simply be seen and viewed as an integral part of every employee's task instead of being assigned as the responsibility of a separate organizational department. This may, in the future of quality trend, blend with every employee's job responsibility.

The purpose of innovating may be for the development of new products or for ensuring that existing products/brands are made more attractive and compelling to buyers, customers, or consumers as well as extending them to new customers thereby widening and expanding their market scope. Innovation therefore helps not only to improve product quality but also enables the products to reach newer markets more effectively and efficiently in terms of delivery time and meeting all other customer (or consumer) needs, requirements, and specifications. Innovation is generally driven by organizational desire to be competitive, maintain, and gain the needed market share ahead of all the others.

The role of innovation in the successful operation of an organization can therefore not be overemphasized. Innovation is a process which can be achieved across most of the organizational activities. The implication here is that innovation can be achieved in the various departmental activities of an organization as highlighted as follows:

- Research and development
- Marketing and sales
- Product development
- Process development
- Product design and engineering
- Product branding and rebranding
- Spare parts production and supplier cooperation
- Production/manufacture or services provision
- Supply/logistics
- Product packaging
- Other related processes throughout an organization

The launching of innovative ideas into reality and/or the provision of required *new solutions* requires the following ingredients if it has to mature to achieve its ultimate desires and goals:

- Knowledge and information about the relevant business atmosphere and market environment in relationship to product and its production activities as well as investments in research
- Access to and the collection of appropriate information and data followed by its effective and accurate analysis
- Management determination to innovate and its capacity for innovation
- Provision of needed resources—human, financial, and materials

- Adequate and proper planning
- Ability to select and prioritize the right areas and processes to carry out innovative activities

The areas and processes selected and the type and nature of innovation must be seen and adjudged to lead to the achievement of competitive edge over contemporary organizations or competitors.

At the pre-innovation stage experimenting, prototyping and brainstorming are some of the commonest sets of tools that may be employed. These set of tools generally help to reduce the cost of failure in the course of innovating. It is better for a prototype to fail than the innovative activities failing after going the whole length. The process of innovating should therefore begin with the idea, brainstorming over it before prototyping and experimenting to assess the possibility of achieving the innovation and its targeted goals/objectives.

It is however, the prerogative of management to select particular areas and processes for any intended innovative activities. The selection must, as a matter of necessity, be on factual basis if the venture to innovate has to be successful. Hence, information and data analysis must be as accurate as possible since the successful execution of innovative activities must be planned on the basis of the realities of issues and all situations at stake. The critical criteria needed for successful innovation are as follows:

- Decisions must be taken on the basis of factual issues, objective and collective.
- Needed information and data analysis must be acquired generally on a broad base, accurate, and of very high degree of reliability.
- Planning must be based on the realities of all the issues at stake.

Any mistake in the execution of innovative ideas could lead to catastrophic results for an organization as money, time, and other resources which were inputs into the process of innovating could be lost, completely lost.

A good example here is the case of the establishment of a multi-million-dollar production plant in Nigeria to produce and sell some *innovative* food item (croissant) which is completely alien to the Nigerian cultural environment or eating habit/taste. The potential sales volume was predicted from pre-project studies assessment to be very fantastic within its first 2 years from where it was expected to rise steadily in subsequent years after. Hence, its entire process design (i.e., including building, raw materials, production capacity, initial staffing (particularly managerial), sales and marketing facilities, and packaging) was based on this extraordinarily optimistic projection. In addition, the product was launched generously with fanfare and outstandingly high optimism and enthusiasm.

The factory which was projected to be selling about 5000 cartons per day of its products in the second year of operations was barely able to sell about 1000 cartons of this product per day which amounted to a mere 20% of the projected. Subsequently, realizable income stabilized practically at about 20% of the originally budgeted (or projected) sales volume. With planned and projected expenditure based on the sales of 5000 cartons per day, the company soon plunged into debt while finding it extremely difficult to meet its obligations to its suppliers, creditors, and other stakeholders so that its operations had to be abruptly closed-down after about 2 years of its establishment to avoid further financial loss.

This is a case of basing the planning and execution of this *innovative* introduction (of an alien food culture on economically weak populace) on an input of *wrong information and data analysis.* The consideration given then to the impact of the people's eating culture and economic status quo of the potential market targets on sales was completely vague and out of tune with the realities of the environment and the eating mentality of her people. Hence, the aims and objectives of setting-up such a capital-intensive food industry on a foundation of unrealistic market information, data analysis, and optimism may never be achievable. Its planning and management by foreign people who lack the ability to adapt to needed environmental and people-oriented production and sales skills ensured the failure of realizing the set-out objectives/goals of this innovation right from the very root and moment its planning began.

Branding and re-branding of products and services have been commonly used as a major quality tool of innovation in various sectors of the presently highly competitive global or world market economy. The forces that most proactively drive innovations are in an organization's physical and economic environment and its planned and/or anticipated changes. Hence, innovations need to be generally aligned with the following:

- The changing trends of consumer behavior
- Societal expectations and sales potentials
- The dynamism of technological growth
- The changing business environment as it relates to its products and business activities

Organizations that want to be successful on a continuous basis in running its businesses need to try as much as is possible to embrace and acknowledge innovation as a strong quality management instrument that will enable them continuously meet customer needs, requirements, and specifications. This is made easier today as they can easily have access to a variety of quality management tools and ready availability of quality management experts for advice and guidance.

Managing Innovational Risks

The point at which we find opportunity and potential solutions represents the creative phase of innovation. Selection of the preferred solution and making it user friendly before the delivery of the solution to the market serves as the linking point between the creative and execution stages.

Innovation or trying something new is, on the basis of the above-stated example, often times overburdened with risks and overshadowed with the fear of the following:

- The unknown
- Financial losses
- Failure
- Risk taking

This is so because innovation itself is a risky business. The risk in innovation comes at different levels. The risk which increases significantly at the execution stage is relatively lower at the creative phase. The risks of whether the product would work or not is restricted to the developmental stages. The most critical risks of them all are those that are affiliate with third parties. An example here is the risk associated with both the suppliers and distributors or marketing partners. These risks include but are not limited to the following:

- Level of acceptability of the new product by customers (downstream risk)
- Ability of new business partners or others involved in product distribution to deliver (upstream risk)
- Supplier risk (risk attached to product assembly)

Failure to make any innovation or new product user friendly also poses the threat or risk of poor market/customer acceptability. It follows here too, that customers must glaringly be able to identify and assess the level of product perceived values which must be seen as having increased appreciably over and above those of other products. Innovators must have a very good understanding of product users so as to be able to create practical user interfaces that will really work for people.

Both supplier and distribution risks can be drastically minimized or mitigated against. In the case of the supplier, you can use the ISO 9001 QMS audit processes to measure and monitor the eligibility, suitability, and sustainability of suppliers' products and processes. This can be used as a quality management tool for achieving effective management of your suppliers. We should realize here too, that supplier relationship must have to be adequately managed at all levels as this is generally a complex situation which requires some levels of sophistication such as organizational emotional intelligence, alignment of organizational goals and directions, and affiliated styles just to mention a few.

As for the marketing partners and distributors, you need to work closely with each other even to the extent of attaching a dedicated staff of yours all issues at stake and other marketing decisions are well communicated between the two of you.

It is the responsibilities of the innovator to ensure that adequate plans are put in place to ensure the following:

- Risks are analyzed, prioritized, and mitigated against
- Products are user friendly
- Product users are excellently understood
- User interfaces that practically work for people are created

Innovators must in addition have the understanding that there can be no innovation without accompanying risks; hence, risk should be seen as an integral part of innovation particularly in business. With the present level of competition in the global market, it can easily be said that future business potentials can only be grabbed by bold and courageous business entrepreneurs willing to take risks.

Improvement/Innovation Inter-relationship

While it may be said that any innovation is an improvement in the activities of an organization, the same cannot be said of the term *improvement*. It follows from here too, that not all improvements are innovations. While it is obvious that information and data form an interface between improvement and innovation, distinguishing between the two terms is not all that easy as they both overlap.

The International Organization for Standardization (ISO), however, solved this problem in its definition of both terms in its ISO 9004:2009 international standard. ISO defined in clause 9.1 that "*improvement applies to something that already exists (for example, current products and processes) while innovation implies development of something new (for example, new products and processes)*."

The role of organizational top management in achieving business success is, on a general basis, quite huge. But at these times of economic meltdown and hardship, there seems to be no other choice than to turn to management innovation and the use of effective quality management systems as the major rescue route for the success of any business/enterprise.

A major key to business success today is strongly hinged on a foundation of strong total quality management with continued and effective emphasis on management innovation across the length and breadth of organizational activities or processes. This will undoubtedly result to the capability of an organization and its management to build the competitive quality leadership strength needed generally for its growth and improved performance.

Generating and Executing Innovative Ideas

While innovative ideas may result from an organization's internal efforts (e.g., contributions through its own internal research works or investment in research by external sources), such may also be purchased from third parties and other intellectual property owners of such ideas. While the latter may be purchased or obtained under special agreements in the form of licenses/rights or even technical know-how. Sourcing innovative ideas internally offers the opportunities of the following:

- Good and technical control of information, processes, and product
- The room for the modification and further enhancement of the innovation
- Implementing the innovation under the most suitable conditions and timing in line with the organization's activities

For example, the use of the technical know-how agreement fees granted by the Federal Government of Nigeria to most foreign organizations in Nigeria that are involved in the production of innovative items/goods or "technology transfer" using imported technical know-how of a third party serves (or in most cases overseas partners) in one way or the other as an added incentive to their original owners as it enables the Nigerian partner to make approved payments of certain percentage of net sales or profit before tax (PBT) in annual remittances to its original owners. The author was involved in implementing and assuring compliance with the statutory guidelines and regulations covering both the acquisition and execution of such rights and agreements.

In order to successfully execute an innovative project, it must be planned and effectively carried out stage by stage. To achieve this, the planned steps of action must be well defined, adequately documented, and properly measured. Adequate care must be taken to ensure as much as is possible that the execution is carried out without making mistakes as this may lead to the failure of the entire innovation process. The innovation process must be carried out with due consideration for or in line with the following:

- Trends in technological growth and development
- Changing trend in consumer response to market dynamics
- Societal expectations in relationship to product
- Any other developmental trends that are likely to affect product

Innovation has its own rewards directly or indirectly.

Innovation as Competitive Tool

The World Economic Forum (WEF) defines competitiveness as "*the set of institutions, policies, and factors that determine the level of productivity of a country*" while noting that "*the level of productivity sets the sustainable level of prosperity that can be earned by an economy.*" The same definition is applicable to organizational competitiveness.

The experience of the author showed, however, that cost control coupled with product and service quality only lead to the achievement and sustenance of a minimum competitive advantage. The competitive advantage that results from product and service *innovation* far outweighs that which is achieved through cost control and product quality.

A practical example here is the case of an international glass packaging manufacturing organization for which the author led its quality teams to install and obtain certification to the requirements of the international ISO 9001 QMS standards, where some innovative ingenuities were brought into the production of "*user specific*" or "*customized*" recyclable glass beer bottles for the two biggest and most popular breweries of the highest brewing standards and quality not just in the West

African subregion but from my own perspective and taste, in the entirety of African continent, the Nigerian Breweries PLC, and Guinness PLC in Nigeria.

Excellence of Customer/Supplier Cooperation

This innovation, which was in close collaboration with the respective customers, was based on *marketing analyses* interests of the author who was academically involved in Nigeria's recycling industry that actually provided work for thousands of Nigerians at that time. At that time, each beer brewing plant in Nigeria used the same types of bottles. It is as a result of this universality or common use of the then existing nationally re-useable recyclable glass beer bottles by every brewer in the Nigerian beer market that created serious production bottle necks for big-time brewers. The big-time brewers were thus held to ransom by smaller ones which lack the needed capital to invest in glass bottle production.

Such big Nigerian beer brewers are the Nigerian Breweries PLC and Guinness Nigeria PLC. Although they regularly invest massively in quality beer bottle production for their own use, they still faced the difficulties of not having enough returned bottles on their production lines because most of the recycled beer and malt drink glass bottles found their ways to the plants of the smaller breweries, and in the hands of fake/nonexistent beer brewers who, due to Nigeria's large beer market, profiteer from adulterating various brands of drinks.

On the other hand, small-scale brewers and nonexistent breweries which avoid heavy capital investments in the production of glass bottles rely heavily and solely on the freely available recyclable glass beer bottles of universal application in the Nigerian beer market, as their primary source of bottles for their operations and production lines.

The universal use of the same type of glass beer bottles by various bottlers in Nigeria also encouraged and motivated product faking and adulteration to the disadvantage of the original beer brewers and bottlers in Nigeria.

Quality Branded Beer Packaging

The *innovation* of introducing product branded or customized bottles in the same way that it had already existed for the soft drinks bottling industries such as the Nigerian Bottling Company PLC, bottlers of the popular Coca Cola products—Fanta, Sprite, and Coca Cola soft drinks—therefore helped to restrict the use of such bottles to the brand owners.

Investigations in the beer market showed then that the development of *customized* recyclable glass beer bottles designed and engineered with the respective company logo and peculiar dimension, color, and shape, different from the common ones in the Nigerian beer market, actually restricted the use of these bottles strictly to owner companies and helped to boost the image of such companies as well as serve to promote and boost organizational integrity, brand, and product sales.

This singular action immediately spelt doom for bottled beer adulterators and the sudden collapse of the then booming adulterated beer market both in Nigeria and the West African subregion, so that beer consumers were given the assurance of getting their most favored and most valued beer brands, such as those brewed and marketed by the Nigerian Breweries PLC and Guinness Nigeria PLC. These are two of Nigeria's breweries exhibiting the highest quality standards in the brewing industry and maintaining such quality standards at all times for all their products.

This innovative act, which was implemented in close collaboration with the glass bottle producers, resulted to a massive competitive advantage even for the glass bottle producers and its customers both in Nigeria and outside Nigeria, particularly in the entire West African subregion.

The two ISO 9001-certified Beta Glass PLC Plants located in Agbara and Ughelli, both in Nigeria, produce excellent high quality glass bottles. These two glass bottle production plants inherited from the era of the author an excellent quality culture in all ramifications of its processes and glass bottle production activities and maintained the same. Beta Glass PLC, a member of the Leventis Group of companies, is today known for its sustainability, adaptive capabilities, and consistency of tapping into the opportunities of all their resources to innovate. Globally creating and integrating the quality mindset among employees while maintaining one of the highest levels of commitment to corporate social responsibilities (CRS) have, in the opinion of the author, been major and critical factors for their sustainable and consistently improving performance, especially in an industrial production-unfriendly country of a failed state like Nigeria.

Making Quality an Organizational Culture

Cultivating quality, as organizational culture, is highly rewarding. The author is particularly very proud here to share his quality leadership experience and successes at these two plants with quality minds across the globe. Working for Beta Glass PLC as a quality management leader in both their Agbara and Ughelli glass production plants where the quality culture was inculcated and planted to achieve the organizational tradition of quality marked the aspirations of a transformational leadership. The organization-wide quality cultural practices of the Beta Glass Plants in Agbara and Ughelli made it very easy for them to cooperate and collaborate with their customers to achieve excellent outcomes.

Seizing the opportunity of organizational excellence in glass bottle production to cooperate with Nigeria's original beer brewers and bottlers to make this innovation quite successful is an example of the expected outcomes of an organization which gives and pays attention to quality and quality management. Certification to the requirements of the ISO 9001 QMS standards is thus an excellent route not just or for achieving high quality products and services, but also for the overall purpose of ensuring customer satisfaction, loyalty, and confidence. An organization billing itself as being ISO 9001 certified simply means that the organization has met the stipulated quality management systems requirements of the standard.

Apart from its maintenance of a strong organizational quality culture, Beta Glass PLC has always been known for its strong commitment to always and responsibly addressing its corporate social and environmental responsibilities (CSER) by giving back to its immediate environment and community in various ways.

Achieving the Quality Culture with ISO 9001

The implementation and certification of both glass bottle production plants to the requirements of ISO 9001 QMS international standards played vital and key roles in the competitive strength of Beta Glass PLC in the buoyant beverage and beer bottle market. This is the way some Nigerian bottle brewers and bottlers used *innovation* most appropriately to boost their sales in Nigeria, growing the beer bottle market to ensure and maintain the quality of their products to the satisfaction of their millions of customers, in a country with rapid population growth like Nigeria which population grew from 60 million at independence in 1960 to over 200 million in 2020. Even with Nigeria's fluctuating economic health, the beer brewing industry enjoys continued growth. The strict focus of Beta Glass PLC on the continuous improvement of the quality of its product contributed and still contribute largely to its success and dominance of the glass bottle market in Nigeria and the West African subregion, of over 400 million people, since the 1990s till the beginning of the twenty-first century.

It is therefore highly imperative here for any organization to function efficiently and to continue to be relevant and show optimum growth, it must consistently and effectively implement and maintain some types of continuous improvement systems, programs, and some types of organizational standards with suitable organizational quality management initiative. As competition gets keener and keener in the global market place, organizational management must be accentuated with some innovations or innovative ideas.

Quality and Innovation

Quality and innovation simply hold the key for opening the doors for future global market penetration of most products and services. Today's competitive market structure is a determinant factor portraying the trend of future economic dynamism. While the global market competition is going to be keener than ever, quality will likely be wholly embraced as the dominant skeletal back bone structure for sustaining virtually all products and services. It is therefore likely that any business/enterprise, small or large, managed with the intention to capture the market may have to focus more on qualitatively and innovatively differentiable products and services in order to catch the attention of current and potential customers/buyers.

Even the emerging markets (Turkey, Brazil, Indonesia, Malaysia, Nigeria, South Africa, etc.) are today placing more and more emphasis on product quality to achieve customer satisfaction. As more and more organizations embrace quality and its market penetration benefits, quality may likely grow in the future to generally become organizational-wide fundamental principles of successful business operations.

Quality Is Universal

Discipline of All Disciplines

There are no professional interests whatsoever, that ever wished to have a break with quality and quality management practice culture. It does not really matter what profession line one may think of, quality, its principles, tools, and techniques are generally available and applicable to achieve better outcome. This is one of the reasons of the author's advocacy for quality management education in all areas of human endeavor. Doing this at the undergraduate level shall undoubtedly help to promote improvement in the career of every graduating student irrespective of the course of studies. Quality is therefore viewed globally as a very strong attribute of human life improvement measures. Quality is an all-round-applicable discipline, hence, of universal deployment.

As confirmed by Payne [22], "Quality is universal in the sense that it can make or break your business—any business. Even your child's lemonade stand, must exemplify the perfect balance of water, lemons, temperature and sugar to ensure it's of the best quality to serve as a refreshing treat on a hot summer day."

The most successful sectors of the global economy have been known to embrace and acknowledge the role of using standards and conformity assessment activities to lower costs and reduce wastages for performance improvement. The universality of quality is thus never in contention.

Global Changes and Quality

Today, technological, economic, human, and environmental changes have resulted to the most dramatic, turbulent, and challenging times of the world global economy. All these changes and the challenges that accompany them have impacted heavily on quality in business and enterprise all over the world. Some of the impacts here include aggressive quality competitions, high economic value of products and services, consumer and customer demands, for higher and higher standards of quality value of products and services and the global access to expanse IT facilities which enable buyers/consumers/customers to easily and quickly and globally obtain needed information about products and services in order to be able to take a decision.

Global market competition has therefore driven most organizations to the realization of the fact that quality is highly relevant—more relevant than anything else because if the customers are not given the right quality of products and services to meet their needs, requirements, and specifications they will simply go elsewhere. This is particularly so since there are fewer and fewer markets where customers cannot switch to other suppliers and service providers within a very short time in these internet and GSM-dominated business era. This situation has led to the realization by various organizations and business enterprises in the international arena that quality is a worthwhile and endless journey to follow by any business or enterprise—small or large—that has the intention and determination not just to remain relevant but to have an appreciable control of the market which dynamism can easily throw any unprepared organization or enterprise out of balance in the global market competition where quality has gradually become the global language of virtually all businesses and customers.

The situation is particularly so in countries which depend solely on only one economic product (mono-cultural economy) as a source of income. This is the case for countries like Nigeria which currently depends solely on its crude oil as the major source of economic livelihood thereby forgetting her history of how she had survived solely on her now neglected agricultural produce such as cocoa, cotton, groundnuts, rubber, coffee, plantain, and yams. This dependence solely on crude oil coupled with the high rate of corruption in government businesses, has in turn, made her business activities highly susceptible to unprecedented price movements generally dictated by the crude oil market dynamism.

It follows therefore that for any organization to survive in the aggressive global market arena, it must have to deliver high quality value products and services consistently to its customers by making quality a fundamental culture of its day-to-day activities an operational strategy. Without this, the organization will not be able to face the major challenges that are now influencing most organizations in the global market place. These challenges include among others the following:

- The demand of customers for increasingly higher standard of quality and value for products and services.
- The rapidly changing business cycles and fluctuations in the global market demand for goods and services.
- The need to effectively match the rising response speed, number, and the aggressiveness of competitors in the global market.
- Growing changes in the processing methodologies/techniques for product manufacturing, development, and service deliveries to meet the needs, requirements, and specifications of the customer.
- The effectiveness in the use and application of high technologies to the supply chain management, for example, computer-based global distribution and purchase of goods and services.
- The current meltdown of the world economy.

It must be mentioned here that quality is generally compromised by corruption and corrupt practices as quality is usually generally thrown to the dogs in corruption-plagued economies of the world (e.g., Nigeria). Compromising quality in this way obviously leads to the exclusion of what would have been the universal effect or influence of quality on economic activities. Here costs of goods and services are generally higher than normal because of the extraordinary cost of quality (also referred to by the author as unnecessary costs of quality, UCoQ), resulting from corruption. This does not, however, result in better qualities of services. Instead, services provided with taxpayers' money are at the lowest ebb, or not at all visible or accessible to those for whom the services were supposedly provided for. Business owners operating in any corrupt enclave must therefore take note of the caveat emptor, hidden in the proclaimed value of goods and services. Corruption is anti-quality hence its absence in the corruptly corrosive and toxic business environment of an extremely and highly corrupt country like Nigeria.

Quality Management Systems/Concepts

Quality tools are instruments or techniques that are used to support and improve the activities of process quality management and improvement, while quality management (QM) itself is, according to the American Society for Quality (ASQ) [23] and ASQ quality glossary (ASQ) [24], "*the application of a quality management system (QMS) in managing a process to achieve maximum customer satisfaction at the lowest overall cost to the organization while continuing to improve the process.*"

Advances in quality management techniques over the years have resulted in the availability of a range of quality management systems, tools, programs, concepts, criteria, technique, or standards from which any interested organization or entity can pick or make a choice to adequately manage its operations. The mostly talked about of these quality management systems/concepts/programs/ or ways of providing quality products in the global market or in the international community include among others the following:

- ISO 9000 Quality Management System (QMS) International Standards
- Six Sigma
- Total Quality Management (TQM) Concept
- Circle—4 Quality System
- Malcolm Baldrige National Quality Award Criteria
- Lean Quality Philosophy
- World Class Quality Concept/World Class Manufacturing
- 5S Total Quality Environment (TQE)
- Kaizen Concept
- Just-in-Time (JIT) Technique
- Integrated Quality Management Systems/Programs (e.g., Lean Six Sigma)
- Other Quality Improvement Methods/Programs/Criteria/Philosophy/Points

Common among these quality improvement methods or concepts are the following:

- The Deming's 14 Points.
- Juran 10 steps for Quality Improvement.
- Feigenbaum's Philosophy of Quality Control.

- Philip Crosby Concept of Zero Defect.
- The Plan-Do-Check-Act (PDCA) Cycle or the Plan-Do-Study-Act (PDSA) Cycle (also commonly known as either the Shewhart Cycle or Deming Cycle/ Wheel). Shewhart created the cycle while Deming was the first to use it in Japan.
- Quality Circle.

The PDCA improvement cycle is, for example, a simple model that can easily be implemented. The implementation of the PDCA or the PDSA allows for the achievement of incremental improvements as it enables the entire system or its individual processes to be reviewed over and over again. The PDCA assumed the name, Shewhart Cycle after Walter A. Shewhart, who carried out the pioneering works (Shewhart straight-line process and the Shewhart cyclical concept) that led to its (PDCA) evolution. The Japanese call it on the order hand the Deming Cycle, after W. Edwards Deming a quality guru who first described the cycle to them.

The design, development, and implementation of any of the above-specified quality management systems/concepts/programs can be easily achieved if handled as a company-wide project.

A major prerequisite for achieving the set quality goals and objectives generally begins with the willingness of the top management of your organization to select and implement an appropriate one. Hence, the full cooperation and support of top management is a key condition necessary and vital for the initiation, implementation, and sustenance of a viable quality initiative. For your management to achieve this, it must have some understandings of the system to be implemented. Here it is important too for your management to gain sufficient knowledge or have enough information to enable it to appreciate or understand the advantages and benefits derivable from this quality journey.

The next important step is that of adequate planning. Thereafter, the new system can be installed or implemented on a gradual basis to avoid drastic changes while ensuring adequate flow of information and the proper training of staff.

The task of achieving the desired quality goals for your production system using a quality management tool of your choice may therefore generally be premised on the following fundamental principles:

- *Top management support*—management support is very crucial to the success of any quality initiative.
- *Planning*—securing the commitment of top management team; getting information about an appropriate quality concept; selecting a QMS or concept or a combination thereof; setting of quality goals and objectives, training, identification of quality team leadership and members; and preparing implementation schedule and implementation. It is important here to have at the back of your mind sufficient information about your customers and customer base.
- *Change management*—the team leadership must in cooperation with your top management team ensure that the process of implementing a new quality management program is steady, gradual, consistent, and total. Poor change management methods may actually lead to failure or at times unsustainable success.

- *Performance*—carrying out all planned activities as planned in the manner of "doing it right the first time" as and when due.
- *Performance measurement*—measure achievement against set out milestones using adequate key performance indicators (KPIs) to assess the stage-by-stage achievement.
- *Corrective and preventive actions*—introduce corrective/preventive measures as and when needed.
- *Review*—using internal and external audit results, customer feedback, experience, process/technique/technology upgrade/improvement measures, corrective and preventive actions, any other input from the customer, changes in statutory regulations that may affect concerned organizations and their products, outcome of both processing and product benchmarking, rebranding, etc.
- *Improvement on a continual basis*—through innovation and the implementation of the review outcome including new ideas.

The following vital points are as such considered by the author as critical and important in your installation of any QMS or improvement program of your choice in your organization:

- *Selection, designing, and development of a system considered most appropriate for your organization to ensure that customer needs and requirements and specifications are met and surpassed to the delight of your customers.*
- *Implementation, management, sustenance of the system, and its dynamism.*
- *Continually review the system to put preventive and corrective measures in place while adding innovation and innovative ideas to ensure that the system undergoes continual improvement on a regular basis.*

Improvement Focus

One of the critical aspects of quality management is the need for the continual improvement in the performance of products and/or services as well as those of the processes for achieving them. Some key areas of focus to achieve performance improvement are as follows:

- Customer (satisfaction/dissatisfaction) feedback
- Products/services performance review
- Review of processes for achieving products and/or services including machinery and equipment
- Ability to anticipate or predict business or market direction in terms of competitiveness (e.g., through regular benchmarking)
- Gap analysis of staff skills/competencies and then bridging it
- Market status of product

The global manning of the recent global economic downturn is actually a pointer toward the fact that in most cases the role of quality is misplaced usually during the times of economic crisis. Instead of focusing on quality (long-term financial gain) for business improvement, most managers wrongly resort dogmatically to calls for cost savings (short-term financial gains) by constantly evoking measures such as the following:

- Staff reduction (often times beginning with quality assurance departmental staff)
- Reduction or total cancellation of research activities/funds
- Reduction or at times suspension of all or part of staff training schemes

This is actually a wrong focus of attention at times when the production of quality products/services (long-term objectives) ought to have been strongly emphasized. Deming [25] recognized these facts a long time ago in his "Out of Crisis" that short-term profits are not an indication of management ability.

Management Commitment

Management commitment goes beyond management just talking about quality whenever customers complain or merely mentioning quality concerns often in meetings with staff. Management commitment is much more than that. Management commitment must be seen, felt, and experienced by all. To support this, I wish to mention one of my personal experiences here.

As the new general manager of a crown cork manufacturing plant, I frequently visited and witnessed production activities on the factory floor as soon as I took over from my predecessor whom I was later told visited the production floor only once in a while. The frequency of my stay on the production floor gave me the opportunity to witness what the workers were doing in terms of quality and very often witnessed and acknowledged most of the things they were doing to sustain and improve the quality management system. This in turn motivated other management staff to show their presence too on the production floor. The whole involvement of the management team in production activities in this way was seen by the workforce as a motivational factor as quality significantly improved while wastages which used to be about five (5%) when I took over was reduced within 2 months to about two (1–2%). Productivity which went up from the previous 60–65% to about 75–80% within the same period was even acknowledged by the workforce as soon as this was made known to them, for the first time, through a production feedback system similarly introduced by my management team as a part of a series of quality measures and initiatives to improve the system.

Management commitment is defined in the words of Summers [26], as "participation of the highest-level officials in their organization's quality improvement efforts. Their participation includes establishing and serving on a quality committee, establishing quality policies and goals, deploying these goals to lower levels of the organization, providing the resources and training that the lower levels need to achieve the goals, participating in quality improvement teams, reviewing progress organization-wide, recognizing those who have performed well and revising the current reward system to reflect the importance of achieving the quality goals."

The ISO 9001:2008 QMS standards similarly specifies in clause 5.1 of its requirements the following lines of action to be taken by top management as evidence of its commitment to the development and implementation of the quality management system and the continual improvement of its effectiveness:

- Communicating to the organization the importance of meeting customer as well as statutory and regulatory requirements.
- Establishing the quality policy.
- Ensuring that quality objectives are established.
- Conducting management reviews.
- Ensuring the availability of resources.

It is therefore apparent that top management, including the CEO/MD, must clearly be seen and loudly heard on a continual basis, to be involved in, and committed to an organization's quality initiatives. In fact, the CEO/MD must be at the forefront of the quality improvement efforts and initiatives. This is the only way to ensure that the entire organization shall be seen as believing in and supporting the concepts of continual quality improvement, focusing on customer, are productive and able to create an enjoyable work environment, teamwork, collaboration, and open communication at all levels.

As succinctly put by Deming [27], "*the quality of the output of a company can't be better than at the top. Top management makes quality. Job security and jobs are dependent on management's foresight to design products and services that will entice customers and build a market; and their foresight to be ready, ahead of the customer, to modify products and services.*"

Quality Development

The development of quality can generally be traced back to man's desire to improve his standard of living (i.e., improvement) and his ability to make a choice of what he wants and needs (i.e., product specification) coupled with his ability to afford or procure them (i.e., value).

Talking in terms of production, the issue of quality as it is known today, did not actually surface until the advent of the industrial revolution in Europe when specific workers were given the responsibilities of executing particular jobs in the concept of the division of labor.

Quality in the way it is known and understood today can therefore be said to have begun with product inspection and gauging. From here, the manifestation of quality shifted to production monitoring using statistical quality control chart and statistical sampling techniques. From here, quality grew to total quality management (TQM) before its advancement to the quality management system (QMS) concept of today.

Common Quality Management Concerns

There are certain aspects of quality management that top management and their CEOs always take for granted or are oversights on their parts despite their concern and critical view of the need to increasingly achieve healthy financial performance. Some of these issues are enumerated as follows:

- Poor intra- and inter-departmental communication. Intra-organizational communication from top to bottom or vice versa could also result to poor management response to problem handling.
- Poor and/or unclear communication with customers in terms of specifications, needs, and expectations.
- Poorly defined problems and agreement ambiguities that may likely have negative impacts on the abilities and capabilities of your organization to fulfill your obligations to the customer.
- Poor or lack of adherence to certain aspects of quality planning. For example, the violation or even the lack of the use of the organizational structure (or organogram).
- Poor communication among top management staff including the CEOs. At times, they are told only the things they would like to hear.
- Excessive overlapping of responsibilities which may lead to duplication of responsibilities and wastes of human and materials resources input.
- Poor process measurement and monitoring activities which in some cases may result to the unnecessary and uncontrollable flow of your products or in-process products around the factory for one reason or the other. An example here is the situation in mobile phone production organizations where in certain cases thousands of the handsets remain within the production system for days and months without identification and further processing.
- High staff turnover at both managerial and workers levels.
- Poor quality management documentation and organization which at times result to the muddling up of procedures guides, work instruction, and other supporting documents.
- Poor work supervision.
- Competition, envy, and poor communication among management staff and between management staff and top management staff.
- Poor management response to customer enquiries or demands.
- Inability of management to detect workers' incompetency on the job.
- Self-alienation of the CEOs from production processes and activities.
- The failure of CEOs and other management-level personnel to recognize that effective and efficient quality management activities are integral parts of product and service delivery that deserve to be a top organizational priority.
- The focus of CEOs primarily on profit making without recognizing the fact that it is *customer satisfaction,* the target of quality that directly and indirectly brings the profit for any organization especially in the current situation of high global market competitiveness.

Quality Education

It is the view of the author that in order to facilitate the general improvement of products and services as well as to improve the quality of life of the masses all over the world including the poorer nations of the African and South American continents, there may be the need, an urgent need to integrate quality education into all institutions of higher education all over the world.

This is particularly so in the African continent, where poverty and highly corrupt political leadership have jointly combined to impoverish the masses.

Embracing quality management principles and implementing quality management requirements in the business of governance in a country like Nigeria portends rapid and steady improvement in the life of the masses as the huge extra cost of quality (ECoQ) consumed presently by corrupt practices may finally find their way back into capital projects when, through effective quality management, government business shall be *done right the first time* and always. For example, the magnitude of the ECoQ has driven government businesses in a country like Nigeria, the pinnacle of corruption and corrupt practices in Africa, to a situation where the budget for recurrent expenditure is almost at par with that of the capital budget. At the end of the day, there would be nothing left to fix the dilapidating roads, bridges, universities and other higher institutions of learning, electricity power supplies, poor utilities provision, and other welfare services that are taken for granted in the developed economies of the world.

The promotion of massive quality education in the African continent seems to be the panacea for igniting the flame to get rid of corruption in Nigeria to give way for people improvement-oriented governance.

References

1. Olunloyo, V. O. S., Ibidapo, T. A., & Dinrifo, R. R. (2011). Neural network-based electronic nose for cocoa beans quality assessment. *Agricultural Engineering International: CIGR Journal, 13*(4), 1–12.
2. Wilson, A. D. (2018). Applications of electronic-nose technologies for noninvasive early detection of plant and human diseases. *Chem, 6*, 45.
3. Lehman, D. W. (2017). Organizational culture theory and research administration knowledge management. *Journal of Research Administration, 48*(2), 52–66.
4. Schein, E. H. (1984). Coming to a new awareness of organizational culture. *Sloan Management Review, 25*(2), 3–15.
5. Katz, D., & Kahn, R. L. (1978). *The social psychology of organizations* (2nd ed.). Wiley.
6. Lee, J. Y., Gowen, I. I. I., Charles, R., & McFaden, K. L. (2018). An empirical study of U.S. hospital quality: Readmission rates, organizational culture, patient satisfaction, and Facebook ratings. *Quality Management Journal, 25*(4), 158–170.
7. Luria, G. (2008). Controlling for quality: Climate, leadership and behavior. *Quality Management Journal, 15*(1), 27–40.
8. Mishra, S., & Delgado, D. (2021, June). Engineering engaged employees – Power to your people to add strength to your quality program. *Quality Progress*, pp. 16–24.
9. Burns, J. M. (1978). *Leadership*. Harper & Row.

10. Jabnoun, N., & Al-Ghasyah, H. A. (2005). Leadership styles supporting ISO 900:2000. *Quality Management Journal, 12*(1), 21–29.
11. Kujala, J., & Ullrank, P. (2004). Total quality management as a cultural phenomenon. *Quality Management Journal, 11*(4), 43–45.
12. Naveh, E., Katz-Navon, T., & Stern, Z. (2011). The effect of safety management systems on continuous improvement of patients: The moderating role of safety climate and autonomy. *Quality Management Journal, 18*(1), 54–67.
13. Belohlav, J. A., Cook, L. S., Olson, J. R., & Drehmer, D. E. (2010). Core values in hospitals: A comparative study. *Quality Management Journal, 17*(4), 36–50.
14. International Organization for Standardization, ISO 9004:2009. *Managing for the sustained success of an organization – A quality management approach.*
15. Scriabina, N. (2011, June). Organize how you innovate. *Quality Progress*, p. 16.
16. Lee, S. M. (2015). The age of quality innovation. *International Journal of Quality Innovation, 1*, 1. https://doi.org/10.1186/s40887-015-0002x.
17. Lee, S. M., Olson, D. L., & Trimi, S. (2012). Co-innovation: Convergenomics, collaboration, and co-creation for organizational values. *Management Decision, 50*(5), 817–831. https://doi.org/10.1108/00251741211227528
18. Reid, R. D. (2011, December). Know your future. *Quality Progress*, p. 70.
19. Merrill, P. (2020). *ISO 56000: Building an innovative management system*. Quality Press.
20. International Organization for Standardization, ISO, Innovation management – Innovation management system – Guidance (ISO 56002:2019). https://www.iso.org/standard/
21. International Organization for Standardization, ISO, Innovation management – Fundamentals and vocabulary. (ISO 56000:2020). https://www.iso.org/standard/
22. Payne, T. (2020). Quality is universal. November 19, 2020. Blog Article, IACET, https://www.iacet
23. American Society for Quality, ASQ. www.asq.org
24. ASQ. (2007). Quality glossary. *Quality Progress*, pp. 39–59.
25. Deming, W. E. (1986). *Out of the crisis*. MIT Press.
26. Summers, D. C. S. (2000). *Quality* (2nd ed.). Prentice Hall.
27. Deming, W. E. (1995). Quality leadership. In *Search of quality*. Executive Excellence Publishing.

Managing Quality

3

Essence of Quality Management

The management of quality to ensure that goods produced or services rendered meet the needs, requirements, and specifications of the customer as well as those of statutory and regulatory requirements generally requires among others that the following are carried out:

- Production processes must be carried out under controlled conditions; hence, there is the need for the adequate monitoring of these processes.
- Appropriate techniques/technology need to be employed in the monitoring and measurement of activities.
- Processes and other significant activities must be documented to ensure consistency and product reproducibility.

These activities serve to ensure that adequate checks and balances are put in place so that the quality of products and/or services themselves are as desired and can be consistently achieved.

Quality Control and Quality Assurance

Quality control and *quality assurance* are two terms that feature prominently in the world of quality. In spite of this, prominent people still assign various meanings and implications to them. Reasons for this are not farfetched. Quality control remained a dominant factor in quality for a long time.

Examining the literary meanings of the terms "control" and "assurance" also shows that multiple meanings can be given to them. Hence, in order to have a full understanding of quality, it is critical to know their exact meanings in terms of quality and the concept of its management.

T. A. Ibidapo, *From Industry 4.0 to Quality 4.0*, Management for Professionals,
https://doi.org/10.1007/978-3-031-04192-1_3

One definition given by the ASQ [2] in its Quality Glossary (ASQ [3]) to ***quality control*** is *"the operational techniques and activities used to fulfill requirements for quality"* while ***quality assurance*** is defined here and also by Pyzdek [22] as *"all the planned and systematic activities implemented within the quality system that can be demonstrated to provide confidence that a product or service will fulfill requirements for quality."*

Quality control is defined by ISO [13] in ISO 9000:2015 as *"a part of quality management focused on fulfilling quality requirements."* In a similar manner, ISO defined quality assurance as *"a part of quality management focused on providing confidence that quality requirements will be fulfilled."* The usage of these two terms by the author is in accordance with these definitions.

Quality Control

In practice, quality control activities include all the checks and balances put in place to monitor, control, and regulate the quality of production processes so as to ensure that such processes are performing within specifications or under acceptable specified conditions. Hence, quality control can simply be seen as activities put in place to ensure the conformance of a process to predetermined specifications. Here, relevant processes are monitored and assessed and/or measured usually on a regular basis to check if they are working under specified controlled conditions or specifications. Quality control generally leads to the minimization of variations in processes vis-à-vis their output. The advent of modern technology has actually enabled organizations to design or install in-built quality monitoring systems/devices into various processes rather than using the manual sampling methods to assess the conformance of processes and their outputs. Verifying the *quality of conformance* or carrying out the *quality control* checks of a process often requires inspection and/or testing of samples.

In the case of smaller organizations that cannot afford automated or built-in quality control system, there is the alternative of using the more manual process inspection method. For cost-effectiveness, inspection points within the production flow system have to be carefully selected. While the proliferation of inspection points may be too costly, insufficient inspection points may lead to error of product quality assessment which will end up raising the cost of quality beyond that of proliferation of inspection points. As a result of the importance and relevance of quality control, the management itself must ensure the adequacy of the inspection points, sampling and sampling methods, monitoring and measurements, and the assessment to be carried out in obtaining information about the degree of conformity of intermediate and final products. There are three key areas of consideration when it comes to process inspection, monitoring, and measurement:

- *The inputs or raw materials*—to ensure that the process is not started with scraps and also to ensure that things are done right the first time.

- *During production (or process control)*—to ensure that the conversion of input into output is proceeding within acceptable or specified boundaries at every production stage so that only minimal input and/or added value would be expended on in—process-defective outputs that would ultimately be scrapped either during or after production. This generally leads to production cost reduction.
- *Post-production products or outputs*—to ensure that products are in conformance with specifications and that only products that meet customer requirements and specifications are passed on to the customer.

Here it is important to "*do it right the first time*" by ensuring that your processes are not started with scraps; hence, there is the need for inspection of raw materials before the commencement of production. This inspection can, however, be skipped if the suppliers of such inputs are reliable and give the assurance as to the reliability of the product. This is more so if the supplier has a good record with your organization. No matter what considerations are at hand, it is highly imperative to ensure that your inputs are in conformance with your production specifications.

If the results of measurements or tests carried out and/or samples taken show that the product is not acceptable, the process is stopped immediately for corrective action to be affected. If on the other hand it is a process that cannot be immediately stopped due to the nature and type of process, for example, in hollow glass bottle production, the output of the process obtained before the implementation of corrective action must be separated for recycling (culets) or discarded. It must, however, be noted here that preference has to be given to opportunities for reuse by putting defective products back into the production cycle (if applicable) for recycling until output conforms with specifications.

Quality Assurance

While quality control focuses on and emphasizes all operational techniques, processes, and other activities to ensure that products/services meet required standards, specifications, and expectations at the respective stages and levels of production and/or processing, quality assurance encompasses the planning and implementation of all the planned activities to ensure that the product/service will meet the needs, expectations, specifications, and requirements of the customer.

The focus and emphasis of quality control on the identification and selection of defective products have been with us since the advent of manufacturing. *Quality assurance* mainly emphasizes on preventing the production of defective products and in identifying and correcting them before delivery to customer or sales evolved at a later stage.

Quality Development Phases

In the Beginning

The end of the Second World War globally marked the official beginning of what may appear today to be the global quality movement. The foundation of quality was, in the beginning, focused on the improvement of manufactured products on the basis of the philosophy, which *makes consumer needs the focus of attention while empowering employees in evaluating product quality for the purposes of improving it.* The subsequent evolving phases of quality management development resulted in making its improvement needs a permanent feature by making it a continuous/continual occurrence.

The building of the mechanism of continuous improvement in quality and its management system, undoubtedly, represents an important leap forward in product/services quality. Since continuous improvement cannot be achieved without measurable evidence, the need for quality measurements became obvious and critical in the evaluation of quality. Today, quality practitioners have universally accepted the essentials of the constant evaluation of how well or qualitatively consumers' or customers' needs are met. Evaluation itself is a critical quality management tool needed to put necessary plans in place to effectively adjust and perfect various processes or process stages to achieve performance excellence.

The Growing of Quality

Apart from quality control and quality assurance, there are various other concepts of quality such as, *total quality control* (TQC), which evolved from quality control; and *zero defects* reared their heads in the evolution of quality before total quality management (TQM) and the now popular strategic approach of quality management systems (QMS). One of the quality gurus, Armand Feigenbaum emphasized the need for TQC to be enlarged beyond the primary concept of its application mainly to manufacturing to include design and incoming raw materials as well as the need for greater involvement of top management in quality.

With the trend moving from quality control to TQC, TQM, and QMS approaches, the searchlight of quality began to focus mainly on the general needs of meeting the needs, requirements, and specifications of the customer to achieve customer satisfaction with the full involvement and participation of all employees. The approaches of TQM and QMS concepts were successively recognized as being adequate for achieving or meeting the requirements of the customer irrespective of the degree of variation of such requirements.

Achieving the desires of the customer, in turn, requires that the voice of the customer (VOC) has to be heard, deployed, and integrated into the product or service development processes. This strategy generally known as the *quality function deployment* (QFD) ensures that customer specifications and requirements are put into consideration at every stage of the product design, planning, and implementation. QFD is defined by the American society for quality as a *"structured method in which customer needs or expectations are translated into appropriate technical requirements for each stage of product development and production."* In simple terms, therefore, QFD is tantamount to "listening to the voice of the customer (VOC)."

The movement of quality beyond quality control which may be said to have been the cornerstone of quality as it is known today is as a result of tremendous efforts, ingenuity, and persistent hard work and commitment by various apostles of quality. It will therefore be unfair to talk about the development or evolution of quality without making mention of the various entities that made things to happen.

The history of the development of quality and quality management the way we know it today owes a lot of credit to a lot of quality organizations of individual countries (e.g., the USA, Japan, Germany, Great Britain, and Canada) and global organizations such as the ISO, ASQ, IEC, and the military quality gurus such as Edwards Deming, Joseph Juran, Armand Feigenbaum, Kaoru Ishikawa, Genichi Taguchi, Philip Crosby, and their teams; and various research institutions. The industries themselves have been key movers and drivers of the global quality vehicle which they definitely will continue to drive, pilot, and direct. Here we have a host of organizations that cannot be completely enumerated in this book. Some of the major players here are the Ford Motor Company, General Motors, Mercedes Benz, Volkswagen AG, Toyota Motors, and Motorola. Some of the quality gurus actually made contributions not just generally to the development of quality but also with emphasis in particular areas of quality.

For example, *Deming* may be said to be the architect of modern quality management system approach through his enormous contributions to organizational-wide quality management system and his early acknowledgment and appreciation for the system. He was known for stressing the need to reduce variation in product output, the need for management responsibility to correct the system and a lot of other improvement initiatives in quality management system (QMS) particularly in post-World War Japan. His identification of key points (Deming's 14 points) needed for achieving quality and improvement in an organization and the establishment of the fact too that the causes of inefficiency and poor quality is in the system and not the employees are prominent among his works.

The work of *Joseph Juran*, an architect of quality and one of the most revered leaders of quality management in the twentieth century, is immense, spreading from his belief that an organization can "*manage for quality*" to his view of quality as "*fitness for use.*" The belief of *Juran* that about 80% of quality defects can be controlled by management may be seen as one of the early pointers to today's well known, quality management system which is an organizational-wide activity. This statement is strengthened by his description of quality management in terms of a trilogy [18] made up of the following:

- *Quality planning*
- *Quality control*
- *Quality improvement*

Feigenbaum on his own part advanced the philosophy of TQC and the "cost of nonconformance" approach.

Crosby developed the concept of "zero defects," the phrase "do it right the first time" and promoted "prevention."

Ishikawa developed the "cause -and-effect diagram" and emphasized the internal customer concept (i.e., the next person(s) in the work process).

Taguchi devised the concept for determining the "cost of poor quality."

The role of the International Organization for Standardization (ISO) in the overall field of quality is enormous. The ISO whose main objectives include the development of international standards has been very critical to the development of worldwide acceptable standards of various types, applications, and categories. It is worthwhile to mention here some of the industry-/application-specific and generic standards developed by the ISO. Hence, ISO in its development of standards has focused its attention on the needs of a wide variety of business sectors of the global economy. For example, ISO 14001:2004 which may be said to be a hybrid of the ISO 9001:2000 generic model and the EMS standards addresses special requirements of quality of the environment. Though each of the two standards is implemented separately, organizations could complement them with each other to achieve both product/services quality and environmental quality management.

International Quality Standards

Examples of Sector-Specific Quality Management System Standards (MSS)

The International Organization for Standardization (ISO) has so far established some sector-specific management systems standards which provide additional requirements or guidance for the general application of a generic management standard in specific sectors of the global economy or business sector.

The industrial- and application-specific standards developed by the ISO (iso.org) include but are not limited to the following (ISO [14]):

- **AS9100**—Was last revised (Rev D) in 2016. It is the international Quality Management System standard for the Aviation, Space, and Defense (AS&D) industry. Certification is usually with respect to AS9100D, hence, "AS9100 Certified."
- **IATF 16949:2016**—(Replaces and supersedes ISO/TS 16949:2009). This Management Systems Standard is for the Automotive Sector. It is not a standalone quality management standard; hence, its implementation is aligned or complemented with the latest version of ISO's quality management systems (QMS) standard which is, as at now, the ISO 9001:2015 QMS. It was introduced by the International Automobile Task Force (IATF) and is one of the world's mostly used international standards for quality management in the automotive industries by both the OEMs and their suppliers. One of its major requirements

is that all companies shall ensure the compliance of all products, processes, parts, and services, including all of those that are outsourced [10].

- **ISO 10002:2018** —Quality Management—Customer Satisfaction—Guidelines for Complaints Handling in Organizations.
- **ISO 10012:2003**—Quality Measurement Management Systems—Requirements for Measurement Processes and Measuring Equipment. This standard includes ISO 9000:2015; ISO 9001:2015.
- **ISO 10014:2021**—Quality management systems—Managing an organization for quality results—Guidance for realizing financial and economic benefits. This document provides guidelines for realizing financial and economic through the application of a top-down structured approach. This structured approach uses the quality management principles and quality management systems as described in the ISO 9000 family quality management systems standard.
- **ISO 10018:2020**—Quality management—guidance for people engagement.
- **ISO 13485:2016**—Medical Devices—Quality Management Systems—Requirements for Regulatory purposes Standards for Medical Devices. This gives for regulatory purposes. It is the quality management requirements for the medical device sector.
- **ISO 14001:2015**—Environmental Management Systems —Requirements with Guidance for use.
- **ISO 18091:2019**—Quality Management Systems—Guidelines for the application of ISO 9001 in local government.
- **ISO 19011:2018**—Guidelines for auditing management systems.
- **ISO 19600:2014**—Compliance management systems—Guidelines. This standard has, however, been replaced with ISO 37301:2021 [17].
- **ISO 22000:2018**—Food Safety Management Systems—Requirements for any organization in the food chain. This standard gives the requirements for food safety management systems.
- **ISO/TS 22163:2017**—Railway applications—Quality management system—Business management system requirements for rail organizations.
- **ISO 22301:2019**—Security and resilience—business continuity management systems—requirements. This is used to specify the structure and requirements for maintaining a business continuity management system (BCMS). This standard [12] can be used by materials' suppliers to effectively meet the International Automotive Task Force (IATF [11]) 16949 Clause 6.1.2.3 requirements [23] in terms of the need for maintaining a business continuity management system (BCMS).
- **ISO 26000:2010**—Guidance on Social Responsibility.
- **ISO 28000:2007**—Specification for Security Management Systems for the Supply Chain.
- **ISO 29001:2020**—Petroleum, petrochemical, and natural gas industries—Sector-specific quality management systems—Requirements for product and service supply organizations. This new management system standard (MSS, [15]) was previously ISO/TS 29001:2010 (ISO). This document which is used as a supplement to the latest version of ISO's QMS specifies quality management

requirements for organizations that supply both products and services to the petroleum, petrochemical, and natural gas industries. Hence, it is designed to work hand-in-hand with ISO 9001for the management of supply chain risks and opportunities in the petroleum, petrochemical, and natural gas industries.

- **ISO 31000:2018**—Risk management—Guidelines. It provides risk management guidelines on the management of all types of risks, including those associated with decision-taking, for the use of all organizations. In its definition, the ISO views risk as an essential step in the improvement process proposed under ISO 9001:2015 QMS. Risk in an organization thus represents the effect of uncertainty on objects (ISO Guide 73:2009 [16]). Its management is therefore an essential step which enables the optimization and improvement of the processes of a quality management system. In their risk management modeling research works, Akkiyat and Souissi [1], affirmed the absolute need for risk management to be "integrated in the life cycle of each process" to facilitate researching into potential solutions to problems that may arise.
- **ISO 35001:2019**—Biorisk management for laboratories and other related organizations.
- **ISO 37001:2016**—Anti-bribery management system. This is a specific standard focusing on guidance for a system to prevent, detect, and address bribery and comply with anti-bribery laws. This is an international standard suitable for anti-bribery management systems (ABMSs) for "organizations of various types and sizes" [7]. It is available to the global community where there is the honesty and sincerity of people *commitment to anti-bribery policies and controls.* Unfortunately, the predetermined condition of *people commitment* may have, from the onset, ruled out most of the African countries from benefitting from the use of the standard, especially Nigeria, which is today not just gasping for debt-free quality oxygen, but sinking under the heaviest imaginable burden of bribery and corruption in a heavily insecure atmosphere of deteriorating mis-leadership. One would, however, have expected all African countries and people to overwhelmingly embrace the standard.
- **ISO 37301:2021**—Compliance management systems—Requirements with guidance for use. This standard, apart from specifying requirements, provides the guidelines to enable organizations establish, develop, implement, evaluate, maintain, and improve an effective compliance management system within the organization. It thus replaces ISO 19600:2014.
- **ISO 45001:2018**—Occupational Health and Safety (OH&S) Management Systems—A practical guide for small organizations. Requirements with guidance for use. (OHSAS 18001 was replaced with ISO 45001 though OHSAS 18000 remains valid till end of 2021). This standard is adequate and suitable for employee safety, reducing workplace risks and for creating better and safer working conditions. As claimed by Gasiorowski-Denis, [9], the International Labor Organization (ILO) "2.78 million fatal accidents occur at work yearly" and "374 million non-fatal work-related injuries and illnesses each year." This is why there is the general hope that the standard would lead to transformational

changes in reducing this tragic toll of work-related accidents and illnesses among the people of the global communities.

- **ISO 50001:2018**—Energy management systems. This management system basically provides a framework of requirements to enable organizations develop adequate policies for the efficient use of energy to achieve improved and better use. As demonstrated by Mkhaimer et al. [21], ISO 50001cannot only be used on its own as a management system of the PDCA approach but can also be integrated with Lean Six Sigma (LSS) which follows the DMAIC (Define, Measure, Analyze, Improve, and Control) approach.
- **ISO 6385: 2016**—Ergonomic principles in the design of works systems.
- **ISO/IEC 27001:2013**—Information security management systems standard. This standard gives the requirements for information security management systems (ISMS).
- **ISO/IEC/IEEE 90003:2018**—Software engineering—Guidelines for the application of ISO 9001:2015 to computer software. This document gives guidelines for the use and application of ISO's QMS ISO:2015 to the acquisition, supply, development, operation, and the maintenance of computer software and any other related services.

The ISO has thus made tremendous progress in achieving the objectives of its supporting/promoting nations evidence of which is always available or provided on its website. You can read more about the ISO in subsequent chapters of this book.

Quality Metrics

Agricultural Produce

Quality measurement is generally a factor of the product or service. In some cases, numbers and alphabets are used to denote the dimension of quality of the product.

For example, in the case of cocoa, a major cash crop grown largely in the Southern States of Nigeria, Ghana, Ivory Coast, Indonesia, and some other countries of the West African subregion and South America, the quality of the seeds is measured in terms of the grade classification with Grade 1 representing the best quality. Since quality is defined on the basis of the type and nature of the product/services, there are varieties of dimensions in which quality can be reported. Some of the dimensions emanate simply from some of the characteristics of the product and services.

Examples here are as follows:

- Product durability. Here the focus is on the length of time the product/service remains useful. For example, the hours of operation of electricity generating plants, mileage of cars and other vehicles, and flight hours of pilots.
- Value of product.
- Product reliability/performance.

- Degree of conformance/compliance of product with stated specifications or requirements.
- Product safety both in use and when idle or not in use.
- Appearance/aesthetics—color.
- Taste/smell.
- Customer or public perception of product/service quality. This is related to the indirect measurement of quality using its reputation. For example, German products generally have the reputation of good quality in Nigeria.
- Any other characteristic feature of product/service that may be required by or agreed with the customer.

Some of the *"dimensions of quality"* may be relative to individual customers as well as to the use and application of the product. For example, garri (processed cassava), a staple food produced from cassava common in the West African subregion could be of a sour or flat taste and in white or yellow coloration. Some buyers prefer the sour tasting ones to the ones with flat taste and vice versa, while some people rate the yellow ones as their own premium grade. The grain size of garri is another measure of its quality. While some buyers prefer the fine ones, others go for the less fine-grained ones. The quality grading of the different varieties of garri also dictate the variations in their prices/values.

In the case of palm oil, color and viscosity take the front seat in the measurement of its quality while for textiles color fastness is one of the prominent determinants of quality.

In order for the agricultural produce of the West African subregion (particularly Nigeria) to remain relevant in the growing global market, there is the urgent need to introduce methods and principles of enumerating their quality on a global level and to apply modern QMS in their production systems. This is particularly important now that massive research work in the western world is gradually focusing on ways of finding artificial substitutes for some agricultural produce (e.g., cocoa) which are the main stakes of the economic well-being of the ECOWAS countries in this subregion.

The use of internationally acknowledged QMS in the production of agricultural commodities coupled with adequate political will power may serve as the needed impetus for the reversal of the current trend in which the prices of agricultural export produce of the West African subregion such as timber, cocoa, cotton, coffee, rubber, and plantain are more or less dictated by end-users which is not the case for manufactured goods imported into the West African subregion from other parts of the world.

Quality Metrics in Industrial Production

KPIs generally represent the basic and critical metrics for measuring the outcomes of quality management improvement efforts as it helps generally to track the performance of individual process, or groups of processes and their respective workgroups. The outcomes here are in turn linked with overall organizational business vision and its comparison with the overall business performance. While the KPIs are most commonly used for internally quality performance among internal customers for the purpose of achieving products and services that meet overall customer SNEaRs, other major broad-based metrics deployed for product quality measurement are among others listed as follows:

- Customer satisfaction/dissatisfaction complaints obtained from various feedback sources
- Product returns and call backs
- Record of customer retention
- Audit reports showing product services compliance with customer SNEaRs and regulatory body or standards SNEaRs
- Feedback of customer experience
- Organizational productivity and/or employee output
- Employee satisfaction
- Employee retention and turnover
- Stakeholders' satisfaction/dissatisfaction scale

Role of Management

The task of selecting the quality system considered most appropriate and relevant and the design and development of the appropriate systems (i.e., quality management system, manufacturing/production processes/technology) to achieve products and services that meet customer SNEaRs and values is on the one hand the primary responsibilities of the top management team of any organization.

The desired product quality cannot be achieved without the commitment of top management. That is why it is better not to start implementing any quality management system at all, than to start without the full and total commitment of top management. Even a fractional support of management is not enough to commence the implementation process of an organizational quality and improvement programs. The selection and implementation of any quality management system/concept for implementation must therefore be at the discretion of top organizational management. It is therefore highly imperative that top management commitment to quality must be seen in their *words, actions*, and *deeds*, else the successful implementation and maintenance of any QMS requirements and improvement measures may never be achieved.

In fact, thinking of an improvement program should therefore be restricted to the dreaming level if top management is not committed. It must, however, be mentioned here too that, securing that crucial support can be difficult as it is a factor of the leadership's level of quality commitment. In order to get the needed backing of the top management, it may be necessary to actually illustrate the benefits derivable from the implementation of the quality initiative using methods that impact management.

Top management must *say* it *loud* and *clear* that it is interested and willing to implement a QMS or quality initiative of choice. The management team needs on its own part to openly show and demonstrate its commitment to quality by implementing some or all of the following guidelines:

- Be convinced about the need for the implementation of a quality management system or quality initiative.
- Get information/briefing on the quality management system of choice.
- Demonstrate and show to the employees that top management is in full support of the quality goal thereby making the improvement initiative an organization-wide desire and commitment.
- Mandate or appoint a senior member of the management team with good leadership qualities as the quality management system representative or team leader.
- Clearly define and circulate the organization's quality policy and quality objectives.
- State in clear terms the roles of its employees in the drive to implement the desired quality system.
- Be proactive in all matters relating to the implementation of a chosen and already identified QMS.
- Willingly and timely provide necessary resources (human and capital) needed for the installation and maintenance of the desired QMS.
- Take quality-related issues with the outmost seriousness and sense of responsibility.
- Manage the implementation of the QMS as a project.

The responsibility for the implementation and management of the quality management system is, on the other hand, that of the entire organization (i.e., all employees) under a capable team leader. It is therefore obvious that a vital prerequisite for the successful and effective implementation and management of a QMS is commitment. The commitment to the implementation of the QMS can therefore be put into perspective from two important points of view:

- Total commitment of top management
- Commitment through the entire organization

Quality Management System Administration

Quality Planning

The administration of the QMS can, for practical purposes, be viewed from two perspectives:

Leadership with the outmost commitment, motivation, and inspiration to provide the dynamism needed for the implementation and management of the quality management system to achieve set out goals. The leadership here must embrace and promote team working.

Quality system administration to ensure the effective establishment of the various quality routines such as documentation, record keeping, control of records and document, preventive and corrective actions, monitoring, taking, and recording of measurements, regular production/operational (review) meetings, provision of work instructions, and work procedures, auditing, management review, and archiving is key to achieve the successful implementation and maintenance of a QMS.

Having identified the leadership and administrative quality segments as vital elements for achieving the desired quality goals, it is necessary to highlight the assignment of responsibilities for achieving them.

The first administrative option is the assignment of both the leadership and administrative roles to a management staff with the support and active participation of other members of the organization's management team (i.e., unit/departmental/sectional heads, group leaders, and supervisors). The quality system implementation and management team will then be built around him with the total and unalloyed support of top management so as to achieve the all-necessary team work. This responsibility may, for example, be borne by your Quality Assurance Manager/Engineer based on the status, confidence, and the level of responsibility assigned to him.

The second administrative option is the separation of roles with a top management staff (e.g., the Technical Manager/Director) assuming responsibilities for the QMS leadership while another management staff (e.g., the Quality Assurance Manager) takes up the quality system administrative responsibilities.

Although the issue of the option is a matter of choice, it is of extreme importance for you to take note of the fact that a successful quality management system can only be established and maintained with an effective *team* built around a *dynamic leadership* with the capability to organize, motivate, and inspire other members of the implementation team and those of other members of staff.

The choice of a particular option depends generally on factors such as the size, structure, and culture of your organization as well as the complexities of your operational processes and the nature of your products.

Since products and services are generally obtained from the combined results of the activities (i.e., cross-functional) of every phase of the total processes of an organization or company, quality management can be seen to assume interdisciplinary functions.

Monitoring, planning, and preventive measures are effective quality management activities that enable the identification of interrelationships and interdependencies of processes and other operational activities for the purposes of putting in place suitable and appropriate measures necessary for preventing the occurrence of nonconformities and/or nonconforming activities.

Modern quality management system anchors itself on the prevention of nonconformities, a deviation from the previous practice whereby nonconformities that already occurred were identified, analyzed, and rectified or separated and sold as second-/third-class products. This definitely results generally in a loss as the total cost of production may never be fully recovered. In addition to this, the input into the identification, analysis, and separation of the nonconforming products results in additional costs. Hence, the investment on the production of nonconforming products is a waste of resources and time (i.e., avoidable costs). This is a constituent part of the cost of quality.

The establishment, implementation, and maintenance of an effective and functional QMS should therefore be seen as an essential and vital requirement for every business interested in remaining relevant and in the economic and proactive delivery of quality goods and services. Quality management affects all areas of the business so that it can be recognized as the primary function of business management.

Using the appropriate quality tools, top management can easily achieve its responsibility to ensure that due diligence is exhibited in all areas and segments of the business operations from planning, design, production, logistics, storage, transportation, sales, product, and customer information to the monitoring of the position of the product/service in the market (i.e., customer feedback) and necessary post-sales services.

Apart from the fact that adequately planned and implemented QMS is essential for consistently achieving quality products and services, it also provides business partners and other associates/third parties (e.g., creditors, bankers, insurance brokers, and suppliers) with confidence in an organization's ability to fulfill quality obligations and meet customer and other requirements including those of the regulatory bodies.

Quality Improvement Outcome

The way the economy has recently been driven and shaped by products with effective considerations for meeting customer SNEaRs in the twenty-first century is amazing. Improved customer awareness has been appreciably strengthened through improved customer information across the globe. This most probably spurred organizations to react accordingly to the needs of informed customers.

The buying habits of the consumers are therefore grossly influenced by being informed thus positively impacting quality organizational performance and profitability trends because they had to deploy quality. This, in turn, triggered most businesses—small, medium, and large—to infuse the quality mindset into virtually all organizational processes. The major outcome therefrom quickly impacted the business world gathering momentum from 2016 till date in the following ways:

- Retail outlets were gradually driven to extinction.
- Online purchases soared remarkably.

Maintaining Improvement Gains

Implementing a QMS

The major task in the implementation of a QMS lies mainly in the ability and capability of an organization to sustain the improvement gains that were achieved through the implementation process. This is a problem the author encountered during the implementation of the ISO 9000 QMS in one of the plants under his supervision.

Here the attention of the entire management team was focused strictly on achieving the requirements of ISO 9000. It was not until we have gone half way through the implementation process that it was realized that we may not be able to sustain the improvement of ISO 9000 QMS even if we were able to achieve it.

The two members of staff selected for training in Quality Audit and in the implementation of ISO 9000 QMS with a view to assigning to them, respectively, the responsibilities of that of the Management Representative and Quality Assurance were found to be inadequate in terms of talent, leadership skills, and dedication. Due to other interests, most of the things done by them were only carried out half-heartedly. They were actually not engaged.

They were not able to carry the top management team of their organization along. Review meetings were never held. Internal audit meetings of the QMS were irregular. The improvement gains we made midway into the implementation exercise were unsustainable as they melted away within the twinkle of an eye. They were highly indifferent to organizational progress, moving perhaps toward sabotaging management efforts.

The mistakes made were respectively at the strategic and tactical levels. To correct this mistake, two top talented and engaged senior members of the management team, with good leadership skills and high sense of responsibility, were selected, respectively, to be Quality Assurance Manager and Management Representative in a new beginning of the implementation of the ISO 9000 QMS. The two top management team members were able to get the full involvement and cooperation of the top management team among which they command respect.

The implication here is that in order to successfully implement, achieve, and sustain the desired benefits of a QMS:

- Strategic and tactical plans must be put in place before the beginning of the implementation exercise in terms of people, structured approach to problems, and analytical techniques. Tactical correction may be made based on initial results 3–4 months into the implementation of the program.
- The A–Z of top management must be fully involved because the success of an organization actually starts from the top. They must be fully involved by their actions, words, and deeds in terms of their time, attention, and provision of necessary resources. Management must play a leadership role.

- Employee engagement is quite critical, hence, the need to embrace it, in furtherance of the confirmation of Mishra and Delgado [20], who stated that "Engaged employees go beyond what simply is required for the job and expend energy to solve problems, delight customers and reach organizational goals."
- The selection of top talents to manage the implementation of the QMS is a critical issue especially for the fact of Drucker and others' agreement on the concept of people being the foundation of any concept [19].

People engagement with respect to the contributions of the employees, which may be seen and viewed as an organization's intellectual capital, is particularly very critical in any operational mode, to improve organizational performance and maintaining whatever gains made on a continual basis for sustainability.

Cultivating the Quality Culture

When viewed from the perspective of quality, the word culture, from its dictionary meaning, refers to "the behaviors and beliefs characteristic of a particular social, ethnic or age group."

A major achievement of the author as a quality leader, for a chain of industrial manufacturing packaging and food industries which comprises of two millions-of-dollar glass bottle manufacturing plants, two bottle crown production plants, a cooling system assembly plant, plastic crates injection molding plant, PET preform bottle injection and blow molding production plant, and two food processing plants, is the massive proliferation of quality management and improvement principles, quality tools, quality thinking and mindset, among the workers and their management team members, to the extent that workers were able to talk quality, dream quality, think quality, and joke with various quality concepts, terms, and principles.

Talking about and using the terms "*customer satisfaction,*" "*customer focus,*" "*customer is king,*" "*customer says it all,*" "*continuous improvement is my process,*" "*team work is my goal,*" "*I am compliant,*" "*no defects,*" "*avoid wastes,*" "*it is my responsibility,*" and other expressions dominated worker gatherings. The achievement of developing the mentality among all employees that commitment with customer (internal and external) is a critical quality-focused culture [5], which has been found to greatly help in inculcating the quality culture generally in all operations of the companies and organizations particularly, because of the simplification of the supplier/customer relationships in terms of the organization's internal processes. It is particularly intriguing to see how enthusiastic most employees are, when they get to know that they have responsibility for the work they do and the processes involved. This statement often drives them and their performance beyond expectations. It is therefore very important indeed to ensure process ownership for each step or phase of work, an action which readily and willingly puts the responsibilities of self-work, self-process supervision on every individual employee to achieve performance excellence with minimum oversight.

Factory workers were happy, enthusiastic, and actively involved in the quality drive craze of the entirety of the employees for the particular reason that they had the rare opportunity of mingling with the members of the management of each of the factories on an equal basis. Yes, on an equal basis which they never experienced before because one of the key impacts of the principles and practices of quality is the ability and tendency to put all factory or plant staff members on the same level of equality with every other personnel. Engaging the employees in this way proved extremely beneficial. Quality is, when viewed from this aspect of achievement, a strong unifying force in the environment in which it is seen, viewed, and experienced as a *culture*.

The factory floors were usually generally dominated by the astoundingly resonating language and vocabularies of quality, gave me all needed assurances and satisfaction that quality behaviors and beliefs have become characteristic of each and every one of the workers and members of staff. Cultivating the culture of quality in this way gave me the general sense of appreciating my envisioned accomplishments, just as it made quality management systems implementation in those factory environments, look like a child's play.

It is, however, very important here to mention the fact that these accomplishments have been made possible by full reliance on key quality principles and practices such as active involvement of leadership and management team members, supplier or supply chain communication and involvement, focusing on the customer, strategic planning and its management, adequate management of processes, continual improvement, and providing opportunity for staff involvement in suggesting innovative ideas as if the quality process belongs to them.

The success recorded by the author further confirms the identification by Baros et al. [6] of the exhaustive list of quality principles and practice globally used by quality-driven companies to include among others the following:

Quality Principles

- Leadership
- Customer focus
- Employee involvement and commitment, including top management
- Human resources management
- Strategic planning management
- Process management
- Supply chain management
- Continuous improvement and innovation

Quality Practices

- Quality tools
- Quality standards
- Business and operational excellences models

There is no doubt here too that, from the experience and accomplishments of the author, creating the culture of quality in organizations and maintaining it, generally influences and facilitates its effective use of quality management principles and practices in line with the suggestions of Sampaio and Saraiva [24].

Strategies for achieving quality as organizational structure are, based on my experience in the manufacturing sector, the following:

- Conviction of organizational top management team that the organization is prepared and ready to permanently change the status quo, and prepared to completely focus business attention on customer satisfaction, needs, and values, as well as stakeholders.
- Management commitment and leadership of organizational resources to the continued provision of all the required resources—human, financial, and materials —needed to change the status quo.
- Embrace ab initio, full organizational partnership with customers and supply chain and recognition of and commitment to the environment and society at large, in anticipation of organizational corporate social responsibility (CSR).

It therefore a priority for top organizational leadership to cultivate a culture of quality organization wide, and ensure that adequate resources are devoted quality and quality management processes in a holistic sense of strategic planning, risk control and management, measurements and reliability, and product and/or services warranty.

Cultivating organizational quality culture can be achieved by organizations when, for example, "each and every employee from entry level to the seat of chief executive embraces the company's quality vision, values and goals as a way of life" [8]. The issue of organizational culture was illuminated in a global survey of the partnership between the ASQ and Forbes Insights in August 2014.

Inspiring Excellence: ASQE Inspire Excellence

While it may not be easy for individual organizations to single-handedly initiate and drive its quality cultural practices, professional organizations such as the American Society for Quality (ASQ) are highly endowed and adequately equipped to provide the needed quality ingredients, empowerment, energy, and dynamism to support every organization to achieve, cultivate, and sustainably maintain in all ramifications that great culture of quality to excellently drive the business.

In affirming the preparedness and capability of the ASQ [4] here is the recent founding of the ASQExcellence (ASQE) in January 2020, as "a trade association to set the standard for quality-driven offerings and insights worldwide," to empower the organizations it renders its services to, in achieving well-rounded excellence of products and services. ASQExcellence thus represents a professionally and ethically carved route for any organization across the globe to focus on and advance the business culture of quality-based practices suitable "for accelerating business value and drive growth."

The Impact of Culture

The role of culture in organizational management is easily seen, for example, from the purview of a new hire seeking new opportunities in joining an organization. It is, at times, quite exciting and challenging. On the other hand, it may more often than not, be confusing or disorienting to create fear and anxiety. The author has experienced a few situations when newly hired employees found it extremely difficult settling down to work and decided not to take up the job. The fear was in each of these few situations quite understood. In one particular situation, it was discovered that the other members of the team were from the same ethnic cultural background which made it impossible for a free flow of ideas among the new composition of the team.

The language barrier also resulted in the new member not understanding the team dynamics thereby hindering relationships growing into themselves. This type of situation thrives in the complexities of diversity, easily experienced in organizations operating in most parts of the countries of Africa particularly due to its multiethnic settings. My personal interest in this issue in understanding and explaining the team dynamics and the individual members of the team helped a great deal to imbibe organizational team culture in the context of teamwork and team performance output. Culture is thus very critical as it exhibits the unique opportunities of making or breaking an organization [25].

References

1. Akkiyat, I., & Souissi, N. (2019). Modelling risk management process according to ISO standard. *International Journal of Recent Technology and Engineering (IJRTE), 8*(2), 5530–5835.
2. ASQ. (2007). Quality glossary. *Quality Progress*, pp. 39–59.
3. ASQ. Quality glossary, www.asq.org. Retrieved 2 Mar 2021.
4. ASQ. Excellence Organization Membership. *Inspire excellence*, www.asq.org. Retrieved 2 Mar 2021.
5. ASQ. (2015). *Future of quality report*. American Society of Quality.
6. Baros, S., Sampaio, P., & Saraiva, P. (2014). Quality management principles and practices. Impact on the companies' quality performance. In *Proceedings of the International Conference on Quality Engineering and Management*. Guimaraes, Portugal, pp. 237–247.
7. Field, A. (2017). *ISO 37001: An introduction to anti-bribery management systems*. IT Governance Publishing, JSTOR. www.jstor.org/stable/j.ctt1wn0smd
8. Forbes Insights, ASQ. (2014). *Culture of quality: Accelerating growth and performance in the enterprise*. American Society of Quality, August 2014, www.forbes.cm. Retrieved 2 Mar 2021.
9. Gasiorowski-Denis, E. (2018). *ISO 45001 is now published*. ISO News. www.iso.org
10. Gruszka, J., & Misztal, A. (2017). The new IATF 16949:2016 standard in the automotive supply chain. *Research in Logistics and Production*. https://doi.org/.10.21008/j.2083-4950.2017.7.4.3.
11. IATF 16949:2019, Quality management system requirements for automotive production and relevant service parts organizations.
12. International Organization for Standardization, ISO 22301:2019. Security and resilience – Business continuity management systems – Requirements.
13. International Organization for Standardization. (2015). *ISO 9000:2015, Quality management systems – Fundamentals and vocabulary*.
14. International Organization for Standardization, ISO. http://www.iso.org/iso/iso

15. ISO. (2020). *Guidance for use of ISO 29001:2020, (version 2019-09-13)*, committee.iso.org, pp. 1–2.
16. ISO. (2009). *ISO Guide 73:2009, risk management – Vocabulary*. https://www.iso.org/standard/4465.html
17. ISO. *ISO 37301:2021, Compliance management systems- Requirements with guidance for use*.
18. Juran, J. M. (1986, August). The quality trilogy. *Quality Progress, 10*(8), 19–24.
19. Krivocuca, M. (2021). Catalysts for change – Achieving organizational excellence in post-COVID-19 industry 4.0 process performance. *Quality Progress*, pp. 32–37.
20. Mishra, S., & Delgado, D. (2021). Engineering engaged employees – Poer to your people to add strength to your quality program. *Quality Progress*, pp. 16–24.
21. Mkhaimer, L. G., Arafeh, M., & Sakhrieh, A. H. (2017). Effective implementation of ISO 50001 energy management system: Applying Lean Six Sigma approach. *International Journal of Engineering Business Management, 9*, 1–12. https://doi.org/10.1177/1847979017698712
22. Pyzdek, T. (2003). *The six sigma handbook* (p. 728). McGraw-Hill.
23. Reid, D. R. (2020). Be ready – How business continuity planning helps organizations plan for emergencies. *Quality Progress*, pp. 48–51.
24. Sampaio, P., & Saraiva, P. (Eds.). (2016). *Quality in the 21st century*. Springer Nature.
25. Veyera, J. (2020). *Culture is everything*. Quality Press.

4 Quality Management Trends

Quality Milestones

The tremendous progress made in quality, especially over the last half of the twentieth century, has created great awareness among the people of the world. People have thus realized how important quality has grown to become in their own individual lives. There is no doubt therefore that quality shall continue to revolve around man – his life, socio-economic, and political activities to help preserve his resources and ensure his needs are handy. Hence, quality shall continue to increasingly serve most effectively as a bridge linking man with the various facets of his life – healthcare, technology, education and training, transportation, risk management, etc. The integration of quality in our lives will continue to gain more grounds year in and year out especially with increased risks and exposure to environmental pollution, extreme weather conditions, climate change, and other unexpected disruptive factors of life.

The role played by quality management principles in attending to the challenges of the COVID-19 pandemic reportedly detected for the first time in the USA in January 2020 was a significant demonstration of the relevance of quality in our lives. This is the extent to which quality has evolved and shall continue to evolve.

Quality has thus been transformed to become a part of the everyday life in a great number of businesses, institutions, and organizations. Quality roles in processes, people, products, and services, as well as its close link with innovation and innovational landmarks, can today not be overemphasized. Quality has thus far evolved to become the oxygen for ensuring the survival of businesses, enterprises, and other institutions of interest, across the globe both today and the years ahead.

The global community turning swiftly to the philosophies and principles of quality, to save millions of lives and safeguard the other interests of man, during the globally ravaging deadly threats of the COVID-19 in the year 2020 is a pointer to man's sudden realization of quality in his value chain and the need to perpetrate quality in all ramifications of his life.

T. A. Ibidapo, *From Industry 4.0 to Quality 4.0*, Management for Professionals,
https://doi.org/10.1007/978-3-031-04192-1_4

The trending in quality is thus encompassed in the wider adoption, integration, use, and application of quality improvement concepts and methodologies, quality philosophies, and quality management principles across the length and breadth of industries, businesses/enterprises, and a wide range of service organizations including the public service sector, from the perspectives of total quality management (TQM) and sustainability.

Most African countries are today giving their economies and perhaps the people's quality of life a kiss of death to guarantee their people the lowest quality of life anywhere on the surface of the earth, not because they have not officially embraced quality and its practices but simply for the general lack of the willpower among the people and government to promote both corporate and public ethical culture, a situation that has so far most conspicuously resisted the impact of quality on the lives, economy, and culture of about 1.4 billion people of the continent. Neglecting quality and its principles in governance as well as in all decision-making, processes and infrastructural provision is on its own a risk for the people of the continent.

While acknowledging the in-depth effect of the eight TQM underlying principles of the ISO's most popular QMS series of international standard – supplier relations, systems approach, customer satisfaction, leadership, people involvement, decision-making and problem solving, continual improvement, and process approach – on quality in its trending roles, it is vital here to identify some more details of key critical areas of its impacting trends.

Key Trending Factors of Quality

Some top management entities of small- to mid-size manufacturing companies are yet to have a full understanding of the total implications of quality other than in the number of products that are shipped to the customer. Top management entities therefore need to realize the realities of both the present and future that quality must have to be viewed and seen as an integrated system within the totality of organizational processes.

Experience showed here that training top members of organizational management team at all levels makes it easier for assimilating quality into the entirety of the business processes, their management styles and practices. Continuous learning and improvement are thus critical organizational values that keep trending in quality management both now and in the future, hence the need for quality leadership's appreciation and acknowledgment of quality as a key component of organizational growth potentials. Future organizational commitments in both the overall and technology-specific quality investment remain a highly imperative option for organizations to remain competitive now and in the future. Quality leadership is however pivotal in deciding whether an organization survives or not. Mis-leadership in the political governance of the countries of Africa is a key factor affecting the quality of life of the people.

Quality Leadership

Quality leadership is a key and critical factor needed to support the trending of quality and its management systems. The following are guides helpful for achieving leadership objectives of any organization.

- Maintain and focus on quality as basic foundational principles for accomplishing and maintaining organizational competitiveness at all organizational levels – people, processes, product/service, community and society, local, national, and international.
- Take responsibility in assessing and placing organization in the most competitive position at all times through benchmarking, innovation, gap analysis, and other organizational comparative assessment models to identify weaknesses and upgrade organizational competitive status so as to continuously achieve customer satisfaction.
- Ensure organizational maintenance of customer satisfaction in all ramifications including regulatory requirements and other product-/service-compliant needs even when not specifically stated by customer but found necessary.
- Ensure organizational sustainability in all aspects of quality system selection, adaptation, integration, and implementation by providing necessary funds and resources.
- Have responsibility in getting advice and selection of the most suitable quality programs, principles, concepts, QMSs, or an integration of a combination of them.
- Promptly harness employee creativity, ingenuity, and other resources in adjusting to and effectively managing disruptive changes and any other ensuing or envisaged emergencies and risks.
- Willingly and readily facilitate adaptive activities necessary to facilitate organizational adaptability to disruptive changes through the creation of adaptive space needed for ideas and insights to be more actively explored and developed [2, 3, 28].
- Ensure quality programs are built around customer/market value chain through adequate interconnection and integration of all relevant quality work processes.
- Ensure the maintenance and improvement of technical emphasis.
- Recognition and appreciation of the growing customer/market integration of quality with and as a part of organizational value.
- Believe in the relevance of transforming management orientation and quality systems to match organizational quality strategies with successfully emerging operations of the future time.
- Since success is optional it is advisable that leadership recognizes the need to achieve cultural improvement with Netherton's [34] three-legged stool approach – resources, training, and accountability. While resources must be available and functional, trained personnel must be available to attend to, run and maintain, and measure the processes adequately and effectively to ensure products/services meet customer expectations and are customer compliant. Every

employee and team members where necessary must be held accountable. This is one of the reasons to avoid high employee turnover especially in key highly critical operational processes.

It is of great importance too that organizational top management must have to put as one of the top priorities of organizational values the need to continuously train and develop organizational human resources, the intellectual capital, at all levels to grow the organization. This thus makes it highly imperative for the organization's top executives to constantly engage in leveraging learning to positively impact their organizations and their QMS.

Employee training can therefore not be overemphasized especially in the post-COVID-19 transitional era of many changes including those that are anticipatedly embedded in achieving the vision of integrated industry, also known as Industry 4.0, or 4th Industrial Revolution.

Application: Specific Quality Standards

Customer Compliance Measures

With increased market competition it is highly important that suppliers pay particular attention to relevant supplier or supply chain standards so as to ensure strict compliance of supplied products and/or services with customer and relevant regulatory requirements with extension to environmental protection demands. Failure to adhere strictly to any product/service compliance or regulatory requirements, whether stated or not, may subsequently lead to higher costs of quality (CoQ) in various ways as highlighted below:

- Avoiding recalls which on its own leads to a high cost of quality (CoQ)
- Avoiding wastages due to the need for replacing recalled items, products, or services
- To avoid heavy costs of quality (CoQ) due to failure to comply with regulatory/mandatory requirements, especially in relationship to environmental management systems and protection, a critical aspect of business quality management trends in the twenty-first century

The dynamism of quality trending, in the use and application of product-/service-specific standards and/or management systems, and their integration with other relevant systems/standards in the twenty-first century cannot be overemphasized or stopped, as it shall become more and more in demand across the globe during this time.

These standards, which may be promoted by government and its agencies, private institutions and organizations, individuals, or any other entity, shall not only be made available mainly by the ISO but also by other similar organizations and/or affiliated groups of organizations such as the group of pharmaceutical organizations' Asia Pacific country affiliates – Australia, New Zealand, China, Singapore, South Korea, and Taiwan [30] – which has reportedly established the *good affiliate practices* (GAP), implemented by the group's affiliate organs.

The pharmaceutical sector of the economy is like others in the healthcare industry, heavily regulated and justifiably so too. This however makes it extremely difficult to adhere to and rely solely on a single platform of quality management system. This is so for the good reasons that the products and services of this sector of the economy center exclusively on people's lives – diagnosis, treatment, and well-being, hence the need for extreme caution and the need for stringent quality measures.

Pharmaceutical organizations therefore have to face the challenges of a combination of different regulatory guidelines, such as those for good manufacturing practices (GMP), which in the USA incorporates the Code of Federal Regulations (CFR), 21 CFR (quality system regulation rules of the Food and Drug Administration (FDA), [40] or those of the International Conference on Harmonization Q10 Guideline [9], a description of a model for the effective management of a product over its life cycle.

Complicating the situation in the healthcare sector of the economy is the fact too that there are several definitions of the quality management systems (QMSs), each with a different quality focus. While the manufacturing sector of healthcare focuses on product consistency, hospitals are on patient needs. The readily available ISO 9000 series of quality management system standards, which due to its generic nature could have been able to take care of quality management in the entirety of the healthcare sector as a whole, focus on customer requirements and certification to qualify suppliers. According to Bangert [5, 6] these three routes to quality management only address the principles of quality management to varied extents, hence the need for the establishment of an adaptable QMS named *good affiliate practices* (GAP) by a group of pharmaceutical companies for implementation among its organizations across all functions in their locations worldwide. As reported by London et al. [30] GAP are a good practice-based quality system by design, whose structure and function are patterned along the "eight principles of QMSs that underpin the ISO 9000 series of standards" [13, 14, 15] as highlighted below:

- Process approach
- Supplier relationships
- Systems approach
- Customer satisfaction
- Leadership
- People involvement
- Decision-making and problem solving
- Continual improvement

In order to ensure that the GAP system is both effective and efficient, matters relating to continuous improvement in terms of self-review and internal audits are highlighted. In conclusion, it was affirmed by London et al. that the adaptable *good affiliate practice* (GAP) quality system stood the test of time in the pharmaceutical industry; hence, the possibility of the applicability of the principles developed for implementation and the quality by design approach may be applicable to other industries.

This is a noteworthy example of a quality trend that can be copied by other organizations or conglomerates of industries not just in developing their own adapted suitable quality management systems like the GAP but in integrating existing standards with their own ideas and product regulatory requirements easily, to establish product-/service-specific quality management systems, concepts, and principles for the entirety of their organizational systems or a part thereof. The GAP are found particularly interesting here because the features of the GAP system, as reported by London et al. [30], are all embracing:

- *Healthcare compliance* – Corporate conduct and healthcare compliance
- *Critical components* – Document control, training, management review, internal review, excursions and corrective action preventive action
- *Secondary GAP components* – Business continuity, data privacy and integrity, risk management, vendor qualifications, technology transfer, audit hosting, employee relations, and regulatory affairs
- *Good practice – specific components* – Customer complaints, recalls, change control, pharmacovigilance and risk management, quality risk assessment, good clinical practice, distribution, and logistics

With these combinations of quality system components, the GAP adaptable QMS represents a very strong and promising quality management system for industry-specific application, here in the pharmaceutical sector of the global economy.

With the ISO [4] at the forefront of application-specific quality management standards, many more organizations will follow the example of the GAP adaptable QMS to establish their home-made quality management systems adaptable to their in-house cross-functional requirements.

Some of the already-established application-specific quality management standards which should immediately catch the attention of most African and South-American countries where there is the urgent need for good governance are listed immediately below:

- **ISO 37001:2016** – Anti-bribery management systems.
- This is a quality management system which focuses on guidance for a system for preventing, detecting, and addressing bribery laws.
- **ISO 37301:2021** – Compliance management systems – Requirements with guidance for use. Replaced ISO 19600:2014 [17], hence withdrawn, as of April 13, 2021.
- **ISO 37000** – Governance of organizations – guidance.
- This standard which is based on the principles of good governance of organizations is in the final stage of its approval as an international standard, FDIS (final

draft international standard). If approved, its publication is set for *September/October 2021* (ISO, [21]). The intent of this international standard is in accordance with the provisions of the relevant ISO committee, to help in reflecting "the identity, mission, or purpose of the organization with respect to society and stakeholders."

Both ISO 37001:2016 [22] and ISO 37301:2021 (replaced ISO 19600:2014 [17]) are highly recommended for use in most African countries, especially in Nigeria where bribery is the only incontrovertible culture of the people, and organizational governance is in complete and total states of disarray.

Quality Management Research Exploits

Establishment and Development of Adaptable QMS

An extensive research vacuum in quality management begging for the attention of researchers and the academia lies fallow in various sectors of the global economic platform particularly, in the healthcare systems. The example of London et al. [30] is demonstrative of what could have been the potential vision and objectives of individual and collective researchers across the globe, especially in the continents of African and South America, instead of abandoning the responsibility of quality management system's establishment and development solely in the purview of the International Organization for Standardization (ISO).

London et al., whose work the author greatly admires, successfully "established an adaptable QMS called the "*good affiliate practices, (GAP)*"" for specific application to the pharmaceutical industry though "there is no reason why the principles developed for implementation and the quality by design approach can't be applied to other industries" [30]. The GAP system has its basis rooted on five critical components representing the common major elements of a QMS listed accordingly:

- Document management
- Training
- Excursion and corrective and preventive actions
- Management review
- Internal review

The cross-faculty opportunities and research facilities which are already in existence in today's global research and academic worlds easily bring out the unused academic and research resources in the field of quality management begging for research exploits to establish and develop adaptable QMSs missing in healthcare system management, resource management, agricultural produce management systems, quality management in governance, international trade, transportation and transport system management, etc.

For example, the author's experience in the use and application of the electronic nose odor recognition systems for agricultural produce quality assessment is another research area of quality management waiting for further development and exploitation by interested researchers [25, 35, 45–47]. Higher institutions and research institutes across the globe can easily work together to develop application-specific standards for global use and application.

It is high time too that we all come together as quality management enthusiasts, teachers, practitioners, followers, and professionals to consolidate and bring the widely spread knowledge domains of quality together under an umbrella as a field of study, *Science of Quality* or *Quality Management Sciences*, in which quality management and quality engineering are merged despite the skepticism that these "two areas are not easily brought together (quality Engineering and Quality management)" [38].

Whether we are thinking of tracing the elements and functions of the twentieth-century development of quality management, courtesy of the quality *gurus* to their possible scientific basis and/or rooting, or developing new standards and expatiating on the existing concepts of quality, quality management remains a reservoir of research interests.

Sustainability and Corporate Social Responsibility (CSR)

It is a natural self-defensive instinct for humans to immediately react to mitigate any disruptive situation. If there is one lesson that the COVID-19 pandemic taught organizations in the business world, it's the value of building the preparedness, agility, and capacity to immediately respond to and mitigate the impacts of disruptive situations such as the pandemic.

According to Madhav et al. [31] and Jones et al. [24], "Pandemics are large-scale outbreaks of infectious diseases that can greatly increase morbidity and mortality over a wide geographic area and cause significant economic, social, and political disruption. Evidence suggests that the likelihood of pandemics has increased over the past century because of increased global travel and integration, urbanization, changes in land use, and greater exploitation of the natural environment. These trends likely will continue and will intensify."

The experience of the 2020 COVID-19 pandemic coupled with Reid's [37] suggestion of expert opinion of a possible increase in the frequency of pandemics jointly makes the need for organizational continuity plans to protect resources and ability to uninterruptedly meet customer supply responsibilities highly imperative.

This is one of the reasons why organizations and their leadership need to closely consider the underlisted critical issues for survival and success in the near and long term of the twenty-first century. Organizations need to ensure that:

- The organization's resistance to failure is strengthened by empowering it to be always ready and prepared to withstand unexpected environmental changes, no matter the magnitude, and still remain functional.

- Supply chain management strategies are frequently reevaluated from time to time to keep it strong, always in use, and not disrupted by any future unforeseen changes, risks, and circumstances whatsoever.
- Supply chain risks are avoided or adequately managed by engaging multiple supply sources. The whole world, having to rely mainly on China for the supply of personal protective equipment (PPE), has proved to be a near catastrophic option, during the onset and prevalence of the COVID-19 pandemic particularly throughout the year 2020. There is therefore the urgent need for global economic quality management entities, spread all over the countries of the world, especially in the Western world, to have some re-thinks about the need to help in developing and empowering the establishment of alternative supply chain facilities in nations in other parts of the world, especially in the continents of Africa and South America.
- Uncertainty and disruption are "incorporated" in and "embraced" as an "integral" part of organizational operating models, to maintain organizational preparedness when next the world is upended in whichever way it may happen.
- There is a business continuity plan in place to avoid operational disruption and protect organizational resources and the ability to uninterruptedly fulfill product and service obligations to the customers and the market.

In the words of Reid [37], *business continuity planning* (or business continuity and resiliency planning, or emergency preparedness) is "the process of creating systems of prevention and recovery to deal with potential threats to a company. In addition to prevention, the goal is to enable ongoing operations before and during execution of disaster recovery."

The ISO, in appreciation of the quality need for business continuity, has established a generic standard intended for use by any organization, or parts thereof, irrespective of type, size, and nature. This international standard, in the latest version, is the **ISO 22301:2019** – Security and resilience – Business continuity management systems (BCMS) – Requirements. ISO 22301:2019 is therefore a generic standard applicable to any organization that is generally interested in:

- Implementing, maintaining, and improving its own *business continuity management systems* (BCMS).
- Seeking to achieve and ensure that it is operating in conformity with stated business continuity policy, either for sustainability or in response to customer needs or requirements. A very good example in the latter case is found in one of the key requirements of the automotive industry's business continuity requirements, as reported by Reid [37]. One of the clauses of the International Automotive Task Force (IATF) 16949 stipulates the need for their direct material suppliers to "define and prepare contingency plans according to risk and impact to the customer to provide for continuity of supply in the event of the following: key equipment failures, supply chain interruption, recurring natural disasters, fire, utility interruptions, labor shortages or infrastructure disruptions."

- Strengthening their ability to continue to deliver products and services uninterrupted to the customers and/or marketplace at the rate predetermined or acceptable to them during the disruption.
- Enhancing their resilience through effective application of a reliable business continuity plan or BCMS.
- Assessing organizational ability to meet and fulfill its own business continuity needs, plans, and objectives.

This generic standard, as established by the ISO, which brings to the fore the need to focus attention on risks and how to mitigate the risks, specifies the requirements to implement, maintain, and improve a management system to protect against, reduce the likelihood of, prepare for, respond to, and recover from disruptions when they arise. Since it is not possible to simply eliminate all risks, ISO 22301 also emphasizes the need for organizations to analyze the business impacts of any potential risk or emergency, in order to be able to determine the priorities and requirements for business continuity.

Quality-minded people and organizations have thus come to realize from the outcome of the COVID-19 pandemic that it is now a world of disruption and uncertainties, hence the general need for strategizing for a future of uncertainties.

Building Resilience with Innovation

Naden [33], in an ISO news report, "Innovate… or Break!", rightly identified climate change, cyberattacks, and business disruptors as key threats to business sustainability. Interestingly too is the identification of *innovation* as "a common tool to build resilience against these business threats."

The question then remains as to how innovative organizations should be "in order to roll with the punches of an increasingly uncertain world." Using innovation to adapt risks is thus a strong quality path to thread by organizations that see survival as a key part of organizational business vision.

Threats to businesses in our fast-changing world encompass challenges of various kinds and types including those traceable to digital technology. Most of such challenges call for innovational dynamism to remain afloat, or else a lot of organizations risk going aground, disappearing from the highly competitive business world.

The constantly emerging introduction of new technologies thus requires organizational abilities to quickly adapt newly introduced technologies or innovations. The threats in the power and quality impact of the fast-emerging innovative e-commerce marketplace have unfortunately not been immediately recognized and appreciated by most merchandizing or retailing businesses until recently, when it was already almost getting too late for most of them to react effectively to the then emerging competition. Innovation played key roles too in the dramatic changes experienced in recent years in global consumer behavior, which was similarly also critically influenced or if you like "disrupted" by the global impact of the COVID-19 pandemic.

The need and ability for organizations to innovate therefore remains part of the key trends for the quality management systems of organizations that are keen on and interested in surviving and surviving very well too. This is a further affirmation of Lindborg [28] in his adaptive space that "In today's disruptive environment, we must ensure that our organizations and institutions are agile-they must be able to respond to change instantly and effectively. The only way this can happen is if *novel ideas* flow freely among teams, across departments and throughout an organization."

Risk Management

What Is Risk Management

In their extensive treatment of risk management, Waring and Glendon [42, 43] gave it an all-embracing definition of being "a field of activity seeking to eliminate, reduce and generally control pure risks (such as from safety, fire, major hazards, security lapses, environmental hazards) and to enhance the benefits and avoid detriment from speculative risks (such as financial investment, marketing, human resources, IT strategy, commercial and business risks)."

Moon [32] presented the in *Foundations of Quality Risk Management* the purpose of risk management as being the accurate appraisal of organizational objectives, achievement paths, and continual improvement, the prevention of undesirable outcomes, and adding or sustaining organizational value.

Although risk management is executed to varying degrees by different organizations, there is no doubt whatsoever that risk management has, explicitly or implicitly, become a strategic component of organizational survival and development. It is this survival instinct that has pushed risk management to the forefront of quality efforts to business continuity plans in organizational quality management system (QMS) standards.

In hitting the nail on the head Norman Foster, architect, rightly reminded all quality-minded people of the global community that "As an architect, you design for the present, with an awareness of the past, for a future which is essentially unknown." This is not to say however that existing quality management systems never considered planning for uncertainties and business risks but not in the magnitude of the disruptive changes brought about by the COVID-19 pandemic, especially in the year 2020.

For example, Clause 6.1 of ISO 9001:2015, a significant addition to this international quality management system standard addresses risks and opportunities. Some of the benefits of risk management include but are not limited to the following:

- *It serves to increase both organizational and employees' consciousness* – organizational employees begin to think about risks in their everyday activities – operational processes, handling of materials, interacting with each other and general response to and handling of products and services, and other matters of customer relationships. In this way employees become better partners in organizational success and managing and protecting organizational resources.

- *It helps in creating and cultivating the culture of risk prevention and the ability to effectively and successfully manage risks* – the culture of risk managing though should not prevent risk taking but will lead to informed and carefully considered risk-taking. Since a risk management culture has the potentials to affect the way every employee thinks decision-making is most likely going to be carried out with strong understanding of the inherent risks and the consequential outcomes.
- *It enables focus of attention on how to control and mitigate potential organizational risks* – this will in turn allow for the concentration of attention on issues that matter most to maintain and sustain organizational existence and sustenance, hence no time wasting as it prevents the use of efforts in firefighting potential problems.
- *It promotes organizational business success* – organizations with effective risk management process are open to the opportunities of avoiding crisis management and the cost and time that would have been spent on handling blown-out problems created by unattended risks.
- *It foresees what may go wrong, preempts, prevents, and reacts promptly to avoid risks* – risk management thus in this way serves as the cornerstone of business continuity as well as crisis management, discovering opportunities and reducing liabilities.

The ISO [11] explicitly requires that organizations shall "determine risks and opportunities that need to be addressed." The risks to be addressed are thus the ones considered by any organization implementing the requirements of ISO 9001:2015 as being the most critical or significant, hence the need for organizations to evaluate the risk and opportunities.

There are risk management standards, some of which are:

- **IEC 31010:2019** – Risk management – Risk assessment techniques [20].
  This standard [12] is a joint IEC/ISO supporting standard for ISO 31000 [19]. It provides guidance on the selection and application of techniques for assessing risks, in a wide range of situations even though it is not meant for certification, regulatory, or contractual use. It is a generic risk management standard. The techniques help to assist in making decisions in situations where there is uncertainty, in providing information about particular risks and as part of a risk managing process.
- **ISO 31000:2018** – Risk management – Guidelines (ISO, [19]).
  This international standard provides guidelines on managing the risks faced by any organization. Hence, it is neither industry nor sector specific. It is applicable for use to any organizational activity at all levels, including decision-making.

The COSO Framework

The model for evaluating organizational internal controls developed by the Committee of Sponsoring Organizations of the Treadway Commission (COSO) [36] has been reported as being accepted, not just as the general framework for organizational internal control but also as a standard against which organizations can measure the effectiveness of their systems of internal control. The five components of this framework do not just work to support the achievement of an entity's mission, strategies, and related business objectives but help in routinely identifying and assessing various risks facing any organization at all levels and within all of its functions. The five components for effective internal control system are specified by COSO as follows:

- Control environment
- Risk assessment
- Control activities
- Information and communication
- Monitoring

Governance, Risk, and Compliance (GRC)

GRC, according to Lindros [29], is a strategy for the management of an organization's overall governance, enterprise risk management, and compliance with regulations. In explaining the risk management capability, the GRC reportedly makes sure that any risk associated with organizational activities is identified and addressed in such a way that it supports the goals of the organization's business or enterprise. It emphasizes too that in terms of IT, GRC represents a comprehensive IT risk management process capable of rolling into an organization's enterprise risk management function.

The GRC can accordingly be implemented by both large and small organizations, public and private, interested in aligning its IT activities to its business goals, to effectively manage risk and stay on top of compliance requirements.

Business Continuity Planning

It is obvious from the assertion of Waring and Glendon [42, 43] that "A framework for strategic risk management encompasses strategies for avoidance, deferment, reduction, retention, transfer, sharing and consequence mitigation," thus making it extremely difficult to manage unimaginable, unforeseeable, and unpredictable risks of the type that caught the whole world unawares in 2020 – the COVID-19 pandemic.

COVID-19 taking the business world by surprise in 2020 did not only shock the people of the world, but incited their quality consciousness and mindset, while at the same time leading to prompting the question whether businesses and other organizations could have been better prepared for the emergency situations, such as social, economic, and political disruption, created by the pandemic.

Prepared for Change?

Change is a permanent phenomenon in the life of humans as well as in the lifespan of any business or organization – small and large – irrespective of products and services, thereby constituting a major but inevitable quality trend, of all times. Change is therefore a constant phenomenon. The rate of change in our current world is on the increase from day to day with technological advancement in various usages and applications playing critical accelerating roles.

This dynamism of change thus in turn calls for organizational management leadership dynamism and agility, readiness, and preparedness to react promptly and appropriately to any uncertainty and disruptive environment to avoid possible negative impact on the organization and business so as to achieve their functions undisturbed. It is from the perspective of the constancy of *change* that the adequacy of change management should be viewed and seen as an integral component of an organizational or business quality management system so as to achieve organizational or business adaptability.

Adaptive organizations have the ability to understand "the power of social interactions in facilitating the flow of ideas, information and insights" as much as they know the ways for bridging gaps between the operational systems which are critical for driving efficiencies "and the entrepreneurial activity that is critical to reinvention" [28]. The need for innovational management thus differentiates traditional change management – managing, coordinating, and controlling activities – from disruptive change management, which requires the ability to quickly and instantly and effectively respond to changes for quick adaptation. Understanding change management requires according to the ISO that the organization:

- Understands the sources of organizational changes, or where the stimulus for change generally emanates from
- Identifies change context and the links to the closely interested parties and their relevant requirements
- Determines the processes which support the linkage
- Identifies the risks and opportunities associated with such processes

Achieving the benefits associated with the determination of the risks and opportunities often calls for change which may in one way or another be related to the process – its inputs and outputs, people and other resources, controls and measurements, feedback, and any other aspects of it.

Sources of organizational quality management changes fall into a broad spectrum, too many to enumerate, hence the need for focusing of attention on key extra-organizational operating environmental factors and their perceived implications for and effects on the product/service market, labor market, costs, etc. Some of the important issues that can trigger significant organizational changes are among others the following:

- Technology deployment – software, robotics, automation, artificial intelligence, digitalization, and other advancement-induced changes which may necessitate purchase or changes in equipment and processes that may call for the adoption of new methods and/or tools
- Important changes in raw materials or other supplies
- Economic factors such as market forces, customer feedback, recalls, and other complaints
- Changes in social patterns and structures
- To achieve compliance with new or existing regulatory or mandatory rules or guidelines (even when not mentioned by customer)
- Forced or sudden changes due to various risks and catastrophic situations, such as that created by the unforeseen circumstances of the COVID-19 (coronavirus disease 2019) pandemic in the year 2020
- Other natural disasters that may impact the environment and people

The ISO [15] on its own identified the following situations as capable of triggering changes to organizational QMS:

- In reaction to customer feedback and complaint
- Putting corrective and/or preventive actions in place as response to product/service failure
- Implementing feedback from employees and other interested parties
- Innovational purposes
- Determining risks and opportunities
- Implementing audit – internal and external results
- Implementing the outcomes of management review
- In compliance with identified nonconformity
- Implementing identified opportunities for improvement

Although there was a casual mention of change in ISO 9001:2008 in Subclause 5.4.2., the ISO, in appreciation of the relevance and criticality of change management to an organization and its QMS, soon made up for this in its subsequent version *ISO 9001:2015* in Clauses:

- 6.3. – Planning of changes
- 8.1. – Operational planning and control
- 8.3.6 – Design and development changes
- 8.5.6 – Control of changes

These clauses of ISO 9001:2015 [16] have given needed relevance to change management requirement to greatly enhance organizational QMS.

The need for adaptive change management was demonstrated among various sizes of organizations and businesses during the 2020 COVID-19 pandemic attacks on both humans and organizational and business settings. The aviation sector of the economy was equally shocked by the coronavirus pandemic as well as small businesses especially in the tourism sector of the global economy.

Corporate Social and Environmental Responsibility (CSER)

The subversion of corporate social responsibility (CSR) in the oil mining Delta region of Nigeria and its environmental implication for both people and ecology are strong portrayals of how critical corporate environmental responsibility (CER) has grown to become to the people of the global community. Supporting this assertion is the 2020 global lesson learned from the impact of the COVID-19 pandemic. We the people of the world have been taught the bitter lesson that we are all (equally) subjected to global environmental impact, no matter where we live on the surface of the earth. From China, Africa, North America, other parts of Asia, South America, Europe, to Australia, we have all been subjected to equal doses of the coronavirus.

Hence, the responsibility for the quality of the global environment belongs to all of us, thereby putting corporate environmental responsibilities (CER) at par with CSR, a reason for the incorporation of both the CSR and CER to be incorporated here as the CSER.

Intersecting the past experience of quality with the outlook of quality for the future therefore brings to the fore the need for handling issues of both organizational corporate social and environmental responsibilities (CSER) with utmost care and seriousness or else we shall put the quality of life in our global place in serious jeopardy. This is particularly so in this constantly changing world.

There is no doubt whatsoever that, even when the fundamental and foundation still remain unchanged, environmental concerns as well as the culture of organizational practices and available quality tools for achieving set objectives are daily changing. Coping with this dynamism emanating from the growing changing trends of our time generally results in creating various kinds and types of societal and environmental challenges critical to the quality of life and human survival on the global platform.

Gutner and Adams [10] rightly identified and highlighted "Environmental concerns and social responsibility" as one of the four primary trends, among which are globalization, customer sophistication, and talent management and leadership that affect the worldwide economy. The quality of keeping the global place safe and habitable is as important and critical as harnessing relevant tools, resources, and technological-driven solutions, to sustainably meet and surpass customer needs, requirements, and specifications.

While from the business perspective, environmental issues and quality are coterminous [27], social responsibility and quality management are bridged together through ethnical principles, organizational integrity, trust, and people commitment. Leveraging quality generally with both socially oriented and environmentally oriented corporate social responsibilities (CSERs) shall therefore protect the global community from the negative impact of organizational activities on the environment.

The full commitment of organizational quality management system (QMS) to both socially oriented and environmentally oriented corporate social responsibility (CSER) governance shall undoubtedly help organizations and business entities establish their legitimacy in their business societies. Their full commitment to their business environment shall in turn result to their full acceptance too by the people and society to earn them strong recognition and societal patronage and respect coupled with the likelihood of utmost results of good returns on their investment (ROI). This argument is supported by an empirical research study which investigated environmentally oriented CSR and socially oriented CSR. In this study, the effects of CSR outcomes and CSR governance on organizational financial performance were investigated by Wang and Sarkis [41] and they established that:

- Organizations desire to adopt CSR governance mechanisms in order to achieve both social and environmental outcomes in building their legitimacy within their business society.
- In order to generate superior CSR outcomes "through sufficient resource allocation and business structure changes," rigorous CSR governance must have to be implemented.
- "Superior SCR outcomes assist companies achieve and maintain social legitimacy, and thus contribute to enhanced business environment and greater financial returns."

It thus becomes apparent from the results of this study that organizations must be prepared to fully and most effectively implement CSR governance mechanisms if economic benefits are desirable in line with the thinking of Alexander Pope: "A little learning is a dangerous thing; Drink deep, or taste not the Pierian spring." CSR governance is particularly relevant in taking care of the global place and environment, thereby protecting lives.

Modes of CSR/CER

The early denials and blame shifting associated with the sources of the novel coronavirus COVID-19 pandemic are anti-quality. It is perhaps the most living evidence to demonstrate how devastating CSR/CER denial could be for mankind and the planet of its inhabitant. Imagine that if the insurgency of the COVID-19 pandemic had been immediately confessed to as soon as it was noticed, like the case of Ebola, the whole world would most probably have adaptively reacted swiftly to cage the coronavirus in place, in order to prevent it from spreading its wings of death to other countries of the world. This situation practically helps us to appreciate the role of sincerity in CSR and/or CER commitment.

CSR commitment thus begins with the sincerity of purpose, about the impact of organizational business processes and activities on its immediate and distant environment to include the entirety of the global community. Apart from weighing the direct impact of organizational activities on its business environment, thinking about the positive influence of a business organization on the people of their immediate communities comes next.

This is an area the author has a very good experience too, working for the Leventis Group of companies. At A.G. Leventis Group of organizations worldwide, CSR/CER is viewed and treated with utmost importance, hence the integration of corporate social responsibilities and corporate environmental responsibilities in organizational daily activities. Commitment to CSR/CER is practically a constant reoccurrence in budgetary commitments or allocations of all A.G. Leventis-affiliated organizations all over the world. The author experienced and lived it.

For example, the Beta Glass PLC community was involved in providing critical social amenities such as utilities and portable water to people living in the community of their operational activities in both Agbara and Ughelli (both in Nigeria). These are some of the facilities which were considered highly essential for the quality of the peoples' lives.

Performance Improvement and Competitiveness

Continuous/Continual Improvement (CI)

Continuous improvement which is rooted in manufacturing is an aspirational quality management principle which is expected to constantly drive the ability to positively make positive changes to the status quo of an organization and its processes to constantly improve them. Never being satisfied with or changing the status quo [5, 6] should conveniently incite organizations and businesses to constantly search for areas of improvement, as well as being able to identify the most appropriate methods for achieving and driving improvements across an organization from time to time with the involvement of employees. It is also known or referred to as continual improvement.

Making an organization and its processes better than they currently are is an incremental process which often requires taking many small steps of activities at a time, except perhaps through huge breakthroughs or innovational leap.

Ever since the world of Kaizen, which means continuous process improvement, the manufacturing industry has consistently experienced unprecedented degrees of change particularly since the last decade of the twentieth century. Such changes encompass according to Singh and Singh [39] drastic changes in:

- Management approaches
- Product and process technologies
- Customer expectations
- Supplier attitudes
- Competitive behavior

In their broad and expansive literature review of the continuous improvement philosophy, they were able to identify critical basis for implementing continuous improvement. They include some of the underlisted:

- To change and maintain organizational competitiveness through improved productivity, customer satisfaction, product reliability, cost-effectiveness, and product/service quality, elimination of wastes of all kinds and types, and resource conservation
- For achieving improved organizational work culture and mindset, to effectively monitor, control, regulate, and synchronize production processes and activities while eliminating machine downtime, man-hour losses, duplication of activities and processes, etc. to achieve optimum output
- To minimize setup time and eliminate downtime, defects, and delayed production
- Maximize the effective use of human resources by supporting employee personal growth potentials and competencies through adequate and effective training and education as well as other types of incentives
- Getting rid of problems encountered by organizations with regard to internal factors such as productivity, customer complaints, defect rates, non-adherence to delivery time, and production losses
- To ensure smarter and simpler job processes, safer work environment with motivated employees
- To keep organizations at world-class standard by satisfying global customer needs, requirements, and specifications to achieve organizational adaptability, growth, and sustainability in a highly disruptive and unpredictable global business world of uncertainties

While they claimed the phrase, CI is used in association with different types of organizational improvement activities which include "the adoption of "lean manufacturing" techniques, total quality management (TQM), employee involvement programs, customer service initiatives and waste reduction campaign," Bhuyan and Baghel [7] referred to CI simply as "a company-wide process of focused and continuous incremental innovation."

The current globalized economy has created a global marketplace in which businesses constantly found themselves under increased pressure from both customers and competitors, especially in the manufacturing and service sectors of the global economy, hence the continued trending of continuous improvement approaches to organizational improvement. In order for organizations to rapidly respond to changing customer needs, desires, and tastes, there is the need to maintain:

- Low costs of quality goods and services
- Constant waste reduction
- Trimmed production line
- Accelerated production for prompt delivery and maintaining competitive edge

Coping with most of the above-specified challenges if not all can be accomplished through the implementation of *continuous improvement* (CI), which is defined here as:

> The organizational management culture of constantly and consistently improving organizational quality management systems and processes with effective employee involvement, to increase its values while taking advantage of innovative and technological opportunities to strengthen and maintain its adaptability and sustainability.

This definition deviates slightly from its more common or general literature definition bearing in mind the current disruptive environment of many unpredictable challenges and uncertainties in an environment of constant changes – predictable and unpredictable. Experience showed here that simply identifying the sources of organizational bottlenecks or problem areas could easily create the opportunity for the deployments of continuous improvement tools.

The pressure to gravely conserve and use resources most efficiently, in an industrial environment such as Japan, with relatively low levels of natural resources, contributed largely to the general growth and sustenance of most continuous improvement tools such as just-in-time (JIT) production, which facilitates a constant reduction in waste, and Kaizen, which according to Karkoszka and Szewieczet [26] means "gradual and continuous progress, increase of value, intensification and improvement."

The major goals and focus of CI tools are principally in pursuit of organizational economic efficiency or as commonly said profitability through:

- The optimization of machine/equipment performance, eliminating breakdowns and unscheduled downtime, achieving improved utilization, better product quality, and higher throughput
- The achievement of lower operational costs
- Improved equipment/machine maintainability

On a general basis, therefore, continuous improvement may be viewed generally as a culture of sustained organizational improvement, involving everyone participating to eliminate all aspects of waste in all the systems and processes of an organization.

Principles of Continuous Improvement

The general and basic principle of continuous improvement is the achievement of targeted or planned performance improvement in order to consistently meet customer SNEaRs and to remain highly competitive in the global marketplace. Targeted improvements can only be achieved and maintained by prioritizing the quality and integrity of processes, inputs, machinery, and human resource skills and management. It is very critical too to ensure that each improvement criterion is measurable. Measurable improvements are therefore some of the most critical principles of organizational improvement.

Vehicle for Continuous Improvement

The principles of engaging in continuous improvement are generally customer-driven, with organizational-wide efforts centered mainly on customer satisfaction by continuously improving the performance vis-à-vis quality of both product/service and process. Hence, CI can easily be seen as an integrative quality management philosophy for continuously impacting organizational-wide activities with everyone's participation.

The extensive research of Singh and Singh [39] has established the facts of the many prospective research opportunities in defining and establishing needed methodologies for researching into system-wide and customer-perspective benefits of Kaizen strategies for accomplishing continuous improvement objectives. In addition is the report of their research findings that past investigations have been focused on defining:

- The nature of continuous improvement
- The tools for implementing continuous improvement
- Organizational issues that that are required or needed to support continuous improvement initiatives
- The ability to apply continuous improvement processes to various types of organizations, their processes, and activities
- Issues that affect the implementation of continuous improvement tools
- The critical success factors of implementing continuous improvement measures (Table 4.1)

Continuous Improvement: Prospective Research Opportunities

In an extensive literature review about continuous improvement (CI) philosophy, Singh and Singh provided sufficient literature with excitingly varied information about the roots and rooting of continuous improvement processes and methodologies. They have been able to provide researchers, educationists, and quality practitioners useful information which include among others the underlisted:

- Historical evolution and development of continuous improvement (CI) processes and their relevance in the world of quality management systems
- An overview of various continuous improvement practices and methodologies from the perspectives of the manufacturing sector of the economy, prominent of which are the Kaizen, lean, JIT, quality control circles, Six Sigma, PDCA ("plan-do-check-act," or Deming Wheel or Cycle, continuous quality improvement (CQI) process), PDSA ("plan-do-study-act"), SDCA ("standardize-do-check-act"), ACE (Achieving Competitive Excellence), CIIPM (continuous improvement of international project management), and the Swedish manufacturing companies' balanced scorecard – BSC

Table 4.1 Principles of the approach to continuous improvement

Principles of continuous improvement	Main focus	Targeted results or accomplishments for organizational work processes and activities
Customer-driven	Customer and market	Understanding both existing and future customer needs, specifications, and requirements so as to effectively meet and even strive to exceed them
Leadership	Achieve set goals/ objectives	Lead organization to maintain and sustain unity of purpose and direction, to create most suitable and adequate environment to accomplish organizational goals/objectives with people involvement
Peoples' full participation	Employees' active and full involvement	Employees at various levels must be adequately empowered and motivated – job training/education, exposure, individual growth opportunities, developmental programs, incentives such as financial, job rotation, opinion sharing opportunities – to optimize their individual job contributions and recognition
Process approach	Managing related resources and activities as a process	Effectively achieving desired results is strongly enabled by managing related resources and activities as a process. Resource wastages are effectively minimized or completely ruled out
Systematic approach	System of interrelated processes	The identification, understanding, and management of a system of interrelated processes to achieve a targeted improved output contribute effectively and efficiently to improve the QMS and the overall organizational performance improvement
Design improvement to prevent waste and problem prevention	"Design it right first time" and "do it right first time" to achieve quality products	"Designing it right first time" helps to build quality in individual process stages at project level. "Do it right first time," at every process stage, for internal processes, leads to achieving improved quality products/services while avoiding problems, bottlenecks, and preventing waste. Prevention at the design stage helps to prevent defective products/ services while saving costs
Making factual decision	Gathering and analysis of data and information to evaluate processes	In order to take effective actions and decisions for achieving product/service quality and organization's overall performance improvements, relevant factual data and information about activities and processes must be identified, collated, and analyzed. Sources of these data and information include, among others, customers and customer feedbacks, supply chain, project and process performance records, competition and benchmarking, audit outcomes, subcontractors, management reviews, production reports, etc. A detailed evaluation of acquired information and data is critical to support and decide improvement measure for every stage of organizational processes and activities

(continued)

Table 4.1 (continued)

Principles of continuous improvement	Main focus	Targeted results or accomplishments for organizational work processes and activities
Internal and external partnership development	Effectively building a coalition of all participating parties and alliances	Developing strong organizational business relationship both internally (unions and employees) and externally (suppliers, consultants, regulatory bodies, subcontractors, immediate society, and environment) is highly imperative for accomplishing organizational improvement goals and objectives. Of great importance here are business partnerships and strategic alliances

- Highlights of the suggestions of various researchers and continuous improvement practitioners regarding a number of sophisticated methodologies for implementing continuous improvement processes

Despite this long list of accomplished research solutions to the many questions bothering generally on the applicability of continuous improvement processes, the organizations that deploy those processes, and other issues surrounding them, the researchers [39] have reportedly stressed the need for more critical analysis of continuous improvement, as well as emphasizing the importance of researching more rigorously on the "theoretical basis for conducting research in the field."

There are therefore no doubts whatsoever that the authors have opened up the opportunities for others to exploit the latent academic and research potentials in the field of continuous improvement processes, an ever-trending arm of quality and its management principles to:

- Researchers
- Quality and quality management students
- Improvement professionals
- Other users of improvement programs in various arms of the industrial sectors of the global economy

ISO 9001:2015 and Continual Improvement

Putting processes in place to drive and achieve small incremental improvement across a wide swath of organizational processes and activities with the involvement of people is highly inherent in the requirements of the ISO 9001:2015 [16] quality management system standards. Meeting these requirements surely assures and strengthens organizations from becoming more effective in meeting set goals and objectives.

Common QMS continual improvement processes constitute among others examples such as:

- External and internal audits
- Setting quality objectives and planning to achieve them
- Analysis and evaluation
- External and internal audit nonconformity corrective action
- Management review
- Risk management

The need for continual improvement measures is already an integral part of the ISO 9001:2015 in *Clause 10.3.*, [18] as an equivalent of Subclause 8.5.1. of ISO 9001:2008. For organizations implementing the requirements of ISO 9001:2015, meeting the requirements stated in Clauses 9.1.3. (Analysis and evaluation) and 9.3. (Management review) sort of helps to identify any opportunities for implementing continuous improvement measures and/or projects in organizational QMS as well as its overall performance.

Continually improving organizational QMS should normally ensure the overall improvement of an organization's overall performance – process and production efficiency and effectiveness, qualitatively and quantitatively meeting customer satisfaction, financial, regulatory requirements, etc.

ISO 9001 improvement processes exist within virtually every requirement phase of the QMS standard; hence, using every improvement process such as quality objectives, internal audits, analysis of data and information, corrective actions, and management reviews correctly serves to collectively assure overall performance improvement.

Realities of Quality

While it is acknowledged that quality has grown dramatically since product inspection commenced, it is a reality too that the ISO standards have most recently grown to be one of the fastest growing international quality reference points of our time. Today the ISO quality management systems have become a household name in the manufacturing and service provision industries all over the world. Part of the credit here goes to the ISO and its member countries particularly for its introduction of generic international standards. Most common among these are:

- ISO 9000 series of international QMS standards
- ISO 14000 series of international EMS standards

According to the ISO in its website [11] the subscription to the use and application of ISO 9001QMS standard requirements was as at 2010 over one million organizations spread all over the world. This figure was led by Europe which constituted about 49.0% followed by the Far East with about 37.0%; Africa/West Asia, 6.0%; Central and South America, 4.0%; North America, 3.0%; and Australia/New Zealand, 1.0%.

China tops the list of ten (10) top countries home to organizations that have been certified to the requirements of the ISO 9001 QMS standards as of 2010. This was followed by Italy, Russian Federation, Spain, Japan, Germany, UK, India, USA, and the Republic of Korea. The top ten (10) countries for ISO 9001 growth in 2010 are led by China which is followed by Russian Federation, Italy, Brazil, UK, Germany, Czech Republic, Malaysia, Republic of Korea, and Indonesia. It is interesting here to highlight the fact that some of the emerging markets fall in the top ten (10) in terms of growth in the implementation of the requirements of ISO 9001 QMS standard. It goes to say here that quality vis-à-vis quality management system implementation will continue to be a good competitive tool for achieving competitive edge in the global market economy.

Product Competitiveness

The term "quality product" is, in recent years, frequently used in the global marketplace to express individual and/or collective desires in the acquisition of various goods and services, hence the common emphasis of various organizations and companies on quality and their equal recognition of the fact that the survival of an enterprise is to a large extent dependent on the quality and values of its products and services more than anything else. The role of quality as the strategy for the survival of an organization is further strengthened in the present globalization of the world market economy where competition has become more critical than it has ever been.

Since customers have the opportunities to choose from a wide range of products and services vis-à-vis suppliers, they will simply go elsewhere if those (i.e., products/services) offered to them by a particular supplier do not meet their specifications, values, and requirements. They will also react in a similar manner if they are generally not satisfied with the way, manner, and when the products and services are offered and/or delivered to them. This is particularly so since markets where customers cannot easily switch to other suppliers are gradually becoming fewer and fewer due to the effective privatization of businesses which has increasingly resulted to the depletion of monopoly in the entire business environment in a world that is being brought closer and closer through advancements in technology.

This was brought to bear on the Nigerian economy when the Federal Government of Nigeria sold its shares in most of the oil marketing companies, thereby reducing the monopoly which had previously made both the automotive gas oil (AGO) and petroleum motor spirit (PMS) scarce commodities that purchasers had to beg for. It must however be mentioned here that people in the West African sub-region particularly Nigeria must be very cautious in the way businesses are privatized to avoid creating a new set of monopolies from them. It is therefore very critical here that the act of privatizing businesses must not just be fair and transparent but must also be seen to be so.

In addition to this is the fact that increased emphasis on product quality has, in turn, transformed quality to a benchmarking factor particularly in the international market. For example, any company intending to market its products and services in

Europe and other quality-conscious economies of the world may find it easier to achieve this if it has successfully implemented and maintained a quality management system of world standard or a combination of them. Such systems include ISO 9000 QMS international standards, Six Sigma, World Class, 5S, etc. At the same time your organization and its products/services must meet or comply with other quality requirements that may emanate from:

- Government regulations/guidelines
- Regulatory body/agency prescriptions/guidelines
- Professional body requirements/guidelines/prescriptions

Organizations therefore have to do the best they possibly could to ensure that they survive by providing products and services of utmost quality and values that meet the specifications and requirements of their customers as well as those that comply with those of the relevant professional bodies and government or statutory regulations. The only situations where an organization can probably afford not to meet the specifications/requirements of the customer are those in which survival is neither compulsory nor necessary or in the case of charitable or nonprofit organizations. Even in the case of charitable organizations quality is at play in the value of its achievements.

Government setups or public governance is often managed like charitable organizations to the benefit of the few people in government particularly in the third-world countries of the world where bureaucratic norms are often the order of the day and the paraphernalia of office used to rob the masses of their own basic needs of life.

The understanding of the word *quality* generally begins and ends with the total satisfaction of the product and/or service recipient (i.e., customer) with what has been provided for him in terms of its values, performance requirements, and delivery schedule. Meeting customer specifications with the necessary *precision* and *timing* is therefore highly imperative if a business has to survive. Prompt delivery is, for example, one of the factors of vital importance to delight your customers.

The good news for all organizations, entities, and entrepreneurs wishing to provide goods and services that represent or meet the aspirations of their customers in terms of product quality and value is the fact that a range of quality management packages and guidelines are today available to choose from in the management of their various systems.

Quality consultants are springing up even in the underdeveloped economies such as Nigeria and the other countries in the West African sub-region. This will make the implementation of quality management systems easier to achieve.

Some of such management tools are even specialized or dedicated to particular arms/sectors of the economy. This class of quality tools is, for example, available in the defense, automotive, aeronautic, and food and beverage industries. Examples here are the automobile supplier quality standards (e.g., the Ford Motors Q1, General Motors Target for Excellence (TFE), and the German Automotive Industry (VDA) Non-obligatory Standard Recommendation). For the food industry the hazard analysis and critical control point (HACCP) is a food safety system designed to prevent biological, chemical, and physical hazards in food.

ISO 22000:2018 – Food Safety Management Systems – Requirements for Any Organization in the Food Chain is an international standard focused specifically on food safety [23].

In addition, there are presently quite a number of assistance and guidance available through consultancy services at various levels for organizations willing to implement a quality management tool of its choice. The consultants have the capability to provide training resources and information. Various types of software suitable for use with particular quality management tools are also available in the market of your choice.

Competitive Challenges in the Global Market

The removal of national barriers, particularly through the global democratization process and the global telecommunication system (GSM), will continue to have important competitive effects and impacts on the global economy and market so that quality may gradually assume the role of a major and critical deciding factor but objective tool for the marketing and sales of various products and services. We can therefore not rule it out that quality may, in the nearest future, feature most prominently in taking decisions that affect product/service sales and marketing both within and outside national borders. As the world is brought closely together through technological advancement, dynamic organizations realize the need for the extension of their global reach so that the quality management leaders of various organizations are exposed to constant challenges.

The consequences of the world global market competition for organizations and businesses vis-à-vis entrepreneurs in the least developed countries of the world are enormous. Organizations in the third-world countries therefore need to prepare themselves for challenges of various types and dimensions if they have to keep themselves afloat and also remain competitive at both the national and international levels. Failure to do this may have grave consequences for such countries and their leadership.

Two of the most critical quality challenges that faced the Nigerian financial industry in the most recent time are the 2005 recapitalization regulation of the Central Bank of Nigeria (CBN) which made it mandatory for Nigerian banks to raise their minimum operational capital to 25 billion naira (=N = 25,000,000,000 or US$193million at an exchange rate of US$1.0 to Nigeria naira, N = 130 at that time) and the recent cases of huge non-performing loans which were traced partly to the abuse of office by some of the CEOs and directors of these banks who threw their integrity to the dogs.

The increase in capital when viewed from the quality perspective ensures that the banks are elevated to a position or situation whereby they can have the opportunities to actively and adequately participate in the world global banking/financial activities. This is proactively a quality move to ensure that the banks will be in better positions to meet the needs and requirements of their customers. While the banks have to do more to maintain their new status quo and even surpass it in terms of capital and also to ensure that they provide quality services to their numerous customers on a continual improvement basis, other business organizations/enterprises (e.g., airlines, insurance companies, health management services including private hospitals, shipping companies, tourism and hotel industries, electricity-generating and energy distribution industries, etc.) in Nigeria and the West African sub-region have to take a cue from this to improve their capital base as a catalyst for achieving customer satisfaction. They have to do so with integrity, due process, and openness. This will enable enterprises/organizations from the less developed economies of the world or the third-world countries to remain relevant in the global economy where quality may remain a critical deciding factor for achieving competitive edge for a very long time. Top management integrity is highly essential in quality management as failure to manage with integrity can easily lead an organization aground. Some of the challenges for the third-world economies could emanate from or result in any or some of the following situations/scenarios:

- External opposition to national/regional trade protection laws or codes of practice so as to open up national trade to global competition for which some or most of the indigenous businesses/entrepreneurs in the third-world countries of the West African sub-region may not be adequately prepared due to their level of industrial development, poor capital (financial and human) base, and the general lack of adequate basic infrastructure such as electricity, water, roads, law and order, etc. and the democratic norms known generally to promote human and economic development.
- The global and regional development of trade agreements. A good example here is the General Agreement on Tariffs and Trade (GATT) which involves over one hundred and twenty (120) countries that have agreed to open up their economies, reduce tariffs and subsidies, and expand the protection of intellectual property. This type of agreement is in one way or another against the underdeveloped countries of the world that are very weak both in manufacturing and production and in the ownership of intellectual property. Apart from turning them into eternal product/service buyers, they shall eternally remain in economic bondage and enslavement, hence a life of abject poverty that will neither promote nor encourage quality living for their people. This agreement has already been signed by most of the countries in the West African sub-region without adequately addressing their capabilities to cope with the ensuing competition and the consequential impacts on their economic development and balance of trade. Most of them are carried away by the bait of the promise by the developed economies that they will be given some development aid.
- Removal of trade boundaries/barriers which may lead to the dumping of goods in the countries of the sub-region as is presently experienced by Nigeria where all sorts of inferior quality goods including waste and scrapped items (tires, computers and electronics, textiles and clothing, machinery and equipment, motor vehicles, etc.) are dumped into the market, thereby giving rise to unfair competition with

locally produced goods whose quality can easily be regulated. This has, for example, crippled the previously vibrant Nigerian textile industries to death while the plastics industries are gasping for breath. The two tire manufacturing industries in Nigeria have also closed down their production lines in Lagos and Port Harcourt.

- Need for multi-company/business mergers and acquisitions to meet the global market capital/financial challenges.
- Need for multinational cooperation particularly on sub-regional basis and in facing challenges of trade tariff imposition and collection.
- Need for focused and consistent national economic planning to allow for continuity irrespective of administrative changes in the public sector of the national economy as well as changes in government.
- Need to *transparently,* effectively, and objectively privatize government-owned businesses to achieve effective performance and also to allow governments to concentrate strictly on the provision of infrastructure and governance and commit to the continual improvement of quality of its fiscal responsibilities. Hereby, the concentration of businesses in a few hands must also be avoided since this may also lead to a type of monopoly as well as negatively influence the quality of its services.
- Need to democratize governance to avoid ethnic rivalry and ethnic clashes/wars so as to achieve political stability and maintain law and order in order to improve the quality of the lives of the people. Political instability and tribal frictions have posed serious challenges to development in the West African sub-region in the last two decades and it has not allowed the focus of attention on key economic issues (e.g., productivity, provision of fundamental infrastructure for industrial development, education, capacity building, etc.) of national interest.
- Changes in the status of nations previously seen as business/trade allies to that of competitors in the global market.
- Switch of roles from importers to exporters.
- Increase in the lifespan of products.
- Need to adequately manage and sustain changes.
- Introduction and enforcement of trade agreements that favor national economic developmental programs.
- Need to gain the confidence of customers in the global market and the ability to do clean business in an open and least complicated/complex manner. Here the complexities of multiple and competing taxations between one level of government and the other must be avoided so as not to dwarf the growth of industrial development in the West African sub-region.
- Need to ensure the free flow of goods and services across national borders (at sea- and airports) to ensure prompt product delivery whether through importation or exportation. Goods have to be cleared without tears, a situation that is predominant in most of Nigeria's ports at the time of writing this book.
- The need to eradicate corruption and corrupt practices in the entire public sector. This is one factor that contributes largely today to the high costs of goods in Nigeria where corruption seems to have been adopted as an art, a culture of pro-

fessional practice particularly woven into the uniform of the men and women of the Nigerian Customs Services, the Police, Civil Service, and those of some members of other law enforcement agencies.
- Ability to secure the adequate/necessary capital sufficient enough to do business at the global market level.

Once corrective measures are put in place to address the issues discussed above, the use of quality as a major tool for product and service selection and benchmarking would take its place in the third-world countries, particularly in the West African sub-region, thereby putting them at the same pedestal or competitive level with other developed countries of the world. It follows from here that organizations may, at the end of the day, have no alternative than to adhere strictly to the use of quality as the true and most objective tool for benchmarking in the marketing and sales of their agricultural produce, services, and manufactured products.

For nations and the businesses therein the theme of survival therefore lies in an organization's ability to provide quality products and services of highest values and those that can endure the tests of time in the fast-emerging borderless global market where local markets are shrinking day in and day out due to the growing advancements in technology particularly in the areas of communication, transportation, and product/service delivery.

The need to be relevant in the global trade has consequently led to the globalization and implementation of some comprehensive quality management tools. There are today a range of quality management tools which emanate from the ISO that, various enterprises and organizations can choose from, as they strive to provide quality products and services for their respective customers. It has completely revolutionized quality management on a global platform. This approach that has served to catalyze enterprise growth and development in recent years is quality assurance through the implementation of a series of quality management system standards (ISO 9000) developed by the International Organization for Standardization (ISO, iso.org) [11].

ISO 9000 is a series of international QMS standards that is gradually gaining worldwide or global acceptance since its initial introduction in 1987, hence the present urge of various organizations all over the world to implement its requirements and get certified to the contractual standard, ISO 9001.

Quality and International Trade

Role of Quality

One of the negative impacts of trade globalization is dumping, a process which actually has no respect and recognition for quality and competitiveness in all ramifications. Dumping is practiced in such a way that all sorts of products are arbitrarily dumped in the economically weaker countries of the world without consideration for product quality and the safety and fitness of product for use.

Nigeria and some West African countries are victims of dumping from the international community especially goods from China and India. This practice (dumping) which has more or less bastardized and compromised the Nigerian economy, was grossly encouraged by the corrupt practices of government officials (customs and excise, immigration, police force, and other economic regulatory ministries and agencies of government); and the entire public sector due to a general lack of good education among the majority of the Nigerian end-users/consumers. The practice of dumping is further aggravated by poverty, and the generally high inflation rates that have ravaged the country particularly in the last four decades, precisely from September 26, 1986, when economic measures introduced by the then Nigerian military government turned a sour pill for all Nigerian citizens, as the quality of life actually deteriorated throughout the country.

The war-ravaged countries (Liberia, Sierra Leone, and lately Ivory Coast) of the West African sub-region are worse off. Poverty coupled with war has therefore jointly combined to blindfold and prevent most consumers in the sub-region from recognizing and acquiring relatively good quality products and items of value. In most cases they are left with no other choice than to buy whatever is offered to them – good or bad – take it or leave it, thereby sustaining the West African sub-region wholly or partly as a seller's market.

The amount of money that has been lost in the importation of substandard goods and products (e.g., drugs, tires, scrapped cars, machinery and equipment, textiles and clothing, spare parts, electronic wastes, etc.) and other manufactured or semi-manufactured products imported into Nigeria over the past two decades is huge and of enormous magnitude.

Poor-quality drugs and medication have particularly inflicted the untold hardship on the entire people of Nigeria and her environment which has also borne the hazardous consequences (at times causing untimely deaths/mortalities) resulting from the use of fake drugs and other inferior quality products dumped into the country.

In order to stem dumping and product quality risks and environmental degradation generally associated with dumped products (e.g., batteries, electronics scraps, drugs, chemicals and chemical products, packaging materials, films, used tires, etc.), there is the urgent need for mass education and enlightenment of the general public (i.e., consumers/end-users) in the sub-region so as to arouse their consciousness to willingly assess and query the value and quality of the products and services offered them. This will in turn strengthen the potentials of the consumers to dictate and query the quality of the products and services that are offered them. In addition, it will also enable and empower them to condemn dumping and reject dumped items so that the quality of the West African sub-regional environment and her environmental management capabilities can be enhanced.

Consumers in the West African sub-region need to be conscious of their own potentials and right to dictate the quality of items that are offered to them whether they are imported or produced within the sub-region. It goes to say here that any product/service considered by individuals as not meeting customer requirements/needs or of poor quality and/or low value should be outrightly rejected and not purchased.

There is also the need to ensure that the quality of items imported into the country and the entire sub-region is controlled and the quality assured particularly those products imported from the Asian countries. This could, in turn, lead to the uplifting of the standard of living of the people in the sub-region.

Nigeria has in this regard introduced the SONCAP (Standards Organization of Nigeria Compliance Assessment Program) to control the quality of imported items and MANCAP (Manufacturers' Compliance Assessment Program) for products that are locally manufactured.

Product Specification

The role of product specification in defining quality cannot be over-emphasized particularly in the international trade. A specification can generally be described as *a* "description of that which is to be provided" *or* "functionality/performance of product" in terms of its ability to meet the expectations of the customer:

- Value of product to customer
- Safety for use
- Safety of disposal or specification for disposal after use (if applicable) to maintain the quality of the environment
- Reliability
- Durability
- Dimensions
- Absence of defects
- Tolerances
- Aesthetics/appearance/odor/taste
- Compliance with legislative and regulatory (i.e., legal) requirements
- Other customer requirements

The ISO on its own described specification in ISO 9000:2015 [13] as the "document stating requirements." From its own point of view, it described specification as "a document that states the requirements to which a given product or service must conform."

Specifications are on a general basis related to the following.

Materials

- Components
- Processes
- Products

Hence, transmitting the details or specifications/requirements of desired products/services to the supplier is an important task that has to be carried out with utmost:

- Precision
- Timeliness
- Adequate documentation
- Diligence and integrity
- Responsibility
- Effective customer/supplier communication
- Clearly without any ambiguity

Specifications need to be validated and revalidated from time to time especially in issues or cases which involve design. In a similar way the desires of end-users or consumers must be put into consideration when taking the decision of producing items for sale in the international market.

Customer Specifications

There are dimensional and quality specifications. Dimensional specifications define *product form and shape* and serve the major functions of achieving interchangeability of components and parts as well as the simplification or reduction of the range of sizes needed to cover general usage. Quality specifications are on the other hand concerned mainly with the provision of the details of manufacturing processes and the level of performance.

Customer specifications/requirements should normally be provided by the customer and must have to be agreed upon at the time the contract is signed, reviewed, and revalidated from time to time. Specifications must be adequately documented without any ambiguity. Specifications which may be in the form of drawings and other forms of documentation may include among others:

- Technical specifications for inputs and products
- Regulatory requirements related to input and product
- Delivery requirements
- Inspection procedures
- List of product specifications
- Number of products
- Mode of packaging
- Contact person
- Agreed mode of communication along with the exact identification of the VOC
- Any other relevant information
- Change or alteration made to any of the above issues

Benchmarking Process

Strengthening Economic Competitiveness with Quality

There are no doubts however that benchmarking has been an important quality tool deployed massively to grow China into the present industrialization status that she is today enjoying. This is without further narration a great step for all aspiring countries of the world, especially the countries of the African continent to achieve economic greatness. They all have to set out to aspire for economic greatness benchmarking to set achievable goals.

The way to achieve this is however left for each country to devise and pursue, bearing in mind that for the purposes of competition the industrialized countries of the world may never support the desire, plan, and objective of any African country getting industrialized. This in turn catalyzes poverty in Africa as the quality of life may never improve at an appreciable rate. Hence there is the possibility too, that the developed world may not hesitate to deploy whatever means possible, including various regulatory measures, obstacles, tactics, diplomatic antics, innovative ideas, and philosophies - economic and political alike, to permanently frustrate the industrial development of African countries.

It must however be stressed that to achieve or move towards industrialization, the people of the African continent must embrace the elements of quality management in its entirety. Otherwise, Africa and its population of about 1.3 billion may never be able to accomplish the industrialization status needed to push the continent out of its present state of economic woes. Failure of the African people to massively transparently deploy quality management tools and principles into all business, governance, and public services activities shall continuously make the people vulnerable to underdevelopment and the persistent and constant designation of being the world's epicenter of poverty.

Benchmarking has been previously defined by various authors as Westcott [44] and Camp [8] and the ASQ. It has been used and viewed by the author as an excellent and strong comparative tool to place a business or an organization at a desired level among its peers. But usually, it is a comparative knowledge acquisition process to identify the best organizational practices, processes, and general ways of doing things, among relevant sectors or peers. Understanding the *best of the best* practices and processes, for the purposes of comprehending them, in order to be able to adapt the same, for the purposes of getting better than them, is therefore the ultimate goal of *benchmarking.*

Benchmarking can therefore be said to be "a process of comparative knowledge acquisition among peer organizations across the globe, deployed to identify, comprehend and adapt processes and practices of excellent and outstanding quality (or best-in-class) ratings to aid and motivate an organization for upgrading and improving its processes, practices and product performance level."

Hence, benchmarking is a methodology used in searching for the best practices among the best-in-class organizations and/or practitioners. It can therefore simply be said to be a process by which an organization measures and establishes its own quality standard practices (e.g., strategies, policies, products, organization structure, operations, and processes) against the best examples in the global market or against the best practices of other organizations or of prevailing standard practices. Hence, it is a process that is continuously used for measuring products, services, and practices against those of the toughest competitor or those of the organizations that are recognized as industry leaders.

Benchmarking actually enables you to learn from the best, so as to also enable you to place your products and services in the league of the best ones in the market. The purpose of benchmarking is therefore to learn from others by seeking out and studying the best practices associated with high performances and/or best results for the purpose of emulating them to achieve that level of performance and even surpass or exceed it. Benchmarking seen from this point serves as a tool for creating needed momentum for improving the performances of your organization. You can among others benchmark your strategies, operations, processes, procedures, machinery, products, services, etc. The process of benchmarking includes among others that you:

- Identify and determine the prevailing product/service standards in the market so as to be able to exactly place the standing of your organization and your product/services in the market scale.
- Analyze your own products, operations/processes, technology/equipment, marketing activities, etc. so as to be able to determine and place it among and within the prevailing product/service standards in the market. Assess and measure your current level of performance.
- Identify the organizations that are meeting the standards or are the industry leaders and what makes them thick.
- Carry out a gap analyses to identify the gap between your organization and those against which you are benchmarking your own organization, products/services, and activities against. Know how much the gaps are and where and when they occur.
- Interact with those organizations (i.e., market leaders) that have achieved the standard performance levels to obtain and/or exchange information (where possible).
- Determine how the organizations achieved their performance levels.
- Use the totality of the information obtained from this benchmarking process to improve your own performance, or to close the identified gaps to achieve superior performance.
- Ensure that all the measures put in place for the improvement of your system are effective and sustained so that your organization remains in the achieved benchmarked position and also continue to improve on it.
- Incorporate benchmarking practices into normal work processes even at the internal level.
- Since quality itself is an endless quest, attaining the market standard through benchmarking must not be seen as the only ultimate goal. Instead, your organization should seize the opportunity to set new quality goals and targets that will

take the organization to the level of market leadership or sustainable superior position which shall be retained and even expanded beyond the previous market scope. This pace must be maintained and continuously improved upon, so as to keep the organization ahead of all other competitors.

Benchmarking process – local, national, and international – offers the opportunity for the realistic assessment of an organization in comparison with other similar organizations or competitors, for the main purposes of defining and redefining the processes, to achieve continual improvement.

The ASQ [1, 4] gives a vivid description of what a best practice implies. "A best practice *is a technique, working method or activity that has proven itself more effective than any other technique, method, etc.*"

The use of *best practices* is perhaps an excellent idea, as knowing the best in your business sector, or industry sector of the economy, or among organizational peers enables an organization to avoid or minimize problems, unforeseen circumstances, and possible complexities. In addition, it enables organizations to get an understanding, idea, and picture of what it desires to achieve, that is, desirable outcomes and results.

Stage by Stage of Benchmarking

While each organization is free to adapt its way of benchmarking its products, processes, and practices, it is generally understood that it could similarly be deployed as suggested below:

- Identify and understand your organization's own processes to know and decide the exact processes, practices, or approaches that may need to be benchmarked.
- Carry out a detailed but diligent mapping of the relevant process(es), practice(s), and approach(es) to know the boundaries of the planed benchmarking.
- Carry out necessary measurements to exactly define the measurable performance factors related to or identifiable with the process, practice, and approach.
- Identify organizations, processes, or practices found to be the best processes, practices, or approaches within the relevant industry or peer organizations.
- Identify ways and modes of getting contact to arrange for the benchmarking process.
- Proceed to achieve the goal.

There are various types of benchmarking as listed below.

Types of Benchmarking

Four types of benchmarking occur frequently in literature [8, 44]. These are *generic*, *functional*, *competitive*, and *internal*. These are highlighted as follows:

- Generic benchmarking – identification and understanding of organizations with the best-in-class processes and practices for the purposes of using the knowledge gained to improve one's own processes and practices.
- Functional benchmarking – identify, comprehend, and adapt the processes of other organizations that may be outside your sector but operating similar processes in similar functions.
- Competitive benchmarking – identify, comprehend, and adapt best processes and practices among competitors and organizations in the same sector or industry setting.
- Internal benchmarking – identify, comprehend, and adapt best-in-class organization's practices and share among the others within the organization.

While *generic process benchmarking* (i.e., comparing your organization with organizations in unrelated or different sector) focuses generally on innovative work processes, *functional benchmarking* deals with comparisons of methods across organizations that carry out the same type of functions.

Competitive benchmarking makes comparison with direct competitors as against *internal benchmarking* which focuses attention on best practices within an organization's own activities. The process of benchmarking should therefore be seen and viewed as a route for achieving the continual improvement needed by your organization in its arduous task of consistently meeting customer SNEaRs for product performance improvement.

References

1. American Society of Quality. (2007). *Quality progress, glossary of quality terms*, pp. 39–59.
2. Arena, J. M. (2018). *Adaptive space: How GM and other companies are positively disrupting themselves and transforming into agile organizations*. McGraw Hill.
3. Arena, M., & Uhl-Bien, M. (2018). Leadership for organizational adaptability: A theoretical synthesis and integrative framework. *Leadership Quarterly, 29*, 89–104.
4. ASQ. www.asq.org
5. Bangert, M. (2019). The principles of quality management. *Quality Magazine*. 2 Apr 2019, https://tinyurl.com/principles-qm
6. Bangert, M. (2019). Principles of quality management: Continuous improvement, Quality Info Center. *Quality Magazine*, https://www.qualitymag.com, 31 May 2019.
7. Bhuyan, N., & Baghel, A. (2005). An overview of continuous improvement: From the past to the present. *Management Decision, 43*(5), 761–771.
8. Camp, R. C. (1995). *Business process benchmarking: Finding and implementing best practices*. ASQC Press. ISBN 0873892968.
9. European Medicines Agency. ICH Q10 Pharmaceutical Quality Systems, https://tinyurl.com/y37w63t9
10. Gutner T., & Adams, M. A. (2009). *Leadership prescription for the future of quality*. Report of the Conference Board Quality Council.
11. https://www.iso.org
12. IEC 31010:2019. (2019). Risk management – Risk assessment techniques. https://www.iso.org
13. International Organization for Standardization. (2015). *ISO 9000:2015, Quality management system – Fundamentals and vocabulary*.

14. International Organization for Standardization, ISO 9004:2009.
15. International Organization for Standardization. (2015). How change is addressed within ISO 9001:2015: To explain the requirements for "change", https://www.committee.iso.org
16. International Organization for Standardization. *ISO 9001:2015, Quality management system – Requirements.*
17. International Organization for Standardization (ISO). *ISO 19600:2014-Compliance management systems- Guidelines,* www.iso.org/standard/62342.html
18. International Organization for Standardization, ISO. (2015). *ISO 9001:2015, Clause 10.3.* https://www.iso.org.
19. ISO. (2018). *ISO 31000:2018 – Risk management – Guidelines*, https://www.iso.org
20. ISO. (2019). *ISO 22301:2019 – Security and resilience – Business continuity management systems – Requirements*, https://www.iso.org
21. ISO. (2021). *ISO/FDIS 37000, Governance of organizations – Guidance*. https://www.committee.iso.org. Retrieved 2 July 2021.
22. ISO. *ISO 37001-Anti-bribery management systems,* www.iso.org/iso-37001-anti-bribery-management.html
23. ISO 22000:2018. (2018). *Food safety management systems – Requirements for any organization in the food chain*. ISO.
24. Jones, K. E., Patel, N. G., Levy, M. A., Storegard, A., Balk, D., et al. (2008). Global trends in emerging infectious disease. *Nature, 451*(7181), 990–993.
25. Karakaya, D., Ulucan, O., & Turkan, M. (2020). Electronic nose and its applications: A survey. *International Journal of Automation and Computing, 17*(2), 179–209.
26. Karkoszka, T., & Szewieczet, D. (2007). Risk of the processes in the aspect of quality, natural environment and occupational safety. *Journal of Achievements in Materials and Manufacturing Engineering, 20*(1), 539–542.
27. Kubiak, T. M., & Feigenbaum, A. V. (2005, November). Feigenbaum on quality: Past, present and future. *Quality Progress*, pp. 57–62.
28. Lindborg, H. J. (2020, November). Employee engagement: Adaptive space: How organizations can harness employee creativity to adjust to disruptive changes. *Quality Progress*, pp. 5–7.
29. Lindros, K. (2017). C10 from IDG, https://www.cio.com, 11 July 2017.
30. London, C., Comeros, R. C., & Nguyen, A. (2020, November). Quality management systems. *Quality Progress*, pp. 32–37.
31. Madhav, N., Oppenheim, B., Gallivan, M., Mulembakani, P., Rubin, E., & Wolfe, N. (2017). Pandemics: Risks, impacts, and mitigation. In D. T. Jamison, H. Gelband, S. Horton, et al. (Eds.), *Disease control priorities: Improving health and reducing poverty* (3rd ed.). The International Bank for Reconstruction and Development/The World Bank. https://doi.org/10.1596/978-1-4648-0527-1_ch17. 2017 November 27, Chapter 17.
32. Moon, J. (2020). *Foundations of quality risk management*. Quality Press.
33. Naden, C. (2020). ISO focus: Your gateway to international standards. International Organization for Standardization, https://www.iso.org. 15 Sept 2020.
34. Netherton, G. S. (2020, November). Back to basics: A refresher on a quality tool, concept or method – Achieve cultural improvement with the three-legged stool approach. *Quality Progress*, p. 56.
35. Olunloyo, V. O. S., Ibidapo, T. A., & Dinrifo, R. R. (2011). Neural network-based electronic nose for cocoa beans quality assessment. *Agricultural Engineering International: CIGR Journal, 13*(4), pp. 1-17.
36. Protiviti KnowledgeLeader. (2020). https://www.info.knowledgeleader.com, 12 Mar 2020.
37. Reid, D. R. (2020, November). Business continuity plan: How business continuity planning helps organizations plan for emergencies. *Quality Progress*, pp. 48–51.
38. Sampaio, P., & Saraiva, P. (2016). Quality: From past perfect to future conditional. In P. Sampaio & P. Saraiva (Eds.), *Quality in the 21st century, perspectives from ASQ Feigenbaum medal winners* (p. 18). Springer.

39. Singh, J., & Singh, H. (2015). Continuous improvement philosophy – Literature review and directions. *Benchmarking: An International Journal, 22*(1), 75–119. https://doi.org/10.1108/BIJ-06-2012-0038
40. U.S. Food and Drug Administration. *Code of federal regulations – Title 21-food and drugs.* https://tinyurl.com/CFR-title-21
41. Wang, Z., & Sarkis, J. (2017). Corporate social responsibility governance, outcomes and financial performance. *Journal of Cleaner Production, 162*, 1607–1616. https://doi.org/10.1016/jclepro.2017.06.142
42. Waring, A., & Glendon, A. I. (2008). *Managing risk, critical issues for survival and success into the 21st century* (pp. 3–19). TJ International.
43. Waring, A., & Glendon, A. I. (2008). *Managing risk, critical issues for survival and success into the 21st century* (p. xxii). TJ International.
44. Westcott, R. T. (2006). *Quality/organizational excellence handbook* (3rd ed., p. H1264). ASQ Quality Press.
45. Wilson, A. D. (2012). Development of an electronic-nose technology for the rapid detection of agricultural pesticide residues. *Phytopathology, 102*, 136.
46. Wilson, A. D. (2013). Diverse application of electronic-nose technologies in agriculture and forestry. *Sensors, 13*, 2295–2348. https://doi.org/10.3390/s1302022295. www.mdpi.com/journal/sensors
47. Wilson, A. D. (2018). Application of electronic-nose technologies for noninvasive early detection of plant, animal and human diseases. *Chemosensors, 6*, 45.

Basics of Quality

5

Understanding Common Quality Terms

Various terms and expressions are used in quality management. Most of these terms and expressions which are necessary for your understanding of the subject matter "quality" are highlighted by the ASQ (American Society of Quality) in its "quality glossary," which was published in the July 2002 Quality Progress. In the case of the International Organization for Standardization (ISO) 9000 family of standards (i.e., ISO 9000, ISO 9001, ISO 9004, and ISO 19011), one of its members, that is, ISO 9000, describes the fundamentals of quality management systems and specifies the terminology for quality management systems.

The provision of the quality glossary by the ASQ and the dedication of ISO 9000 to QMS fundamentals and terminology are joint indications of the need to generally provide a platform by which an accurate and good understanding of quality and its application can be assured.

The term "standard" comes up very frequently in quality so that its understanding becomes highly imperative in the teaching and understanding of quality itself. People generally refer to products and services of their choice or those that they wish to acquire as *standard* items to indicate the goodness or excellent nature of their quality. This is confirmed by its dictionary meaning (the DK Illustrated Oxford Dictionary) as "an object or measure, serving as a basis or, example, or principle, to which others conform or must conform or by which others are judged." Apart from the term "standard," other important fundamental terms of quality include but not limited to the following:

- Quality tools
- Quality policy/quality objectives
- Measurement and calibration
- Leadership/teamwork
- People involvement/empowerment

T. A. Ibidapo, *From Industry 4.0 to Quality 4.0*, Management for Professionals,
https://doi.org/10.1007/978-3-031-04192-1_5

- Continual/continuous improvement and process improvement
- Cost of quality (CoQ)
- Customer focus
- Strategy
- Vision
- Value
- Innovation
- Customer requirement/specification/needs

Standards and Benefits

Most people know and associate the word *standard* with products and services that to them are of some measures or degrees of what is expected in terms of use and/or application. Hence, people generally adapt the term standard to qualify their expectations of a product or services of interest.

According to the ISO, a standard is "a document established by consensus and approved by a recognized body that provides for common and repeated use, rules, guidelines or characteristics for activities or their results…." The characteristics of the product referred to here may be in terms of size, shape, composition, mass, color, etc. In modern quality terms, these characteristics may simply be the requirements, specifications, or needs of the customer.

The ASQ in its quality glossary defined standard as "the metric, specification, gauge, statement, category, segment, grouping, behavior, event or physical product sample against which the outputs of a process are compared and declared acceptable or unacceptable."

Most common standards as we generally use to know them are product specific. Standards can be said to have generally evolved from national applications to what we know of some standards today in the global market. The credit of the massive global application of some generic standards known to us today goes mainly to the ever-growing number of the member countries of the ISO. With over one hundred and sixty (160) countries of the world championing the course of the ISO today, the uses and application of standards in various aspects of the world market economy have played critical roles in assuring and ensuring that products/services focus generally on the need to meet customer needs, requirements, and specifications. Two of the most commonly used global standards are the ISO 9000 QMS and ISO 14000 EMS.

Standards may be generated at both the national and international/global levels to cover a wide scope or variety of situations ranging from quality, occupational health and safety (OHS), risk management to even corporate social responsibility (CSR). The use of standards has the advantage that they:

- Are developed through an elaborate and comprehensive decision-making process which involves many parties/entities with a broad scope of relevant expertise and competencies. Such expertise and competencies are not likely to be easily available and affordable for the use of a single entity.

- Provide reassurance to their users.
- Can be produced without the requirement to pass legislative or statutory acts or laws.

Standards are on a general basis used for various purposes which are of immense value-added benefits to their users and the products provided by them. These include but are not limited to the following:

- It helps to ensure that systems work well and safely too.
- Improves work efficiency, product characteristic predictability, and the ability to plan and make products that are affordable to the customer(s).
- As a tool for achieving conformity to regulatory requirements and set-out specifications.
- As a model from which a disciplined management system and good management practices can be developed, achieved, and implemented.
- As a mechanism for providing evidence to potential and existing customers that an organization has the capability and ability to consistently provide products and services that meet the requirements of the customer; hence, standards can serve as confidence building tools and serve to safeguard consumers and product/service users.
- To facilitate trade among countries and make trading fairer than usual.
- As a platform for sharing technological advances and disseminating innovation and innovative ideas.
- As a platform to provide solutions to common problems.
- Provide governments all over the world with a solid technical and technological base for promulgating health, environmental, and safety legislative/regulatory acts.
- Make the development, production/manufacturing, and supply of products/services more efficient, environmentally friendlier, or safer and cleaner.

It is very clear from the above that when an organization conforms to and it is also assessed on the basis of conformity to international standards, that organization's access to global market could be facilitated. The use of standards coupled with the value it adds to your products could similarly make your products more attractive in terms of their quality, reliability, reproducibility, safety of their usage and application, and their being environmentally friendly.

Just like the borderless global trade that has united the world into an enlarged global marketplace so also has the previous era of national standards been transformed today mainly into that of international standards. Instead of the standards being restricted for use in a particular country, we now have international standards that are developed by a combination of many nations with similar interests using diverse expertise and competencies. For example, ISO standards are international standards developed by and used in over one hundred and sixty (160) countries of the world today. Standards may also be product specific or generic in their mode of application.

Joint International Standards

Apart from the development of international standards by the ISO, international standards may be primarily developed through the initiative and collaboration of more than one body or organization, that is, jointly. Such international standards are commonly known as joint international standards. Examples of some joint international standards are given below where the prefix generally gives an indication of the collaborating bodies/organizations or entities:

ISO/CIE – Joint international standards jointly developed by the ISO and the International Commission on Illumination (CIE)
ISO/ASTM – Joint ISO and American Society for Testing and Materials (ASTM) International Standards
ISO/IEEE – Joint ISO and Institute of Electrical and Electronics Engineers (IEEE) International Standards.
ISO/IEC – Joint ISO and International Electrotechnical Commission (IEC) International Standards

It is important here to stress the fact that the organization initiating any standard has the right to invite contributions or inputs from professional bodies or organizations that are considered relevant to the preparation of a specific standard.

Conformity Assessment

The term *conformity assessment* finds common application generally in the management of quality to ensure that the products/services provided meet customer needs, specifications, and requirements on the one hand and regulatory requirements on the other.

The word conformity is defined in the dictionary as "action in accord with prevailing social standards, attitude, practices, etc." The ISO in its own definition claimed that conformity assessment is;

> The name given to the processes that are used to demonstrate that a product (tangible) or a service or a management system or body meets specified requirements.

Conformity assessment therefore refers to the measurement of products, services, systems, processes, activities, and even personnel in relationship to given or referenced relevant specifications or standards or requirements. Precisely put by the ISO "conformity assessment means checking whether products, services, materials, processes, systems and personnel measure up to the requirements of standards, regulations or other specifications."

The processes that needed to be followed in order to be able to demonstrate that products/services meet requirements are provided, for example, in ISO/IEC standards and guidelines. The use of ISO/IEC standards and guidelines for conformity assessment processes generally makes it possible for the global harmonization of conformity assessment processes to the advantage of facilitating both national and international trades by giving product or service end-users the confidence that it meets requirements. Hence, conformity assessment plays highly critical roles in achieving sustainable quality management improvements vis-à-vis organizational development.

To make conformity assessment more purposeful and meaningful for your quality system, the results of this assessment must be closely followed up. This is to say that all recommended corrective actions emanating from conformity assessment must be put in place promptly and effectively. The frequency of product conformity assessment can be decided by your management or on the basis of applicable standards or as mutually agreed with the customer. Hence, the management of any organization may need to be asking itself very frequently the following question:

> Does our quality management system or production system (i.e., products/services, employees, and processes) measure up to the required specifications?

Most organizations today carry out tests on products or specific items:

- To evaluate and confirm their conformity with specifications and/or features such as the ones defined in standards, regulations, and other requirements. Hence, conformity assessment serves to ensure that products and services meet the needs of the customers or end-users.
- For their compliance with safety and/or other regulations before offering them to the customers or market.

ISO standards and guidelines for conformity assessment processes actually defined the processes and good practices that will enable you to check and ensure that product requirements, needs, and specifications are met. Conformity assessment may be achieved through the use of any one or more of the following activities:

- Product sample testing
- Product inspection
- Product certification
- Certification of personnel
- Process evaluation
- Supplier's declaration of product/service conformity
- Certification/registration to or implementing a relevant management system to ensure that products/services resulting from the system and its production activities are reproducible and consistently meet customer specifications and requirements
- Other mutually agreed conformity assessment arrangements

The ISO/IEC conformity assessment standards and guidelines are quite useful and beneficial to all concerned entities, that is, manufacturers and service providers, customers or consumers, regulatory agencies, and the international communities involved in international trade. The ISO which works both on the principles and practice of conformity assessment has been promoting the international harmonization of conformity assessment activities and the worldwide acceptance of the results.

Customers or consumers are provided with a good basis for selecting products or services as they are likely to have confidence in products/services with a mark or certificate of conformity attesting to product quality and/or other customer-desired characteristic features.

The regulatory agents on the other hand may use conformity assessment as a means for the enforcement of national regulations relating to public policy objectives in the regulation of public health, safety, and the environment.

The global harmonization of conformity assessment procedures through the use of international standards is generally of immense benefit to international trade. Here international standards such as those of the ISO have helped cross-border trading to harmonize trade barriers that have been resulting from multiple product testing and/or product certification.

Customer Confidence

Conformity assessment as indicated above provides confidence for you and your customers. You are sure of the reproducibility and reliability of your products and that they will meet the requirements, needs, expectations, and specifications of your customers as you directly or indirectly promised your customers in your contract agreement. This is so because products and services must be seen as if they are promises to customers. Such promises which are generally in terms of the fulfillment of customer expectations are more or less embodiments of product/service values relating to features such as quality, safety, economy, environmental impact, reliability, compatibility, regulatory requirements, and effectiveness.

The confidence of your customers in your products is assured once they realize or know that their SNEaRs will always be met within the ambient of the law and any other regulatory requirements.

Organizational conformity with established laws and professional ethical practices, even when not stated in the contract, goes a long way to build customer, consumer, or market confidence. This is particularly so in the healthcare and pharmaceutical sectors or industries, areas in which the quality of products of services rendered could be defined with the term *death*.

Measurement and Calibration

Measurement is defined by the ASQ as "the act or process of quantitatively comparing results with requirements." It is also the process of determining a quantitative value of an item. Measurements as well as the tools and methods for achieving them are hence major parts of the basics or fundamental elements of quality management.

Measurements are therefore generally critical in quality management especially for purposes that include but are not limited to the following:

- Quality control measures for ascertaining whether measurable customer specifications and/or requirements are met at every production stage, e.g., in the monitoring and measurement of product to verify conformity to specifications and the identification of nonconforming products.
- As process control measures for the monitoring and management of processes, e.g., statistical process control, control chart, measurements of temperature and pressure during processing, etc.
- Assessment of improvement measures using suitable key performance indicators (KPIs) at various organizational process/activity stages (including after sales) or units and for the entire organization at the end product stage. KPI can therefore simply be described as a statistical measure of how well an organization or process is doing. KPIs generally help in depicting organizational performance at selected stages including final product.
- As quality evaluation and control measures for environmental conditions, medical diagnosis for illness detection, and food products vis-à-vis agricultural produce.
- Organizational financial performance.

Measurements in quality can generally be classified into two groups:

- Physical measurement
- Process-related measurement

Under *physical measurement* physical parameters are measured with the aid of test, measuring, and inspection equipment which must be calibrated to ensure that the ability of the inspection, measuring, and test equipment is verified. Hence, *calibration* is one major aspect of measurement that must be put into consideration when using any measuring equipment or else figures obtained from poorly calibrated or non-regularly calibrated measuring equipment may not be reliable and in effect misleading.

Criticality of Quality Measurements

Pumping money into any business is usually generally catalyzed by the level of brightness of the horizon of its potential financial returns, which either makes the business feasible or not. Stakeholders in businesses often base the sustenance of such investments on current and future potentials of continuously improving return on investment (ROI) or organizational performance. Organizational performance and its potentials to continue to improve therefore constitute the heart beat that keeps many businesses or entities well and alive, successful or failing, sickly or dead. Afterwards business and/or organizational success is optional.

Keeping businesses, organizations, and other profit-oriented systems alive is highly inherent in the dictate of its performance. It is for this purpose that according to Netherton [8], organizational management embarks on hiring consultants, trains their employees, and expands organizational "charts to include newly minted "experts."" The role of quality management can however not be overemphasized. In affirmation of the critical role of quality in business successes are the examples of lean implementations by General Electric [7] and Parker Hannifin and Intel [9]. Similarly, Smith et al. [12] claimed that many top-performing businesses that implemented "sound and well-maintained quality management system (QMS)" have achieved "superior levels of success and sustainability." There have also been other literature claims correlating business successes with implemented QMS [2, 10].

These jointly portray the criticality of the growing impact of quality on organizational and business successes from the last century to the current one. There is no doubt however about the continued influence of quality in virtually all business and organizational processes and activities except such entities fail to embrace quality for continual performance improvement and sustainability, especially during the twenty-first century. Performance improvement therefore remains one of the major goals and objectives of any organization. In order to achieve these, organizational processes and activities must have to be measured because according to physicist Lord Kelvin ((a.k.a. William Thompson), "If you cannot measure it, you cannot improve it."

Since business health and sustainability can be strongly influenced by quality performance, a factor governed mainly by the efficacies and efficiencies of processes, productivity, competitive abilities, improvement measures, return on investment, etc., the role of measurement activities in quality management systems becomes highly imperative. This opinion is supported by the remarks of Sampaio and Saraiva [11] that "quality development must take place at the same time good use of proper metrics, instrumentation, and measurements, including those related with new scopes of application (e.g., nanotechnology, big data, genomics)," as well as both physical measurements and the application of metrology and its tools.

In acknowledgment of the importance of measurements in organizational QMS, the ISO highlighted the criticality of "Performance Evaluation" in section 9 of its ISO 9001:2015 [4] or Clause 8.1 of ISO 9001:2008. Evaluating organizational performance requires the monitoring and measurement of processes, hence the need for the prior consideration of *what*, *how*, and *when* to measure as well as the exact identification of the *points of measurement* and *whose responsibilities* it is to carry out the measurements.

Like most of the ISO's international standards, ISO 9001 QMS international standards provide the foundational framework for QMS measurements which most organizations can build upon to achieve their measurement objectives for processes and overall performance improvements. That is the beauty of generic standards. This is obvious due to the differences as well as variations among businesses and organizations.

The absolute quality of measurement equipment and their regular calibration in the healthcare system are quite significant and critical to the life of the customers, hence the need for their reliability and effective use and application.

Calibration

Calibration is the process of comparing a measuring device with a measurement standard to determine how true or accurate the reading is relative to the definition of the measurement unit. The ASQ puts the definition of calibration succinctly as "the comparison of a measurement instrument or system of unverified accuracy to a measurement instrument or system of known accuracy to detect any variation from the required performance specification".

Calibration can be based on either analysis or on comparison. Calibration based on analysis is the process by which the accuracy of a measuring instrument is based on an analysis within the operating environment. When based on the other hand on comparison the accuracy of one measuring instrument is compared with that of another measuring instrument of known accuracy (standard or gauge) for the purpose of adjusting the accuracy of the subject instrument.

Calibration is an important aspect of reliability engineering which must be taken very seriously by all organizations in the management of their measuring systems in quality management. Failure to do this may result to unimaginable catastrophic ends in terms of the accuracy of:

- Processing parameters
- Results of tests
- All decisions based on measurements or measurable parameters
- Machine and equipment operating conditions
- Meeting customer needs, requirements, and specifications

Calibration is therefore, on a wider basis, a critical aspect of metrology that must be strictly adhered to. Failure to calibrate your measuring equipment simply results to taking some risks. An effective calibration is hence a risk management measure which is used generally to control and manage some of the risks associated with measurement and measurement result reliability. You can imagine the life risks involved in the use of, for example, medical equipment (e.g., sphygmomanometer, glucometer, etc.) whose results fall erroneously within the normal range when they are actually out of range due to poor calibration or lack of it.

Measurement Process

Measurement is a critical operation in the management of quality; hence, the measurement process itself is an integral part of the QMS. The measurement process which is defined according to the ISO as "a set of operations to determine the value of a quantity" is useful in various ways from the measurement of inputs, processing conditions to that of the individual process products and then finished product (or output).

The measurement process therefore plays very vital roles generally in:

- The determination of the ability of the QMS processes to achieve planned results
- Defining the characteristics of in-process sub-products at the respective production stages to ensure that the end product will ultimately meet specifications
- Defining end products themselves against requirements and specifications
- Assessing process status
- Assessing and improving the effectiveness of the QMS

For example, the measurement of key performance indicators (KPIs) can be used to assess product and/or process status as well as for assessing the effectiveness of the QMS. It is the right of every organization to determine its own set of key performance indicators but it is very useful if organizations select the KPIs that hold the greatest potential for improvement and give most information about where the organization is in its pursuit of customer satisfaction.

Measurement Management Systems

The measurement management system (MMS) is "a set of interrelated and interacting elements necessary to achieve metrological confirmation and continual control of measurement processes." The measurement management system is essential and necessary in any quality management system. The MMS is very critical in the areas of product and process measurement, monitoring, and analysis to know and assess the exact situation/condition/state of measured products and processes and to assess whether they are capable of meeting specifications, needs, and requirements of both the internal and external customers or not.

Monitoring and measurement of processes and products for compliance to requirements and customer specifications is also a critical way of assuring customer satisfaction.

The various types of measurements to be made, the intervals of measurements, and the nature of measuring equipment or devices to be used within the QMS are at the discretion of each organization type. But it is better for your organization to select those that are adequate and suitable for the purposes for which they are meant. Maintaining your measuring and monitoring devices and/or equipment in its optimal measuring status is very critical for ensuring that they give reliable results. Here the recommendations and guidelines of equipment manufacturers (see product manual) in the use, storage, application, and handling of the equipment are vital and critical for their reliability; hence, they need to be strictly adhered to.

In order to ensure a good understanding of measurement variability such as in the measurable characteristics of products and processes, the *statistical technique* can be employed to solve problems and improve the effectiveness and efficiency of the QMS.

The use of statistical techniques can help, for example, to measure, describe, analyze, interpret, and model variability. The importance of the use of the statistical technique in a quality management system is provided by the ISO in its ISO/TR 10017.

Equipment Reliability

The potentials of the use of inspection, measuring, and test equipment cannot be fully realized on a continuous basis except they are given adequate maintenance and protection. This is because the reliability, that is, *the probability that a product will perform its intended function(s) under stated conditions without failure for a given period of time,* for this equipment is also subjected to one deterioration factor or another as they are used day in and day out. It follows therefore that all inspection, measuring, and test equipment are subject to change over a period of time due to various causes which include but not limited to the following:

- Mechanical wear
- Electronic drifting
- Changes in the environment (e.g., weather changes, humidity, etc.)

The importance of a good measuring system in the management of quality is highlighted by the ISO in ISO 9001:2008 Clause 7.6 by recommending that "the organization shall determine the monitoring and measurement to be undertaken and the monitoring and measuring equipment needed to provide evidence of conformity of product to determined requirements."

There are organizations that calibrate inspection, measuring, and test equipment all over the world whose services you can easily assess from any part of the world due to the present advances in telecommunication systems. Check within your own locality the organizations that are in the calibration business as you may need them from time to time. For example, in Nigeria, the Ministry of Employment, Labor and Productivity has some statutory responsibilities to ensure that weighing scales used by various organizations within the country are calibrated and are functioning accurately. The effectiveness of this activity of the ministry is understandably below expectations. In other parts of the world where such services are offered by private organizations, the results are more effective.

One advantage of calibration is that it helps to protect the consumers of goods and services from being cheated by service/goods providers who may want to compromise them. There are also international reference laboratories to which calibration references can be made.

The acceptability or reliability of individual organizations in the business of calibration can be verified through their accreditation to the requirements of, for example, ISO/IEC 17025:2017 [5], as well as their fulfillment of local regulatory guidelines available in each country. The ISO/IEC17025:2017 specifies the general requirements for the competence, impartiality, and consistent operation of laboratories. Hence, it is applicable to organizations engaged in performing laboratory activities irrespective of size.

For example, the Federal Ministry of Employment, Labor and Productivity in Nigeria has its own guidelines governing the use of measuring scales. These guidelines are focused on the adequate maintenance of measuring scales to ensure that consumers are well protected against any type of malpractices.

The need for *process-related or process-oriented measurements* cut across every aspect of any QMS. On a general basis all measuring systems must be properly and adequately managed to ensure that:

- A high level of accuracy of the measuring equipment is achieved
- Correct measurements are being made at any time

The ISO, in one of its standards, ISO 10012:2003[3], has given some guidance for the management of measurement systems. The standard actually provides the necessary guidelines for the management of all measurements that take place during the product realization processes irrespective of the stage. The application of this standard can aid the achievement of the following results among others:

- In the determination of the necessity and relevance of every measurement
- In the determination of the use of appropriate measuring instrument for every measurement
- To ensure that every measurement made is accurate and done correctly
- To ensure the regular review of every measurement

All in all, accurate and correctly applied measurement made with adequately calibrated measuring equipment irrespective of wherever it is made is an essential element of the requirements of various QMS standards.

One of the basic quality ways of the Toyota Motor Corporation of Japan is its culture of measurement. According to its Chief Executive Officer (CEO), Watanabe [13], "Toyota's way is to measure everything – even the noise that car doors make when they open and close as workers perform their final inspections on newly manufactured automobiles." This assertion, coupled with the long-standing success story of Toyota, is an evidence of the practical demonstration of the basic role of measurements, in the culture and practice of quality.

When viewed as an entity, measurements are critical for ascertaining or assessing the performance of processes and activities involved in the provision of goods and services either as suppliers or manufacturers. In order to ensure the quality of the products and/or services emanating from your organization or enterprise, the following measurements are considered helpful:

- Measurement of the input provided by the suppliers to ensure that set standards for inputs are met.

- Measurement of organizational performance in terms of its processes and output using key performance indicators (KPIs).
- Performance goals that are set for processes are measured and managed to assure compliance and improvement, thereby achieving process optimization, while outputs are measured to ensure that they meet customer requirements.
- Measurement of customer feedback to determine whether customers are getting what they need and require and to determine the level of customer satisfaction. This in turn enables the assessment of the need to put corrective actions in place and which corrective actions are necessary.

The issue of calibration needs to be taken very seriously not just because of its impact on the product specifications but also because of its effect on the *cost of quality (CoQ)*, here mainly the *appraisal costs*. Hence, it is important that the management of your measurement systems give adequate considerations to the following critical points and questions:

- Determining the types of measurements that are necessary to ensure that the quality of your products, both at the processing or intermediary and final stages, meets the requirements, specifications, and needs of the customers (internal and external)
- Determining where, when, and how frequently those measurements have to be taken
- Determining and providing the needed measurement equipment
- Ascertaining the required range, resolution, precision, and accuracy that are required for the achievement of necessary measurements
- Ascertaining that the measuring process is error proof and that effective preventive and corrective action processes are put in place to achieve high accuracy and precision measurements
- Ascertaining the suitability and impact of the environment and/or area of location of equipment (critical for weighing scales) on its stability vis-à-vis the accuracy of the measurements
- Are the operators or members of staff involved in carrying out measurement activities and handling inspection, measuring, and test equipment adequately trained to use and handle them most appropriately?
- Identification of the influence of measurement uncertainties and how to account for these uncertainties
- Is it necessary to calibrate the measurement equipment or has it been calibrated? What is the frequency of calibration needed to maintain all measurement equipment and where and how are they going to be calibrated?
- Is the calibration traceable to the appropriate measurement unit of the International Systems of Units?
- Protection of all measurement instruments by ensuring that they are used and kept under controlled conditions so that they are protected from unauthorized and unnecessary alterations or adjustments

- Reviewing and evaluating from time to time the number of equipment to be calibrated or simply determining the inspection, measuring, and test equipment that need or have to be calibrated
- Determining the tolerances or degree of accuracy of the specifications of your products and sub-products to assess the need for the calibration of the inspection, measuring, and test equipment
- Ensuring that the operations needed to assure that the measuring equipment conforms to the requirements for its intended use are reviewed at defined or regular intervals
- The need for the monitoring and auditing of the entire measurement management system at appropriate intervals considered suitable to ensure that your measurements are correct, accurate, reliable, and precise at all times

Continual/Continuous Improvement (CI)

Continual improvement is a recurrent trend in issues relating to quality management. Continual improvement stresses the unending quest to continuously meet the demands, requirements, specifications, and needs of your customers so as to remain in business. As defined by the ISO [6] continual improvement is "recurring activity to increase the ability to fulfill requirements." In a similar manner the ASQ [1] defines continuous improvement, sometimes called continual improvement in the American perspective, as "the ongoing improvement of products, services or processes through incremental and breakthrough improvements." Hence, continual improvement is an important driving force in quality management as you have to aspire at all times to exceed what has already been achieved both in terms of the product/service quality and performance and meeting the requirements, needs, and specifications of your customers. Improvement here refers to improvement in all aspects of organizational quality activities.

The improvement of product quality alone is no more adequate or good enough if you want to remain relevant and competitive in the present global marketplace in which business activities are facilitated through the use of fast communications systems such as the Internet, GSM, etc. It therefore becomes highly imperative for all organizations and enterprises that intend to remain in business to ensure that all aspects of its business activities are continually placed on the course of improvement. This brings us to the fact that *continual improvement* of your business in all its ramifications is highly critical to your survival. It is only businesses that have no plans to continue to exist and progress that can afford to ignore the need for the continual improvement of their activities. This is definitely the reason why the most internationally acclaimed organizations always place so much emphasis on the consistent needs for the "continual improvement" of their businesses.

It is necessary here to point to the fact too that some authors and other quality practitioners use the term "continuous" in place of "continual," thereby creating some gaps of understanding between continual and continuous improvement. In order to clear the air about any ensuing confusion, there is the need for these terms to be given some clarifications here and to state in clear terms the understanding of the usage of the term continual improvement by this author.

Here it is important to ask what is understood by the term continual improvement. The ISO in its definition states that continual improvement is the "recurring activity to increase the ability to fulfill requirements." A continual improvement process can therefore be said to be one in which objectives are established and tested and opportunities found and explored for improvement. This can usually be achieved through activities or measures which include but are not limited to the following:

- Audit findings and conclusions
- Production meetings
- Management reviews
- Analysis of data
- Customer feedback
- Technology update
- Innovative measures or innovation
- Any other process improvement measures

They all generally serve as input to the continual improvement process.

Quality Use of the Terms Continual and Continuous

The word *continual* is oftentimes usually confused with the word *continuous* though in the context of the US English, there seems to be no difference between continual and continuous improvement. The difference here as stretched in the definition of the ISO can be found in the *recurring* nature of the activities that lead to *continual* improvement. Here you put a system in place, work with it for some time, review the system, and use your review to improve the system. The continual improvement measure can also be demonstrated with the principles of Shewhart Cycle, PDCA, which vividly summarize your activities for improvement, **p**lan your improvement activities, **d**o according to your plans (or execute your plans), **c**heck (or study) your system, and then **a**ct (or take action).

The cycle of occurrence is then repeated as frequently as is necessary. The difference in meaning can further be explained with the dictionary (DK Illustrated Oxford Dictionary) meanings which state that *continual* means "happening frequently" (but with breaks in between each occurrence), while *continuous* means "uninterrupted, incessant."

The two words are more often than not used interchangeably though the ISO in its international standards ISO 9000 quality management system (QMS) and ISO 14000 environmental management system (EMS) keeps its faith only with the terminology *continual* which is so commonly used in both international standards to define the need for an ongoing improvement of your management system (or even in your business activities). Contrary to ISO 9000 and ISO 14000 standards, the

American version, QS-9000, is more or less restricted to the use of the term *continuous* in its first, second, and third editions [14].

Irrespective of the differences in the meaning and usage of the two terms in terms of quality management and the confusion generated, the objective of their usage to precede the word improvement either as "continual improvement" or "continuous improvement" should be understood and seen from the perspective of the need to make the improvement of your system an ongoing process. The author however sticks to the use of continual improvement in line with the definition provided by the ISO throughout this book.

To survive the competitive pressures in the present and future global business environment, you must therefore operate your business with the basics of continually improving your products/services with the main objective of offering at all times t*otal customer satisfaction* (TCS).

Some basic guidelines which can help you stay in business as seen from the perspective of meeting the requirements and needs of your customers with continual improvement include but are not limited to the following:

- Make your customer (or product consumers, or service receivers) the major focus of your activities at all times in your business goals/objectives.
- Know your customer, its processes, and products as much as is possible irrespective of the age of the relationship.
- Treat every customer issue as if the life or survival of your company is solely dependent on it.
- Renew your knowledge of your customers as often as there are changes in your customer's processes, products, and market.
- Meet customer expectations, needs, requirements, and specifications at all times.
- Uphold a constant review and update of the requirements of your customer.
- Identify and listen to the voice of the customer (VOC) at all times.
- Ensure effective communication is maintained with your customer at all times even under difficult situations such as when the delivery schedule cannot be met by you for one reason or another. The earlier your customer knows about this, the better it is for your organization, customer, and their relationship with you. The information provided to the customer must be accurate, concise, and devoid of any ambiguities.
- Identify and provide all the resources (human and capital) needed by you to meet customer needs, specifications, and requirements.
- Embrace appropriate and adequate skill upgrade of your personnel to assure and improve their level of competency. The dynamics of the business should actually dictate the nature and types of skill upgrade needed for your organization and its personnel from time to time.
- Motivate your personnel.
- Benchmark, identify, and provide the best (in terms of technological advancement) and most economical processes to meet the needs and requirements of your customer.

- Constantly review, refine, and update your processes to ensure you can always meet customer expectations, needs, specifications, and requirements and that your products too remain competitive in the market.
- Improve your entire organizational processes on a continual basis through adequate reviews of your processes, techniques, and equipment in line with your customer satisfaction objectives.
- Be innovative.
- Maintain your customer-focused culture at all times.
- Manage supplier relationship very effectively.
- Support your suppliers to help them meet your expectations.

This chapter treats some fundamental terms and basics of quality which generally serve to help in the understanding and enlightenment of those that have quality management skills as well as those that are just getting involved with quality and quality management systems for the first time, that is, quality beginners. They provide beginners in the area of quality management the opportunity to gain a quick insight into what quality entails and to be able to understand or follow the subsequent issues treated in this book.

References

1. ASQ. (2007). Quality glossary, (2007), Quality Progress, pp. 39–59.
2. Fons, S. (2011). Measuring economic effects of quality management systems. *The TQM Journal, 23*(4), 458–474.
3. ISO 10012:2003. (2003). *Measurement management systems – requirements for measurement processes and measurement equipment*, ISO, www.iso.org
4. ISO 9001:2015. (2015). *Quality management systems – requirements.*
5. ISO/IEC 17025:2017. (2017). *General requirements for the competence of testing and calibration laboratories*, ISO, www.iso.org
6. ISO/IEC Guide 2:2004. (2004). *Standardization and related activities - general vocabulary*, International Organization for Standardization, www.iso.org
7. Nayab, N. (2011). *Six Sigma and GE: A story of successful Implementation, "The story of Six Sigma and GE,"* BrightHub Project Management,. https://www.brighthubpm.com
8. Netherton, G. (2020). A Leg Up – Achieve cultural improvement with the three-legged stool approach. *Quality Progress*, 56.
9. Parker Hannifin., & Intel. (2017). *Top 10: Lean manufacturing companies in the world*, Manufacturing Global.
10. Rusjan, B., & Alic, M. (2010). Capitalizing on ISO 9001 benefits for strategic results. *International Journal of Quality and Reliability Management, 27*(7), 756–778.
11. Sampaio, P., & Saraiva, P. (2016). Quality: From past perfect to future conditional, p.10. In P. Sampaio & P. Saraiva (Eds.), *Quality in the 21st century*. Springer International.
12. Smith, R. A., Bester, A., & Moll, M. (2014). Quantifying quality management system performance in order to improve business performance. *South African Journal of Industrial Engineering, 25*(2), 75.
13. Watanabe, K. (2007). The HBR interview, Lessons from Toyota's long drive, interview by Thomas A. Stewart and Anand P. Raman. *Harvard Business Review*, 74–83.
14. West, J., & Cianfrani, C. (2009). Expert answers, Quality Progress, page 8.

Quality Teamwork

6

Introduction

The successful implementation of any quality management system standards or quality management concepts depends generally on the positive contributions and engagement of all concerned or relevant entities – management, employees, customers, suppliers, investors, and other stakeholders – who must all move in one direction with one and the same goals and objectives. Each and every one of the entities must play their respective roles adequately and promptly while key or core quality management activities must be carried out under committed, dedicated, effective, and dynamic leadership.

Another important area of quality team working that is critical for, and strongly impacts businesses and their growth potentials is firstly, the collaboration among organizations despite the competition, and secondly, between regulatory bodies and suppliers/organizations.

Quality Leadership

The ASQ in its quality glossary [1] defined leadership as "an essential part of a quality improvement effort." Leadership is, according to Forster [10, 11], "the process by which an individual influences a group to move toward the attainment of a superordinate goal" which he claimed "benefit groups instead of simply individuals."

Achieving the quality goals of your organization requires proper and adequate utilization of resources (human and materials), machinery and equipment, tools, processes, and other resources. The proper management of these resources and the need for effective coordination of activities therefore call for good leadership with integrity, focus, and direction or else the acquisition and possession of these resources may be in vain. Since leadership involves power sharing relationships,

T. A. Ibidapo, *From Industry 4.0 to Quality 4.0*, Management for Professionals,
https://doi.org/10.1007/978-3-031-04192-1_6

good leaders need to be fair and effective in the use and sharing of power. In relating these needs to quality management systems, the *Baldrige Criteria for Performance Excellence* [17] state clearly that:

> Your leaders should ensure the creation of strategies, systems and methods for achieving performance excellence, stimulating innovation, building knowledge and capabilities and ensuring organizational sustainability.

The aims of leadership in quality management as professed by W. Edwards Deming [8], a renowned quality guru, are to:

- Improve the performance of man and machine
- Increase output
- Improve quality
- Bring workmanship pride to the people

In the case of service provision such as consultancy, the aim of leadership is embedded in the three traits of effective leaders given by Zeithaml et al. [22], and they are:

- *Service vision,* that is, the ability of the leader to have a vision of how to provide great services.
- Maintaining *high standards* which must be communicated to others for them to emulate.
- *In-the-field leadership style* stresses leaders that get out in the field to make things happen or involvement of leaders in activities. This is leadership by example.

On a general basis the primary role of leadership in quality management is to create a clear vision for the success of whatever QMS or quality management concept that is to be installed or already in place and to communicate their vision clearly, consistently, and repeatedly throughout the entire organization, thereby leading the efforts. Hence, quality leaders must establish a vision which must be communicated to the employees with the provision of adequate tools and knowledge necessary for its realization.

In contrast to the above views of good leadership traits, bad or ineffective leaders are in most cases:

- Without vision or goals/objectives.
- Fond of assigning blames to subordinates.
- Not usually involved in activities.
- Believe in the removal of employees seen or viewed by him as being problematic or in opposition to his views.
- Do not consider the opinion of others.

- Claims all successful achievements are made by him; hence, in his report of success stories the pronoun "I" occurs most frequently as opposed to the usual word "we" which is indicative of the collectiveness of purpose and the general portrayal of team working.

From the perspectives of Juran [13] it is highly imperative that quality leaders must have to pay adequate attention to:

- *Quality planning*, that is, learning about the customers and finding all the ways to satisfy them. It is therefore highly imperative here for an effective leader to ensure that customer specifications, needs, and requirements are defined and met.
- *Quality control:* to ensure that actual product performance is compared with set-out product goals in order to effectively eliminate any gaps found between them.
- *Improvement of quality:* the planning of ways to improve quality and ensuring that resources for achieving the planned objectives are made available as and when needed.

In conclusion therefore a leader may be effective by:

1. Directing the ways the works of employees are carried out to achieve set-out goals/objectives
2. Helping employees to discover and achieve their potentials

Leadership roles are so important in quality management that it cannot be overemphasized.

Leadership Roles in Quality Management

Trying to get a good example of excellent leadership roles and activities in quality management actually brings to my memory some of the observations I made about ants in my grandmother's cocoa plantation during my secondary school days in the 1960s. It was amazing and perhaps inexplicable how effectively and efficiently these insects of the Formicidae family effectively mobilize and organized themselves with the utmost discipline, to face and accomplished tough challenges. These are all exhibited in the excellent ways the ants execute their collective business of sourcing for food and their emergency management capabilities as demonstrated in the way they rescue each other at times of risks or in emergency situations.

For example, when an ant finds any food item, others quickly gathered around it to move the food item which may be many times their individual sizes to safety. Similarly, when they find preys, they quickly surround and capture it before moving it collectively to a safe location for consumption. Whenever their pattern of movement in a row is disrupted, they quickly regroup in the same pattern shortly thereafter. Even when one of them is injured, they quickly moved it jointly into a safer location. The attitude of the ants led me then to think as a child that they probably were taking instructions in their own language from their unidentifiable leaders that most likely maintained an open communication system similar to that of the town crier with them.

Although my late grandmother was not able to answer most of the numerous questions that I asked her about the ants and their strong philosophy of working together with diligence and focus to achieve tasks of various types and kind, all the same she managed to dampen my curiosity each time I asked such questions with the statement that they were created by God to be disciplined, focused, and organized, diligent, strategic, and cooperative with one another if they must survive in an environment in which they are easy preys to many other creatures. Although she did not mention anything about their ability to plan their activities, it is obvious from their achievements that ants too must have the ability to adequately and effectively plan their activities before they execute them.

The quality management lessons that can be learned from the case of the ants can generally be viewed from the perspective of:

- *Leadership*
- *Followership*
- *Communication*
- *Teamwork*

The ingredients of the success of the ants are therefore undoubtedly embedded mostly in their:

- Trust in each other
- Good communication system
- Partnership and unity of purpose
- Sharing of and focusing on common goals and objectives
- Diligent approach to their individual responsibilities

The inference could then be made about the approach of the ants to life and their achievements that they adequately plan, build trust in one another, maintain effective communication, and focus on the set goals. Using the activities of the ants as a good reference point, the role of a good quality management team leader can be said to include but are not limited to the following:

- Planning and devising strategies (including the choice of appropriate quality management program/concept/system)
- Building trust in team members
- Maintaining an effective and efficient line of communication with team members
- Ensuring cooperation and partnership of team members
- Focusing on set-out goals and objectives
- Working diligently to achieve set-out goals

Leadership Styles

Going by the distinction of the leadership scholar James MacGregor Burns as reported by Eagly and Carli [9], leadership styles fall into three groups, namely:

- Transformational
- Transactional
- Laissez-faire

Transformational Leadership

The concept of transformational leadership was introduced by Burns [7], a leadership expert, who claimed that transformational leadership can be seen when "leaders and followers make each other to advance to a higher level of moral and motivation."

There is no better and practical way of presenting the attributes of a transformational leadership here than to talk of the way I headed my quality management team members to achieve positive changes in the group of companies (seven in all) for which I had the opportunity to lead to greater heights. We successfully implemented the requirements of the ISO 9001:2000 QMS international standards and achieved astonishingly improved productivity and appreciable reduction in wastages in all affected plants to meet the SNEaRs of our then increasing number of customers.

As soon as I was delegated to lead the group in the task of improving product quality and productivity through the implementation of the ISO 9000 series of international quality management system (QMS) standard, I took full control of the project by:

- Defining and communicating in the most unambiguous and easily understandable terms the vision, quality policy, and quality objectives/goals of the company to group members.
- Passionately charging and energizing the group members that the project belonged to every individual member; hence, the glory of a successful implementation at the set-out completion time would be the success and glory of every individual group member.
- Putting an implementation plan in place with identified relevant milestones to be achieved at specified times.
- Ensuring that all needed tools and implementation infrastructure are made available to group members in each of the plants as and when needed.
- Emphasizing the benefits of the successful implementation of the project to both the organization and individual employees.

Just as demonstrated in the example above, a transformational leader sets out goals and puts plans in place for their realization and even goes on to innovate, irrespective of the success already achieved by the organization being led. This type of leaders does not only mentor and empower the group members or employees but also encourages them to develop their full potentials. Hence, transformational leaders easily gain the trusts and confidence of their followers or in terms of quality, the employees, who readily accept and see them as role models. Transformational leaders are generally more effective just as they lead their followers or employees to contribute more effectively to their organizations.

The role of leadership in project management to accomplish set-out objectives is so important that this deserves special attention and consideration at all times. In order to help you in the selection of a transformational leadership to execute your organizational quality management or other projects, the components of transformational leadership are as spelled out by Bass [5] highlighted here:

- **Intellectual Stimulation** – expresses the intellect of the transformational leader in challenging the status quo to encourage group members to be innovative and creative in finding new ways and opportunities of doing things.
- **Individualized Consideration** – is an expression of the ability and involvement of the transformational leader to keep open communication lines to foster supportive relationships and encourage individual members of the group to freely share or make their individual and unique contributions available to the group.
- **Inspirational Motivation** – this defines the ability of the transformational leader to articulate a clear vision of the task to group members while at the same time helping group members to experience the same passion and motivation to fulfill set-out goals.
- **Idealized Influence** – defines the situation whereby the transformational leader is trusted and respected that group members emulate and internalize his ideas as a role model.

Transactional Leadership

The transactional style of leadership, as the name implies, gets the cooperation or compliance of his group members just to get things going through both rewards and punishments. This exchange model leads to rewards being given to group members for good work or positive results, while poor work or negative results may be rewarded with punishment. A transactional leader can therefore be said to be established on the basis of give-and-take relationship between leader and followers which is more attractive to the latter (i.e., followers). The conventional mode of management is used here for the clarification of the responsibilities of employees who are rewarded when they meet set-out goals/objectives. In cases when the employees do not meet set-out goals/objectives, they are corrected.

The transactional leadership generally concentrates more on finding faults and deviations. As against the situation in the case of proactive transformational leadership where attention is focused on future or long-term development, transactional leadership focuses attention more on getting immediate results. Hence, this type of leadership is usually more suitable and effective for managing situations where immediate results are exempted. Examples here are in emergency or crisis situations and others when identified tasks have to be carried out in a specific way and manner. Transactional leadership which is responsive thrives well in the athletics world when rewards are emphasized to promote success with the end results that group members become highly committed to the extent that they are ready to even take risks to accomplish the outcome asked for by the leadership.

Laissez-Faire Leadership

Laisser-faire which implies "completely hands-off" simply defines leadership without involvement. In the case of the laissez-faire *leadership* style, the leader's group members are given little or no guidance and hence they take little or no responsibility in managing people. Instead, group members are given the freedom to take their own decisions in solving problems or managing projects. Handing off the decision-making activities of a group to its leader pre-supposes that members excel when they are left alone to respond to their responsibilities and obligations in their own ways.

The only situation in which laissez-faire leadership could be of good effect is when the group members are:

- Highly skilled/competent
- Highly motivated
- Capable of working independently
- Disciplined to follow and maintain planned project schedules

The leadership here must however ensure that all needed tools/inputs are available to the group members.

My experience in the manufacturing sector of the economy showed however that this is still the leadership style resulting in the lowest productivity. This may probably be seen as an indication of the general need for somebody to coordinate group responsibilities. At times responsibilities may have been carried out by individual group member but results may not be coordinated and/or delivered at the right time.

The lackadaisical nature of the laissez-faire type of leadership is not likely going to give you the positive changes that you may be looking forward to get in your change management structure as you implement your quality project.

Good Leadership Qualities

In most cases most leaders adopt the features that are common to both the transformational and transactional leadership modes. Irrespective of the type of leadership, it is important that any good leader must:

- Be patriotic
- Have integrity

- Be honest, sincere, transparent, and trustworthy
- Be prepared to lead by example, i.e., do what I do and not just what I say
- Be objective
- Possess good analytical mind
- Be prepared to hire and fire whenever it becomes necessary
- Not shy away from any of his responsibilities

Impact of Leadership Styles in Quality Management

There are no doubts whatsoever that the literature is awash with evidences which massively and strongly suggest generally that management is key to a successful quality program implementation, management, and sustainability. There are however fewer research works to identify the roles of leadership models/types and/or profiles that are more or less supportive of the implementation and sustenance of quality. The author's personal experience however showed that leadership model plays important roles in the success, efficacy, and rate of quality program introduction and implementation. All in all, leadership matters so much in quality management that it may even be considered impossible without leadership vis-à-vis management support [14].

That leadership matters in the quality management world is most distinctly accentuated by the US Congress which, in 1987, took a global leadership role to raise awareness of quality by recognizing US companies that have successfully implemented quality management systems with a yearly award, the MBNQA (Vinyard [20] and Blazey and Grizzell [6] and ASQ [2]). This exemplary national leadership annual quality award, the Malcolm Baldrige National Quality Award (MBNQA) [16], and its accomplishments since inception in 1987 are a living evidence of the excellent roles of leadership motivational efforts in quality management.

The creation of the Armand V. Feigenbaum Medal by the ASQ in 1997 for encouraging the early career development of others in the field of quality is another excellent recognition for the general need to maintain a stream of leadership reservoir for quality management as a whole [21]. Leadership is the singular most critical criteria for organizational quality management, hence the additional need for leadership passion and enthusiasm for the success of any quality program.

In their studies to establish a correlation, if any, between leadership models and quality management principles, Barbrosa et al. [4] showed most interestingly that both transformational and transactional correlate positively with the principles of quality management even though transformational leadership style tends to have a slightly better trend.

Similarly, in their extensive research work carried out primarily in the manufacturing sector of the economy, Hirtz et al. [12] evaluated the leadership styles among the range of *transformational*, *transactional*, and *non-transactional* relative to organizational performance using the criteria from the Baldrige Quality Award:

- Leadership
- Strategic planning

- Human resource development and management
- Process management
- Customer focus and satisfaction
- Measurement, analysis, and knowledge management

The outcome of their works similarly suggests that transformational leadership is positively related to the successful implementation of quality management vis-à-vis higher performance. On the other hand, passive leadership styles, such as laissez-faire, have a negative impact.

Above all is the generally known fact that "a leadership approach that has affinity to quality management is servant leadership which emphasizes an increased service to others, a holistic approach, promoting a sense of community and the sharing of power in decision-making." Transformational leadership thus exhibits the potentials for implementing quality management vis-à-vis achieving higher organizational performance levels.

Teamwork

A team is "a group of individuals organized to work together to achieve specific goals/objectives or to get a job done." Hence, a team can be said to be put in place to get results of the various tasks given to the team to achieve.

How well a team performs in achieving its goals is however a factor of many variables which include among others the following:

- Team structure
- Interpersonal relationship among team members
- Quality of the team leadership
- Empowerment (i.e., have the authority, information, and skills to take necessary decisions as may be needed for achieving set-out goals)

For a team to be successful team members must jointly brainstorm to:

- Identify decisions to be made or problem to be solved by the team
- Choose or identify sub-teams to work on and make each decision
- Assign responsibility of achieving results to one member of the sub-team
- Select the mode of achieving results for each decision and give a deadline for members of the larger team to make input
- Implement decision as soon as it is made or concluded and announced it to the larger team

The major characteristics of a good team leadership therefore include among others the following:

- There should be a clear strategy for decision-making in order to give team members a sense of purpose and direction.

- Operational goals should be clearly specified and defined to avoid losing track of set-out goals or targets.
- The roles and responsibilities of every individual member must be clearly identified with dates (time) of completion, documented and jointly agreed upon to avoid passing the buck and blaming each other.
- Business should be transacted in an open and transparent manner.
- The way and mode of decision-making must be agreed upon from the onset. Here it must be agreed whether decisions will be made on the basis of "majority carries the vote or by one person alone (i.e., unilaterally)."

The success of a team depends generally on the willingness of the individual members, their cooperation, and the ability of the team leader to move the members in the right direction at the right time with the right pace. It is my belief that a good and balanced leadership breathes, in turn, a set or group of good followership.

Nurses' Leadership Skills in Healthcare

The healthcare sector is one the most critical aspects of human activities that goes a long way to define the quality of his life, even though this fact was not recognized until the middle of the twentieth century or thereabout.

The registered nurse (RN), apart from leading other cadres of nursing care personnel in the healthcare sector of the economy, such as certified nursing assistant (CNA) and licensed vocational nurse/licensed practical nurse (LVN/LPN), coordinates all other patient care activities across the hospital system to facilitate the effective treatment of the patients in order to achieve planned or intended outcomes.

The experience of the author also attests to the fact too that nurses are overall the absolute leaders of quality imagery of not just the hospitals but the entirety of the healthcare systems in the following ways:

- Nurses are usually the first patient care contact hence, the first patient/ customer experience in healthcare hierarchy.
- Nurses generally exhibit the professional skills to advise and reassure patients in order to give them the hope of healing apart from the doctor.
- Nurses exhibit the longest customer or patient contact time.
- Nurses use their competencies in various aspects of patient advocacy and teaching to holistically enhance patient care.
- Nurses provide the most critical patient guides and guidelines about patients to facilitate the often brief or perhaps "swift" and hurried attention of the doctor.
- Nurses are the most down-to-earth teachers or educationists of both patient and relatives.
- Situated at the frontline of patient care activities, nurses are silently "forced" to endure emotional shocks and suffer psychological damages emanating from their first encounters with customers/patients in the state of patient arrival at the hospitals or other healthcare facilities.

- Nurses are often made to endure the leadership pains of small healthcare facilities such as nursing homes, memory care, rehabilitation centers, etc.
- Nurses are in the forefront and general coordination of correctional healthcare system managing clinical operations of inmates' healthcare in correctional facilities.

The quality management leadership's pivotal role in healthcare quality management is generally inherent in the training of nurses. As precisely summed up by Sullivan [19], "all nurses are managers." This strong affirmation is made irrespective of the areas of the nurses' professional practices which include among others the following areas of interest:

- Freestanding clinics
- Ambulatory surgical centers
- Critical units in acute care hospitals
- Hospice care for home care agencies

The nurses' leadership position in the healthcare industry is thus quite expansive and far beyond direct patient care to include the management and dealings with other healthcare staff members – other nurses, unlicensed assistive cadre of staff, customer management, and at times the management of nursing home clinical operations.

In some other situations nurses as leaders have to effectively manage the costs of quality (CoQ). The need for and maintenance of excellent teamwork among nurses in the healthcare industry can therefore not be overemphasized. The nurses' team working expectations are quite enormous and at times overstretched.

Team Structure

From my experience in the manufacturing setup, the objectives of setting up teams vary from situation to situation, of which the most profound of them are to:

- Proffer solutions to problems and provide consistently efficient action plan for the implementation of suggested solutions
- Execute projects which may vary in nature, type, and form
- Bring innovative ideas to organizational activities

In my years as the Plant Manager of the biggest glass bottle crown manufacturing plant in Nigeria and in the West African sub-region (Frigoglass Crown Division, Ijebu-Ode, Nigeria) and windshield manufacturing plants (TSG Limited, Ibadan, Nigeria), I had the opportunity to lead, select, and work with teams of various structures which include:

- Team members selected on the bases of *background diversity,* that is, with people of different age groups, gender, ethnic groups, etc.

- Team members selected on the basis of *functional diversity*, that is, people of different skills, job experience and/or number of years of service, part-time staff, full-time staff, job hierarchy, etc.
- Team members of *cross-functional or mixed diversity*, that is, comprising a mixture of both the background and functional diversities – age, gender, ethnic groups, mixed skills, job titles, job hierarchy, part time, and full time

Quality teams of the *background diversity* types are in most cases generally usually very close to each other, more friendly, less argumentative, and seemly cohesive and always quick at getting results due to efficient and easy coordination and their resilient and perseverance. It is however noteworthy here that solutions proffered by this group of people to quality problems were usually shallow and lack in most cases the necessary depth and innovative ideas.

Background diversity teams are on the basis of my experience very good for solving quality problems which emanate from process interfaces, customer satisfaction problems, and interpersonal issues.

Technical, processing, and other skills-related problems are easily solved by the *functional diversity* quality teams using the appropriate skills and experience of the team members. They are very argumentative and usually come up with solutions of adequate depth and some degrees of innovation. It must however be mentioned here that on a few occasions there were strong disagreements that led to the production of opposing results due to interpersonal conflicts.

In-depth and consistently good decisions full of innovative and creative ideas were usually obtained from *cross-functional* or *mixed diversity* groups which suggested or recommended solutions to problems that were generally usually based on wide perspectives and broad considerations. The likelihood of formation of subgroups within the group was noticed here a few times but did not in any way hinder the production of efficient decisions. This group was used extensively by me for solving complex and difficult quality problems which had existed in the two Crown Plants managed by me between 1993 and 1997. A particular case here is that of the smooth operational merger of two different crown production plants located across the country, Nigeria, that is, the merger of a crown production plant in Kano with one at Ijebu-Ode.

It must however be mentioned here that other external factors such as level of education and its differences among group members, degree or level of maturity, and cultural upbringing have roles to play in the success of each team structure. All in all, leadership has a tremendous role to play in the way quality management groups achieve set-out objectives/goals.

This is strongly demonstrated in the case of a country like Nigeria which has refused to grow and develop in spite of her oil wealth and other natural endowments because of her extremely poor leadership hierarchy over the years which had been centered mainly on "individualism" and individual interests rather than national development and growth.

My experience with teams of functional diversity does not however preclude the fact that collaboration among diverse professionals is usually smooth and without difficulties. Collaboration does not usually occur naturally; there are difficulties that one has to tackle within the team. The problems here are diverse and according to Rees [18] include the following:

- Lack of buy-in to group goals
- Personal agendas that adversely affect member behavior
- Decisions and actions that are not recorded and are therefore later abridged
- Poor attendance by one or more members

To tackle this problem Rees suggested the focus of attention by leaders or facilitators on three dimensions of teambuilding which are:

- Tackling the assigned problem
- Maintaining an effective group dynamic
- Winning the personal buy-in of each individual

Team leaders or facilitators must have these problems at the back of their minds and then focus attention on Rees' [18] three dimensions of teambuilding highlighted above.

All in all, the roles of team leaders and/or team facilitators are highly critical in the effective use of teams/groups to achieve successful results. The success of a team depends generally on the way that team is led and managed; hence, there is the need here to closely look at the role of team facilitators or team managers in group activities.

Role of Facilitators in Team Management

The impact of facilitation skills on the ability of quality teams to solve problems and resolve conflicts is enormous. Hence, team facilitation skills remain one of the most critical human resource skills that managers of quality must not just possess (or acquire through training) but also put into use in team management. It is as a result of this that it has become necessary to identify this trait or ability in whosoever your organization is selecting to lead any of its quality management or other teams.

In addition to having the traits to facilitate, there is also the opportunity for you to provide suitable training in facilitation skills and traditional project management skills. Training is very important in the sense that it is at times very hard for your managers to change their own (old) ways and processes to follow the path of standard problem-solving methodology with which they are not familiar. Once they are properly trained, they can easily assume leadership roles in the problem-solving structure adopted by your organization and help your quality teams with the use of appropriate problem-solving methodologies or techniques, train team members, lead meetings, and ensure that teams achieve the objectives for which they were established.

The way facilitators are generally seen is put together by Mallory [15] "as guides for the problem-solving process, who can assist with the technical skills of group interactions and problem solving." The traditional functions of facilitators as given by him include the following:

- Keeping the team focused
- Keeping all team members working together as a group
- Ensuring that all team members participate
- Ensuring the effective utilization of meeting times
- Ensuring that assigned responsibilities are made with time ultimatum for completion and documented

Since most of the activities of facilitators revolve around problem solving, it becomes obvious too that "helping the team use appropriate decision-making techniques" is a major role for them.

Vision and Strategy

From the quality glossary of the ASQ [3], vision is:

> An overarching statement of the way an organization wants to be; an ideal state of being at a future point

while strategic planning is:

> The process an organization uses to envision its future and develop the appropriate strategies, goals, objectives and action plans.

Since vision refers to the desirability of an organization to be at a particular point in the future, organizational leaders have the task of not just establishing a vision but must communicate the same to all its employees and at the same time provide the needed tools, knowledge (training), and resources necessary for the accomplishment of the vision.

In the present world economy business is gradually being dominated by:

- Globalization
- Just-in-time (JIT) delivery
- Empowered and enlightened consumers
- Frequent changes in technological advancement
- Stiff market competition
- Innovation
- Supply chain management

Any organization that has to survive must be far ahead of the market to plan the needs and requirements of its customers (or consumers) and potential customers on a long-term (i.e., upwards of 5 to 10 years) basis. Limiting your vision to short term may not be the best for your organization. In addition, your vision must be accompanied by the most adequate strategy for achieving it.

Evolving a long-term vision and strategic planning does not however imply that your responsibilities to your current customers and those of the immediate future should be compromised or jeopardized or else you may never be able to realize your long-term vision. Hence, your strategic planning must have incorporated in it the need to meet all current obligations to all your customers/consumers.

In planning your strategies attention must be focused on the dynamism of business and other world events particularly those that are likely to impact on your business. This is necessary since changes in global events may likely necessitate your changing or modifying your business strategies to be able to accommodate new changes, thereby falling in line with the dynamism of the business.

To achieve your quality vision, it is pertinent to:

- Identify your vision and make it the cornerstone of your activities
- Share your vision with the relevant stakeholders
- Communicate relentlessly with your employees
- Respect your employees
- Hold your customers in high esteem
- Train your staff and motivate them through adequate reward and promotion
- Make policies that will empower your employees
- Identify achievable goals/milestones and the period to achieve them
- Measure performance
- Give employees the relevant sense of ownership
- Share the joy of every achievement with your entire employees

References

1. ASQ. (2007). Quality glossary. *Quality Progress*, 39–59.
2. ASQ. What's the Malcolm Baldrige National Quality Award (MBNQA)? www.asq.org
3. ASQ. www.asq.org
4. Barbrosa, F. M., do Gambi, L., N., & Gerolamo, M. C. (2017). Leadership and quality management – A correlational study between leadership models and quality management principles. *Gest. Prod., Sao Carlos, 24*(3), 438–449. https://doi.org/10.1590/0104-530X2278-16
5. Bass, B. M. (1985). *Leadership and performance*. Free Press.
6. Blazey, M., & Grizzell, P. (2019). Insights to performance excellence, 2019–2020. Using the Baldrige Framework and Other Integrated Management Systems.
7. Burns, J. M. (1978). *Leadership*. Harper and Raw.
8. Deming, W. E. (1986). Out of the crisis, MIT CAES.
9. Eagly, A. H., & Carli, L. L. (2007). Women and the Labyrinth of leadership. *Harvard Business Review*, 65.
10. Forster, S. T., Jr. (2007b). Leadership. *Quality Progress*, 35.
11. Forster, S. T., Jr. (2007a). *Managing quality: Integrating the supply chain*. Prentice Hall.
12. Hirtz, P. D., Murray, S. L., & Riordan, C. (2007). The effects of leadership on quality. *Engineering Management Journal, 19*(1) ABI/INFORM Global, 22.
13. Juran, J. (1989). *Juran on leadership for quality*. Free Press.

14. Leonard, D. (2016). The future of quality: Strategy, leadership and an opportunity to improve quality of life on a global scale there to be seized or lost. In P. Sampaio & P. Saraiva (Eds.), *Quality in the 21st century* (pp. 33–45). Springer.
15. Mallory, R. E. (2008). Facilitation skills remain a critical ingredient of world-class performance. *The Quality Management Forum, 34*(1).
16. MBNQA. http://www.baldrige.nist.gov
17. National Institute of Standards and Technology, (NIST). (2007). *Baldrige national quality award criteria for performance excellence*. ASQ Quality Press.
18. Rees, F. (2005). *The facilitator, excellence handbook*. Pfeiffer Publishing.
19. Sullivan, E. J. (2012). *Effective leadership and management in nursing* (8th ed., pp. 1–10). Pearson.
20. Vinyard, J. (2019). *Baldrige users guide, 2019–2020. Organization diagnosis, design, and transformation* (9th ed.). Wiley.
21. Watson, G. H. (2016). The contributions to quality development of young practitioners. An introduction to the ASQ Feigenbaum Medal. In P. Sampaio & P. Saraiva (Eds.), "*Quality in the 21st century – Perspectives from ASQ Feigenbaum medal winners" foreword 2* (p. ix). Springer.
22. Zeithaml, V. A., Parasuraman, A., & Berry, L. L. (1990). *Delivering service quality*. Free Press.

Economics of Quality

7

Quality – Ground Zero to the Twenty-First Century

Growing from the prosperity of being able to separate defective products from non-defective ones, or good products from bad ones, through inspection, quality was able to convincingly demonstrate to the entirety of the people of the world its ability to strongly dictate business or organizational economic growth potentials.

Manufacturing industries using quality to optimize their financial performance with first-grade (or first-choice) products actually inspired and motivated businesses and organizations to improve their economic growth potentials. They initially relied on product *inspection* or product *quality control* to identify and separate first-grade/first-choice products from second and subsequent grades, depending on organization and product types. The choice of customers then was therefore to make their product choices from different product grades for certain items, with the most expensive products being the first-choice/first-grade products. For luxury items, such as cars, choices were just as we have it today mainly based on brand differentials. This clearly demonstrates the economic-driven potentials inherent in product quality.

My first experience in quality began as a quality line- and end-product inspector in the *quality control* department of one of Germany's biggest chemical and textile processing organizations, in Krefeld. This opportunity gave me the insight as to the losses generally incurred by manufacturing organizations then, in selling finished second- and third-choice products far below the prices of those classified as first-grade/first-choice products. These losses can only be imagined after the realization of the fact that each product, good or bad, has been transformed generally going through the same processes with the same inputs (energy, utilities, equipment, etc.) and resources (human and materials).

It follows therefore then that the issues responsible for making products other than the first-grade/first-choice ones are not just "agents of organizational losses" (e.g., defects, oil stains, weaving faults, dyeing irregularities, repeated job

T. A. Ibidapo, *From Industry 4.0 to Quality 4.0*, Management for Professionals,
https://doi.org/10.1007/978-3-031-04192-1_7

processes, etc.) but non-quality agents working against organizational economic values. Recognizing and eliminating these uneconomic causes of value losses to outrightly make *only* first-grade/first-choice products constitute then what is known today as *quality*. Quality is thus responsible mainly for the effective:

- Removal of product defects to ensure its "fitness for use" by end-users or customers
- Elimination of defective products/services to assure the production of defect-free products/services in "conformance to the requirements" of the customer or market
- Maximize operational process efficiencies in terms of time and resource inputs – human and materials to ensure there are no wastes

All in all, and considering the above, *quality* has grown to become the harbinger of "the characteristics of any product or service that bear on its ability to competitively and continually satisfy stated or implied needs, specifications and requirements of the customer/market." Hence, quality has distinguished itself, ab initio, with its ability and capability to promote organizational or business economic gains, advantages, and survival.

The clear choice here belongs to individual businesses and organizations. It is however apparent that business survival instinct of individual organizations makes quality-driven economic gains/advantages the clearest survival option for businesses and entrepreneurial organizations.

The economic advantage of quality has also been ascertained by the confirmed correlation "between customer-perceived quality, market share, and return on investment," in "the Profit Impact of Market Strategy (PIMS) study sponsored by General Electric and conducted by the Wharton Graduate School of Business" [24].

Hence, quality earned as from its early developmental stages appellations such as "fitness for use," "conformance to requirements," "pursuit of excellence," etc. It is therefore for the reasons of making products or process outputs fit for use or conforming with customer/market predetermined conditions or state of product excellence for use and application that the quality concept was brought into existence firstly, among the manufacturing industries, from where quality tentacles have since spread to all sectors of the global economy including servicing, healthcare, pharmaceutical, and public and governance sectors, just to name a few.

Quality has thus evolved from one phase of economic relevance and application to another (see Table 7.1), galvanizing along the way the professional skills of the manufacturing sector-evolved quality "gurus" of the twentieth century and growing stronger and stronger in use and application through various sectors of the global economy.

It must however be emphasized here that, although quality may have been viewed and seen as an evolutionary offshoot of manufacturing efforts to achieve "fit-for-use" products or conforming outputs, there is no doubt however that the academic world made its own contribution, no matter the magnitude, to the evolutionary stages of quality.

Table 7.1 Viewing quality evolutionary phases from a global perspective – concepts and emphasis

Quality phases	Emerging quality concepts	Emphasis of quality practices
Quality 0.0 (1300s to early 1900s)	Work organized by unions of "craftsmanship" that later evolved into "guild"	Just emerging practices of *measurement* and *product inspection*. Emphasis more on production volume or product *quantity*. Goods were produced by the same person or set of people
Quality 1.0 (1920s to 1940s)	*Quality control* of finished product to ascertain level of product conformity through *measurement* and *inspection*, to detect finished product defects by sampling. Separating good products from defective ones. Defective products scrapped or reworked	Rise in *mass production* and the emergence of industrial revolution. Evolution of quality concept. Emergence of *team working*. Recognition of product variation and quality as vehicle for controlling *process variation*. *Standardization* of designs and components. Putting *statistical quality control* (SQC) and sampling techniques in use to maintain product standard. Focus on process outputs and/or final product quality
Quality 2.0 (1940s to late 1980s)	Widening the principles of *quality control* activities to include organization-wide processes to assure final product quality culminated into *total quality control* in the 1950s. *Quality assurance* evolved to optimize process outputs to achieve fit-for-use products, as required by customers and the market. Introduction of audit functions to enhance quality effectiveness	Use of QFD from the 1960s enabled listening to the voice of the customer (VOC). Popular use of individual national or product standards – military- and application-specific industry standards. Development of quality concepts through active involvement of quality "gurus." Appearance of generically applicable ISO 9000[vii] series of "Quality management and quality assurance standards – Guidelines and section for use" in 1987. Popularization of quality audit, preventive and corrective measures, meeting customer needs, requirements and specifications, and customer or market feedback

(continued)

Table 7.1 (continued)

Quality phases	Emerging quality concepts	Emphasis of quality practices
Quality 3.0 (1980s to early 2000s)	*Total quality management (TQM)* – systematically planned quality assurance activities, at every process stage across all levels of organizational activities to assure product or service quality requirements are achieved. Transformation of quality management into quality management systems (QMSs) in the year 2000	Taking cue from US military standards and BS 5750 (1979) standard as precursor to the development of ISO 9000 family. Focus on cross-organizational quality management assurance confidence – internal and external – that quality requirements are met. Leadership commitment to ensure organization quality management is documented with a focus mainly on manufacturing systems, but with continuous improvement potentials to embrace the services and public sectors. Formalizing the quality system in terms of documenting its structure, responsibilities, and procedures for effective quality management. ISO 9000 series of standards redesignated "ISO 9000:2000 – *Quality Management Systems*" with a focus on continual improvement, customer satisfaction, leadership, process management, and wide applicability through its generic nature. Use of certification
Quality 4.0 (2015 till the emergence of a newer quality paradigm likely dictated by industry 4.0)	Risk-focused, research-attracting, digital technology-enhancing, artificial intelligence (AI)-based *quality management systems (QMSs)* with opportunities for broad-based academic and industrially experienced professionals. Automated system with controls shifting more to process designers than process operators	With the ISO in the steering wheel of the global quality vehicle to face the challenges of the twenty-first century, ISO 9001:2015 QMS was introduced in 2015 with emphasis on *risk management and sustainability* to provide an enduring framework to achieve long-term business product/service excellence and customer satisfaction. Use of *artificial intelligence* (AI) to achieve machine self-regulation of productivity and product quality. High organizational interconnectivity through Internet of things (IoT)

This thus brings to the fore the exemplary roles of one of the quality gurus of the twentieth century, Dr. Armand V. Feigenbaum (1922–2014), who according to Watson [24] published as early as 1945 his doctoral dissertation on quality: *Quality Control: Principles, Practice and Administration; an Industrial Management Tool for Improving Product Quality and Design and for Reducing Operating Costs and Losses.* This academic input actually culminated into the publication of the birth of "Total Quality Control" in 1956.

Ability to Update and Evolve

The ability of quality and its application to update and evolve from time to time remain its strength for its global acceptance and acknowledgment for use in all sectors of the global economy. For example, the ability of quality management (QM) to update and evolve has been reported by Fundin et al. [11]. The need for quality or quality management to update and evolve is a living phenomenon which is undoubtedly traceable to the general desire for meeting the changing context and needs of global organizations to achieve product and service quality that meets customer needs, requirements, and specifications.

While Hermel [13] identified four great periods, with inspection as first and total quality as fourth, between the early 1900s and the 1980s, Dahlgraad [6] assigned three phases of quality evolution from the mid-1940s to the early 1990s. Deleryd and Fundin [7] proposed Quality 5.0 following their already identified four major generations of quality management (QM). In proposing Quality 5.0 as a new paradigm, its focus of attention was claimed to have been mainly on organizational *sustainability*.

In its relationship of quality evolution with industrial advances from the 1800s till date, the ASQ [1, 3] came up with four generational phases of quality in parallel with equivalent industrial evolutionary phases:

- **Quality 1.0** – Quality assured through measurement and inspection with emphasis on volume of production and worker productivity rather than on quality. Tallies with ASQ's Industry 1.0, for the period prior to 1890
- **Quality 2.0** – Maximization of productivity with adherence to minimally acceptable quality standards, scrap generation, and rework. Tallies with ASQ's Industry 2.0, for period 1890 to 1940
- **Quality 3.0** – Era in which quality remains a business imperative with a focus on achieving customer satisfaction using continual improvement processes and relying on standards such as ISO 9000 series of standards [15]. Tallies with ASQ's Industry 3.0, for period 1940 to 1995
- **Quality 4.0** – Digital era of quality management oriented in the shifting of operational tendencies from focusing on process operators to process designers. Automation to facilitate machines in self-regulating and interconnectedly managing productivity and quality. Tallies with Industry 4.0, though with additional need for quality data collection and analytics. Evolving along with Industry 4.0 initiatives

According to the ASQ, "*Quality 4.0* brings together *Industry 4.0* advanced digital technologies with quality excellence to drive substantial performance and effectiveness improvements."

Quality 4.0 aligns, according to the ASQ, quality practices with digital environment, in correlation with the ASQ's *Industry 4.0*. In its Quality 4.0 enlightening forum in 2020, the ASQ successfully organized "The 2020 Quality 4.0 Virtual Summit."

Keynote speakers addressed various issues including those that may, according to Connelly [5], impact organizations' "ability to manage uncertainty" and "effectively identify how trends could have significant impacts to one's business."

The presentation of Gale [12], "Excellence in a Digital Age: Where Quality Evolves in a World of Uncertain Opportunity," tells it all.

This innovative educational summit of the ASQ is undoubtedly an excellent effort proposed to be repeated on an annual basis to ensure no organization is left behind, even though when, according to Gale, 28% of companies are already thriving as of today, with their digital transformations. The ASQ leadership role here is highly acknowledged and appreciated.

As of today, quality has tremendously grown to assume a strong position in economic considerations, globally representing one of the few available options, for accomplishing sustainable business and organizational competitive well-being, in different parts and regions of the global community, on the basis of socio-economic sustainable developmental paradigm. Quality shall continue to evolve based on the changing context and application of quality.

Impact of Quality on Economy

Correlating Quality with Economic Growth

The evolution of quality has proven to be somehow in correlation with economic growth. The impact of quality on the economy is thus evident in their synonymity with one another. The evolvement of quality from Ground Zero, **Quality 0.0** to **Quality 4.0** (Table 7.1) has been accomplished along with the global economic growth. Quality has thus proved today to be a vital and key driver of economic growth. The fact of the bilateral relationship and positive correlation between quality and the economy has been ascertained by various authors in various arms and sectors of the global economy.

This fact and "The Economics and Value Impact of Quality" are reported in detail in the reports of the research studies of the US Department of Energy, prepared by Home Innovation Research Labs for the National Renewable Energy Laboratory [23] in the new home construction sector of the economy.

In their studies to detail the value of quality management in general but particularly in the home construction industry, they found that many builders using quality management tools and techniques have seen dramatic improvements in energy and quality performance, profitability, and customer satisfaction.

In a similar vein, Rodchua [19] in studying 63 manufacturing organizations found that *failure costs* amount to between 70% and 80% of the total cost of quality (TCoQ), while the total cost of quality itself ranges between 8% and 10% of expenses or between 2.6% and 4% of sales revenue (Table 7.2).

The work of Evans and Jack [10] also confirmed the fact too that improving quality management positively impacts financial performance. Further evidences to support the fact that quality management helps to appreciably enhance return on

Table 7.2 The percentage representation of the total cost of quality (TCoQ) in both small–/medium- and large-sized organizations [19]

Costs of quality	Small–/medium-sized organizations [%]	Large-sized organizations [%]
Preventive costs	10	11
Appraisal costs	17	9
Internal failure costs	47	38
External failure costs	26	42

investment (ROI) were also reported by Schiffauerova and Thomson [20]. They based their conclusion on the fact that organizations which introduced quality management were able to reduce the total cost of quality, TCoQ. They indicated in their report that the underlisted organizations succeeded in reducing their total cost of quality by specified percentages at specified times:

- PC manufacturer (Hewlett-Packard – 25% in 1 year)
- Electronics (Raytheon – 65% to 15% in 8 years)
- Semi-conductors (Philips – 35.8% to 18.1% in 4 years)
- Telecommunications (United Technologies – 23.3% to 17.3%)

Return on investment (ROI) is highly influenced by the economy of its management.

The Economics of Quality Management

The economics of quality generally requires that a product is produced with a very high probability that the product shall be accepted or is acceptable by the targeted customer or market; otherwise the planning and production of such a product may be worthless, thereby leading to financial loss. It is for this reason that manufacturers and other product makers or service providers actually present their products/services with very strong consideration for customer values. This is however not done without consideration for the organization's own values such as profitability and employee motivation, awareness, integrity, and morale boosting. This consideration translates directly into the need for every organization to focus attention on its customer(s)/consumer(s) and their values. Organizational values may also be reflected in the values of its own employees.

Investments in businesses are generally made for the purposes of getting some returns. Hence, quality management helps in ensuring that investors or organizations generally achieve increased revenues and higher productivity. These are achieved by the implementation of quality management tools which facilitate:

- Customer loyalty
- Improved businesses
- Increased cash flow

- Satisfied employees
- Healthy workplace

Economic Importance of Quality Management

Quality management helps in ensuring:

- Excellent or superior products and services as measured in terms of performance, durability, and reliability which meet customer and/or market needs, requirement, and specification
- Customer loyalty to attract and bring existing customers back again and again
- Reduction of wastes and inventory through the use of appropriate quality management tools
- Increased revenues or higher return on investment (ROI)

Why Is the Need for Quality Initiatives?

Quality initiatives can be said to be *the efforts or drive put in place to promote or implement quality requirements, continuous improvement, performance excellence, and allied quality management-related activities.*

You may at times like to ask yourself the question, "why the need for quality initiatives?" Or you may want to know why the fuss about quality. The answer here is simple. The bottom line for every business is simply to provide products/services that:

- Meet customer SNEaRs to ensure that they are satisfied
- Are attractive and of value to customer
- Command customer patronage and loyalty
- Dominate the market
- Have the ability and dynamism to consistently maintain sustainable market leadership
- Are of good value and profitability so that their manufacturers/producers will always be in the best position to effectively sustain themselves and their activities

In order to consistently achieve the above-listed objectives, most organizations have committed their resources to the implementation and sustenance of one quality management system/improvement concept or another. An organization's investment in quality and quality management such as the implementation of the requirements of the ISO 9000 series of international QMS standards, Six Sigma, lean manufacturing, etc. therefore has a lot of advantages which include but are not limited to the following:

- The creation and maintenance of efficient and effective operational systems
- Assuring the reproducibility of products/services on a consistent basis

- Increasing customer satisfaction and your ability to retain your customers/market share
- The enhancement of your marketing activities
- Promotion of trade generally and internationally particularly as the latter aids your organization in gaining international recognition.
- Increased potential of achieving better return on investment (ROI) vis-à-vis profits
- Reduction in wastes and wastages in virtually all aspects of input
- Improvement of employee motivation, awareness, and morale
- Assure transparency of organizational management
- Promotion of the effective documentation of processes
- Ensuring the continual improvement of processes

The financial power that is realizable from the effective implementation and execution of quality management processes is enormous. It is in recognition of this fact that companies must have to measure and manage the economics of quality and its costs. The globalization of the world market economy actually puts some economic and cost pressures on organizations. Hence, there is the need for top corporate quality leaders to pay close attention to the measurement and management of these new internationally driven challenges.

Mistakes Are Costly

The efforts to ameliorate mistakes and the consequent cost of quality incurred had earlier motivated quality initiatives in the healthcare management system.

Value System

Value

Value according to the dictionary meaning is simply "the worth, desirability, or utility of a thing, or the qualities on which these depend." Pyzdek [18] in his own terms referred to "value" as that which one acts to gain and/or keep.

Values as defined in the ASQ [2] glossary refers to "The fundamental beliefs that drive organizational behavior and decision making." Values therefore represent goals.

The term value as applied to or used in quality is of fundamental importance in quality management. This is so since the worth, desirability, or utility of products/services or the qualities on which these depend are jointly critical factors that determine the acceptability of the product and/or services to the customers or intended customers.

Hence, value can be said to be a fundamental "goal" of quality that must be achieved or felt in any product/service resulting from the implementation of any QMS. It is therefore a matter of common sense and not just economic sense that very strong considerations must be given to the *value of products and services* as a part of the various ways to achieve customer satisfaction. Customers on their own part generally base their decisions of supplier patronage on critical issues such as:

- Relative gains in the economics of products and services (i.e., economic benefits that are derivable)
- Relative gains in the performance of the product
- The overall economic value of the product (i.e., related costs)

The implementation of any QMS or improvement concept must therefore give strong and adequate considerations to the economics of the entire production/manufacturing or service provision systems.

It is therefore highly imperative that people involved in the management of quality or quality systems should be proficient enough to be able to effectively measure and communicate the economics of quality. It is in pursuance of this objective that the ISO [17], in its "ISO 9004:2018, Quality Management Systems – Guidelines for Performance Improvement" emphasized the fact that the economics of quality is a means for the measurement and monitoring of processes, analysis of process data, and an integral part of management review.

In furtherance of the issue of the relevance of economic consideration in quality matters, top management must appreciate at all stages the need to put economic considerations side by side with all quality measures that are put in place to ensure products and/or services comply with customer specifications, requirements, and needs just as they represent value.

In response to the need for the measurement of quality costs, the ISO [16] issued *ISO 10014:2006, Quality Management – Guidelines for Realizing Financial and Economic Benefits*.

The top management and all those responsible for the implementation of any QMS must first of all recognize the fact that available resources must be maximized to ensure that the total economic values of products and services are achievable. It therefore goes to say that the economic sense in every activity must be given the needed consideration at all times. It must therefore be recognized that activities should be considered and weighed in terms of business vis-à-vis economic sense. Whether an activity makes economic sense depends principally on the:

- Economic benefits that would be obtainable from the activity and/or its resultant impact
- Related costs
- Benefits derivable from the alternative uses and/or applications of resources

In realization of the task of achieving an impressive return on investment (ROI), your top management needs to ensure the maximization of the economic values of the resources that are at its disposal or under its control.

Normal Production Costs

If you effectively and efficiently implement a suitable quality management system (QMS) or improvement concept(s)/program(s) and things are done right the first time so that your products and/or services are most likely to meet customer satisfaction or market needs without incurring extra costs or additional input vis-à-vis money, you will be talking of a straightforward or normal production costs. The implication here is that when things are done right the first time, you are not likely to incur extra costs in your production system; hence, the *cost of quality* (CoQ) is *zero* or you have simply avoided incurring the costs of quality (CoQ). The implication here is that the costs incurred in making your product right the first time to achieve the right quality or full customer satisfaction or if you like the *costs of attaining quality* can also be said to be equivalent to your normal costs of production. The components of the costs of attaining quality or your normal production costs may therefore be summed up thus:

- Costs of preventing losses that may be due to poor quality
- Costs that are of value to your organization
- Costs of all planned activities, that is, all controlled activities

Your normal costs of production can be simply classified into three major groups:

- Costs associated with *preventive activities* (i.e., costs that result from activities for ensuring that processes do not fail such as preventive and predictive maintenance costs)
- Costs that emanate from *appraisal activities* (i.e., costs that result from process and product verification activities such as testing and inspection)
- Costs of all other planned activities

Prevention costs are those related to activities concerned with reducing or even eliminating the potentials for or possibilities of having quality problems. Hence, prevention costs result from or are associated with the costs of:

- Design
- Monitoring
- Collection and collation of data
- Data analysis
- Training
- Planning
- Quality administration
- Quality control measures
- Working closely with suppliers
- Defect prevention measures
- Any other preventive measures taken to ensure product quality and its improvement

Appraisal costs are those costs related to measures put in place to ensure quality or detect defects or defective products/services and they include activities such as:

- Inspection
- Testing
- Test equipment and its calibration
- Laboratory
- Quality audits
- Inspection (and cost of inspectors)
- Other appraisal measures put in place to ensure product/service quality or its improvement

Extra Production Costs

The costs of activities that are not of direct value to an organization result to additional production costs. In order to ensure that such activities are of value, they either have to be carried out again (rework) or the products involved may have to be replaced. Hence, extra costs are incurred on poor-quality activities vis-à-vis products/services which have to be replaced, compensated for, or reworked. It is obvious here that losses due to poor quality, work, and any other operational activities that do not add value to the business and all other system deficiencies result to extra costs. Here one may put the sources of extra costs together as:

- Costs traceable or related to *failure* which occur during production or service provision (e.g., costs of unplanned machine breakdown). The failure may result from defective parts or products or faulty services. Such costs may be internal (i.e., failure identified before product/service gets to the customer) or *external* (i.e., failure that is detected after a product/service has been delivered to the customer or already in the market). Here, costs of product recalls or warranty/guarantee claims are good examples.
- *Delayed action* and/or *wrong decision costs* that result from *delayed* actions and/or *wrong* decisions (e.g., costs resulting from the violation of contractual agreement including penalty clauses such as those resulting from failure to meet delivery schedule or delayed project or product/service delivery).

Failure costs which could be internal (i.e., costs related to products and services that are found to be defective before they are delivered to the customer) or external (i.e., products and services found to be defective after delivery to the customer).

Internal failure costs include among others those that are affiliated with:

- The loss of production time
- Defect investigation and defect-problem-solving activities
- Production wastages/scraps

- Rework and the costs of all affiliated inputs such as energy, equipment, materials, and labor needed to put corrective actions in place
- The wrong use of defective inputs such as the use of defective materials received from supplier and the downtime resulting from sorting such inputs

External failure costs related to products/services found to be substandard or defective after delivery would have been made to the customer (or at times the marketplace) or defective products not detected until they have been delivered to the customer. These costs are related to returned goods, reworking and handling of complaints, warranty/guarantee, recalls, loss of goodwill, loss of confidence in product and services, litigation, replacement of products/services, breach of some agreements, etc.

The addition of costs resulting from *delayed action* and/or *wrong decision* is obvious since this can easily lead to incurring substantial costs that may in some circumstances even be higher than those of prevention, appraisal, and failure costs put together. Delayed action may result from various factors which include among others the following:

- Sudden changes in or inconsistency of government policies/statutory regulations (a common phenomenon in a country like Nigeria and some other poor economies of the world) that may suddenly result to product use/application noncompliance. Here immediate communication with the customer either directly or through the VOC is imminent to avoid unnecessary costs.
- Poor and wrong implementation of government policies that may result in unplanned increases in cost of inputs and subsequently production costs.
- Bribery and corruption, also a common phenomenon in a country like Nigeria and some other economies of the world where corruption still thrives.
- Use of untrained or incompetent staff.
- Wrong use of discretion by organizational staff in touch with the customer or VOC.
- Inability to take decisions as and when necessary.
- Failure to plan or inadequate planning.

How Costly Is Leadership Failure?

Costs resulting from delayed action and/or wrong decision are still highlighted here despite the fact that they easily could have been aligned with failure costs. An example here as experienced by the author is the decision of a CEO to appoint a manager to a position at par with that of the General Manager of a manufacturing plant in Nigeria, thereby creating a situation/scenario of having two captains in a boat. The damage done by this singular act to the quality management system and employee relationship at all levels of the production plant management is left to your imagination.

It crippled the plant and its quality assurance activities for about 18 months, after which it had to be restructured to put it back on the path of recovery. It must be mentioned here too that this singular act of top-level *mis-management* almost led to the liquidation of that plant as it made unimaginable production or business losses. This type of scenario is very common in some factories or organizations in the developed economies of the world where positions (or responsibilities) are either duplicated or even proliferated for one reason or another.

Costs emanating from unethical behaviors (e.g., stealing and corruption) of some employees may directly or indirectly result, in some cases, to the incurring of extra costs of production or service provision for an organization. Although an issue of this nature may not be common in the developed parts of the world, it still poses serious quality management challenges in some underdeveloped parts of the world.

Poor or lack of coordination among organizational management teams is one of the most probable and common quality problems in the developed economies of the world. Unnecessary costs most likely incurred here include but are not limited to the following:

- Duplication of personnel and unnecessary overlapping of responsibilities
- Duplication of documentation and their unnecessary proliferation within the quality management system

Avoiding these problems would in fact help to ward off your organization from incurring some unnecessary costs.

Value-Added Activities

Value added is defined according to Stevenson [21] as "the term used to describe the difference between the cost of inputs and the value or price of outputs." Operational functions are generally used in adding value to inputs. The operations or production functions which are employed for achieving the goods and/or services produced by an organization are hence some of the major activities of an organization. Workers and other human resources are generally rewarded for the time spent by them in adding value to products and/or services.

Non-value-Added Activities

Transportation and storage are examples of some of the most common *non-value-added* activities in some production systems. When viewed in terms of time and manufacturing processes, value-added activities consume less than about 10% of the time taken by non-value-added activities such as storage and transportation. Hence, the overall *lead time* which is represented by the addition of the time consumed by both value-added and non-value-added activities is consumed mostly by the non-value-added activities. Any time-based improvement strategy therefore may have to be focused mainly on the non-value-added activities.

This brings to the fore the economic relevance of the now popular *supply chain management* principles which has the ability to reduce your lead time and increase your profitability.

Value of Time

The activities and life of man are generally tied down to time. In a similar way and manner, we all, no matter what role we play or what position/status we hold in an organization, COO/CEOs, managers, employees, customers/consumers, or suppliers, generally trade our time for money or value it in terms of money. In an attempt to do this, we put our time under some measure of control to ensure that we put it into qualitative use.

Every worker, no matter the status, in an organization gets a monetary (e.g., dollar, naira, euro, etc.) reward for the time spent in an organization to add value to the products or services rendered by that organization to its customers. It is obvious therefore that in order to get needed values from employees, economically reasonable or productive organizations pay a lot of attention to *value-added* services or activities. With most organizations concentrating more on its core business activities, most of the non-value-added activities are contracted out.

In a country like Japan where the Toyota quality system emanated from the just-in-time (JIT) delivery system, it helps to reduce the non-value-added component of raw materials storage and those of process input. In order to improve your lead time, it is important to focus on ways to reduce the non-value-added component of your lead time. This brings to the fore the role of time and the need to save it in the overall economics of quality and its management.

A reduction in the time taken to achieve or accomplish any QMS activity or planned production task therefore represents value-added. Any improvement in the time taken for achieving a product/result or in carrying out a task in the QMS can even be used as a key performance indicator (KPI) such as:

- Productivity per unit time
- Task achieved per unit time

At the same time this can be used as a means for assessing the effectiveness and improvement of processes as well as that of the quality management systems.

Waste and Waste Reduction

Managing Waste

Waste, often referred to in Japanese as *muda*, is an enemy of productivity; hence, there is the need to avoid it as much as it is possible. *Time* and *resources* are two key elements that could be subjected to *waste* or *muda*. The way we manage both elements are as critical to productivity as they are to the whole economy of quality management. Hence, if things are "done right the first time," there will be no need for putting corrective actions in place or spending time to implement corrective measures or sorting the good products from the bad ones, thereby saving time vis-à-vis money.

If we view the entire production system from the perspective of wastes and waste generation, the following sources or potential causes of waste and/or waste-generation acts are common:

- Machine production time wastage through breakdown maintenance or unplanned maintenance
- Poor regulation of production or processing machines/equipment
- Double handling
- Overstaffing
- Poor material planning
- Use of incompetent or unskilled employees
- Poor training
- Disorganized working environment
- Late product delivery

Putting these two elements into consideration and looking at the way some organizations allow the use of GSM telephones in some countries during office or production hours, one wonders how and why such organizations choose not to put this wasteful act under control. The author also believes very strongly that the use and charging of GSM telephones without adequate control during office hours contribute to the ineffective use of time. This act was a common feature or occurrence in some Nigerian organizations. Apart from time and energy wastages the uncontrolled charging of GSM telephones in factory environments also exposes such organizations to the risk of fire.

The provision of very poor-quality GSM services (low efficiency) due to whatever reason is another cause of *muda* calling for the attention of the respective regulatory agencies to avoid further exploitation of innocent customers by GSM providers particularly in the West African sub-region or the African continent.

Muda oftentimes is caused by the national government of Nigeria when it shifts public holidays which fall on Saturdays and/or Sundays to Fridays and/or Mondays or Mondays and Tuesdays. This is particularly so for religious holidays. The negative impact here is actually on the overall national productivity as well as on the private organizations that have to pay salaries for those days employees have to go on unplanned holidays.

Some examples of the various ways in which *muda* can be experienced include but are not limited to the following:

- Poor quality of final/intermediate products which may require rework
- Repeated handling (e.g., double handling) of same tasks

- Time spent on corrective action which ought to have been prevented in the first place or failure to do it right the first time
- Staff duplication or overlap of responsibilities or carrying out the same tasks by different staff
- Failure to embrace the lean philosophy

Healthcare Quality Improvement and CoQ in the USA

Although commercial interests of the capitalist world may not have noticed the wastes resulting from the healthcare sector of the USA, the eagle eyes of quality cannot but glaringly spot this. Mistakes generally contribute to such wastages which, in turn, result in the escalation of unnecessary costs of quality to the detriment of the customers, that is, the patients.

The causal factors of poor service quality to the detriment of the customers/patients in the healthcare system, in terms of waste generation and the high cost of quality (CoQ), can be divided into three root causes:

- Mistakes
- Medication prescription
- Poor affordability of healthcare by its customers due to high costs of patient care

According to Sullivan [22], the Institute of Medicine (IOM) (1999) reported at that time a yearly 98,000 deaths from what was termed "preventable medical mistakes" including among others [14]:

- Falls
- Wrong-site surgeries
- Avoidable infections
- Pressure ulcers

The aftermath of such wastes is borne unfortunately by the victims of these avoidable quality management mistakes, the patients who are generally impacted, even after leaving the hospitals [9].

The recognition of how critical quality management is to the healthcare system and the general need to meet customer SNEaRs have today resulted generally in bold steps being taken to achieve further effectiveness in patient care in the USA and elsewhere.

The following key measures have reportedly been critical factors thus far used to ensure quality improvement in healthcare:

- Public reporting of healthcare organizations [4]
- Institution of an agency, the "Agency for Healthcare Research and Quality" (AHRQ, [22]), for improving healthcare quality, safety, efficiency, and effectiveness [8]

- Making hospitals absorb the costs incurred by medical mistakes or in quality terms unnecessary CoQ
- Private sector quality initiative such as that of the Leapfrog Group
- Benchmarking
- Evidence-based practice strategy for quality improvement
- Magnet status certification

Quality in healthcare across the global platform of human activities is highly imperative, as demonstrated during the COVID-19 pandemic. While quality management in the industrial sector centers around products, that of healthcare systems targets human beings and their quality of life.

References

1. American Society for Quality, The Evolution of Quality 4.0, https://www.asq.org. Retrieved on 23 Jan 2021.
2. ASQ. (2007). Quality glossary. *Quality Progress*, 39–59.
3. ASQ., www.asq.org
4. Christianson, J. B., Volmar, K. M., Alexander, J., & Scanlon, D. P. (2010). A report card on provider report cards: Current status of the health care transparency movement. *Journal of General Internal Medicine, 25*(11), 1235–1241.
5. Connelly, S. (2020). "Confessions of a Corporate Futurist: Coming Trends that Will Revolutionize Your Business," *ASQ Virtual Summit Presentation,* "The 2020 4.0 Virtual Summit," https://www.asq.org. Retrieved 23 Jan 2021.
6. Dahlgaard, S. M. P. (1999). The evolution patterns of quality management: Some reflections on the quality. *Total Quality Management, 10*(4–5), 473–480. https://doi.org/10.1080/0954412997424
7. Deleryd, M., & Fundin, A. (2015). *The fifth generation of quality concept, [Paper presentation].* The World Quality Forum of International Academy for Quality (IAQ), Budapest, Hungary.
8. Dunton, N., Gonnerman, D., Montalvo, I., & Shumann, M. J. (2011). Incorporating nursing quality indicators in public reporting and value-based purchasing initiatives. *American Nurse Today, 6*(1), 14–18.
9. Encinosa, W. E., & Hellinger, F. J. (2008). The impact of medical errors on ninety-day costs and outcomes: An examination of surgical patients. *Health Services Research, 43*(6), 2067–2085.
10. Evans, J. R., & Jack, E. P. (2003). Validating key results linkages in the Baldrige performance model. *Quality Management Journal, 10*(2), 7–24.
11. Fundin, A., Ilja, J., Lagrosen, Y., Bergquist, & Quality 2030. (2020). quality management for the future. *Total Quality Management and Business Excellence.* https://doi.org/10.1080/14783363.20201863778
12. Gale, M. (2020). Excellence in a digital age: Where quality evolves in a world of uncertain opportunity, *ASQ Virtual Summit Presentation,* "The 2020 4.0 Virtual Summit," https://www.asq.org. Retrieved 23 Jan 2021.
13. Hermel, P. (1999). The new faces of total quality in Europe and the U.S. *Total Quality Management, 8*(4), 131–143.
14. Institute of Medicine, (IOM). (2010). *The Future of Nursing: Leading change, advancing health,* Reported by Sullivan, Eleanor J. (2012), Effective Leadership and Management in Nursing, Eighth edition, pp. 1–10, Pearson.
15. International Organization for Standardization, ISO 9001:2015., https://www.iso.org.

16. ISO. (2006). *ISO 10014:2006, Quality management – guidelines for realizing financial and economic benefits.*
17. ISO. (2018). *ISO 9004:2018, Quality management systems – guidelines for performance improvement.*
18. Pyzdek, T. (2003). *The six sigma handbook, revised and expanded* (p. 98). McGraw Hill.
19. Rodchua, S. (2009). Comparative analysis of quality costs and organizational size in the manufacturing environment. *Quality Management Journal, 16*(2), 34–43.
20. Schiffauerova, A., & Thomson, V. (2006). A review of research on cost of quality models and best practices. *International Journal of Quality and Reliability Management, 23*(4).
21. Stevenson, W. J. (1999). *Production/operations management* (p. 7). Irwin McGraw-Hill.
22. Sullivan, E. J. (2012). *Effective leadership and management in nursing* (8th ed., pp. 1–10). Pearson.
23. U. S. Department of Energy, National Renewable Energy Laboratory, (NREL). (2013). *The economics of quality: The implementation and economic impact of quality management in the homebuilding industry*, http://www.homeinnovation.com
24. Watson, G. H. (2016). The contributions to quality development of young practitioners: An introduction to the ASQ Feigenbaum Medal. In P. Sampaio & P. Saraiva (Eds.), *Quality in the 21st century, foreword 2* (pp. ix–x). Springer International Pub.

Process Management 8

Process Approach

ISO 9001:2015

The adoption of a process approach was promoted by the ISO for the development, implementation, and improvement of the effectiveness of a QMS in order to enhance meeting customer SNEaRs. The use of the process approach to understand and manage interrelated processes as a system is therefore claimed by the ISO in ISO 9001:2015 [7] as contributing to an organization's effectiveness and efficiency for achieving intended outcomes.

A process can simply be defined as "any activity or a set of interrelated work activities that uses resources (i.e., people, tools and materials) in value – added tasks to transform inputs into outputs."

Organizational activities can be more effectively managed if its major production activities are broken down into simpler processes or, simply put, into sub-processes. To achieve this numerous interrelated or interacting processes are systematically identified and managed individually at the sub-process level, thereby leading to the achievement of effective organizational management. It is the process of the identification and management of the processes used by an organization in achieving its products, particularly the interactions between its processes that are referred to as the "process approach." In most cases the output of a sub-process (or process stage) directly forms the input into the next sub-process (or process) stage. A good management at each of the basic sub-process levels, namely, sub-process stages 1,2,3,4, ……*n*th, that eventually leads to an effective management of the main process itself as the output from one sub-process (or process stage) forms the input into the subsequent processing or sub-process stage.

T. A. Ibidapo, *From Industry 4.0 to Quality 4.0*, Management for Professionals,
https://doi.org/10.1007/978-3-031-04192-1_8

Managing the Process

Process management is defined by the ASQ [1, 2] as:

"The pertinent techniques and tools applied to a process to implement and improve process effectiveness, hold the gains and ensure process integrity in fulfilling customer requirements," while process improvement is "the application of the plan-do-check-act (PDCA) cycle to processes to produce positive improvement and better meet the needs and expectations of customers."

The use of the process approach in the management of quality is one of the latest developments of the QMS. This is critical to the implementation of the requirements of ISO 9001:2015 which specifically requires an organization to apply a process approach to:

- Management
- Product/service realization
- Measurement, analysis, and improvement

In order to ensure the effectiveness of an organization's QMS using the process approach, the following guidelines are important and critical so that they can be of good use to you for improving your product or service quality:

- *Identification* (using, e.g., process mapping) *of all individual processes* involved in achieving or realizing products/services.
- *Definition of the interrelationship* of individual processes and their interfaces.
- *Assignment of personnel* responsible for each process or combination of processes and interfacial activities. Take note of the fact that problems most often arise at process interfaces so that process interfacial phases may have to be given special attention and proper focus.
- Flowcharting of each process.
- Specification of the standards for the measurements needed to control and record the outputs and the effectiveness of each process, that is, process performance.
- Identification of appropriate KPIs for the assessment of the level of performance improvement achieved by the process or process stage.
- Assessment of the impact of each process and their interaction with each other.
- Assessment of the effects of each process on the overall organizational output.
- Identification and implementation of continual process improvement measures.

Documentation is an essential part for achieving effective quality management systems; hence, it must be effectively deployed to all processes involved in:

- Product/service realization
- Measurements and analysis of measurement results
- Analysis and improvement

- Procedures or standard operating procedures (SOPs)
- Work instructions (WI)
- Quality plans
- Results of process audits
- Objectives of process
- Improvement measures and their results

The management of quality also requires that the in-process and finished products be monitored and/or inspected to make sure they meet the needs, requirements, and specifications of both the internal and external customers. The full implication here is that the product of every individual sub-process must be monitored and inspected at that process stage (preferably by the concerned or relevant employee) to make sure that it represents the specifications of the customer (internal and external) so as to avoid making products that shall be rejected after the completion of the entire production processing stages, thereby ensuring that unnecessary costs are avoided by ensuring that things are "done right the first time." Here it is strongly recommended that every operator be trained to be able to inspect the products of his activities before passing them to the next process stage rather than assigning this responsibility to separate workers. To say this loud and clear, every employee must act as the quality controller of his own work result or product. It is however critical too that the quality control department should also independently ensure that random (using tested and regular time intervals) quality checks are carried out on a consistent basis.

Improvement management therefore has to do with making sure that the quality of in-process products vis-à-vis final products gets better and better from one processing stage to another and also from time to time. This brings us to the underlying principles and basics of quality management to achieve improvement which can be summed up thus:

> Quality management when effectively deployed, enables or leads to the achievement and sustenance of measurable and consistent product/services improvement that is usually generally rewarded with customer vis-à-vis market satisfaction.

Measurements are therefore very critical for the assessment of any achieved improvement.

There are various methodologies available for achieving process improvement within your QMS or as a part of your TQM system. Some of the most prominent here include but are not limited to the underlisted:

- The plan-do-check-act (PDCA) or plan-do-study-act (PDSA) methodology.
- Problem identification and problem-solving methods or techniques such as *root cause analysis*.
- ISO 9000 quality management system standards.
- Six Sigma – using the "define, measure, analyze, improve, control" (DMAIC cycle) continuous improvement process/methodology.

- Knowledge management and professional development systems – hereby a training requirement matrix can be developed so as to identify all personnel and their respective training requirements. The matrix is then used to ensure that each of the involved personnel is able to achieve his/her required level of training.
- Innovation.
- Technological update in terms of both equipment and processing methodology to achieve improved products/services.
- Benchmarking, that is, the process of evaluating, comparing, and measuring the products, services, and processes of an organization against that of other leading organizations in the same area of business with the intention to improve an organization's products and services to at least the same level or even to a higher level. In order to optimize the gains of benchmarking, you should actually aim at making your organization to supersede that of the company or organization with which your organization has been benchmarked or compared.
- Measurement and measurement processes.
- Auditing processes.
- Process and system review.
- Gap analysis.
- Training, staff motivation, and other competency improvement measures.

It is useful too to note the fact that training and continuous development of your members of staff in various skills considered necessary for your production is critical to your entire process development and improvement schemes just as the role of the management team is vital and necessary. Role modeling also plays a good part in your quality management system. Hence, management must not just stress to all levels of your organization that quality is the cornerstone for the long-term survival of its operations but that continuous improvement is the keyword for success. Here management members of staff must lay good examples by behaving in ways that their subordinates can easily see them as good role models.

For personnel training to yield good results to both the organization and the trained staff, appropriate challenges (e.g., improved productivity) must be added to the responsibilities of any trained personnel or else the entire investment in the training may not be worthwhile for the organization while at the same time the personnel may get frustrated. This is because it is a common assumption by workers that training is associated with improvement in status and/or competencies, responsibilities, and work challenges. However, when there is no change in status the trained personnel must be made to realize the fact that the purposes of the training have to be achieved. Managers and/or supervisors must be able to identify the potentials of a staff that is to be trained or else you may end up sending the wrong set of people to the right training, thereby sending wrong signals to those members of staff.

Process Variation

Usually, the focus of attention generally by organizations is mainly on two key components of their activities to avoid or reduce variations in their product realization processes:

- Process control
- Process improvement

One easy way to achieve process control is the strict adherence to documented, established, and proven standard operating procedures (SOPs) coupled with the use of effective process measurement and analysis systems. From the general point of view, the impacts of process control and process improvement can be briefly summed up as follows:

- Process control generally serves the purpose of keeping variations within predictable levels or limits.
- Adequate process measurement enables you to identify and take necessary actions against unpredictable deviations in order for you to be able to maintain a given process in its standard state or optimum performance level.

Process Control

The implication here is simply that process control does not completely exclude variations from processes. This is in line with Shewhart's definition of control which says that:

> A phenomenon will be said to be controlled when, through the use of past experience, we can predict, at least within limits, how the phenomenon may be expected to vary in the future. Here it is understood that prediction within limits means that we can state, at least approximately, the probability that the observed phenomenon will fall within the given limits.

Assuring process control through strict adherence to the SOP does not in any way preclude the further or continued improvement of the system. The important thing to do here is firstly to identify improvement measures, plan the ways to implement them, and then put them in place.

Process Improvement

Improvement Tools

Since quality itself can be seen as an *endless journey*, continual improvement has become very critical as the only and major tool needed to grease and keep the wheels of quality continuously in motion within your manufacturing/production setup. Without this vital tool the wheels of quality would break down and your journey to meeting the needs, requirements, and specifications of your customers (or market) will be brought to a standstill or an abrupt end. We all know the implication of this to your different businesses or enterprises. Hence, continual improvement of the entire business, enterprise, or service provision is critical for the achievement of continuity and ensuring the survival of your business/enterprise.

Process improvement can, from a general perspective, therefore be said to be a *gradual or systematic* approach for achieving the improvement of a process. In order to fully appreciate the full implication of continuous improvement on your business or enterprise, it is necessary here to put the history of the industrial growth and development of Germany and Japan from the pre-World War I era till the post-World War II period into perspective. Their journeys and those of their companies to achieve their present industrial greatness and the quality that is today generally associated with their products (e.g., Mercedes, Volkswagen, Audi, Krupp, BMW, and Bayer as few examples from Germany and Toyota, Honda, Nissan, and Mitsubishi from Japan) have been very rigorous and tortuous ones accentuated with intent, zeal, commitment, dedication, continual improvement, innovation, consistency, dynamism, and very strong drive.

The improvement efforts of German, Japanese, and other Western companies as evidenced in their endless strive to achieve top quality products and services have jointly crystallized into today's global market competition. The emphasis of Japanese manufacturers on quality particularly since the 1980s has been of tremendous contribution to the global process vis-à-vis product improvement achievements. This is most visibly demonstrated in the fact that you cannot be involved in the science and technology of production and quality today or narrate its history without mentioning, learning, knowing, and talking about some Japanese concepts and phrases such as:

- Kaizen quality philosophy
- 5S Total Quality Environment
- JIT
- The muda concept/lean production system

neither would you be able to narrate the history of quality in today's global concept of quality without acknowledging the contributions of quality gurus such as:

- Lord Edwards Deming
- Joseph M. Juran
- Kaoru Ishikawa (known for the development of the cause-and-effect diagram or fishbone diagram)
- Philip B. Crosby
- Walter A. Shewhart

and the influence of other Japanese manufacturers in their provision of competitive environment or healthy rivalry in a global competitive arena in terms of products and services as well as for their general focus of attention on modern global quality approaches which emphasize increased productivity of operations, continual improvement, teamwork, employee empowerment, innovation, customer satisfaction, and *muda*.

The contribution of Japanese companies to the growth and development of quality and quality products, flexibility, and time-based competition or in simpler terms the "quality revolution" of all times has become a major driving force for competition in the recent trends of the global market. These achievements have impacted positively on manufacturing and service provision in the USA, European Union, and within the continent of Asia itself. The likelihood of the continuity of this role by Japanese companies and their capability to maintain this quality trend in manufacturing and service provision industries vis-à-vis foreign trade in the foreseeable future are not at all in doubt and may continue to impact positively on global product quality competition.

One of the basic requirements needed for the successful performance improvement of a process on a general basis is hinged on the fact that the system must be well understood and known inside out. As a result of this the improvement of a process may oftentimes require input and contributions of in-process participating personnel or members of staff so that adequate ideas can be generated towards achieving process improvement.

There are various ways for generating ideas for process improvement. Some of these include but are not limited to:

- Meetings
- Interviewing
- Brainstorming
- Benchmarking
- Quality circles
- Asking questions such as why, what, when, where, how, what, which, etc.

The following quality management principles which form the basis for the ISO 9001:2015 QMS international standards can, according to the ISO, be used by an organization and its management team towards the achievement of improved performance. Hence, implementing this quality management system is a strategic decision, needed to successfully drive an organization's improved performance. There are seven (7) fundamental quality management principles underlying the application of ISO 9001:2015:

- Process approach
- Customer focus
- Leadership
- Involvement of people
- Continual improvement

- Evidence-based decision-making
- The management of relationships

Benchmarking as Performance Improvement Tool

Weigh your product/service, process, and organizational performance with those of selected organization in your area of activities and assessed by you as being the best and with product(s) performing better than yours. Benchmarking can therefore be seen as a very valuable continuous improvement tool used by organizations to identify, according to ReVelle [14], areas that need improvement by showing where others are doing a better job. It is therefore advisable for your organization to take benchmarking as a self-mandatory continuous improvement requirement that is needed, from time to time, to assess the level of performance of your product among those of its peers or competing organizations.

You may actually have to choose or decide the units of measurement most useful and suitable for you to be able to achieve the most adequate comparative results needed for you to drive your product or organizational performance improvement. This may range from resource input productivity to sales volume or business profitability. At the end of the day, you need to ensure that your comparative units are fairly chosen and worthwhile. Hence, you just have to compare apples with apples, dollar for dollar, or naira with naira.

Benchmarking could actually be used along with other management tools such as strategic planning, customer relationship management, vision statements, TQM, lean, Six Sigma, etc. as a tool for achieving operational cost-reduction targets and repositioning of your business from time to time. Read more about benchmarking in Chapter 4.

Improvement Concepts

Improvement in whatever we do and/or plan to do should normally be a common desire of every businessman. Product and services are not left out here; hence, you will come across various improvement statements, concepts, and ideas in the management of quality. The objectives of all improvement concepts or statements are generally and conjointly to achieve positive results or improving trends in meeting the needs, requirements, and specifications of the customers, inclusive of consumers, as well as those of other operational and financial performance expectations.

The conceptual basis for achieving process or system improvement continually is embedded, for example, in the plan-do-check-act (PDCA) cycle also known as (aka) the Shewhart Cycle because Walter A. Shewhart [16] discussed this in one of his books, *Statistical Method from the Viewpoint of Quality Control*, and in the Deming version, plan-do-study-act (PDSA), or the Deming Wheel or Cycle because W. Edwards Deming introduced it in Japan.

The PDCA cycle is a four-stage process for the improvement of quality. The four stages are fully indicated in the words *plan, do, check*, and *act* which are actually verbs that point out the actions that are expected to be taken in sequence:

- The first stage *(plan)* requires that ways for effecting or implementing improvement concepts are thought of and developed.
- The second stage *(do)* specifies that the plan be implemented. This may be achieved firstly on a small scale before application to the entire process.
- The third stage *(check)* implies that the impacts or effects of the plan on the process are observed or assessed.
- In the fourth and last stage *(act)*, the results or resultant effects of the plan on the process are studied in order to deduce conclusions and know things that can be predicted.

The cycle is repeated as often as it is desirable to achieve continual improvement of a process. Each improvement cycle must however bring out some elements of improvement relative to the previous cycle.

W. Edwards Deming's 14 Points

Deming's 14-point management practices help organizations generally to improve their quality and productivity. These points [4] are as listed below:

1. Create constancy of purpose for improving products and services.
2. Adopt the new philosophy.
3. Cease dependence on inspection to achieve quality.
4. End the practice of awarding business contracts on the basis of price alone; instead, minimize total cost by working with a single supplier.
5. Improve constantly and forever every process for planning, production, and service.
6. Institute training on the job.
7. Adopt and institute leadership.
8. Drive out fear.
9. Break down barriers between staff areas.
10. Eliminate slogans, exhortations, and targets for the workforce.
11. Eliminate numerical quotas for the workforce and numerical goals for management.
12. Remove barriers that rob people of pride of workmanship, and eliminate the annual rating or merit system.
13. Institute a rigorous program of education and self-improvement for everyone.
14. Put everybody in the company to work to accomplish the transformation.

The use of the Deming's 14 points and other quality improvement concepts for quality improvement is at the discretion of every organization and its management. It is only organizations that do not have to grow that can avoid the continual improvement of their QMS.

Risk Management

Survival Instinct Factor

It makes common sense for every organizational management team to view and see risk management with the natural mindset of a survival instinct. Risks generally create states of many uncertainties in the life of an organization. This is the main reason why there is the general need for organizations to use the experience of the 2020/21 COVID-19 pandemic to:

- Understand and anticipate possible risk sources
- Understand major risk mitigation strategies and how to apply them to prevent and control errors in adaptive situations
- Leverage organizational strengths and preparedness in order to overcome uncertainties of the type of disruptive environment created by the sudden surge of the COVID-19 pandemic
- Maintain an adaptive organizational environment of enabling leadership with needed flexibility to facilitate and enable immediate responses to uncertainties
- Understand that it is only organizations and businesses that successfully mitigate ensuing risks that shall survive and thrive particularly in the current situation and environment of various kinds and types of uncertainties that generally call for effective organizational risk vis-à-vis change management capabilities
- Understand the need for organizations to become resilient and flexible in its processes, supply chain partnership, and customer culture in order to be able to strengthen and guarantee strong customer relationship

We are today living in the full glare and realization of a world full of risks and uncertainties, to which no organization is immune to attributive risks and disruptive environment, particularly in this age of organizational immersion in digitization.

Organizations are today open to a wide scope of risks, creating organizational-wide uncertainties which in turn make operational processes, employees, and technologies highly vulnerable. Presently, the world is faced with uncertainties of various types and contexts which include among others those resulting from the following:

- The COVID-19 pandemic
- Industry 4.0-/Quality 4.0-induced changes – interconnectivity, technology integration, digitization, automation, big data, data analytics, etc.
- Changing regulatory compliance landscape

- Increasing market competitiveness of a globalized market economy
- Supply chain challenges and issues
- Globalization and geopolitical matters

The caveat here is that effective risk vis-à-vis change management is the only panacea for organizational and business survival and sustainability.

Pure and Speculative Risk Management

Risk (pure and speculative) management is a very strong and reliable approach for enhancing and improving the quality management system. Risk management can, from a general perspective, be said to be all activities that are directed towards the assessing, mitigating (to an acceptable level), and monitoring of risks [19].

Waring and Glendon [18], in a more elaborate form, defined risk management as:

> A field of activity seeking to eliminate, reduce and generally control pure risks (such as from safety, fire, major hazards, security lapses, environmental hazards) and to enhance the benefits and avoid detriment from speculative risks (such as financial investment, marketing, human resources, IT strategy, commercial and business risks).

Risk management can therefore be seen as the process of analyzing and assessing the exposure to risk and determining how best to handle any of exposures either to completely avoid the risk or at least minimize its impact.

In businesses however, risk management encompasses all the organized activities employed in managing uncertainties, potential failures, hazards, and threats, and it involves ensuring that employees are following the standard operational procedures and safety guidelines and using applicable tools and taking necessary measures to ensure conformity with organizational risk management policies. Since it may not be possible to operate in an environment that is completely free or devoid of all types of risks, the acceptable level of risk may have to be defined per risk type.

Benefits of Integrated Quality Management Systems

There are many standards that may be integrated to achieve higher efficiency and effectiveness of organizational objectives in the delivery of products and services that meet customer SNEaRs (specifications, needs, expectations, and requirements). An example here is the case of the aviation, space, and defense (ASD) industries which, by virtue of the nature of their operations, are extremely sensitive to risks, hence the general requirements to creatively manage risks and change, in order to meet the ever-changing requirements and expectations throughout their supply chain. This brings out the creativity of the benefits derivable by the ASD industries from integrating quality management systems (QMSs) with safety management systems (SMSs) [3].

It is good to take note here that for some organizations and some types of risks, the acceptable level may be zero (e.g., the aviation group of industries). The aviation, space, and defense (ASD) organizations which operate in a complex landscape of contractual, regulatory, and statutory requirements operate on the quality management principles of zero risk tolerance. This is perhaps one of the major reasons why "the relationship between a QMS and a safety management system (QMS) is nothing new – especially in ASD organizations" [3]. As confirmed here, the benefits of aligning a quality management system (QMS) with a safety management system (SMS) help in the effective management of risks as it sort of extends the scope of safety management far beyond the conformity of working practices with safety expectations towards the thorough identification and proactive mitigation of hazards.

Financial Risk Vulnerability

The overall intent of quality management tools is to motivate organizational performance which at the end of the day is translated to the return on investment (ROI). It is for this reason that the quality management of the banking institutions is of great importance in the society at large.

The Central Bank of Nigeria's accusation of five Nigerian Banks for grossly violating the risk management measures applicable to the banking industry in Nigeria, which has a population (an estimated 150 million as of 2009) equivalent to about half that of the entire West African sub-region, sometimes ago led to the sacking of some CEOs of the affected banks. This act of poor-quality management by the affected CEOs led according to the Central Bank of Nigeria to huge unpaid loans totaling about 500 billion naira or three billion three hundred and thirty-three million US$ (or $3.333 billion) at an exchange rate of one hundred and fifty naira (= *N* = 150.00) to the US$1.00 at that time. The resultant impact of the banks' failure to operate at the prescribed or advised level of risk or their failure to consider the risk factors in their operational activities coupled probably with other operational issues led generally to the depreciation of their real values as well as the values of their stocks at the stock market. For example, their prices in the Nigerian Stock Exchange (NSE) actually crashed to the detriment of all their shareholders and other investors including the author. The action taken by the then Governor of the Nigerian Central Bank is commendable as it was ensured through his quality management skills that no direct customer of the affected Banks lost money as had happened earlier on in that country.

The successful management of an organization requires that risks which are normally associated with business activities be promptly identified, evaluated, and appropriately managed to forestall possible losses and/or damages. Risk management either in quality or in project management therefore involves looking ahead proactively during planning stages to identify potential future problems.

To ensure quality services adequate and proper management of risks can always be achieved using the following general guidelines:

- Identification of risks, i.e., threats and/or hazards
- Assessment/analysis of risks, i.e., evaluate/assess impact of risk on operations and/or business
- Evaluation of risks

The examination of the framework of enterprise risk management (ERM) shows, according to Meier et al. [11], that quality and project management concepts play integral roles in the way risks are identified, analyzed, evaluated, and managed. The aim of enterprise risk management (ERM) is mainly for the improvement of organizational performance through the coordinated and systematic identification and assessment of significant risks [21].

Risks are generally embedded in organizational activities at various levels and activities. Technological developments too also bring some risks along with its developmental impacts. For example, the development of nuclear energy has its side effects on both the people and environment. Even the use of the Internet is not excluded from risks to its users. The recent act of information leakages through WikiLeaks is an open demonstration of the risks involved in the use and application of technology or technological (internet) development.

These facts go to demonstrate the fact too that every activity or nearly all activities of man are laden with its own risks which may at times be glaringly seen or imagined (i.e., pure risks), while in other cases it may have to be speculated (i.e., speculative risks). The pure risks in the life of man actually begin from his immediate environment (including domestic) through to his activities (including transportation and professional) and the way he handles them all. Hence, issues of risk and its management are closely related to both human and organizational and management factors. In most cases too, risk issues are very closely related to health and safety matters to the extent that at times one may not be able to sharply demarcate matters of safety from those of risk and their management. It follows from here that in most cases matters pertaining to risk border closely with risk and its management.

Some major safety and risk matters, traceable or relating to human factors, include but are not limited to the following:

- The level of suitability or adequacy of process operational procedures
- The degree and level of the adequacy of maintenance processes and how such maintenance requirements are met
- All the factors (i.e., environmental, physical, legislative, etc.) that have the potentials to impact on either individual or organizational performance
- Ability to adequately and properly analyze and/or interpret tasks/responsibilities and the risk of human error
- Efficacy of process management and supervision
- Identification of potentially suitable and qualified candidates and recruitment
- Assessment and training of employees in needed areas of competencies

- Climatic factors
- Level of safety consciousness/awareness

Some major safety and risk management systems/concepts or schemes relating to organizational management are well articulated in some ISO international standards such as:

- ISO 9000 family of quality management system (QMS) standards.
- ISO 14000 series of environmental management system (EMS) standards.
- ISO 45001 – Occupational Health and Safety (OHS). This standard was established building on the success of OHSAS 18001.
- ISO 22000 Food Safety Management System (FSMS).
- ISO 26000 Guidance on social responsibility.
- ISO 35001 – Biorisk management for laboratories and other related organizations.

Risk management measures include but definitely not limited to the following:

- Practical and realistic organizational risk and safety policy, objectives, and adequately planned systems
- Adequate, appropriate, and suitable processes
- Determination and provision of needed resources
- Defined and well-communicated responsibility and authority
- Adequate risk assessment procedures using the most suitable methods
- Detailed and an all-enhancing engagement of employees
- Effective measurement and monitoring of processes
- Effective people involvement in safety, risk, and communication

COVID-19 Pandemic Risk Quality Management

Supply Chain Risk Management

Quality management has overwhelmingly demonstrated the strength of its ability to drive high performance in the manufacturing, services, public, and other sectors of the global economy. It is definitely for these reasons too that quality management measures were immediately deployed by most healthcare institutions, organizations, and the public sector to immediately ameliorate the impact of the COVID-19 on the global community. Such measures include frequent quality meetings, effective quality management team communication, social distancing, washing hands, wearing face masks, etc. Effective quality management communication was of extreme importance because so little was known about the coronavirus, especially at the onset of the pandemic.

The risks inherent in the pandemic or any other once-in-a-lifetime risk situation require therefore that, on a general basis, organizational quality leadership must have to ensure that they exhibit the necessary agility and preparedness to enable organizations respond very swiftly and effectively to disruptive changes or emergencies, such as the one created by the COVID-19 pandemic.

COVID-19 Assault on Quality Tools

While one may not necessarily lay blames of quick depletion of needed manufacturing inputs on lean, or just-in-time (JIT) inventory, the experience of the immediate impact of the COVID-19 pandemic on industry is devastating. Panic of the fear of the unknown actually created panic-buying, leading to scarcity of some consumer goods, such as paper products – toilet paper, paper towels, and other items.

The role of quality in convincingly creating a one-sided equilibrium between product/service provider and consumers/customers has continuously evolved from the beginning of the last century till date and shall continue to evolve in line with the growing context and changing needs of the human society. The provider has constantly applied the tools of quality to ensure that it is able to meet its obligations of maximally meeting the *specifications, needs, expectations, and requirements* (SNEaRs) of the customer/consumer at costs which allow for some profits.

Two of the key quality tools in which integrity has been directly assaulted by the sudden disruptive challenges of the COVID-19 pandemic are *lean manufacturing* and *just-in-time* (JIT) inventory, both of which have been referred to as "the culprit that may have triggered and exacerbated problems of product delays and shortages" [6]. There are no doubts however that *lean* and *JIT* have jointly or individually played key roles in organizational (providers') abilities to consistently eke out more profits over several years. As an ardent follower of both lean and JIT, their effectiveness is not in doubt, bearing in mind that the COVID-19 pandemic created, on a global platform, unprecedented abnormal and complicated situations.

Since abnormal situations require abnormal solutions, organizations have to be swiftly and quickly get adaptive to disruptive emergencies or disruptive environment. There is therefore the need for precautionary measures based on the unpredictability of potential emergency situations, such as the coronavirus pandemic of 2020 and unexpected environmental hazards.

Whether lean or JIT, possible delays in supply chain due to unforeseeable future of unpredictable circumstances may need to be viewed cautiously as quality management risk factors, which require adequate planning measures.

Organizations operating in developing economies have a good understanding of the need to, on a normal day, adequately plan for the rainy day because of the frequent occurring of:

- Supply chain delays due to shipment and possible clearing delays, or other shipment problems at the ports, on normal days. Despite that, they need to be more effective and adaptive in putting adequate planning in place for a global pandemic risk emergency situation of the magnitude experienced all over the world in 2020.

- Disruptive environment of political instability that may result to or create unrests which in turn may lead to port and road closures.
- Risk associated with daily rising of unexpected increases in foreign exchange values and unpredictable higher inflationary rates and other poor economic planning measures.
- Unplanned incidences of environmental uncertainties and insecurity.

On a general basis however, the following emergency risk factors may likely emanate from disruptive or emergency situations:

- Poor and overzealously managed inventory.
- Too tightly controlled supply lines.
- Unreliable supply chain system.
- Overextended supply lines.
- Overreliance and concentration of Western world organizations and countries on China as a major source or originating supply chain pose potential threats for the future of the global community. Spreading out the global supply chain across all the continents of the world, Africa, South America, and Oceania will definitely lead to the avoidance of the looming shock the world's sole reliance on China for their supply chain may cause at a later date.
- Lean and JIT may need to be deployed with strong consideration for possible supply chain risks as witnessed during the global COVID-19 pandemic. According to Sorensen and Wells [17], "Lean manufacturers maintaining low inventory levels were unable to respond adequately to the COVID-19 demand spike." Afterwards nobody ever expected the COVID-19 pandemic at the time it surfaced on planet Earth.

My experience with lean and JIT shows generally that the impact of any disruptive or emergency situation on them is not adversely too different from that of other systems or quality tools, especially when viewed from the perspectives of their traditional, cost-saving advantages. While taking necessary precautions to minimize risk exposure, *excessively* padding the inventory may also threaten organizational sustainability, especially in emergencies of global dimensions, as the demand for products/services may also be otherwise impacted too.

Looking at the future of supply chain risk management measures therefore requires most importantly that organizations have to build and rely on resilient supply chain systems and also establish supply chain outlets at the closest locations as may be possible. Accomplishing this requires organizational leadership to pitch their tents of risk management in the case of lean in the middle, "striking a balance between surplus and lean manufacturing" [15].

COVID-19-Imposed Quality Norms

Some of the changes made in organizational quality management systems to minimize the impact of the COVID-19 pandemic which caught the global community unawares in the early parts of 2020 may subsequently become permanent quality management phenomena, thereby resulting in a post-COVID-19 era of entirely new norms. The impact of the COVID-19 pandemic is today strongly and heavily reflected in the ways we socialize and interact with each other, do our shopping, our recreational habits, manage our resources, how our kids acquire knowledge at schools and colleges, and where and how we work, just to name a few.

In short, the COVID-19 pandemic may have disproportionately altered to a certain extent the quality of the lives of the global population. The impact on businesses may however be more far reaching than had been envisaged. Apart from the impact of the pandemic on employees' lives, there are going to be marked changes in production management systems.

Flexible Job Option

The revelation of the COVID-19 era in year 2020 and beyond has brought to the fore the perks that make working remotely, or from home, highly attractive to some employees who value flexible job routines as a more effective way to balance work with life [5]. This will most likely create the opportunity of a flexible job option for interested employees in the foreseeable future [20].

Automation and Digitization

Going by the prediction of the World Economic Forum (WEF) in its report, "The Future of Jobs Report 2020," the year 2025 is going to witness the displacement of 85 million current jobs which would similarly be replaced with 97 million jobs due to organization's automation and augmentation scheme [20].

This is particularly so, bearing in mind the needs arising from workers being forced by the COVID-19 pandemic to embrace remote working. The problem here is that the jobs planned to be created may be entirely different from the ones lost due to organizational embrace of process digitization and automation, which raises the questions of both reskilling and/or upskilling their employees, or in the alternative employ new ones with adequate experience in digital technology. Existing employees therefore have to quickly get adaptive in their digital capabilities or learning abilities.

It is evident from the reports of Pietenpol [13] that a lot of "organizations have increased their adoption of robots, chatbots and autonomous vehicles." The extent of automation has also been widened to include the use of robots in the cleaning and sanitization of surfaces, in the delivery of foods and medical supplies without contact with the service recipients, and in analyzing grocery store stocks (Peterson et al. [12]). Organizations with reasonable number of employees working remotely may be motivated to speed up the digital transformation of their working processes.

The adaptive technological innovations embarked on by businesses to effectively cope with the COVID-19 challenges are not without needed investment implications and risks. Most important of the risks here include those of cyberattacks.

Quality Biorisk Management

Gentilli et al. [22] rightly and promptly called the attention of the global community to biosafety and biorisk as emerging areas of safety that are not quite understood by the public. This opinion emerged from the then reported lapses of safety at federal laboratories and other research institutions [23]. The devastating impact of the COVID-19 pandemic, especially its lingering repercussions of socio-economic woes on man's daily activities, makes it glaringly visible to the people of the world how desperate we should be to urgently unite to find appropriate quality management solutions vis-à-vis standards, for addressing and managing biological risks from the perspectives of organizations engaged in the management of biological materials. This is particularly so for the mere fact that virus testing is at the center of many COVID strategies [24]. The COVID-19 pandemic and its global impact on life created a pressing need and awareness for a relevant standard of the nature of the ISO's ISO 35001.

ISO 35001:2019 [8] builds, according to the report of Lewis, on the elements of ISO 45001 though with emphasis on "the unique aspects of bio-risk management." As affirmed here, ISO 35001 is available in helping to "mitigate the acute risk of COVID-19 now," while "its benefits are long-lasting: "implementation of ISO 35001 will help organizations prepare for all future risks, from simple laboratory-acquired infection to future pandemics.""

Biorisk management is defined by the ISO as the coordinated activities to direct and control an organization with regard to biorisk (ISO Guide 73:2009, [10]). The role of quality organizations and their professional members in quality management can generally not be overemphasized, if we have to keep planet Earth safe for human existence, hence the need for the expanding roles of interconnectedness of quality management in all ramifications of our lives:

ISO 35001:2019 – Biorisk management for laboratories and other related organizations
ISO 31000:2018 – Risk management – Guidelines [9]
ISO Guide 73:2009 – Risk management – Vocabulary

References

1. ASQ. (2007, June). ASQ quality glossary. *Quality Progress*, pp. 39–59
2. ASQ. www.asq.com
3. Daniels, A. (2021, March). The next level of success – The benefits of integrating QMSs with SMSs. *Quality Progress*, pp. 56–58.
4. Deming, W. E. (1986). *Out of the crisis*. MIT CAES.
5. Dhaliwal, G. (2020). How the pandemic is changing the future of work. *Forbes*, October 27, 2020. https://www.forbes.com/sites/forbestechcouncil/2020/10/27/hoe-the-pandemic-is-changing-the-future-work/#67d508886841
6. Edmund, M. (2021, January). Laying into lean. The progress report. *Quality Progress*, pp. 8–9.

7. International Organization for Standardization. (2015). *ISO 9001:2015. Quality management systems – Requirements*. https://www.iso.org
8. International Organization for Standardization. (2019). *ISO 35001:2019 – Biorisk management for laboratories and other related organizations*. https://www.iso.org.
9. International Organization for Standardization. (2018). *ISO 31000:2018. Risk management – Guidelines*. https://www.iso.org
10. International Organization for Standardization, ISO Guide 73:2009. (2009). *Risk management – Vocabulary*. https://www.iso.org
11. Meier, R., Williams, M., & Singley, R. (2008, Spring). Merging the bodies of knowledge in quality, project, and risk management. *The Quality Management Forum, 34*(2), 1.
12. Peterson, E. R., Toland, T., & Huddard. *Robots vs. COVID-19: How the pandemic is accelerating automation*. Kearney. www.de.kearny.com/web/global-business-policy-council/article/?/a/robots-vs-covid-19-how-the-pandemic-is-accelerating-automation
13. Pietenpol, L. (2020, December). The times they are a-changin. A glimpse into the future of work. *Quality Progress*, pp. 6–7.
14. ReVelle, J. B. (2004). *Quality essentials from A-Z*. Quality Press.
15. Schell, C. (2020). Here's how we need to change global supply chain after COVID-19. *World Economic Forum*, September 30, 2020. www.weforum.org/agenda/2020/09/covid19-crisis-change-global-supply-chains.
16. Shewhart, W. A. (1980). *Economic control of quality of manufacturing*. ASQ Quality Press, 1931.
17. Sorensen, E., & Wells, A. (2020). Lean manufacturers blamed for paper towel shortage. *Industrial Equipment News,* September 14, 2020. www.ien.com/video/video/21175204/lean-manufactureing-blame-for-paper-towel-shortage
18. Waring, A., & Glendon, A. I. (1998). *Managing risk*. Thompson Learning.
19. Wikipedia. http://en.wikipedia.org/wiki/Risk_management
20. World Economic Forum. (2020, October). *The future of jobs report 2020*. https://www.weforum.org/reports/the-future-of-jobs-report-2020.
21. Young, P. C., & Tippins, S. C. (2001). *Managing business risk: An organization – Wide approach to risk management*. American Management Association.
22. Gentilli, S. M., Potts, J. M., Clarkson, A. J., & Jacobi, H. B. (2016). An overview of the NIH biorisk management program. *Applied Biosafety: Journal of ABSA International, 21*(1), 26–33.
23. Young, A. (2015). Safety experts slam lax safety practices at CDC Labs. *USA Today*, March 19, 2015.
24. Lewis, B. (2020). International Organization for Standardization – Managing Biorisk: Why we need ISO 35001. *ISO News,* December 15, 2020.

9 Dictates of Quality

Implication of the Quality of Customer Satisfaction Concept

Attention is focused here on the relationship between quality and customer satisfaction. In an attempt to understand the term "quality," itself it is very important for you to try to define it in your own words and terms. Thereafter, I would like you to compare the definitions provided below by various authors with yours.

Both Juran [15] and Deming [5] who are some of the most widely celebrated authorities and role models in quality management have long before now recognized and acknowledged the role of the customer in quality management. This opinion is very well accentuated in their respective definitions of quality as summed up below in the words of some of the most widely known quality experts:

> Quality is, in the opinion of the author, the total composite product and service characteristics of marketing, engineering, manufacturing, and maintenance through which the product and service in use will meet the expectations of the customer.

- Juran [15]: "Quality is fitness for use."
- Lord Deming [5]: quality is the "economic manufacture of product that meets the demands of the market."
- For Feigenbaum [7], in his working definition, he viewed quality as being "What the user, the customer says it is."
- In the words of Crosby [4]: "Quality is conformance to specified requirements."
- For Ishikawa [10] the extent of quality is determined by how well the true quality characteristics (customer needs, expressed in customer language) match substitute quality characteristics (product specifications, expressed by a producer in technical language).
- On its own part the ISO in recognition of the role of the customer in quality defines it in ISO 9000:2015 [12] (Quality Management System – Fundamentals and Vocabulary) as the "degree to which a set of inherent characteristics fulfils requirements."

T. A. Ibidapo, *From Industry 4.0 to Quality 4.0*, Management for Professionals,
https://doi.org/10.1007/978-3-031-04192-1_9

~C__________SC__________SC__________SC__________S~

C=Customer

S=Supplier

Fig. 9.1 Poly-customer/supplier chain

It is obvious from the definition of Juran that quality is the fitness for use by the customer or end-users since every product is made specifically for certain users or user categories who, at the same time, represent the market which is being referred to in the definition of Deming. The full assertion of the vital role of the customer is highlighted in the general definition of the term quality. The word "requirements" which appears frequently in the definition of quality here refers to both customer and statutory requirements, needs, and specifications.

Apart from its definition of quality, the ISO in its contractual standard (i.e., ISO 9001:2015, Clause 5.2 [13]) categorically requires that "top management shall ensure that customer requirements are determined and are met with the aim of enhancing customer satisfaction."

It follows therefore that the concepts underlying quality center principally around and on:

- Meeting both the stated and implied needs (including those relating to regulatory/mandatory/legal) of the user (i.e., customer requirements and specifications)
- Achieving products that meet the requirements, needs, and specifications of the customer at costs that represent value to the customer
- Continual improvement of the product and the entire production system

In my own words quality can be described as the:

Ratio or quotient of product performance (P_p) in all ramifications of customer specifications (including product performance, appearance, reliability, durability, conformity with customer and regulatory requirements, ease of use, delivery time, etc.) to the customer's total product performance target (P_t). Hence quality can simply be described as "the degree to which a product or service conforms to the overall specifications (implied and intended), requirements, and expectations of the customer in all ramifications."

In mathematical terms therefore this ratio is, in the case of an assumed situation of a product/service with perfect quality, expected to give a value that is equal or nearly equal to 1 (one).

$$Q = P_p / P_t \sim 1$$

In reality the ratio of P_p to P_t is not likely to be equal to one (1) since meeting the exact specifications, needs, expectations, and requirements (SNEaRs) of the customer in all ramifications for all products at all times may never be completely achievable. Hence, the value of the ratio or quotient tends to be 1. The only exception here is the case of internal customers in which the ratio of product (here a sub-product is actually in question) performance/specification (P_p) to the internal customer's product specification or performance target (P_t) must be equal to one (1) assuming that a zero %-variation tolerance has been planned:

$$Q = P_p / P_t = 1(\text{tolerance of zero} - \%\text{variation})$$

However, if your quality management system allows a planned V% variation from specification, that ratio must be put into consideration at the particular production stage. On the one hand whatever value of % deviation acceptable for a sub-product at particular process stages must be planned and agreed upon, but on the other hand it must not in any way prevent the final product from meeting the specifications, needs, and requirements of the customers or else such a deviation must not be tolerated at all.

From the view point of this definition of quality, the deduction can be made that quality remains a moving or shifting target that every product/service provider continually strives to catch up with. This unending task therefore explains the frequent needs or calls for the continual improvement of any system. This brings out glaringly the need for measurable factors.

Poor Product Quality

Apart from the issue of increased costs, poor/unsatisfactory product quality or faulty services have various other adverse effects or impacts on the performance of an organization. Poor design or inadequate choice and mixture of materials could easily lead to product failure that may, in turn, result to accidents and various degrees of catastrophes. For example, some lives have been lost in Nigeria in the last few years when some poorly designed buildings constructed with substandard materials, faulty approvals, and poor supervision design collapsed. The two tragic accidents of Boeing 737 Max are still fresh in our memories, while the dark shadows of those memories are still highly reflective in the core values of Boeing – safety, quality, and integrity.

This may under normal conditions consequently have resulted to the increase in insurance liability of the construction company involved through the payment of compensation to the families of the deceased and heavy fines/penalties to regulating agencies with the possibilities of facing the rigors of court cases that may not be concluded many years after the respective incidences.

Poor-quality products also lead to the loss of productivity which may have resulted from the time lost in replacing defective parts, repeat jobs, or in product rework/repair and even in cases of accidents. Guarantee/warranty commitments are also costly ventures just as product recalls are not cheap undertakings. The most grave and serious repercussion of poor-quality product/service is the creation of dissatisfied customers which has the potentials of driving away potential customers since the information of their dissatisfaction would not only end with them but will be transmitted to others who, in turn, will also pass the same information to others and so on. The company's reputation of making unsatisfactory products will spread by word of mouth so that it will not be patronized by other customers. If we assume that the initial customer tells ten other potential customers about this incidence, and each of these ten potential customers tells another ten potential customers, then the loss of future customers could theoretically count and rise in the value of the exponents of 10. It is important here therefore for you to take note of the fact that quality is one of the key decision instruments that will always drive your business.

With the recent rise in the price of crude oil (getting to peaks in 2008 and also in 2012), energy costs, if not included in quality plans, can have devastating effects on a company's ROI.

The production and the provision of services just have to be "done right the first time" in line with the quality principles of Crosby [4] who also devised the concept of "zero defects." Manufacturers and other service providers must avoid "muda," repeating jobs not just to improve the value and quality of their products and services but also to ensure customer satisfaction.

Fundamentals of Quality

The quality of a product or service is dictated by some basic fundamental factors which include among others the following:

- Product design
- The degree to which the products/services and their features conform to the expectations and intent of its design
- The ease of use or application of product
- The degree or level of user friendliness of products and services
- Product performance after delivery
- Easiness of product packaging or product disposal as and when necessary

Using the examples of the collapsed buildings mentioned above as examples, it can be said that the design (vis-à-vis planning) stage is the foundation stone for the level of quality achieved by any product. The decisions taken at the design and/or planning stages must therefore be critically considered and revalidated before the commencement of construction works, manufacturing, or execution of a project:

- The needs and expectations of the customer
- Costs
- Product performance
- Conformance of product to relevant regulatory/statutory requirements
- Production and process capabilities
- Product durability
- Safety of use

- Mode of disposal after use and consideration for its impact on the environment
- Other necessary or relevant considerations

Design criteria must therefore be carefully selected and considered to ensure feasibility so that intended products or services are achievable in terms of production process, equipment, adequate human capital, impact on the environment, and the availability of all other necessary inputs. Inadequate or poor design can hinder the achievement of products and services irrespective of the degree of adequacy of other material and human input.

Another critical issue that is fast becoming fundamental in the manufacture or provision of products is that of the disposal of the product after its usage. The disposal of products and their impacts on the environment after they would have completed their life cycles are today becoming more and more important as the issues of the preservation of the environment continue to attract the attention of man. The issues of scarce land resources for landfills, groundwater pollution, air pollution, and ozone layer depletion are some of the grave consequences staring at man.

For a product to conform to all the intended desires, all other inputs such as human and material resources must similarly be adequate and suitable, while the equipment and process/technology must be capable, efficient, and effective. In addition, monitoring and measurements must be effective and timely, while corrective and preventive measures have to be put in place to ensure continual improvement.

The design of products and services must also consider the use and application of a product or service adequately to ensure the ease of use and achieve effective post-sales performance.

One way of getting one sort of assurance or another that the product or service to be contracted out would likely meet stated specifications, needs, requirements, and expectations is the use of organizations or companies that are certified to the requirements of the ISO 9000 series of international quality management system standards or their national equivalents. Here reference is made to organizations that have gained certification to the requirements of its present version, ISO 9001:2008 (or the national equivalents such as the AS 9100), and as they may be modified from time to time. The list of certified organizations is maintained by the ISO in its directory of ISO 9000 certified organizations.

Customer Satisfaction

Since customer – internal and external – satisfaction is actually an expression of the feelings of the customer towards the goods and/or services it receives from a supplier, the measurement of the feelings or impressions of the customer about the goods and services and the way they (i.e., goods/services) are received are strictly left in the hands of the customers who are the only ones that can objectively decide through available *feedback system* whether they are satisfied or not. Both the customer (i.e., receiver of goods/services or the marketplace) and the organization (i.e., supplier of goods and/or services) need however to ensure that goods and services are provided in line with relevant statutory/regulatory guidelines and regulations. This is an obligatory responsibility for the goods and/or services provider as it must ensure that its products and/or services are compliant with applicable regulatory/ statutory requirements, be they stated or generally implied.

The indication here is that it is only the customer that can confirm his level or degree of satisfaction with the products/services at his disposal. This brings to the fore the need for a supplier/customer partnership which is a very important and critical issue generally in the QMS. It is for this and various reasons that the needs, specifications, and requirements of the customer must ab initio be specifically defined both qualitatively and quantitatively.

There is therefore no doubt that the issue of customer satisfaction is very important and paramount in assessing the services already rendered by an organization. The measurement of customer satisfaction does not actually bring to the fore nor does it in the real sense emphasize areas that need to be improved upon and the actions to be taken. It is however possible to generally use the feedback from the customer to shape or design the mode and nature of the future services of an organization to its customers.

Customer satisfaction should be treated by an organization in such a way that it is capable of attracting the attention of potential customers and also to demonstrate that the *voice of the customer* (VOC) is heard and agreeably complied with at all times.

Customer satisfaction thus refers to the things that customers appreciate in an organization's past performance in the form of goods/services provided with little or no focus on the areas where improvement is needed or required. The product supplier or service provider can however use the information made available by the customer/consumer/end-user, i.e., customer feedback to plan and put corrective actions in place to (further) achieve customer satisfaction. This has to be done on a continual basis since quality itself is dynamic.

It is therefore relevant at this point to stress the fact that while you are measuring customer satisfaction, you may have to pay attention to the following critical points and issues which are necessary for you to be able to focus your balanced attention on areas where there is the need for improvement:

- Accurate survey of the areas perceived by the customer as requiring improvement. This can be obtained through a questionnaire prepared specifically for the attention of the customer. This is a general practice in the USA today where customer feedbacks are achieved in most cases through the request of customers to complete the prepared questionnaires online. Also relevant here is the recording of customer telephone conversation with organizational representatives similarly for quality purposes. It must however be mentioned here that even in the USA feedback from internal customers still need a lot of improvement within the quality management system of various organizations.
- Request to the customer to please inform you as a supplier about any concerned issue and all areas found to be below expectation in products and services already rendered so as to use them to improve future deliveries.

- Identification of areas noticed by the organization (i.e., supplier) as requiring improvements during the provision of goods and services.

Customer satisfaction with identified areas of improvement will therefore give the most beneficial survey to actually measure the degree/level of customer satisfaction for both the services rendered or products offered.

The results of the survey to assess customer satisfaction therefore need to be designed to cover a wider scope or perspective of the use and application of the product. For example, if the case of the products/services provided by a hotel has to be critically screened by the guest/customer, issues to be examined for satisfaction are vast and they include among others the following:

- Food provision and its quality
- Cleanliness of the hotel environment
- Comfort of the guest
- Clean beddings
- Noise
- Closeness to areas of interest to hotel guests/customers
- Noise level
- Entertainment facilities
- Provision of other services considered important by the guests, e.g., laundry, exercising facilities, shoe-cleaning facilities, Internet, newspapers, etc.
- Safety of the guests and his belongings – provision of firefighting equipment such as water hydrant and fire extinguishers, fire exit, fire protection guidelines, etc.
- Provision of first aid (medical) services
- Accessibility and transportation
- Behavior and attitude of hotel staff to the guests particularly the way they attend and respond to customer requests, questions, needs, and other requirements.
- Prompt response to calls, needs/requirements, and inquiries of the guests
- Provision of firefighting equipment
- Clear indication of the location of fire assembly point
- Conspicuous location of fire exits and the provision of clear access to them
- Provision of luggage room
- Orderliness
- Amount of leisure at the disposal of the guest
- Provision of hot/cold clean water
- Strict restriction of smokers to particular zones or areas of the hotel
- Ability to give the customer the confidence of being in a safe environment

It follows from the above that the degree of customer satisfaction or dissatisfaction can generally be assessed on the basis of the experience gained from past products and services. And the lessons learned from this can be used to improve the quality of future ones so that it can also be used as an input to the review of the QMS.

In order for you to achieve customer satisfaction, it is highly imperative for you to put a customer assessment mechanism in place to monitor and measure the feelings of your customer particularly their complaints on a continual basis. When viewed from the general perspective, it will be seen that customers generally appreciate the following:

- Recognition.
- Trust and integrity.
- Loyalty.
- Provision of products and services of good value to them.
- Reliability of products and services as well as the ability to provide them on a continually improving basis.
- Prompt response to inquiries.
- Prompt delivery of goods and services.
- Regular communication even when you are in a difficult position that you may not be able to deliver as per your agreement.
- Customer services devoid of states of anxiety.
- Adequate post-delivery services and prompt response to problems and other issues of interest.
- Low risk products/services.
- Access to key or relevant staff in the form of a customer contact point. This is of particular importance to the banking industry and other service provider organizations/industries.
- Safety of customer resources kept with or under your jurisdiction.
- Product or services with adequate consideration for compliance to legislative or statutory guidelines.
- Products with adequate consideration for the impact of its post-usage handling on humans and the environment
- Provision of product usage information guidelines stressing areas of risks with emphasis on necessary precautionary measures.
- Friendliness and courtesy.
- Respect.

No matter what we do to maintain and install a suitable quality management system or concept, the objective remains the same and it is to achieve customer satisfaction. For example, the ISO 9000 series of international QMS standards generally emphasize the need to focus on customer satisfaction in achieving quality, hence its constant emphasis on customer:

- Needs
- Requirements
- Specifications

There is sufficient evidence in ISO 9000 documents to support the fact that this series of international QMS standards places the customer as the overall goal/target of quality. This is vividly expressed in some of the clauses of the requirements of ISO 9001:2008.

Examples of these are cited below:

- Management commitment in ensuring that an organization is conscious of the importance of meeting customer requirements is very well spelled out in Clause 5.1.
- Focus on the customer whereby top management are required to ensure that customer requirements are determined and are met with the aim of enhancing customer satisfaction. This is one of the main provisions of the QMS standard (see Clause 5.2).
- One of the major responsibilities of the QMS management representative is to ensure the promotion of the awareness of customer requirements throughout the organization (Clause 5.5.2).
- The inclusion of both the customer feedback (Clause 5.6.2.) and improvement of product related to customer requirements (Clause 5.6.3) as major input of the management review processes.
- The determination and provision of resources that are needed to enhance customer satisfaction by meeting customer requirements (Clause 6.1).
- Determination of *all* product requirements (including statutory/regulatory as well as delivery and post-delivery activities) related to the product irrespective of whether they are specified by the customers or not (Clause 7.2.1).
- Review and confirmation of all the requirements related to the product, including changes made to product requirements, prior to the organization's commitment to supply a product to the customer (Clause 7.2.2).
- Determination and implementation of effective arrangements for communicating with customers, at any required time, in all matters relating to product. Such matters may include among others any information, inquiries, contracts, or order handling, including amendments and customer feedback/complaints (Clause 7.2.3).
- Ensuring the adequate safeguard/protection of customer interests and property that are kept in the custody of the organization so as to ensure that they are properly kept and utilized to the benefit of the customer (Clause 7.5.4).
- Ensuring that the performance of the quality management system is monitored and measured so as to be able to determine the customer perception of the extent to which customer requirements have been met (Clause 8.2.1).
- Analysis of data providing information relating to customer satisfaction (Clause 8.4).

It is therefore obvious from the requirements of ISO 9000 that once the customer is placed as the focus of an organization's quality activities, there is the likelihood that the customer will receive the needed attention and focus which will in turn result in the provision of products and services that meet customer requirements and specifications.

Customer Satisfaction from Within

Whether unionized or not, the satisfaction of employees which make up organizational internal customers is very critical to both organizational performance and improvement. The fact that employees make things happen within organizational activities further brings out the relevance and criticality of employees as internal customers. Yee et al. [21] in realizing the role of employees as internal customers concluded in their studies that "Employee satisfaction is significantly related to service, quality, and to customer satisfaction, while the latter in turn influences firm profitability, leading to a satisfaction-quality-profit cycle." The results of various research activities further reinforced the need for customer satisfaction to start from within. For example, Brown and Lam [3] described the relationship between customer satisfaction and employee satisfaction as "positive and statistically and substantively significant."

Customer Role in Quality Management

The term customer is, as defined by the ISO in ISO 9000:2018, an "organization or person that receives a product." For example, end-users, clients, patients, consumers, spectators, congregation, passengers, commuters, retailers, students, and purchasers/buyers constitute various forms and categories of customers.

The masses by their own rights as voters to elect people in government constitute the customers in the business of the governance of a nation. Their abilities to duly play the role of customers depend however very largely on the democratic values at their disposal and their consciousness of the roles they have to play as well as their willingness to play such roles.

The role of the customer in any business undertaking is so vital that no business can sustain itself without the customer except in situations where survival is not compulsory or in the case of charitable or "father-Christmas" organizations whereby return on investments (ROI) are neither expected nor necessary. Hence, the customer can simply be described as the most fundamental element or requirement for the establishment, sustenance, and even the overall existence of any business enterprise.

This is the reason why feasibility studies are usually carried out for new businesses to define and estimate among others the availability of potential customers for which the products and/or services could be targeted. There can be no business if there is no customer; hence, the customer is the alpha/omega or the beginning/end of any business enterprise/organization.

When the products and/or services of an organization do not satisfy or meet the requirements of the customer, the customer automatically becomes dissatisfied. The dissatisfaction of a customer generally has very negative impacts on the market performance of the products and services of an organization. The news of a dissatisfied customer spreads generally like a bush fire in the dry season or harmattan.

Creating dissatisfied customers has very serious and grave consequences or repercussions on any organization since such a customer will consciously or subconsciously spread the news of its ill feelings to other people or entities. On the generally assumed basis that one dissatisfied customer tells ten other people who in turn will also pass the same information to same number of people including potential customers, the organization may actually find it extremely difficult to maintain its position in the market.

Once an organization loses a customer it is costly and difficult to reverse the situation. This is to say that winning back unsatisfied customers is an uphill task that requires a lot of effort. Winning back lost customers can in the real sense only be attained with very huge advertising budget coupled with improved product/service.

Dissatisfied customers can easily be created, for example, when on a general basis, products and services fail to meet the overall customer and regulatory requirements and specifications.

Apart from the fact that the customers desire quality, they expect:

- Performance
- Reliability
- Competitive prices through the provision of goods/services of value
- Credibility
- Dependability
- Good to excellent services
- Correct services
- Clear and correct documentation
- Quick response to all inquiries and generally excellent communication
- Timeliness in product and service delivery
- Doing things right the first time

It therefore becomes highly imperative for all business managers who want to succeed to strive to delight the customers at all times or else somebody else shall not only do it but also take the business away.

Quality Failure

Quality failure is an unpleasant experience that no organization wishes to go through; hence, it is an evil that has to be avoided at all costs. Quality failure whether internal or external has negative impacts on an organization and its products and/or services. The case discussed below is a good example to explain the implications of quality failure.

A practical example here is the situation of a food industry (De United Foods Ltd) in Otta, Ogun State, Nigeria, in which three batches of its major products were, as made known to the Nigerian public in various newspapers, ordered for recall by the NAFDAC (National Agency for Food and Drug Administration and Control) sometime in May 2004 as a result of quality complaints in terms of meeting regulatory requirements.

Regaining Customer Confidence

The case in question actually showed that regaining the confidence of lost customers is not cheap, not even in a country like Nigeria which has a very high level of illiterate population who are quite gullible.

The company aggressively mounted massive marketing and sales campaigns using the following channels:

- Electronic media.
- Billboard advertisement.
- Newspaper advertisement.
- Outdoor/street musical promotional rallies and campaigns whereby product samples were freely distributed to the public, that is, both previous and potential customers.
- Television interviews and demonstrations (the CEO of the organization actually was shown on one of the television programs eating the product so as to demonstrate its safety to the entire public probably based on the saying that "seeing is believing").
- Distribution of free products to the public in mass procession in open vehicles with dancers particularly to catch the attention of the youths and children who are known to be one of the major consumers of the products in question.
- Public consumption (openly on the television) of some of its products by its members of staff.
- Sponsorship of various community development seminars, debates, youth programs, and other gatherings particularly at the secondary school level.

These were all done with a view to:

- Persuade its numerous customers of the fitness of its products for consumption
- Restore the confidence of its numerous customers in the product and in the organization itself
- Assure the general public about the quality of its product
- Gain back all lost customers and even win new ones so as to regain its market position and status
- Gain back the lost integrity, goodwill, and corporate image of the organization

It is left for you to imagine the budget (*cost of quality, CoQ*) for such an exercise which would probably have been avoided if things have been done right the first time or from source to ensure that product quality is maintained, sustained, and improved upon continually. The example referred to here is a practical demonstration to show that the *cost of quality* is actually that of not doing things right; hence, it is an avoidable cost. You can read more about the cost of failure in Chap. 8.

Another example that is still fresh in our memories is the resultant effect and impact of the avian flu simply known as bird flu on the Nigerian tourism industry and the Nigerian economy and the increase in the price of fish which went up by about one hundred percent (100%). The poultry sector of the Nigerian economy was more or less brought to a standstill or near collapse. Fish farmers took advantage of the pressure in the fish market to market all their stocks irrespective of their sizes.

Some poultry farmers actually took their campaigns to the media where they openly demonstrated the safety of chickens by eating them for television viewers to openly see that there was nothing wrong any more in eating chicken.

It goes to say therefore that customer dissatisfaction if not nipped in the bud could, in turn, spell doom for any organization since there is the likelihood that both the survival and existence of the affected organization would be under a very serious threat of poor patronage.

Most organizations therefore spend a substantial part of their annual budget on advertising so as to gain more and more customers and also to sustain the number or simply the volume of its existing customers, thereby retaining and at the same time improving on its market position/strength.

A business enterprise will gradually move in the direction of liquidation/extinction or receivership whenever the level of customer patronage begins to diminish or fall below its economically viable level. The issues of customer satisfaction vis-à-vis meeting customer requirements must therefore be seen as fundamentally vital aspects of organizational survival/existence, hence the key to its quality management system.

Customer-Supplier Relationship

There are generally two types of customers involved in transactions at both the micro- and macro-levels of any business activities and these are the internal (or on-the-job customers) and external customers (or the customers of the organization itself). Operations at the micro-level of transactions involve the internal staff of an organization, whereas the external customers are the organization's customers whose requirements have to be met by the totality of an organization's activities.

In order to have a good understanding of the concept of customer satisfaction, it is very important to understand the term "customer" itself. From the definition of the ISO in ISO 9000:2015 [12], a customer is an "organization or person that receives a product."

Using a process as an example, it is directly visible that the concept of customer crops up at various stages of the process or activities so that in any process or activity there is a chain of customers, thereby making this concept actually synonymous with a polymer chain that is made up of many individual monomer-repeat units.

The individual customer within a process falls generally under the class of internal or on-the-job customers. It follows therefore that within any process there is a quality system poly-customer/supplier chain where there are numerous customer-supplier relationships. Virtually every one in an organization is a customer to at least one other person in the business chain and its activities just as he also is a supplier to another one. Hence, every individual involved in any process or business activity is at one stage or another acting both as a customer and a supplier at the micro-level.

The quality system supplier-customer chain relationship will be broken or simply de-polymerized when one internal supplier fails to satisfy his internal customer. The resultant effect in the QMS chain is that the product or service in question may subsequently fall short, in one way or another, of the requirements of the external customer. It therefore goes to say that failure to effectively satisfy the internal customer within a process or business activity may in turn have very serious consequences on product/service delivery to the external customer, thereby putting the satisfaction of the customer at risk. Satisfaction within the chains of internal customers and suppliers ultimately leads to the satisfaction of the final customer. The advantage of this is that it results to an effective QMS in which the commitment to quality is shared throughout an organization.

Since the success or failure of the business transactions in the chain of internal customer/supplier relationship ultimately manifests itself in the satisfaction or non-satisfaction of the external customer, it is particularly important to ensure at all times and at every stage of manufacturing or service rendering/provision that everyone involved in a process plays very proactively the roles of a customer that consistently provides a feedback to its supplier to express and define the extent or degree of satisfaction.

Customer satisfaction at the micro-structural level of the QMS is therefore a fundamental and vital building block for the building of a solid and impregnable foundation to achieve the confidence, trust, and the satisfaction of the external customer. The customers are thus the final referees/umpires/judges of the quality of the products and services that they receive. The dissatisfaction of the customer which may lead to the termination of a product from the market could be viewed in a similar way as the referee of a football match showing the red card to a player that has violated the rules on the football field.

A customer that is not satisfied may either express its dissatisfaction directly to the suppliers or withdraw its patronage. In most cases, a customer that is not satisfied will not inform the supplier of its ill feelings. Rather, they simply switch to competitive suppliers or products. For example, a study reported by Stevenson [19] claimed that a satisfied customer will tell a few people about his or her experience, while one that is not satisfied will tell an average of 19 others. The withdrawal of the patronage may subsequently lead to the loss of sales and market share. In some cases, the organization may totally lose the business.

In a brief summary the delivery of substandard product has the likelihood of affecting an organization in the following major ways:

- Increased costs of doing business
- Loss of customers, hence loss of business which could, in extreme cases, result to the liquidation of an organization/enterprise
- Loss of productivity
- Increased liability

Role of Supplier in Customer Satisfaction

As mentioned under TQM there is the need for the supplier to also work closely with the concept of focusing attention on meeting the needs, requirements, and specifications of the customer. One way this can easily be achieved is through close *partnership with the customer* or in simpler terms partnership between supplier of goods and users/consumers of such goods.

Producer-consumer partnership can therefore help the organization to achieve the maximization of its efficiency vis-à-vis productivity which in turn has a positive impact on the profitability of the organization. This can be achieved through the reduction of wastages and other non-value-added activities such as inspection of supplied items to identify products that are below-prescribed standards. The cooperation here ensures that the supplied items are used directly for production without the need for further inspection other than the one which has been carried out by the supplier.

One major objective of the supplier-organization partnership therefore is to completely or greatly reduce the inspection of incoming materials. The implication here is that the supplier who takes on the additional responsibilities of product inspection simply bears the burden of the inspection, the processes of which may have been integrated into its production system. This can be achieved through the use of some quality tools given by Ericson [6] as:

- Process capability assessment
- Intelligent supplier qualification
- Material qualification and assessment
- Measurement correlation

The cooperation or partnership of a supplier with the customer in this way may, if well managed, even result in the customer receiving the materials as "direct to stock" or "ship to stock," thereby bypassing the process of an in-house inspection (i.e., lean inspection) to go directly to the warehouse of the customer or in some situations as a "just-in-time" (JIT) delivery in which case the supplied items are used directly as supplied on the production line.

For this to happen there is the need for the customer or the organization receiving the products or services to have confidence in the QMS of the supplier whose responsibility is to inspect all supplied items which are delivered with all the inspection data and numbered using the lot numbering system.

The level of cooperation or partnership needed here may have to stretch to situations whereby both the supplier and customer embrace the following:

- Having similar quality goals
- Sharing their quality objectives/goals with one another
- Exhibiting and promoting the practice of the concept of continual improvement of their production processes/systems
- Mutually negotiating prices, services, and delivery agreement that are of benefit to both supplier and customer

Supply Chain Management

Global outsourcing is now a current trend in products and service provision, hence the need for assuring the quality of activities involved in all aspects of supply chain management. Many big organizations with integrated supply chains have already adopted large-scale integrated models in their operations to ensure effective performance measurement and strategy. This is very important since global outsourcing actually plays strategic roles in organizational activities particularly the large organizations which cannot afford to be self-contained in all aspects of its activities.

In order for an organization to be sure of the quality of the inputs coming into its system through the supply chain, there is the need to make the supply chain management an integral part of the organizational QMS. Hence, the suppliers in the supply chain need to be handled beyond merely measuring compliance. Similarly, the change or transition from a centralized structure to a more modular form which the supply chain represents needs to be properly managed or else the employees may become confused, disoriented, and disillusioned.

The change from the usual centralized system to the supply chain structure requires you to have sufficient information and knowledge of the suppliers and their adaptive ability as well capability to manage risks and execute projects. For example, high technology organizations such as those of the oil sector, aerospace, and automobile industries rely heavily on the supply chain to get high levels of quality inputs needed by them to achieve their expected performance objectives and product quality so as to be to meet customer SNEaRs.

It is for these reasons that the ISO developed some application-specific standards, most of which could be used with or integrated with standards based on the principles of generic management systems. While ISO 9000 QMS and ISO 14000 EMS families of international standards are generic standards, ISO/TS 16949:2009 is application-specific for the automotive industries.

Since *knowledge management* is a core element in building and providing quality products and services, it is important that in integrating the *supply chain management* into organizational QMS, it is necessary to have a very good understanding of how knowledge and information are effectively used throughout the supply chain network. This is particularly important in the era of digital transformation with the rollout of Industry 4.0 initiatives.

It is therefore obvious here that knowledge management is a key element in any management system but particularly so in the management of the supply chain if quality products and services have to be supplied to customers as, where, and when needed. Due to the exigencies of business orientation towards return on investment (ROI) supply chain management in business organizations, supply chain management quality is rarely deliberately compromised. This is contrary to supply chain management in government and public services, especially in the corrupt-ridden countries.

Quality in Public Supply Chain Management

The supply chain structure in government and public services is often subsumed in the complexities of bureaucracy. Additionally, public supply chain is used in some countries as an avenue to incur unnecessary costs of quality (CoQ) due to corruption and corrupt practices. In the Western world and other economically advanced countries of the world, it serves as a source of politically corrupted patronage in terms of political party or electioneering campaign financing.

In the highly corrupt countries of Africa and elsewhere, it is a drain pipe used to compromise the quality of people's lives.

The quality of supply chain management is thus as critical in public service as in business organizations. This is very critical in the award of government contracts generally but particularly in the developing countries, such as Nigeria, where government contracts are not only overinflated to incur unnecessary cost of quality, but awarded in most cases on the basis of politics and power play instead of relying on the application of knowledge management to award contracts to make them relevant to the improvement of people's quality of life and societal improvement.

Using knowledge management for supplier selection and supply chain management is thus the quality path of choice, hence the application of knowledge of suppliers and their products and services to improve the quality of analysis for decision-making in respect to the award of contracts to qualified contractors. The choice of suppliers must therefore be analyzed on the basis of the record, ability, and capability to promptly deliver goods and services of quality. This is a way of ensuring that contract awardees are committed to quality in line with the acknowledgment of Wruck and Jensen [20] that:

> In addition to improving the quality of analysis for decision making, the application of knowledge reduces the odds that politics, power or fear will interfere with effective decision making.

Quality Control Requirements

Two things that may be considered highly imperative for your organization to consistently and satisfactorily meet customer SNEaRs are:

- Strict adherence to internal controls, most of which are manifested in your QMS
- Stringent control of suppliers and supplies in your supply chain which play expanded roles in your final product quality

While it may be easier for you to put modalities in place for achieving strict adherence to your internal controls which may be based on your QMS (e.g., ISO 9001, Six Sigma, Lean Six Sigma, etc.), getting suppliers to provide you with their goods and services under stringent control measures may sometimes be more difficult. There is no doubt therefore that effective supplier partnership through the integration of your supply chain management into your QMS is a critical supply chain management approach.

One of the best ways for integrating the supply chain management into your system is the building of industry standards on the principles of TQM and the partnership with suppliers that believe and practice the same principles. It is only in this way that solid and very strong "organization-supplier" links can be established and achieved to the benefit of the quality of organizational products and services.

Integration of the Supply Chain Management

Integrating the supply chain management is likely to continue to pose newer and newer challenges in the business world particularly in the areas of the need for the realignment of organizational structures and cultures. This may be necessary if supplier-organization partnerships are intended to lead to the realization of the full potentials, benefits, and advantages of supply chain integration.

Reports of some researchers in the recent past highlighted the following features of organization-supplier relationship [18]:

- Joint planning
- Shared control of inventory
- Electronic data interchange
- Shared visions and goals

The reliability of the supply chain management is very critical to the success of organizations that depend on supply chain management. Hence, the research assertion here is that organizations dependent on supply chain management must:

- Formulate relevant criteria to appraise the performance of its supply chain
- Negotiate the performance parameters
- Give rigorous and continuous measurements

Effective supply chain management can, on a general basis, be achieved by giving adequate consideration to the following key issues in respect to the integration of the supply chain and its management:

- Every link in the supply chain is critical and must be so considered.
- Expansion of the scope of information and delivery technologies.
- Ensuring that strategies are effectively communicated between the suppliers.
- Concerned parties must show commitment.
- Sharing of information on costs and other relevant issues with the suppliers.
- Ensuring that the supply chain is managed with precision.
- Organizational performance goals must be aligned between the supplier and the customer.
- Ensuring that effective risk management measures are put in place.

The role of information in supply chain management is so critical that organizations that are dependent on supply chain must have to acquire or build an adequate information support structure/data bank needed to effectively manage the supply chain. Supply chain management is for obvious reasons easier to achieve in developed economies than they are in the developing or poorer nations of the world in which supply chain security has to be closely monitored and managed.

There are limitations as to the type of products and services that could be outsourced in an economy that is mainly import oriented, that is, consumer nations like Nigeria and most of the other countries in the West African sub-region. This is very much so despite the now large global market that has been brought closer through the Internet and the global telecommunications system (GSM).

Security, logistics, maintenance and spare parts, power generation, personnel recruitment, canteen services, cleaning, and training are some of the most commonly outsourced services today in Nigeria. Most of the oil companies operating in Nigeria maintain supply chain networks to achieve needed operational efficiencies.

Role of Supply Chain Security Management System

The recognition of the need for organizations to adequately and effectively manage and secure their supply chain by the international community has in no doubt motivated the ISO in the establishment of an international standard, the *Supply Chain Security Management Standard, **ISO 28000:2007*** [11].

ISO 28000:2007 is a global security management standard which can be used to establish your supply chain security management system (SMS). ISO 28000:2007 defines a series of supply chain security management system requirements provided in its Clauses 4.1–4.6. The standard is similar to the ISO 9001 QMS standard in its generic nature. Some of the major requirements of ISO 28000:2007 which are highlighted below represent some of the critical issues or actions needed to be taken or put in place to ensure the effective management of your supply chain security [11]:

- Establishment, documentation, implementation, and maintenance of a supply chain security management policy
- Identification of supply chain security threats and assessment of risks
- Identification of supply chain security management control measures
- Establishment of procedures to manage legal, statutory, and regulatory security requirements
- Establishment, implementation, and maintenance of supply chain security management targets
- Establishment, implementation, and maintenance of supply chain security management programs
- Creation of a supply chain security management structure
- Ensuring personnel handling supply chain security is competent and well trained.
- Development of procedures to ensure that pertinent supply chain security information is communicated

- Establishment and maintenance of a supply chain security management documentation system
- Establishment of procedures to control the documents, data, and information of the supply chain security management system
- Implementation of operational supply chain security management system control measures
- Preparation of emergency supply chain security management plans and procedures
- Monitoring and measurement of supply chain security performance
- Evaluation of supply chain security management system plans, procedures, capabilities, as well as compliance with regulations, best practices, and conformance with supply chain security policy and objectives
- Investigation of supply chain security incidents and taking necessary action
- Controlling of the supply chain security management system records
- Auditing of supply chain security management system
- Review of the supply chain security management system by examining inputs, assessing reviews, and generating management review outputs

The standard provides an orderly, effective, and consistent way of managing your supply chain security.

Making Customer the King

Since the customer holds the ace for the survival of an organization, the customer can simply be tagged or referred to as the alpha and omega of any business enterprise interested in surviving. The survival of an organization can as well be seen as a factor of the quality of its products and the quantity of its customers as well as that of its ability to maintain and sustain them.

The issue of customer satisfaction is therefore of paramount importance in that without the customer an organization providing goods and services cannot even take off with any of its own activities, let alone surviving and sustaining them. The only way a customer can be satisfied is to ensure, at all times, that the goods and services provided for that customer completely represent and even surpass the customer's specifications, requirements, and values in all ramifications.

Achieving customer satisfaction at all times however requires that an organization should make the art of quality product and services a culture and way of life. To achieve this task the *quality mindset* has to be developed in its human capital.

Quality Leadership Focus

The focus of quality leadership on the customers helps to enhance not just the quality of your products and services but also that of the overall quality of your organization. One issue found by the author to be very critical to customers is the commitment by organizational leadership at all levels to keep customers in their sights. Demonstrating a real commitment to customer is a tool used by the author to ensure that one of the companies, a windscreen manufacturing organization, managed by him recorded its first profits in several years. This was achieved through regular monthly visits to the markets to see the product distributors and witness for a good stretch of time at each market location the interaction of the customers with our products. This singular act resulted to:

- The establishment of a link between what we do and the results we obtain
- The demonstration of the level of management concern for its customers and its products
- Making customer focus practical and visible to all employees and customers
- Driving home to the employees the issues at stake
- Promoting the business and concerns of the customers
- Gaining the confidence of the customer

Keeping your customers within the sights of your entire management team including those of your supervisors can also help to motivate your employees in keeping their attentions focused on your customers.

Purpose of the QMS

While there is the need for leadership focus on the QMS implementation, there must be the general assurance by leadership that whatever quality management systems, tools, principles, and techniques deployed, they are suitable and adequate for an organization's operations and processes. The focus of leadership must be within the understanding that:

- The quality system is effective for lowering the risk of defective product issues.
- Quality requirements and performance are adequately communicated.
- Organizational and departmental performance indicators are adequately and effectively communicated to enhance organizational global performance.
- The organization has not missed out on quality improvement plans and initiatives that may be inherent or manifested in the dynamics of technological advancement.

Visible leadership focus and involvement in the implementation of a chosen QMS often intoxicates the emotions of employees to the extent that they start having the inner thinking of seeing their workplace from the perspective of being owned by themselves.

Customer Feedback

When talking of customer satisfaction, one is actually referring to a broad range of issues that cut across the entire activities of an organization. In order to ensure the relevance of the feedback of the customer to future activities of the organization, it is important to look at some of the areas of interaction between an organization and its customers.

Some of such supplier/customer inter-phase activities suitable for use in devising ways and modes of measuring customer satisfaction are identified as listed below by the author based on his experience in industry and enterprise management:

- Communication with the customer in terms of response to inquiries and provision of relevant product features and characteristics
- Timely response to customer enquiries and questions
- Accuracy in the compilation and documentation of orders
- Prompt confirmation of orders
- Accurate and timely invoicing
- Adequacy in the protection and safeguard of customer property/input kept in the custody of an organization for inclusion in the production of the customer's goods/services
- Proper and economic use of customer property
- Competitive prices and good value of products and services
- Prompt/timely delivery/shipment of goods and services to the customer
- Accuracy and timely provision of delivery/shipping documents
- Regularity, prompt, and accurate reconciliation of accounts affecting customer transactions
- Degree of product failure during usage by primary or secondary customers
- Product acceptability/rejection by customer
- Product/service quality rating by customer
- Number of product/service units that had to be replaced by the organization within a defined time limit and the ease with which this is done
- Downtime of machine/equipment or production stoppages emanating/resulting from product/service defect(s) or failure within a specified time frame
- Rating of production environment by customer
- Customer satisfaction with overall product specification as produced
- Provision of technical data/information for product
- Provision of safety guidelines for use of product/services
- Provision of guidelines for the disposal of product or its packaging after usage bearing in mind the need to protect the environment
- Provision of marketing/sales services
- Provision of after-sales services
- Post-delivery inquiries made by the organization about the performance of its product/services
- Prompt implementation of guarantee/warranty commitment as soon as they are due by supplier
- Honoring of all the conditions of the supply as stipulated in the contract agreement

Organizations can actually ask questions about the items highlighted above and then assess the responses from either the customer or from the appropriate unit within the organization and then score the responses with okay or not okay remarks (or good/bad or even rate each answer accordingly). The overall assessment must however lead to the conclusion – satisfactory or unsatisfactory performance of the product/services.

Customer feedback is a very important input into the QMS review activities since it shows the level of satisfaction of the customer in terms of the services already rendered. Customer feedback has to be worked upon in terms of putting in place necessary corrective and/or preventive actions in response to the questions, complaints, and needs of the customer as highlighted in the feedback.

Customer Delight

Customer satisfaction remains the ultimate goal of any business enterprise interested in succeeding through the achievement of good return on investment (ROI). After the achievement of the goals, you don't have to rest on your oars, but rather you should by all possible means ensure that your customers remain satisfied at all times. Quality does not allow for organizational complacency. After consistently meeting the requirements of your customer, your next task would be "to delight your customers."

Meeting the requirements of the customer consistently over a long period of time can actually create an image of good reputation, or image of excellence, for an organization. Such an image of good reputation will in turn give birth to customer loyalty. Customer loyalty, in turn has, as listed below, some positive effects on your organization in terms of your budget, cost of doing business, and profitability:

- Customers generally cost less to retain than to acquire. If in doubt check the marketing budget of your organization.
- Maintaining an excellent relationship with the customer, on a long-term basis, results to higher profitability since marketing costs can be minimized.
- A delighted customer will likely remain loyal and committed to its chosen supplier as long as a line of confidence is maintained.
- New customers can be won through delighted and loyal customers so that savings can be made on customer acquisition costs.

Organizations that delight their customers will definitely find delight in the operational results and ROI to the delight of the shareholders or business ownership. Hence, delighting your customers is delighting your shareholders and delighting yourself. The resultant impact is that you will earn yourself *customer loyalty*.

Customer Loyalty

It is highly imperative that for your organization to remain in business, you must not just keep your customers but also win new customers. To keep your customers, you must be able to consistently satisfy their needs, meet their requirements, and provide them with products and services which do not only represent value to your customers but also meet their specifications at all times. Achieving these stated objectives simply imply that you must exhibit some degrees of loyalty for your customers who in most cases are also ready to be loyal to you.

There are among others two critical issues necessary for you to be able to adequately and promptly meet the requirements of your customers:

- Ability to *listen* attentively to your customers at all times
- Ability to *adapt to circumstances* of diverse disruptive situations times and the variations that accompany each situation

Your customers are quite sensitive to every action you take to meet their requirements; hence, you need to always give them positive signs indicative of your readiness and willingness to meet their requirements no matter how diverse the situations may be and how often they may change. It is in line with this requirement that Goodman and Collier [8] wrote that "for your organization to avoid burdening your customers with the same unsatisfactory experiences, you must excel in three areas." The three areas are given by them as:

- An actionable voice of the customer (VOC)
- A linkage of that VOC to your service process
- A service process that is flexible and can adapt to each customer's particular situation

Eight attributes of organizations that may easily lead them to the achievement of a high-impact and result-oriented system are highlighted by Goodman and Grimm [9]. Key among the achievements of implementing the VOC system as highlighted by both Goodman and Collier [8] and Goodman and Grimm [9] is that you will be able to:

- Achieve a flexible response process that will make you adaptable to and enable you to effectively respond to and handle every situation emanating from your customer needs and requirements
- Improve your commitment to solving customer problems
- Achieve some level of reduction in the cycle time for implementing recommendations by linking the VOC with the needs and other issues of interest to the customer directly with the product/service delivery process

All in all, your adoption of the VOC system shall undoubtedly improve your ability to listen to your customers as well as improve your adaptability to various customer needs and requirements, thereby boosting your ability to satisfy and meet the requirements and needs of your customer which in one way or another help to maximize customer *loyalty*. Achieving customer loyalty goes further to enhance delighting your customer. Loyalty is the reward of loyalty; hence, there is the tendency for your customer to be loyal to you if you are loyal to them and loyalty to them depends on your ability to manage your customers' experience.

Building Customer Loyalty

A systematic management of the experiences of your customers is important and critical for you to achieve customer loyalty. This is because the perception of value by a customer emanates from the customer's overall experience with an organization and the goods/services offered by it. Connecting emotionally with customers requires, according to Berry and Carbone [2], that an organization creates a cohesive, authentic, and sensory-stimulating total customer experience that resonates, pleases, communicates effectively, and differentiates the organization from the competition. Hence, one way to build customer loyalty is through the management and enhancement of your customers' total experiences.

It is obvious from the above that spending time to know your customer will undoubtedly help you to reap long-term benefits in your business performance in various aspects ranging from high turnover, good profitability to lower costs of sales.

Guidelines for Achieving Customer Loyalty

Getting customer – internal and external – loyalty should be the aspiration of any organization wishing to build a reliable and solid customer base. Customer loyalty can be achieved through:

- Making products that are reliable for customer use by meeting customer specifications, needs, expectations, and requirements (SNEaRs)
- In constant communication with your customers – internal and external
- Being there for your customers – internal and external – whenever they need you

Basics of Serving Your Customer

The basics of serving your customer involve you taking actions that are as simple as learning the ABC. Such actions include but are not limited to the following:

- Develop *patient ears*.
- Be generous with the word "please."
- Make "thank you" your watchword.
- Overwhelm your customers with *smiles*; smiles that could even be heard over the phone.
- Provide quick *updates* as a reassurance that you are working on your customers' problems.

These simple actions can even make you stand out among your competitors. Key to your business success therefore lies in your dedication to customer service and your consistent demonstration that you care about all issues relating to them. Treat your customers with concern and compassion particularly since your business is not about you yourselves but about your customers.

Knowing the Customer

You will come across a wide range of customers in your business activities and each of them definitely comes with various characteristics, desires, specifications, needs, and expectations. Your success and capability to satisfy them depends to a large extent on your ability to know each of them as much as is possible. In addition, this will also help to ensure that you are able to offer each and every one of them products and/or services of utmost value to them. Knowing and understanding your customer will help to enhance customer communication and articulate your proposals as building blocks for business trust.

Developing the Customer Strategy

Knowing your customers and their respective products will give you the opportunity to develop strategic plans in dealing with each customer and its peculiar problems or issues. Developing customer strategy will in turn help in the enhancement of customer satisfaction and also lead to your establishment of the areas for improvement.

Employee Education, Communication, and Empowerment

Your frontline managers should be educated about everything that is known about each customer from their product/service characteristics to delivery schedule and any other commitments of your company to the customer. Your workers should in turn be trained on the need and how to achieve products/services that meet and even surpass customer needs, specifications, and requirements.

The empowerment of your employees to be able to respond to the requests and/or questions of the customer will go a long way to enhance customer trust and confidence which ultimately leads to customer satisfaction. Relevant employees especially those that are in contact (even through telephone) with the customers must be trained to know how to respond and react to all situations and questions. Even when they do not know the needed answers, they must be able to say so to the customers and that they will find out and get right back to them or inform their superior who must immediately get back to the customer with the right and appropriate answers. Meeting customer needs, expectations, and requirements is therefore a quality culture and a theme that must permeate your entire organization.

Maintaining Organizational Integrity

Maintain a high level of trustworthiness and integrity with your customers by ensuring that you always deliver on your promises to your customers, thereby assuring them that you can deliver the goods/services at the value they ascribed to them. The combination of your credibility, reliability, and integrity will undoubtedly lead to the development of very strong attachment to your customers and their getting delighted.

Customer satisfaction is today the baseline expectation in the global market where competition is not just keen but a major dictate of quality product and services.

Boosting Governance with QMSs – Organizations and Public

Adverse Impact of Governance Without Quality

The role of quality management in the governance (QMIG) of organizations is of great importance for human survival. While attention has been mostly focused on business organizations, high-profile organizations such as FIFA, Lehman Brothers, and others have hitherto been out of the quality management radar. The same faith has similarly befallen public services and governance, or governments, especially in the underdeveloped countries of the world like Nigeria.

Bringing governance – corporate and public – under the radar of quality thus daily becomes extremely necessary and important, in order to realize quality outcomes similar to those of business organizations. This will, in turn, help to reduce the immense adverse effect of such organizations and ill governments on people and society.

The International Organization for Standardization (ISO) is so adequately placed to establish some relevant international guidance standards for high-profile organizations/world bodies and public governance because of its experience, ability of pooling expertise, and other resources among its membership cadres across the globe.

While the lessons of, for example, the Lehman Brothers and FIFA still linger in our minds, the unending democratic tragedy and pathetic threats to democratic elections and governance in many of the 54 African countries and recently in the USA are begging for the attention of relevant quality bodies, organizations, and professionals for the prescription of appropriate QMS guidance standards to:

- Effectively remove and prevent "perceived abuses of authority"
- Highlight and identify the objectives, mission, and organizational roles and commitment to their immediate surroundings, society at large, and stakeholders
- Effectively and continually improve organizational performance measured from the purview of sustainability, fairness, responsibility, and accountability

- Avoid major incidences and abuses, in order to maintain organizational integrity and positive organizational projection
- Ensure organizations are appropriately focused to accomplish set goals/objectives in fulfillment of the purposes for which they have been established
- Improve the quality vis-à-vis integrity of election procedures and operations, to promote appreciable progress for achieving a peaceful environment, human development, civic engagement, human rights, and economic growth and above all to facilitate general human development and innovation

Hence, it is very critical here that the general consideration for quality management (QM), total quality management (TQM), or any elements of quality principles and techniques is completely lacking in most African countries which are generally being recklessly governed aground. For example, the failure of the Nigeria State is due to the absolute lack of quality considerations in both governance and in public services, a situation worsened by the general lack of accountability, which daily escalates the unnecessary cost of quality (UCoQ), in an environment rooted heartlessly in the growing culture of corruption and corrupt acts.

Nobody in government and public services in that part of the world seemed to have realized the importance of customer/supplier relationship at all, let alone thinking of how to meet customer SNEaRs, in a continent plagued by mis-leadership pandemic on the one hand and littered by herds of quality-blind misleaders on the other.

Do we therefore wonder why there is extremely low quality of life in a country like Nigeria, which is perhaps beyond any human imagination, despite the country's enormous resources, which have been squandered all over the years? Effective quality management in all ramifications of life is the most likely solution to upgrade the people's quality of living, in a continent torn to shreds by its ineffective management and its bedevilment by the bounty of its own natural resources, its natural endowments.

Quality Management: Panacea for Public Governance Mis-leadership in Africa

Hence, there is a call here for an urgent turnaround for Africans to massively focus their attention on ways to:

- Develop the quality mindset among the people of the continent.
- Create and sustain the quality management culture among its uncontrollably escalating population. This is perhaps the best panacea for the sustainability of most African countries, or else the continent shall end up towards the end of the twenty-first century to be a continent of miniature countries, numbering over 100 with a population it cannot feed.
- Embrace the teaching of quality management in all ramifications of life and other activities in this continent with a growing 1.3 billion people.

African universities, research institutes, and other relevant institutions need to urgently embrace "quality" as necessary knowledge base for developing the continent and its people or else all may have been lost. Quality is your answer; embrace it though survival may not be compulsory!

Quality Management Panacea to Restoring US Election Integrity

The unprecedented "manufacturing" of falsehood and the massive deployment of conspiracy theories in last year's historic US presidential election have showed to the entirety of the global community the new face of America's democratic nightmare and the need for the deployment of quality tools.

"Claims of election fraud, assertion of suspicious recounts and charges of vote dumps. Cyberthreats to the election process, partisan litigation disenfranchisement, gerrymandering and misinformation campaigns" have reportedly "created an unprecedented level of public mistrust around U.S. elections and contributed to the perceived decline in the integrity of the U.S. electoral system" [1].

The negative perception of the US electoral system has been reinforced by some research outcomes. According to the report of Kulke [16], "38% of Americans Lack Confidence in Election Fairness," while from the findings Lardieri [17], "Majority of Americans Don't Trust Elections, Poll Finds."

Using their quality management experience and exposure, the ASQ Election Excellence Group quickly identified "quality management" as one of the best ways to address the situation so as to restore some faith in US elections. In a similar vein, the author is quite confident that, if implemented with needed transparency and sincerity, the people of the African continent stand to gain from the deployment of electoral quality management system to achieve political stability. The advocacy of the ASQ Election Excellence Group for the adoption of an ISO/TS 54001- and ISO 9001-based election quality management system (E-QMS) in US jurisdictions portends a great future for political stability in democratic settings by boosting election integrity.

ISO Standards on Global 9-1-1 Calls

The role and importance of the International Organization for Standardization (ISO) in the achievement of quality outcomes for virtually every aspect of human endeavor, or activities, are again brought to the fore with the establishment of ISO/TS 54001:2019 [14] as a complementary QMS to ISO 9001:2015 [13] in this case.

ISO/TS 54001:2019 [14] Quality management systems – Particular requirements for the application of ISO 9001:2015 for electoral organizations at all levels of government.

According to the ISO, this international standard "specifies requirements for a quality management system where an electoral organization: needs to demonstrate its ability to manage elections by secret ballot, to provide reliable, transparent, free and fair results that comply with electoral requirements; within the established legal framework, aims to enhance the trust and confidence of citizens, candidates, political organizations, and other electoral interested parties through the effective implementation of electoral quality management system, including processes for continual improvement."

Whether in the developed economies or not, there are needs all over the globe to preserve and continuously improve on our democratic processes through the fostering of greater election integrity generally to enhance democratic processes and boost global political stability and sustainability.

References

1. ASQ. (2021, June). Electoral QMS needed to boost election integrity. *Quality Progress*, pp. 10–11. https://www.asq.org/quality-resources/research
2. Berry, L. L., & Carbone, L. P. (2007, September). Build loyalty through experience management. *Quality Progress*, ASQ, pp. 26–32.
3. Brown, S. P., & Lam, S. K. (2008). A meta-analysis of relationships linking employee satisfaction to customer responses. *Journal of Retailing, 84*(3), 243–255.
4. Crosby, P. B. (1979). *Quality is free*. McGraw-Hill.
5. Deming, W. E. (1986). *Out of the crisis*. MIT CAES.
6. Ericson, J. (2006). Lean inspection through supplier partnership. *Quality Progress*, pp. 36–41.
7. Feigenbaum, A. V. (1983). *Total quality control* (3rd ed.). McGraw-Hill.
8. Goodman, J., & Collier, C. D. (2007, March). Deliver great service by listening and adapting. *Quality Progress*, pp. 22–27.
9. Goodman, J., & Grimm, C. (2004). Eight factors for an effective voice of the customer process. *Competitive Advantage* (a publication of the Service Quality Division of ASQ), Summer, p. 7.
10. Ishikawa, K. (1985). *What's total quality control? The Japanese way*. Prentice-Hall.
11. ISO, International Quality Management Systems Standards, ISO 28000:2007, Specifications for Security Management Systems for the Supply Chain.
12. ISO, International Quality Management Systems Standards, ISO 9000:2015, Quality Management Systems – Fundamentals and Vocabulary. https://www.iso.org
13. ISO, International Quality Management Systems Standards, ISO 9001:2015, Quality Management Systems – Requirements.
14. ISO, ISO/TS 54001:2019 – Quality management systems – Particular requirements for the application of ISO 9001:2015 for electoral organizations at all levels of government.
15. Juran, J. M. (1989). *Juran on leadership for quality*. Free Press.
16. Kulke, S. (2020, December 23). 38% of Americans lack confidence in election fairness. *Northwestern Now*. https://tinyurl.com/3zskkh43
17. Lardieri, A. (2020, February 13). Majority of Americans don't trust elections, poll finds. *U.S. News*. https://tinyurl.com/k6hku8n7
18. Neuman, J., & Samuels, C. (1996). Supply chain integration: Vision or reality? *Supply Chain Management, 1*(2), 7.
19. Stevenson, W. J. (1999). *Production operations management* (6th ed.). Irwin McGraw-Hill.
20. Wruck, K. H., & Jensen, M. C. (1998). The two key principles behind TQM. *European Financial Management, 4*(3), 402.
21. Yee, R. W. Y., Yeung, A. C. L., & Cheng, T. C. E. (2008). The impact of employee satisfaction on quality and profitability in high contact service industries. *Journal of Operations Management, 26*(5), 651–668.

People Involvement 10

Categories of People Involvement

The people are generally the most important asset of any organization or business hence [8] the need for their involvement, engagement, and empowerment. People are therefore there to cultivate and sustain organizational quality culture. People involvement is in two stages, management leadership and employee levels. Organizational survival or sustainability depends largely on the commitment and interrelationship of both.

At the senior/management level, quality leadership and commitment must be glaringly seen and visible. In doing so it must provide necessary resources for organizational quality management. These include among others:

- Quality policy/objective
- Leading by visible examples by following organizational quality policies/objectives to the letter
- Establishing and fostering a no-blame engagement environment
- Budgeting for organizational and employee improvement programs such as quality training
- Commitment to implementing a suitable and adequate quality management system of choice
- Putting in place a sustainable mechanism for employee engagement, involvement, consultation, and participation
- Maintaining an effective communication system in place particularly focusing on organizational-wide key performance indicators (KPIs)

Both members of the management team and employees should actually see themselves as being on the same pedestal of organizational commitment. The role of management in employee engagement cannot be overemphasized.

T. A. Ibidapo, *From Industry 4.0 to Quality 4.0*, Management for Professionals,
https://doi.org/10.1007/978-3-031-04192-1_10

Engagement of People

Organizations need their employees to create value, which generally takes place in an organization when the people feel that they are engaged particularly, when they have the understanding of their individual contributions to create organizational value.

Drucker [13] taught us all that, "In a traditional workforce, the worker serves the system: In a knowledge workforce, the system serves the worker." All in all, is the additional fact too, that the foundation of any enterprise is its people. These jointly bring forward the importance and relevance of people engagement in organizational activities. The importance of people (intellectual capital) continues to grow, becoming a critical and major business resource [31]. This is further ascertained by Sopadang et al. [49], in their research studies which suggested that, "The employee is the core element [8] of Industry 4.0."

In order to appreciate this, it is very important to realize the critical value of employees performing the task, that they know and understand, most importantly, the essence of a quality problem reduction as well as the general need for continuous improvement of processes and performance. This thus makes it critical to involve employees in the major tasks of achieving quality products/services as explicitly emphasized in ISO 9001 international standards.

In the author's experience implementing the requirements of ISO 9001 QMS, every employee writes their work instructions themselves and works together within their respective units to participatively finalize quality policies and work procedures to achieve standard operating procedures. Employees engaged in establishing their own quality targets and action plans for corrective and preventive measures. Employees when allowed to formulate product/service improvement plans and discussing all quality problems and providing corrective and preventive measures actually send them to the rooftop of organizational commitment leading to emotional attachments to their work and workplace.

ISO 9001, beginning with the year 2000 revision, provided seven principles which include people engagement. The role of the ISO in promoting employee engagement goes beyond mere people engagement clauses of a standard but now the theme of a newly released ***ISO 10018:2020 –*** *Quality Management – Guidance for people engagement* [22].

This new standard provides general guidelines rooted deeply on the ways in which organizations can build, develop, cultivate, and nurture the kind of culture capable in promoting people engagement (ISO).

Looking back into the evolutionary history of quality management brings out the visionary perspectives of one of the world's "father of quality," W. Edwards Deming, in his 14 principles of effective management. These principles, when closely viewed, reveal the need then for improving employee engagement [11].

It is important therefore to highlight the fact that effective collaboration within an organizational setup results generally in more productivity especially when it comes to the application of technology.

Collective Responsibility

The involvement of people or people engagement is thus a key factor in quality management. An adage in Yoruba, a Nigerian language, says that *agbajo owo lafi nsoya* meaning that you can only beat your chest effectively with the collective responsibilities of the palm and fingers. So also are the objectives of implementing any quality management system/program/concept which can only be achieved through the collective responsibilities, efforts, and inputs of all the stakeholders involved in the running of an organization and its operational activities. By stakeholders, reference is being made to the following key players, in the activities and management of any business enterprise/organization:

- *Shareholders/promoters/financiers*
- *Management*
- *Employees*
- *Suppliers/supply chain*
- *Customers*

Shareholders as represented by the Board of Directors or other shareholder/stakeholder representatives may have to give approval and/or guidelines to management which in turn has to implement and provide the resources necessary for the implementation. The need for teamwork among the employees of an organization as well as among the management team; the management/employees; and suppliers/organization cannot be overemphasized.

Apart from ensuring, too, that all regulatory requirements are fulfilled, there is also the need for various enterprises and organizations to be mindful of their corporate social responsibilities (CSR) particularly to their immediate operational environment and the people therein. With the achievement of the appropriate teamwork, the implementation of the requirements of ISO 9000 or any other QMS or quality improvement concept/program would be made easier.

The following elements are some of the vital features that must be exhibited by an effective organizational team if the requirements of international standards or other QMS standards/programs must be adequately and effectively implemented to harvest the maximum benefits of conformance to their respective requirements:

- Conviction that the contribution of every individual member is very relevant towards achieving set-out goals and objectives.
- Each team member must be committed to the achievement of the common goals/objectives and that all everybody must move in the same direction.
- Each team member must see the goals as belonging to him (as an individual).
- There must be an effective communication among team members. All relevant information must be made available to all team members irrespective of his position in the organization. In order to achieve this, it may be necessary to provide adequate number of notice boards at appropriate locations within an organization to ensure that all employees have access to matters affecting the implementation

of the requirements of the standard. More effective still is the use of electronic communication systems to dissipate information.

- There must be mutual trust among team members. Members must be able to express themselves freely irrespective of the positions occupied by them in the organization.
- Team members must jointly agree on achieving "excellence" as goals of their respective responsibilities in the organization.
- Each team member must be ready to cooperate and make the necessary sacrifice at the interface of their activities with one another and between one department/unit and the other.
- All achievements of the team must be seen and recognized as that of every member of the team. Hence these achievements must not be seen or perceived as that of an individual (e.g., the leader or manager) the common pronoun must be "we."

Teamwork must therefore be seen as another vital tool for realizing the full benefits of the requirements of any standard such as the ISO 9000 series of international QMS standards or any other quality management program or concept. Hence the involvement of people is one of the eight quality management principles that form the basis for the QMS standards within the ISO 9000 series.

Quality Team Members

The composition of the team members implementing a QMS must be viewed basically from the entire sphere of a total quality system implementation to ensure that the aspirations of TQM objectives are achieved. When viewed from this perspective, it becomes obvious that members of the quality team extend generally beyond the organizations implementing a QMS or quality program. It includes the enlarged quality team players ranging from suppliers to quality regulatory bodies. These wider range team players who must similarly work together or cooperate with each other to achieve set-out quality objectives are listed below:

- Suppliers
- Entity or organization implementing a QMS
- Customers (or consumers)
- External quality auditing agencies/consultants
- Quality regulatory bodies/agencies

Each of these team players must carry out its responsibilities diligently, timely, and appropriately with the outmost integrity.

For example, there is the need for strong collaboration and strategic partnership alignment between various organizations and their suppliers particularly on planning and forecasting. This will go a long way to strengthen the supply chain and make it more reliable so as to completely remove any skepticism that may be plaguing the supply chain management.

Quality regulatory bodies/agencies, particularly in the emerging democracies of the world, and quality consultants (including auditing organizations) as well as quality associations/societies need to work together to back up organizations with aspirations to meet customer requirements through effective auditing and offer of training opportunities in all ramifications of quality and the entrenchment of the production of goods and services that meet customer requirements.

Quality Management Leadership

Defining Leadership

Various definitions have been given to the term leadership by different authors. Leadership is, as defined by the ASQ [5, 6],

> "The act of directing and managing a project, group, or an organization." Reitz [41] defined leadership as "a process of influencing a group towards the achievement of a goal," while in the words of Jacobs and Jacques [26], leadership is "a process of giving purpose (meaningful direction) to collective effort, and causing willing effort to be extended to achieve purpose."

Apart from the military, leadership is from the general perspective not the sole responsibility of people of higher hierarchical levels. Quality management leadership in an organization therefore calls for people of high interest in an organization's success and improvement. This thus makes it highly imperative therefore that employee involvement in leadership constitutes one of the most effective and fundamental ways for building organizational success.

There is the need to differentiate.

Leadership, which is defined in the context of a dynamic process and viewed as an influencing process, portrays some key behaviors which include among others:

- Relationship to a purpose (or goal) through vision, mission, objectives, core values, targets, or specifications whereby the vision of jointly accomplishing (or achieving) the common purpose/goal is shared by a group of people who are individually committed.
- Collectiveness about leadership and its pursuance by a group of people.
- Existence of decision discretion in the leadership process so as to ensure that the opportunity to exercise leadership can exist.

Hence leadership is a purpose-related role behavior which can be displayed by any member of a group of people or assembly of people or an organization, and it can be directed towards equals/peers, juniors/subordinates, or superiors/seniors. Leaders are therefore people who are willing to achieve set-out goals with all their energy, strength, and efforts and at the same time are committed individuals. Leadership therefore can be seen as a dynamic process, involving a group and a decision context, expressed through role behaviors [29].

It is obvious from the definition of leadership and the need to jointly attain the common goals/objectives that have united to bring to the fore the following critical points:

- Need for common direction and jointly moving towards it
- Team working in all ramifications
- People engagement and empowerment

The role of the entire workforce in the management of quality or in the implementation of a QMS in an organization under an effective leadership can therefore not be overemphasized. Even in situations where highly automated production systems are put in place and efficient process control flow are assured through integrated process control systems, the use of people still remains a critical aspect of achieving quality products and services. The amount of PC-based workstations deployed to the production floor notwithstanding the contributions of the workforce still remains critical for the:

- Attainment of quality products and services
- Implementation and maintenance of a QMS

It must, however, be mentioned at this stage that in addition to contributions of the workforce, the role of a top leader who must visibly support and enable the implementation of a QMS is a catalyst towards achieving quality. The leader must be the forerunner and torch bearer of quality within an organization. A quality leader must not just pay lip services to quality but lead the implementation process in the position of a role model and fulfilling the requirements of the saying "do what I do" and not just what I say. The open demonstration of a good and focused leadership in quality system implementation earns in return a good, devoted, and dedicated followership to achieve performance excellence. People actually make a difference.

Even when a good QMS has been successfully put in place or implemented, the human element still cannot be pushed aside. This is particularly so when it is considered that the implementation of a QMS actually needs some shifts in decision-making responsibilities.

Fundamental Principles of Quality Leadership

The fundamental principles of quality leadership are set where quality principles become "a basis for guiding, empowering and supporting the constant pursuit of excellence by employees throughout the organization" [15]. A quality management leader is therefore not just responsible for improving the quality management system but need to ensure, on a continuous basis, that every employee is engaged in executing all tasks with greater satisfaction. Capping it all with the prescription of Deming [11], a leader is not a judge; hence, he must see himself as a colleague and counsellor leading his people on a day-to-day basis while making room for himself to learn from them and with them [11].

Leadership Selection

Selecting a leader is a critical decision in quality management; hence, it has to be taken very seriously. In order to ensure the successful implementation of a QMS of your choice, a leader must be chosen at the various levels of the organization. Two critical issues here are:

- The leader must be fully supported by team members.
- The management must have full confidence in the leadership.

In choosing a leader for the implementation of your selected QMS, consideration should be given to some of the following characteristics and capabilities:

- Visionary
- Knowledge of process and product
- Technical skills
- Good listener
- Ability to motivate
- Teacher
- Humility
- Level of discipline
- Ability to organize and move people
- Humanitarian leaning or ability to care about people
- Temperament
- Objectivity, fairness, and sincerity
- Ability to strategize
- Ability to communicate effectively
- Ability to manage people to achieve results

Quality in Transition

Hence, quality is today obviously going through a leadership transitional phase. Similarly, quality is experiencing another transition from pre-COVID-19 pandemic quality management practices to that of post-COVID-19 pandemic-induced change management due to the newly evolved norms of the pandemic, such as remote working. There are no doubts therefore that quality is really in transition. The roll-out of Industry 4.0 no doubt represents another transitional phase of quality, the digital transition in line with Industry 4.0 initiatives to create Quality 4.0.

Making of Leadership in Quality

Leadership in quality by the *quality gurus* of the twentieth century was by individuals evolving through strong commitments into positions of leadership. The demise of the *quality gurus* therefore opened up the challenges of leadership in quality, just as it provides opportunities for quality bodies and their followership to reshape leadership of quality as dictated by the current business exigencies and in line with general leadership trends and knowledge demands.

Quality is going through an exceptional and unprecedented transitional stage – leadership, COVID-19 pandemic, and digital transitions. Quality presently exhibits strong potentials of a fourth transition, that of transforming quality to an undergraduate discipline by its own merit. All these jointly unite to accentuate how critical and necessary the making of leadership in the field of quality, has become in the 21st century.

The role of quality professionals and bodies as well as quality organizations in the making of leadership in the field of total quality management can therefore not be overemphasized. A very important factor here is the need to urgently facilitate and coordinate the qualitative transfer of total quality management knowledge/skills and relevant leadership experience to newly evolving leaders of quality across the globe. The roles of the world's quality leadership bodies such as the ASQ and others in Europe and all over the globe are of extreme importance to accomplish this. For example, the ASQ [6] has, in preparation for facing the challenges of leadership making in the future of quality, developed an "Emerging Quality Leaders Program" (EQLP, [5]).

Most importantly, too, are the various national awards of the ASQ, which help tremendously to motivate and inspire new cadres of quality leadership. Such awards include but are not limited to ASQ [4]:

- Philip B. Crosby Medal
- George D. Edwards Medal
- Armand V. Feigenbaum Medal
- Richard Freund-Donald Marquardt Medal
- Hromi Medal
- Spencer Hutchens Jr. Medal
- Kaoru Ishikawa Medal
- E. Jack Lancaster Medal
- Walter Shewhart Medal

The beauty of these highly motivational national quality awards and the most impactful of the opportunities they offer to quality leadership potentials is the memory of those quality gurus who used their experiences and working life to develop quality to the level that it is today. As recipients of these awards, they will be able to easily recognize that there is reward in quality leadership.

Leadership/Followership Flow

One of the most critical issues in the interrelationship between a leader and the followership is the need for the two parties to accept that they:

- Are moving in the same direction
- Share the same vision and mission
- Are both working to achieve the same goals, targets, and objectives
- Are all working for the same purpose
- Jointly bear the outcome (good or bad) of their enterprise

The acceptance of the joint purpose will in turn lead to the personal willingness of each individual member of the team to be involved in pursuing the set-out goal using all their time, intellect, energy, and all other resources available to them. The process of leadership attaches people to particular aims and purposes/goals; hence, people involvement requires that people must have to cooperate and communicate with each other. This is a demonstration of the acceptance of their common purpose.

Handling People

The success of an organization could easily be achieved by the leadership, cooperation among members of staff, teamwork, and the level of empowerment of its workforce. You cannot, however, think of empowerment, cooperation, or teamwork without meeting the fundamental needs for handling your workers. Basic among these needs include the following:

- Genuinely give respect and honor to every worker as a human being.
- Showing of heartfelt concern to your employees.
- Exhibiting high regards for their individual self esteem
- Show commitment to every single employee.
- Recognition of every employee as a critical part of the organizational team and its achievements.
- Giving recognition and acknowledgment to every employee in terms of their skills, ideas, personality, and any other contribution they have made to an organization. In most organizations in the less developed economies of the world, teamwork is usually proclaimed mainly at the stage of achieving a task. This situation is then usually reverted no sooner than the task has been achieved.
- Acknowledgment of their efforts and contribution.
- Provide relatively good reward [12].
- Share feedback and other necessary information with employees irrespective of its status, that is, corrective, negative, or positive.

The management of people with attention paid to these fundamental issues and other related matters would likely help in bringing out the best in your employees [17] who actually are the driving forces behind the success of the quality of your products and/or services.

The observation of these fundamental needs coupled with development opportunities and encouragement offered to employees under honest, impartial, and objective decision-makers or management would likely help greatly to develop the needed team players capable of producing employees that would willingly assume the needed decision-making responsibilities, hence very good leadership positions.

Skills acquisition is an essential and critical part of employee empowerment and promotion of the QMS to achieve products and services that represent customer values and meet customer needs, requirements, and specifications; hence, it has to be given the necessary attention at all levels and cadre of work. Apart from skills, the people also need vision, incentives, resources, and an action plan.

Human Resources Practices

Your human resources practices which include recruitment, training, evaluation, promotion, counseling, compensation, and disciplinary action are very important for the success, firstly, of your quality management system and in the overall organizational performance indices. It is therefore critical for organizations to generally appreciate the important roles of human resources for their sustainability, adaptability, agility, and innovation, which are key requirements for organizational performance in the years ahead. This will help to ensure on a general basis that:

- The most qualified people are recruited.
- A training and development policy is put in place and implemented.
- Relevant members of staff are given access to training so that they can perform their jobs well especially in today's constantly evolving global market environment.

Job Competency and Training

The implementation of any QMS actually begins with the competency (i.e., the knowledge, skills, and behavior needed to perform tasks) of your human resources. There is therefore the need to establish the level of competency needed for particular jobs and to ensure too that the skills, knowledge, and behavior for each level of competency are specified. It follows from here therefore that a development process for staff must be put in place to ensure that they can meet job expectations. This thus brings us to the critical role of training and its roles in a quality management system. Training is a critical aspect in the quality management system of any organization irrespective of its size and status. Skills acquisition is generally facilitated through effective training. Hence training must be given its due recognition at all stages of quality management spreading across the under-listed areas:

- QMS training
- Skills acquisition and improvement of the competency of the workforce
- Knowledge acquisition about process, process management, and process improvement
- Know-how of new technologies and technological update
- Measurements and equipment calibration
- Process control
- Ability to operate new software, machines, and equipment
- Leadership and leadership improvement
- Team working and creation of a sense of teamwork
- Improvement in communications skills
- Computer training
- Project management

Technological Knowledge Update

Quality organizations must put themselves in positions that they can easily recognize the impact of technological changes on the development of their businesses. It is particularly important here, too, that we are sensitive to the ways such changes affect our employees. It is worthwhile to note here that technological changes generally evoke two types of emotions in the workforce:

- Excitement
- Fear (or technophobia)

The only ways to overcome such fears which if not arrested in time may result to a loss of confidence by the workers even in themselves are to adequately plan and execute suitable and necessary trainings for all affected employees before the introduction of a new technology or processing methodology. By doing this, the workforce would have been prepared to succeed. Appropriate consideration for this human element which is the most critical part of our continual improvement equation is highly essential to the success of any organization. Among other things, training serves to ensure that our employees/teams are prepared to:

- Deal with the daily increasing demands and challenges of the highly competitive global market to accomplish their tasks.
- Adequately handle the constant technological changes in tools, equipment, work environment, manufacturing, and/or servicing methods.

Training, a part of the responsibilities of management, should actually be seen and viewed primarily as a long-term benefit to organizations while aiding the success of the affected employee. In order to fully reap the long-term benefits of training from your employees,' situations in your environment may demand that, trained employees are put under company bond for a specified period of time, with considerations for factors such as total investment, easy availability of replacement personnel, ease of retraining new staff, nature of technology, etc.

People Empowerment

Sharing Responsibilities

Empowerment can, according to Miscikowski and Stein [35], be defined as:

> The shifting of decision- making responsibility downward within an organization from the management staff to the factory or shop floor level.

Here making decisions within an organization becomes more widely spread among the generality of the workforce vertically than just among the management staff or a few favored members of staff.

Spreading or shifting decision responsibility across an organization vertically down the organization has, from the experience of the author, more advantage than the concentration of authority in the hands of only one or a few members of staff.

An example here is the situation in a multimillion-dollar glass packaging industry in Nigeria where the Chief Executive Officer (CEO)/Managing Director (MD) overzealously shifted the factory operational and quality decision-making responsibilities, respectively, from the factory General Manager (with his management team) and the quality management representative (QMR) to a non-team player technical staff who up till that time was actually reporting to the General Manager. This is in spite of the fact that this decision is contrary to the tenets of ISO 9000 QMS standards which was implemented shortly before then by the author and his quality management team with the commitment, approval, and strong support of the same CEO/MD.

There was an appreciable decrease in quality communication between the QMR and the other key top management staff. Quality review meetings were no more regular. Some ISO 9000 QMS maintenance assignments were missed. What ensued thereafter is left for your imagination.

ISO 9000 standard requirements which had been a culture within the organization since its implementation were abandoned in terms of most controls and approvals as he now de-empowered virtually all the other management staff and supervisors to make himself the "super star manager" and the only staff with the sole authority to approve:

- Purchases
- Store requisitions
- Supplied items
- Production planning
- Finished products
- Delivery

- Staff promotion
- Staff recruitment
- Deployment of staff

This led to a state of division and confusion in the factory as virtually all decisions related to glass bottle production operations and other production management and product delivery issues had to be delayed waiting for the attention of the "super star manager." On the other hand, he too was running from post to pillar to be able to cope with his newly self-acquired "super human" status at the glass factory.

Day in, day out, there was increased delay in production and allied activities due to delays in decision-making by the one-man management staff. Some of the major quality problems encountered within the organization were as follows:

- Deliveries to customers were delayed.
- Machine downtime for the annealing process was running much below the projected time.
- The customers were finding discrepancies in the products they received.
- Production goals were falling short of target.
- There was a drop in production efficiency from an average of about 82% to below 50%.
- Wastages increased by about 33% which means that about a third of the products are recycled as culets.
- Staff supervision was no more effective as only a few people are favored by the "super star manager."
- Cooperation among the workforce broke down completely as only favored members of the workforce got the attention of the one-man management.
- The team spirit for which the company was known for during and after the implementation of the ISO 9000 international QMS standards completely disappeared as he proclaimed in most cases that every good result was his personal achievement while other people outside his friendship circle were responsible for bad results.
- There was a complete breakdown of communication.

This led to a state of confusion which took over the management of the factory as the implementation of the ISO 9000 QMS standard requirements was dethroned and quality issues thrown to the dogs. The high degree of empowerment of the workforce and the self-supervision mechanism achieved during the implementation of ISO 9000 QMS were almost completely lost to the confusion that ensued.

The entire situation took its toll on the activities of the factory within that year and in the subsequent year. Meeting the requirements of the numerous customers became an uphill and difficult task to achieve. Customer requirements and specifications could no more be met due to a drop in productivity from an average of about 80–84% to 45–55%, and product rejects (or wastages) increased by about 33%, while there was a dramatic drop in sales.

In the following year, there was a dramatic drop in the turnover and operational profit vis-à-vis financial performance of the glass company. This eventually led to the subsequent disengagement of the CEO/MD and his "super" manager to restore sanity to the company which restructuring began with a new management team that had to face some of the consequences and impacts of the management misadventure of the overzealous CEO/MD.

The company lost a major customer which, as a result of its dissatisfaction, decided to patronize other glass bottle manufacturers. Other customers seized the opportunity and that of the hostile manufacturing environment in the country (multiple taxation by all three arms of government (i.e., federal, state, and local)), bad roads (more of trenches than roads), very poor public supply of energy, lack of water, lawlessness, astronomic increase in fuel (i.e., AGO, DPK, Gasoline, etc.), prices, unreasonable increase of taxes, unstable and frequently changing tariff, unstable polity, etc. to import glass bottles from Asia.

The empowerment of the workforce to take some critical decisions related to his individual work such as that of initiating corrective actions without instant recourse to the Quality Assurance Manager (QAM) or a superior officer therefore represents a major leap in the maintenance and sustenance of the QMS. The empowerment process must however put individual staff capability into consideration so as to ensure that they are able to take the right decisions at the right time. For example, machine operators can be trained to be able to take some critical corrective actions without having to wait for the foreman or supervisor which would have slowed down his productivity and responsiveness. The results of people empowerment in quality have, from the experience of the author, more than proved the fact that it is the engagement and involvement of people and their empowerment that actually move quality. Hence, one can categorically say that both employee engagement coupled with effective and purposeful leadership are key factors in any result- or performance-based quality system management.

Workforce Empowerment

Empowerment can generally be said to be an act of power sharing or spreading of responsibility and authority among employees so as to be able to act on behalf of an organization.

One of the most important routes for the achievement of any QMS and its effective maintenance is the empowerment of the workforce. The empowerment of the workforce actually begins generally with training and skills acquisition, particularly in relationship to the acquisition of knowledge in operational or processing data (i.e., statistical analysis and analytical results). Hence each organization needs to maintain a certain level of widespread operational data which can easily be captured, interpreted, and displayed for the use of relevant workforce or operators in taking crucial quality decisions whenever necessary. Hence operational data must, for the purposes of effectiveness, be documented and distributed to all relevant members of the workforce. If properly interpreted operators could easily be trained to use the operational data interpretation for taking necessary actions for making corrective actions whenever required without recourse to the supervisor or manager.

Operational knowledge which can be acquired from manuals, documents, and experience comprises mainly of tactics, theories, and concepts and is more abstract than operational data; hence, they cannot easily be captured through the use of common analytical tools for display and use by the workforce (i.e., operators). Operational knowledge is however very vital and critical for effective decision-making in the successful operation of a QMS. Hence most of the quality systems in operation today emphasize this, while attention is focused on the acquisition of such knowledge by the workforce.

A combination of operational knowledge and operational data with adequate skills for interpretation is therefore part of the adequate tools necessary for the empowerment of the workforce. The implementation of knowledge-based systems (e.g., software that is capable of delivering both operational data and knowledge to users) which are designed to capture and make operational knowledge available as and when needed is also of good value in empowering the workforce. Knowledge-based systems include document management systems, neural networks, or case-based reasoning systems though only rule-based expert systems deliver explicit knowledge [37].

In order to effectively provide the necessary information to empower the workforce, organizations can easily introduce PC-based work stations to provide knowledge-based operational information to various cadres of staff to enable them initiate and take corrective action decisions independently without recourse to management staff. Knowledge-based systems on a general basis include neural networks and document management systems.

Expert systems [28] can similarly be employed as tools to empower the workforce as they can be applied in the following areas of production to support and aid the implementation of any QMS.

- Carrying out the gap (know key steps to bridge the gap between current state and desired state) analysis in the implementation of a QMS standard, such as ISO 9001
- Designing of products and services
- Production of products and services
- Product and service delivery
- Logistics application for the management of supplier performance [14]
- Management of other production and service-related issues

The involvement of people in QMS implementation is therefore desirable irrespective of the nature and type of QMS involved. A major way to achieve this is through the empowerment of all categories of the workforce. People empowerment will, in turn, lead to operational empowerment. This can be realized by an organization through:

- Investment in the training and skills acquisition processes on a continual basis
- Investment in the procurement and deployment of knowledge-based and expert systems including desktop- and web-based facilities to provide the needed operational knowledge

The engagement of employees in finding solutions to customer problems after they have been given adequate tools to achieve this is a motivating factor which may enable the employees to make customer focus an integral part of their activities. Giving authority to or empowering the employees to solve customer problems may give them not just a sense of fulfillment but also that of employee satisfaction which may in turn drive productivity. Productivity in a chain-like reaction has the capability to give birth to value which in turn drives customer satisfaction which subsequently leads to customer loyalty to achieve profitability and growth.

Magnet Status and Employee Engagement

Quality and Relying on People

Directly or indirectly, the Magnet concept, which originated as an outcome of a study to investigate nursing shortages and high turnover rates in US hospitals, has ended up to assume the values of quality role modeling structure for people motivation and people empowerment [1, 43].

People and their involvement are perhaps the most conspicuous aspects of any quality management system or concept, tools, principles, and their application. People therefore remain on a general basis, the nucleus of quality management, in virtually all aspects and ramifications of its use and application, irrespective of the areas of use.

The ISO in IO 9001:2015 glaringly brought to the fore the importance and criticality of people to all aspects of the implementation of the requirements of this international standard. ISO 9001:2015 in its appreciation of people role in quality actually provides high levels of requirements on people. Clause 6.2 of ISO 9001:2008 [25] and ISO 9001:2015 (Clauses 7.1.2.; 7.1.6.; 7.2; 7.3; and 7.4., [24]) adequately spell out the need to determine and provide the people that are required for the QMS and the operational activities and processes of an organization. People's roles in ISO 9001:2015 are highlighted in terms of their knowledge about the organization, competency on the works executed, awareness about organizational quality policy and objectives among others, and the need for people's proactive approach to organizational communications strategy. It goes to say that people must be engaged, motivated, and empowered to be able to fully meet organizational quality management requirements of their employees. People engagement is thus promoted by ISO QMS international standards.

Employee Engagement

Employee engagement is, from the definition of Canada Human Resources Centre [9], "the level of commitment an employee has towards the organization." They went further to identify the primary behaviors of engaged employees as:

- Speaking positively about the organization to coworkers, potential employees, and customers
- Having a strong desire to be a member of the organization
- Exerting extra effort to contribute to the organization's success

Wikipedia similarly defines an engaged employee as one who is fully absorbed by and enthusiastic about their work also taking positive actions in furtherance of the organization's reputation and interests.

Employee engagement is a very crucial aspect of an organization's success which is the main reason why organizations need to invest in their workforces [2]. Keeping employees happy generally triggers their engagement and passion for the work. These, in turn, elevate them to a different level of thinking about the job, making them emotionally connected to their work and responsibilities. This subsequently leads to improved process output quality, to create in an environment of sustainable quality culture.

The author used this approach of employee engagement, to quickly root out the previous culture of unengaged employees always ready to embark on disruptive union activities, stealing of company assets and other acts of sabotage to frustrate and extract money from the previous management team. As the new CEO of a bottle crown manufacturing company and a toughened glass processing plant (Leventis Group) in Nigeria, employees showing interests in their jobs were identified and engaged. It worked like magic. However, to achieve this goal, a lot of worker-information activities were immediately deployed, to know my new work environment from the perspectives of the employees. The "outcomes" resulted in getting the true opinion of every 1 of the 210 workforces. These varied opinions were handled on the openly expressed basis that every employee is seen and viewed on the platform of equal relevance to the organization. Some of the measures taken include among others the following:

- Employee pulse survey.
- Detailed employee satisfaction survey.
- Every employee's anonymous suggestion carried out within a specified time frame for moving the company forward. This was collated personally by the author to know every employee including the supervisors.
- Get to know each employee interactive face-to-face meetings to exchange ideas.
- Productivity feedback based on individual units/processes and overall factory performance.

The outcomes were not merely a book of revelations about how the quality of work relationships and values of the company interact with each other, to impact the work outcomes, but served largely as the foundation of the author's quality management successes and the enormous and dramatic performance improvement achieved by the organization when compared with the era prior to the new era of the author's leadership. Some of the author's experiences of the outcomes are shared with you as listed below:

- Identification and appreciation of employees' personal resources and their exploits to engage them with the company.
- Detection of employee gang-up-ism and the opportunity to eradicate the gang of employees involved in company assets looting undetected.
- Recognition and appreciation of employee's positive contributions and immense importance to company sustainability and growth to create awareness about individual employee contributions and potentials to grow with the company. This factor alone led to the employee's perceptions of how important their jobs are, to create unprecedented levels of loyalty and commitment. Engagement was discovered here to have led to loyalty and "extreme" commitment of employee to the organization.
- With the introduction of individual work instruction and documentation of work procedures, employees' expectations were no more beclouded in the ego of supervisors but clear and "visible."
- The identification of the unfortunate fact that, supervisors inclusive, the last time an employee in the company went outside of the factory premises to mingle with other people, or on interactive training, or participatory classroom knowledge exposure was 16 years. Hence, the employees had the least opportunities and capabilities to make any plant improvement moves, suggestions or contributions whatsoever. Their understanding of the need for change was buried in the preservation of their jobs by any means possible. Change, though looming, was in the perception of every worker a step closer to their exits. This battle against change was dramatically won by the author through massive training opportunities – in-house and external – and the employee-involved competency assessment education which led to the peaceful reduction of total staff from 210 to about 110 within 6 months, to achieve an unprecedented performance improvement in the history of the organization, 250%.
- Regular departmental meetings, sectional meetings, effective feedback systems, and inclusive management practices did not only improved but also strengthened to a great extent employees' relationship with peers, supervisors, and subordinates alike.

The author observed, too, that engaged employees often concentrate more on their jobs than is usually the case, to ensure problems are appropriately solved as they surface, to the extent of putting in performances that exceed expectations while engaging in self-supervision. The self-supervisory aspect is amazing and highly rewarding. The only exception here is perhaps in the experience of the author being accused of plotting to take over a business he managed for his brother-in-law because of his "extreme engagement." This is however an extreme case which in no way negates the values of an engaged employee. In fact, an engaged employee can be measured in the extent of regarding what (s)he is doing as her/his own.

This observed trend is further affirmed by Mishra and Delgado [36] that, "Engaged employees go beyond what simply is required for the job and expend energy to solve problems, delight customers and reach organizational goals. And the best part is they do it because they want to."

This brings out the fact that employee engagement process must be led by the very top management hierarchy, who has a full understanding that employee engagement is of extreme relevance and importance in achieving planned business results and performance improvement. The importance of employee engagement to organizational quality management is widely reported in the literature.

Quotes from Richard Branson says it all, "Clients do not come first. Employees come first. You take care of your employees they will take care of the clients." In his deduction of three major factors influencing organizational performance measurements, Dornbrook, [12] claimed that, according to Jack Welch that, "There are only three measurements that tell you nearly everything you need to know about your organization's performance: employee engagement, customer satisfaction and cash flow."

To crown it all is the correlation of quality with employee engagement by Mishra and Delgado [36] in, "Furthermore, the relationship between quality and employee engagement is highly correlated, and the quality of any service or product depends greatly on how engaged employees are. Creating an emotional connection to the work is at the heart of taking employees from simply being satisfied to being engaged." It goes to say too that people are undoubtedly the most important asset of an organization. From the words of Mishra and Delgado [36], "Employee engagement is key to a strong sustainable culture of quality."

In the words of Rosenblatt and Peters [44], engaged employees are so effective that they could be readily seen and viewed as the most effective evangelists and ambassadors of organizational brand hence the need for nurturing employee engagement. However, if these religious and diplomatic accolades about engaged employees are not convincing enough, the reported affirmation of Mishra and Delgado [36] that "Research shows that engaged employees return 120% of their salary in value to the organization" must more than convince you to always give "Power to your people to add strength to your quality program."

Magnet Status and Employee Engagement

The focus of the ANCC's Magnet Recognition Program (MRP) on demonstrating "Nursing Excellence" no doubt in hospitals must definitely demonstrate and represent a different but extraordinary commitment to achieving an exemplarily excellent employee engagement. The origin of the concept of the Magnet hospital, from a study carried out by the American Academy of Nursing, to investigate *nursing shortages* and *high turnover* in American hospitals tells it all (ANCC). The

"Magnetic forces" found to be exhibited by some hospitals during the study distinctly separated or, in comparative terms, identified about 41 hospitals characterized by their greater success rates (or when viewed in terms of nurses being employees, *nurses' engagement*) in three key areas of:

- The hiring of nurses
- Retention of the services of nurses
- Job satisfaction of nurses

These 41 hospitals caught the attention of the researchers who were perhaps immediately attracted, like a magnet, to those outstanding fourteen (14) common characteristic features separating or filtering them out of the great lots of hospitals in the USA. These 14 organizational attractive "forces of magnetism" represent these hospitals generally as embodiments of "nursing excellence."

The ANCC consequently used the knowledge and experience of the research outcomes of the American Academy of Nursing (AAN) to *innovate* what is known today as the Magnet Recognition Program (MRP), in recognition and certification of healthcare organizations or systems that demonstrate "Nursing Excellence" [42, 43]. Currently, the MRP, which was updated in 2008, is reportedly structured to encompass five (5) critical or essential components inherent in the original model's 14 strengths as indicated below:

- Transformational leadership
- Structural empowerment
- Exemplary professional practice
- New knowledge, innovation, and improvements
- Empirical quality results

For any hospital or healthcare system to acquire the "Magnet status," it is highly imperative to meet the stipulated eligibility requirements provided by the MRP. Findings in the literature [27, 30, 32, 50, 51] generally associate and link Magnet hospitals with the following common achievement levels:

- High-quality care
- High nurse retention
- Better work environment
- Higher nursing job satisfaction
- Less burnout
- Decreased intent to leave
- Less nurse turnover
- Lower hospital mortality
- Lower patient-fall rates
- Greater patient or customer satisfaction

The evidence for the impact of Magnet recognition on nurses and patients [39] and the healthcare organizations [46] are accordingly identifiable in the literature.

This is not to say, however, that there are no literature reports proving the Magnet status to be otherwise or comparative with non-Magnet status, even though they may be very few. While Goode et al. [20] were reported by Rodriguez-Garcia et al. [42, 43] as the only one reporting worse outcomes in Magnet facilities, Clement-O'Brien et al. [10] and McLaughlin and Fetzer [34] reported only slight or no comparative differences.

In a more comprehensive and systematic review to analyze current evidence regarding the impact of Magnet status on nursing professionals, patients, and healthcare organizations, Rodriguez-Garcia et al. [43] considered two issues: first, a comparison of Magnet with non-Magnet hospitals and, second, to find out whether Magnet hospitals show different outcomes with regard to nurses, patients, and healthcare organizations.

Their findings showed generally that on the overall, Magnet hospitals achieved better nursing, patient, and organizational outcomes, as well as better nursing work environments, than non-Magnet hospitals.

Without any doubts whatsoever, evidence available in the literature overwhelmingly address the role of the Magnet status in defining the quality of hospitals with Magnet status particularly in terms of better:

- Nursing (care)
- Patient (care)
- Organizational outcomes
- Nursing work environments

Quality in the healthcare system is defined by far numerous criteria or factors than in any other single entity or organization in the service of humanity. This is mainly because healthcare generally operates in a very complex, dynamic, always changing environment where decisions often depend to a large extent on interdepartmental collaboration [16].

The achievement of the Magnet status, as reflected generally in the literature, in engaging hospital nursing employees is an outstanding result that glaringly demonstrates the beneficial outcomes of employee engagement.

The Magnet status is therefore not just worthy of emulation by other organizations in the healthcare sector and beyond but also deserves more focus and greater attention from the academia and the research world. It is a fertile area that commands multidimensionally diverse research interests. For example, it will be interesting to know the impact of Magnet status on readmission rates, an important area of measuring the actual quality of hospital care [45].

Employee engagement is an enormous part of any organizational quality culture. It must therefore be identified as a criterion to promote the healthcare industry quality management system, which makes highly imperative to openly view and pursue it as such. There are no doubts, too, that the Magnet status program should always be kept on the track of continual improvement without complacency until the full realization of its potentials to outstandingly and excellently facilitate the quality of hospital patient care across the globe.

While employee engagement as initiated and pursued by the ANCC is poised to advance the quality of nursing care worldwide through continual improvement measures, other areas of the healthcare industry, such as the doctors, pharmaceutical employees, technical support employees, etc., should quickly understudy this enviable quality management program, with the intent of engaging all of their employees as a great stride to improve the overall quality of our hospitals. It is viewed too by the author as the universal panacea for professional burnouts in the healthcare industry and far beyond.

The cultivation of the culture of the Magnet status across hospital professional cadres of employees is not only for the admiration of hospital customers/patients and mankind as a wholebut also in the interest of hospitals; in terms of meeting patient and stakeholders' SNEaRs, employee satisfaction, sustainability, adaptive capacity, and growth. Sustainability is in the present disruptive environment that we all live in of extreme relevance.

The proliferation of quality principles, tools, and techniques in hospitals all over the world is definitely going to grow in the twenty-first century. Hence hospitals across the planet earth may have to embrace the Magnet status program and other quality improvement standards, systems, and other opportunities to improve healthcare on the global basis. Quality tools and professional are available in abundance to maintain quality management dynamism; hence, complacency must not be allowed to set in.

COVID-19 Pandemic Quality Management Leadership

The uncertainties which envelop the advent of the COVID-19 pandemic call for cooperation among employees and people of the communities and society at large. We in the USA suffered severely in 2020, as a result of the general lack of full cooperation and the incoherently and inadequately coordinated handling of the pandemic among the executive arm of the government, the states, and the scientific world.

Scientists had to expediently engage themselves in the most obvious quality management approach. They accomplished this through urgently gathering needed information about the novel coronavirus through extensive research activities and strong interconnectivity, so as to facilitate the understanding of the biology and human impacts of this novel coronavirus, in all ramifications – its behavior, characteristic features, impact on people, vaccination against the virus, and hundreds of others – while at the same time establishing and consolidating the testing for its detection.

Various organizational management team members, especially in the healthcare systems, quickly took the deployment of quality management tools and methods [47, 52] to protect society, people, and organizations' resources and ensure business continuity and recovery (ISO 22301:2019 [23]). For example, the constraint management method or theory of constraint (TOC) [21] was used in the healthcare systems sector of the economy to determine the "most constricting links holding back the treatment of more people" when hospitals' intensive care unit (ICU) capacities were overwhelmingly outstretched "by an exponentially massive caseload of COVID-19 patients, resulting in some patients being turned away or not receiving proper care" [48].

COVID-19 Pandemic Impact

Adaptability

The unexpected and unplanned challenges witnessed by the people of the global community during the COVID-19 pandemic are unprecedented in the recent history of quality from the mid-twentieth century to the twenty-first century. Both employer and employees have been affected in various ways, in their respective roles to their organization. Workplaces changed, the way people work was fundamentally impacted, and nearly everyone has been affected in one way or the other. Quality approaches to confront the pandemic such as social distancing, wearing facial masks/coverings, working from home, and lately inoculations resulted into new norms for all stakeholders – local communities, government officials, customers, employees, and the society at large. The COVID-19 pandemic has actually succeeded in disrupting businesses and the work of quality management professionals, especially when we think of the workplace, travel restrictions, and the way they impact quality auditors, supplier management, and many other issues [48]. Some small and retail businesses had to close down.

The lockdown restrictions of the COVID-19 pandemic may, on a general basis, have changed some of the quality practices in human lives, vis-à-vis work culture on a semi-permanent to permanent bases. This is particularly so, since according to Whitacre [53], "The quality "person" is physical, emotional, mental, and spiritual." And if these do not match, we may be unable to deliver quality work output. Hence, there is the need to appreciate the fact that applying quality tools to our work and personal lives can help us all in making things manageable after the defeat of the pandemic, and in any subsequent unforeseen disruptive situations.

It is interesting to note from the work of Lindborg that, "The COVID-19 pandemic has forced many people to work virtually from home, and it also has led to an unanticipated outcome – improved productivity" [33]. This is further ascertained too by Gelles [19] in his reported survey by the Deutsche Bank, which claimed that, "on average, workers in the United States are more productive today than before the pandemic." Leapfrogging to accept this conclusion as a new post-COVID-19 norm may be highly deceitful, as it may be undermining the quality culture of team working and the collective abilities to innovate.

The roles of organizations and their leadership, post-COVID-19 era, are all embracing, especially due to the manner of the uncertainties created by the pandemic, particularly to the supply chain systems. The fragile nature of the supply chain system makes it highly susceptible to any nature of disruptive environment full of uncertainties. Learning from the experience of an upended world, due to the impact of the pandemic therefore, requires that organizations "should embrace the uncertainty as part of their operations model, since agility and the ability to adapt quickly will be far more important than sticking to a plan" [7].

In addition is the fact too that digging deeper into digital technologies has been frequently acknowledged in the literature as a way to overcome the challenges of unplanned disruption. There have also been renewed interests to urgently embrace automation and the use of robotics in mitigating against the COVID-19 disruptive environment resulting from the restrictions on the movement of people and their impact on the supply chain. The advantages here are due to the fact that, "Robots work tirelessly across shifts and can complete certain tasks faster and more accurately than humans, while not requiring raises or benefits" [38].

Organizations are, in this respect, faced with the challenges of employees' reskilling or upskilling in areas such as data analytics, digital technologies, artificial intelligence, machine learning, robotics, etc. The resultant impact of any ensuing economic recession emanating from the impact of the COVID-19 pandemic will be felt for sometimes to come not only by both employers and employees but also by the immediate community and global communities at large. While some sectors experienced declining wages, a few others saw some growth [40].

Industry 4.0, People, and Productivity Gap

While Industry 4.0 is principled on organizational competitiveness, it is doing so discriminately and segregationally right from the conceptual stages of this marvelous initiative at the German Research Center for Artificial Intelligence (DFKI, "Deutsches Forschungszentrum für Künstliche Intelligenz") to its delivery at the Hannover Messe Halle, in 2011. This is perhaps most vividly reflected, directly or indirectly, in the ASQ's Quality Progress (QP) Report in its, "Workplace - Bridging the Productivity Gap" [3].

The 12 deadly horrifying months of the 2020 COVID-19 pandemic distinctively revealed the two faces of organizational reality in how "many organizations have accelerated efforts around digital transformation to stay in business and keep pace with competitors" while "some are able to capitalize on the latest technology to collaborate effectively and efficiently, becoming more productive." These two faces jointly unite to create the third face of real-life organizational experience.

This face is no other than that of organizations that neither have the technology nor investment capability! Since competitiveness is not just a universal desire of all organizations but also a driving force needed to keep organizations in business, organizations that have neither the technology nor investment potentials are ab initio automatically excluded from implementing the initiatives of Industry 4.0. This is the corporate gap, inherent in the ideas of Industry 4.0 initiatives. This is not to say, however, that Industry 4.0 initiatives are not achievable but that they are not meant for every organization but those with the resources and the need for higher productivity and competitive challenges. This is the corporate gap inculcated in the initiative ab initio. The other obvious gap that may likely spring up in Industry 4.0 initiatives is that of the skills vacuum for the development of adequate skills to cope with the evolving digital challenges as technology advances, to create organizations' greatest assets, for sustainable future and continued business growth and improvement.

It is very obvious from the above that the future of business success will likely be influenced by the level of organizational ability to collaborate and/or invest in relevant technological advances in a catch-up process.

Corporate Productivity Gap

One of the greatest assets deployed by the author in turning around the fortunes of one of the organizations quality-managed by him in a heavily unionized setting of about 40% productivity was that of the *active engagement and inspiration of the employees* to immediately double productivity and exceed set business goals within 1 year.

Deploying the continuous improvement tool, "theory of constraints" (TOC) helped to quickly identify the weakest link in the manufacturing system of the factory [21]. A quick survey of the credentials of all employees gave a general reflection of a high number of employees in dire need of training and reeducation. With 210 employees, the objective was to reduce the number of employees to 110 without the corrosive reactions of the union members, as soon as possible (ASAP).

We immediately set up a productivity improvement team (PIT), with members from across various factory units charged with the responsibilities of writing individual work instructions (WI) and standard operation procedures (SOPs) and setting daily (24-hourly) departmental productivity goals, monitored by individual employees with the proviso that each employee training needs be exactly identified and documented with the consent and agreement of the concerned employee.

The quality team, in its findings, identified and recommended over 110 employees for necessary training to be able to effectively carry out their responsibilities in line with their new WIs and SOPs. The author immediately made provision for their training with the option to immediately go on retirement with full benefits to anyone that may want to.

The outcome was the biggest surprise I ever experienced in my working career. Ninety employees immediately opted for retirement, and 20 opted to be trained, while other interested employees were offered in-house training opportunities to facilitate their productivity in an environment of employee participation, inspiration, and engagement.

With 120 employees achieving and superseding the usual productivity level of 210 employees, the previously identified impossible task was so easily accomplished, without the factory being burnt down by the union members.

The individual "thank you" cards from enthusiastic employees and expression of "gratitude and appreciation" received from the impacted employees made nonsense of the union banner, accusing me of turning the factory into an "institution of learning."

Turning the factory performance around in such a short time, despite top management fear of unionized reactions, is as a result of employee engagement and inspiration. This was the best way to bridge this *corporate productivity gap* (CPG), encapsulated in 120 employees accomplishing and surpassing the productivity record of 210 employees.

In its recent research reports, the Harvard Business Review actually uncovered the concept of "corporate productivity gap." While stressing the productive time benefits of 5 to 8%, for companies collaborating effectively during the lockdowns and disruptive environment of the COVID-19 pandemic, the researchers identified organizations with productivity reduction of between 3% and 6%, or even higher, "due to inefficient collaboration, wasteful ways of working and overall decline in employee engagement" [18]. In elaborating the relevance of employee engagement to achieve relatively higher productivity, Garton and Mankins [17]) identified three factors – *time*, *talent*, and *energy* – in relationship to the relative productivity of large organizations. How these three key factors impact productivity is explained accordingly as follows:

- "Time" committed by each employee to productive work on a daily basis, without being distracted by excessive e-communications, unnecessary meetings, and other bureaucratic procedures and processes
- "Talent" inherent in each worker that can be brought to use in their respective jobs and the ways by which organizations tap into their best talents in terms of deployment, team utilization, and leadership
- The discretionary "energy" willingly invested by each employee in their work and dedicated to the success of the organization as well as its customers and other stakeholders

There are no doubts, however, that these three quality management factors – time, talent, and energy – constitute a major combination of the momentum driving workforce productivity vis-à-vis organizational performance. Appropriately tapping into the opportunities of these three factors is at the discretion of top organizational management. Hence, their ability to realize the essentials of minimizing wasted employee time and keeping them engaged and focused appropriately could be deployed as a strong competitive tool.

This is especially so because according to Garton and Mankins [18] in their research work, "The companies that are the very best at managing scarce time, talent and energy – that is, the average of the top quartile of companies in our research – are 40% more productive than the rest (the average of the remaining three quartiles)." This thus creates a *productivity gap* claimed by the researchers as "a key source of competitive advantage for the very best companies."

It goes to say therefore that the better your employees are engaged, inspired, and focused on their jobs, the better their outputs are, to the global benefit of organizational performance. According to a research report published by the ASQ [3], an engaged employee is, in terms of measurable findings, 45% more productive than a merely satisfied worker.

References

1. American Nurses Credentialing Center (ANCC). About magnet: History of the Magnet program, https://www.nursingworldorg/organizational-programs/magnet/about-magnet
2. ASQ IoE (Insights on Excellence). (2021, June). Employee engagement: IoE report: Leadership is key. *Quality Progress*, p. 24.
3. ASQ. (2021, March). The progress report, "workplace – Bridging the gap". *Quality Progress*, p. 6. https://tinyurl.com/hbr-corporate-gap
4. ASQ. (2021, May). ASQ award recipients. *Quality Progress*, p. 7. https://www.asq.org/about-asq/asq-awards
5. ASQ. www.asq.org
6. ASQE Insights on Excellence. 2020 IoE annual report, https://insightsonexcellence.org
7. Bauer, H., Burkacky, O., Kenevan, P., Mahindroo, A., & Patel, M. (2020). *How the semiconductor industry can emerge stronger after the COVID-19 crisis*. McKinsey & Co. 18 June 2020. www.mckinsey.com/industries/advanced-electronics/our-insights/how-the-semiconductor-industry-can-emerge-stronger-after-the-covid-19-crisis
8. Branson, R. *Goodreads*. https://www.goodreads.com/quotes/7356284-clients-do-not-come-first-employees-come-first-if-you
9. Canada Human Resources Centre. *Employee engagement*. https://www.canadahrcentre.com/solutions/employee-engagement
10. Clement-O'Brien, K., et al. (2011). Innovativeness of nurse leaders. *Journal of Nursing Management, 19*(4), 431–438.
11. Deming, W. E. (1986). *Out of crisis*. MIT Press.
12. Dornbrook, J. (2015, April 30). Three questions with former GE CEO Jack Welch. *Kansas City Business Journal*. https://www.bizjournals.com/kansascity/news/2015/04/30/jack-welch-leadership-analytics-advice.html
13. Drucker, P. (2002). *Managing in the next society*. Macmillan.
14. Eom, S. B., & Karathanos, D. (1996). The role of expert systems in improving management of processes in total quality management organizations. *SAM Advanced Journal, 61*(4), 8–15.
15. Feigenbaum, A. V. (2007, February). The international growth of quality. *Quality Progress*, pp. 36–40.
16. Gardner, J. W., Linderman, K. W., & McFadden, K. L. (2018). Managing quality crossroads in healthcare: An integrative supply chain perspective. *Quality Management Journal, 25*(1), 2–17.
17. Garton, E., & Mankins, M. (2017). *Time, talent, energy: Overcome organizational drag and unleash your team's productive power*. Harvard Business Review Press.
18. Garton, E., & Mankins, M. (2020, December). Motivating people – The pandemic is widening a corporate productivity gap. *Harvard Business Review*.
19. Gelles, D. (2020, June 23). Are companies more productive in a pandemic? *New York Times*. https://tinyurl.com/productive-pandemic
20. Goode, C. J., et al. (2011). Comparison of patient outcomes in magnet and non-magnet hospitals. *Journal of Nursing Administration, 41*(12), 517–523.
21. Gupta, R.. (2021, January). All-inclusive improvement – 5 steps to fine-tune any system with TOC. *Quality Progress*, p. 56.
22. International Organization for Standardization. (2020). ISO 10018:2020 – Quality management – Guidance for people engagement.
23. International Organization for Standardization. ISO 22301:2019 subclause 8.4.4.1.
24. International Organization for Standardization. ISO 9000:2015, Clauses 7.1.2.; 7.1.6.; 7.2.; 7.3. and 7.4.

25. International Organization for Standardization. ISO 9001:2008, Clauses 6.1.; 6.2. and 5.5.3.
26. Jacobs, T. O., & Jacques, E. (1990). Military executive leadership. In K. E. Clark & M. B. Clark (Eds.), *Measures of leadership* (pp. 281–295). Leadership Library of America.
27. Kelly, L. A., et al. (2011). Nurse outcomes in magnet and non-magnet hospitals. *Journal of Nursing Administration, 41*(10), 428–433.
28. Khan, M. K., & Hafiz, N. (1999). Development of an expert system for implementation of ISO 9000 quality systems. *Total Quality Management, 10*(1), 47–59.
29. Kolarik, W. J. (1999). *Creating quality: Process design for results* (pp. 500–510). WCB/McGraw-Hill.
30. Kramer, M., et al. (2011). Clinical nurses in magnet hospitals confirm productive, healthy unit work environments. *Journal of Nursing Management, 19*(1), 5–17.
31. Krivokuca, M. (2021). Catalysts for change – Achieving organizational excellence in post-COVID-19 industry 4.0 process performance. *Quality Progress*, pp. 32–37.
32. Lake, E. T., et al. (2010). Patient falls: Association with hospital magnet status and nursing unit staffing. *Research in Nursing and Health, 33*(5), 413–425.
33. Lindborg, H. J. (2020, November). Adaptive space – How organizations can harness employee creativity to adjust to disruptive changes. *Quality Progress*, pp. 5–7.
34. McLaughlin, A., & Fetzer, S. J. (2015). The perceived value of certification by magnet and non-magnet nurses. *Journal of Nursing Administration, 45*(4), 194–199.
35. Miscikowski, D. K., & Stein, E. W. (2006, October). Empowering employees to pull the quality trigger. *Quality Progress*, pp. 43–48.
36. Mishra, S., & Delgado, D. (2021, June). Engineering engaged employees: Power to your people to add strength to your quality program. *Quality Progress*, pp. 16–24.
37. Nonaka, I., & Takeuchi, H. (1995). *The knowledge – Creating company: How Japanese companies create the dynamics of innovation*. Oxford University Press.
38. Palandrani, P. (2020, September). Global supply chain disruptions driving robotics adoption. *Robotics Business Review*. www.roboticsbusinessreview.com/analysis/global-supply-chain-disruptions-driving-robotics-adoption
39. Petit Dit Dariel, O., & Regnaux, J. P. (2015). Do magnet-accredited hospitals show improvements in nurse and patient outcomes compared to non-magnet hospitals: A systematic review. *JBI Database of Systematic Reviews and Implementation Reports, 13*(6), 168–219.
40. Pietenpol, L. (2020, December). The Times They Are a-Changin' – A glimpse into the future of work. *Quality Progress*, pp. 6–7.
41. Reitz, H. J. (1977). *Behavior in organizations*. Irwin.
42. Rodriguez-Garcia, M. C., Marquez-Hernandez, V. V., Belmonte-Garcia, T., Gutierrez-Puertas, L., & Granados-Gamez, G. (2020). Original research: How magnet hospital status affects nurses, patients, and organizations – A systemic review. *American Journal of Nursing, 120*(7), 28–38.
43. Rodriguez-Garcia, M. C., Marquez-Hernandez, V. V., Belmonte-Garcia, Teresa, Gutierrez-Puertas, L., & Granados-Gamez, G. (2020). Original research- How magnet hospital status affects nurses, patients, and organizations: A systematic review. *American Journal of Nursing, 120*(7), 28–38. https://doi.org/10.1097/01.NAJ.0000681648.48249.16
44. Rosenblatt, H. F., & Peters, D. M. F. (2002). *The customer comes second*. Harper Business.
45. Salinas, S. R. (2017). Examining the relationship between perceived quality of care and actual quality of care as measured by 30-day readmission rates. *Quality Management in Healthcare, 26*(1), 29–32.
46. Salmond, S. W., et al. (2009). A comprehensive systematic review of evidence on determining the impact of magnet designation on nursing and patient outcomes: Is the investment worth it. *JBI Library of Systematic Reviews, 7*(26), 1119–1178.
47. Schnaneveldt, S. J. (Ed.). (2021). *The certified quality process analyst handbook* (3rd ed.). Quality Press.
48. Schvaneveldt, S. J., & Neve, B. V. (2021, March). Proving their mettle – Combating the COVID-19 pandemic with quality tools. *Quality Progress*, pp. 24–31.

49. Sopadang, A., Chonsawat, N., & Ramingwong, S. (2020). Smart SME 4.0 implementation toolkit. In D. T. Matt, V. Mondrak, & H. Zsifkovits (Eds.), *Industry 4.0 for SMEs: Challenges, opportunities and requirements* (pp. 279–300). Palgrave Macmillan.
50. Staggs, V. S., & Dunton, N. (2012). Hospital and unit characteristics associated with nursing turnover including skill mix but not staffing level: An observational cross-sectional study. *International Journal of Nursing Studies, 49*(9), 1138–1145.
51. Stone, P. W., et al. (2007). Nurse working conditions, organizational climate and intent to leave in ICUs: An instrumental variable approach. *Health Services Research, 42*(3, Pt. 1), 1085–1104.
52. Tague, N. R. (2005). *Quality toolbox* (2nd ed.). Quality Press.
53. Whitacre, T. (2020, December). The whole package – Taking care of yourself in turbulent times matters more than you may realize. *Quality Progress*, pp. 10–11.

Quality Tools and Techniques 11

Achieving Performance Improvement

Continuous improvement is one of the most critical aspects of quality management, on which the long-term health of most organizations depends, hence the need for organizations to commit to it. Quality management (QM) is in itself viewed broadly from various perspectives by different authors. For example, Dean and Bowell [5] see QM as consisting of a comprehensive organizational philosophy which is embodied in the principles, practices, and techniques that strive to effectively meet customer specifications, needs, expectations, and requirements (SNEaRs). Sitkin et al. [24] view the principles of QM from the perspectives of customer satisfaction, continuous improvement, and system.

The affirmation of Kovach [12] that improving existing business processes calls for a true understanding of how the process or system works thus brings to the fore, the importance of learning and knowledge creation as vital components of quality management. Similarly, continuous improvement also requires creativity. The purpose of learning is obviously to generate and create knowledge, while continuous improvement naturally involves learning and the creation of knowledge [16, 24].

There is the need for organizations to understand the mechanisms for learning and cultivating knowledge because knowing how to effectively harness and apply organizational knowledge assets to improve its performance can always lead to competitive advantages [2, 14].

Available research works in the literature similarly portray the fact, too, that learning provides inputs that often lead to the successful implementation of improvement projects [1, 3, 11]. Knowledge outputs generally constitute specific practices that are generally needed for improvement projects. For example, the scientific methods for systematically:

- Identifying and reducing sources of customer dissatisfaction such as flowcharts, cause and effect diagram, etc.
- Tools used to monitor and analyze work processes such as control charts, Pareto charts, etc.

T. A. Ibidapo, *From Industry 4.0 to Quality 4.0*, Management for Professionals,
https://doi.org/10.1007/978-3-031-04192-1_11

The importance of exploring organizational knowledge through the learning process and taping into individual employee ingenuity is that it can easily lead to organizational creativity and innovation, as critical improvement measures. This is particularly critical in today's world of uncertainties and disruptive environment as the one created by the COVID-19 pandemic in the global community in the year 2020. It is for this reason, too, that organizations must allow "novel ideas flow freely among teams, across departments and throughout an organization." This is particularly so going by the words of Lindborg [13] that, "Everybody wants to more fully engage and share their ideas." Each organization thus have the discretional option to effectively harness employee creativity not just to adjust to disruptive changes but also as a component of its improvement measures.

The ISO 9001:2015 [8], the latest version of the international QMS standards, specifically requires that organizations determine and select opportunities for improvement. Improvement requirements are specified in sections 10.1, 10.2 and 10.3, hence a key component of the requirements for certification to its requirements. These may among others include the following:

- Improving the quality management system (QMS) itself
- Action items emanating from QMS review
- Corrective actions
- Improvement projects
- Actions for the reduction of risks
- Actions needed to address matters of customer feedback
- Planning for achieving organizational quality objectives
- Measures for products and/or services improvement
- Correcting, preventing, or reducing any undesired effect

There are, on a general basis, quality management improvement tools and techniques that organizations can choose from. Some of them are listed hereafter.

Using Quality Tools

Achieving Process Efficiency

Quality tools represent a major and essential activities interface in the management of quality. For example, an auditor needs to use many types of quality tools to plan and perform an audit and also to analyze and report the results. Hence it is very important for auditors to understand such quality tools and their application for them to be able to carry out effective quality audit in terms of assessing how adequately and effectively the auditee is using the quality tools. Similarly, the auditee also uses various quality tools and techniques for various purposes which include but are not limited to the following:

Definition of Processes

Identification, quantification, and characterization of problems (e.g., product defects) so as be able to effectively implement and achieve relevant corrective actions.

Analyzing and Reporting Results

It follows therefore that both the auditors and auditees need to have sufficient knowledge of the application and uses of various quality tools and techniques. You are introduced to the use and application of these quality tools and techniques in this chapter.

Quality tools and techniques are generally used to test and make processes effective and efficient for the benefit of the customer or end users in ensuring that product/service requirements are met. The application interface of these tools and techniques falls within the purview of three key entities of your quality management system – the customer, the process, and the employees.

Customer

It is a product or service receiver (or according to ISO 9000:2018 "an organization or person that receives a product"), and there are various types of customers. Some examples of customers are listed as follows:

- Consumers
- Retailers
- Hotel guests
- End users
- Clients
- Congregation
- Spectators
- Students/parents
- Passengers
- Patients
- Public or voters (here as an entity in terms of governance and the provision/usage of amenities/utilities and services such as water, electricity, and telephone)
- Market

It is the customer that actually defines desired product/service, quality expectations, and requirements in terms of performance, reliability, value, competitiveness, time of delivery, packaging, shape, post-delivery service provision, ability of product to conform to regulatory guidelines, aesthetics features, dimensional specifications, customized features requirements of the customer, etc.

The ability of any product or service and their application to comply with regulatory or legislative guidelines and requirements is on a general basis taken for granted by the customer; hence, the supplier or organization must have to take this into consideration at all times.

Process

Process, which is defined in ISO 9000:2018 as a "set of interrelated activities which transforms inputs into outputs," is the combination of equipment, people, methods, and processes (including the use and application of quality tools), raw materials, and environment that work together to produce the product. How well the process performs in terms of quality of output and productivity is a factor of the way the process has been designed and is operated and the quality of all input – human and material.

Hence, the right process technique/technology must be selected right from the beginning, accurate product design made, process monitoring devices adequately provided, relevant quality tools selected and employed in process and product testing, sound production scheduling made and qualified, and adequately trained staff used to ensure prompt delivery, defective products avoided, wastages minimized, excellent productivity assured, machinery and equipment downtime minimized or completely avoided through preventive and predictive maintenance, and other necessary actions put in place to avoid process failure and achieve products and services that meet customer specifications.

In addition, processes must have to be constantly examined and reexamined to achieve the complete removal of activities that do not add value to the process and reduction of cycle time so as to improve product quality and meet or even exceed customer requirements and expectations.

The need to improve the quality of work processes must, from quality concepts and perspectives, be seen as an endless task desired by every quality process. Work process improvement can generally be achieved through the following sequence of actions or activities:

- Definition of the process for quality improvement
- Analyses of the process
- Definition of the ideal process
- Testing of any new process to ensure and confirm desired results are obtained
- Put new process in place

Employees

Employees are the workers of an organization. They actually make things happen. They are involved in teamwork to create results and ensure that things are "done right the first time" through training in:

- Production and quality management-related strategies
- Quality control/quality assurance methodologies
- The use and application of applicable quality tools and techniques
- Systems documentation and the appropriate use of relevant quality documents as and when needed
- Process monitoring using necessary tools and techniques
- Holding review meetings (e.g., unit/departmental, production, technical, sales/marketing, management, etc.)
- The ways and methodologies for meeting customer (internal and external) requirements, needs, and specifications
- Process efficiency and productivity
- Wastages minimization/reduction to the barest possible level or even zero wastes
- Effective communication both within and outside the quality system
- Quality audit (internal and external), documentation, etc. so as to completely imbibe the quality culture in every employee

In order to achieve these, employees must be motivated in every facet of their work for them to effectively focus their minds, talents, and energies on ensuring that outputs satisfy and meet customer needs and requirements.

A factory survey is carried in eight manufacturing industries in Nigeria to determine the expectations of the factory workers. The results of the survey showed the following findings as their topmost desires:

- Job security
- Recognition
- Reward for performance (measured in terms of better pay/financial reward)
- Position in organization (also measured in terms of increased pay)
- Opportunity to develop and follow an identified career path in line with their respective jobs
- Opportunity to have challenging jobs/responsibilities

While the customer provides the specifications and allied product/service requirements, the employees work with the needed team spirit to operate and document the required processes while at the same time using quality tools to monitor the processes to ensure that things are done right the first time to minimize product and material wastages to achieve customer satisfaction.

C*ustomer satisfaction* is defined in ISO 9000:2015 as the,

> Customer's perception of the degree to which the customer's requirements have been fulfilled.

The use of some quality tools and techniques can greatly affect your organization's ability to consistently provide your customers and/or consumers with:

- *What they want or desire*
- *When they want it*
- *Using the most efficient quality method/tools or technique to achieve them at a cost that is affordable to respective customers*

Various tools and techniques [17] are at the disposal of the various cadres of quality system personnel and organization to ensure and guarantee the quality of various products and services at the various stages of production. These tools may be used to plan, analyze, and report quality systems results.

In order to ensure the effective use of these quality tools, there is the need for an effective understanding of their use and application. This chapter provides some information on the use and application of some of these tools and techniques some of which have been advanced over the years by most of the acknowledged and distinguished gurus of quality such as Shewart, Deming, Juran, Feigenbaum, Ishikawa, Crosby, and many others.

In order to improve any system using a systematic approach, there is the need to understand the processes using the knowledge of simple quality tools and techniques. The development of the quality tools and techniques available today for use in the management of quality systems witnessed at its earlier stages among others the seven basic quality tools which comprise mainly of cause and effect diagram, check sheets, control charts, histograms, Pareto analysis, scatter plots, and stratification. Some of the other useful quality tools and techniques are arrow diagrams, affinity diagrams, matrix data analysis, matrix diagrams, relations diagrams, process decision program charts, and tree diagrams.

Key Quality Tools

Catalyzing Sustainability

The effective use of these quality tools and techniques similarly requires that they must be applied by people who have a good understanding of the ways they are used or applied to achieve quality products and services; hence, there is the need to adequately train all those involved in their use and application. The support and commitment of management in the provision of adequate training at all times is hence of immense importance to organizational survival. The following is a list of some of the quality tools and techniques that are available for your use and application:

- Affinity diagrams
- Arrow diagram (aka activity diagram/chart, network diagram, node diagram, or critical path method chart)
- Brainstorming – a way for generating free flow of ideas among groups of people in solving problems and in implementing projects

- Building consensus
- Cause and effect diagram/analysis (or Ishikawa diagrams aka "fishbone" diagram)
- Check sheets
- Checklists, guidelines, and log sheets
- Control charts
- Defect measurement
- Descriptive statistics
- Failure modes and effects analysis
- Flowcharts
- Histograms
- Interviewing – a means of identifying both internal and external problems and gathering information about such problems with the intention of improving on them vis-à-vis product/service quality
- Matrix data analysis
- Matrix diagrams
- Pareto analysis/plots
- Pattern and trend analysis
- Process decision program charts (PDPC)
- Process mapping
- Quality circles – which comprises of a number of workers who meet at regular intervals to discuss modes and ways of how to achieve process and product improvements
- Relations diagrams
- Roof cause analysis
- Sampling
- Scatter plots
- Statistical process control (SPC)
- Stratification
- The **5W2H** approach of Robinson [18] – a technique in which the questions **w**hat, **w**hy, **w**here, **w**hen, **w**ho (5 "W" words), **h**ow, and **h**ow much (2 "H" words) are asked about an existing process with the sole aim of identifying its weak point and ways of improving it
- Theory of constraints (TOC) analysis
- Tree diagrams

The main impact of the use of these quality tools and techniques is on a general basis for the overall improvement of the products and services by improving processes and operational tasks. The key quality improvement areas of application of these quality tools and techniques include, among others, the following areas:

1. For the definition of processes
2. Identification, characterization, and grouping of problems in order to prioritize and find solutions to them
3. Presentation of results

Quality tools and techniques are, on a general basis, organizational or analytical techniques which aid or assist in the understanding of a quality problem. A quality tool/technique can, according to the ASQ, be described as,

> An instrument or technique to support and improve the activities of process quality management and improvement.

They help in the understanding and provision of solutions to problems hence their use and application for the understanding of problems and the provision of solutions for the improvement of quality.

Various quality tools have emerged over the years of which some are numerical while others are not. Some of these quality tools and techniques are described below.

Cause and Effect Diagrams (C-E Diagram)

The cause and effect diagram – also known as *fishbone diagram* or *Ishikawa diagram* – enables brainstorming about the root causes of quality management problems. The cause and effect (C-E) diagram which was invented by Ishikawa is a method for analyzing the factors from which a given effect emanates so as to establish the relationship between the various causal factors and the quality effect. The C-E diagram is therefore constructed to identify and organize all the possible causes of an identified effect in a rational way.

The cause and effect diagram is also referred to as either the *Ishikawa* diagram (a name it acquired after its inventor) or the "fishbone" diagram because of its shape which resembles that of the skeleton of a whole fish.

The diagram has a stem which represents the effect or the quality characteristic feature(s) that is (are) intended to be controlled and improved. Major branches and sub-branches are attached to the stem. While the primary stem represents the origin (i.e., root cause) of the unfavorable effect(s) (i.e., the quality characteristic intended to be eliminated, improved or controlled), each of the major branches corresponds to a major cause or class of causes.

Check Sheet

A check sheet is simply a data recording sheet custom designed by the user for the collection and analyses of data. The check sheet which is a pre-prepared structured form is designed in such a way that it enables the user to readily interpret results.

Control Chart

It uses a graph to study how a process changes per unit time.

Histogram

This is a graphical representation showing frequency distributions or how often each different value in a set of data occurs. It is one of the most commonly used quality tools used to obtain a graphic summary or representation of variation as it occurs in a set of data. Using it for analyzing the frequency of items in a set of data ensures that we get a pictorial view of the patterns or trend of a set of data thereby enabling the ease of understanding of such sets of data.

Pareto Diagram/Analysis

A Pareto diagram is a graphical tool that is used in the ranking of problems and their causes from the most important to the least important. The Pareto chart aids the prioritization of bar charts in the determination of the order in which problems can be tackled or solved. The Pareto chart is named after the nineteenth century Italian economist, Vilfredo Pareto, who suggested that most effects come from relatively few causes. This is to say, for example, that 80% of the effects come from 20% of the possible causes [18].

The Pareto diagram thus represents a quality tool, applicable in differentiating between "the vital few" improvement opportunities and "the trivial many," through a distinction between categories with different frequencies of occurrence.

In Juran's [10, 19] suggestion for differentiating the "vital few" from the "trivial many," it was the assumption that 20% of the quality or improvement opportunities is accountable for 80% of the overall available quality improvement opportunities. This is often referred to, in the literature, as the "80/20 rule" which subsequently resulted in the 80th percentile, being turned into a significant cutoff points in decision-making [6, 15, 23].

One of the major shortcomings of the Pareto analysis identified by Rudisill and O'Connor [19] is the subjectivity created by the fact that there were actually no tests for statistical significance. These two researchers, however, corrected this in their research work, as listed in their results.

Scatter Diagram

A scatter diagram is a graphical technique used for analyzing the relationship that exists between two variables or for the identification of correlations among variables.

Stratification

It is used for the separation of data that are gathered from a variety of sources to discern patterns.

Flowcharts

Flowcharts can simply be described as a graphical representation of the various steps of a process. They are tools used for depicting sequential activities. Standard drawing symbols are typically used to represent the individual activities of a process. They are of good use in process visualization hence the understanding of a process. They can be used to describe an existing process/system or used in designing a new one.

This is a specific tool used to illustrate or give the pictorial representation of a process or system. They are used to describe how things are done to enable the visualization of the entire process or system and identify the respective areas of strength and weakness in the process/system. Hence flowcharts are used to *depict the various steps or events in a process or system* thereby simplifying the analysis of the system to identify or obtain some indications about which activity or event that may be negatively impacting on the process or system. Apart from the use of flowcharts to describe an existing process or system, they are also used to design a new one.

In brief, flowcharts are generally used for the:

- Identification of inspection and checkpoints for making important decisions in the quality system
- Identification of employees/personnel executing/performing specific job steps based on job title thereby helping in the recognition of the contributions and responsibilities of the individual employee
- Identification of areas that are potential sources of problems, bottlenecks, repetitive or unnecessary steps, and rework loops so as to improve process/system efficiency
- Identification of opportunities for changes and improvements
- Assistance in the identification of root causes, defects, and the development of potential corrective actions and solutions thereby enabling the reduction of defects and at the same time achieving improved cycle time
- Assistance in obtaining review inputs for changes and improvement of the system
- Provision and development of a good understanding of the overall process/system and the depiction of the sequence of activities and processes/operations using standard drawing symbols

Flowcharts are also useful to quality auditors who may use them for the purposes of understanding both production and service processes when carrying out quality system audit.

Although various symbols are used in flowcharting depending on the type of industry and application, the following are some of the commonly used ones.

- *Rectangle* – The activity symbol with a brief description of the activity within the rectangle.
- *Diamond* – This is the decision symbol which designates a decision point from which the process branches into two or more paths.

- *Rounded rectangle* – This is the terminal symbol which identifies the beginning or starting point of a process flow, "START," and ending or stopping point of a process flow, "STOP."
- *Lines with arrowheads* – This is the flow line which represents the process path connecting process elements such as activities, decisions, etc. The arrowhead on a flow line is used to indicate the direction of the process flow.
- *The circle* – This is the connector symbol which is used to indicate flow diagram continuation.

There are various types of flowcharts which include some of the following:

- Matrix flowchart
- Activity sequence flowchart
- Top-down flowchart

Process Mapping

Process maps are flowcharting that may or may not use the standard flow symbols. Otherwise process mapping serves the same purpose as flowcharts.

Arrow Diagram

The arrow diagram which is also known as *activity diagram*, *network diagram*, *activity chart*, *node diagram*, or *critical path method chart* is a type of planning tool used to show or illustrate the required order (schedule) in which a task is carried out in a project or process. The use and application of the arrow diagram covers both simple and complex activities as it is used nowadays even for scheduling, organizing, and monitoring complex projects and situations.

A historical background provided by Natalia Scriabina [21] showed that the further development of the arrow diagram by the US Navy was propelled in the 1950s by the use of the two project management techniques, the program evaluation review technique (PERT) and the critical path method (CPM). The use of the arrow diagram with both the PERT and CPM enables the provision of more detailed information about individual activity within a complex process structure.

Affinity Diagrams

An affinity diagram is a visual tool or technique used in quality management to systematically organize, align, group, or classify a pool or a large number of issues, data, ideas, items, or observations into related categories or classes for easier understanding and further analysis.

Tree Diagram

A tree diagram is a treelike diagram used to break down wide categories of problems into finer levels or stages of detail. It is used by management as a tool for depicting the level or hierarchy of tasks and subtasks needed for the completion of an objective.

Matrix Diagram

It is a planning tool used for the organization of knowledge in the form of a matrix, to show the relationship among information groups or sets of data.

Process Decision Program Chart

This is useful in the identification of the things that might go wrong in plans that are under development.

Relations Diagram

The relations diagram is deployed for the determination of the cause and effect relationships.

The use of any of the above-specified tools to characterize any quality problem and then finding the solution to it becomes easier and achievable. These quality tools may be used in a single form or in combination with one another.

Some of the abovementioned tools belong to the group of the "seven tools of quality" defined by the ASQ as "the tools that help organizations understand their processes to improve them." They are the cause and effect diagram, check sheet, control chart, flowchart, histogram, Pareto chart, and scatter diagram.

Root Cause Analysis

The root cause generally refers to the ways and system by which the primary or root cause of an unfavorable effect(s) or problem(s) is (are) identified or recognized.

The root cause which is directly or indirectly responsible for the effect is controllable such that its elimination results in getting rid of the effect(s). This is the original reason for nonconformance with a process. Once the route cause is identified and removed or corrected, the nonconformance will be eliminated. This can be presented in the cause and effect diagram, which is also referred to as the Ishikawa or fishbone chart.

Control Charts

Graphs used to monitor variance in a process over a period of time so that unexpected variance (i.e., change in a process or business practice which may lead to the alteration of the expected outcome) cause defects in products and services can be immediately detected and corrected.

Theory of Constraints (TOC) Analysis

Theory of constraints is a strategic tool that can be used to achieve continuous improvement of organization's QMS. It was reportedly developed by E.M. Goldratt in 1980 [7]. The theory views organizations as a system of interlinked individual elements or basic links which collectively work together as an integrated chain with a focus on achieving a common performance goal. The optimum performance of each of the linking elements or basic links results generally to maximum efficiency or full productivity, a situation referred to as an infinite return on investment (ROI). If, however, one of the links or elements becomes weak or performs worse than the optimum expected of it, it is termed a *constraint* or as commonly referred to, on the factory floor of a manufacturing system, a *bottleneck* hence the need for its immediate identification, correction, and the element quickly returned to state of full performance; to achieve performance improvement [25]. The TOC improvement strategy is based on a five-stage approach of identifying the constraint, exploiting the constraint, subordinating everything else to the constraint, and elevating the system's constraint, and if a constraint is broken, repeat the cycle [7, 22].

The TOC analysis was, for example, used in the identification of the constraints – number of ventilators, ICU beds, skilled healthcare personnel, and personal protective equipment (PPE) such as face masks and respirators and gowns, which hindered the treatment of more COVID-19 patients in hospitals' intensive care units (ICU) both locally and internationally in the early parts of the pandemic [20].

Collectively Generating Ideas

Solving Quality Problems

The following quality tools are used also for solving quality problems as well as for process improvement:

- Brainstorming
- Quality circles
- Interviewing
- Run charts
- Benchmarking

Brainstorming

Brainstorming is a technique or quality tool that is used by teams or group of people to generate a free flow of ideas in a group of people to examine all aspects of problems with the intention of finding solutions to them. The problem referred to here may be in the form of a new project or for an existing one where improvement is required or targeted. Brainstorming is generally carried out in a relaxed atmosphere where every participant has the freedom to express his opinion. The implication here is that people share thoughts and ideas on problems to generate ideas and proffer solution to particular problems or subject matter or for achieving other set-out objectives.

The goal here is therefore to:

- Generate a free flow of ideas from a group of experts or experienced employees/personnel in various areas of the processes involved in achieving the set objective or target on identifying problems
- Find causes to problems
- Find solutions to problems
- Find ways to implement a solution

At the end of the first brainstorming exercise, all ideas generated in each area or unit (e.g., human resources, technical, information technology, facilities, engineering, etc.) being considered are collated and listed by one person and presented to the unit or group participants to identify solution milestones. The solution milestones for the various areas or units are then listed for the entire project and responsibilities assigned to capable individuals with specific dates of completion.

The major focus of brainstorming can therefore be generally summed up as being for the:

- Identification of problems
- Classification of problems
- Analyses of problems
- Identification of the causes of the problems
- Proffering of solution to problems including system requirements
- Identification and summation of solution milestones
- The identification of needed resources (capital and human)
- Identification of the lines of communication
- Assignment of the timing requirements (i.e., number of days/weeks/months) needed for the completion of each assigned solution
- Assignment of responsibilities to capable individuals based on the identified solutions
- Assignment of dates (or in some cases frequencies) of completion of assigned responsibilities
- Identification of the review period for the entire project and/or fractions of it

Each participating member of the brainstorming team is required to think in a creative way and manner to generate as many ideas as possible about the entire project/problem and the set objective/goal. These ideas and the ensuing solutions are then discussed, implemented, and reviewed at the end of the brainstorming exercise.

Brainstorming can be carried out by firstly writing the specific objectives on the writing board or on a flip chart. Response from each brainstorming participant must be one at a time. All ideas generated during the brainstorming exercise are noted and documented. Usually there is no criticism of ideas during the brainstorming session.

Once brainstorming has been completed, the results can be analyzed, and the best solutions can be selected either for further brainstorming or through the use of other quality technique or tools.

The following guidelines are useful for ensuring the best results:

- The brainstorming session needs to have a member playing the leading or leadership role.
- Active participation in the brainstorming session by all members of the brainstorming team must be encouraged and assured.
- Do not criticize or evaluate ideas during the brainstorming session since this may introduce an element of risk for the group member involved.
- A record of the brainstorming session must be kept for studying purposes and subsequent evaluation.
- Both individuals and groups may be engaged in brainstorming.
- No single member is allowed to dominate sessions.
- All ideas are welcomed (including crazy and seemingly stupid ones).

Quality Circles Idea

Quality circles comprise of groups of people/workers who meet together to discuss ways of improving products and/or processes. Although quality circles are not properly structured, they have the capability to motivate workers if they are well handled. It gives workers the opportunity to contribute valuable input into the quality system. This could be of good use to an organization if well managed as the workers remain the major and direct contact with their respective jobs and the problems emanating from them from time to time.

It is however worth noting here that since the quality circle is not a formal structure in an organization, the authority or empowerment given to the team is quite minimal, and as such only minor changes can be implemented by the group. This is not to say, however, that useful suggestions by the team to improve the quality system must not be given adequate consideration by the management. This approach which originates from Japan emphasizes the training of workers, that is, employees of the basic or lowest cadre in the organizational hierarchy, in the use of basic quality tools. For success to be achieved here, there must be focus and effective leadership to direct the employees and the deployment and use of quality tools towards broad-based activities for process improvement. The deployment of the idea of quality circle was used successfully in Japan where it was used as an integral part of established organization-wide process improvement activities.

Care must however be taken in the developing parts of the world to ensure that quality circle activities are not hijacked and turned into those of the labor union. It must however be stated that whatever joint action that is necessary to be implemented as a part of the group activities should be by consensus of opinion of the members of the quality circle.

Interviewing

Interviewing is a tool that is suitable for the identification of problems and gathering information. Employees may be interviewed to solve internal problems or get information about internal issues, while customers or end users may be interviewed to solve external problems or obtain information from outside an organization.

Benchmarking Process

Benchmarking is, according to Chow et al. [4], the "process of evaluating, comparing and measuring the products, services and processes of other organizations." This comparison simply provides the opportunity for an organization to weigh its own activities down from its performance to its process operations, products, and services against those of other organizations with superior performance or those of the best-in-class organization(s) or competitor(s) to ascertain its own weaknesses; hence, benchmarking is used for "identifying areas that need improvement by showing where others are doing a better job of meeting customer needs." Using the performance of organizations identified as leaders in product/service quality and continuous improvement as a benchmark platform your organization can identify the gap between it and the best in the sector (i.e., carrying out a *gap analysis*) so as to be able to improve its system with the goal or objective of getting better to being the best in the sector.

Benchmarking is a topic of general interest in quality management irrespective of the QMS and/or QMS standards you may be using or considering for use. In benchmarking, the organization carrying out the benchmarking exercise searches using comparative studies to identify the competitor (or company) with the best product and/or best practices determines the *competitive gap* with the sole objective of using the findings to project and develop action plans for achieving future performance levels that is most superior among competitors. The gap analysis needs however to be carried out with the focus of attention also on innovation, latest and most effective technological developments, and most recent and relevant machinery and equipment that may be necessary to firstly create value addition to customer needs and requirements and then to achieve the leadership performance in its class of industries. This is to say that benchmarking alone must never be viewed narrowly as the sole and primary improvement strategy as this alone may never give an organization a sustainable competitive advantage.

Hence benchmarking which, on its own, is more or less a learning and discovery process may be seen, too, as a very good methodology for measuring the performance of your process operation against those of the most outstanding or best in class, for specific operations or processes. Benchmarking can be done on the basis of:

- Best practices in your industry or sector of the economy
- The quantification of the effect of installing the best practices
- Delivery schedule fulfillment
- Billing system.

Setting operating targets based on the best possible industry practices is highly critical to the success of every organization. Just like the PDCA methodology of quality management improvement, the process of benchmarking needs to be carried out using specific process approach which can be broadly classified into the **PAIAM** phases – **p**lan, **a**nalyze, **i**ntegrate, **a**ction, and **m**onitor as explained below:

- *Planning* the benchmark to know the exact activities to be benchmarked and determine the data and method of their collection for selected comparative organizations of superior performance.
- Carry out a gap *analysis* of your current performance with a projection for future performance expectations.
- *Integrate* the results of the gap analysis through adequate and proper communication to gain organizational acceptance.
- Take necessary *action* to establish needed functional goals, to develop and implement appropriate action plans to ascertain leadership position, and to reassess benchmarks.
- *Monitor* the progress of operational processes to ensure that the best practices are fully integrated and organizational set-out leadership position attained and maintained.

Going into the details of achieving the benchmarking processes therefore requires further implementation guidelines as suggested below:

- Ensure first of all that you have an in-depth knowledge and understanding of your performance in the marketplace as well as those of your operational processes and their strength and weaknesses.
- Investigate and identify the leaders and best-in-class competitors in your sector of the economy for the purpose of comparing your system with theirs from relevant operational processes to the best practices that made them the best in class in the industry.
- Carry out a gap analysis to identify all areas that are actually separating you from being the best in class.

- Communicate the benchmark results as necessary to organizational wide support and assure cooperation in setting and achieving planned goals.
- Define the goals.
- Develop and implement appropriate lines of action to be taken to achieve set-out best practices and leadership or best-in-class position.
- Monitor the progress of implementation to achieve full integration of best practices in your system.
- Reassess benchmarks.
- Maintain leadership or best-in-class position.

The author advises that every organization irrespective of its size and range of products/services should regularly engage in the benchmarking of its processes, products, and performance to ensure that it is not left behind in terms of its performance and processes. Benchmarking will help to determine an organization's current competitive gaps to enable it to collect data and information necessary for projecting future performance goals and objectives for achieving performance levels to put it above all competition.

Identifying Best-in-Market Products

Organizational global self-assessment activities need to be integrated into the quality management system rather being made just a marketing departmental responsibility. This is not to say, however, that the department cannot be the coordinating unit for product comparative benchmarking to know how competitive the products are and whether there are better products in the marketplace in terms of quality, price, demand, and other necessary criteria. Depending on circumstances at hand, benchmarking could be extended beyond products/services to include the quality management system itself, management team performance, machinery and equipment, technology and techniques of production/processing, materials input, and quality of staffing, among others.

Challenges in Developing Economies

For the less developed or developing countries of the world, it is very easy to know the best products/services in the market just by having a good and honest feel of the market and/or through market surveys and analyses. This may, however, be somehow subjective if the study is initiated by your organization. If the study is however carried out by an independent organization with the necessary expertise in doing the job, and the criteria for the analysis and judgment is adequate and suitable for your sector of the economy then, one will surely get an objective and reliable analysis of the leadership position in the sector of the economy for which the study and analysis has been made.

The use of awards to decide market elites in the developing world may not be good enough to yield the best results since manufacturing activities or outfits are relatively very low. In addition, too, is the fact of the prevalence and dominance of corruption. Although there are some quality awards in some of those countries, competitiveness is not usually motivated by the “seller’s market” nature of the economy. Hence the reliability of awards to select processes and products/services to be benchmarked may not just be sufficiently objective and reliable.

The only way awards could be used in the underdeveloped countries of the world is probably to rely on those that are directly obtained by individual organizations directly and their processes and products/services from outside the country. The few criteria cum awards available for you to consider in Nigeria for selecting the best in your sector for the purposes of benchmarking your processes and products/services are on a general basis:

- ISO 9000 Certification
- ISO 14000 Certification
- Occupational Health and Safety Assessment Series (OHSAS) 18000 or the new ISO 45001 [9]
- The NIS Award of the SON
- The MANCAP Award of the SON
- Registration to NAFDAC or other National Regulatory Agencies/Bodies
- The National Universities Commission (NUC) Accreditation Awards to Universities (only for higher institutions of learning in Nigeria)
- Financial Sector Organizational Ratings by Rating Agencies such as Agusto & Co., Fitch, etc.
- The Nigerian Stock Exchange (NSE) Annual Awards (e.g., the NSE’s Annual President’s Merit Award for the best financial report in the banking industry)
- Any awards given on a regular basis in various countries of the world to reward product/service quality and effective organizational quality management

Since the economy of most of the developing nations is more of import-based than manufacturing, it is important and critical for you to benchmark your product/services against the best ones in the global market so that you may have no alternative than to tailor your processes in such a way as to be able to achieve the benchmarked products.

The story is different in the developed economies of the world which are more of manufacturing/production. For the developed countries of the world, there are choices of various ways by which you can assess the leadership positions of various organizations in the various sectors of the economy since there are already a host of compendia of business awards and citations of merit received by organizations for quality products/services and also for business process improvement. Such awards which include those regularly given by professional bodies such as the ASQ are numerous just as they vary from country to country as well as from one continent to the other. From the purview of various literature sources, some of such considerations include the following:

- Industry Week's Best Plant's Award
- National Institute of Standards and Technology's Malcolm Baldrige Award
- USA Today and Rochester Institute of Technology's Quality Cup Award
- European Foundation for Quality Management Award
- Fortune Magazine
- Competitiveness Forum
- Deming Prize
- Federal Quality Institute
- United States Navy's Best Manufacturing Practices

Irrespective of the nature of your economy, the other area of interest for you to get more information about the performance of your contemporaries is through research – market and academic – findings from the academic sector.

References

1. Anand, G., Ward, P. T., & Tatikonda, M. V. (2010). Role of explicit and tacit knowledge in Six Sigma projects: An empirical examination of differential project success. *Journal of Operations Management., 28*(4), 303–315.
2. Choo, A. S., Linderman, K., & Schroeder, R. G. (2007a). Method and context perspectives on learning and knowledge creation in quality management. *Journal of Operations Management., 25*(4), 918–931.
3. Choo, A. S., Linderman, K. W., & Schroeder, R. G. (2007b). Method and psychological effects of learning behaviors and knowledge creation in quality improvement projects. *Management Science, 53*(3), 437–450.
4. Chow, A. F., Bowman, R., & Wittenberg, L. C. (2007). Six Sigma, achieve compliance through CI. *Quality Progress*, ASQ, 28–33.
5. Dean, J. W., & Bowen, D. E. (1994). Management theory and total quality: Improving research and practice through theory development. *Academy of Management Review, 19*(3), 392–418.
6. Grosfeld-Nir, A., Ronen, B., & Kozlovsky, N. (2007). The Pareto Managerial principle: When does it apply? *International Journal of Production Research, 45*(10), 2,317–2,325.
7. Gupta, R. (2021). All-inclusive improvement – 5 steps to fine-tune any system with TOC. *Quality Progress*, 56.
8. International Organization for Standardization. (2015). *ISO 9000:2015, International Quality Management Systems Standard, Quality Management Systems – Fundamentals and Vocabulary*.
9. International Organization for Standardization, ISO 45001, Occupational Health and Safety.
10. Juran, J. M., & Godfrey, A. B. (1951). *Juran's quality handbook*. McGraw-Hill.
11. Kovach, J. V., & Fredenhall, L. D. (2013). The influence of continuous improvement practices on learning: An empirical study. *Quality Management Journal*.
12. Kovach, J. V. (2016). The role of learning and exploration in quality management and continuous improvement. In P. Sampaio & P. Saraiva (Eds.), *Quality in the 21st century – Perspectives from ASQ Feigenbaum medal winners* (pp. 75–89). Springer.

13. Lindborg, H. J. (2020). Adaptive Space: (2020), How organizations can harness employee creativity to adjust to disruptive changes. *Quality Progress*, 5–7.
14. NIST. (2009). *Malcolm Baldrige National Quality Award: 2009–10 criteria for performance excellence*. National Institute of Standards and Technology of the United States Department of Commerce.
15. Ochoa, J. J. (2014). Reducing plan variations in delivering sustainable building projects. *Journal of Cleaner Production, 85*, 276–288.
16. Osterloh, M., & Frey, B. S. (2000). Motivation, knowledge transfer, and organizational forms. *Organization Science, 11*(5), 538–550.
17. ReVelle, J. B. (2004). *Quality essentials from A to Z*. Quality Press.
18. Robinson, A. (1991). *Continuous improvement in operations, a systematic approach to waste reduction* (p. 246). Productivity Press.
19. Rudisill, F., & O'Connor, J. (2020). Making the cut – Critical values for Pareto comparisons remove statistical subjectivity. *Quality Progress, 2020*, 38–43.
20. Schvaneveldt, S. J., & Neve, B. V. (2021). Proving their Mettle - combating the COVID-!9 pandemic with quality tools. *Quality Progress, 2021*, 24–31.
21. Scriabina, N. (2012). Beyond the basics, arrow diagrams. *Quality Progress*, 18–29.
22. Singh, R., Gupta, R., Verma, P. L., & Bajpai. (2018). Theory of constraints: Strategy for continuous improvement. *International Journal of Mechanical and Production Engineering, 6*(1), 66–69.
23. Singson, M., & Hangsing, P. (2015). Implication of 80/20 rule in electronic journal usage of UGC -Infonet Consortia. *Journal of Academic Librarianship, 41*(2), 207–219.
24. Sitkin, S. B., Sutcliffe, K. M., & Schroeder, R. G. (1994). Distinguishing control from learning in total Quality Management: A contingency perspective. *Academy of Management Review, 19*(3), 537–564.
25. Urban, W. (2019). TOC Implementation in in a medium-scale manufacturing system with diverse product rooting. *Production and Manufacturing Research, 7*(1), 178–194. https://doi.org/10.1080/21693277.2019.1616002

Cost of Quality (CoQ)

12

Counting the Costs

The economics of quality requires that you make products or provide services which meet customer needs, requirements, and specifications (quality products/services) at the lowest possible cost.

Except for philanthropic organizations, every other one setup for business purposes operates their businesses or enterprises mainly with the drive for getting returns on investment (ROI), that is, to make profit. The only way to achieve this objective is for the management team to strive to ensure that quality products which meet the needs, requirements, and specifications of the customers are achieved in the most effective way with the least cost.

The cost of production can be classified into two major parts:

- Unavoidable costs – Buildings, machinery and equipment, materials, labor (as long as employees are not in excess of what is normally required adequacy), electricity, and water
- Avoidable costs – Cost of error/defect prevention and detection, cost of error/defect removal and rework, extra delivery costs incurred in the delivery of products rejected by customers, warranty costs resulting from product failure, fines/costs incurred for the violation of statutory/regulatory requirements relating to product, and costs incurred on recalls due to product failure

Categorizing the Cost of Quality

Minimizing the Costs

The cost of quality is probably one of the most controversial terms in the theory of quality management. It is most often misconstrued by most people as referring to

T. A. Ibidapo, *From Industry 4.0 to Quality 4.0*, Management for Professionals,
https://doi.org/10.1007/978-3-031-04192-1_12

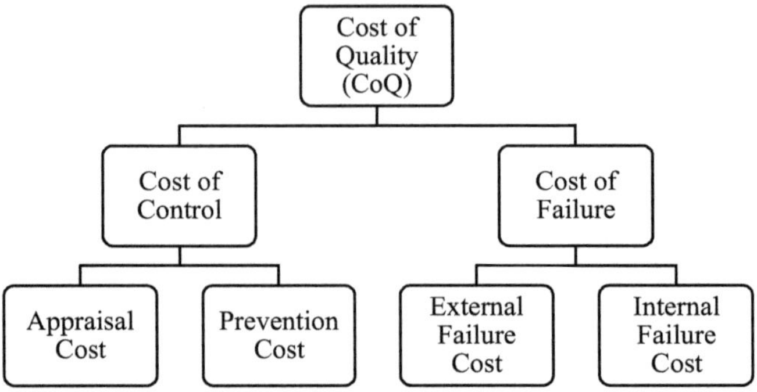

Fig. 12.1 Categorization of the costs associated with "quality" or "no quality"

the price of creating a quality product/service or putting quality processes and procedures in place. Converse to this misconception, the cost of quality (CoQ) is the cost of "not creating a quality product/service the first time." Since you are likely to achieve quality products and services the first time if you operate with a QMS or quality improvement process/program/concept in place, CoQ may also be seen in this perspective as the cost incurred for not putting quality procedures or quality management systems in place. It is therefore obvious from here that CoQ is actually the costs that are associated with the provision of poor-quality products, or services, hence the obvious reference as "cost of poor quality" (CoPQ). It is one of the quality gurus, Philip Crosby, that used the term "cost of quality" for cost of poor quality. CoQ has stayed with us since then.

The cost of quality is generally made up of:

- Appraisal costs
- Failure (internal and external) costs

The cost of quality is very significant for any organization no matter the nature and type of business or project one may be involved in executing (Fig. 12.1).

Price of Quality

Cost of control is equivalent to conformance, while *cost of failure* represents non-conformance. Achieving conformance through products and services that meet customer SNEaRs (specifications, needs, expectations, and requirements) remains the ultimate quality goal, hence the importance and need for emphasizing prevention and appraisal processes to avoid product failure, especially in the hands of the end user or customer within a specified limited period. An important statement that may constitute a rule of the thumb is that, "the nearer the failure is to the end-user, the more expensive it is to correct" [1]. Imagine the costs of returned products/services which had to be replaced/repeated.

It is interesting, firstly, to discuss the price of quality so that the way can be cleared for ensuring a good understanding of the term "cost of quality" (CoQ) itself.

For an organization to be able to ensure the production of quality products or rendering of quality services, that is, those that conform with the requirements and specifications of the customer and relevant regulatory guidelines, there is a price to be paid. This can easily be termed the conformance price, that is, the price involved in your aiming to assure the quality of your products and services or in "doing it right the first time" as well as "designing it right from the onset." This cost emanates from the actions and mechanisms put in place to achieve products and services that outrightly meet the requirements and specifications of the customer without any complaints. Hence, we have the prevention and appraisal costs.

To understand the theme "cost of quality" (CoQ), there is the need to look at quality very closely from the point of view of producing goods and rendering services to the customer. Cost of quality is an issue difficult to understand because it results mainly from indirect expenses. Hence various questions come to mind whenever a quality system is about to be implemented or whenever the issues of quality is brought to the attention of management. Some of these questions are as follows:

- What is the cost of quality?
- Does the cost of quality raise the cost of goods and services?
- Can savings be made by implementing the requirements of a QMS?
- What is the amount involved in implementing a QMS?
- Is the money spent on implementing a QMS recoupable?

From a general perspective, the cost of quality can be viewed as "the expenses incurred when things are done wrong" or "as the cost of nonconformance" which may also be translated to mean "the cost of poor product/service quality." The cost of quality can therefore be said to be the amount of money lost directly or indirectly by a business enterprise because of the following:

- The realization of its products and/or services was not done right the first time.
- Malfunctioning or defective products/services were delivered to the customer.

The issue of cost of quality is very vital to all the stakeholders of an enterprise or company, that is, the shareholders, customers/end users, organization, and its employees and suppliers. It is obvious indeed that the purpose of setting up any business enterprise is to make profit or in other terms to get good ROI. It is therefore not surprising to hear the voice of the shareholder in the market wilderness crying "ROI…………ROI…………………ROI…................................"

It is necessary to consider the financial aspect of an enterprise when dealing with an organization's QMS for the following reasons:

- Quality of the product/service or on the other hand their non-quality has considerable effect and impact on product patronage vis-à-vis the profit and loss account of a company and its organizational units.
- Losses are reduced when customer satisfaction is improved through the improvement of the effectiveness and efficiency of work, process, technology, and human capital performance.

It is therefore obvious that the effectiveness of the quality system can be measured in economic terms so that there is a direct relationship between the cost of quality and ROI. Good quality products are likely to attract good patronage by customers hence good sales vis-à-vis good ROI particularly since:

Sales minus Costs equal Profits or:

$$\text{SALES} - \text{COSTS} = \text{PROFITS}$$

Since the primary objective of every manufacturer/industry or service provider is generally to meet the overall requirements/specifications (i.e., product/service and regulatory/statutory) of the customer, the cost of quality can be figured from the points of view of:

1. Planned system to assure quality hence the conformance of product and/or services to customer and statutory requirements (i.e., cost of control)
2. Unplanned system or uncontrolled work with the resultant effect of producing goods and services which do not generally conform with the requirements of the customer such that nonconforming products and services are generally produced (i.e., cost of failure to control) and/or delivered to the customer/consumer

Some examples of the components of the cost of quality are widely reported in literature such as by Cokins [1], and in most cases, they are categorized as shown below:

1. *Conformance*

   Prevention
   - Quality training and manpower development
   - Process design
   - Defect cause removal
   - Quality audit
   - Preventive maintenance
   - Risk mitigation/prevention

   Appraisal
   - Test
   - Measurements
   - Evaluation and assessments
   - Problem analysis
   - Inspection
   - Detection

2. *Nonconformance/Noncompliance*
   Internal Failure
   - Scrapped products
   - Rework
   - Repairs
   - Unscheduled and unplanned service
   - Defect removal
   - Processing time lost

   External Failure
   - Returned products
   - Product cost reduction resulting from customer complaints
   - Warranty expenses
   - Compensation or liability claims
   - Product malfunctioning
   - Replacement costs
   - Poor safety of product
   - Cost for administering customer complaints

Cost of Control (Conformance)

The costs of conformance are costs that are related to prevention and appraisal so as to meet requirements. It can be grouped generally into two parts which are prevention and appraisal costs.

- *Prevention Costs*

Costs Related to the Prevention of Failure or Prevention Costs

These comprise mainly of all the direct and indirect costs associated with the implementation of an appropriate QMS to ensure that products and services conform to the requirements of the customer. These costs include among others those that may result from the following activities:

- Quality education and training – The training/retraining of personnel, on-the-job training, quality training, etc.
- Quality improvement schemes/projects – Documentation (i.e., writing quality manual, work procedures guide, work instructions, job description, technical instructions), quality improvement teams, meetings, etc.
- Inspection, monitoring, and measurements.
- Data collection and analysis.
- Process capability evaluations and change – Costs of process evaluations and changes made to the process to achieve conformity of product to customer requirements.
- Process design – Costs of design.
- Quality auditing costs.

- Costs related to measures taken to remove the causes of defect.
- Preventive maintenance costs.
- Supplier capability assessment/surveys.
- All other costs related to the planning and fault prevention to reduce the potentials for achieving defective products and services.
- Provisions are made to adequately prevent and minimize, as much as possible, the potential impacts of *unforeseeable risks* and *circumstances*, such as that of the COVID-19 pandemic.

- *Appraisal Costs*

Costs Related to the System and Product Appraisal or Appraisal Costs

This is made up mainly of all the costs involved in or associated with the testing, measuring, auditing of materials/spare parts, inspection, and examination/testing of the system to assess whether or not quality standards/requirements are complied with or fulfilled.

The composition of this includes among others the costs of:

1. Hiring quality personnel
2. Product, process, or service quality audits
3. Equipment and materials in the testing laboratories
4. Maintaining and calibrating testing equipment
5. Certification bodies/agents/registrars, etc.
6. Inspection
7. Measurements, tests, evaluations, and assessments
8. Problem analysis
9. Detection

Cost of Failure to Control (Nonconformance)

The cost of failure which is also known as the cost of poor quality or cost of nonconformance are costs that are related to external or internal failures and associated with the provision of poor-quality products/services.

- *Internal Failure Costs (Costs Associated with Defects Found Before the Customer Receives the Product/Service)*

Cost of Internal Quality-Related Processes or Internal Failure Costs

This includes the cost of internal losses incurred by an organization prior to the delivery/shipment of product or the handing over of services to the customer. The costs here may be incurred through:

1. Scrapped products/wastages
2. Re-inspection, rework, retesting, and/or defect removal
3. Redesign
4. Product downgrading
5. Unplanned modifications
6. Any other corrective action
7. Material losses
8. Downtime due to production problems, defective products, and the time required to solve or rectify such problems
9. Downtime resulting from unacceptable quality before their delivery to the customer
10. Concessions
11. Overtime resulting from the need to carry out corrective actions

Sources of costs due to internal losses may generally be summed up as follows:

- Failure to achieve development objectives/targets
- Unplanned rework and sorting activities
- Rejects/scraps
- Value reduction of products
- Re-inspection and testing of products
- Deviation in product quality
- Investigation of problem
- Downtime due to failure
- Energy costs involved in producing and reworking defective/rejected products particularly now that the cost of energy is high in most countries due to the continued increase in the price of crude oil and the expansive search for new sources of cheaper energy

External Failure Costs (Costs Associated with Defects Found After the Customer Has Received the Product or Service)

Cost of External Quality-Related Processes or External Failure Costs

These are costs that are borne by the product manufacturer since they emanate from the delivery of defective, substandard, or poor-quality products/services (or faulty services) to the customer or end user. When viewed from the total amount of input into a product/service, it would be understood that the nearer a product/service failure is to the customer/consumer/end user, the higher the costs of putting corrective measures in place and vice versa. This is usually reflected in the individual components of the costs of failure which comprise mainly of the following tangible costs:

- Returned products
- Replacement costs
- Complaint administration

- Warranty expenses
- Cost of product shipments for replaced items
- Cost of sorting and repair/reworking of products
- Product liability claims
- Downtime
- Cost of investigating the causes of failure/problem
- Cost of recalls, warranty/guarantee commitment
- Administrative costs in dealing with failure and loss of goodwill
- Penalty clauses/compensation costs
- Extraordinary marketing costs to regain lost customer and/or regain market share that is lost to competition due to one reason or the other emanating from external failure
- Legal exposure and costs

The intangible costs resulting from here are as follows:

- Goodwill
- Company image

The loss of goodwill and image may, at the end of the day, result to the loss of the customer(s) which if not abated or handled with the outmost care and attention could, at the end of the day, lead to the liquidation of an organization or business enterprise.

Sources of costs due to external losses are summed up as follows:

- Loss of image/goodwill
- Loss of customers and the loss of future sales
- Increased advertising budget
- Investigation of nonconformities
- Product liabilities
- Transportation of retuned goods
- Recalls
- Warranty
- Compensation to customer
- Loss of market status
- Other penalties imposed on nonconforming products/services especially those that are statutorily regulated

For products that are obtained by doing it the way of the concept of Philip Cosby, that is, "doing it right the first time" or in cases of "zero defects," quality costs would more or less be restricted to those of appraisal and preventive measures since the costs of failure would then have been completely or to a large extent avoided/eliminated or reduced to the barest minimum.

Profit-making therefore requires that customer requirements be met through adequate appraisal and preventive measures to ensure that quality is delivered at the least cost and in the most efficient way. An analysis of the costs involved in the achievement of a product or in the delivery of a service can therefore generally be classified into two types – *unavoidable* and *avoidable* costs.

Unavoidable costs include among others those of:

- Labor and personnel
- Machinery and equipment
- Facilities/utilities
- Appraisal
- Preventive measures
- Other necessary inputs to produce or render services that are acceptable to the customer without recourse to or with minimal rework and failure costs

Avoidable expenses/loses that are mainly made up of internal and external costs of failure are as follows:

- Preventable costs that are incurred directly and indirectly on the detection and removal of errors during production.
- The cost of materials and other inputs expended in the production of products with errors (or scrapped products).
- The costs incurred in the transportation, maintenance, and repair of products that failed to meet the requirements of the customer after such products may have been delivered (i.e., post-delivery corrective actions).
- The warranty and liability costs of such products.
- In addition, the delivery of products that failed to meet customer requirements/satisfaction may afterwards result to the eventual loss of goodwill and the customer, the value of which cannot be quantified.
- The costs of advertisement to win back lost customer and for the restoration of product image to the market.

The losses resulting from the production of unacceptable product or product failure are so huge that they may in extreme cases even result to the loss of business and its eventual collapse and liquidation.

The implementation of an effective QMS has, on the other hand, the capability of actually providing the opportunity of keeping prevention costs at the barest minimum or at least at a reasonable level just as it appreciably helps to avoid unnecessarily high appraisal and failure costs. This in turn leads to the following:

- Improved product value
- Increased competitive advantage
- Improved product reliability
- Increased productivity
- Lower scrap and rework costs
- Low customer service problems
- Decreased time-to-market cycles

Quality costs can therefore be summed up under the following headings:

- Prevention costs – investments put in place in advance to ensure conformance of products/services to requirements
- Appraisal costs – costs incurred to identify defects or faulty products
- Product failure costs – internal (or internal error) costs-costs of rework and repairs carried out on product before delivery to customer
- Product failure costs – external (or external error) costs-costs of rework and repairs carried out on product after delivery to customer

Quality costs can be measured so that they can actually be said to be central to the installation and implementation of any total quality management (TQM) system. The cost of quality therefore becomes a core issue in the business strategic planning of any enterprise/organization hence the need for its elimination and/or reduction to the barest minimum.

It is obvious from the foregoing that in order to ensure effective management of your organization, organizational leadership must take necessary measures to ensure that all:

- Processes are error free
- Products and services are free of defects
- Wastages are eliminated
- Adequate management of risks and unforeseeable circumstances as far as humanly possible

Factors Influencing the Cost of Quality

People Engagement

No matter the level of technological development and advancement, the role of human beings to the quality management system in the workplace is highly critical and inevitable. Hence, the role of humans in the workplace is of extreme importance. It therefore goes to say that whether it is process engineering, quality management, or manufacturing processes, people in the workplace share the responsibilities of detecting and preventing errors, to avoid defective and below-quality substandard products and services in protection of innocent consumers or customers to achieve their satisfaction. It is for these reasons, too, that most quality management systems standards focus on measures and processes to avoid errors in organizational quality management systems.

Some of the shortcomings or defects with their sources traceable to errors are listed by Sherman [2] as follows:

- Omitted processing
- Processing errors

- Missing parts
- Errors setting up machinery or workpiece
- Using of wrong parts
- Processing of wrong pieces
- Mis-operating equipment
- Equipment adjustment errors
- Failure to properly set up equipment
- Improper preparation of tools and jigs

Some of the sources of errors traceable to humans are among others the following:

- Forgetfulness
- Misunderstanding
- Misidentification
- Lack of experience
- Willfulness errors
- Slowness to react to situations
- Lack of standards
- Surprise errors, such as when equipment is allowed to run differently from the way it is designed or expected to run

The problem with human errors resides in the fact that while many continuous improvement tools are successfully deployed to reduce other quality-related costs, those resulting from human errors remain a persistent and intractable problem for organizations (Sherman [2] and Evans [3]). Two examples most conspicuously remembered in our recent past are the two reported by Petkovski [4] which are as follows:

- Challenger space shuttle explosion in 1986
- The two Boeing 737 Max airplane crashes

Failure costs in these two cases together are reportedly beyond the catastrophic level of billions of dollars but also involved unquantifiable number of hundreds of human lives. In reference to the former, "This tragedy cost NASA several billion dollars, and seven astronauts died," while in the latter example, "Boeing suffered a direct loss of about $10 billion," and "in the deaths of 346 innocent people [4]."

As for the Challenger, as reported by Sherman, "The root cause, however, was human error." And "Like the Challenger, the problem with the Boeing 737 Max was well-known but not solved timely or properly." The lessons from these two cases bring out the obvious fact and reality that product or services failure is at a cost, hence the need for organizations to completely embrace quality as the obvious choice to enhance their existential potentials and sustainability.

Investment in Quality

The first question you, as a business owner, would always like to ask regarding the quest to implement or introduce a QMS is that which directly relates to the impact of the QMS system on the financial health of the business as well as its ability to meet the requirements of the customers.

It is good for your organization to keep CoQ as low as possible, but it will be of high benefit to the entire organizational setup and its shareholders if more money is invested in:

- Conformance activities so that prevention and appraisal measures are effectively implemented
- Processes to ensure things are done right the first time
- Employees to ensure they have the capability and ability to carry out their responsibilities efficiently and effectively to avoid internal and external failures bearing in mind the fact that it is less expensive to implement corrective measures earlier in the business process
- Tracing and assigning indirect expenses on the basis of a one-by-one cause and effect relationship

Most of the quality systems in use today emphasize both direct and indirect ways of adding value to the business for which they are applied or implemented. Although many quality indicators are not expressed in common financial terms, some fundamental business management concepts, including financial principles, can be applied to enable the expression of quality indicators in common financial terms. Hence, it makes a good sense for your management to integrate quality costs with operations by measuring the financial implications of quality and making it an integrated part of an organization's regular accounting report.

For example, unplanned downtime or breakdown time can be converted to the number of products that would have been produced or that are lost using the productivity data. The value equivalent of the lost products can then be obtained. Defective products can easily be quantified. Once each root cause is identified, quantification of the loss associated with them can easily be obtained.

Project-Based Cost of Quality

The impact of the CoQ in the case of project-based businesses or in project management could be devastating though there is no particular model for describing all projects. There is variation in the CoQ from project to project. Despite this difficulty, it is possible to look at projects on a global basis to assess the CoQ.

Since the CoQ for projects could be very high, it is highly imperative that a project must be carefully planned and cautiously executed with particular attention paid to:

- Planning
- Design and design control
- Control of design changes
- Selection of materials and materials control
- Training of manpower
- Use of experienced personnel at all stages of the project from the planning stage to the execution stage
- Project scheduling/timing of execution
- Project execution
- Project assessment and measurements
- Risk assessment

Unlike the mass production and manufacturing systems which can tolerate a certain level or degree of failure, the project business cannot afford any deviation from the originally programmed goals at every stage of its execution else the cost of failure vis-à-vis CoQ may escalate beyond imaginable limits. Hence, adequate care must be taken particularly with all types of projects to ensure that every aspect of the project is given sufficient consideration at both the planning, design, and development stages so that once the execution begins there will be no errors to avoid incurring higher CoQ due to design failure [5]. This is the reason why the ISO in one of its QMS standards (ISO 9001) gave so much prominence to design planning and development requirements as provided in clause 7.3. of ISO 9001:2008.

The guidelines provided by ISO in ISO 9001 generally highlight all critical measures that have to be put in place to ensure problem-free design planning and development to avoid or even dramatically reduce incidences of design failure vis-à-vis higher CoQ. These are provided under the subheadings listed below:

- Design and development planning
- Design and development inputs
- Design and development outputs
- Design and development review
- Design and development verification
- Design and development validation
- Control of design and development changes

The use of inexperienced staff may lead to higher prevention costs due to retraining, while redesigning due to design variations resulting from working with inexperienced staff may lead to higher failure costs. The need for additional measurements or testing results to higher appraisal cost. Material failure and project completion time variations generally increase failure costs. Poor project execution resulting to rejection of project or its outcome by the customer leads to higher failure cost.

A project with high risk leads generally to an increase in prevention and appraisal costs. Failure costs here too may result into the escalation of CoQ. The creation of quality costs models to fit economically similar project groups allows a manager to take action to prevent failure costs without waiting until the project is completed.

Hence the control of failure costs remains the primary objective of quality cost measurement[2].

Extraordinary Cost of Quality (ECoQ)

Unmerited Value-Added Cost

It is worth mentioning here that some organizations operating in some underdeveloped countries of the world as well as some pockets of those operating in the advanced countries incur some extraordinary costs of quality (ECoQ) with or without any "true value" added to the products and/or services rendered or to be rendered. Apart from the fact that ECoQ may add some "pre-assumed or imaginary values" to the products or services in question, it may after all end up not having any true value added to the product or services for which it was incurred. Consequentially therefore the ECoQ may also:

- Result in the relegation of merit to the background particularly in the selection of suppliers and in the acceptance of supplied items both in terms of quality and quantity
- Lead to compromising the quality and integrity of the product and/or services rendered as well as that of the organization and its management
- Result in the abandonment of organizational procedures
- Give a completely negative image about the organization and its management team
- Derailment of the status of any QMS
- Send a wrong signal to potential customers
- Lead to unnecessary increase of the price of products and services thereby reducing their competitiveness in the market

These costs which are code-named mainly as "public relations fees," "facilitation fees," and "kickback," (or "egunje" in most parts of Nigeria) simply lead to increased costs of products, tangible and intangible, just as it may give room for very poor/low-quality products to be sold in place of high-quality products after the palms of the personnel responsible for the order and/or acceptance of supplied items would have been greased.

The bribery scandal which rocked Siemens (Germany) which, as revealed by a court in Muenchen (Germany) in the last quarter of 2007, affected the businesses of Siemens in Nigeria, Libya, and Russia falls under the ECoQ. Bribery given to organizational personnel to gain undeserved favor/consideration or to avoid or reduce compliance with procedures, guidelines, and regulatory requirements or pervert the course of justice is a classical example of source of what could be termed as ECoQ.

Siemens was similarly reported to have been fined "a record $800 million yesterday to settle a long-running bribery and corruption scandal [6]." This amount is tantamount to the ECoO. The overall cost of what can be said to be the consequences of not doing things right the quality way or simply being noncompliant reportedly runs into billions of US dollars.

In cases where there are claims of "added value," it is a value of deceit which in most cases actually overstates the value of poor-quality products that would have been sold at either reduced costs or scrapped as unfit for the use of the customer or end user. Hereby the personnel responsible for customer's product verification and acceptance may have, in collaboration with the appropriate staff of the supplier organization, compromised their own integrity and that of the quality of the products involved in this shady transaction with both parties gaining some advantages, in kind and/or cash, to the detriment of the quality of the product or services concerned. In all cases, competitiveness of product and/or services would have been thrown to the dogs and due process abandoned.

This corrupt practice which is endemic in a country like Nigeria and some other African, Asian, and South American states just to mention a few has appreciably reduced the competitiveness of the products of organizations where such practices have been allowed to flourish unabated especially in cases where some top management employees are themselves involved. This situation is particularly critical when it is practiced along the entire supply and production chains involving even the internal customer relationship.

The more the number of people involved, the higher the cost of sales and the less the competitiveness of the products/services involved. This situation must have to be stopped to ensure that the interests of shareholders are adequately protected while the product or service is allowed to effectively compete in the market strictly on the basis of the customer perception of the affected products/services.

CoQ in Government Establishments/Undertakings

Although the implementation of any CoQ program may, in no doubt, be unique to each level of government and their agencies, there is no evidence to show that any attempt has been made in a country like Nigeria, with her huge earnings from crude oil, to measure the total cost of quality (TCoQ) which is the summation of prevention, appraisal, and failure costs. Attempts by the author to establish the understanding and implications of the CoQ among the operatives of some Federal Government of Nigeria institutions met with mountains of bureaucratic obstacles. Daily occurrences and information available in Nigerian newspapers however spurred the author to the estimation of the TCoQ in government or service sectors of the Nigerian economy to a current value of between 40 and 50% of her total earnings if not more.

Most of these costs result from corruption and corrupt practices as well as the following:

- Very poor project planning
- Extremely poor project implementation
- The overinflation of contracts

- Wastage of resources
- Payment for contracts that did not actually exist or fake contracts
- Award of contracts to organizations and/or individuals that do not have the necessary wherewithal, competency, capacity, and capability of executing such contracts which are usually of large magnitude to encourage embezzlement of funds
- Abandonment of contractual agreements midway into the contract
- Poor project execution
- Lack of budget guidelines and poor budget implementation
- Collusion of supervisory parties such as the civil servants with contractors to defraud the government and the people of Nigeria of project funds
- Insincerity and lack of integrity on the part of government officials and civil servants and a host of other wasteful activities
- Extremely poor maintenance culture resulting in inability to manage and sustain amenities and other basic infrastructural provisions
- Lack of fiscal discipline

Product Safety and Liability Protection Costs

Reducing the CoQ

Assuring product safety and protecting product liability can go a long way to reduce the CoQ. One of the best ways to achieve this is to ensure that production processes are done under controlled conditions with adequate focus on customer needs and requirements. One of the easiest ways therefore to achieve product safety and reliability protection is to look inwards rather than just relying on overseas suppliers who are not within your control. Apart from the fact that overseas suppliers are not under your control, there are certain problems that are associated with overseas suppliers and their associated economies. For example, the purchase of products or materials from untested or unproven suppliers in places such as China or India is, according to Goodden [7], not the same as doing business with established suppliers in places such as Europe.

Another way for achieving product safety and liability protection for products from overseas suppliers is through the presence of the receiving organizations in the plants of the suppliers to ensure that the products meet the exact product specifications. Consideration here may also be given to products and/or services made under the controlled conditions stipulated in some product-specific and/or other international standards such as ISO 9000 by certified suppliers from overseas. Here references to the applicable standards must be made available to the customer who should also be given the opportunity to view organizational quality reports.

Some components commonly used in achieving product safety and liability protection include, but are not limited to, the following:

- *Warning labels and instructions* printed or stamped on product or its packaging. Product warning label designs and the provision of instructions on their packaging are in most cases done to some prescribed international standards requirements which should normally be used by your organization and your design engineers as may be dimmed necessary. There is the need to give consideration to such international standards from the product design stage. Of particular interest and consideration here is most importantly the post-consumer or after-use handling of product packaging materials. Here information or guidelines about materials composition/component must be provided by product manufacturers specifically for the use of post-consumer recycling entities to the advantage or benefit of protecting the environment. For example, the use of plastic packaging materials without the provision of the component materials name code, as provided in the ASTM International Resin Identification Coding (RIC) System, must be discouraged. The RIC system provides polymeric materials as identified as follows: PETE [1] for polyethylene terephthalate, HDPE [2] for high-density polyethylene, LDPE/ LLDPE [3] for low-density polyethylene/linear low-density polyethylene, PP [5] for polypropylene, PS [6] for polystyrene, and [7] or [O] for other polymeric or plastic materials.

- Put appropriate *contracts and agreements* (between an organization and its customers, suppliers, dealers, manufacturing, and product representatives as well as other services providers) in place so as to limit and/or specify the limitations of the level of commitment of an organization's potential exposure to product liability. When suppliers are concerned, the contract agreements must provide adequate protection for your organization against the negligence of suppliers. An example here is the protection of insurers by underwriters against adverse selection.
- Avoid the use of defective components by entrusting your supplies into the hands of capable and reliable or known suppliers by enthroning a procedure for the *selection and control of suppliers*. It is necessary here to select suppliers with liability insurance against any potential problems while indemnification clauses are properly inserted into your supply contracts and agreements.
- Put *recall procedures* in place to equip you with the needed preparedness to effect and implement a recall as soon as is necessary. The procedure needs to specify ways of reporting product problems, who and where to report to, ways and means of handling of a recall, and provision of the resources needed for handling a recall.
- Implication of *product warranties*. Adequate clarification and appropriate education of concerned management and other relevant members of staff (e.g., sales, marketing, product representatives, etc.) on the types and (e.g., full, limited, etc.) of warranties and implied warranties.
- *Procedure for product design reviews*. Adequately reviewed and sufficiently tested and reviewed design to ensure product quality, reliability, safety, fitness for intended use, and application.
- *Procedure for reliability testing of new products*. New products need to be adequately and sufficiently tested for their safe and reliable use. The procedure must be particularly explicit on the ways to handle all products after the test especially those that are below quality expectations and specifications.

- *Safety review of products*. Hazard analysis and risk assessment of all new developed products must be adequately carried out at all times to ensure they are safe and free of hazards both during and after usage.
- Avoid making claims and statements that may subject your organization to unnecessary liability claims in your products *marketing and advertising statements* through videos, billboards, packaging designs, and brochures. This is particularly critical in developed economies where the average consumer is conscious of his/her rights as dictated by the consumer protection acts and other societal norms and values. This is probably less so in the poorer and less developed parts of the world where consumer protection laws are either nonexistent or subverted.
- Since legal disputes or lawsuits may result in defense of product liability, it will be necessary to put a good and readily retrievable *records retention procedure* in place. The period of archiving your documents must be defined and may be tailored along the requirements of national legislative acts or regulations or that of the guidelines of relevant professional bodies so that you can easily provide them as and when needed by the law court.

Product Recalls and Cost Implication

Product recalls due to reasons which may result from the product and process design stages contribute largely to the CoQ not only in terms of the original costs for making them but also the cost of fines and penalties inflicted on the manufacturer or importer of the recalled items by the consumer agencies of affected nations and in terms of all the costs usually associated with nonconforming external failure of product which according to Cokins[1] are:

- Returned product
- Billing reduction from customer complaints
- Field repair call
- Warranty expenses
- Legal exposure and costs
- Liability claims
- Poor availability
- Malfunction
- Replacement
- Poor safety
- Complaint administration

Huge attention, particularly those of consumer product safety agencies, was drawn to the massive product recalls world over in the year 2007. Prominent among these recalls were those of children's toys which as reported by Goodden [7] were spearheaded by 473 recalls, involving 110 million products, of the US Consumer Product Safety Commission (CPSC). Product recalls then were reported to include toys, household, outdoor, sports, and recreational items. The risks and hazards associated with these products are the potential hazards of lead paint, choking, swallowing, cuts, and strangulation for the toys, while for the household wares, there were concerns about fire, burns, shock, and carbon monoxide poisoning.

As a result of the high CoQ emanating from recalls and the damage to the integrity of both product and producer, it is apparent that manufacturers need to pay good attention to all possible causes of product failure from product and process design through in-process quality control to product testing, safety, and hazard analysis before being made available to the customers.

To avoid producing items that may end up being recalled or that may generally lead to product failure, manufacturers need to pay particular attention to some of the following critical issues that are likely to result in product failure:

- Failure to Implement and maintain any relevant QMS standard or any other effective quality management program. Reliability on quality program may actually be on its own a liability or counterproductive here if, for example, documented audit records show that an organization is nonconforming with its own quality procedures or guidelines.
- Lack of effective in-process quality control.
- Lack of appropriate product risk analysis.
- Failure to carry out product hazard analysis.
- Poor process control.
- Lack of consideration for regulatory requirements in country of product designation and/or usage.
- Poor correlation between new product design and product specifications from the design stage.
- Avoid design defects or safety hazards in the development of new products.

Impact of CoQ on Organizational Management

It is often believed by the management team, especially those of small-scale industries that are mostly one man or family businesses, that quality is an expensive venture which they cannot afford. The only exceptions here are situations when quality problems are directly making it impossible for them to sell their products or put them in the market.

Managing the CoQ

The proper measurement and management of the cost of quality play a critical role in the successful operation of any organization. This is particularly so in a global market where businesses and companies have to constantly expand their global reach in order to maintain their business standings and even achieve growing improvements. This is, however, a factor of the way and manner corporate quality leadership uses CoQ as a tool for facing the increasingly ensuing global business challenges.

Rising costs coupled with the need for competitively lower prices are some of the critical challenges that companies and other businesses have to cope with if they have to survive and achieve good ROI. The impact of quality costs on your bottom line cannot be overemphasized particularly because it is an activity that can be felt company-wide or across the various spheres and facets of organizational operations or activities.

Measuring quality costs affords us the opportunity to identify and track down failure costs from which opportunities for improvement can be more easily identifiable.

References

1. Cokins, G. (2006a). Measuring the cost of quality for management. *Quality Progress*. ASQ, *2006*, 45–51.
2. Sherman, M. (2020). Minimize the negative – How negativity bias affects human error, and what management can do to prevent it. *Quality Progress*, 58–62.
3. Evans, J. M. (2006). Look for trouble. *Quality Progress*, 56–62.
4. Petkovski, K. (2021). Don't leave it to chance – Prioritize risk by its potential to increase your risk maturity level. *Quality Progress*, 22–29.
5. Wood, D. C. (2008a). Project oriented cost of quality. *The Quality Management Forum, 34*(1), 5–7.
6. Gow, D. (European Business Editor), (2008). "Record US fine ends Siemens' bribery scandal", Cost of case to German firm totals European Euro 2.5 billion, *The Guardian,* December 15, 2008. www.theguardian.com, retrieved on 7 March 2021.
7. Goodden, R. L. (2008). Better safe than sorry. *Quality Progress*. ASQ, May, 28–33.

Purchasing and Supplier Roles 13

Supply Chain Impact

Purchasing and the entire supply chain is a very critical aspect of any quality system of any organization hence the need for its effective and efficient management. The impact of the supply chain can make or mar the quality of your product as well as the level of satisfaction of your customers. The reason here is pretty clear particularly because purchasing fully encompasses what is defined by the ISO as "externally provided processes, products and services." This is provided by the ISO [6] in Clause 8.4 of ISO 9001:2015 with its equivalent in subclause 7.4.1. of ISO 9001:2008 [7].

As highlighted by the ISO and Cochran [1], the scope of purchased or procured items – processes, products, and services – is broad and wide that it includes some of the following classes of products:

- Raw materials procured directly from their original sources or indirectly through contractors or other suppliers in the supply chain
- Processes you get from direct owners or through subcontractors
- Products/services
- Others items such testing facilities used to inspect and confirm or verify the quality status of your products

Even if the products are not made directly by you but by a contractor or any external sources must be controlled by you to fully enhance the quality of your products and the integrity of your organization.

T. A. Ibidapo, *From Industry 4.0 to Quality 4.0*, Management for Professionals,
https://doi.org/10.1007/978-3-031-04192-1_13

Elements of Purchasing

Market Players

The market has today become a globally institutionalized platform for two key interactive players – s*uppliers/providers* and *consumers*. These two major market players operate with two different goals and expectations. Petkovski [13] views these goals as being encapsulated in the product's quality which may be viewed as a sum of attributes. While market providers aspire to maximize its profits, consumers strive to attain the maximum fulfillment of their intrinsic SNEaRs. To achieve these different objectives, the provider/supplier creates desirable or *quality* products at minimum costs, while consumers seek after what it gets out of a product, the quality of the product.

Purchasing therefore represents an important interface that is very critical for product quality hence the need to look at some of the key elements of purchasing as listed below:

- Is a procedure for the regular evaluation and selection of suppliers in place?
- Question of whether the supplier's financial capabilities has been verified and found suitable.
- Has the supplier have the necessary machinery, equipment, human capital, and process capabilities to produce or provide services to meet the demand of the customer in terms of quality, quantity, and value?
- Ask the question whether the premises of the supplier have been visited, in order to verify and/or ascertain the capabilities of the supplier to provide the products or services in question.
- Is there a list of qualified and proven suppliers maintained?
- Is there a system or procedure in place to ensure that incoming materials conform to specified requirements and specifications?
- Are there procedures or ways of verifying the quality and quantity of the supplied materials/items?
- Are your members of staff at the interface for receiving incoming materials honest and sincere?
- Are checks and balances put in place for the verification and recording of all incoming materials?
- Has the supplier have a quality system in place?
- How effective and reliable is the supplier's quality system?
- Are purchasing documents put in place for easy identification and traceability of supplied items?
- Are procedures put in place for the verification, storage/preservation, and maintenance of supplied product?
- Are sample tests for the verification of purchased products defined?

Supplier Relationship

A close cooperation of both the supplier and its customer organization, that is, the organization implementing the requirements of ISO 9000, is a necessity in realizing the product/services. This is to ensure that the products or materials purchased from third parties, that is, suppliers, as input for product realization correspond with specified purchase requirements and specifications including delivery schedule. This is necessary because the quality of the final product in any process is partly a factor of or dependent on the input from outside.

There is the need therefore for organizations to establish a good rapport with its suppliers so as to be able to monitor and control outside supplies effectively. This can be achieved through a combination of various other activities that include among others the following:

- Determination and the exact description of the materials or products to be supplied
- Provision of adequate definition, specifications, and requirements of product to be supplied
- Objective evaluation and selection of suitable and appropriate suppliers through the establishment and implementation of an adequate supplier selection process
- Control and maintenance of a register of approved and reliable suppliers
- Establishment and implementation of all activities necessary for the verification of the supplied product in terms of specified purchase requirements
- Agreed and approved mode of packaging
- Other delivery conditions such as mode of transportation particularly in parts of the world where rail and air cargo transportation are not readily available for used
- Definition of the delivery schedule

The need to control suppliers and purchases is a major element of the requirements of the ISO 9001:2015 (Clause 8.4) [6].

A tight control is particularly necessary here mostly in situations or countries where corrupt practices are known to hinder the objectivity needed for the selection of suppliers and the quality of products delivered. It is pertinent here to stress the fact that in order for organizations to be able to effectively control its suppliers and purchases both the organization and its suppliers must have to work closely together with the team spirit and with mutual honesty and sincerity whereby strict confidentiality is duly respected in terms of:

- Patent
- Product or trade secret
- Process technology
- License or know-how protection

The nature and types of cooperation as well as the implementation of agreed procedures and contract must be given adequate consideration and attention by both parties. Other environmental and relevant factors (e.g., legislative or regulatory requirements, economic policies, political instability, etc.) that are capable of affecting the contract and product delivery must also be given thorough consideration and documentation.

Control of Supplier Movement

One way of achieving a good control of the movement of suppliers in your premises is to clearly mark out a defined route for supplier movement. The use of the route by the suppliers must also be monitored to ensure compliance. Areas which suppliers are not allowed access must be clearly marked as such to ensure strict compliance.

Apart from this there is the need, too, to agree on specific modes of communication and period of meeting with the supplier so that there will be the assurance that nothing can go wrong, and if it does happen, preventive measures can easily be put in place.

Purchasing Information

Each organization needs to generally get sufficiently adequate information about the overall performance and capability of all suppliers so that they will always be available at all times that they may be needed. Such information which may include among others the following may also include the outcomes of the most recent supplier audit:

- Establishment and maintenance of documented procedures to ensure that purchased product conforms to specified requirements
- Evaluation and selection of suppliers on the basis of their ability to meet product requirements (including the quality system and specific quality assurance requirements)
- Definition of the exact controls that the supplier exercises over
- Establishment and maintenance of the quality records of acceptable suppliers
- Provision of purchasing data that clearly describe the product ordered in terms of the type class, grades, drawings, process requirements, inspection instructions, and other relevant technical data or any other precise identification of the product
- Review and approval of purchasing documents to ensure that the products are adequate and also conform to specified requirements prior to the release of the product for use
- Verification of purchased products at subcontractor's premise by both supplier and customer

There is the need to establish and put a process in place for the gathering, collation, and processing of information relating to the facilitation of the identify.

Control of Customer-Supplied Product

- Establishment and maintenance of documented procedures for the control of verification, storage, and maintenance of customer-supplied product which are provided by the customers as input or provided for incorporation into the supplies or for related activities.
- Ensure that all such products found unsuitable, lost, or damaged are recorded and promptly reported to the customer.
- Ensure the recording and reporting to the customer of all products that are found to be unsuitable.

Supplier Evaluation and Selection

A company must as a matter of necessity evaluate its suppliers prior to their acceptance. This has thus made it highly imperative to define the requirements, assessment criteria, and selection mode of suppliers. With the recent experience gained from the disruptive environment created by the COVID-19 pandemic, there is even the need to *reevaluate* the entirety of the supply chain to understand potential supply delays and disruption so as to be adequately prepared for any challenges whatsoever. Though planning for unforeseen uncertainties may be difficult it is quality-driven.

It is the responsibility of the top management of an organization to ensure that suppliers are adequately evaluated and selected on merit based on verifiable evidences that sure suppliers have the capabilities to deliver products or services that represent the organizations' requirements. It may therefore be necessary to put a procedure in place for the evaluation and selection of suppliers.

The following are some of the vital criteria that may be put into consideration by the organization in the evaluation and selection of suppliers:

- Ability to understand purchasing information, that is, product quality requirements, specifications, and expectations and ability to comply
- Financial capability
- Technical competence
- Ability to supply quality product that meets the requirements of the organization and specified product performance specifications
- Economical consideration (product value)
- Logistics requirements (product packaging, delivery schedule, transportation, etc.)
- Regulatory/legislative requirements
- Previous experience with evidence (i.e., records) generally in the supply business but particularly in relation to product concerned

The selection of suppliers must be early and timely to allow them sufficient time to understand the requirements and prepare and plan for product realization before delivery. There are various ways by which the suitability of a supplier can be demonstrated. These include among others the following:

1. Assessment of the quality system of a supplier can be assessed through:
   - Systems and process audit
   - System audits report of other customers of the supplier
   - Certifications through accredited certification bodies
2. Assessment of the product quality through:
   - Product audits
   - Sample testing
   - Quality assessment

Special attention may have to be paid to the selection of suppliers for products with special and complex characteristic features. A list of approved suppliers should at the end of the verification exercise be maintained. A reevaluation of suppliers can be carried out as may be found necessary particularly for new products/services, in cases of repeated supply of defective items and when suppliers relocate their own production lines.

Verification of Purchased Product/Goods/Services

The verification of supplied product is as critical as the evaluation of the supplier so as to ensure that supplied items actually meet the stated purchase requirements and expectations. The verification may at times be carried out in the premises of the suppliers or in that of the organization that is being supplied. In both cases the procedure for verification and acceptance of product has to be agreed upon as a part of the purchasing agreement. If the items are to be inspected in the premises of the supplier, there must be the assurance that the inspected products are the ones delivered after the verification exercise.

The control of outside supplies is therefore a very important process for achieving an organization's quality objective. That is the reason why there may be the need to put a procedure in place for achieving this on a regular basis.

Responsibilities for the verification of supplied items may be given to the purchasing manager, quality assurance manager, and a responsible member of staff of the user department of the item supplied. With this verification team, there is the likelihood that nothing will go wrong.

Waste Reduction Foundation

One way to maximize efficiency and optimize profitability is the reduction of wastes and all non-value-added activities. A good example here is the inspection of supplied items or inputs provided by the supplier. Since the inspection of incoming materials do not necessarily improve a product but only lead to the identification of products that do not meet the required standard, it is generally advisable to completely avoid it if possible or in the list reduce inspection time and all costs associated with this activity. See cost of quality.

One way to achieve the objective of reducing the inspection of incoming or supplied materials is to wholly or partly shift the responsibilities of inspection to the supplier. It is however necessary for you to evaluate the capability of your suppliers. In order to ensure the reliability and high quality of the products to be supplied by your suppliers, you must ensure that they (your suppliers) are not only committed to quality but understand your:

- Products and their values
- Processes
- Organizational environment
- Cultural environment

In order to adequately manage the supply chain, it is necessary that every organization must have a very strong supplier relationship. The features of such a strong organization/supplier relationship may include among others the following:

- Development of joint production planning
- Having joint visions between organizations and suppliers
- Alignment of the performance goals and objectives of an organization and its suppliers
- System integration
- Joint control of inventory
- Interchange of software and other electronic data

The adequate management of your supply chain requires, too, that measures should be put in place to assess or appraise the performance of the supply chain itself. In doing this both the organization and its suppliers must as a matter of necessity:

- Jointly agree or establish the most suitable criteria for appraising the supply chain performance
- Identify the parameters for the measurement of the supply chain
- Agree on the frequency of measurement of such parameters to ensure continual improvement
- Ensure continuous improvement of the supply chain so as to enhance customer or consumer values
- Share information on costs

The general need to meet the requirements and specifications of the customer in a highly competitive global market place where customer satisfaction is becoming more and more prominent and of high importance requires that organizations and their suppliers must work hand in hand to effectively and efficiently manage the supply chain. For example, big organizations cannot provide everything they need on their own; hence, they have to rely on a supply network (i.e., a set of economically dependent manufacturers/producers, transporters, distributors, and sales outlets that provide goods and services needed by other organizations) to be able to meet the requirements and specifications of their customers.

RFID Application in Supply Chain Management

Gotmare et al. [5] view the Radio Frequency Identification (RFID) as "an intelligent object tracking system having exponential applications in various industries."

RFID has as at today gained tremendous application in virtually every aspect of human endeavor where identification is required. Its major application in product traceability has actually gone beyond manufacturing systems and supply chain management to include among others the healthcare sector [18] quality management.

The RFID thus represents the source of an automated and very reliable data capture system. It is today being rapidly deployed to improve patient safety by supporting staff and patient workflow in various ways which include but are not limited to the ones listed below (Coustasse et al., [2, 3]):

- Authentication of healthcare quality and sterilization processes
- To achieve general improvement in the efficiency of healthcare provision by providing automated reliable data capture system for improving patient safety
- Management of surgical instruments
- Automation of replenishment and billing
- Streamlining the process of bed assignment
- Managing medical equipment location
- Automation of supply chain inventory management
- Pharmaceutical tracking and traceability
- Patient identification
- Accuracy of medication tray restocking

Its growing application in the healthcare sector is a strong factor of RFID's economic potentials in saving organizations their highly valuable resources – time and money. This is particularly so when it is recognized that RFID provides real-time traceability, identification, communication, temperature, and location data for people and resources [12].

Some critical issues in the tracking management of the supply chain are the challenges of theft and those of keeping the supply chain visible. One of the most common problems of the supply chain management in Nigeria and some of the world's underdeveloped or developing economy is theft. The use of the Radio Frequency Identification devices (RFID) in solving these two problems comes very handy since, according to the RFID Study Group at Pennsylvania State University [16], the two most commonly cited advantages of the RFID are supply chain visibility and theft reduction. The use of the RFID in the West African sub-region just like anywhere else is not without its challenges which include:

- Ability to effectively handle the volume of data resulting from the use and application of the RFID
- The need to have the expertise for exploiting and using the RFID data for the purposes of improving product quality and reducing costs
- The general problem of corruption, especially in the developing economies of our globalized economies

Product Packaging

Product packaging is one of the most important and critical aspects of customer satisfaction. Some quality assurance problems often emanate from supplier inability to meet their customer packaging and/or shipment specifications. Some of the common problems here include but are not limited to the following:

- Mix-up of packaged materials which make it cumbersome and uneasy for them to be handled and processed when receiving them
- Damage resulting from poor packaging
- Damaged packaging resulting from poor handling both during loading and in-transit and when off-loading

These and other packaging and shipment problems will definitely not make the customer happy with the supplier.

What are some of your customer expectations in terms of product packaging and shipment?

On a general basis, your customers often require that:

- All materials/items are protected against damage and manhandling during shipment
- Packaging of products/materials must be carried out in such a way that allows for easy and efficient handling
- Packaging must ensure the safety and protection of materials during handling
- All packages must be easily identifiable and traceable to enable easy and accurate processing of received items into customers' materials received processing (MRP) system

In order to achieve part or all of the above, various organizations in the USA and Europe usually have and maintain a list of trucking suppliers who already have knowledge of customer products and handling/shipment requirements.

Product Identification and Traceability In-Transit

Most suppliers are today required to provide barcode labels on their boxes, crates, and skids. Fortunately, technological development has provided us with various software options in the global market. It is thus easy for you to easily set up your barcode systems. Usually, the barcode system offers the opportunity of providing product- or order-specific references and any other information considered relevant for your transaction. For some organizations the purchase order (PO) or local purchase order (LPO) number is a key or significant requirement of the barcode format. Examples of other important information include but are not limited to the following:

- The quantity of products or materials shipped.
- Part number.
- The purchase order line number.
- Part number description.
- List of contents.
- Serial number giving a clear picture and reference to the total number of cartons/boxes. For example, if a product is in five boxes/cartons, it is preferable to label the first, second, third, fourth, and fifth in the series, 1 of 5, 2 of 5, 3 of 5, 4 of 5, and 5 of 5. This y of y mode of numbering will help your customers easily organize its MRP.

Quality Assurance Agreement

It is a general quality management practice for organizations to enter into a quality assurance agreement (QAA) with its suppliers. The QAA as the name implies generally stipulates the quality assurance measures provided for the purpose of having an agreement between contracting parties or in a business/supplier relationship. The QAA generally describes the requirements of the contracting organization to the supplier's management system just as it regulates the rights and obligations of both parties in relationship to the quality of the products/services to be supplied.

In most cases the QAA usually forms an integral part of the supply agreements between an organization and its suppliers. A typical supply agreement may comprise among others the following schedules:

- Products/services involved in the agreement.
- Prices of products/services.
- Packaging and shipment.
- Change management process.
- Code of conduct.
- Contingency plan.
- Quality assurance agreement.
- Payment and reconciliation.
- Clear definition of required specifications.

- Nonconforming products and their mode of identification which may be by inspection of received items or incoming inspection, in-process quality control checks, final testing, or any other suitable method. Level of tolerance must also be defined.
- Quality representatives actually serve as the voice of both parties as far as quality issues are concerned. The quality representatives are responsible for coordinating the implementation as well as the maintenance of the QAA. They shall also be the ones to adopt the decisions necessary for the implementation of the QAA; hence, a change in person by either party must be immediately made known to the other.

Post-COVID-19 Pandemic Supply Chain Norms

Creating New Norms

Apart from wrecking unprecedented havoc on human health, the COVID-19 pandemic has completely messed up man's social life. The psychosocial impact on man apart, the pandemic has largely devastated the global economy with developing countries severely affected [15]. This is evidently reflected in the estimation of the World Bank (2020) that the real growth rate of the global economy for 2020 is at −5%. Apart from the stagnant distribution of organizational products and services, there was a sharp drop of sales since the pandemic struck the people of the global community.

Although most of the existing supply chain structures in the globalized economy have some degrees of resilience against contingencies, the unexpected impact of the COVID-19 pandemic actually rubbished most, if not all, of them. Organizations using supply chains that had no protection against contingencies have been greatly impacted. Most businesses were directly or indirectly impacted by the level of disruption suffered by the supply chain. This is supported by Montshiwa et al. [11], in their survey which showed that supply chain corporations significantly impact business continuity planning (BCP) in times of disasters.

The COVID-19 pandemic demonstrably brought the people of the global community and their supply chain systems on their knees. It was a practical demonstration of how vulnerable the current globalized supply chain is while at the same time creating the awareness of the urgent need for reevaluating supply chain management strategies. This is supported by the findings of Ishida [8] that, "the spread of COVID-19 has indeed had a severe impact on the supply chains of companies." Businesses that rely on global sourcing faced hard choices in managing the crisis that resulted from the supply chain disruptions due to the COVID-19 pandemic. In their summative assessment of the impact the coronavirus pandemic had on global supply chains, Kumar and Mishra [9] viewed the situation generally from the perspective of an earthquake, or a tsunami.

The obvious lessons that should be taken away from the COVID-19 pandemic onslaught are the simple fact that organizations must not just be innovative but inventive and adaptive if sustainability is critical. Organizations need to urgently gain the consciousness to boldly manage disruptions and potential disruptions of the future, hence the need for strategizing.

Organizations may have no choice in some cases other than to move their supply chains closer home while at the same time decentralizing their concentrations and huge reliance on supplies and productions from China and other low-cost supply jurisdictions in the far east. The western world may be putting their lives and economies in a tighter corner by overreliance on China and the far east countries by ignoring the golden opportunities and quality of Africa's labor force. The opportunity of the current digital transformation should be seized by western economies to restructure the supply chain system to use sources as close to their bases as possible.

The insincerity and general lack of transparency and corporate social responsibility with which the origin of the coronavirus has been beclouded are enough reasons for caution among the people of the global community. Transparency and commitment to corporate social responsibility (CSR) are values or qualities that must not be toyed with else we may all perish in it. There is therefore a call for caution about the threatening quality of our environment in the future – another pandemic, nuclear plant accident, nuclear war, environmental degradation risks, and natural disaster – we must "be prepared."

Reevaluating Supply Chain Strategies

There is therefore the need for organizations to urgently subject their global supply chain management under the microscopic loop of operational uncertainties and reevaluate management strategies, in order to effectively restructure their supply chain for the post-COVID-19 pandemic era hence the call for a shake-up of the supply chain [19]. Both short- and long-term management strategies are at stake.

There are, however, many questions to be answered, as organizations examine their supply chain strategies for reevaluation, to ensure that organizations are repositioned and strengthened, in order to enable and make them sufficiently agile to be able to react promptly and swiftly to, and cope with, future emergencies and disruptive situations emanating from unknown and unplanned supply chain uncertainties, disruptions, and interruptions. Some of these numerous questions are, among others, the following:

- What are the different conceptual and tactical options available to organizations in order to ensure that their supply chain management activities remain strong, unhinged, and effective to face the challenges of future disruptive and interruptive eventualities or situations?
- How agile must organizations become to create needed enabling environment to immediately respond to next business crisis for *sustainability*?
- Whether they are due to the pandemic, environmental emergencies, digitalization or digitization, robotics, automation, 5G wireless technology, or any future emerging technological revolutionary changes, are there going to be supply

chain management strategies, including new investment requirements, in place for achieving immediate adaptability?

The first step to create the needed dynamism for reevaluating supply chain management strategies is undoubtedly that of organizational management, shifting to the realization of a new mindset. This mindset includes among others, the need for embracing a new norm of the business world that, "*uncertainty and disruption always will play a pivotal role in any supply chain equation*," as ascertained by Edmund [4], and the fact too, that uncertainty has become a part of any organization's operating model. This thus keeps the people of the world in suspense as to the timing, hence the big question remains, when? When would it happen next?

The lessons of the coronavirus pandemic bring us to the realization that it is not an overstatement to assume that future global business uncertainties may swing between extremities. Hence, the future aspirations of businesses across the globe should actually be for the repositioning of a post-COVID-19 pandemic supply chain systems that are flexible, agile, and proactive.

A part of the solution is the general need for the diversification of the present globalized supply chain from its present mono-structural practice of sourcing mainly from China-based manufacturing suppliers to structures capable of withstanding any disruptive change or emergency situations. Hence, the general need to recognize the fact that, the diversification of sources of supply is a vital and critical alternative here [17].

The studies of Ishida [8] in three different industrial settings – automotive equipment, personal computers (PC), and home furnishing – showed generally that supply chain management strategies could actually be fashioned along industry-specific lines of operations. This is in order to derive strategies for overcoming the negative impacts of a pandemic or disruptive environment on the supply chain as was the case with the COVID-19 pandemic which shook the global supply chain structure. Based on a "distributed management and centralized management of a single location," and the "dynamic capability of organizational theory derived from supply chain risk assessment studies," Ishida arrived at the following results for each of the three types of industrial settings studied.

While the automotive industry is claimed to be "shifting to a model that takes advantage of its inherent closed-integral strengths by increasing proximity to the country of production sites as much as possible," that of the PC industry is reportedly "shifting to a model that takes advantage of its global supply chain while maintaining transactions with local suppliers." The option of a "tighter vertical integration" is reported as being required for the home furnishing industry. Researching into possibilities in other groups of industrial settings is a challenge to the academia!

In a brief summary, the following strategies could be of good use to organizations regarding the need to maintain an effective supply chain system, irrespective of the level of disruption or interruption:

- Reevaluation of the supply chain to devise meaningful overall strategies to overcome and resolve issues that arose during the COVID-19 pandemic, and how to solve them in case and when the next crisis hits.
- Diversification [17] of sources of product supplies with focus on increased proximity rather than relying strictly on mono-structurally globalized supply chain system, as China was for world's globalized economy, in the year 2020.
- Constantly get engaged with the supply chain for updates as one of the modes for achieving continuous improvement to ensure organizational preparedness and sustainability.
- Improved organizational agility to enable management ability to swiftly and quickly respond and adjust to changes.
- Organizations need to embrace technological advancements and perhaps invest in relevant ones to support the efficiency and reliability of the supply chain, such as digital supply chains, transportation management systems, warehouse management systems, and global trade management systems [10].
- Top organizational management should consider investments, where possible, in the technology to integrate preemptive risk management and more in-depth data analytics into supply chains.
- Following the advice of Reid [14], "It's also top management's responsibility to have a plan to protect the organization's resources and meet ongoing interested party needs and expectations in the event of an emergency."

Organizational management therefore needs to use whatever is within its capabilities to prepare for, and surmount, potential disruptions and interruptive environment when next it hits. Be prepared by not underestimating the probability of another era of a pandemic, another tsunami, or earthquake or any other human challenges in the supply chain. The dynamism of today's environmental changes thus calls for cautionary measures, realism, and preparedness rather than mere egocentrism and outrageously unrealistic political braggadócio which played itself out in the USA from 2016 to 2020.

References

1. Cochran, C. (2015). *ISO 9001:2015 – In plain English* (p. 150). Paton Professional Books.
2. Coutasse, A., Cunningham, B., Deslich, S., Willson, E., & Meadows, P. (2015a). Benefits and barriers of implementation and utilization radio-frequency identification (RFID) systems in transfusion medicine. *Perspectives in Health Information Management, 12*(Summer), 1d.
3. Coutasse, A., Meadows, P., Hall, R., Hibner, T., & Deslich, S. (2015b). Utilizing radio frequency identification technology to improve safety and management of blood bank supply chains. *Telemedicine and e-Health, 21*(11), 938–945. https://doi.org/10.1089/tmj.2014.0164
4. Edmund, M. (Ed.). (2020, November). Defeating disruption – Strategies to maintain supply chain when the world is upended. *Quality Progress*, pp. 10–11.
5. Gotmare, A. V., Bokade, S. U., Inamdar, Z. Z., & Bhirud, S. G. (2019). A systematic literature review on RFID application in manufacturing and supply chain management. *Industrial Engineering Journal, 12*(10), 1–12.
6. International Standards Organization, ISO. (2015). ISO 9001:2015, Clause 8.4.

7. International Standards Organization, ISO. (2008). ISO 9001:2008, subclause 7.4.1.
8. Ishida, S. (2020). Perspective on supply chain management in a pandemic and the post-COVID-19 era. *Engineering Management Review, 48*(3), 146–152. https://doi.org/10.1109/EMR.2020.3016350
9. Kumar, R., & Mishra, R. S. (2020). COVID-19 global pandemic: Impact on management of supply chain. *International Journal of Emerging Technology and Advanced Engineering, 10*(04), 132–139.
10. McCrea, B. (2020, May 11). The current state of digital supply chain transformation. *Supply Chain 24/7.* www.supplychain247.com/article/the_current_state_of_digital_supply_chain_transformation
11. Montshiwa, L. A., Nagahira, A., & Ishida, S. (2016). Modifying business continuity plan (BCP) towards an effective auto-mobile business continuity management (BCM): A quantitative approach. *Journal of Disaster Research, 11*(4), 691–698.
12. Paaske, S., Bauer, A., Moser, T., & Seckman, C. (Summer, 2017). The benefits of and barriers to RFID technology in healthcare. *Online Journal of Nursing Informatics (OJNI), 21*(2).
13. Petkovski, K. (2021, January). Don't leave it to chance – Prioritize risk by its potential to increase your risk maturity level. *Quality Progress*, p. 24.
14. Reid, R. D. (2020, November). Business continuity plan, "Be ready – How business continuity planning helps organizations plan for emergencies." *Quality Progress*, pp. 48–51.
15. Reuters. (2020, April 9). World Bank downgrades outlook for developing countries in Europe, Central Asia. *Business News.*
16. RFID Study Group at Pennsylvania State University. (2006, November). Challenges in RFID enabled supply chain management. *Quality Progress*, pp. 23–28.
17. Sheedy, C. (2020, September 1). Supply chain management: Diversifying sources of supply. *In the Black.* www.intheblack.com/articles/2020/09/01/supply-chain-management-diversifying-sources-supply
18. Wilkerson, B. Top 5 ways RFID Technology is being used in healthcare. *Healthcare Solutions, RFID.* www.smsolution.com. Retrieved on March 8, 2021.
19. Wiriyapong, N. (2020, September 21). Supply shake-up. *Bangkok Post.* https://www.bankokpost.com/business/1988911/supply-chain-shake-up

Customer Focus 14

Quality Reflection

Reflecting back on the earlier days of the ground zero of quality (Quality 0.0) and its evolving trend to Quality 4.0 (Table 7.1.) in the twenty-first century gives the opportunity of appreciating how much humanity has appreciated and benefitted from quality management. The people of the world have been extremely blessed with quality management benefits in various ways – industrial growth and development, healthcare, water supply, food safety, transportation, environmental management, and facing pandemic challenges as witnessed particularly in the year 2020 to the early parts of 2021.

There are no doubts whatsoever that, for the future, quality and its application may continue to evolve with the likelihood of "new fields and emergence of existing ones: of technologies, areas of study and disciplines (for example, genetics, biology, physics, biophysics, electronics, software, microfluids, human development and learning). There are going to be interdependencies that were previously never imagined" [1]. The fields of polymer science, engineering, and technology and its daily expanding nanotechnology base shall continue to widen the scope of quality and its application. These widening scopes of quality and its application shall, as we move into the future, definitely continue to grow and expand the ambits of quality's principal focus, that is, the *customer*.

Product Quality Responsibility: Who Bears the Brunt?

He who plays the piper dictates the tune just as the referee determines the results of the game! These jointly say the obvious truth that, according to Drucker, providers need to be aware that consumers are the market referee who determine what quality is.

T. A. Ibidapo, *From Industry 4.0 to Quality 4.0*, Management for Professionals,
https://doi.org/10.1007/978-3-031-04192-1_14

The current market dynamism which continues to be driven by the customer, in terms of maximizing the fulfillment of its specifications, needs, expectations, and requirements (SNEaRs), cannot be overemphasized. This thus makes the consumers, or customers, the product/service referees on a global market platform. The only exemption to this rule is highly reflected in the western subversion of customer/consumer rights, in the underdeveloped parts of the world such as Africa. It is the only part of the world that customer rights are subdued and suppressed, in that the prices of both export and imported items are not functions of either the market or the customer. As customers or consumers, the prices of imported goods are forced down the throats of the African people, by the western world and now by China, irrespective of product quality. Mis-leadership and corrupt leadership jointly turned consumer and customer roles on their heads to undermine the importance of product quality.

Else, it is highly imperative that organizations or suppliers/providers remain highly concerned about their products/services being of good quality and value to the customer at all times. The fact therefore that customers/consumers determine what quality is brings to the fore the inevitable role and momentum that customers bring along with them to the global marketplace.

This is understandable, too, because it is the customers/consumers that bear first and foremost the brunt of the repercussions of defective or poor products/services quality, irrespective of the terms of warranty or guarantee, while the unnecessary costs of quality (CoQ) shall be incurred by the supplier or organization.

There are two critical factors, goals and expectations, encapsulated in the product/service quality, which separate the aspirations of suppliers from that of consumers:

- Providers/suppliers aspire to achieve *maximum profit* through the creation of desirable products at minimum cost.
- Customers/consumers aspire to achieve the optimum *fulfillment* of their intrinsic *specifications*, *needs*, *expectations*, and *requirements* (SNEaRs) in terms of product/services.
- Both customer and supplier views on the meaning and implication of product/services quality don't necessarily tally. While quality issues are always "very obvious" for the customer or market, it is not necessarily the same with suppliers. This opinion is similarly ascertained and shared by Petkovski [2].

The implication is that suppliers/providers must carefully decide precisely whether to put a product or service in the market or not and at what stage and condition, too, the product or service shall be made available to customer, or in the market. The market equilibrium between the supplying organization (or supplier/provider) and the customers (or consumer/market) is driven heavily by quality, such that it (market equilibrium) tends more towards the customer (or consumer). This is obvious, since customers only pay for what is useful, and of value, vis-à-vis "quality" to them.

Complacency in Quality Management

Complacency is an issue that must never be taken for granted or allowed, in whatever form or shape, into the quality management systems and its activities. Complacency must never be allowed to especially creep into the following:

- Internal quality auditing activities at all levels of organizational quality management internal processes. This is a dangerous negligence which may easily creep into the quality management system. This is especially so when involved personnel from both customer and supplier may have been used to each other, trusted one another, so much so that product quality may easily be *assumed* or *taken for granted*, or perhaps compromised, instead of being physically subjected to objective and adequate evaluation and testing. This attitude could subsequently lead to catastrophic product usage outcomes. This is so because of the general lack of the assurances by the relevant personnel from both sides – customer/supplier or supplier/regulatory body – that the product adequately meets both internal and external customer SNEaRs. This is a costly nature that could creep up in human negligence as it may easily lead to compromising not just the product quality integrity but also the supplier commitment in its responsibility of ensuring that the products meet relevant regulatory requirements. Management members of an organization must be adequately and responsibly audited irrespective of organizational position. Respect for leadership is entirely different from negligence of auditing responsibilities and must therefore neither be mixed up nor undermined. Internal quality auditors must therefore *never* allow management to be more concerned with cost and delivery schedule than product quality attributes such as *safety* and *reliability*.
- External quality systems auditing and regulatory product inspection, both of which must similarly be properly and responsibly conducted, must never be compromised, no matter the situation. The tragic incidences of Boeing 737 Max have taught the people in the quality world – auditors, inspectors, and other regulatory enforcement personnel inclusive – that they must always fulfill their primary roles and responsibilities of independent quality accessors or supervisors objectively and adequately without fear or favor. Regulatory agents and quality professionals must under no circumstances whatsoever rely completely or partially on supplier organization's employees or personnel vouching for product quality and safety conformity or compliance without the self-evaluation and self-conviction of the adequacy of product performance and compliance, through appropriately predetermined and agreed evaluation and testing, to decide whether a product meets the relevant specified/stated quality criteria or not.

The consequences of supplier shortfall in not always taking quality as an obvious issue could be of extremely grave and tragic consequences, not just for the customer/consumer but for the entirety of humanity at large. To understand the essential roles of quality in our lives, we need not go far but to consider the tragic incidences of human tragedy and error, which resulted from the two Boeing 737 Max airplane crashes, in Indonesia and Ethiopia.

According to the widely spread media information and in the report of Petkovski [2], "The effectiveness of Boeing's internal quality - and safety-control mechanisms failed due to decisions made by management, which was motivated by maximizing profits at the cost of the aircraft's safety." This is further reinforced by the report of the US House Committee on Transportation and Infrastructure, Rep. Peter DeFazio, in "how Boeing – under pressure to compete with Airbus and deliver profits for Wall Street – escaped scrutiny from the FAA, withheld critical information from pilots, and ultimately put planes into service that killed 346 innocent people." He further reiterated that, "What's particularly infuriating is how Boeing and FAA both gambled with public safety in the critical time period between the two crashes" [3].

In this situation, the supplier, Boeing, lost billions of dollars, being cost of quality (CoQ) resulting from the consequences of nonconformance, for not doing it right the first time, while the customers' losses are far beyond the dollar values, to include lives, 346 lost lives altogether. This is unfortunately a good, but tragic, example to illustrate the situation of the customer bearing the brunt of poor-quality products and services, based on wrong decisions traceable to the fact that quality issues are not always being seen as an obvious issue to provider/supplier organizations.

Organizations often forget that without customers, there can be no businesses, except in the case of charitable organizations. That is how important the customer and its roles in the business community are, hence the need for organizations to *focus* on their customers/consumers and the market at large with the utmost efficacy.

Customer Concern

The customer is defined by ISO [4] as

> "the organization or person that receives a product" and customer satisfaction as the "customer's perception of the degree to which the customer's requirements have been fulfilled" (ISO 9000:2015).

The implication here is that quality is in the mind of the customer; hence, it is very critical and important for an organization to produce the goods or render the services wanted by the customer, in line with its SNEaRs. It follows from this definition that the various types and ways services and/or products are rendered to those receiving such services and/or products actually spell out the various types of customers that exist. Consumers/end users, clients, students/pupils, congregation, and patients are examples of customers that are common in the society. Analyzing the various areas of customer concern to an organization and the quality of its products gives you vivid demonstration of not just the need to focus on the customer, irrespective of the nature and type of business, but also getting closer to them. Getting closer to your customer should not be seen narrowly from the perspectives of:

- Installing a better customer relations management system
- Finding better ways to measure and increase the levels of customer satisfaction
- The activities of the marketing departments alone

Instead, it should actually be seen and treated as the responsibility of your organization in its whole entirety. You therefore have to go beyond mere obtaining:

- Customer feedback
- Emphasizing customer satisfaction
- Preaching customer delight
- Treating customers as kings

You should actually view your numerous customers from the point of view of your:

- Being the source of your business sustainability and profitability
- Understanding the customers
- Obtaining information about them (and their businesses where necessary)
- Being agile and adaptable to be able to adjust quickly to overcome uncertainties and disruption to sustain and maintain the ability to meet customer SNEaRs
- Focusing on the voice of the customer (VOC)

To achieve these objectives, there is the need to get as close as possible to your customers and critically look at customer information in totality to ensure that you have a good understanding of their activities as well as their SNEaRs.

All customer interaction information, including those of customer needs in the past, present, and future, must be *collated*, *consolidated*, *analyzed*, and *made available*, for the purposes of rendering services and/or providing products for the customers, to employees that may need them.

Doing this shall provide your organization with the opportunities of:

- Detecting inefficiencies
- Correcting inefficiencies
- Gaining insight into customers from past behavior
- Knowing more about customer SNEaRs

There is no doubt, however, that the efforts of your organization in understanding the business of your customers would be appreciated by a variety of your customers, who in most cases naturally expected that their product suppliers and service providers should care about them, value their businesses, and give them their due respect and recognition.

It follows from the above, too, that achieving the customer focus mindset throughout your organization is the beginning of the road towards achieving excellent customer focus.

ISO 9001 QMS Standard and Customer Focus

Customer focus has been described as the awareness of who the customers are, their strategic importance, and their needs and expectations, as well as being the reason for the organization's existence [5].

The role of the ISO and its international QMS standards in the globalized economy cannot be overemphasized. That is the reason why it is very important to share the concerns of the standard with readers especially when it comes to the issue of "customer focus." However, the entirety of the requirements of the standard focuses generally on the customer and the processes, procedures, and activities for meeting its SNEaRs. In its present version, ISO 9001:2015 (Clause 5.1.2) addresses the requirements of an organization in terms of customer focus. It was also required in the 2008 version, ISO 9001:2008 (Clause 5.2).

Due to the relevance and importance of customer focus in the area of achieving customer satisfaction, the responsibility to achieve customer focus is placed conspicuously at the doorstep of organizational top management, who are expected to "ensure" in all circumstances that customer focus is accomplished. While they may not necessarily perform these relevant tasks themselves, they can always ensure the requirements are met through their oversight or communications role. These top management responsibilities to ensure *customer focus* are summed up as follows:

Top management will make sure that:

- Customer SNEaRs and applicable statutory and regulatory requirements are determined and met
- Risks and opportunities affecting products, services, and customer SNEaRs are determined and acted upon
- The organization focuses on creating customer satisfaction

All of the requirements also connect with other stronger requirements and tasks, in the other sections or clauses of this QMS international standard, and they can be met simply through oversight and effective communication.

All that top management need to do is to ensure that necessary information, data, and feedback are received and analyzed by the appropriate personnel and consequently disseminated among the relevant and concerned members of the organization. This also goes to stress the role and importance of effective communication across the length and width of organizational activities.

Voice of the Customer (VOC)

The role of the VOC [6] is highly imperative for suppliers irrespective of the products or services involved. It is, however, particularly very critical for new businesses, especially in manufacturing or in situations where a new relationship is just being established.

The VOC, therefore, provides detailed and in-depth understanding of the customer's requirements, a common language for an organization's team moving forward in the product development process, which is an essential input for planning and setting appropriate design specifications for the product or service as well as a very useful springboard for product innovation [5]. Similarly, a study by Rini [7] claimed that the VOC has the most substantial impact on new product development. The ASQ [4] similarly defines the VOC as "the expressed requirements and expectations of customers relative to products or services, as documented and disseminated to the providing organization's members."

In some special cases as practiced by the author, in a glass bottle manufacturing plant for a new product, the VOC is brought so close to the supplier through the presence of the customer's employee at the supplier's production plant, to ensure that the VOC is not only clearly and loudly heard but verified to be "visible" as well. It became very clear to the customer here that the author's organization keeps truth with every "voice" and word of its contract without disguising any information. The news of Beta Glass Company's abilities and capabilities to manufacture excellent beer and beverage glass bottles that meet customer SNEaRs as well as regulatory requirements spread then across the manufacturing world like wildfire. The hybrid quality tools deployed by the author then were mainly a combination of the ISO 9001 QMS standards, "cautious" lean, and 5S, along with the implementation of the requirements of the ISO 14001 EMS to ensure adequate environmental conditions.

The outcome of listening to the VOC cannot be overemphasized as it was great and highly rewarding as the supplier easily builds the needed trust and confidence which may result to decades of closer relationship than can be imagined. The most interesting thing is the fact, too, that the VOC may thereafter result to resonating the voice of the supplier (VOS) in the competitive market.

Product Market Dynamism

While the market is torn apart by competitive forces, product quality galvanizes its forces of attraction. The momentum created by a product's forces of attraction therefore dictates its market dynamism among customers or market. The important role of the customer is strongly embedded in this market dynamism which makes customer or consumer the center of any business attraction.

While the market forces of suppliers are often entangled in its phantasmagoria, those of the customers or consumers are constantly devoured by their silence. The level of customer satisfaction tends, therefore, to tilt the market equilibrium between the supplier power and that of the customer or product receiver, more towards the latter, the *customer*, hence its dictates of the tune in the business market.

Under normal operational circumstances and expectations, a supplier should create an environment and circumstances suitable for it to be able to put a high-quality product or service in the market in such a way that they are in compliance with the following:

- The fulfillment of the intrinsic SNEaRs of the customer, in relationship to the appropriate product quality attributes as generally defined by their functionality, safety for use, reliability for use, aesthetics, their feel, and other customer-desired special attributes.
- Applicable regulatory requirements whether in the contract or not, though I prefer it being mentioned or even exactly detailed and spelt out in the contract. These include, among others, individual country regulatory requirements, such as those of the Federal Aviation Administration (FAA), US Food and Drug Administration (FDA) regulations, the regulations of Nigeria's National Agency for Food and Drug Administration and Control (NAFDAC), etc.
- The supplier accepting necessary responsibility such as the expectations of the society as a whole both morally and ethically. These are highly inherent in corporate social and environmental responsibility such as water, air, and ground pollution, deforestation to promote erosion disasters as common in the African continent, human rights abuses, employees' underpayment, unnecessarily exposing, and subjection of employees to danger and avoidable risks.

Suppliers do not just exhibit the power to make critical and important decisions but also to enforce them irrespective of their effective consequences and outcomes – negative or positive. The decision to put Boeing's 737 Max in the air despite its shortfall has been reportedly traced primarily to the supplier as shown above.

Petkovski [2], in his interesting and extensive work on the prioritization of risks, identified the silent power of consumers and the limitless decision-making power of providers (or suppliers), with the characterization of three of their important characteristics. That of the supplier includes those of:

- Being "intentionally (hierarchically) organized" with an internal structure which makes its responsibilities and decision-making authorities rationally and consciously constructed with the clarity of purpose
- Giving each individual the opportunity to enable them to independently take decisions irrespective of the impact on product and organization
- Being "institutionalized by the law," that is, by the legislative provisions of the society

Three of Petkovski's important characteristic features of "the silent power of consumers" or customers are exhibited as follows:

- The collectiveness of consumers, since in most cases the individual impact of a single consumer's decision is more or less negligible or has far less impact, whereas their collective decisions to patronize a product or service or not, of a supplier or provider, could be more impactful and perhaps disastrous for the supplier or organization.
- Customer or consumer's decision-making being more controlled by emotions than being rational.

- The daily increasing power of the consumers or customers due to the facilitation of customer feedback opportunities traceable mainly to the information technology revolution of our time. The transparency resulting from online product/service information availability and the proliferation of competitive product/service providers jointly unite to enhance consumer or supplier power. The opportunity of online feedback for sharing experiences about product quality performance has further strengthened consumer power.

At the end of the day, it is extremely important for organizations not to take quality and its management potentials for granted no matter the confidence and trust already built in the marketplace because one day of complacency or negligence could be so tragic and catastrophic to destroy your quality imagery of a century. Keep quality the only trusted and reliable effort which must never be betrayed or compromised.

The dynamics of today's market dynamism makes it generally mandatory for organizations to appreciate the fact that it is no more enough for suppliers/providers to come to the realism and that it is no more sufficient for organizations just to understand the things that customers want but to anticipate customers' SNEaRs for the future [8]. Similarly is the fact too that we are now in the era when it is no more enough just for organizations to have a good product/service but one of realisms that it is actually a mandatory requirement for remaining in business.

Customer Satisfaction Culture

Fundamental Unit of Reference and Analysis

Getting closer to the customers can be said to be a major task for any organization that has the ambition of remaining in business through the continuous achievement of a good ROI. Customer focus should therefore be seen and viewed by you, as an endless task which must be accomplished by the entire members of your organization, if survival is of importance. This journey must not just be undertaken by the information technology (IT) and/or marketing departments alone but must be taken as a task that cuts across all sections of your organization [9].

The first step towards accomplishing this onerous task is to make the customer "a fundamental unit of reference and analysis" similar to the way logistics, accounts, products, and sales are being handled in the conventional management culture that we know. To achieve this there is the need for you to get and collate information on a regular basis about:

- How your customers are treated at each of your product outlets and all other customer/organization and customer/product interfaces?
- What your customers care about and their values?
- What are the needs of your customers?

- What do your employees know about the roles of your customers and the way they (employees) are affected by them?
- How your employees handle the properties of your customers that are kept in your custody either for keeps, or as product or service input?
- What is the impression of your customers about the products/services offered them?
- Are your customers happy with the conditions and timing of product/service delivery?
- Is there a feedback mechanism through which changes in customer SNEaRs are channeled or conveyed?

These are some of the ways to cultivate the customer, market, or consumer quality culture, across the length and width of organizational activities.

Experience of Customer/Consumer Culture

The experience of the author shows that in some cases, where some or part of the information required to answer the questions listed above are available, they are left within the confines of the marketing department alone. And they are used discretionally by the marketing personnel to their individual benefits, usually to justify their level of performance or non-performance rather than being put to use by the entire organization to improve organizational fortune.

This is a situation which is quite common and predominant particularly in developing economies like Nigeria and some other countries of the African continent, where individual interests more or less overshadow those of the entire organization and team-working grossly undermined.

The author has some experience to share with you in this case. In this experience which was observed in a big international bakery in Lagos, Nigeria, the marketing manager completely shielded the management of her department away, not only from the rest of the bakery personnel but also from the attention of her supervisors – the Director of Operations and the General Manager of the bakery. The marketing department was more or less a "no-go" area for her superior officers, contemporaries, and others she felt may easily get the picture of what is going on in the bakery market. All the marketing activities including budgeting were kept strictly to the chest of the marketing manager who believed that any contribution from any personnel outside the marketing department is nothing but an intrusion, which must be nipped in the bud, no matter how good the advice or input may sound.

For example, the implementation of the requirements of ISO 9000 QMS standards in the marketing department of the same organization was very strongly resisted by the same marketing manager. The abolition of this closed-door type of management which restricted all customer information strictly to the marketing department was accomplished by the author during the implementation of the requirements of ISO 9001 QMS which led to the exit of the marketing manager, who vehemently resisted the implementation of the QMS, at the first instance.

It was at the commencement of the implementation of the requirements of ISO 9001 international standard, specifically after the second management briefing sessions which coincided with her exit from the company, that the door to all marketing information became opened and accessible to other departments and other members of the production plant. The marketing department was now represented in the wide activities such as production meetings and ISO 9000 training sessions.

Immediately after her exit and as soon as marketing activities are included in the regular productivity meetings and other company-wide brainstorming activities, loopholes and marketing defects were identified and corrected. Product sales increased almost immediately by about 30%. This positive result was obtained mainly as a result of:

- The availability of customer information to the management team and improved company-wide dissemination of information
- The complete integration of the marketing department and its activities into the mainstream of the bakery activities
- Teamwork
- Management by people involvement
- Documentation of processes
- Identification of marketing defects

Hence, it is important that the entire organization must be diversely and completely customer focused. This is to say that virtually everything about customer SNEaRs at the most basic level – past, present, and future – must be known or, in case of the future, anticipated.

The lesson for you and me in this case is that all information about the customer must be gathered holistically across the organization in a central pool where every department can have access to it.

The following suggestions can be of good use to you in achieving customer focus vis-à-vis customer satisfaction:

- Gather, consolidate, analyze, and standardize customer interaction information to learn everything about the customer and its products from the most fundamental to the most complicated, so as to create a comprehensive picture and information pool about the past, present, and future needs of your respective customers.
- Process, simplify, and standardize the collated information, to bring them to a level that they can be easily used in the provision of products/services to the customer.
- Information flow should be properly managed on a company-wide basis, to ensure they are used for the benefit of the customer and the organization.
- Use the information and data collated in taking decisions relating to products or services, organizational structure, strategy planning, management review, and continual improvement basis for developing an understanding the likely behaviors and needs of the customer.

- Make the customer the fundamental unit of analysis along with those of accounts, product/services, and sales figures.

My long relationship with the incredible success of the international organization for standardization (ISO) and its ISO 9000 series of QMS international standards began in the mid-1990s, when I was entrusted with the responsibilities of getting the manufacturing conglomerate of some Coca Cola packaging products in West Africa – crown cork plants, glass bottle plants, PET preform and bottle blowing plants, and plastics crates molding plants – certified to the requirements of ISO 9001 QMS *generic* standards. It completely engulfed my interests when it was established that this standard actually represents and presents the fundamentality of quality assurance practices that can be applied across organizational activities by any organization anywhere on the globe.

This capability is strongly entrenched in its gross representation of an excellent foundation for any business or organization to successfully plan, control, and continuously improve its wide range of activities in a systematic and organized manner. Above all is the broad approach of the ISO in guiding organizations to the realization of the business fact that the customer is the most critical aspect of any business enterprise, through its general focus of attention on the customer.

As reported by Marimon et al. [10], the certification and implementation of the requirements of the ISO 9000 series of QMS international standards stand out as one of the standards which application and use in all aspects of business management has accelerated in recent years in an "environment characterized by economic globalization and integration."

The popularity of this international QMS has since swelled across the globe. Based on "the ISO survey of manufacturing system standards certification" [11], China is ahead in the list of ISO 9001 certified organizations as at 2019, with 280,396 organizations, followed by Brazil (17,952), Nigeria (351), and South Africa (3464).

Monitoring Customer Satisfaction

Market Dynamism

Product market dynamism is, on a general basis, highly influenced and propelled by the level of customer satisfaction. The customer therefore is at the dictates of quality. Since quality is a strong prevalent factor in whether a customer is satisfied or not, it is highly imperative to pay adequate and needed attention to customer satisfaction in organizational quality management systems.

According to Alghwery and Bach [12], customer satisfaction is "a core determinant factor for the survival of business organizations," with the ability of "affecting different organizations in need of providing the fast analysis of the customer's demands." It is obvious, too, that customer satisfaction deteriorates with poor services, lack of organizational cooperation, unfavorable prices, and general product dissatisfaction.

Alghwery and Bach's explorative review and meta-analysis research findings have been established, through the generation of "a model that conceptualized product pricing, trust, product quality, and services as the driving forces for customer satisfaction." Product quality has, in an earlier report of Vanhuele and Dreze [13], been deducible from the analysis of the issues of reputation, price, warranty, services, features, and performance.

It becomes highly critical that organizations must, as a matter of necessity, have to set up and maintain adequate measures and mechanisms, if not already in place, for objectively measuring, assessing, or analyzing the:

- Adequacy of product prices to various levels of consumers or customers
- Level of customer and market trust in both organization and product/services
- Degree of product/service quality as perceived by the customer, the consumers, and the generality of product market
- Adequacy of warranty/guarantee conditions and specifications
- Product performance

Most organizations are today massively involved in getting feedbacks from customers and consumers online and through other avenues. It is important here to ensure the genuineness and originality of such information, due to cyber insecurity and any other shortcomings. Monitoring feedbacks are as important as getting them, hence the need for top organizational management teams to be involved, so as to ensure and facilitate the implementation of corrective measures.

In order to assure the quality of your products and services, therefore, it is highly imperative, too, to look beyond the immediate issue of an unsatisfied customer and seek to prevent and reduce the recurrence of same or similar unpleasant situations and problem from coming up again.

Impact of ISO 9000 Series of QMS Standards

Introduction

The requirements of this series of standards, ISO 9001, generally present organizations with an excellent foundation for any business or enterprise to plan, control, improve, and propel its quality management systems to ensure customer satisfaction and market sustainability, performance improvement, and innovation, if effectively and adequately implemented.

My personal experience, however, goes beyond the ISO 9001 being a quality model for customer satisfaction, market improvement, innovation, and sustainability but as a strong and effective basic model for successfully managing any business, enterprise, or organization. This series of international QMS standards has been at the disposal of mankind since its first version in 1987 leaving in its historical

Table 14.1 The evolution of ISO 9000 family of international quality management systems standards from 1987 till date

1st version (1987)	2nd version (1994)	3rd version (2000)	4th version (2008)	5th version (2015)[a]
ISO 9000	ISO 9000:1994	**ISO 9000:2000**	**ISO 9000:2005**	ISO 9000:2015
ISO 9001	ISO 9001:1994	**ISO 9001:2000**	**ISO 9001:2008**	ISO 9001:2015
ISO 9002	ISO 9002:1994	**Integrated in 9001**		
ISO 9003	ISO 9003:1994	**Integrated in 9001**		
ISO 9004	ISO 9004:1994	**ISO 9004:2000**	**ISO 9004:2009**	ISO 9004:2018
	ISO 8402:1994	*ISO 9011:2001*	ISO 19011*:2011*	*ISO 19011:2018*
Focus on manufacturing with intense documentation	With minor revision. Highly prescriptive with focus on manufacturing	Significant revision. Focus on continual improvement, customer satisfaction, leadership, and process management	Revised with very minor changes. No requirements added or removed	Significant revision. Takes the form of a model for organizational management and improvement

[a]The most current version is the only one valid for certification/registration except otherwise prescribed/allowed by the ISO

tracks hundreds of thousands of ISO QMS-certified organizations all over the globe. It has gone through five improvement developmental stages, with the fifth iteration, ISO 9001:2015, carrying the banner of its excellent accomplishments high in the global world of quality standards (Table 14.1).

Services Quality

The quality of services rendered to customers covers a slightly different sphere from that of a manufactured product. In the case of manufactured goods/products, interpersonal relationships or skills play lesser role than in the case of rendering services where individuals are directly involved with the customer.

The individuals that are directly involved in the provision of services to the customer must be adequately equipped and trained to be able to effectively and efficiently carry out assigned responsibilities and duties to the satisfaction of the customer at all times.

All the necessary and appropriate tools and resources (i.e., instruments and/or equipment) must be promptly provided for these individuals, so as to ensure that the services are provided to the satisfaction of the customer without delay, thereby achieving the quality and excellent services. The following are necessary guidelines that are likely to help in achieving quality services for your customer:

- The organization providing the services must have a good knowledge and understanding of both the customers and their SNEaRs.
- The individual employees that are responsible to provide services for the customer must have the ability and capability to render the services that are assigned to her or him.
- The organization providing the services must exhibit certain degrees of credibility.
- Both the services provided by an organization for the customer and the organization itself must be seen as reliable and dependable by the customer.
- The organization must be prepared to promptly and timely render services to the customer.
- The organization which must maintain an effective line of communication with the customer must be both receptive and responsive to customer SNEaRs questions.
- The customer must be treated with dignity, respect, and politeness during the period of service provision and at any other interactive periods.
- Individuals rendering services to the customers must be adequately provided with all necessary tools and equipment to enable rendering the services satisfactorily.

The guidelines referred to above, if maintained, are likely to lead to improvement in the quality of the services rendered by any business or organization. The role of customers or consumers cannot be overemphasized in the lives of various organizations and businesses across the globe, hence the general need for organizational focus on customers or consumers or the market generally, to make them daily organizational reference points. There are various approaches to organizational or supplier focus on the customer/market.

There are national, sectorial, and international management systems standards available to businesses, as critical approaches for accomplishing adequate but also consistent focus on customers or the market in terms of providing quality and excellent products that meet their SNEaRs. The ISO 9000 series of quality management systems standards is a key representative in this group.

Impact of ISO 9000 QMS International Standards on Businesses

Q 9000 was sponsored jointly by the American Society for Quality Control (ASQC) and the American National Standards Institute (ANSI). Unlike in Europe and Nigeria where quality has mostly been made a national and international policy, quality in the USA is a private sector affair.

Presently the use of ISO 9000 QMS standards is mandatory in Europe for certain regulated products in critical industries, such as those of the medical equipment, commercial scales, and industrial safety machines. This could be seen as a pointer generally towards the possible direction and trend of future development in international and multinational trade and business relationship between the European Union and other countries.

This development could have serious repercussions for the poor developing countries of the West African sub-region which economies and present governance structures can hardly support the provision of machinery/equipment, technology, energy, roads, and other basic infrastructure requirements necessary for providing products and services that meet the market requirements at the international level. No matter how this is viewed, the developing countries of the world may be alienated from international trade activities if they fail to progress along with other nations of the world in embracing industrialization, and doing so with adequate focus on products/services quality.

The desirability of ISO 9000 certification or registration is year in, year out on the increase worldwide. ISO 9000 presently enjoys a high level of acceptance and degree of public awareness in Europe, the USA, China, Australia, Brazil, Czech Republic, and others, while some companies in southeast Asia are spending considerable resources on developing quality management systems based on the ISO 9000 series of international standards to sustain and keep their own products and services on the platform of international trade. African countries have no alternative than to follow this trend to achieve tangible economic growth.

The massive embrace of the ISO 9000 QMS standards and its wide acceptance in the economically advanced countries of Europe, China, and North America are a unique feature which may turn ISO 9000 to an acceptable international scale for the measurement and rating of quality for both national and multinational businesses not only in the European Union but also in the USA and other parts of the world.

If the present pace of acceptance in the use, certification, and application of ISO 9001 is sustained, there is the likelihood, too, that it would during the twenty-first century become the most definitive and most widely accepted international QMS standards irrespective of the degree of fear and skeptics that may have been initially associated with the introduction of this series of international QMS standards by any organization anywhere on the globe. See Table 14.2 to see a number the ISO standards for which certifications have been achieved by various organizations across the globe.

Industries and other organizations in the developing countries of the world which may have been caught unawares, by the status which ISO 9000 QMS and other application-specific standards are gradually assuming on the international trade platform, particularly in Europe, need to emulate such quality trends.

Noting that ISO 9001 QMS requirement may, at the end of the day, voluntarily turn out to be a universal quality policy or mandate, African countries and their organizations should, at all costs, do everything possible to keep up with this pace of quality management development so as to remain relevant in the global market. Failure to follow this trend may turn out to be a disadvantage to them on the international trade platform.

Table 14.2 List of 2019 Global Management System Standard Certifications [11]

ISO standard	Use and application and (year) of last revision	Total valid certificates	Total no. of sites
ISO 9001	Quality management systems – requirements (2015)	883,521	1,217,972
ISO 14001	Environmental management systems – requirements with guidance for use (2015)	312,580	487,950
ISO/IEC 27001	Information technology-security techniques-information security management system – requirements (2013)	36,362	68,930
ISO 22000	Food safety management system – requirements for any organization in the food chain (2018)	33,502	39,651
ISO 45001	Occupational health and safety management systems – requirements with guidance for use (2018)	38,654	62,889
ISO 13485	Medical devices-quality management systems – requirements for regulatory purposes (2016)	23,045	31,508
ISO 50001	Energy management systems – requirements with guidance for use (2011 and 2018)	18,227	42,215
ISO 22301	Societal security-business continuity management systems (2012 and 2019)	1693	6231
ISO/IEC 20000-1	Information technology-service management-part I: service management system requirements (2011 and 2018)	6047	7778
ISO 28000	Specification for security management systems for the supply chain (2007)	1874	2403
ISO 37001	Anti-bribery management systems – requirements with guidance for use (2017)	872	4096
ISO 39001	Road traffic safety management systems – requirements with guidance for use (2012)	864	1852

ISO 9000, the European "CE" Trademark and International Trade

The acceptance of ISO 9000 as the universal language of the culture and management of quality which transcends all national borders may be seen as a cause for concern for organizations in the poor economies of the world. Even now, when the economic doors of Europe, which houses the European Economic Area (EEA) and comprises of about 400 million consumers then in 25 countries, are not statutorily shut on the products and services of non-ISO 9000 certified organizations or firms, it is important to embrace world product standards as they evolve. This is more so when viewed from the fact that Europe has more or less used ISO 9000 standards to harmonize the European market.

The EU which grew from 6 countries (Germany, France, Belgium, the Netherlands, Italy, and Luxembourg) in January 1958 to 27 members now introduced the **CE** mark in January 1996, as a mandatory symbol that a manufacturer fixes to a product so that it can be sold in Europe. The **CE** mark which stands for "Conformite Europeenne," a French word meaning "European Conformity," actually covers the EU, Turkey, and Israel.

In appreciation of the quality and trade relevancies of the European **CE mark**, other countries have similarly established equivalents such as the FCC in the USA, CCC in China, VCCI in Japan, RCM in Australia and New Zealand, and KCC in South Korea. This trend obviously puts African countries on the edge and, as usual, again in an economically and product quality disadvantaged position on the global trade platform. All these constitute the different quality levels of leadership/mis-leadership parading itself in the world's political makeup.

It is, however, envisaged that international geopolitical and competitive economic pressures (i.e., competitive threats) may (or may not) in the not-too-distant future result to ISO 9000 becoming a major and paramount hallmark of international trade requirements, particularly because of its emphasis on customer satisfaction, except in the African continent where perhaps because of corruption, greed, and mis-leadership, customer or consumer rights have been constantly undermined.

Future Outlook of Quality in International Trade

If and when ISO 9000 certification becomes mandatory in Europe or elsewhere, it could directly or indirectly assume the status of a trade regulatory barrier which may turn out to be suicidal for the industrial development of the already poor and economically weak nations of the world, most of which cannot even afford the basic infrastructures (i.e., law and order, roads and transportation, social services and healthcare, provision of food, education, stable electricity supply, employment, telecommunications, clean environment, provision of potable water, etc.) which are, fundamentally, the basic ingredients of industrial development and are actually taken for granted in the already developed parts of the world.

This would be particularly so if the QMS standards requirements are, at any time in the future, emphasized for agricultural produce and other raw materials which form the economic backbone structure for the sustenance of the economies of such nations. Even if the standards are not emphasized for agricultural produce for now, situations may arise in the nearest future when substitutes of such products (e.g., cocoa, coffee, maize, timber, etc.) produced to meet the requirements of international quality standards may be widely accepted and subsequently introduced into the European market, thereby reducing the need for the importation of such agricultural produce to the European market. This would, in turn, spell doom for the foreign exchange earning potentials and capabilities of the underdeveloped countries, which economies solely rely on these commodities for survival.

It is therefore to the interest of enterprises and farmers in the various sectors of the economies of countries in the West African sub-region to take advantage of ISO 9000 QMS standards to improve the quality of their products and agricultural produce (e.g., cocoa, banana, plantain, coffee, tomatoes, beans, yams, rubber, maize/corn, timber, etc.). Subscribing to the use and application of this series of generic international QMS standards shall therefore help to enhance the quality of their produce or products while, at the same time, boosting the confidence of their customers in them, particularly in the international market. The cocoa market is already being threatened by the use of "other substitutes for the cocoa bean." West African political misleaders must therefore wake up to the global realization of the total relevance of quality in agriculture, governance, and extermination of bribery.

Avoiding Economic Marginalization with Quality

In order to avoid being marginalized in the international global market, and to be relevant in international trade, organizations and firms operating in the developing countries of the world (particularly in the poor states of the West African sub-region, ravaged with war in the last few decades) have to reckon with the ISO 9000 QMS standards now. More importantly, too, is that they need to immediately move with the growing tide of this worldwide customer-friendly quality trend by their adoption and implementation of their requirements, even beyond the conventional products and services, to encompass all other human areas of endeavors where transparency, diligence, reproducibility, consistency, continuity, sincerity, continual improvement, and reliability are of daily relevance and social necessity.

It is therefore advisable at this stage that the developing countries should embrace and adopt the ISO 9000 QMS standards in every facet of life including even governance, agricultural produce, water supply, energy generation and distribution, public administration, school management, etc. so as to facilitate the efficient performance of their economies, both at the national and international levels.

The failure of organizations or firms operating in the developing countries to deploy meeting the requirements of ISO 9000 QMS standards for either certification or implementation purposes may frustrate and puncture the attempt and potentials of such firms to offer products and services at the international level, particularly to markets where ISO 9000 certification or other quality standards may eventually become mandatory requirements, or competitive pressures.

It can also not be completely ruled out that products and services from some countries may be rejected or downgraded under the pretext of not meeting customer SNEaRs, CE mark, or ISO 9000 standards requirements when actually they would have been simply rejected for political or geopolitical reasons. This is to say that the use of ISO 9000 QMS standard requirements or other similar quality management systems or standard requirements as documents of trade embargo, or political weapon, cannot be completely foreclosed or ruled out in the future.

It must, however, be stressed here, too, that on a general basis, the merits of ISO 9000 quality management system standards certification far outstretch and surpass any shortfalls that may be discreetly or indiscreetly associate with it. Its adoption and implementation, by any organization or business whatsoever, shall undoubtedly benefit from it whether they are affected by competitive threats and/or any other forms of pressures, or not.

Scope of Quality Management Embrace

It is noteworthy here that the implementation of the requirements of ISO 9000 as well as any other quality management system standard such as those listed in Table 14.2 generally calls for key changes in the structure of the implementing organization to support some of its major activities which include the following:

- Rewarding systems
- Decision-making
- Performance measuring systems
- Customer feedback systems

The popularity of ISO 9000 is demonstrated by the number of organizations that have certified to the requirements of ISO 9001:2015 QMS international standards, across the globe with China boasting of 280,386; France, 21,696; Germany, 47,868; Spain, 30,801; Australia, 7184; India, 34,397; Czech Republic, 12,439; Brazil, 17,952; South Africa, 3464; Morocco, 1066; and Nigeria, 351 certificates, as examples, based on the ISO Survey of Management System Standard Certifications, in 2019 (ISO).

Impact of ISO 9001 QMS Certification on Developing Economies

Africa's Poor Embrace of Quality Management

The poor representation of the African continent in the list of countries that are certified to the requirements of the ISO 9001:2015 is obvious – poor economic development. It is a general reflection of the low level of industrialization in an economic environment of a very high level of economic mismanagement of resources, overburdened with unprecedented corruption, undemocratic governance, and misleadership. Nigeria which, for example, has the wherewithal to tower Africa's industrialization drive is today sinking in gross mis-leadership of all times and drowned in leadership and people corruption, terrorism, and ethnic warfare and genocidal threats. The outcome is extremely poor quality of life.

Poor Quality of Living

The Nigerian economy presently suffers from the general lack of the most basic infrastructural amenities such as public electricity and water supplies, good roads, mass transit system, healthcare, reliable pension fund, and access to low-interest funds, usually taken for granted, in most of the developed countries of the world.

Instead of relying on public services provision, each organization operating in the Nigerian economy is more or less forced to directly accept responsibilities for the provision of its own utilities, roads, drainage, and the generation of electricity, to meet its immediate requirements. In some cases, such as with Beta Glass Company Ltd, where the author worked, electricity provision is provided for the community in which it carries out its operations, in a magnanimous act of corporate social responsibility (CSR).

The roads needed for the movement of goods and the transportation of goods and personnel are in extremely poor conditions. In addition, the Nigerian economy is saddled with multiple taxation, high energy costs, and erratic price movements vis-a-vis high inflationary rates and dramatic changes of government tariff and budgetary and economic policies thereby leading to low productivity and high prices of goods and services.

The industrial and economic development of most African countries has been plagued with the general lack of security, a problem which solution may only be found through the enhancement of adequately implemented quality management measures.

Despite the low productivity of the Nigerian economy, the few available locally manufactured products and goods have to compete with imported ones at home and with others on the international market (particularly in the West African sub-region). This has subsequently led to the urge to offer good quality and competitive products, to satisfy customer SNEaRs, both nationally and internationally. It is this quality drive that suddenly prompted suppliers in Nigeria to seek registration to the requirements of ISO 9000 series of QMS standards in the middle of the last decade of the twentieth century, almost a decade after this family of QMS standards was introduced in Europe.

The number of firms/organizations certified to the requirements of the ISO 9001 requirements in Nigeria rose from 1 in 1996, 3 in 1997, 12 in 1998, to 351. There were 36 certified organizations in 2000 and 65 between 2003 and 2005 in Nigeria. It has since grown to 351 in 2019. China is a contrast to Nigeria in the way the organizations have embraced the ISO 9000 family of international quality management systems standards. The strong surge of China has obviously resulted in China being turned into today's global chain supplier for thousands of products and services.

The implementation of ISO 9000 QMS standards in the underdeveloped or developing world should, on the basis of the international or global level of quality awareness, be taken up as a major project, necessary for the enhancement of African countries' foreign exchange earnings and improved domestic production.

Some Chief Executive Officers (CEO) of some industries in Nigeria had, in the early stages of the standard, openly criticized the ISO 9000 QMS standards for not focusing enough attention on product quality reliability. Most others actually don't have enough information about ISO 9000 QMS standards, their concept, and how it is expected to impact on their businesses and organizations. Some of them even thought that ISO 9000 is a quality recipe either for the blue chip companies or those organizations that have the money to give out. Many organizations are, however, still in doubt, as to the relevance of these international QMS standards to their business activities. Some small businesses in the USA still doubt the role of quality in their businesses because of their strong belief in personal relationships and its impact on product acceptability. Prioritizing personal relationship for product quality may temporarily help product acceptability, but the quality in such decisions is definitely short-lived and without solid rooting. The same product poor quality will continue unstoppably.

Initially some firms do not even have a clear understanding as to which of the then contractual quality system models of ISO 9000:1994 was applicable to, or relevant to, their operations. These shortcomings and misunderstandings notwithstanding at that time certification to ISO 9000 in Nigeria grew by 1800% from 1 in 1994 to 23 in the third quarter of 1999. The number has since been growing though slowly.

All in all, the universal acceptance of the ISO 9000 QMS standards as a major and definitive international quality "language" and "culture" has no parallel. The awareness of the use and application of the ISO 9000 continued to soar and appeared to be unstoppable up till date, no matter the degree and extent of criticism.

Even if an organization is not interested in obtaining the certification to the requirements of the Nigeria's adopted NIS ISO 9000 QMS standards, it would be worthwhile for organizations operating in this region of the world to consider the implementation of the QMS requirements. They could consider doing so for the purposes of improving their product quality and productivity. These they can do to the advantage of being able to market their products/services competitively in the daily expanding global market. For the developing countries of the world, investments in quality are worthwhile except for those that survival is not a necessity. A major factor mitigating against the deployment of quality tools in most African countries is the unfortunate upending and usurpation of consumer rights, by making most African markets into "the sellers' market."

The standards organization of Nigeria (SON) has the legal mandate of the Nigerian government to implement the accreditation of organizations with quality systems that meet the requirements of ISO 9001. Nigeria is a member state of ISO.

Certification Agencies/Registrars

As at the time of this publication, the Standards Organization of Nigeria (SON) is the only effective governmental third-party entity, with such responsibilities in Nigeria. SON has so far been able to cope with the demand probably due to the slow pace of certification/registration to ISO 9000 in the country and its overall slow pace of economic development.

How long the SON will be able to continue to singularly play this vital role of a registrar or ISO 9000 assessment body in a country of over 200 million people will definitely be decided firstly by the rate of demand for registration or certification and, secondly, the ability of SON to effectively and efficiently execute its responsibilities. Its level of integrity, credibility, discipline and of course the ability to shield or prevent its officials from Nigeria's epileptic corruption, a known hallmark of government (military and civilian alike) businesses, in a country grossly misgoverned and mismanaged by its own people, without any consideration for quality of people's lives are very critical factors that may also impact its success

The SON may, on the long run, not have any other alternative than to introduce the use of private registrars, like it is the situation in the USA and Europe, so that it would only be saddled with the responsibilities of monitoring and regulating the performance of such bodies in the country.

Impact ISO 9000 Reviews

The regular review of ISO 9000 QMS standards for continual improvement purposes is on its own a welcome exercise. The frequency of the ISO review of its QMS standard may however result in organizations being frustrated, depending on both its frequency and the degree/extent of changes or modifications resulting from each change. No matter the depth of the changes coming out of its reviews, users are definitely going to be impacted. So far, the reviews have been well taken by users though there have always been one criticism or the other. This is the reason why too frequent review changes of these international standards will, however, not be in the best interest of Nigeria and the entirety of the developing nations of the world, particularly because of the cost of installing and managing the QMS itself, in a sellers' market.

The same thing applies to small-scale industries that may be frustrated, particularly if more frequent changes are made, soon after the implementation of an existing version of the standard. Frequent changes shall obviously generate more criticisms, and the ISO has to be careful to avoid this, so as to maintain the integrity of this set of international standards outside Europe and probably also to maintain its internationality.

It must, however, be mentioned here, too, that the flexibility allowed in implementing the requirements of the standard further enhances its generic or fit-all status, thereby making it easily adaptable to organizations all over the globe.

In Nigeria, the SON, an ISO member body, plays the role of a third-party assessment body with authority to issue a "certificate" after a satisfactory audit of the requirements of the QMS standards. The surveillance audit is carried out on a half-yearly basis while recertification audits after 3 years of initial certification.

References

1. Kimberlin, C. (2016). Quality in the 21st century: Perspective from ASQ Feigenbaum Medal winners. In P. Sampaio, & P. Saraiva (Eds.). Foreword 1. Springer Nature.
2. Petkovski, K. (2021, January). Don't leave it to chance – Prioritize risk by its potential to increase your risk maturity level. *Quality Progress*, pp. 22–29.
3. Kesslen, B. (2021). 737 Max crashes that killed 346 were 'horrific culmination' of failures by Boeing and FAA, House report says. *U.S. News*, September 16, 2020. https://www.nbcnews.com. Retrieved on 28 Jan 2021.
4. International Organization for Standardization. https://www.iso.org
5. Fuadah, P. A. T., & Prasetio, E. A. (2019). Capturing the voice of the customer for paper-notebook product development. *EJBMR, European Journal of Business and Management Research, 4*(5).
6. Ezumba, C. (2017, March 1). Voice of the customer: A tool for continual improvement. *Quality Magazine*. https://www.qualitymag.com
7. Rini, A. S. (2018, May 9). Manufaktur. https://ekonomi.bisnis.com/read/20180509/257/793560/pasar-buku-tulis-masih-menjan. Retrieved from bisnisekonomi.com
8. Sampaio, P., & Saraiva, P. (2016). Quality: From past perfect to future conditional. In P. Sampaio & P. Saraiva (Eds.), *Quality in the 21st century: Perspective from ASQ Feigenbaum medal winners* (pp. 1–22). Springer Nature.
9. Novella, A. (2012). Linking individual resource organizational practices and purchaser satisfaction on merchandise quality. *International Journal of Human Resource Management, 23*(18), 3906–3924.
10. Marimon, F., Casadesus, M., & Heras, I. (2010). Certification intensity level of the leading nations in ISO 9000 and ISO 14000 standards. *International Journal of Quality & Reliability Management, 27*(9), 1002–1020. https://doi.org/10.1108/02656711011084800
11. International Organization for Standardization. (2019). The ISO survey of management system standard certifications. https://isotc.iso.org. Retrieved on 28 Jan 2021.
12. Alghwery, H., & Bach, C. (2014). Customer satisfaction. *International Journal of Innovation and Scientific Research, 3*(2), 193–198. ISSN 2351-8014. http://www.ijisr.issr-journals.org/
13. Vanhuele, M., & Dreze, X. (2002). Measuring the price knowledge shoppers bring to the store. *Journal of Marketing, 66*(4), 72–85.

15 Change Management

Catalysts of Change

Who of all living beings would, during the Christmas or thanksgiving celebrations of 2019, have thought, or even belief the mention of it, that people all over the world would in the following year be condemned to involuntary lockdowns, working from home, school closures, restaurant closures, social distancing, and mask wearing to compromise the quality of human life and living? And may be some of those alive then in 2019 never heard or read about the Spanish flue of 1918 until the COVID-19 pandemic year 2020 rolled in.

The COVID-19 pandemic and the experience of the global community, though shocking to the marrow, taught us some painful lessons, from the ensued disruptive environment – remote working, social distancing, and mask wearing – to the worst of all things, losing loved ones through the poorest unimaginable but lonely "quality of death." We all witnessed how volatile, disruptive, and uncertain our world suddenly became.

While the healthcare industry was qualitatively overwhelmed, gasping for oxygen and personal protective equipment (PPEs), air travel was in limbo, cruising boats were parked in desserts, businesses closed, and the people of the global community abandoned in the recklessness of hopelessness. Managing the changes of a disruptive environment by quickly adapting to achieve sustainability was a common denominator of individuals, organizations, businesses, and governments across the globe, from China to Italy and Spain, the USA to Brazil and Chile, and the UK to Johannesburg. No nation was practically left unscathed.

All the while, quality and its management principles, tools, and techniques were on global 911 calls. The outcome of "quality-managing" the fight against the pandemic finally brought back some hopes of relief to the people as vaccines of varied effectiveness were produced. Some accepted the inoculation, while others refused the opportunity of this quality outcome.

T. A. Ibidapo, *From Industry 4.0 to Quality 4.0*, Management for Professionals,
https://doi.org/10.1007/978-3-031-04192-1_15

We all witnessed practically how disruptive our world and environment could suddenly become and the necessity to be adaptive in the face of the inevitability of the ensuing change. We saw how divisive human beings are in their reactions to resist change even when their lives seemed to depend on it. The value of quality and its management tools were glaringly visible in efforts to minimize the deadly impact of COVID-19 pandemic.

Key quality management lessons here are as follows:

- We are today living in a world of frequent changes. Change which is inevitable is probably catalyzed by "today's world of volatility, uncertainty, complexity and ambiguity" [30]. It may be difficult, hard or arduous, unpredictable, or nonlinear.
- No matter how change is managed, it is most likely going to be resisted in one way or the other.
- Though we may not be in the position to completely eliminate resistance to change, it can be successfully managed to reduce it and the impact on organizational activities.

The success of change management is inherent in the way it is managed as vividly put by Drucker [9] that, "People are not stressed because of too much change in organizations but because of the way change is made." Hence, the role of top management in change management cannot be overemphasized. The research findings of Prosci [33] further highlighted this, in identifying the fact that senior management should not only participate in change management but also get involved with it, a factor which has consistently been at the top of the success criteria for 20 years.

Managing Change

Manufacturing industries are today faced with the challenges of implementing the digital transformation necessitated by *Industry 4.0* or SmartFactory initiatives using technology-based solutions (see Chap. 19). This is a revolutionary change in industrial practices motivated by the recent dynamics of technology. Managing organizational transformational changes for achieving *Industry 4.0* initiatives is very critical for shaping and advancing the future of organizations of the global economy hence its relevance and importance in discussing change management.

There are various organizational approaches to change management; hence, managing change is neither rigid nor of a specific approach. For example, digital transformation generally requires extensive change management practices, efforts, and strategies. This is especially so, because the concerned changes here are involved with a combination of advanced manufacturing practices, internet of things (IoT), artificial intelligence-based tools (AI), and data and analytics into integrated production operations systems. Implementing these new technological changes will help organizations to increase their production level, reduce manufacturing costs, and be more competitive to achieve organizational excellence.

It is as a result of this that there is the obvious need for cross-organizational cooperation with focus on the change being implemented or managed. Hence, change must have to be made and managed from the purview of being driven by everyone, with focus on serving the changing SNEaRs of the customers. It is therefore critical for organizations to constantly seek ways to make beneficial changes. There are various possibilities for organizations to transform their operations or manage changes, some of which may be as follows:

- Change implementation in a way that produces incremental improvements.
- Change implementation through the project approach, that is, as formal project management processes.
- Manage change as ad hoc projects in the same way as organizational planned strategic projects are managed.
- Change implementation in such a way and manner that motivates or encourages innovative or breakthrough improvements.

Just like in the case of the changes involved in digital transformation, there is often the need for financial investment which must be adequately planned and executed. This calls generally for adapting a financial-first approach.

ISO 9001:2015 QMS and Change

Change management is also emphasized by the international organization for standardization in its popular ISO 9001:2015 QMS standard. ISO 9000:2015 defines "change management" in its focus on four major elements:

- *The purpose of the change and its consequences* – need to have consideration for the planned changes and the possible extent of its implementation in all ramifications
- *Integrity of the QMS* – having consideration for the impact of the change on the QMS and the ways to maintain it during the change
- *Availability of resources* – consideration for all the resources needed for executing the change, their clear specifications, and how they will be acquired or procured
- *Responsibilities and authority* – consideration for defining who has responsibilities for "what" and "when" to ensure accountability during the planned execution of any change and authorities

Rather than allowing oneself to be overwhelmed by change, the better option is managing the change. Hence, it is the guidance of the standard that expected changes should be carefully and deliberately planned. Systematically addressing changes by defining it, studying it to understand its effects, and identifying its interactions hold the panacea for effective change management.

Although change management first appeared in ISO 9001:2008 (subclause 5.4.2.), [18] organizational requirements were neither emphasized nor required. The concept of change management is, on the contrary, fully realized in ISO 9001:2015, clause 6.3., [17] which emphasized planned changes.

Although the standard has not specifically emphasized change process documentation and record keeping, it is the belief of the author that they are both critical for the QMS and its integrity.

What Is Change Management?

The ASQ defines change management as:

> The method and manners in which a company describes and implements change within both its internal and external processes.

This includes, according to the ASQ preparation and supporting employees, the establishment of necessary steps to making changes and the monitoring of both pre- and post-change activities to ensure successful implementation of the change in question.

Examples of processing factors relating to internal changes include among others:

- Technological changes
- Changes due to operational exigencies
- Changes in processes
- Organizational policy requirements
- Organizational improvement and/or modernization initiatives
- Chances that may be generated by organizational management

Factors originating from outside the organization that may warrant changes include but are not limited to the underlisted:

- Initiatives resulting from globalized economic pressures
- Technological advances
- Competitive pressures
- Legal requirements
- Regulatory requirements and/or enforcement needs
- Environmental forces
- Economic necessities

Implementing changes could be very tasking and complex too, especially because in most cases, changes in an organization demand the cooperation of people at various levels of organizational activities, as it usually involves different independent entities. The human element is generally very critical for the success or failure of a change. Two considerations for accomplishing the planned outcome of changes are as follows:

- Planned benefits of the transition
- Identification and mitigating all possible disruption that may potentially be associated with the change in question

The implication here is the necessity and criticality to develop a structured approach to change if the objectives of the change are to be accomplished. Organizational changes are usually generally intended for improvement purposes for the organization, hence the constant and frequent recourse to change. All in all, organizational changes are intended to work, irrespective of whether it is internal or external.

This goes to confirm the famous saying by Francois de la Rochefoucauld that the only thing constant in life is change [11]. This emanated from the doctrine of Heraclitus which elaborates the fact, too, that things change continuously in life [21]. Fortunately, or unfortunately, change comes as two sides of the coin. It is unfortunate in the sense that people can take several years to make significant differences, but time may quickly deteriorate all of those efforts in no time [13]. This tells us, too, that change may also be a decline of something that is good, from good to bad.

Why Change?

Both the growth and life experience of man are constant reminders to us all that change is a permanent feature generally in the affairs of man. Hence, change may even be seen as one of the most prevalent features man has to cope with, in all his day-to-day activities. Change in the life of man begins with those generally associated with growth, education and educational development, general life experience, career/working life, marriage and married life, parenthood, health as he grows up, changes in his physical features, etc. The change referred to here may be physical or structural.

An organization may decide to change its equipment, or machinery, and it may change its processing methodology/techniques, policies, and management style. It may decide even to change its management team/team member, or other key personnel. Changes in an organization may be from a state of one quality management system to another, or a state of no quality management system to one of implementing and maintaining a particular quality management system/improvement concept, or a combination of some QMS standards or programs. All in all, changes have to be focused generally on efficiency and quality.

One of the most common organizational changes is that which emanates from the introduction, or implementation, or engagement, of any quality management improvement tool. For example, the change from a situation where an organization has no QMS in place to that of implementing ISO 9000 QMS or that of deploying Six Sigma. Organizations engineer substantive changes generally to achieve:

- Cost-effectiveness in all operational aspects (economic and market factors)
- Reduction in staff burdens and ineffectiveness (labor market)
- Modernization of machinery/equipment and other plant facilities (technology change)

No matter the type and nature of change, there is the likelihood of a certain level or degree of resistance either consciously or subconsciously by those (i.e., employees) that are affected by such changes.

This is actually in fulfillment of Newton's first law of motion which states that "everybody continues in its state of rest or uniform motion in a straight line except acted upon by a force." The change ensuing from here results from an external force acting on the body. In the case of quality organizations, changes may be induced by various factors which may include any of the following:

- ***Market competition*** – Changes become necessary when the products and/or services offered by competing organizations are better or they provide higher value than yours. You are then compelled to make changes; else the resultant impact on your business may be grave, as you may lose your customers and sales/revenue. If care is not taken, the entire business may go on bankruptcy, collapse, or fail.
- ***Maintaining industry leadership position*** – For organizations with the business culture of maintaining product or service leadership position, making changes from time to time is understandably a routine activity.
- ***Introducing new ideas and innovation*** – Situations whereby new ideas and/or innovation are introduced call for appropriate management system changes, to match those innovative ideas towards the realization of the intended objectives of the innovation.
- ***Training needs*** – Organizations should be prepared for changes that are expected to be made in realization of the full benefits of any training scheme undertaken by its members of staff. This is necessary to avoid frustrating or dashing the hopes of the employees.
- ***Responding to technological advancements*** – The integration of new technological developments, e.g., in terms of operating processing technology/methodology, machinery/equipment, etc. which often help to achieve higher productivity, improvements in quality, and increase in processing efficiency, is a good driving force for making changes in your management systems.
- ***Regulatory guidelines and laws*** – Changes may be forced on you through mandatory rules and regulations by government agencies or regulatory bodies. The introduction of SONCAP and MANCAP by the SON, respectively, for the regulation of the quality of imported items and locally manufactured products in Nigeria and the imposition of sewage management guidelines to protect the environment in Lagos State (Nigeria) are good examples of changes that definitely

will impact on the management of organizations operating in Lagos State and its environs which presently houses an estimated 66–70% of Nigeria's industries. Organizations generally need to pay particular attention to future mandatory environmental and other statutory guidelines that are likely going to be formulated on a global basis to protect the daily deteriorating environment, particularly those conditions that emanate from global warming and ozone layer depletion. It is particularly important here also to mention the needed dynamism of organizational management in an environment like Nigeria and other emerging markets, where operational conditions are actually on the move as a result of frequent changes, generally caused by unstable government policies, constantly changing customs and excise duty/tariff, unstable tax regime, political instability, deteriorating infrastructure such as energy provision, utilities, roads, etc.

- ***Changes mandated through the requirements and demands/complaints of the customer*** – Some of your good customers may demand for some changes in your policies and the way you do things which, in order to retain them, you have no alternative than to oblige. Do not forget that some customers that do not feel committed to you in anyway may not even complain but just would shift patronage to your competitors. Changes usually experienced here may affect your policies, procedures, and even management systems.

Since most intended changes are generally geared towards achieving improvements over the current status, changes are unavoidable and are necessary in our everyday activities. Hence, there is the need to adequately manage changes to the benefit of an organization, its people, stakeholders, and other affiliated entities. Very critical in the management of change are the abilities to successfully:

- Define the problems or reasons/needs for the change
- Identify the changes to be made using necessary measurements and analysis
- Identify and select potential solutions
- Permanently integrate into the existing system or daily activities the new changes or improvements

Failure to fully and adequately consider all factors relating to and affecting the full integration of identified solutions/changes or improvements into the existing system may render the whole exercise useless and unrewarding.

Risks Associated with Change

Making changes at all is as risky just as failure to make the change is. Managing change itself is not without its own risks as well. Failure to or not seeking to manage change is similarly an embodiment of risks. The strategy and methodology used for implementing changes is extremely critical in the management of associated risks [14, 19]. Hence, it is very important to critically examine all the risks associated with or related to organizational changes. This will in turn help in the selection of the right strategy and methodology for managing change to achieve expected or anticipated results.

When viewed from the perspective of risk management, it becomes glaring that change management strategies may be classified as risk strategies since the objectives of such changes are generally to avoid unwanted consequences while the intended improvement of existing conditions is achieved or enhanced.

Resistance to Change

Employee Predisposition to Accepting Change

Research works in literature showed generally that, "executives cannot simply impose change on an organization, yet grassroots change is unlikely to be sustainable without strong executive support" [22]. There is therefore the general need for a top-down support for any organizational change to be successful and effective else it may be hard. The implication here is that successful organizational change may have to be facilitated by "a sufficiently powerful coalition" [25]. It was similarly claimed here that, "the predisposition of employees to embrace, accept and tolerate change can be objectively accomplished by applying various quality tools and methods" such as an objective survey. Awareness, education, and brainstorming to get employee contribution could, as well, do the trick.

The recent COVID-19 pandemic-induced changes in the workplace, from in-person to virtual work from home, created polarized views among some employees. While some completely embraced a virtual approach, others were reportedly said to have strongly opposed it [25].

People Psychology in Quality Management

When viewed from the general perspectives of human existence, one may assume that people are generally positive. This, however, does not in any way imply that they are willing to accept change. The evidence that people are resistance to change has been reported by Bourne [4] and Bourne et al. [5]). That uncertainty which is the hallmark that bars people's willingness to embrace change has long been established by Fukuyama [10].

Newton's First Law of Motion

Resistance to change can simply be ascribed to obstacle that impedes the implementation of any change. Resistance to change could come in different ways and may be due to:

- Human beings or a group of them, such as the union
- Organizational systems or processes that are obsolete or no more suitable for current business activities

Resistance to change is a human attitude that, more frequently than not, obeys Newton's first law of motion. Hence, resistance to change is a natural response or phenomenon which requires proper handling if the change has to yield successful results or outcomes. The causes of resistance to change are apart from obeying Newton's laws of inertia, also a natural phenomenon.

People that have been working on existing systems, or involved in the current process for which changes are now required and planned, actually grew and developed their skills along with existing system or processes through its various developmental stages. Consequently, the individual employees or workers concerned with changes have similarly grown and developed themselves and their skills and competencies. In doing so, they have acquired some psychological pictures of their relevance and confidence to the system or process. Some may even have developed some emotional attachments to their jobs and job status, which they are afraid may be lost through the implementation of new changes and/or improvement schemes, hence the need and natural urge to resist whatever changes that are planned so as to maintain their assumed levels of job security. Change may therefore be viewed by such people as creating some job instabilities for them.

These, coupled with the mindset of the employee, about his existing job structure and relationships as well as the attached benefits, may lead to the creation of the impression and thinking that the impending changes or improvements, as threats to their existing job and work positions, are in line with the common saying that the "devil you know is better than the one you do not know."

The fear of the unknown, and the thought too, about the anticipated task of acquiring new skills and knowledge needed to properly fit into the new process or operational modes may strengthen the feelings of self-doubt. This, in turn, creates a strong feeling of anxiety and job insecurity in the concerned employees. This line of thinking and the mindset about the impending changes may therefore result to an internal revolt of one type, or the other, in the minds of employees, to such extent that they might put up very strong and damaging resistance to frustrate or even sabotage the implementation of any new change(s). It may be individuals or group(s) of employees.

Kegan and Lahey [23], however, found out in their research work that, "resistance to change does not reflect opposition nor is it merely a result of inertia. Instead, even as they hold a sincere commitment to change, many people are unwittingly applying productive energy toward a hidden competitive commitment. The resulting dynamic equilibrium stalls the effort in what looks like resistance but is in fact a kind of personal immunity to change." They explained further that competing commitment is a subconscious, hidden goal that conflicts with their stated commitments that make people personally immune to change.

The signs of sabotage that you are likely to notice may include among others the following:

- Poor productivity
- Poorer quality products
- Generation of higher amounts of scraps
- Absenteeism
- Equipment damage
- Poor maintenance
- Slow work rate
- Stealing
- Poor measurements and unreliable metrics

Resistance to change, if not well managed from the planning to implementation stages, could actually lead to the failure of a newly introduced QMS or any other form of improvements or organizational changes, to the frustration of management, and its ambition, objectives, and targeted goals. This can consequently lead to financial loses, waste of time, and other efforts already put into implementing and achieving the change.

The major causes of resistance to change include but are not restricted to the following factors:

- Job security and ability to retain position after the changes would have been made.
- Fear and anxiety of the overall impact of the changes to be made on employees.
- Inability to cope adequately with job requirements due to changes in technology/methodology/technique or new processes introduced after changes would have been made, that is, technophobia. This is particularly threatening to older staff members who are not easily retrainable, due to their educational level and their perception of the nature of change and its requirements from the employers.
- Concern about the loss of some, or all of the existing benefits, such as the ego or status quo, the prestige of individual employees, present position in the organization (i.e., power), pecuniary rewards, and any other perceived benefits of the current system.
- Perception or awareness that the proposed changes are faulty and are likely going to cause or create operational problems that may negatively impact on the existing processes, operations, and/or the employees.

As recently reported by Krivokuca [25], some employees were found to be resistant to COVID-19 pandemic-imposed remote or virtual working while others with embrace. Among those resisting this change were "many older employees who were only moderately comfortable with technology, along with others who found virtual workplace imposing on their social lives."

It is therefore very important that changes have to be made with care and good consideration of the impact on your organization and the employees, particularly those that have been loyal to your organization for several years. This group of employees and other members of staff must be given the confidence right from the onset of the introduction of new changes that the changes are not targeted at their jobs; rather, they are to enhance the job quality and performance.

Imperative of the Atmosphere of Trust to Change

Scholarly publications in the literature already affirmed the relevance of trust in change management. For example, Lewicki et al. (2006) and McAllister (1995) discussed trust from the perspective of cognitive, affective, and behavioral domains, while Covey [6], the author of *The 7 Habits of Highly Effective People*, has long seen trust as the glue of life. The importance of creating trust in change management is highly emphasized in the literature. Trust has thus been referred to in different ways and forms. Trust is thus viewed as the social bond that allows for all forms of cooperative human existence. It is an essential ingredient of effective communication as well as the foundational principle holding all relationships [13].

Whenever a looming change is announced in an organization, the level of trust rises on the platform of communication and relationships. Trust then becomes very critical in several ways, such as:

- How employees think with respect to the envisaged or proposed change
- The way they feel about the change
- Their action towards the change
- The way they process available information in the process of reassessing organizational management

According to Deutsch [8], trust is involved in people's ability to juxtapose their loftiest hopes and aspirations with their deepest worries and fears. Similarly, it is highly imperative to realize the simple fact that organizational change leads to the awakening of emotional reactions with respect to the way employees are committed to, or resist, change, especially with respect to both the processes involved and the envisaged outcomes [31, 37]. It goes to say generally therefore that both the employee perception of leadership roles coupled with their trustworthiness jointly unite to contribute to the effective response of employees to change [38].

Change is the ultimate goal of any business organization except when profitability and sustainability are out of the business formulae.

Barriers to Change

Apart from resistances to change, there are other factors that may constitute barriers to transformational changes. A good example here are factors that may constitute into barriers for implementing the digital transformational changes associated with the current *Industry 4.0* initiatives (see Chap. 19).

The highlights of a recent ASQE's research work identified five major factors that are viewed as barriers to an organization's digital transformational changes related to, and resulting from, implementing the initiatives of *Industry 4.0* rollout. Such barriers include concerns revolving around cybersecurity, obsolete infrastructure, shortfall in digital skills, siloed or fragmented data, and organizational resistance to adopt new technologies [3].

Achieving the Objectives of Change

In order to achieve planned objectives of change, it is essential to create, as a precedent to implementing any new change, an atmosphere:

- Of trust and openness in which people can be trusted and can freely express their minds. Hence the intention and purposes of the proposed changes must be clear and certain so as not leave any doubt in the minds of the affected people.
- Where the voice of employees can be heard.
- In which the problems, concerns, and needs of those affected by the changes can be understood and measures put in place to address and convincingly resolve them.

In order to alleviate the fears of your employees about pending changes, and to remove any doubts from their suspicious minds, there is the need to clear any uncertainty from the minds of your employees, particularly about the causes, intention, and consequences of the proposed changes or improvement measures. Communication with your employees must not just be timely and effective but also must be handled or done with some degrees of tact and effectiveness; else the issue of resistance to change may even escalate.

It is therefore of paramount importance that the perspective and approach of the individual agents, or leaders of change, must just be right. Rumors must be avoided right from the onset; hence, the timing for employee information must be right and adequate. The technique for passing information to employees and all those affected by the change, as well as the exact choice of words, must be effective, distinct, and unambiguous.

To accomplish this, there may be the need to select appropriate and capable personnel, or agent of change, to deal with the situation. The issue of dealing with the resistance to change as treated by Lawrence [26] gives more details on the handling of this delicate but vital theme of quality management in any organization. In order to be able to successfully implement changes or implement improvement, management must put appropriate measures in place to ensure that:

- Mistakes are avoided at any stage of implementing new changes
- Employee concerns are adequately and satisfactorily presented and handled
- Necessary information is properly and carefully communicated to the employees and all those concerned

Strategies for Dealing with Resistance to Change

According to the suggestions of Kotter and Schlesinger [24], the following strategies can be employed for dealing with situations where there is resistance to change.

- Education and communication
- Participation and involvement

- Facilitation and support
- Negotiation and compromise

In order to ensure that stakeholders are given accurate and undistorted information of good analyses about the impending changes, or quality improvements, there is the need for them to be directly educated and promptly informed, about the changes and their full implications for the organization and its employees. This will help to get rid of rumors and unnecessary speculations about the proposed changes or quality improvements.

The involvement of those that are going to be directly or indirectly affected by the new development can be invited to make inputs, take decisions, and make necessary contributions both at the planning and implementation stages to give them the impression that:

- The new dispensation belongs to them
- They themselves are parts of the decision-making

Bridging the Skills Gap

Envisaged gaps in employee skills that are needed for the new dispensation must be timely identified and closed through training and exposure as a part of the confidence building process to remove perceived barriers. The concerns and problems of affected employees must be identified and solved.

Any loses envisaged to result from the changes or quality improvement may have to be negotiated and compensated for. Disruptions and losses must be avoided or at least minimized to the barest minimum to make any change worthwhile.

Based on the culture of respect for elders and superiors as it exists in some third world or underdeveloped countries of the world, two other approaches highlighted by Schultz [34] that could be used to overcome and reduce resistance to changes are as follows:

- Manipulation and co-optation
- Explicit and implicit coercion

These two approaches described by him as coercive and top-down in nature are often used as a last resort or option. It must however be mentioned that some cultures of respect for elders or superiors may unquestionably encourage their ordinary use. The risks involved in the use of these two approaches are akin to forcing the changes down the throat of the affected people, rather than by conviction, which may have some negative impacts on the sustainability of the changes or improvements.

Changes Resulting from Quality Improvement

Change is a necessity for most organizations with the intention to grow, prosper, and meet the dynamism of the global market. The changes brought about by the transition from one quality management system to another, or from a situation where there is no QMS in place to the implementation of quality management system requirements, need to be adequately managed to avoid rocking the boat.

It therefore goes to say that any entity or organization that has the intention of setting up, or implementing, for example, the requirements of the ISO 9000 QMS standards for the first time, that is, a situation in which there is no quality culture in place, or as a replacement for an existing one, needs to adequately plan, design, and implement the system in a systematic way. This is necessary to ensure that the organization and its workers can easily cope with the impending drastic changes. Of the utmost importance is the issue of the mindset and attitude of the individual employee, both of which have to be worked on if the quality management system has to be successfully implemented.

In order to achieve this, each organization must ensure, first of all, that it has the capability of imbibing in all its employees, across every level of each operational stage, the ability of:

- Quality thinking
- Process thinking
- Team working

Impact of Interpersonal Relationship

The absence of "quality thinking" is actually a major obstacle usually experienced at the beginning of the implementation program and change process. In some cases, the implementation program is unnecessarily opposed at times even by the top management hierarchy of an organization implementing the requirements of the new QMS standard, hence this precautionary measure.

A situation that may sometimes arise was experienced by the author when, at the beginning of the implementation of the requirements of the ISO 9000 QMS standards in a food manufacturing company, a senior management staff challenged him for trespassing into her department. She did this, in line with her policy of keeping everybody away from her department for reasons best known to her. This type of attitude at the level of top management is likely to be encountered frequently in some underdeveloped economies of the world where cultural influence practices still dominate the minds of the people.

This attitude has not been very useful to the organization as most of the workforce working with her, including even some management staff under her, were very reluctant to take decisions in operations even when it is obvious that such decisions are potentially useful and helpful for the organization, for fear of retribution by this management staff. Individual "steer clear off my area of responsibility" attitude surely has no place in quality management hence must not be tolerated in any part or aspect of quality management.

This opinion was, however, reverted at the end of the second management briefing session to explain the advantages of implementing the requirements of the standard to the management team. In fact, the implementation of the requirements of these QMS standards revealed that all inputs to product marketing were misused and misplaced by the staff in question.

The implementation of the requirements of the ISO 9000 QMS standards in the plant resulted to a fifty percent increase in the monthly turnover from 90 million Naira (=*N* = 90million or US$692,308 at an exchange rate of US$1.00 equals *N* = 130.00) to 135 million Naira (=*N* = 135million or US$1.038 m) just by allowing access to her department, getting input or contribution from other team members, and the implementation of the team spirit which deluded that unit of the production outfit, since the management staff was employed. Field sales officers were now able to contribute to all sales decisions without the fear of retribution. There was general increase in the level of confidence for one another.

The task of introducing and implementing the system may, for the purposes of effectiveness, have to be taken as a project with the approval and active involvement of the top management, if the venture has to succeed. It should even be discussed in the budget preparation sessions and, of course, included in the budgetary activities for the period planned for the implementation of change.

Key Considerations in Change Management

Self-Assessment for Change

Using the digital transformational changes, one of the major changes to happen in the history of most of the existing industrial manufacturing organizations, as a change management example, helps in understanding some of the management processes involved in change management. Digital transformation is now gradually emerging from the early stages of the rollout of Industry 4.0 initiatives.

As ascertained by Krivokuca [25], "An organizational self-assessment is a quality method frequently applied as the first step to implement a major process change." This is undoubtedly so, despite his confirmation, that, "Unfortunately, as of yet, the digital maturity self-assessment is not widely applied by organizations as an element of their Industry 4.0 quality management systems" (see Chap. 19 for information about Industry 4.0).

In the case of the digital transformation, organizational self-assessment of its digital maturity should normally be the first logical and reasonable step to be taken. As defined by Kane et al. (2021), organizational self-assessment of digital maturity is:

> A flexible process by which the organization can continually adapt to a changing technologies environment, realigning its people, culture, tasks and structure in response.

Organizational Leaders and Managers

Organizational leaders and managers have critical roles to play, generally, in instituting change. They therefore have to exhibit the attributes of role models in order to effectively manage the change. According to Jalagat [20], in order to successfully implement change initiatives, management and organizations need to be convinced that the planned change(s) align well with corporate goals and objectives. This goes further to strengthen literature findings of what appears to be the general relationship between change, change management, and achieving corporate goals and objectives. Karmarck [] also stressed the fact that there is a positive direct relationship between organizational change and achieving organizational strategic objectives.

Aligning Change with Organizational Goals/Objectives

As part of his definition, Armstrong [1] views change from the perspective of changes in structure, management, employees, processes, and other related activities of the organization. Additionally, it is purposeful to align changes with organizational goals and objectives as stressed by Lucey [28].

No matter how much you planned the change or the amount of supervision ability put into it, there will be no meaningful result, if the people operating in the new environment are *not aware of the need for the change* or are, on the other hand, *not willing to participate*. It is therefore obvious that without a good understanding of the reasons why there is the need for a change, there may be no commitment to put it in place and make it work. It follows therefore that the dynamics of change management begins generally with the:

- Identification of the need for change
- Conviction of the stakeholders that change is needed
- Willingness of people affected by, and involved in, the environment in which the change is taking place, to participate in the change process(es)

Once these are achieved, the change process can be commenced, albeit with the assurance that all those relevant to it are carried along. All in all, there are about eight key considerations that are of particular relevance and importance in driving people for the successful introduction of a change, or implementing a quality improvement program, and these are as follows:

- ***Vision*** – The vision simply gives a clear and communicated view of what an organization should look like after the change or quality improvement relative to the existing situation. Hence, existing shortcomings or problems must be identified and appropriately and objectively defined.

- ***Communication*** – Adequate information should be provided to all affected people (i.e., shareholders, customers, employees, suppliers, etc.) in easily understandable and very clear and unambiguous terms of the:
  - (i) Present problems and difficulties
  - (ii) Need for the anticipated changes
  - (iii) Set-out goals and objectives
  - (iv) Need for the input of all stakeholders as well as their active participation in fashioning and implementing clearly realizable and achievable solutions
  - (v) Overall benefits derivable from the quality improvement, or change
- ***Training to acquire skills*** – Providing the employees the necessary skills needed for them to work collectively as a team, and to adequately use the appropriate tools, provides the necessary confidence and empowerment to confront the change without fear and anxiety. Managers and supervisors must be trained to lead by example, so that they can boldly and openly be able to proclaim the saying "do what I do."
- ***Incentives*** or as is commonly expressed by the workers themselves "what is in it for me?" (WIIIFM). Incentives here do not only necessarily refer to financial implications but also to the acknowledgment of efforts, recognizing whatever has been achieved, as well as provision of feedbacks for results and preventive and/or corrective actions. Financial incentives are surely of positive impact after the change has been accomplished and the situation stable.
- ***Provision of resources*** – Provision of all necessary resources including finance must be properly planned and made available at the time they are required and/or needed.
- ***Planning*** – An action plan must be put in place. This is critical since, according to the common saying, "failure to plan is planning to fail." This actually brings to the fore the relevance of planning in whatever we do. The use of a time-phased project plan can always be used in educating your quality and improvement team members, for achieving short-term goals.
- ***Measurement, analyses, and assessment*** – Measure, analyze, and assess the results of the implementation of the quality improvement or change, to bring out evidences and facts to demonstrate its impact on your processes and/or operations as well as any other relevant activities.
- ***Consolidation and standardization*** – As soon as targeted improvements have been established as already achieved, the entire activities, processes, and operational steps resulting from the changes, or quality improvement, must be fully integrated into the daily turn of operational events, to ensure the new improvement measures are permanently installed until a further improvement becomes necessary in the future.

The planning and execution of any change require on a general basis adequate information and proper planning. The following guidelines are suggested for your use in the implementation of the requirements of the ISO 9000 series of international QMS standards, or those of other quality management systems/concepts/programs or any other improvement tools of choice:

- Get information about the new system and the expected changes and pass same to every relevant employee and other stakeholders including the suppliers. Communication with employees must be effective and consistent.
- Put an action plan in place stipulating planned achievements at specified times.
- Involve employees in the interrelationship of all the processes involved in the impending changes, so as to create a unified course and purpose, in order to empower them.
- Involve relevant employees in making decisions that relate to the impending changes so as to demonstrate their participatory roles, and shared responsibilities, for achieving the set-out goals and targets. This should help to openly demonstrate the fact, too, that the changes are made through collectivity of the organizational team. This will give employees the confidence that the changes taking place in the organization actually belong to them. This is very important so as to be able to change the mindset of the employees which could sometimes be very difficult to accomplish.
- Train employees on their individual roles and responsibilities as provided in their job description/work instruction so as to empower them.
- In cases where a junior staff has been given the responsibility to take decisions in issues that were the traditional responsibility of management, that is, *status quo trap*, efforts must be made by management to ensure this is avoided.
- Assure employees of job security despite the changes.
- Project the impending changes as a positive tool for the future growth and development of both the organization and its people.
- Introduce changes on a gradual basis, that is, stage by stage or phase by phase, to ensure that most of the employees, if not all, are carried along.
- Use measurable and analytical parameter to assess the outcome of the new change, or quality improvement, with reference to those of the pre-improvement era, or in the old system.
- Specify and circulate the benefits resulting from the changes, i.e., improvement of quality, ability to meet customer SNEaRs, economic utilization of materials, increased confidence in both the organization and its workers vis-à-vis products/services by the customers, marketing tool, etc.
- Acknowledge and celebrate the achievement of the change or quality improvement in terms of the hard work, cooperation, and commitment of the stakeholders and those that were involved in making the switch a fruitful one.
- Standardize the results of the outcome of the change along with any other subsequent improvement measures, so that the new changes or improvements become embedded in the day-to-day work routine.
- Benchmark the new system, from time to time, and implement needed corrective and preventive actions, to ensure that there is continual improvement.

The advice of ISO 9001 QMS experts, registrars, and consultants will, as much as possible, be of value, especially in the areas of top management briefing and the training of the employees.

Apart from training and the provision of adequate resources, there has to be a proper coordination of all activities relating to the new system or, in the case of the introduction of the ISO 9001 QMS, the implementation of the requirements of the standard. It goes to say therefore that the implementation of the requirements of the QMS standards demands that all activities must be well administered with the appropriate motivation of all participants, through the provision of a highly responsible, responsive, and dedicated quality management leadership.

It then becomes the responsibility of the QMS implementation leadership, supported by the Quality Assurance Manager (QAM), to lead the organization's implementation teams to the set target and objectives – the promised land of quality for the organization and beyond. Here it is important to take note of the reality that quality is an endless journey which cannot be terminated. It is therefore left for the ISO 9001 implementation or change management team leadership of an organization implementing the requirements of the standard to ensure that the:

- Enthronement of the ISO 9001 QMS standard is planned and orderly, systematically, and properly organized
- Routine of implementing the requirements of the standard is followed diligently so that activities such as documentation and its control, monitoring, measurement and data collection, auditing, corrective and preventive actions, customer feedback, and continual improvement measures are well organized and put in place as and when necessary

The quality management lead(er) (QML), who must have the confidence and trust of the top management, is generally expected to assume the vital role of leading the implementation team to a successful installation and sustenance of the requirements of the standards. Failure to produce a strong management leadership may spell doom for the achievement of the implementation of the ISO 9001 QMS standard requirements or any other quality management system/program/concept and the benefits associated with them.

ISO 9001 Change Management Lead(er)

The question that immediately springs to mind here is that of who should bear the leadership mantle of implementing the requirements of the ISO 9000 QMS standards or any other QMS or other process improvement measures.

From the experience of the author, the role of the quality management lead(er) and that of the QAM or Quality Engineer (QE) (in the case of ISO 9001 implementation) when combined in a responsible member of the top management team often proves very effective for achieving the set-out quality goals and objectives. This is not to say, however, that the situation whereby two individuals act separately as the quality management lead and QAM/QE is not effective. This is strictly the responsibility of top management to decide which way to go. The size and activities of an organization and its activities need to be brought to play here.

The use of quality management system consultants for the installation or implementation of the QMS standards has also been observed to lead to timely and successful implementation of the requirements of ISO 9000 though at a higher cost. Whether implementation is in-house or not, achieving the ultimate organizational goal is paramount. But learning from the experience of the author, the involvement of employees in implementing the requirements of any quality management systems standards is far beneficial to an organization and its activities.

People Involvement

Overreliance on consultants must therefore be minimized or avoided to a certain extent, since a "turnkey" type of certification has the capability to partially alienate or exclude the employees from actively participating in the implementation exercise.

It also has the possibility of casting some doubts in the minds of the employees, since they would, in most cases, not be involved in making key quality management decisions. Maintaining the QMS after implementation may, in this case, be slightly more difficult, since the mindset of employees may still remain largely unchanged.

In order to reduce costs and also to ensure that employees are adequately acquainted with the new system, it is necessary to reduce the level of dependence on external consultants, by restricting the activities of consultants to training and the supervision of the implementation process. The involvement of the consultant is critical and vital in driving the implementation process until the new quality culture is attained and sustained.

Employee participation is therefore critical for the installation of the requirements of, for example, the ISO 9001 QMS standards. The more involved the employees are in the implementation process, the better it is for the organization. The involvement of employees is therefore a very vital factor in the evolution of appropriate mindset vis-à-vis quality thinking, since whatever changes are achieved in this way would be seen as their own changes thereby making its sustainability an easier task.

The mode of massive employee participation in the implementation of ISO 9001 QMS standards requirement, or other quality system/concept, or in the implementation and management of any change, or improvement tools, was used by the author in the implementation of the requirements of ISO 9001, ISO 14001, and OHSAS 18001 (now replaced by ISO 45001) in various manufacturing plants – glass bottle production plants, crown cork manufacturing factories, PET preform injection and blow molding plants, plastics crates production plants, truck bodybuilding manufacturing plant, cooling system manufacturing factory, food production factory, and flat glassing processing company.

For the reality of its inevitability, change stands out distinctively as catalyst to organizational improvement and sustainability, hence the need for its total embrace and preparedness.

Sustaining the Change

Preparedness to Embrace Change

Making changes, improving a system, or even implementing a QMS requires tact and skillful management in:

- The identification and definition of problems
- The selection of appropriate solutions and/or suitable QMS
- The creation of an atmosphere of trust and feeling of job security for the employees
- Embarking on confidence building
- Strengthening team working
- The provision of adequate resources
- Adequately empowering employees
- Careful and appropriate management of the transition
- Communicating effectively with employees at every stage of the change
- Measurement of the impact of change on processes and operations
- Convincingly changing the culture, attitude, and thinking of the employees so as to accept the new quality culture or level of achievement of the organization

It is one thing to put a structure in place; it is another to be able to maintain and sustain it. In fact, sustaining or managing success is a difficult task and oftentimes more difficult than achieving it. In the case of maintaining a QMS, it is very easy to slip into failure, as demonstrated by the anatomy of a failure witnessed and investigated by the author.

In order to be able to sustain the level of achievement after every change and also to improve on it, or to maintain a QMS already in place, leadership of such changes needs to be on their toes. They have to be innovative and proactive and must not allow previous or present successes to go naively into their heads.

Leadership must not just have a very good understanding of the new system/situation but also must acknowledge and appreciate the team spirit and effort, which are actually the foundation of that achievement. Leadership must be able to maintain and sustain the pace of improvement and even improve on it.

The following suggestions may be of good use for an organization to be able to maintain and sustain changes already put in place:

- Standardization of the new improvement or change to ensure full integration into the work routine and monitor it.
- Assess the new system at regular intervals to determine its status, using data obtained from measurements carried out at defined intervals, to determine key performance indicators (KPIs) on which you can rely on, and to know whether the system is improving or deteriorating.
- Put preventive actions in place as and when needed, to ensure that the system is sustained and improving.

- Benchmark operational processes, and products, against the best in the market, or industry through gap analysis, to know the placement of your organization in the competitive market.
- Implement on a continual basis necessary corrective actions, to maintain a system or process that is always on the path of improvement.

23-Universal Business Improvement Guide (23-UBIG)

Change Management Tool for Top Management

Based on the author's working experience gained at various business management levels in a variety of manufacturing organizations (crown cock production, plastics crate injection molding, PET bottle preform injection and blow molding, plastics recycling, glass bottle production, and windscreen/windshield manufacturing) and retail experience in the food and automotive businesses over the years, the following **23-Universal Business Improvement Guide (23-UBIG)** is considered as helpful for your enterprise/organization (both for existing and new) to achieve the common quality objectives through the use, implementation, and sustenance of a quality management or improvement initiative of your choice (e.g., ISO 9000 QMS standards, lean manufacturing, Six Sigma, etc.).

The 23-Universal Business Improvement Guide (23-UBIG) brings out the fact that an organization is free to even carve out a niche for itself by developing a systematic QMS for its use to achieve comparatively suitable improvement measures for its product and/or services. It is also applicable to new investment projects of any type and kind, in a step-by-step mode, depending on the level identified as suitable for your objective.

1. **Define** and **describe** your organizational mission and vision and strategize before setting out on your business improvement/establishment journey or in case of change new mission, vision, and objective.
2. **Identify** all customer complaints (or for new organizations your customers or potential customers, including consumers or markets) and establish their value chain by fully understanding their specifications, needs, expectations, and requirements (SNEaRs) and through various sources of reliable information/data, particularly through the integration of the sources and deployment of the voice of the customer (VOC). If an unplanned change occurs, swiftly identify adaptive measures and new strategies for sustainability and move forward.
3. **Analyze** your level of preparedness or maturity for the change. Assess your business/enterprise and operational environment to get information about the general situation regarding your level of preparedness (if unplanned change), your competitors, and the best-in-class organizations within the relevant industrial/business sector to build your **adaptive capacity**. Listen to government guidelines and actions taken depending on the magnitude of change and use information to move forward (if unplanned disruptive change). Prepare and

assess the feasibility of your business (new enterprise) or proposed improvement measures among existing ones. Make yourself **adaptive** as quickly and effectively as possible if it is an unplanned disruptive change.

4. **Benchmark** your business processes (see the definition of a process) vis-à-vis products/services and performance against the "best in class" within the same group/class of businesses, industries, or enterprises. Or if unplanned change occurs, **benchmark** your situation and actions planned, with similar organizations going through the same situation, regionally, nationally, and internationally.
5. **Measure** their processes and products/services. Know their processes and techniques. Identify what makes them tick and whether their products are best in class or different from your situation since the change has equally affected you.
6. Determine and review existing gap through the use of **gap analysis** all the issues separating you or your product from the best in class and identify complementary considerations needed to make your organization or product the *newest best in class* among its business group or peers, with reference to your processes, machinery and equipment, product packaging, and other necessary parameters. Areas for consideration here should also include but not limited to resources – human (i.e., competencies and training needs) and infrastructure (i.e., process machinery/equipment including hardware and software, workspace, and other utilities) as well as other supporting services; processes (including flow chart) and processing technology as well as other product realization activities (e.g., customer processes and customer communication); design and relevant developmental processes; and measurement, monitoring, analysis, and improvement activities/processes, and all these with considerations for sustainability within Industry 4.0. Hence, particular attention need to be paid to issues such as digital technology and initiatives, artificial intelligence (AI), Internet of Things and machine learning on shop floors, big data, getting suppliers closer to home, and taking advantage of the latest in technological advancement.
7. **Set** organizational-wide and *specific*, *measurable*, *achievable*, *relevant*, and *timely* (SMART) **goals/objectives** in terms of your intent and aspirations to be the best in class and your ability to meet customer SNEaRs. This should normally be done by the entire management team with employees properly informed. Do not forget that setting wrong goals and objectives will automatically lead to a derailment or a crash of your efforts. This is like starting your production system with trash; the resulting products/services are left for your imagination. In addition, the hopes and aspirations of your employees who have reposed some confidence in the top management echelon would have been dashed. Also of good importance here is your consideration of the costs of failure and the need to minimize them.
8. **Get** sufficient **information** about available quality management or quality improvement initiatives/concepts, mode of their implementation, and the results you are likely to get after implementation as well as the needed time schedule for achieving anticipated results and the implication (including costs) of the resultant changes to your organization and its stakeholders. This can today be

sourced using the internet and/or the services of quality resource personnel, or through the use of quality management consultants.

9. **Select** the quality concept/initiative/program/system (e.g., ISO 9000 QMS international standards, 5S Total Quality Environment (TQE), TQM, Six Sigma, Lean Manufacturing, etc.) or a combination of quality management systems/concepts (i.e., integrated quality management systems (IQMS)) that you intend to introduce and implement in order to achieve your set-out objectives. Your selection could be based on either your perception or the advice of the quality management professionals/consultants that are advising you.
10. Map out a most realistic **quality plan/destination** for moving your organization, enterprise, or business forward by setting achievable goals/objectives. Base your plan on experience, previous management review vis-à-vis QMS review, reliable data, information about contemporary industries/businesses, problems, and difficulties. Follow your plans through both logically and sensibly.
11. **Communicate**, inform, and engage, as and when necessary, your employees and other relevant stakeholders about management's intention and preparedness to implement selected quality management concept(s) or system and highlight organizational goals/objectives with the convincing demonstration of full management commitment and readiness to provide needed resources while openly demonstrating top management's willingness and determination to achieve same with their support and input.
12. Select an organizational broad-based quality management implementation and team building **leadership** to implement the project. S(he) should preferably be a member of the organization's management team. The team leader must have to be given the free hand to implement the concept and objectively select the members of his implementation team. To be successful members spread across the various units and departments of the organization is key. The team leadership must, as a matter of necessity, have the ability and capability to manage change, promote teamwork, and be tactful, dependable, courageous, loyal, objective, and knowledgeable about the activities of the organization and the quality program to be implemented. Being decisive as well as a good team player with good reputation and integrity to drive the team in the quality journey shall effectively propel the team. The project leaders should also be able to maintain/sustain whatever achievements that are accomplished as the implementation progresses. Here the use of the 14 leadership traits – *justice*, *judgment*, *decisiveness*, *integrity*, *dependability*, *tact*, *enthusiasm*, *initiative*, *bearing*, *unselfishness*, *courage*, *knowledge*, *loyalty*, and *endurance* – come very handy as criteria for the selection of quality leadership.
13. Carry out **competency evaluation** of your members of staff particularly those that perform work affecting conformity to product requirements through profiling and performance evaluation. Assess the competency gap, if any, in order to identify the training needs of your personnel from time to time and to ensure, too, that quality management gains are adequately maintained and organization sustained.

14. Put a **training** plan in place now and again not just to bridge any ensuing competency gap but also to improve the skills and competencies of the employees. This will most likely strengthen and improve individual skills and competencies, thereby enabling them to adequately and promptly perform their duties and responsibilities and also to empower them. Training could also help in promoting teamwork. Since IT is the order of the day, your employees would appreciate it if they are trained and given access to the use of computer terminals even during breaks, lunch periods, and specially arranged training sessions, to update their communications skills. This will also help to get rid of the phobia for technology particularly among your older members of staff and those that rose through the ranks and file.
15. Take necessary **actions** to achieve the set-out quality policy, goals, and objectives in line with the selected quality management system/methodology and spell out distinctly what are to be accomplished globally within the organization and departments with identified and specified milestones of achievements.
16. **Document** your activities in line with the requirements of the quality management system/concept that you are implementing and as may be found necessary by your organization. This may include your company-wide and departmental quality policy and objectives, interrelationships of personnel (organizational structure) and processes (process flow or workflow), their respective responsibilities (job description or work instruction (WI)), work procedure/standard operations procedure (SOP), forms and other process monitoring and control measurements, safety measures, performance measurement, data collection and analysis, etc. For example, key quality documents in the implementation of the requirements of ISO 9001 QMS include but are not limited to the quality manual, procedures, work instruction, calibration data sheet, and process monitoring forms.
17. Regularly **measure** and **monitor** organizational performance using appropriate key performance indicators (KPIs) and statistical data to assess accomplishments and determine the impact of the ongoing changes on organizational performance, such as costs reduction, defects and waste minimization/reduction, improved safety and downtime, improvement of the bottom line, overall process improvement, improved customer satisfaction using customer feedback information, increased turnover and accompanying growth in profits, as well as any other organizationally recognized improvement measuring tools.
18. Provide internal **feedback** mechanisms using relevant KPIs to let employees know the impact of their efforts and contributions towards the realization of organizational-wide and departmental objectives including customer (internal and external) satisfaction (e.g., using productivity data, line efficiency, %-waste, etc.). This will serve as a sort of motivation to employees. It may also serve to sustain the QMS by promoting necessary continual improvement activities and employees' cooperation. Feedbacks could be presented through various means which may include during regular departmental and organization-wide meetings (e.g., production or departmental). Feedbacks may at the discretion of

management include, among others, the outcomes of management reviews, quality audits, and innovational inputs.

19. **Continually review** your system, through regular departmental and organization-wide meetings (e.g., production or departmental, management reviews, quality audits, etc.) on the basis of the following parameters – the level of achievement of customer (internal and external) satisfaction, innovations, processes and productivity, production techniques improvement or modernization, technological advancement and challenges, training needs, market requirements (decide on the need for new products and services), experience gained from organizational-wide activities and the overall needs for continual improvement and ability to continue to meet customer needs, market and environmental challenges, and other challenges of the business.
20. Put **corrective and preventive actions** in place as may be needed or necessary based on the results of regular production meetings and measurements carried out in item 15 above – customer feedback, review meetings/activities, internal audit output, etc. – to ensure the continual improvement of your quality management system/concept/methodology so that set-out objectives and goals are not just achieved but surpassed.
21. **Control** all work processes including work procedures/standard operations procedure and work measurements, performance measurements and calibration of equipment, documentation, maintenance of records and their mode of storage, training, predictive and preventive maintenance, and customer feedback vis-à-vis customer complaints to ensure that the QMS itself is maintained in good order.
22. **Renew** your system from time to time and as the need arises by the introduction of innovations and innovative ideas (e.g., product rebranding or relaunching), introduction of customized/new products, product packaging and services along with consideration for needed changes in the marketplace (global and domestic), customer needs, specifications and requirements, customer spectrum, and other general business challenges.
23. **Reevaluate** the value and standing of your products/services in the market from step 1 above with the necessary sustenance and repeat cycle as often as you consider it necessary or as long as you may want to maintain market leadership.

The 23-UBIG continuous improvement approach is very simple to use for all businesses and interests as often as it may be necessary to achieve sustainability and build adaptive capacity. It also gives the top management team a picturesque overview of change and its management, going ahead.

Managing COVID-19-Induced Changes

COVID-19 Pandemic Experience

While some organizational changes – internal and external alike – could be adequately planned for, changes emanating from the situations of a pandemic, like that of the COVID-19, cannot be planned for because of its sudden disruptive nature. Such emergencies therefore require instant, quick, swift, and rapid organizational responses to minimize ensuing damages. Unfortunately, the real-life reaction across the globe was slow, blame shifting, and underpinned with denials and uncertainties at various national and international government and people accountability levels. The best and most qualitative reaction then would have been to swiftly freeze the virus in place, that is, limit it to its originating location. Before quality measures were effectively imposed, COVID-19 has already devastated and dealt damaging impacts on both businesses and the society at large. Lessons learned here should normally help to mitigate the impact of a future pandemic and similar emergencies especially now that it has already been speculated that, "These trends likely will continue and will intensify" [29, 33].

Most of the people who were forced to take adaptive decisions in attempts to defeat the swift and sudden disruptive blow of the pandemic on organizational, economic, and social activities probably heard of the 1918 pandemic for the first time, as the novel coronavirus ravaged our planet in the infant days of the COVID-19-year, 2020.

Pandemics are, from the report of the National Center for Biotechnology Information, US National Library of Medicine, "large-scale out-breaks of infectious disease that can greatly increase morbidity and mortality over a wide geographic area and cause significant economic, social, and political disruption" [29]. And as reported by Reid [33], available evidence shows that there is an increase in the likelihood of pandemics over the last century and may likely continue to be so. The reasons for future anticipation of increased pandemic resurgence are assigned to the situations highlighted below:

- Increases in the rates and frequency of global travel
- Increases in people integration across the globe
- Increases in urbanization of the global community
- Changes in land use
- Overexploitation of the natural environment

The COVID-19 pandemic caught humanity, government and individuals alike, unawares, thereby "catalyzing" or "forcing" organizational, societal, social, and people interactive changes. This immediately resulted in a lot of constraints in healthcare capacity which were overwhelmed. As reported by Schvaneveldt and Neve [35], some of the challenges of the pandemic-catalyzed changes constituting critical capacity constraints of quality healthcare facilities were identified as listed herein:

- Excessive hospital intensive care unit (ICU) capacity
- Number of ventilators
- Inadequate availability of ICU beds
- Inadequate provision of personal protective equipment (PPE) such as respirators, surgical masks, and gowns
- Inadequate number of skilled healthcare personnel

These constraints constitute itself into a list of prioritized decisions that have to be taken very expediently to be able to manage these forced changes emanating from the pandemic. In addition to these are the other damages the pandemic immediately bequeathed to both the people and the environment:

- Profound levels of stress and anxiety among the people of the world.
- People living and working in states of needless uncertainties regarding human health and safety.
- Alteration of work culture due to employees' forced implementation of virtual operations. Suddenly turning homes to their new employees' workplaces due to social interactive restrictions and other safety measures has been taken with mixed feelings.
- Unplanned but also "poor quality lonely deaths" of thousands of people leaving their loved ones in grief among the people of the global community.

In these ways, the COVID-19 pandemic forcefully created some critical but unplanned changes for organizations, society, and people, some of which may turn out to be more permanent than planned ones, thereby creating what may be termed "post-COVID-19 evolving normal."

Mitigating COVID-19 Changes with Quality Tools

These changes obviously called, most expediently, for immediate *change management* and measures.

Some quality management tools (personal protective equipment (PPE), quarantining or sorting, social distancing, and traceability/contact tracing) were quickly deployed to rescue organizations and society at large, both nationally and internationally.

The immediate quality management steps to mitigate or at least minimize the impacts of the COVID-19 pandemic on the people and environment include among others the following:

- Equipment sharing
- Reconfiguration and creating make-shift ICUs from existing hospital facilities
- Use of temporarily recruited medical personnel
- Using the military as bridging gap for medical personnel requirements to care for the surging cases of patients requiring hospital care

- Manufacturing companies' emergency reconfiguration of available capacities to enable the production of more ventilators and other PPEs to bridge the gap
- Prioritization of COVID-19 patients ahead of elective surgeries
- Encouraging social distancing and the use of facial coverings

The immediate recourse to capacity constraint management helped in finding some solutions to enable the immediate *management* of the *change* immediately resulting from the COVID-19 pandemic. The growing application of quality management tools and techniques in the healthcare system is again brought to the fore, in *change-managing* the changes emanating from the pandemic, hence the affirmation of Schvaneveldt and Neve [35] of the deployment of "the same tools that quality professionals use when a rash of defects occurs: containment, materials segregation and traceability." There is no doubt, too, that the *plan-do-check-act* (PDCA) cycle played an active role as "the guiding principle for implementing and improving COVID-19 countermeasures."

Just as in the cases of businesses, the work of Schvaneveldt and Neve et al. [35], Goldratt and Cox [12], Schvaneveldt [36], and Tague [39] showed generally that quality management comes with many tools, techniques, and methods, such as the process decision program chart (PDPC) and the constraint management/theory of constraints (TOC), needed to combat the disruptions and other changes brought about by the COVID-19 pandemic and any future pandemics in future times.

Apart from the potentials of globally increasing trends of recurring pandemics, other causes and sources of global, regional, national, and international emergencies are also looming, in the environment, hence the need for organizations and people around the globe to embrace quality management tools and methods in their emergency preparedness and business continuity planning, as critical elements to rely on for sustainability. It is therefore worthwhile for also making these major survival measures a new culture of organizational quality management.

The ability of the pandemic, or other disruptive environmental situations, to catalyze *disruptive changes* requires that organizations need to continuously plan for the rainy day, so as to guarantee business continuity and resiliency. The COVID-19 pandemic thus poses one of the highest possible risks not just to organizational sustainability but also to existential threat to the global community, at large. The COVID-19 thus remains a big existential or *sustainability risk*, for both businesses and people of this planet, hence must be treated accordingly.

It is for our ongoing COVID-19 pandemic experience that we must all understand the disruptions portended in our ever-changing world, hence the general call here for organizations, businesses, and the people of the world to develop the quality mindset of being prepared to view risk mitigation very seriously, irrespective of the origin of the disruption be it pandemic induced, technology pivoted, natural disaster, economic, or political upheaval. Risk mitigation strategies, measures, processes, and procedures may need to be integrated into organizational annual budget planning to avoid being taken unawares, and/or unprepared.

ISO's Biorisk Management Standard

It is important to mention what might appear to be a good coincidence with the current needs of the global population to appropriately respond to curbing the threat of biorisk to human existence and quality of life. The ISO [15] established in 2019 the ISO 35001:2019 – Biorisk Management for Laboratories and Other Related Organizations.

The biorisk management system was like its ISO 9001:2015 counterpart, also based on a management system approach, enabling an organization to effectively identify, assess, control, and evaluate the biosafety and biosecurity risks inherent in its activities.

Post-COVID-19 Change Perspectives

Apart from the generally envisaged public health recommendation of the need to repeatedly inoculate people against the coronavirus to mitigate its health impact on the populace, at intervals yet to be properly ascertained, the future perspectives about post-COVID-19 era are highly uncertain. Further decisions regarding vaccination frequency are highly dependent on the outcomes of many research works going on now, about the novel coronavirus, around the world, particularly in medicine, academia, pharmaceutical companies, and the public health sector, at large.

One thing is, however, certain in terms of the workplace and team working. The future normal for tomorrow's workplace may likely be split between virtual operations and in-person traditional mode of work, which is hybrid, due to the experience gained from COVID-19-related restrictions. Organizational team working mode may not be the same again, splitting into the *virtual employee team* (VET) and *in-person traditional team* (ITT) members.

There are the additional possibilities, too, that the advent of *Industry 4.0* practices may sooner than later lead to a total embrace of virtual operations to the obliteration of the traditional mode of working, especially among the bigger organizations in the developed economies of the world. This is likely going to constitute into what is perceived by the author as the post-COVID-19 operational normal. Going this route in the future calls generally for training because effective virtual teams are highly essential to accomplish this level of virtual operations irrespective of organizational size and product.

This is supported by the affirmation of Levit [27] that, "Highly effective virtual teams are comprised of employees with the 'Three As' – assertiveness, accountability and the ability to work independently." One of the advantages the author derived from implementing ISO 9001:1987 with its high focus on documentation was its self-supervisory tendency which led to employees being assertive, accountable, and able to work independently without any interface problems. Working at home generally calls for the ability to work independently while at the same time *self-supervising* one's own work.

The virtual workplace is also not without its own shortfalls, varying from individual to individual in different ways and manners. For some it is an excellent fit into their lives or lifestyles, while for others, it may be seen and viewed as "imposing on their social lives" [25].

Similarly, virtual learning may likely gain more admiration in higher education, among professional organizations and its members, and among organizational activities holding virtual meetings with its customers, suppliers, and other stakeholders. Post-COVID-19 era shall most definitely boost e-learning and virtual meetings across the globe, in all ramifications of its application and usage.

That the COVID-19 has greatly disrupted in-person events suddenly draw people's attention to virtual opportunities. Many professional organizations and organizational board meetings and other networking events have been moved online. This may likely impact quality management auditing if the pandemic cannot be effectively controlled or eradicated. Virtual audits are to me not adequate to achieve QM audits which may require physical verification. Then relying solely on what the auditee tells you has its own risks.

US employees are greatly hit by the COVID-10 pandemic in its aftermath. For example, a survey reported in the June 2021 issue [2] of the Quality Progress reportedly claimed, "Workplace stress hits U.S. employees hard." The survey showed 41% of US workers are impacted by chronic workplace stress – exhausted, overwhelmed, and burnt out – since the beginning of the pandemic.

The gravity of the devastation inflicted on mankind by the pandemic is not just what is felt in the economy but also the impact on people's mental health. This is glaringly visible in the outcome of the survey which "found that 87% of employees said their jobs affect their mental health." Thirty-seven percent of those surveyed are of the opinion that the job stress experienced by them is so intense that it has affected their personal lives. That is the extent to which the COVID-19 pandemic has adversely impacted the quality of people's lives. These are life changes that have to be qualitatively managed to achieve improved quality of physical and mental health.

Risk-Based Thinking

Going by the ISO 9001:2015 QMS [16] standard requirements (Clause 6.1.), planning the actions to address risks and opportunities is one of the major requirements of the standard. This thus makes risk-based thinking an essential ingredient "for achieving an effective quality management system." Effective risk management coupled with organizational and employee innovation holds the key perspectives for organizational sustainability. This is affirmed, too, by Daniels in, "Creatively managing risk and change in an organization is key to meeting the ever-changing requirements and expectations throughout the supply chain" [7].

References

1. Armstrong, M. A. (2009). *A handbook of human resources management* (11th ed.). Kogan Page.
2. ASQ Survey. (2021). Workplace stress hits U.S. employees hard. *Quality Progress*, June, p. 12. https://listwithclever.com/research/mental-health-2021
3. ASQE. (2021, March). 2020 Insights on excellence – Annual research reports and association highlights. *Quality Progress*, p. 7. https://tinyurl.com/IoE-2020-Research
4. Bourne, P. A. (2010). Crime, tourism and trust in a developing country. *Current Research Journal of Social Sciences, 2*(2), 69–83.
5. Bourne, P. A., Beckford, O. W., & Duncan, N. C. (2010). Generalized trust in an English-speaking Caribbean nation. *Current Research Journal of Social Sciences, 2*(1), 24–36.
6. Covey, R. S. (1989). *The 7 habits of highly effective people*. Carpetbagger Books, IOBA.
7. Daniels, A. (2021, March). The next level of success – The benefits of integrating QMSs and SMSs. *Quality Progress*, pp. 56–58.
8. Deutsch, M. (1973). *The resolution of conflict*. Yale University Press.
9. Drucker, P. F. (2001). *Management challenges for the 21st century*. Harper Business.
10. Fukuyama, F. (1995). *Trust: The social virtues and the creation of prosperity* (p. 27). Free Press.
11. Fuller, F. (2014). *The only thing constant in life is change*. Emmaus Library.
12. Goldratt, E. M., & Cox, J. (2004). *The goal: A process of ongoing improvement* (3rd ed.). North River Press.
13. Higgins, D., & Bourne, P. A. (2018). Implementing change in an organization: General overview. *Scholarly Journal of Psychology and Behavioral Sciences, 1*(1), 7–18. https://doi.org/10.32474/SJPBS.2018.01.000102. 2018.SJPBS.MS.ID000102. 29 Aug 2018.
14. International Organization for Standardization, ISO 31000:2018 – Risk Management Guidelines.
15. International Organization for Standardization, ISO 35001:2019 – Biorisk Management for Laboratories and Other Related Organizations.
16. International Organization for Standardization, ISO 9001:2015, clause 6.1.
17. International Organization for Standardization, ISO 9001:2015, clause 6.3.
18. International Organization for Standardization, ISO 9001:2015, subclause 5.4.2.
19. International Organization for Standardization, ISO Guide 73:2009 – Risk Management – Vocabulary.
20. Jalagat Jr, R. C. (2016). The impact of change and change management in achieving corporate goals and objectives: Organizational perspective. *International Journal of Science and Research (IJSR), 5*(11), 1233–1239.
21. Kahn, C. H. (1979). *The art and thought of Heraclitus*. Cambridge University Press.
22. Kane, G. C., Phillips, A. U., Copulsky, J. R., & Andrus, G. R. (2019). *The technology fallacy: How people are the real key to digital transformation*. MIT Press.
23. Kegan, R., & Lahey, L. L. (2001, November). The real reason people Won't, HBR's 10 must reads – On change. *Harvard Business Review*, Boston, Massachusetts.
24. Kotter, J. P., & Schlesinger, L. A. (1979, January–February). Choosing strategies for change. *Harvard Business Review*, p. 57.
25. Krivokuca, M. (2021, March). Catalysts for change: Achieving organizational excellence in post-COVID-19 industry 4.0 process. *Quality Progress*, pp. 32–37.
26. Lawrence, P. R. (1969, January–February). How to deal with resistance to change. *Harvard Business Review*, p. 47.
27. Levit, A. (2019). *Humanity works: Merging technologies and people for the workforce of the future*. Kogan Page.
28. Lucey, J. (2008). Why is the failure rate for organizational change so high? *Management Services, 52*, 10–18.
29. Madhav, N., Oppenheim, B., Gallivan, M., Mulembakani, P., Rubin, E., & Wolfe, N. (2017). Chapter 17. Pandemics: Risks, impacts, and mitigation. In *Disease control priorities: Improving health and reducing poverty* (3rd ed.). World Bank.

30. Mishra, S., & Isazada, N. (2021, June). Fear of the unknown – Managing employee resistance to change initiatives. *Quality Progress*, pp. 26–31.
31. Piderit, S. K. (2000). Rethinking resistance and recognizing ambivalence: A multidimensional view of attitudes towards organizational change. *Academy of Management Reviews, 25*(4), 783–794.
32. Prosci. *Organizational agility as a strategic imperative*. https://www.prosci.com/resources/articles/organizational-agility-strategic-imperative
33. Reid, R. D. (2020, November). Be ready: How business continuity planning helps organizations plan for emergencies. *Quality Progress*, pp. 48–51.
34. Schulz, J. R. (2007, November). Process improvement: Eight steps to sustain change. *Quality Progress*, p. 25–31.
35. Schvaneveldt, S. J., & Neve, B.V. (2021, March). Proving their mettle: Combating the COVID-19 pandemic with quality tools. *Quality Progress*, pp. 24–31.
36. Schvaneveldt, S. J. (Ed.). (2021). *The certified quality process analyst handbook* (3rd ed.). Quality Press.
37. Smollan, R. K. (2011). The multi-dimensional nature of resistance to change. *Journal of Management and Organization, 17*(6), 828–849.
38. Szabla, D. B. (2007). A multidimensional view of resistance to organizational change: Exploring cognitive, emotional, and intentional responses to planned change across perceived change leadership strategies. *Human Resources Development Quarterly, 18*(4), 525–558. https://doi.org/10.1002/hrdq.2018
39. Tague, N. R. (2005). *Quality toolbox* (2nd ed.). Quality Press.

Quality Management 16

Bi-relational Burdens of Quality

Quality, in its simplest form, is generally expressed in relationship to how products and services are *perceived* or *valued* by their recipients, or end users, or the market place. The universal or general application of quality today is a global attestation to the fact that quality has grown beyond products and services. Today we talk about the quality of life, quality of a play, quality of work, quality of a presentation, quality of government/governance, quality of teaching, quality of materials usage/application, quality of medical services, quality of response against a pandemic, etc.

Quality is, thus, the value created, or reflected in, or resulting from the outcome(s) of actions or efforts; activity or series of activities; a process or set of processes (e.g., manufacturing); the way things are done; the way things are used; the way resources are used or utilized or managed; the way people are governed; etc. Quality is value attributed with them, by those for whom they are originally made or provided, or those who use them, or, in general, the marketplace. Hence, quality can simply be seen or perceived as a general measure of the level of customer value balanced with culture in determining product/services acceptability or satisfaction. That's the reason why people generally talk of very good quality, good quality, bad quality, or perhaps unsatisfactory quality. Quality is value. But today the definition of quality is, due to globalization of the world economy, growing beyond the scope of this definition in our disruptive environment. Quality has today grown to enhance culture and relationships. Quality is thus a pre-requisite for business success, [1].

In order to achieve quality, therefore, product makers and service providers set out to achieve the critical goal of their products and/or services being able to perform the functions and objectives for which they have been intended, in order to achieve customer or market value. And who determines this?

The end user, the market, or in general terms *the customer*. It follows from here that quality, on the overall, stands for the ability of a product or service to meet, conform to, and represent the functions and expectations (or value) for which they

T. A. Ibidapo, *From Industry 4.0 to Quality 4.0*, Management for Professionals,
https://doi.org/10.1007/978-3-031-04192-1_16

have been intended for use by their recipients – customers, end users, or clientele. It is very clear here that quality begins, on a general basis, from the product and services planning and designing stages, with focus on all ramifications of the ability of products or services to balance their functionalities with those for which they have been intended.

Putting the relative meaning of *quality* into consideration, the ISO defined quality as, "The totality of features and characteristics of a product or service that bear on its ability to satisfy stated or implied needs." It is important here that, in order to enhance product/service quality, it must be emphasized that such products and services must have to be delivered to their respective end users or customers under mutually agreed but customer- or client-specified conditions which include among others the following:

- Product/services cost and mode of payment.
- Time of delivery and other logistics issues.
- Downstream after-sales services such as warranty packages, product/services maintenance opportunities, and effective and prompt response to customer after-sales complaints. This is particularly important in our growing world of e-commerce.
- Product/services recalls as and when necessary.
- Effective customer communication and relationship.
- Other customer enhancing conditions though not mentioned.

Quality Management Guidelines

Any for-profit organization or business is established solely for the purpose of profit-making. It is not just making profit today, or tomorrow, but profit at all times, and profit always, except when survival, healthy survival, is neither a goal nor an option. To achieve this main goal and sole objective of business ownership, promoter, or stakeholder, there seems to be no other alternative than to have a clear vision of continuous improvement established in the deoxyribonucleic acid (DNA) of the organization or business, irrespective of size, product, or the services provided, no matter the location on the surface of the earth. This is to say in the clearest terms therefore that the business, organization, or enterprise must remain healthy at all times, which requires a lasting ability to be focused, constantly competitive, best among the best of its rivals, and ready for maintaining the continuous improvement psyche and mindset among organizational processes and activities.

According to Kovach [2], commitment to continuous improvement, which is a key aspect of quality management QM, holds the key to the long-term health of any organization, across its processes and activities. Quality management, which has its roots traceable back to statistical quality control which was claimed by Barouch and Ponsignon [3], to have been developed by Walter Shewart in the USA and popularized by William Edwards Deming and Joseph Juran, has grown to become a mainstream managerial approach and reliable route, for achieving improved business processes, products, and services, as well lead to the generation of customer satisfaction for achieving organizational market competitive advantage [4].

Although QM was initially focused on the improvement of quality in manufacturing organizations and systems, its use and application have, over time, been widely enlarged to encompass all functions and departments of organizations beyond manufacturing, to include the services sector of the global economy [5].

There have been various literature reports of the successful deployment of quality management among the industrial and service sectors of the economy. It has been reported by Kaynak [6] and Douglas and Judge [7] that the adoption of quality management practices generally results in superior organizational performance, an opinion equally shared by Kovash [2]. This has more or less become the norm for quality management. QM is often used as a generic term to describe or reference both QM and TQM.

Despite the successful application and use of QM in a wide range of global economic sectors, it has attracted a lot of criticisms from research and the academia, mainly because the origin of QM is rooted outside the academic world. Instead, it was fundamentally and outstandingly established in the footprints of the manufacturing sector of the global economy, courtesy of the twentieth-century *gurus* of quality.

The raging scholarly misunderstanding of quality management subsequently ensued, from several years of failed attempts of many researchers to establish the theoretical foundational roots of QM. Their criticisms of quality management thus center most prominently on the fact that QM lacks theoretical foundations.

It is this line of thinking among the people in the academic and research world that led to comments such as QM is theoretically incomplete, and their assumption, too, that QM generally lacks theoretical foundation is ambiguous, or weakly founded [3].

This is probably the reason why Barouch and Kleinhans [8] tried to explain what they termed as QM's failure being due generally to managers' lack of the understanding of the foundations of QM, a reason adduced for the main causes of QM's poor implementation. It must, however, be mentioned here that those of us familiar with the evolution of ISO 9000 series of quality management systems (QMS) standards since inception are in clarity of its QM concepts.

The search for the theoretical underlay of QM has been a catalyst needed to incite and excite the people in academia and other researchers to pay closer attention to quality and quality management. The academic exercise notwithstanding, it is obvious that what is regarded in the above-scholarly arguments of several authors as poor implementation may also be termed as varied implementation efficiencies depending on variables such as:

- Who and who is implementing QM's elements?
- Which elements are implemented and their depth of implementation?
- Participatory levels of leadership and management commitment!
- Level of employee motivation, commitment, training, empowerment, and taking responsibilities.

- Level of supplier-customer relationship, communication, and partnership.
- Degree of process interface identification and management.
- Effectiveness of organizational-wide relationship management.

Since continuous improvement drive is the key momentum propelling organizational performance improvement, customer satisfaction, the dynamism of organizational economic health and well-being, organizational survival, and how it survives among competitions are therein all encompassing, in the frameworks of quality management.

The six concepts of the generic conceptual framework for QM listed immediately below are those that are embodied in the main concepts of ISO 9000:2015 quality management systems – fundamentals and vocabulary [9] and key to the implementation of ISO 9001:2015 quality management systems – requirements.

- Customer focus (stakeholder focus)
- Leadership
- Engagement of people
- Process approach
- Improvement
- Managing relationships with key stakeholders, such as suppliers and stakeholders

These six concepts have been reported by Sousa and Voss [10] to represent the core components of QM, as a field of study.

For further understanding of QM, in terms of its theoretical base, Barouch and Ponsignon [3] introduced a generic conceptual framework for QM, which resulted from the synthesis of combinations of four existing works, beginning with the QM theory of Anderson et al. [11], based on the Deming management method, the Dahlgaard-Park's [4] generic theoretical model for TQM, and the major concepts of ISO 9000:2015 (ISO) quality management systems – fundamentals and vocabulary [9]. As shown by [3], in (Table 16.1), a convergent overall conceptual framework for QM emerged from these three synthesized contributions, to clearly bring to the fore the prevailing concepts of:

- Customer and stakeholder focus
- Management commitment and leadership
- Employee involvement
- Process management
- Continuous improvement
- Partnerships with customers, suppliers, and society

It was thus established by them that these six emerged concepts of convergence "form the theoretical blocks for describing, explaining, and predicting the organizational impact of quality management adoption."

Table 16.1 Barouch and Ponsignon's [3] synthesized theoretical frameworks for QM and TQM

Deming-based theory of QM [11]	ISO 9000:2015 requirements	Theoretical model for TQM [5]	Synthesized generic conceptual framework for QM and TQM
Customer satisfaction	Customer focus (stakeholders focus)	Focus on the customers and the employees (internal customers)	Customer and stakeholder focus
Visionary leadership	Leadership	Strong management commitment and leadership	Management commitment and leadership
Employee fulfillment	Engagement of people	Everybody's participation focuses on training, learning, and education	Employee involvement
Process management	Process approach	Focus on facts (processes and measurements)	Process management
Continuous improvement	Improvement	Customer-driven continuous improvements	Continuous improvement
External and internal cooperation	Managing relationships with key stakeholders, such as suppliers and customers	Building partnerships with customers, suppliers, and society	Partnerships with customers, suppliers, and society

QM is today widely acknowledged as an important strategic organizational management tool which involves the use and application of quality principles and practices at all levels of an organization [12].

There is no doubt, however, that when viewed from the perspectives of varied results of QM and TQM implementation or adoption, quality management, and the often varied challenges of its adoption and application, may continue to attract research and scholarly interests from the academia.

This is particularly so in our present challenging world where the role of technology application cannot but make a difference, especially in the emerging era of the author's "Quality 4.0." (Table 7.1).

The key to effective quality management resides very passionately in the depth of the understanding of the various concepts in its generic conceptualized framework. Needed explanations are provided in Table 16.2.

Quality Management System

Quality management system is defined by the ISO [9] as the "management system to direct and control an organization with regard to quality," while quality management is the "coordinated activities to direct and control an organization with regard

Table 16.2 QM/TQ management concepts and guidelines

Conceptual framework for QM	Quality management guidelines
Customer and stakeholder focus	Long-term organizational survival highly dependent on the dictates of the *customer* and *stakeholder/investor* Balance customer and stakeholder/investor needs on long-term basis to achieve sustainable organizational performance with compliance to all regulatory requirements – responsible waste disposal; clean air, water, and soil; and product regulated compliances *Focus* on and *satisfy customer* and *stakeholder/investor needs* Ensure customer, stakeholder, and investor issues are promptly dealt with, and effective responded to, in order to achieve customer and stakeholder satisfaction Ensure owners/investors receive favorable returns on investment (ROI)
Management commitment and leadership	Visionary and focused leadership with commitment Strong management commitment and leadership to ensure quick and immediate responses to all issues Lead by example; ensure availability of current information for decision-making Ensure the recognition, identification, and effective management of process interfaces
Employee involvement	Employee empowerment, enablement, and motivation to willingly accept process ownership and responsibility. There may be productivity competition among sections Employee training, well-being, and involvement to reflect sense of belonging Fostering and motivating team working among employees and ensure feedback Knowledge sharing among organizational employees in line with the requirements of ISO 9001:2015 to communicate organizational quality policy and ensure its organizational-wide understanding among personnel
Process management	Managing organization as a system of interlinked processes with subsystems Optimize process output through interface management, recognition of, and management of interdependences existing among organizational process components Process measurement and control; calibration, corrective, and preventive measures to reduce undeserved effects

(continued)

Table 16.2 (continued)

Conceptual framework for QM	Quality management guidelines
Continuous improvement	PDCA, using customer communication, customer feedback, process and output feedback, technology innovation, and other necessary inputs Maintain effective customer/supplier feedback mechanism – internally and externally – and use as feedback for improvement processes Using appropriate technology input such as hardware, software, and know-how; reengineering, rebranding, innovation, and market competitive indicators as effective tools to drive up continuous improvement Improve products and services on a continuous basis by implementing changes based on adaptive learning from customers, market place, competitors, organizational experience, relevant research results, and other relevant sources
Partnerships with customers, suppliers, and society	Partnership with the supply chain to create strong customer/supplier relationship with effective communication to avoid disruption and be given prior information about any disruption to enable alternative sourcing Partnership and cooperation with other stakeholders as may be needed or necessary Maintain good relationship with community, which often desires a responsible organization willing to work with its neighbors rather than against them Cooperate with society especially the immediate environment to prioritize and maintain the ethics of organizational corporate social responsibility (CSR) Meet, keep, and ensure product/services compliance with all relevant and necessary regulatory requirements even without customer's request Prioritize corporate social responsibilities to community and the people to avoid risks and protect lives

to quality." The use of a quality management system for the management of an organization's quality system provides a broad stream of activities which include among others the establishment/determination of the:

- Quality policy and objectives
- Customer needs/specifications, requirements, and expectations
- Processes and responsibilities needed for the attainment of the quality objectives
- Resources needed for attaining the quality objectives and their provision
- Methods for monitoring and measuring the effectiveness and efficiency of each process
- Means needed for the prevention of nonconformities and the elimination of their causes

- Process for achieving continual improvement of the quality management system
- Needs and expectations of other interested parties such as the shareholders, suppliers, and employees

Following this approach generally results to the creation of customer confidence in the organization's processes and their capabilities as well as the quality of its products and services. Hence the implementation of a quality management system is to the advantage of your organization and the quality of your products and services. Some of the quality management systems/concepts/programs available for your use and application are discussed below and in subsequent chapters of this book.

Forgetting the Silent/Hidden Customers?

Using the case of a tragic plane crash as an example brings us closer to the realization that there is the need for quality focus on all categories of customers which the author boldly assigns here as secondary (2°) and tertiary (3°) levels of customers. Most often the tertiary customers are either taken care of or put in the forefront of quality considerations.

Total Quality Management (TQM) Concept

The concept of total quality management (TQM) emanated from philosophies which view the component parts, that is, resources – people and materials – processes, and products of the production systems, as entities which interact with suppliers and customers, to achieve a common goal. Hence TQM can be said to be a route for managing quality through a systems approach methodology. In the TQM approach, all organizational quality functions such as the underlisted are managed as integrated systems:

- Product engineering and design
- Maintenance
- Management
- Production control
- Manufacturing
- Research and development
- Operations planning
- Sales and sales forecast
- Marketing
- Finance
- Logistics
- Customer service
- Training or human resources development
- Organization/customer interrelationship

These quality functions are integrated with adequate focus on:

- The objectives of the organization
- Meeting the needs, requirements, and specifications of the customer in all ramifications

The philosophy of TQM therefore is that of an all-inclusive participatory work culture where all parties, that is, organization and all its employees and functionaries, customers, suppliers, and all other stakeholders, are involved in achieving the common goal of improving quality and achieving customer satisfaction. Hence TQM can be said to be a complex quest for quality and continual improvement that involves the participation of everyone in an organization. This simply means that anybody making any input into the workings of an organization must ensure that his own roles are played with the outmost quality. Hence the culture of "doing it right the first time" is required from all the people at all times.

The philosophies of the TQM which involve people, processes, and products have been described by various authors. While Deming [13] emphasized the 14 principles that formed the basic foundation of TQM, Juran [14], Feigenbaum [15], and Ishikawa [16] provided further avenues for a deeper understanding of it.

Although the total quality philosophies described by various authors are diverse, yet they have some common focal points, some of which are highlighted below:

- Define organizational aims, goals, and objectives in the form of a statement which will be widely circulated among all the employees.
- Management openly demonstrates and shows its commitment to the statement through its actions, words, and deeds, that is, leadership by example.
- Create consumer- or customer-oriented culture, that is, customer-driven or customer-centered quality, within the organization.
- Determine who the customers are and their needs.
- Determine product specifications.
- Develop processes that can achieve product features and specifications to the satisfaction of the customer(s).
- Ensure fast response.
- Use facts, data, and statistical methods to evaluate actual product in comparison with product goals and ensure all actions are based on facts.
- Measure process performance to achieve set standards (e.g., zero defects) and process improvement.
- Identify quality improvement actions and improve production and/or servicing systems on a regular basis.
- Establish controls to maintain improvement.
- Empower employees through training, organizational teamwork, and communications.
- Recognize efforts and results in creating quality.

The primary objective/target of TQM is the overall achievement of products/services of value that are wanted or demanded by the customer. TQM was, for any organization therefore, centered basically on meeting the requirements of the customer or, simply said, the delivery of the products to meet customer demand and satisfaction. Hence every organization must, as a matter of survival, focus all its attention, internal operations, and activities on the customer and realign its corporate strategies towards achieving this. The implication here is that first and foremost all employees must be part of all quality activities and system integration aimed at meeting customer demands/requirement.

Achieving TQM requires focusing attention on some important factors which include but are not limited to the following:

- Product quality
- Goal/target setting objectives
- Training of workforce and horizontally integrating them while they must be taken as integral parts of the quality system
- Reducing costs through continuous improvement
- Maintaining the consistency of purpose

TQM should be seen as an important management strategy that lays emphasis on:

- Product quality
- Efficiency
- Knowledge of customers
- Knowledge of the market
- Knowledge of internal processes

While TQM should actually be seen as a quality management concept or program that can be used to improve process vis-à-vis product quality achievement, it is complex and cumbersome. TQM had numerous tools and techniques for its implementation. Although TQM promises results in about 3 years, it may also end up in a lot of cases with frustration. TQM generally impacts on people, including suppliers and customers. Hence the implementation of TQM requires important changes in the structure of an organization to promote and support the following critical activities:

- Taking decisions
- Performance measurement systems
- Compensation systems

Implementing the TQM Approach

Step 1: Establish the values, needs, specifications, and requirements of the customer (internal and external).

Step 2: With the information and data available from step 1, design a product or service of value that shall meet and even exceed the needs, requirements, and specifications of the customer.

Attention should be focused here on the ease and economy of production so as to ensure that products and/or services are of good value to the customer. At the same time, the products/services must be easy to use and apply. Consideration must be given, too, to legislative/regulatory requirements (e.g., environmental regulations) and after use handling or disposal.

Step 3: Design a production process/technique that will result to doing the job or rendering the service to ensure that "the right things are done right, the first time, every time."

Step 4: Put machinery and equipment in place that can guarantee the production of products and services that meet and surpass customer requirements the first time using adequately trained and dedicated employees.

Step 5: Monitor process performance through well-defined measurements to detect defective products and services and the causes. Put preventive actions in place to ensure mistakes are not repeated and the process is free of errors.

Step 6: Maintain a record of the results of management review and those of process monitoring and measurement which should be used to monitor and ensure the improvement of the system on a continual basis.

Step 7: Organization should partner with suppliers to ensure that the concept described in steps 1–6 is similarly implemented so as to ensure that they possess the ability to promptly supply quality items that meet the needs, requirements, and specifications of the organization.

If the distribution of the product is the responsibility of a separate entity, this entity should be encouraged to keep to this guideline. Other elements that are relevant to TQM as provided by Stevenson [17] are as follows:

- Continuous improvement.
- Competitive benchmarking.
- Employee empowerment.
- Team approach.
- Any decision taken by management must be logical and substantiated with factual data.
- Knowledge of tools by employees-members of staff must be trained in the use and application of the relevant quality tools.
- Quality of products and services provided by the supplier.

Here continuous improvement is a philosophy which seeks to improve all the factors, i.e., machinery/equipment, techniques/methods, materials, people, etc. that are concerned with or related to the process of converting inputs into outputs on an ongoing basis.

Although there has been no theoretical formalization of total quality management, it is generally assumed in quality circles as a discipline and philosophy of management which institutionalizes planned and continuous improvement. TQM can therefore be seen as a quality culture that emphasizes quality as the result or outcome of all organizational activities in which all organizational functions and employees (i.e., employee participation) led by top management leadership must partake in so as to:

- Achieve continuous improvement of all operations, processes, and activities as well as ensuring technological and equipment/machinery update.
- Achieve fast and even rapid responses to the needs of customers (internal and external).
- Achieve product quality at source since each employee is made responsible for the quality of his own output; hence, the concept "do it right first time" must be imbibed in them.
- Make TQM the organizational culture and way of life.
- Ensure that facts and objective data obtained from statistical analysis are used as basis for taking decisions, planning, review and performance tracking, improvement of operations, comparative assessment with other competitors, etc.

Advantages of TQM

The combination of technology with the application of a quality management concept of the likes of TQM jointly strengthens both manufacturing and other service providers to suppress or overcome competitive pressures resulting from the ever-shrinking global market which is becoming more and more competitive day in, day out. Using the systems and/or process approach is very useful in managing complex organizational operations. TQM results in a good and rewarding utilization of human resources as it affects all the people, gets them adequately involved in quality management activities, and impacts very strongly on the development attitude and culture towards quality. TQM can thus be seen as a quality concept that gets people involved. The overall advantages of the TQM can generally be summed up thus:

- TQM enables the integration of people to foster good interpersonal relationship between employees.
- TQM enables the effective integration of organizational activities into an overall total system which is very effective.
- TQM leads to the use of systematic approach in finding solutions to quality problems.
- The alignment of efforts to achieve set-out quality objectives is made easy by the use and application of TQM.
- TQM increases the probability and consistency of achieving desired products and services.

The integration of people efforts and organizational activities generally leads to higher productivity.

The consideration of TQM being the classical approach to the management of quality of organizational settings has been expressed by various authors such as Boggs [18], Sebastianelli and Tamimi [19], and Kujala and Ullrank [20]. The research findings of Kujala and Ullrank on TQM and organizational culture actually suggested that quality management "should be studied as a cultural phenomenon with a coherent set of underlying assumptions that form an ideal quality culture." To make TQM compatible with organizational culture they went further to emphasize the need for quality managers to understand the existing organizational culture, in order to be able to identify any existing gaps so as to be able to bridge them, so that TQM will be compatible with the quality culture [21].

References

1. Juran, J. M. (1992). *Juran on quality by design*. Free Press.
2. Kovach, J. V. (2016). The role of learning and exploration in quality management and continuous improvement. In P. Sampaio & P. Saraiva (Eds.), *Quality in the 21st century* (p. 75). Springer International.
3. Barouch, G., & Ponsignon, F. (2016). The epistemological basis for quality management. *Total Quality Management, 27*(8), 944–962. https://doi.org/10.1080/14783363.20161188659
4. Dahlgaard-Park, S. M. (2015). *Total quality management. The SAGE encyclopedia of quality and the service economy*. SAGE.
5. Dahlgaard-Park, S. M. (2011). The quality movement: Where are you going? *Total Quality Management, 22*, 493–516.
6. Kaynak, H. (2003). The relationship between total quality management practices and their effects on firm performance. *Journal of Operations Management, 21*(4), 405–435.
7. Douglas, T. J., & Judge, W. Q. (2001). Total quality management implementation and competitive advantage, the role of structural control and exploration. *The Academy of Management Journal, 44*(1), 158–169.
8. Barouch, G., & Kleinhans, S. (2015). Learning from quality management criticisms. *International Journal of Quality and Service Science, 7*, 201–216.
9. ISO 9000:2015. (2015). *Quality management systems – fundamentals and vocabulary*. ISO.
10. Sousa, R., & Voss, C. A. (2002). Quality management revisited: A reflective review and agenda for future research. *Journal of Operations Management, 20*, 91–109.
11. Anderson, J., Rungtusanatham, M., & Schroeder, R. (1994). A theory of QM underlying the Deming management method. *Academy of Management Review, 19*(3), 472–509.
12. Talib, F., Rahman, Z., & Qureshi, M. N. (2011). A study of total quality management and supply chain management practices. *International Journal of Productivity Management, 60*(3), 268–288.
13. Deming, W. E. (1986). *Out of crisis*. MIT Centre for Advanced Engineering Studies.
14. Juran, J. M. (1989). *Juran on leadership for quality*. Free Press.
15. Feigenbaum, A. V. (1989). *Total quality control* (3rd ed.). McGraw-Hill.
16. Ishikawa, K. (1990). *What is total quality control? The Japanese way*. Prentice Hall.
17. Stevenson, W. J. (1999). *Production operations management* (6th ed., p. 493). McGraw-Hill.
18. Boggs, W. B. (2004). TQM and organizational culture: A case study. *Quality Management Journal, 11*(2), 42–52.

19. Sebastinelli, R., & Tamimi, N. (2003). Understanding the obstacles to TQM success. *Quality Management Journal, 10*(3), 45–56.
20. Kujala, J., & Ullrank, P. (2004). Total quality management as a cultural phenomenon. *Quality Management Journal, 11*(4), 43–55.
21. Mishra, S., & Delgado, P. (2021). Engineering engaged employees – Power to your people to add strength to your quality program. *Quality Progress, 54*(6), 16–24.

Improvement Concepts 17

Kaizen Strategy

Endless Journey

Maintaining product/service quality is an endless task needed for organizational sustainability. This thus makes organizational quality mindset and improvement drive an existential necessity and business lifeline. Quality management sustenance through various strategic approaches is thus equivalent to embarking on an endless journey.

Kaizen is a Japanese word translated to mean "continuous improvement." It is the belief too that all aspects of life should be improved, on a constant basis. Kaizen, which is a registered trademark of the Kaizen Institute Ltd., is thus a philosophy of unending continuous improvement. Kaizen is viewed in Japan from where it originates as being applicable not just to the workplace but also to all aspects of life, whereas in the USA, it is mostly used for work processes in an organization.

The word which was originally used to refer to subtle, steady, and gradual change over time has however metamorphosed to also include quick or fast improvements, Kaizen events. Today people are even talking of *Kaizen* blitzes, quick *Kaizen,* or rapid improvements [1].

The Kaizen strategy emphasizes unending efforts for achieving organizational-wide improvement. This means that improvement cycles have to go on continuously without stopping throughout all phases of the organization.

Application of Kaizen to Life

The application of the Kaizen philosophy when viewed from the point of view of its base and origination in Japan is conceptualized for application in all aspects of life. It is therefore seen as an approach to achieve constant and continuous improvement

T. A. Ibidapo, *From Industry 4.0 to Quality 4.0*, Management for Professionals,
https://doi.org/10.1007/978-3-031-04192-1_17

of all aspects of life. Kaizen can therefore be seen from this perspective as the quality magic wand that could transform the quality of life in the least developed and developing parts of the world such as the West African sub-region where the lack of fundamental infrastructure (e.g., roads, hospitals, electricity, education, etc.) and basic life amenities such as potable water, food, clean environment, access to medical care, etc., generally taken for granted in the developed parts of the world, have stampeded over 200 million people to "eternal" poverty to the extent that what they are thinking of is first of all survival rather than the quality of life. The situation here is complicated by tribal conflicts/wars and accelerated by diseases and hunger. This is irrespective of the fact that Kaizen does not actually concern itself with changing fundamental systems. What is critical here is the use of Kaizen to achieve small improvements with the involvement of everyone. In the USA Kaizen is generally used to achieve continuous improvement in the workplace and in work processes.

The Kaizen concept is itself the root of continuous improvement as it is known and practiced today. Continuous improvement helps to create an environment that aids the achievement of incremental change in an organization or workplace. This is achieved through the joint efforts of the hierarchy of an organization which ranges from top management to the operative. According to Imai [2] the roles in Kaizen are defined for the following hierarchy of workers:

- Top management
- Middle management
- Supervisors
- Workers

For example, it is the responsibility of the top management to drive the implementation of the Kaizen concept by

- Conceiving with determination the idea of introducing the concept
- Making policies necessary for implementing Kaizen
- Providing the support and needed resources
- Establishing the policy for Kaizen and making it an organizational strategy
- Providing the necessary infrastructure for the introduction of Kaizen

The middle management is expected to follow the directives of the top management to

- Implementation and the deployment of Kaizen in line with management directives
- Implement the goals of Kaizen
- Train employees in developing the awareness and consciousness of Kaizen requirements

- Establish, maintain, and carry out an upgrade of standards as well as staff
- Aid employees in the development of tools and the skills needed for solving problems

The involvement of the supervisors includes

- The introduction and maintenance of discipline in the workshop
- The use of Kaizen in their functional responsibilities
- Making plans and providing guidelines to workers for their implementation
- Improvement of communication with workers
- Listening to individual suggestions and support small group activities

For the workers they are to

- Show discipline in the workshop
- Get involved in Kaizen through small group activities and the suggestion system
- Achieve enhanced skills and job performance
- Involvement in continuous self-development to improve ability to solve problems.

According to the Japan Human Relations Association [3], Kaizen Teian is described as "a means to develop abilities, solve problems, and devise measures that deal with causes of problems."

Benefits of Kaizen

The use and application of *Kaizen* or *Kaizen* events is laden with many benefits [4] that can be classified into quantitative (i.e., measurable results) and qualitative (i.e., results are felt more than they can be measured). These quantitative benefits may include among others some or all of the following:

- Savings in time
- Money saved
- Reduction in the number of people needed
- Reduction in cycle time or lead time
- Reduction in the number of process steps
- Improved yield of first pass
- Reduction in inventory
- Reduction in total distance traveled

Since these benefits are quantifiable, it is possible for you to translate them to monetary returns.

The qualitative benefits which include the state of your workplace are

- An orderly workplace
- Ability to locate items easier than it has ever been
- Working with less stress
- Making the workplace safer

A major task before or after the implementation of Kaizen is your ability to sustain the gains. This can easily be achieved by

- The standardization of the processes to the new improved level
- Training all involved personnel to the new standard
- Ensuring results are monitored to be consistent with expectation over a period of time
- Ensuring management commitment
- Giving the responsibility of maintaining and improving on the gains to specific employee

Lean Manufacturing

Misunderstanding Lean Manufacturing

Schonberger [5], the author of the first book to feature *lean manufacturing* (first known then as *just-in-time (JIT) manufacturing*) offered vivid explanations about the erroneous executive misunderstanding of the term "lean manufacturing and its objectives" in a discussion which featured in the "Reaction Gauge" section of the Quality Progress, Seen and Heard [6]. According to him, the term *lean manufacturing* or *just-in-time manufacturing* was over a period of time, renamed the JIT inventory.

It is the application of lean to the inventory, in JIT inventory, that makes people easily forget that the JIT inventory is not the primary essence of lean/JIT. Misconstruing lean manufacturing as the culprit of the early COVID-19 pandemic days' scarcity in paper towels and toilet paper is therefore absolutely wrong, since that was not the sole objective of the JIT Inventory approach. As rightly put by Schonberger [7], "What's solely missing is flexibility to easily and quickly adapt to always unpredictable demand."

Essence of Lean

It is the necessity to overcome the main manufacturing problems of high variety production in post-World War II Japan that led to the development of the lean manufacturing approach by Toyota so as to improve its efficiency. In order to give better products and/or services to the customer, defects and wastes of any type have to be avoided. In fact, the customer must be given products and/or services that represent or are of *value* to them.

The lean approach, as the name implies, utilizes less quantum of certain resources (e.g., fewer number of workers, less inventory, less wastages, etc.) than the conventional mass production system. Lean manufacturing is a generic process management philosophy which emphasizes cost reduction through identification and elimination of all types and kinds of wastes (or *muda in Japanese*) to improve the overall customer value.

Muda includes all types of defective work. Lean thinking therefore focuses attention on flow and the need to reduce nonvalue added activities. Examples here include but are not limited to the following:

- Any defective work
- Time wasted in production
- Wasted materials
- Unnecessary movement of people and wares
- Waiting time of any kind
- Excessive or overproduction
- Inventory or items which could be raw materials or finished products, kept in the warehouse or store because they are not immediately needed or required

In these ways *lean* enables organizations to focus on process speed and efficiency. The Toyota production system (TPS) which contributed to the derivation of this philosophy emphasized three types of waste:

- Nonvalue added work (*muda* in Japanese)
- Overburden (*muri* in Japanese)
- Unevenness (*mura* in Japanese)

Materials based on the TPS are listed, according to Conner [8], into seven major forms of wastes:

- Waste from overproduction
- Waste from waiting, that is, wasted time
- Waste from product defects
- Waste of motion through unnecessary movement of people
- Transportation waste through unnecessary transportation of goods
- Processing waste or unnecessary processing
- Inventory waste both in process and finished goods

On the basis of the lean approach, it is advisable for you to completely avoid any action or activity, from the planning and design stages to the points of delivery to your customers and after-sales services, that will not add *value* to your products and/or services. Based on your own experience in production or manufacturing, it is easy to identify areas of work, or processes in which wastes may be generated.

From my experience in the factory, the following are some of the areas found to have resulted in waste generation in terms of time (i.e., downtime for machine and personnel) and materials:

- Delays in carrying out any activity, thereby resulting in waste of production or productivity hours.
- Poor layout of the facilities which may result in various wastes including energy, operator time, wears and tears on machinery and equipment such as the forklift, poor supervision, etc.
- Lack of training and adequate skills on the part of operators, supervisors, and other employees which may result in time wastages, due to excessive setup times, wrong setup of machinery and equipment, passing on parts and/or products that are defective, etc.
- Poor machine and equipment maintenance resulting in unnecessary downtime and material wastages, due to incapable processes, malfunctioning machines, poorly utilized man hours, etc.
- Lack of, or poor, preventive maintenance and maintenance management, resulting in wastages in operational hours and man hours.
- Lack of appropriate working tools, such as tool boxes which may have been provided by management but mishandled (i.e., may be sold, or exchanged with poorer-quality tools) by employees. That is why it is important to allocate tools by person, with the name of the organization inscribed on them, and subjection of the tools in the toolbox to regular (about once every 2 months) auditing to ensure they are complete and available for use at all times. This is particularly important in the underdeveloped economies of the world.
- Use of wrong or at times fake spare parts which may completely paralyze production activities.
- Lack of work procedures and instructions.
- Poor process controls or uncontrolled work processes.
- Disorganized workplace or poor standard of housekeeping which may result in downtime, excessive time in getting things done, accidents, loss of tools, diversion of attention, etc. Here the implementation of the requirements of ISO 14001 requirements may help to ensure good housekeeping and subsequent reduction in wastages.
- Use of mobile telephones during working hours and in the workplace.
- Lack of accountability which may likely cause a lot of delays in getting things done on a general basis.
- Unreliable suppliers bringing in poor-quality items at delayed times. Here the choice of suppliers should be strictly based on merit, reliability, and integrity of the supplier rather than on personal relationship.
- Over-inflation of supplied items.
- Material wastages.
- Faulty production machine/equipment location or the entirety of the factory layout may be faulty.
- Poor level of communication resulting in poor coordination of activities among internal customers, or poor process interface management.
- Designing goods and services outside customer specification.

- Lack of organizational focus and vision.
- Poor organizational and unit leadership.
- Interruption of power supplies especially in Nigeria and other African countries, which results in unnecessary stoppages, the starting and re-starting of machinery and equipment.
- Voltage fluctuation (also a common feature in Nigeria) which has the tendency to damage machinery and equipment.
- Any non-value-added activity within the work stream.
- Unnecessarily long cycle time.

Manufacturers apart, lean manufacturing, a name commonly applied to the JIT inventory approach, is generally designed purposely for improving process efficiencies through the:

- Minimization of wastes
- Maximization of products (or outputs)

The USC Consulting Group [9], in its broad support for the continued use of lean manufacturing principles, listed the following five critical reasons for sticking with the lean manufacturing principles:

- Lean manufacturing is not just about inventory but about maximizing customer value and minimizing waste.
- Lean can be used to enhance flexibility to improve process efficiencies by optimizing equipment to handle multiple tasks instead of one.
- Lean leads generally to increased employee engagement as it "enables workers to have more say in terms of decision-making as they become stakeholders."
- Lean leads improvement of organizational responses to the behaviors of customers because it helps producers to adapt to and respond to changing customer demands as they happen.
- Lean manufacturing has been widely tested and has proved to be successful; hence it's been termed in many ways as "a way of life" that is "highly prioritized" among some of the world's outstanding organizations.

JIT Inventory Approach

The just-in-time (JIT) inventory approach to manufacturing is a quality concept that, as the name implies, is based on the fundamental principles of getting the right materials in the right, or exact, quantity at the right time. Doing things at the right, or exact, time, so that there will be minimum levels of wastages, stocks/inventory, and space, comes with a lot of advantages. In addition, there will also be a minimization of manpower and transaction time.

This concept which was developed at the Toyota Motor Company of Japan by Taiichi Ohno focuses attention on production systems of small batches in which both the movement of goods and deliveries by suppliers are carefully programmed to take place just as they are needed, thereby avoiding large stocks (inventory) of finished products or work-in-progress (WIP). The practice of the JIT inventory approach may however be hampered in countries of poorer infrastructural backbone structures such as a country like Nigeria. Extra efforts are needed in such countries in respect to the time of product orders to the delivery time bearing in mind erratic changes in government policies, foreign exchange rates, and general insecurity of people, goods, and services.

The JIT inventory approach makes use of inputs supplied mainly at times of need, so that there is little or no need for keeping large stocks of raw materials, or inventory. In this way the processing time is reduced to the minimum or made as short as possible. This is a classical approach good for the preservation of excess materials/inventory and human capital. JIT has, as a result of this principles, earned appellations such as zero inventory production system (ZIPS) and minimum inventory production system (MIPS). Conditions that are critical for the successful achievement of the objectives of JIT are:

- Effective planning in relationship to raw materials' delivery and exactness of all inputs (both human and materials) to avoid excesses and wastes, thereby saving costs and avoiding idle items and excess input.
- Effective process and inventory controls to save on needed space and to avoid tying down of capital.
- Effective timing of the flow of parts and materials through and within the system to avoid idle products and minimize semi-finished products (e.g., work-in-progress, WIP) and downtime.
- Effective timing of various other services to ensure that they are provided for use as and when needed, to avoid and/or minimize waiting or idle time.

The JIT inventory approach is particularly suitable for the orderly and most organized countries of the world, where there are very reliable provisions of services, by organizations with the capability to provide specialized services as may be needed and at the times of need too. The COVID-19 pandemic of 2020, however, showed most critically and perhaps erroneously that the JIT inventory poses some degrees of organizational vulnerability in a disruptive environment; hence, there is a need for some flexibility, quick response, and adaptability.

As far as the author is concerned, the advent of the COVID-19 pandemic is a situation that can be likened to a *once-in-a-lifetime occurrence*, so there are no possibilities whatsoever for manufacturing organizations, whether operating with lean or JIT inventory approach quality management tools, to have prepared adequately to avoid the immediate detrimental impact of the novel coronavirus. The solution for avoiding such detrimental impact of the disruptive environment that resulted from the 2020 COVID-19 pandemic causal is the swift response and adaptability of organizational management team.

Similar thing is the need to stress again and again the fact, too, that the JIT inventory approach is not directly impactful for most parts of the West African sub-region, where industrial development has been marred with the general lack of necessary infrastructural provisions, such as good roads, high level of insecurity, political instability, long processes, and unstable economic policies, to facilitate the use of the JIT inventory approach.

Value Stream Mapping

Waste Occurrence and Identification

There is sufficient information in the literature which shows that *value stream mapping* is a very good tool for the identification of the occurrence of wastes in your system. Value stream mapping which is a visual process for identifying all the activities in the planning and manufacturing process makes the recognition of both value-added and non-value-added activities possible and easy. There are software variations in the market to enable the incorporation of value stream mapping into production systems. For big manufacturers, value stream is built as an end-to-end visibility in the software delivery lifecycle for reducing wastes, hence improving efficiency across organizational activities. In addition, it enables you to utilize and capture most of your key performance indicators (KPIs) to achieve quality products and prompt deliveries.

Value stream mapping can be used to achieve optimum outcomes if:

- There must be good teamwork efforts between product development and operations.
- Customer feedbacks must be put into serious considerations in product development; hence, it must be promptly requested for and received.
- Locations where values are lost must be easily identifiable and promptly prevented in the delivery process.
- Value stream mapping must be transparently and visibly carried out.

In order to facilitate the achievement of planned outputs, it is important and critical to ensure that:

- There is an effective and improved cross-functional collaboration and a system of automated communicational systems in place.

- Production bottlenecks and constraints must be appropriately identified and eliminated in the workflow.
- Development operations performance are effectively managed and are visible.
- Improve build time rates.
- Current and future states for tools and processes must be adequately mapped.

Here, all activities are documented in four main stages of:

- *Product development* based on the identification of the requirements of the customer, definition of the method or of product delivery, and quantity required by the customer.
- *Process design* taking note of and documenting the cycle time, change-over times, number of operators for each process, actual production time, amount of scrap, product variations, batch size, packaging size, etc.
- *Preparation* of the materials needed and then identify critical areas of values to the customer and have trained personnel in place to execute this lean program.
- Effective *planning* is key to achieving set goals and customer values, in value stream mapping, hence the need to put all necessary factors, such as management approval and support in place.

Lean production sets out to define value, creating flow and eliminating waste in every area and stage of work including customer relations, product design, supplier-related activities, and production management so as to significantly improve the manufacturing performance of an organization and sharpen its competitive edge through the achievement of better process speed and efficiency. In order to achieve perfect work flow and minimization of wastes, lean focuses on getting the right things to the right place at the right time in the right quantity.

Process Variability

One of the many ways to avoid wastes is to ensure that there is no variability in the way work is done or executed. Process variability can, for example, contribute to variability of the output. Variability in the skills and training of the employees can also result in variability of the output. Poor information dissemination can also cause or result in the variability of the output.

One way of avoiding variability of output is the use of standard work practices; hence, the introduction and use of standard work procedures or standardized work practices is a good foundation for lean thinking. That is why, according to Locher [10], an initial focus of a lean effort is to implement true standard work practices throughout a business process.

The use of a standard work procedure or practice is particularly important for new employees or for employees that have to relief others that are away on leave of absence. A regular staff may at times also use the procedures guide to update his memory.

Implementing Lean

Since the application of lean is primarily to improve the overall performance of an organization and its ability to compete favorably in the market as regards meeting customer needs and requirements just like any other QMS, there is the need to start its implementation with a vision statement and set out objectives which may include some or more of the following:

- Commitment to continuous improvement with focus on how to effectively use time
- Commitment to achieve high standard of quality with a focus on "doing it right the first time"
- Training of employees as team leaders to facilitate the new culture of waste reduction with the intention of making it an organization-wide attitude
- Commitment to achieve operations capable of reducing wastes
- Elimination of all activities that do not add value
- Commitment to the application of statistical quality tools to identify problems and to find solutions to identified problems
- Completely reduce wastes by eliminating all activities resulting in waste generation
- Training and motivation of employees to be leaders of quality teams and to embrace the team spirit and the idea of working together as a team using as much as possible the consensus decision-making
- Management commitment and provision of necessary resources
- Encouraging the company-wide use of statistical quality management tools for the identification and analysis of problems with the main aim of solving the problems as quickly as possible

Lean Team Selection and Roles

Once objectives and goals have been set, the next line of action for lean implementation is the selection of members of the various lean implementing teams listed below and the definition of their respective roles:

- Steering team
- Continuous improvement coordinator
- Model line team leader
- Model line team members
- Manager and supervisors

In order to ensure the success of the lean program, it is very important to consider the following criteria in the selection of members of the lean teams. Members of the teams must:

- Be willing to volunteer and participate in the lean team activities as long as the project lasts

- Have the knowledge and expertise to tackle the problems and tasks that are within the scope of the team
- Have the capability to represent various organizational levels and function
- Have vested interests and concern in the task areas

Roles of the Steering Team

The major role of the steering committee when viewed from a broad perspective is to ensure the success of the lean program and the achievement of continuous improvement through the creation of the vision statement, ensuring company-wide communication and lean team management to make sure that the set-out objectives are achieved.

Roles of the Continuous Improvement Coordinator

It is the major responsibility of the continuous improvement coordinator to coordinate the implementation of the model line with the steering committee team members to achieve successful implementation. The continuous improvement coordinator serves as the link between team leaders and the steering committee as well as shares results of the improvement process with all those concerned.

Process Flow

The effective timing of the flow of materials and parts through the system is very critical in ensuring the smooth flow of products; hence, everything should be done to ensure that the flow of product is smooth and uninterrupted. The interruption of materials flow may occur through various means which includes:

- Handling method
- Machine setup time
- Unplanned downtime
- Machine breakdown
- Transportation issues
- WIP inventory
- Inadequate staffing

Objectives of JIT

From the point of view of its goals and objectives, the JIT which can be said to be synonymous with *lean manufacturing* is generally for the achievement of a system that:

- Is efficient and balanced
- Is steady and characterized by rapid flow of materials
- Is free of disruptions or in which disruptions are eliminated

- Eliminates wastes
- Minimizes stocks/inventories
- Reduces setup
- Reduces lead time for deliveries

Application of JIT

The JIT approach is not suitable for every organization. JIT is used generally by manufacturers for goods such as automobiles which have attained certain level of quality (including those of trained staff) and needs to respond to the needs and demands of some customers, thereby avoiding the building up of stocks/inventory of finished products. In the case of automobiles, it may just be for the production of a limited number of one or two models, demanded specially by some customers. Hence organizations practicing JIT are limited in one way or the other to smaller sizes of batches.

Organizations in countries that solely rely on the importation of most raw materials are not likely to benefit from JIT especially when government import regulations and customs tariff are not stable. Hence the use of the JIT concept is not likely going to work in a country like Nigeria.

Improvement Measures

Science of Improvement

The great opportunity of working immediately after graduating from the Hochschule at a high quality-based manufacturing outfit of excellence, Eduard Kuesters Machinery Manufacturing Factory in Krefeld, Germany, quickly exposed me to the practical role and importance of *confirmation* studies and validation in the design of experiment (DoE) model projects which frequently involve confirmation runs. It is interesting though tasking waiting anxiously for your models to produce the accuracies of predictions, especially bearing in mind the long-standing saying of Box and Draper [11] that "all models are wrong, but some are useful." This thus stresses the general need for model validation and confirmation.

As identified in Chap. 19, research interests in quality, quality management (QM), and total quality management (TQM) as well as quality management principles, tools, and techniques are going to grow in the future. This is particularly so not just because quality evolved outside of the academia but for the general need to confirm, find, or establish and validate some mathematical and scientific theoretical bases for quality terms and concepts. We all realize here that most of the quality terms and concepts that we are acquainted with today evolved or were deduced from industrial manufacturing experience-based assumptions or realities and also to find new paradigms for quality in the twenty-first century. Confirmation studies are likely going to be of good use in this wise.

Recent publications in the literature, Jensen [12], Stevens and Anderson-Cook [13], and Anderson-Cook and Lu [14], give some highlights of the usefulness of confirmation studies not just in design but also in "solving quality quandaries through statistics."

Whether we are talking of process improvement, predicting process optimum operating conditions, or analyzing study results, "Confirmation and validation using independent data are a characteristic of good science and good analytical studies" (Snee [6]). This goes to highlight the need for validation and confirmation of data in quality measurements and studies.

Summary for Quick Checks

It is mere wishful thinking for the management of any high-performing organization or business enterprise to think that its organization can ordinarily keep or maintain its high level of business performance. Such a wish could only be realistic in an environment where the management teams of other competing businesses have gone to sleep. Fortunately for end-users or consumers nowadays, most organizations are very conscious of the highly competitive nature of the global business environment. Hence, it is very vital and critical for the management team of every organization not to relent, or rest on its oars, by simply relying on its current performance indicators, without thinking of innovative ways and strategies needed, not just to maintain its competitiveness but generally to ensure the sustainability of the business in its entirety. Hence, there is the general urgent need to ensure and maintain improvement measures on a continuous basis. The choice is therefore that organizations have no other alternative than to thread the path of *continual improvement* in order to outwit other competitors.

There are various concepts and programs for continually improving your products and services. The underlisted improvement guidelines are some of the measures for organizational sustainability.

Improvement Guidelines

- Talk to your customer/market and get necessary feedback (through survey, study, questionnaire, feasibility studies, direct meetings, etc.).
- Know and confirm the products or services wanted by your customers with relevant updates from time to time.
- Know their exact SNEaRs as stated directly by the customer, instead of using a third party.
- Define the gaps between your current products/services and customer/market needs.
- Keep your accredited and qualified suppliers or the supply chain abreast of your organizational SNEaRs.

- Improve your production line vis-à-vis your products/services to meet customer/market SNEaRs.
- Create and constantly maintain a strong and frequent communication line with your customer/market to get and update the voice of your customer (VOC).
- Review your production system on a continual basis through regular internal and external audits, production meetings, customer feedback, and any other relevant quality management tools.
- Use your review output to continually improve your products/services, quality management system, and organization.

Improvement Planning for Competitiveness

It is necessary to keep your organization well-equipped for competitiveness in line with market and customer dynamism:

- You can equip your organization for competitiveness, by firstly identifying where exactly you would like your products/services to be in the market. Lay the solid foundation of your improvement goals in your *mission statement.*
- Spell out your *strategies* for getting there.
- List the *actions* or *business tactics* that will take you there.

Picking Your Strategies

Picking the right strategies for achieving your improvement goals is very critical for you. A lot of options are available for you to choose from. Some of the options available include, but are not limited to, the following:

- Quality-based strategies
- Time-based strategies
- Production-based strategies

Quality-based strategies are highly effective in achieving your improvement goals, but adequate measures have to be put in place to ensure that the most appropriate quality management system and/or improvement concept is effectively implemented.

Productivity Improvement

Use relevant performance improvement measurements to identify and ascertain the level of process and performance improvements achieved from time to time, day by day:

- Establish easily achievable goals/objectives.
- Introduce key performance indicators (KPIs) to be used as basis for measuring or assessing improvement.
- Get the support of management.
- Select and develop methods for productivity improvement.
- Develop productivity measures.
- Determine critical operations.
- Measure improvements.
- Give feedback about improvement achievements to employees.

Elements of Competitiveness

Identifying the elements of competitiveness product by product help you maintain your market competitiveness:

- Product/service quality
- Innovation/difference from others
- Price
- Time
- Product maintainability/availability of after-sales services
- Flexibility

Factors Affecting Productivity

Consider factors that may affect organizational productivity to solve any problems inhibiting productivity:

- Product/service quality
- Management ability to provide needed resources as and when needed
- Technology update from time to time as may be relevant
- Provision of capital needed for reinvestment
- Management identification of relevant training for appropriate employees
- Poor motivation of employees

Scope of Conformity Assessment

Conformity assessment, as the name implies, are activities or processes that are used to assess the level or extent to which systems/products/services or even organizational activities are in line with reference guidelines, standards, or other predetermined conditions. Conformity assessment activities can be accomplished by one or more of the under-listed:

- *Inspecting* – Here applicable production processes for achieving products are inspected to ensure that they have been made in safe manners in line reference regulations/guidelines or predetermined conditions.
- *Testing* – With this, products/services are tested to determine whether they comply or perform in line with the specified requirements.
- *Implementing* – This is concerned with the implementation of a quality management system/standard/program/concept to ensure that products or services have been consistently produced or delivered by an organization to meet the needs, specifications, and expectations of the customer.

Key Performance Indicators (KPIs)

Using KPIs

Key performance indicators (KPIs), or key success indicators (KSIs) as they are also being referred to, are quantifiable measurements expressed in simple units to evaluate an organization's level or state of progress/success vis-à-vis improvement toward organizational goals/objectives at regularly defined time intervals. KPIs can therefore be seen as critical performance metrics of an organization. Hence, they are of extreme importance in gauging the overall improvement as well as the success story an organization may want to tell. Some of your KPIs may be measured on a daily, weekly, monthly, quarterly, bi-annually, and/or yearly basis. Your unit of measurement must have to be agreed upon by your management, and it must be chosen to reflect the area(s) or process units of your organization which improvement you may want to be measuring.

You are at will to select your KPIs on the basis of the entirety of organizational activities, or specific process sections/units or departments. But your KPIs must however be defined. The use of KPIs for process units may also help to bring to your notice some of the internal bottlenecks that may have been hindering your improvement. Every organization selects its own suitable KPI criteria based on its strategies, business goals, and objectives. You should, however, ensure that those ones selected by you will give you the best results in the measurement of your improvement either on departmental or organization-wide basis.

KPIs are diverse and they may be financial, internal process performance, or business-level based. Financial performance indicators (FPIs), such as return on investment (ROI) and profitability, are usually organizational-based. Examples of business-level KPIs may be derived from customer satisfaction feedbacks, loyalty scores, on-time delivery, quality defective products, cost of poor quality, employee satisfaction, and other business activity-based metrics [15].

KPI and Competitiveness

Today's market challenges are quite complex especially when viewed from the perspectives of a globalized market structure coupled with the challenges of technological, economic, and environmental dynamisms. The ability of organizations to effectively compete in such a complex business environment requires, firstly, that they engage a proper approach that may help them in the identification, measurement, and understanding of organizational performance, in order to be able to move forward. No matter what quality tools that you may decide to deploy for the improvement of your processes and organizational performance, key performance indicators (KPIs) offer the opportunities for business assessment and management. KPIs are therefore great tools for managing organizational business performance.

KPI measurements may be made to reflect wide organizational business strategies, stakeholder interests, and a reflection of organizational competitiveness with consideration for the factors that impact the employees, too [16].

In their cross-industry study of the use of KPIs in the digital era, Schrage and Kiron [17] established the fact that, "Leadership will increasingly decide which KPIs will inform human behavior and which will inform machine learning. Those decisions will increasingly determine enterprise success." While using KPIs to lead and manage a business in the hitherto customer-centric marketplace, an area in which they have achieved increased relevance, the future potential of KPIs may have to be redefined to broaden their focus on customer experience, due to the globalized and digitalized environment of intensive competitive pressure.

KPIs may be tactical, strategic, financial, operational, or otherwise defined by various organizations as may be suitable for their goals and objectives. It should be noted, too, that performance metrics vary generally in their purpose, definition, and content [18].

Criteria for KPI

The criteria for selecting your KPIs may vary from one process type to another within the same organization just as it varies from one organization to the other. Find below some relevant criteria from which KPIS can be derived:

1. *Productivity* – Man/labor hour, unit time of operations, unit of material input or material yield, raw material wastages, etc. to enable you to know, for example, the improvement made, or otherwise, in your resource utilization.
2. *Product sales* – Sales in dollar values or product units, after sales rejects, etc. This helps to determine change in sales volume per specified time, etc.
3. *Customer satisfaction* (including internal customers) – This may involve KPIs from various organizational units/departments. For example, the number of products rejected during inspection or by quality assurance, number of products re-worked, (production department), etc.

4. *Supply chain management* – Defective materials received from suppliers, inventory, re-order level, etc.
5. *Manufacturing/production* – Machine efficiency using product cycle, downtime, defective products or rejects, product recalls, etc.

Measuring Performance Improvement Using KPIs

- Specify goals to be achieved with respective KPIs.
- Define KPIs for organization's global goals and those for necessary units/departments and/or individual process types in support of the overall organizational goals. Avoid the proliferation of KPIs to avoid unnecessary diversion of employee attention.
- Define KPI units of measurement and ensure it is understood by relevant employees.
- Identify exact mode of measurement.

Advantages of Using KPIs

- Organizational and/or unit or departmental performance management tool
- Give a very clear picture about the improvement factors critical to management and organization
- As employee feedback system which if widely communicated among employees has the capability to motivate them in achieving more and more
- Serve generally as critical focus factors for all employees as targets to achieve and even exceed

Customer-Supplier Partnerships

Customer-supplier partnerships are highly essential ingredients to boost your quality management systems, product quality, market share, and profits. Organizational management often neglects or underrates the importance of good and virile customer-supplier partnerships. This is probably because of the poor recognition of the benefits derivable from it. It is therefore important here to stress the fact that you can positively influence your quality management system, product quality, market share, and profits through effective customer-supplier partnerships. Hence it will be of importance for you to effectively establish, nurture, and keep such relationships alive in your organization. Some important steps that you can take for you to achieve this quality improvement measure are listed here:

- Create a partnership environment between your suppliers and you through the establishment of relevant teams with responsibilities to establish and/or implement supplier capability guidelines, product specifications, product and/or system audit, and supplier certification/registration and de-certification criteria.

- Maintain a system that will enable you to maintain customer-supplier or organization-supplier agreement for supplier capability goals and supplier certification/registration, identify post-certification improvement performance levels and application of benchmarking processes, and establish de-registration or de-certification criteria.
- Identify the mutual benefits of a long-term and mutually beneficial customer-supplier partnerships, in terms of achieving a more cost-effective but satisfactory delivery performance. This would aid the understanding and cooperation of all parties involved.

It will be of great benefit to you too to completely leave the caveat of product inspection to your supplier, thereby making them responsible for whatever problems that may result from defective supplied items. Apart from the fact that you will save money by not having to use your staff to inspect the supplied materials or input, you would be able to put the materials to use just as they are delivered as is the case with JIT approach. Here you will save on inventory and stocks' expenses.

KPI in Government Contracts

Quality practices in government or public service are at a level that is entirely different from the way it is in the private sector organizations. In government quality is defined, based on the subject matter. Quality trends in government rely strongly on the use of KPIs as measurable metrics for evaluating government contracts. KPIs thus "act as the broker for contractors by showing the government they can perform the work outlined in the awarded contract" [19]. It is used to determine a contractor's performance level and eligibility/ineligibility for subsequent contracts.

Benefits of Process/Business Improvement

Process improvement on a continual basis, though not compulsory, is extremely relevant and important to your quality management system if you have to keep pace with the global market economy and remain competitive. The reasons for business are numerous, and it may interest you to learn or know about some of them here. Some of these include, but are not limited to, the following:

- Achieve business success.
- Improve product/service quality.
- Remain competitive and possibly gain competitive edge.
- Promote the sales of your products/services and market relevancy.
- Make more profits.
- Avoid equipment, products/services, machinery, and equipment suddenly becoming obsolete.
- Keep business alive and active as an ongoing enterprise.

Quality Improvement

The continual improvement of your business is very important for its survival and ability to compete effectively in the global market economy. It therefore becomes highly imperative for business owners to embrace process improvement in order to be successful. Quality is as dynamic as technology and the changing pattern of customer expectations hence the general need to keep up with the types of improvements needed to keep pace with technological development and the changing customer requirements.

There are various ways to go about the improvement of your business/enterprise and its quality management system. In order to simplify your improvement process, the approach provided in the author's 23-Universal Business Improvement Guidelines (23-UBig) may partly or wholly be of good use for you to achieve your set-out quality improvement goals.

Selecting Improvement Systems/Concepts/Strategies

Every organizational or business management team has the right to decide whether to improve his or her business. At the same time, the choice of a quality management system or improvement program/concept/scheme/methodology is also yours. There are long lists of choices for you to pick from, and there is no doubt too that many more options for business improvement will continue to emerge in the future too.

The list of some improvement or quality management options is provided below in order to give you a general picture of available opportunities:

- 5S total quality environment
- Circle-4 quality system
- Feigenbaum's philosophy of quality control [20]
- 23-UBIG – 23-Universal Business Improvement Guide
- Integrated Quality Management Systems/Programs (e.g., Lean Six Sigma, Lean Kaizen, 5S Kaizen, etc.)
- ISO 9001 QMS standards [21] series and their equivalents, in member countries
- Juran's 10 steps for quality improvement
- Just-in-time (JIT) technique
- Kaizen strategy
- Lean Kaizen
- Lean production system
- Lean Six Sigma
- Malcolm Baldrige National Quality Award Criteria
- Muda concept
- Philip Crosby's concept of zero defect
- Quality circle
- Six Sigma

- Deming's 14 points
- The plan-do-check-act (PDCA) or plan-do-study-act (PDSA) cycle (also known as either the *Shewhart* cycle or Deming cycle/wheel). Walter A. Shewhart created the basis for the evolved establishment of the cycle, while Deming was the first to use it in Japan. It should be noted that Deming did not invent or originate the PDCA [22].
- Total quality management (TQM) concept
- World-class quality concept/world-class manufacturing

Using 5S Principles

5S quality management methodology or principles was first established by Toyota in Japan. 5S is a methodology which enables organizations to maintain a workplace that is clean, uncluttered, safe, and well organized to help waste reduction, optimize productivity, and improve safety. 5S originates from five (5) Japanese "**S**-letter" words – *seiri*, *seiton*, *seiso*, *seiketsu*, and *shitsuke*.

5S shows how simple the concept or philosophy of quality could be. The actions or activities prescribed by each these Japanese words represent the quality management requirements spelled out with it. When translated into English, we have the intended activities as follows:

- *Seiri* – "organize" or "sort things out" to get rid of anything whatsoever that is not needed (i.e., wastes) from the workplace. It could be materials, tools, machine parts, etc.
- *Seiton* – "orderliness" or "set things out in good order" by neatly arranging everything in such a way that they do not obstruct and are easily traceable and identifiable.
- *Seiso* – "cleanliness" or "shine," that is, the work area must be kept properly cleaned at all times.
- *Seiketsu* – "standardize"
- *Shitsuke* – "discipline" or "sustain"

The 5S quality methodology has been able to withstand the test of time and grown prominently in use in a wide variety of industries [23].

Some Performance Improvement Tips

- Customer satisfaction is the sole objective of quality; hence, it should be your sole business objective.
- Select the most adequate quality management system/concept/program/strategies and implement the needed requirements to achieve customer satisfaction.
- Keep your business alive; meet customer (internal and external) specifications, needs, and requirements at all times.

- Quality planned at source, controlled at processing stages, and continually improved on are building blocks for achieving improved performance.
- Use selected KPIs for the measurement and assessment of the performance of your business on a regular basis. Choose the KPIs that are easily measurable and understandable for you to use in tracking your daily, weekly, monthly, quarterly, or yearly business improvement performance.
- Review and take necessary actions if your expectations are not satisfactory or does not show the expected or planned level of improvement.
- Grow your business through continual performance improvement.

It is worthy of mentioning here that improvements must be glaringly visible and definable in measurement terms. This further reinforces Peter Drucker in: "If you can't measure it, you can't improve it."

References

1. Manos, A. (2007). The benefits of kaizen and kaizen events. *Quality Progress, 40*(2), 47–48.
2. Imai, M. (1986). *Kaizen: The key to Japan's competitive success*. McGraw-Hill.
3. Japanese Human Resources Association. (1992). *Kaizen Teian 1*. Productivity Press.
4. Alukal, G., & Manos, A. (2006). *Lean kaizen: A simplified approach to process improvement*. ASQ Quality Press.
5. Schonberger, R. (1982). *Japanese manufacturing techniques: Nine hidden lessons in simplicity*. Free Press.
6. Snee, R. D. (2021). Statistics spotlight: Thou shall confirm. *Quality Progress, 74*, 54–56.
7. Schonberger, R. (2021). Seen and heard – The reaction gauge. *Quality Progress, 25*, 4.
8. Conner, G. (2001). *Lean manufacturing for the small shop* (Vol. 2001, p. 42). Society of Manufacturing Engineers.
9. USC Consulting Group. (2020). *Empowering performance – 5 reasons why you need to stich with lean manufacturing principles*. March 11, 2020. http://www.usccg.com retrieved on April 11, 2021
10. Locher, D. (2007). In the office: Where lean and six sigma converge. *Quality Progress, 40*(10), 54–56.
11. Box, G. E. P., & Draper, N. R. (1987). *Model-building and response surfaces*. Wiley.
12. Jensen, W. A. (2016). Confirmation runs in design of experiments. *Journal of Quality Technology, 48*(2), 162–177. https://doi.org/10.1080/00224065.2016.11918157
13. Stevens, N. T., & Anderson-Cook, C. M. (2019). Design and analysis of confirmation experiments. *Journal of Quality Technology, 51*(2), 109–124.
14. Anderson-Cook, C. M., & Lu, L. (2020). Statistic spotlight: Why not sequential DoES? *Quality Progress, 53*(11), 44–47.
15. Ramu, G. (2021). To the point – ISO/FDIS 10014 incorporates the language of business to help top management understand its intent. *Quality Progress, 54*(4), 56–59.
16. Kenny, G. (2020). Create KPIs that reflect your strategic profiles. *Harvard Business Review.*
17. Schrage, M., & Kiron, D. (2018). Leading with next-generation key performance indicators. *MIT Sloan Management Review, 16*, 1–2.
18. Villazón, C. C., Pinilla, L. S., Olaso, J. R. O., Gandarias, N. T., & López de Lacalle, N. (2020). Identification of key performance indicators in project-based organisations through the lean approach. *Sustainability, 12*, 5977.
19. Payne, T. (2020). *Quality is universal*. November 19, 2020. Blog Article, IACET, https://www.iacet

20. Feigenbaum, A. V. (1989). *Total quality control* (3rd ed.). McGraw-Hill.
21. International Organization for Standardization, ISO 9001:2015.
22. Pruitt, W. F., & Imam, S. M. W. (2021). The Shewhart cycle: Did W. Edwards Deming invent the plan-do-check-act (PDCA) cycle? *Quality Progress, 56*, 6.
23. Griffin, T. (2021). Best in SHOW: Updating 5S principles for a modern heat-treatment facility. *Quality Progress, 54*, 64.

Quality Management System Audit 18

Audit Concept

Quality Audit

The word audit as is most commonly known to the layman is mainly in the context of its application to financial accounting systems. This is adequately reflected in its dictionary meaning which simply describes audit as "an official examination and verification of accounts and records, especially of financial accounts."

The term *audit* is, however, all-encompassing in the way it stretches the term "accountability." The manufacturing sector, international trade sector, and supply chain systems constitute some of the most frequent traditional auditing havens of human activities apart from accounting.

For example, there are five different types of audits to evaluate your supplier – *social compliance audit* (or social accountability audit), *quality system audit*, *good manufacturing practice* (GMP) audit, *product regulatory compliance audit* and C-TPAT (Customs-Trade Partnership Against Terrorism) security audit [2]. It is obvious from the general application and use of "auditing process" that there is a common goal and objective of the outcome: it is the "quality of the services in question through risk reduction."

The term "quality audit" is, however, used in a broader sense as it extends far beyond the accounting boundaries of organizational activities to include, to a large extent, transparency in various aspects of organizational systems of activities, including the accounting systems itself.

Of course, the principles and objectives of both quality management audit and accounting audit are undoubtedly same as encompassed in the words:

> Evaluation/examination and verification of records, documents of proof to obtain transparent evidences of compliance or conformity with both regulatory and predetermined requirements, guidelines, rules and provisions.

T. A. Ibidapo, *From Industry 4.0 to Quality 4.0*, Management for Professionals,
https://doi.org/10.1007/978-3-031-04192-1_18

When viewed however from a broader perspective or from the view point of quality management, audit is used to indicate a formal or methodical examination, review, and investigation of a system to know the extent to which it is in compliance with planned arrangements or predetermined conditions, standards, and regulatory guidelines generally as a performance improvement measure and organizational sustainability. This is why the author believed very strongly in quality management sciences being sufficiently ripe as a discipline on its own in the new decade.

The ISO in ISO 9000:2015, adequately defines *audit* as:

> A systematic, independent and documented process for obtaining objective evidence and evaluating it objectively to determine the extent to which the audit criteria are fulfilled.

Quality audit which may be first, second, or third party could be seen as a measure leading directly or indirectly to improving the quality management system (QMS). This is particularly so when the QMS in question is subjected to regular auditing with corrective (reactive measure) and preventive (proactive) actions put in place promptly and effectively after each audit exercise [1].

There are no doubts however that every organization has the freedom to select which improvement modes are to be used. It is however advisable that auditing is in a special class of available QMS improvement tools hence the need to make a part of organizational choices of improvement measures or processes. This in turn requires the need for training your own personnel to be able to carry out internal audits (also known as first-party audit) at regular intervals of organizational choice (e.g., about once a year or so).

Third-party audits may be executed by external, independent, auditing firms such as the ones providing certification or registration of conformity or governmental agencies/bodies. Certification or third-party audits may be carried out at intervals recommended by your quality consultants. For example, ISO 9001 certifications audits may be executed about once in 3 years or in some countries as may be determined by regulatory bodies and subject to organizational choice and management abilities to maintain and uphold the QMS.

Generally, yearly internal surveillance audits are okay, depending on the choice of your management. However, organizations in the third world countries where the QMS may easily derail both internal and surveillance audits may assume or call for a higher frequency.

Audit Participants

ISO 19011:2018 – Guidelines for auditing management systems. It provides a full list of vocabularies useful in understanding every bit and aspect of the auditing process. Reference to ISO 19011 such as provided below is therefore important to the understanding of the auditing process [7]

While the organization being audited is referred to as the *auditee* (ISO 19011:2011, section 3.7), the *auditor* (section 3.8) is a person who conducts an audit. The *audit client* (3.6) is an organization or person requesting an audit, while the *audit team* (3.9) refers to one or more persons conducting an audit. While the *audit team leader* manages the entirety of the audit process, the *guide* (3.12) is a person appointed by the auditee to assist the audit team. The *observer* (3.11) accompanies the audit team within the audited premises and throughout the duration of the auditing process without acting as an auditor. The *audit program* (3.13) is a set of one or more audits planned for a specific time frame and directed toward a specific purpose, while the *audit scope* (3.14) which sets the extent and boundaries of an audit generally gives a description of the physical locations, organizational units, activities, and processes.

Performance Review

It is important for you to regularly review the performance of your business on a regular basis to ensure that:

- Business is on course in terms of achieving your planned business goals/objectives.
- Business operations are going on in line with regulatory or statutory guidelines.
- Operational bottlenecks are detected in time before damages are done.
- Necessary corrective actions are put in place as and whenever necessary.
- Business improvement measures put in place from time to time are effective.
- Verify or *ascertain* key performance indicators (KPIs).
- Organizational activities, processes, and products conform with regulatory guidelines, directives, or even laws.

Just as you need to continually carry out your business performance review so also may your customers have the need to do same. In both cases system audit is a very good tool to achieve this as it provides organizational management the opportunity to execute improve organizational performance in all ramifications through the auditors' eagle-eyed findings.

While you need to carry out internal audits often referred to as *first-party audit*, at regular intervals your customer may want to carry out an audit (*second-party audit*) of your system to verify your capability to make quality products or render quality services that you promised to give or render. Your customer may carry out the audit by itself or appoint other persons to do it on their behalf.

Defining Quality Audit

The first questions that you may want to ask here are as follows: "What is quality audit?" "Is it related to accounting audits, if not how is it different?

The ASQ in its Quality Glossary defines auditing as:

> The on-site verification activity, such as inspection or examination, of a process or quality system, to ensure compliance to requirements.

The ISO defined audit in ISO 19011:2011 as:

> The systematic, independent and documented process for obtaining objective evidence and evaluating it objectively to determine the extent to which audit criteria are fulfilled.

ISO 19011:2018 defines an audit as:

> A systematic independent and documented process for obtaining audit evidence – records, statements of fact or other information which are relevant and verifiable – and evaluating it objectively to determine the extent to which the audit criteria – a set of policies, procedures or requirements – are fulfilled.

These definitions show generally that an audit is an independent assessment exercise usually carried out to estimate or determine the degree or extent of conformity of a system, process, or product with prescribed requirements, performance, or expectations. The audit may therefore generally be seen as an information-gathering exercise that aids the determination of the degree of conformities or compliances in a system so that corrective actions can be put in place for the purposes of improving the system.

Common Areas of Quality Auditing

Although there is no limitation as to the applicability or use of quality, the author's years of experience lead to the identification of three common areas of audits – *system audit, product audit, and process audit.*

System Audit

An example here is the audit carried out to examine an *environmental managemental management system* (EMS). For this system, therefore, a documented exercise is carried out by trained auditors to verify, through examination and the evaluation of objective evidences, that applicable elements of the EMS are appropriate and effective and have been developed, documented, and implemented in line and in conjunction with specified requirements.

Product Audit

This area of audit focuses on specific products and/or services. It is carried out for the purpose of examining a particular product or service in order to evaluate and determine whether it is in conformity with appropriate performances standards, regulatory requirements, and customer SNEaRs.

Process Audit

This area of auditing is used mainly to verify or ascertain that organizational work processes are working in line with established limits or predetermined modes. Hence, process audit is deployed to measure the conformity of an operation or methodology against predetermined instructions, standards, or prescriptions and the level of effectiveness with which this is achieved. In achieving this goal, a process audit may therefore be deployed to:

- Examine and check how adequate and effective process control systems are in relationship to established procedures, work instructions, and established process specifications.
- Check process conformity with defined conditions, requirements, and parameters such as time, temperature, amperage, pressure, composition and consistency, component mixture, and responsiveness.
- Evaluate and check overall process performance, in terms of all the resources or a combination of them engaged in transforming inputs into outputs – people, equipment, and materials – as well as the processing environment, processing methods (procedure and work instructions), and the measures, such as the KPIs collected to ascertain or determine the process performance.

The prescribed requirements or criteria for which a system is audited against may, among others, include such examples as:

- Compliance to specific standard/norm
- Product or service performance requirements
- Predetermined condition of any kind and type
- Certification to certain compliance requirements

Quality Auditing Standards

Guideline Standard

Auditing is a skill that has to be acquired generally through training and practice. There are various books and guidelines which you can use for the acquisition of auditing skills. There are, however, auditing standards available for executing auditing – internal and external – exercises in area-specific industries. Examples include:

- *ISO 19011:2018 – Guidelines for auditing management systems* [7]. It provides guidelines that can be used to audit management systems such as the ISO 9001 QMS and the ISO 14001 environmental management systems (EMS) standards requirement. This standard also provides guidelines about the principles of auditing, managing an audit, and conducting management system audits. In addition, the standard gives guidance on the evaluation of the competencies of individuals

that are involved in the audit process, such as managing the audit program, auditors, and audit teams. It is applicable to any organization that require "to plan and conduct internal or external audits of management systems or manage an audit program," (ISO).
For example, a *quality management system audit* is used to evaluate an existing QMS in order to determine the extent of its conformance with organizational policies, regulatory requirements, and customer contract commitments.
- *ISO/TS 22003:2013 – Food safety management systems* [9] *(requirements for bodies providing audit and certification of food safety management systems).* It gives the guidelines useful for bodies providing audit and certification services for food safety management systems (FSMS). This standard can, for example, be used in auditing ISO 22000:2018 – Food safety management systems (requirements for any organization in the food chain).

Principles and Relevance of QMS Audit

Many people may wonder why the need for a quality management systems (QMS) audit when there are many other quality management improvement areas available for use and application. The QMS audit is a highly essential quality management tool available for organizational management to achieve a thorough state-of-the-organization evaluation of organizational performance in terms of production and technical competencies and its exact competitive abilities. From employee satisfaction, resource wastages, process downturn to internal customer satisfaction, the audit is a superlative continuous quality improvement tool to make organizations more productive, more competitive, and more of a better place to work for employees.

Ethical Considerations of Auditing

Since ethical conduct is generally seen as the foundation of professionalism, quality management systems auditors need not just exhibit a high sense of ethical conduct, objectivity, and diligence but must also be seen as such in all ramifications of the auditing exercise. This brings to the fore the general needs that audits are being performed by various auditing bodies, among which are the ones listed below, and must be as thorough and objective as possible:

- Government agencies and/or regulatory bodies
- Accreditation groups
- International standards certification groups
- Private registrars or any other agents involved in organizational auditing (these are the main source of quality auditors in the United States)
- Organizational trained internal auditors

When carrying out audits, it is extremely helpful to be professional and on the basis of ethics. Some of the ethical considerations include the following, among others:

- Build *trust* in the auditee through *competency*.
- *Professionalism* in all aspects of the auditing process.
- *Fair presentation* of the audit.
- Every auditing activity must be handled with the utmost *objectivity* by the auditors.
- *Impartiality* in handling auditing process.
- *Audit evaluation* should be evidence-based.
- Ensure *good and effective communication* and *cooperation* with the auditee.

Purpose of Audit

The primary intention of any audit exercise is for the improvement of the audited system. Hence, auditing is generally necessitated by the need to verify whether a system meets the requirements of a standard and regulatory guidelines or whether a product or a process can achieve the level of performance or set out goals for which they are put in place or made. The objectives of an audit can be understood using the example of the investigation of the conformity of a quality management system with the requirements of a standard by asking the following pertinent questions:

- To what extent is the prescribed standard and/or regulatory guidelines or norm being followed?
- To what degree or extent has the quality system met the requirements of the standard and/or regulatory guidelines?
- To what extent has the quality system contributed to the efficiency and effectiveness of an organization's ability to achieve the set-out goals and objectives, such as customer SNEaRs?

The answers to all three questions can practically be obtained through an audit exercise. In a brief summary therefore, audits may generally be conducted for various reasons including the following:

- As a means and opportunity for performance improvement
- To achieve best practices with reference to accomplishing customer SNEaRs
- To ensure organizational compliance with specific standard requirements, such as ISO 9001 QMS international standard
- To ensure conformity with regulatory requirements and/or guidelines
- To ensure that a QMS is effectively implemented, maintained, and sustained

Audit Classification

There are, on a general basis, various types and classes of audits (Fig. 18.1). In some cases, audits are classified broadly on the basis of the following:

1. Relationship between the auditee (defined in ISO 9000:2015 as "the organization being audited") and the auditor (defined in ISO 9000:2015 as the "person with the demonstrated personal attributes and competence to conduct an audit") and that of the customer-supplier. Hereby, we have internal and external audits.
2. Reason for the audit (may be for the purpose of verification of the compliance or not, status of a process, product, or system) either by the organization to assess itself or by the customer to assess its supplier. Hereby one may be referring to a product audit, process audit, equipment audit, etc.

A further classification of audits results in the following forms based on relationships between the auditor and the auditee.

- First-party audits – Internal audits to evaluate organizational performance in line with its goals and objectives, identification of problem areas, and overall performance improvement
- Second-party audits – External audits such as customer audits of suppliers to evaluate conformance to customer SNEaRs and any other customer interests
- Third-party audits – External (independent) audits. To evaluate conformity to specified standards, predetermined requirements, regulatory requirements/guidelines, etc.

Internal Audit or First-Party Audit

Most QMS regulations or standards generally require every organization irrespective of its size, products, and services to develop and maintain an internal monitoring process to ensure that there is a continual compliance with the regulations and standards.

Internal process or compliance or first-party audits therefore come very handy as major processes used by many industries and organizations as their internal monitoring system to ascertain or determine the degree of compliance of their various units or groups with their QMS.

For a first-party audit, an organization carries out "the auditing of its own activities to assess its procedures, process or system either in fulfillment of a requirement or external standard or for self-appraisal purposes." Internal audit may therefore be defined as:

> An audit performed by, or at the instance of the organization itself.

A first-party audit may therefore be implemented at the request of management to get the assurance that the area or process to be audited is in compliance with specific quality standards and that the goals and objectives/strategies of an organization are being met.

This audit type aids the audit client (defined in ISO 9000:2005 as the "organization or person requesting an audit") in knowing its weaknesses, nonconformities, or non-conformances as may be revealed in the audit findings (defined in ISO 9000:2005 as the "results of the evaluation of the collected audit evidence against audit criteria"); hence, it could also be seen as an in-house motivational factor for the self-improvement of an organization's own QMS. The objective of the first-party audit can generally be summed up as follows:

- For the assessment of the progress of an organization's QMS in terms of its ability to comply with the requirements of a standard or norm as provided in its quality manual (QM) and its procedure guides.
- To review the continuity of implementing an organization's QMS and evaluate its continual improvement opportunities.
- To confirm whether the documentation, document control, and all process monitoring measures are carried out in accordance with planned procedures in line with the provisions of an organization's QM.

As a result of the importance and relevance of internal audits in the maintenance the QMS, it is critical that the personnel (i.e., employees) participating in internal audits must:

- Be familiar with the reasons why an audit is conducted so that they can appreciate why they must be fully prepared to participate in it.
- Understand how the audit is related to ensuring the use of good business processes.
- Be educated to realize and appreciate process improvement benefits achievable through the experience of the internal audit.

From the experience of the author, educating the employees is highly critical since audit (including audit meetings and reports) surveys conducted among the employees over a period of time (1997–2000) actually showed that most of the employees do not actually believe that audits are generally beneficial to the organization. Rather they believed initially that audits are management rituals that have to be carried out to satisfy management and that it is a time-wasting exercise. It was later discovered through the use of a root cause analysis of this fundamental problem carried out by the author that the reasons for the negative impression of the employees were actually due to the fact that most of them had little or no understanding of the audit process, preparation for the audit, and its overall benefits to the operational processes as well as to the organization at large. In order to correct this impression, we decided to carry out some specific training programs as corrective actions to bridge their current knowledge gap. We divided the employees into groups of ten and arranged short training schemes not longer than 15 minutes at a stretch for them.

The design and objective of this training was to effectively enlighten them on:

- The audit process – what it entails, its purpose and importance to the business, objective, role of documentation, and the need for it so as to increase their understanding of the entire audit process.
- Audit preparatory activities and their individual roles in the audit process and expectations of their input into the process.
- How they can effectively participate or be involved in audits.
- The benefits of the audit to their respective units, their individual and collective performance (organizational level), and how this can affect or impact on the attainment of the targeted productivity in terms of quality and quantity as well as how the audit process can influence the monthly productivity bonus.
- Interrelationship between each individual worker (potential auditees) and the auditor.

The gross impact of this training on the employees and auditing process is enormous as listed below:

- Easy and adequate provision of evidence and/or documentation to back up compliance to process requirements
- Appreciation of the role of auditing processes as valuable means of identifying activities for achieving improvements
- Better audit reports
- Appreciable reduction in the number of hours that are needed for internal auditors to prepare for audit meetings and conduct audits
- Willingness and readiness of employees to participate in audit processes
- Easy preparation for the audit process
- Impressive employee involvement in audit processes with great enthusiasm
- Employees voluntarily employing auditing principles to review their own internal processes and the implementation of corrective actions randomly and prior to auditing exercise to ensure continual compliance with the requirements of the QMS
- Voluntary request/demand for internal audit of their departments or units by employees to know and ensure that they are still compliant with the requirements of the QMS standards
- Domestication of the terms, “audit” and “compliance” by workers who use them to express their feelings toward each other in normal conversations

Internal audit usually takes place at the instance of an organization and is normally executed by the organization’s internal auditors or in some cases by auditors specifically engaged or contracted by the organization.

An ethical issue which must be highlighted here is the fact that the internal auditors must in all cases have no vested interest in the areas that are being audited by them. Such internal auditors must be trained quality auditors if good internal audit findings/results have to be obtained.

The use of trained employees as internal audit team (defined in ISO 9000:2015 as "one or more auditors conducting an audit, supported if needed by technical experts") has the advantage that they are conversant with the system and its processes and procedures. In addition, it is more economical than hiring external auditors from outside the organization though a technical expert (defined in ISO 9000:2015 [5] as "(audit) person who provides specific knowledge or expertise to the audit team") may be hired to join the internal auditors.

The author effectively made use of in-house trained auditors in the certification of a group of international manufacturing organizations.

It serves as one of the most vital and necessary tools for ensuring that an organization's quality and environmental management systems conform to planned arrangements and that they are implemented and managed effectively in compliance with the requirements of the respective international standards.

Second-Party Audit

The second-party audit, a form of external audit, is usually carried out at the request of customers (defined in ISO 9000:2015 [8] as an "organization or person that receives a product") on the activities of an organization or at instances when an organization audits its suppliers (defined in ISO 9000:2015 [8] as an "organization or person that provides a product"). The purpose of this audit is on a general basis determined by the purchasing or quality assurance department of the customer or supplier.

The main purpose of this type of audit is to assess the capability and ability of either the organization or supplier to deliver the goods and/or services that comply with stated specifications and requirements of the customer in line with an agreed contract. The assessment here also includes the general evaluation of the totality of facilities (including the QMS and technical provisions) and resources at the disposal of the organization/supplier for achieving the product or services.

The concept of determining whether the supplier is fulfilling the expected contractual requirements enables the purchaser gain confidence in the quality of the goods and services resulting from the customer-supplier relationship.

The purpose of the second-party audit can on a general basis be summed-up as follows:

- For assessing the capability of a supplier to meet contractual requirements through the review of the resources at the disposal of the supplier toward the execution of the contract and the assessment of the commitment of the supplier's management to the quality requirements of the customer's product.
- For the verification of the processes, machinery/equipment, and materials used or to be used for the achievement of the customer's product specifications/requirements as stated in the contract.

In some cases, second-party audit can be conducted to identify the possible causes of nonconformities noticed in the products already supplied or services already rendered. Hereby an assessment audit of the processes, procedures, records, and the quality system documentation is undertaken.

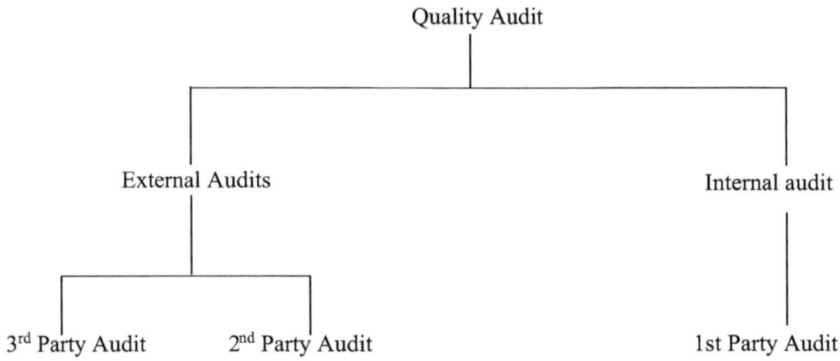

Fig. 18.1 Types of quality audit

The results of the second party audit generally go a long way to influence the relationships, customer/organization, and supplier/organization.

Third-Party Audit

Third-party audits are generally carried out by independent bodies/organizations. Such entities are outside the customer-supplier relationship; hence, we are dealing here with an external audit.

The product, process, or system certification to particular standards and requirements or already agreed criteria may be achieved through third-party audits (i.e., audits by certification bodies or registrars). Examples here are the compliance audit of organizations to the requirements of the ISO 9001 QMS and ISO 14001 environmental management system (EMS) standards. The general classification of audits is illustrated below (Fig. 18.1).

The classification provided here is in no way exhaustive so that other modes of classification could also be used.

Key Aspects of Audit

Participants in the Audit Process

Participants of an audit include a cross section of the personnel of an organization to be audited, those people that are to carry out the audit, and the body that has the responsibility to issue the certificate to the audited organization. The various participants of an audit are highlighted below:

- *The auditee* – the organization which is being audited. Its management team has the responsibilities of providing some inputs into the audit – resources, reviewing the audit results, makes use of the audit output – and provides information about organizational policy, needed documents, customer feedback, quality planning, and previous audit results.

- *The auditors* – The team of auditors have to be trained and provide information and time necessary for the audit.
- The *lead auditor* – is usually the leader of the team of auditors. The lead auditor has the responsibilities to prepare and plan for the audit, manage the audit, and do the preliminary and closing paperwork or documentation. Preparing for the audit requires defining audit *objectives*, *scope*, *resources*, *criteria*, as well as the preparation and distribution of *audit notification* to the auditee. In addition, the lead auditor gathers and understands relevant *documentations* needed for the audit and prepare the *audit plan*.
- The audit *guide* (if necessary).
- The audit *observer*.
- The certifying body or registrar – the body responsible for the issuance of certification to the auditee based on audit outcome.

The *audit scope* encompasses the:

- Time frame of the audit exercise
- General identification of the audit boundaries or limits
- Processes that are expected to be audited
- Organizational functions that are included in the audit
- Emphasis of the audit

The *audit criteria* help to identify some of the exact needs such as adequate documentation that would be referenced for the auditing as shown below:

- Organizational policy directions
- Organizational documentation – policy statement, standard operating procedures (SOPs), quality system procedures, and work instructions; calibration procedures and records/evidence or certification of calibration; training procedures and records; maintenance procedures and records; customer feedback procedures and records; emergency management procedures; specifications and drawings; design procedures; and other necessary reference documents and resources useful for the audit evaluation.
- Any other external audit criteria such as government/agency regulatory requirements, industry codes, customer requirements as provided by relevant contract documents such as that of the supply chain, and any other externally generated documentation used by the organization in its improvement processes.

There is the general need for auditors to review as much adequate documentation as available. And considerations must similarly be given to critical data related to organizational performance within the system and also as provided in previous audits – internal and external.

Professionalism in the Auditor

It is very important, too, for the auditor to identify, ascertain, and clarify the limitations and extent to which the exchange of information with the auditee and its personnel is allowed. Since various auditees have different views and perspectives about the audit process, it is very vital to mention here the need for the auditor to be sufficiently objective, tactful, and professional, especially in cases where the auditees reluctantly accept the audit or somehow skeptical about it and/or the auditors. In such cases the auditor may need to behave in a way that ensures the removal of such resentment or obstacle resulting from the auditee's perception of the audit. Auditors need to remain focused even when faced with other types of difficult situations or hostilities.

Auditors may also come across auditees that may want to reverse the auditing roles by taking over the responsibilities of the auditor so that he does most of the talking. Some auditees may even refuse to talk during interviews or even devise time-wasting tactics. No matter what the situation may be, and no matter how difficult the auditee may appear to be, the auditor should remain focused, polite, firm, and have a grip and complete control of the audit at every stage of the process. It is very important here to mention, too, that the auditor must exhibit self-control.

In addition, an auditor must plan as much as possible to keep within the planned audit program, or schedule, right from the opening meeting through to the closing one. Even the issue of lunch or tea break for the auditors must be kept under strict time control, so that room is not given for the abuse of the audit plan/schedule.

In order to ensure strict compliance of the audit with preplanned schedule, the auditor should be conscious of the following possible time-wasting devices:

- Late arrival of the audit *guide* and *observer/escort* either in the mornings or the beginning of an audit session
- Personnel to be audited not available at the scheduled time of audit
- Delay in the provision of documents, records, safety devices, etc. required by the auditor
- Constant interruption of audit resulting from telephone calls, people going in and out, noise, etc.
- Auditee claiming that he has not been given a prior notice of the audit

Auditors need to bring up such issues at the opening meeting with agreed guidelines put in place between the auditors and the auditees.

Here the auditor may have to stress the need for the punctuality of the observer/escort, emphasize the provision of the audit plan/schedule to all concerned, request for needed supplies such as safety devices, and confirm that employees are aware of the time they are to be audited. Auditors may also have to state the effect of the absence of the personnel to be audited on the length and scope of the audit.

It must also be mentioned here, too, that compliance of the auditor with all relevant guidelines and the upholding of the ethics of auditing coupled with an outstanding conduct/performance of the auditor do not completely preclude or rule out the disgruntled auditee from making false allegations and accusations against the auditor. Such allegations and accusations may include, among others, that of bribe, sexual harassment/misconduct, discrimination, theft, insincerity, and other forms of nonprofessional behaviors. This is one of the reasons for the involvement of an observer.

One way of avoiding these types of false accusations is the use of two auditors as a team to carry out the audit in the presence of the auditing observer/escort usually provided by the auditee. In addition, auditors may arrange for the use of recording equipment to obtain and preserve the transaction between the auditor and the auditee.

The Audit Cycle

The processes or activities involved in auditing can generally be arranged in the following sequence or stages only for the purpose of good understanding since there is no fast rule about this.

- *Stage I – Audit Planning and Preparation (Pre-audit Stage*)
  This stage of a quality audit generally begins with the decision of an organization to get an audit conducted with background information gathered about the auditee and the auditing exercise itself and ends when the auditing process begins. During this audit preparation phase, the auditing team is selected and audit is planned in advance by all interested parties – the auditor, lead auditor, auditee (client) representative, and audit program manager.
- *Stage II – Auditing Exercise Itself (On-Site Performance of Audit Stage)*
  The auditing execution itself is a multi-activity exercise also referred to as the *fieldwork.* This phase which begins in the premises of the client or the organization to be audited for data gathering purposes with the opening meeting and ends when the physical audit is completed and the closing meeting held. Common activities of the audit consist mainly of on-site audit management, holding meetings with the auditees, and gaining knowledge of all relevant auditee activities to have a good understanding of its system controls and processes. Auditors' permitted movement routes within the premises are also agreed with the auditee. Verification to ensure that the controls work in accordance with planned expectation is carried out through communications among team members and with the auditee personnel. In achieving this, necessary documentation such as standard operation procedures (SOPs), quality manual, standards, regulatory guidelines, predetermined requirements, and other relevant tools are used and referred to. Similarly, other physical audit examinations and evaluations are accomplished through physical sighting and experience during the audit.
- *Stage III – Reporting the Audit/Closing Meeting (Post-audit Stage*)
  The closing meeting is the phase in which the documented compilation of all the audit findings is communicated and presented to the auditee. The audit report is expected to provide a compilation of clear and correct records, statement of facts,

and others relevant to audit criteria as *audit evidence*. The audit evidence thus represents a potentially useful resources suitable for the effective use of organizational management for improving the organization by addressing the important issues emanating from the audit.

Although the audit process may be viewed as completed whenever the report is issued by the lead auditor, at the closing meeting, the author believes that the full benefits of the audit shall be fully realized only after the ensuing follow-up actions are put in place or completed to ensure that all nonconformances or nonconformities are rectified. There is however the need for the follow-up stage if all nonconformities have not been closed out at the time of the closing meeting or as may be agreed with the auditee.

- *Final Phase – Audit Follow-Up and Closure (Audit Closure Stage)*
  This phase encompasses the audit follow-up activities whereby actions are taken in response to audit report/findings to ensure that all nonconformities are closed out for the improvement of the system through needed *corrective* and *preventive* actions.

Step-by-Step of Auditing

Although you may be free to execute your audit in any particular way of your choice, you are likely going to get a good outcome in the right time if you choose to go systematically about it with the sequence of activities listed below:

- *Intent to Audit*
  The intent to audit a system is generally the most vital aspect of initiating an audit. This means simply that the auditee has to show or give an indication of its intent to be audited.
- *Audit Planning*
  Planning begins first with a clear definition of the objectives and scope of the audit. It then follows with the identification and assignments or selection of the lead auditor and the other members of the auditing team. Next in the series are the communication of the status of the audit, in terms of the audit plan and timing to the auditee, and collating the necessary work papers needed to guide the auditors in conducting the audit and prepare them. These could include the lists of questions considered for the audit, the work instructions and SOPs, and process flowcharts for processes to be audited if found necessary.
- *Communication and Distribution of the Audit Plan*
  This is where communication and distribution of the audit plan to all concerned parties and individual ensue.
- *Opening/Pre-audit Meeting*
  At the opening or pre-audit meeting, the following process takes place: presentation of the purpose of the audit and review of the audit plan, confirmation of audit logistics, presentation of any special request of the auditee in terms of confidentiality or any other desired restrictions, and areas of exclusion from audit and other concerns of the auditee.

- *Audit Data Collection*
  Data may be physically collected and verified by examination of document, records, interviews, and the physical verification and observation of activities as they are carried out.
- *Documentation of the Audit Findings*
  Findings during the audit must be adequately documented in simple unambiguous way for the ease of understanding using simple language. Audit findings may be classified as *conforming* or *non-conforming.* Non-conformances may further be classified into two categories of minor and major.
- *Analysis of Audit Findings*
  Check for the adequacy of documents and competency of personnel performing works, and check for excellent housekeeping. Audit different areas or processes with the intention of ensuring that they comply with their stated objectives. Get the evidence that processes and activities meet stated requirements through the analysis of data, records, measurements, and visibly on-the-spot evidences at process locations. Evaluate improvement performance and trends through feedbacks from and to customers, as well as from the recorded customer complaints.
- *Closing/Closure Meeting or Post-audit Conference*
  This is where the presentation of the audit findings which should include the summary of nonconformities and their status, presentation of the audit overall results, and the discussion of follow-up actions to ensure close-out of all nonconformities take place.

Authority to Audit

Whether it is an internal or external audit, the authority to carry out an audit has to be generally well defined. The authority to audit varies however with the type of audit that is involved.

In the case of internal audit, the authority comes from within the organization varying from the organization's management hierarchy or defined in its QMS or policy/objective.

In the case of external audit, the authority to carry out an audit may emanate from outside an organization in the form of authority specified by one or more of the following:

- Contract
- Government regulation
- The requirements of a standard or regulatory body

Areas of Concern to the Auditee

There is generally the likelihood that auditees express concerns about certain activities or areas of the audit. This is particularly so in the case of a first-time audit when auditees don't actually have audit experience so they are virtually anxious over various issues including potential deficiencies and the overall outcome of the audit. This anxiety may result in concerns of the auditee over such issues.

It is therefore one of the responsibilities of the auditors to ensure that such matters are duly cleared during the opening meeting. The professionalism of the auditors most especially that of the lead auditor has to be put to use here to allay the fears and anxiety of the auditee so that the audit exercise can be carried out in a relaxed environment where mutual trust between the auditors and the auditee co-exists.

From the experience of the author, an area that is known to create the outmost anxiety or concern is the way the employees of the auditee organization view the audit in its entirety in relationship to individuals. The lead auditor may in this respect make some further clarifications during the opening meeting to emphasize the fact that the exercise is to audit the system and processes and not the individual employee. It may also be useful, too, to stress the fact that the purpose of the audit is basically for the improvement of the system.

Although there may be slight differences in auditee concerns as we move from one type of audit to the other (i.e., first, second, and third party), it will be helpful if lead auditors can during the course of the opening meeting reflect on the following issues which may be seen as possible potential areas of concern of the auditee organization.

- The implication of the audit findings (i.e., nonconformity/nonconformance reporting) as they affect individuals, the overall audit results, and the usage of the results.
- The timing and mode of closing out of nonconformities/non-conformance.
- Movement of the employees during the audit and the arising need to get a consensus to any audit plan/schedule alteration.
- Clarification of any other issues raised by the auditee particularly those that are related to the difficulties encountered in the implementation of procedures and work instructions.
- In the case of first-party audit, there is usually the fear that audit results will affect staff performance assessment. The lead auditor should address this issue and other concerns usually associated with first-party audit in the areas of auditee job performance as reflected in the audit results. Here there is the need to separate the audit from the usual organizational hierarchy if good and objective results are to be obtained.

Achieving a Successful Audit

It is the responsibility of the lead auditor and his auditing team to ensure that the auditing exercise is successfully carried out [12]. The following lines of action and type of relationship with the auditee can facilitate and aid the achievement of a successful audit.

The maintenance of an efficient and regular communication with the auditee both prior to (i.e., at the audit planning stage) and during auditing is vital so that both parties can maintain a mutual understanding in all matters relating to the audit.

Maintaining an open and effective communication channel throughout the various stages of the audit is particularly important since it offers both the auditor and the auditee the opportunity to adequately clarify and explain all issues relating to the audit and identify and implement corrective action.

The ability of the auditor to effectively communicate with the auditee and its management team portends generally a good response and cooperation of the auditee which is a highly critical ingredient for the success of the entire auditing exercise.

It is very important, too, for the auditor to commence the auditing exercise with the establishment of a very good rapport with the auditee. Here, the auditor may even go to the extent of highlighting commendable observations about the auditee. For example, the comment may be on the auditee's facilities, environment, and/or personnel. While being friendly with the auditee is a desirable tool for the success of the audit, being overfriendly on the one extreme and being morose, garrulous, or unfriendly on the other should be avoided. Auditors therefore need to strike a balance between being reserved and excessively friendly to ensure that the seriousness of the audit is not watered down.

Auditors must therefore exhibit and show visible proof of professionalism, objectivity, and efficiency to earn the respect and confidence of the auditee. This can be achieved, for example, through the implementation of an adequately planned audit schedule and the presentations of a report that is more a true reflection of the audited system. It is very important, too, for the auditor to identify, ascertain, and clarify the limitations and extent to which the exchange of information with the auditee and its personnel is allowed.

Since various auditees have different views and perspectives about the audit, it is very vital to mention here the need for the auditor to be sufficiently objective and tactful especially in cases where the auditees reluctantly accept the audit and/or the auditors. In such cases the auditor may need to behave in a way that ensures the removal of such resentment or obstacle resulting from the auditee's perception of the audit.

Auditors may face other types of difficult situations or hostilities. Auditors may come across auditees that may want to reverse the roles by taking over the responsibilities of the auditor so that he does most of the talking. Some auditees may even refuse to talk during interviews or even devise time-wasting tactics. No matter what the situation may be and no matter how difficult the auditee may appear, the auditor should remain focused, polite, and firm and have a grip and complete control of the audit at all times. It is very important here to mention, too, that the auditor must exhibit self-control at all times during the audit.

In addition, an auditor must plan as much as possible to keep within the planned audit program or schedule right from the opening meeting through to the closing meeting. Even the issue of lunch or tea break for the auditors must be kept under strict time control so that room is not given for the abuse of the audit plan/schedule.

In order to ensure strict compliance of the audit with preplanned schedule, the auditor should be conscious of the following possible time-wasting devices:

- Late arrival of the audit escort either in the mornings or the beginning of an audit session.
- Personnel to be audited not available at the scheduled time of audit.
- Delay in the provision of documents, records, safety devices, etc. required by the auditor.
- Constant interruption of audit resulting from telephone calls, people going in and out, noise, etc.
- Auditee claiming that he has not been given a prior notice of the audit.
- Auditors need to bring up such issues at the opening meeting with an agreed guideline put in place between the auditors and the auditees.

Here the auditor may have to stress the need for the punctuality of the escort, emphasize the provision of the audit plan/schedule to all concerned, request for needed supplies such as safety devices, and confirm that employees are aware of the time they are to be audited. Auditors may also have to state the effect of the absence of personnel to be audited on the length and scope of the audit.

It needs to be mentioned here, too, that compliance of the auditor with all relevant guidelines and the ethics of auditing coupled with an outstanding conduct/performance of the auditor do not completely preclude or rule out the disgruntled auditee from making false allegations and accusations against the auditor. Such allegations and accusations may include, among others, that of bribe, sexual harassment/misconduct, discrimination, theft, insincerity, and other forms of nonprofessional behaviors.

One way of avoiding these types of false accusations is the use of two auditors as a team to carry out the audit in the presence of the auditing escort usually provided by the auditee. In addition, auditors may arrange for the use of recording equipment to obtain and preserve the transaction between the auditor and the auditee. The responsibilities of the auditor listed here are shouldered by the lead auditor who is actually answerable for the entire audit exercise.

Audit Process

Process Overview

This is a general overview of the series of major auditing activities as indicated:

- Preparing detailed plans for an audit
- Executing the audit
- Reporting the results of the audit, including conclusions and recommendations
- Performing corrective actions as may be needed
- Follow-up activities to verify and ensure corrective actions are effectively put in place

Roles of Auditees and Auditors

It is the responsibility of both the auditor [12] and the auditee to play their respective roles to make the opening meeting a success. The responsibilities are as highlighted below.

The Auditee

- The auditee must be adequately represented at the opening meeting by an appropriate member(s) of staff who may be a member(s) of the auditee organization's internal audit team. It is however the opinion of the author that the organizations and representatives at the opening meeting should include key management staff selected across the board and the organization's quality management representative. In case of any doubt as to the number and caliber of those that should be present at the opening meeting, an organization is free to ask for the advice of the lead auditor or the auditing organization who would be in a good position to recommend minimum attendance and suggest those representatives that could attend.
- It is the responsibility of the auditee's most senior representative at the opening or closing meeting to introduce the representatives of the auditee organization.
- The most senior representative of the auditee and the co-representatives should be in agreement with the auditors on the following issues that relate to and affect the audit:

    1. The auditee representative or individual that will take decisions on behalf of the auditee organization on all matters relating to the audit and its follow-up activities. This official remains the contact.
    2. Safety and regulatory requirements.
    3. Areas that need to be kept confidential from the auditors or excluded from the audit.
    4. Provision of support personnel such as escorts for escorting the auditors.
    5. The need or necessity for a very brief acquaintance tour of the site to be audited by the auditors ensuring however that the time available for the auditing exercise is judiciously spent and the pre-planned auditing schedule is strictly adhered to.

The Auditor

The voice of the auditors [12] is heard throughout the audit mainly through the lead auditor or his nominee so that the under-listed actions form a part of the overall responsibilities of the lead auditor:

- The entire auditing team must be present at the opening meeting.
- The agenda for the opening and closing meetings must be prepared by the lead auditor who has the responsibility to introduce his team members and makes a presentation of their credentials.
- Gives a description of the auditing process.
- Informs the auditee of the scope and purpose of the audit in clear terms with reference to the standard and the quality documentation used.
- Highlights some of the benefits of the audit to the auditee.
- Presents the details of the auditing schedule to the auditee.
- Ensures that an attendance list for the opening meeting is maintained and minutes are recorded.
- Makes sure that the auditee organization has informed its staff that the audit is being conducted.
- Entertains questions from the auditee.

Roles of the Observer/Escort

The provision of an observer/escort to each auditing group is an important requirement that has to be met during the audit except in the case of internal audits where auditors are already familiar with the auditee organization and its activities and premises. The roles of the escorts are highlighted below:

- Acts in the capacity of a liaison between the auditors and the management of the organization that is being audited.
- Acts as guide by showing the way leading to each department or section to the auditors and ensuring that the auditors do not violate company rules and regulations.
- Introduces the personnel to be audited to the auditors.
- Acts as an observer for the management of the auditee organization.
- Witnesses the data gathering activities in terms of the findings and observations of the auditors.
- May assist in the provision of the documents and records required by the auditors.

The opening meeting is very important in that it opens up a line of communication between the auditors and the auditee just as it provides an avenue for the physical interaction between the auditors and the management team of the organization to be audited. The opening meeting should be made so flexible to accommodate all the questions that any member of the auditee team may want to ask.

There are some slight differences between the opening/pre-audit meeting of an external and internal audit. As a result of the frequencies of the internal audit, the auditors and the auditee are generally more interactive with each other, so the degree of formality is quite low. Hence the opening meetings of internal audits are generally informal and shorter than those for external audits where the auditors are not likely to be conversant with the system that is being audited.

Planning the Audit

Planning an audit actually begins with the appointment of a lead auditor whose responsibility is to manage the entire auditing exercise [12]. The audit plan is on its own a brief document that gives the details of the line of action or program and its timing as they will be followed during the auditing exercise. The auditing plan focuses attention on the:

- Purpose and scope of the audit as defined by the organization to be audited (with specification of the appropriate reference standard).
- Name of the organization to be audited
- Members of the auditing team.
- Standard for which the system is audited against.
- Date and place of the audit.
- The period or duration of the audit (including the timing of the opening meeting).
- Transportation arrangements/schedule.

The auditing plan must be signed by the lead auditor and approved by the appropriate authority of the auditing body/organization before its prompt and effective circulation to all concerned parties.

The selection of the auditing team is generally based on the purpose and scope of the audit. The lead auditor takes over the management of the audit with the preparation of all necessary documentation (to include auditing and audit result forms) and the implementation of the audit plan.

Audit Agenda

An agenda must be prepared prior to the conduction of an audit. The agenda should generally list the areas to be evaluated, the exact types of testing to be observed, and the general audit program itself.

The Opening Meeting

Every audit exercise generally begins with an opening meeting, otherwise termed the pre-audit meeting which is generally conducted by the lead auditor. Present at the opening meeting are the auditing team and the management team of the auditee or the organization to be audited.

At the pre-audit or opening meeting, all pertinent issues relating to the audit are discussed with the aim of achieving the under-listed objectives:

- The introduction of the auditing team and the management teams of the organization that is being audited to each other.
- Identify communication links between the auditors and the auditee personnel.

- Inform the auditee of the plan and scope of the audit with reference to the standards for which the organization's quality management system is audited against.
- Description of the audit procedures and methodology.
- Inform the auditee of the way and mode of documenting the audit findings and the status (major/minor) of the nonconformities and nonconformance.
- Agree on logistics such as the time schedule of audit, auditee contact person(s), records and documents, provision of facilities for keeping confidential documents and records, observer/escorts for the auditing teams, rooms/office space for auditors' use/meetings and daily auditee briefing, provision and location of other necessary facilities (e.g., telephone, fax/photocopy machines, toilet, canteen area, tea break areas, etc.), and other resources that may be needed for the audit.
- Identify areas of confidentiality and/or areas/processes of exclusion from the audit if applicable. In cases where there is an existing confidentiality agreement, necessary explanation is provided to ensure that the audit team has a full understanding of this.
- Identify safety and security requirements and provide necessary safety gadgets for the use of auditors.
- Agree the date and time of the closing/exit meeting and explain the things (i.e., audit report, effecting corrective action, all other audit follow-up matters, etc.) to expect at this meeting.
- Discuss any other issues of concern to the auditee.
- Clarification of the issue of the language of communication among the employees of the auditee. This is particularly important in various parts of the world where there are language differences within a few kilometers and a nationally low literacy level (e.g., Nigeria).

Gathering Audit Data

Audit data collection is generally achieved through examination of document/records; interviewing of relevant employees or personnel; and the physical verification, examination, and observation of work or process activities.

The data gathering/collection phase of the audit is therefore that part of the audit in which auditors

gather *factual* information and *objective* evidence for analysis and evaluation against a reference standard, regulatory requirements, and/or an organization's quality document (i.e., quality system procedures, quality manual, and work instructions) with a view to determining the level of conformity of the system.

Where a supplier is being audited by its customer, analysis and evaluation may be carried out against the customer's own predetermined specifications and relevant legislative or mandatory requirements. The analysis and evaluation are in all cases usually followed by conformance/nonconforming conclusions drawn by the auditors from the comparison.

The information gathered and the evidence obtained by the auditor must be objective, just as they must adequately represent and reflect the exact situation of activities in the system being audited. The professionalism, objectivity, and broadmindedness of the auditor are particularly very important here if objective results have to be obtained. To achieve this, the auditor must recognize and put into consideration the interrelationship between the departments/sections and their processes and activities.

Gathering factual information or obtaining objective evidence can be accomplished through various ways that include, among others, the following:

- Interview of employees
- Observation of process and work-in-progress
- Examination of records, data, and other documents
- Physical examination of product samples

Interviewing Employees

Collecting information through interviewing employees (auditee) is commonly used for gathering information during audits. Such interviews are generally carried out one-on-one and face-to-face though auditors have the freedom to interview auditees in groups too.

The auditor should be in a good position to adequately assess and filter the answers given by the interviewee so as to be able to distinguish the facts from the non-factual ones. The interview method has the advantage of giving insight into the system and at the same time allows for on-the-spot detailed clarification of issues.

In order to get good results, it is important for the auditor to ensure that the interviewee is in no way tensed up. It is therefore imperative for the auditor to begin the interview in a way and manner that will put the interviewee at ease. The auditor could actually start an audit with questions that are not likely to generate tension in the interviewee. It could be merely familiarization questions before moving gradually to more serious ones. The auditor must however not lose sight of the issues and items at stake, that is, documentation, facts/evidence, and activities, and not concentrate on the person.

Closing/Closure Meeting or Post-Audit Conference – presenting the audit findings to include the summary of nonconformities and their status, presentation of the audit outcomes, and the discussion of follow-up actions. A properly conducted audit must have to be thoroughly documented in a way that makes information simple to extract. The audit is completed when all the planned audit activities have been carried out or otherwise agreed with the auditee [6] (ISO 19011:2018, clause 6.6).

ISO's Process Approach and Auditing

The author is personally concerned firstly with the ISO suddenly making the terms "document" and "record" directly irrelevant in the 9001:2015 though they may have respectively and indirectly sneaked in through the back door, "maintaining documented information" to imply "document" and "retaining documented information" for "record." Using the backdoor entrance simply brought in the words maintaining and retaining to differentiate document from record.

Any new version of the ISO 9000 series of international quality management systems (QMS) standards generally calls the wisdom of quality auditors to question, hence the need for their thorough understanding of the version before embarking on their auditing responsibilities if they have to maintain the general needs for their professionalism.

The process management approach was introduced in the ISO 9001:2000 in a significant revision of this international QMS standard. The intention here was to focus attention to widening the scope of top management involvement perhaps, to openly demonstrate their leadership roles facilitating the general and overall effectiveness of the QMS, particularly in areas which include the promotion of the risk-based mindset, process approach, and performance improvement. While this may have, in one way or the other, shifted the leadership of the QMS from the management representative and/or the quality manager to top management, the author's experience still supports the fact that there is still the need for the role of a management representative responsible for the day-to-day management and implementation of the QMS.

The *process approach* which was further reinforced in ISO 9001:2015 enables an organization being seen as composed of linked activities-processes that transform inputs to outputs. The individual components of the process are defined by the standard include inputs, outputs, criteria and methods, resources, responsibilities and authorities, risks and opportunities, and evaluation and improvement [3].

The difficulty of auditors in auditing processes has been reported by Reid [10] as being due to the fact that the ISO has only described but never defined the term process approach. As mentioned too by Reid [10], the issue with the process approach for auditors is strongly embedded in the fact that there is the general need for some level of expertise in relationship to understating the individual components of a process in the QMS, such as inputs, outputs, metrics, controls, risks, and improvements.

The author's experience shows generally that the leeway here to overcome this problem is to make the process owner's functions, responsibilities, and department the sole focus of the audit within the processes in question. In addition, the process owner's expertise and/or conversancy with the process involved is used to the auditor's advantage to accomplish the task.

Layered Process Audit

The major role of the auditing process as generally understood and as mentioned in various parts of this book and in literature is that of aiding the initiation of quality improvement. While the typical audit process described above focuses attention more on the product, the layered process audit (LPA) emphasizes process improvement. It is important here to stress the fact that the LPA must therefore not be confused with the ISO 9001:2015 QMS *process approach* requirements discussed above.

The LPA can therefore be seen as an improvement measure for a process with which you can check to see if the operator is following the defined process to ensure that critical process parameters such as flow rates and gauges were correctly set, thus making it, in one way or the other, another type of process audit [11]. The focus of the LPA on the process is based on the assumption that if defined parameters are set correctly and accurately, there is the likelihood that the products will be good; hence, they will meet customer requirements. This is also in line with the saying in quality of "do it right first time." The LPA may from this point of view be seen as a good source of process control measure.

The implementation of the LPA is carried out by various layers or levels of organizational leadership (or staff/management cadre) through mere on-the-spot verification checks on specific processes or process stages to ensure that they are correctly and adequately followed. This personal verification of processes by various cadre of organizational leadership provides the opportunity of determining whether the process is working as expected or not.

Technology and Virtual Era Auditing

Every COVID-19 era organization quickly embraced sustainability by adaptively resulting in making changes in the way each of them conducts their businesses. Auditing is not an exemption.

Auditing, like any other quality management improvement tools, was significantly impacted by the COVID-19 pandemic. COVID-19 pandemic changes thus led to the rapid introduction of some new norms into the auditing exercise.

This begins with welcoming auditors into the auditees' premises with a temperature scanner, a disposable sticker, and fist or elbow bumps instead of the traditional warm handshake. Seating arrangements during opening or other audit meetings took the pattern of COVID-19 pandemic public preventative settings, which allowed for 6 feet spacings in between seats.

With most audits now virtual, audits are remotely conducted. Here, video conferencing and cloud-based documentations are used. Facility tours are at times carried out using PowerPoint presentations. Similarly, pre-recorded videos and FaceTime or other modes of technology found applicable are deployed.

Examples of permitted remote auditing include, but are not limited to:

- Regulatory bodies/authority.
- Notified body – an organization designated by an EU country to assess the conformity of certain products before they are placed on the market. Notified bodies are thus free to offer their conformity assessment services to any economic operator inside or outside the EU (European Union), [4].
- Internal audits.
- Supply chain audit.
- International Organization for Standardization certification body.

The effect of the COVID-19 pandemic on organizations and businesses is quite significant and will likely continue to change perhaps until normalcy returns or until the changes turn to new norms [13].

Conformity Assessment Audits in Trade

It is the responsibility of organizations which compete in the market or international markets to demonstrate that their products/services or even systems meet the requirements of relevant standards – local or international. This, in turn, helps organizations and their products to gain increased confidence from all stakeholders and customers alike while aiding in assuring regulatory compliance. Conformity audit helps generally to promote international trade.

ISO/IEC 17000:2020 – Conformity assessment (vocabulary and general principles). This document specifies, according to the ISO, the general terms and definitions relating to conformity assessment (including the accreditation of conformity assessment bodies) and to the use of conformity assessment to facilitate trade. On a general basis, conformity assessment interacts with other fields such as management systems, standardization, metrology, and statistics.

References

1. Arter, D. R., Cianfrani, C. A., & West, J. E. (2013). *How to audit the process-based QMS* (2nd ed.). ASQ.
2. Burkhardt, M. (2019). *Manufacturing and QC, "5 different types of audits to evaluate your supplier*," July 23. http://intouch-quality.com
3. Cochran, C. (2015). ISO 9001:2015. In *Plain English* (p. 4). Paton Professional.
4. European Union (EU). (2021). https://www.ec.europa.eu retrieved July 15, 2021.
5. ISO 9001:2015
6. ISO, ISO 19011:2018, Clause 6.6.
7. ISO, ISO 19011:2018, Guidelines for auditing management systems.
8. ISO, ISO 9000:2015, Quality management systems – fundamentals and vocabulary, ISO, 2015, https://www.iso.org
9. ISO, ISO TS 22003:2013, Food safety management systems – requirements for bodies providing audit and certification of food safety management systems.
10. Reid, R. D. (2019). Auditing. "It's all in the Approach – Understanding the ins and outs of the process approach". *Quality Progress*, 54–57.
11. Sittsamer, M. J., Oxley, M. R., & O'Hara, W. (2007). Turbocharge your preventive action system. *Quality Progress, 40*(11), 37–42.
12. Thaller, E., & Bravo, J. (2021). Be the best you can – Tips for becoming a better auditor. *Quality Progress, 54*(7), 50–52.
13. Wrestler, D. (2021). An inside look – The peripheral impacts of COVID-19 on businesses. *Quality Progress, 56*, 12–13.

19 Dynamics of Quality

Redefining Quality

Quality in the Digital World

Quality is by its own right a unified developmental tool available for the entirety of the people of the world to improve their environment and their lives, organizations, enterprises, and businesses. Quality transformed in the twentieth century along with industrial revolution. The industrial revolution assumed important roles in the lives of every individual and among the countries of the world. The criticality of industrialization is reflected today in the way this word has been commonly used as a tool to separate the industrialized parts of the world from those countries that, through their obvious mis-leadership and political corruption, merely turned themselves mainly into the consumers of the products of industrialization. These are mainly countries in the continents of Africa and South America.

The rapidly evolving world of advanced technological revolution, highly inherent in Industry 4.0 vis-à-vis Quality 4.0, may most critically create an economic canyon separating the peoples of the world, far beyond our expectations from the mid-2020s, especially if the present momentum of organizational and business embrace of artificial intelligence (AI) and machine learning (ML) and other 4.0 technologies is maintained.

While the already advanced economies of the world shall grow tremendously more powerful in manufacturing and services provision to dominate the global economy, in product quality, competitive abilities, and global market share, the present underdeveloped economies of the world shall lose out woefully in the catch-up game, especially at a time of the rapidly expanding globalized world economy. Organizations and businesses that are successfully able to move with the digital transformational tide are likely going to dominate global economic competitiveness from the 2030s until and beyond the digital proliferation era. Highly productive

T. A. Ibidapo, *From Industry 4.0 to Quality 4.0*, Management for Professionals,
https://doi.org/10.1007/978-3-031-04192-1_19

organizations and businesses stand in good positions of advantage for sustainability through the digital revolutionary stages and beyond.

Contrarily, the present underdeveloped and highly corrupt countries of the "nth-world" (e.g., Nigeria), most of which may already be viewed as economically failed states, shall completely crash out of the surviving world of digitized and digitalized industrial manufacturers, to absolutely and totally wreck the chances and potentials of their future generations in the era of the "SmartFactory." This is because Industry 4.0 digital manufacturing initiatives may most probably dictate the economic tune of industrial production not just in the next decades of the twenty-first century but for the rest of it.

This is to say clearly here that, with its deteriorating and collapsed infrastructural base, organizations operating in countries dominated by the hyper-religiosity, economic banditry, and corruption stand no chances of guaranteeing their people a good quality of life. Highly corrupt countries such as Nigeria, and some other African countries, may never get the opportunity of dreaming about the "SmartFactory," how much more actualizing its potentials.

Drifting further and further away from the realities of Industry 4.0 vis-à-vis Quality 4.0 initiatives, a lot of retrogressing African countries such as Nigeria may have to resign to merely populating the consumer world of digital products and services, though not without a price! Rather than gradually growing in the catch-up game to achieve higher quality of life for its people to close the gap between them and the people of the developed economies of the world, most African countries like Nigeria get themselves obsoleted in the race for quality life, by fully engaging themselves in tracing their cattle-grazing routes of the eighteenth, seventeenth, and so on centuries.

While it is not the intention of technology and quality to alienate any part of the world from its rapidly growing developmental phases, the inability of some world economies to keep pace with technological phases of advancement due to their own technological negligence, democratic hypocrisy, political brigandage, ethnic rivalry, political bigotry, and hyper-religiosity may, at the end of the day, keep them breathlessly gasping for digital air. The rate at which artificial intelligence is being adopted, especially its skyrocketing adoption mode due to the COVID-19 pandemic, portend the fear of being left behind for those organizations playing the waiting game anywhere on planet Earth.

Wholeness of Quality Considerations

Most of the definitions of quality that we grow up to know have their origins deeply rooted in the use and application of quality in the manufacturing sector of the economy during the twentieth century except perhaps those of the international organizations for standardization (ISO) and the ASQ.

The ISO [30] views quality as "the degree to which a set of inherent characteristics of an object fulfils requirements," while the ASQ [7]sees quality as "the characteristics of a product or service that bear on its ability to satisfy stated or implied needs, or a product or service free of deficiencies." Of course, the stated or implied needs, as well as the requirements fulfilled, are obviously and primarily those of the customer or ultimate consumer, an assumption which has generally led to the populist slogan, "The customer is always right."

Quality in today's world has moved beyond emphasizing mainly the primary (1°) customer to greatly enhance the satisfaction of the silent but secondary (2°) critical customer – the regulatory body and its regulatory guidelines or laws. Viewing quality from the vulnerability of the environment and society to organizational business activities calls, too, for the general recognition of the community and society at large as the tertiary (3°) customers of every business organization and its activities, which requirements must also be fulfilled. And this is mostly achieved by extension mainly through the general fulfillment of the secondary customer SNEaRs.

The vulnerability of the people of the world to the impact of the previously un-envisaged novel coronavirus, in 2020, makes the direct recognition of the tertiary customer in the definition of quality extremely critical to the survival of the human race.

This is not, however, to dwarf or diminish the criticality and importance of meeting 1° customer's (or ultimate consumer) SNEaRs. It is particularly so in the digital world of Quality 4.0 in which, according to Kennedy [35], "The internet has given ultimate consumers phenomenal power while bearing little or no responsibility." The reviews of the primary customer are highly critical since they could create the demarcation line between organizational success and failure.

Today and in future years of the twenty-first century, it shall remain highly critical and essential to emphatically define quality in terms of its apparent primary (1°) and secondary (2°) vis-à-vis tertiary (3°) product/service customers if the planet Earth and the businesses operating within its sphere have to be sustained without unnecessary adverse effects on the people of the world. Or at least we should have them behind our quality minds. The totality of the customer referred to in the definition of quality is therefore on a general basis of the following three categories:

1. *Primary (1°) customer* – End-user, customer (ultimate customer), the market place and internal customers within the organization's production system. Digital transformation will in reality redefine the context of both internal and external customers, mainly due to the interconnectedness and interactive roles among machines, devices, and, perhaps occasionally, humans. While traditional quality management practices are customer centric, Quality 4.0 initiatives in the digital age seem to shift and strengthen the cooperating "organization/customer" culture more toward a co-working environment.
2. *Secondary (2°) customer* – Government, regulatory bodies (or regulator), and the required guidelines, laws, or regulations. Regulations are directed at protecting the people, environment, and planet at large.
3. *Tertiary (3°) customer* – Immediate community of business location, environment, and the planet Earth itself. This has so far been indirectly tucked under the umbrella of corporate social and environmental responsibility (CSER), or corporate social responsibility (CSR) and corporate environmental responsibility (CER).

Failure to meet the SNEaRs of the secondary customer may ultimately result in failure to meet those of the tertiary customers, whether stated or not. Failure to fulfil the requirements of the tertiary customer is however not without subsequent repercussions and impacts.

As powerful as the primary (1°) or ultimate customer is or may have been viewed, it is a high time we realized the fact, too, that they are just one of the parties impacted by the inherent characteristics of the product/service in its life cycle. The COVID-19 pandemic and its deadly impact on the people of the world are lessons learned about the importance of the 2° and 3° customers. The reported repercussion of Volkswagen, Audi, and Porsche for installing a "defeat device" software in certain diesel vehicles prohibited under the Clean Air Act is another case in which the 2° customer SNEaRs were claimed to have been violated.

Achieving Quality Outcome

The desired outcome of quality efforts and initiatives is a tripartite issue of paramount importance to all the parties involved – from *providers* (or creators) and *customers* (or consumers) to *stakeholders* (or complementors). There are generally two major ways for achieving quality outcome and they are:

- Quality outcome based on the exact prescriptions or predetermined dictates of the customer, that is, products/services made exactly to customer *specifications, needs*, *expectations*, and *requirements* (SNEaRs).
- Quality outcome thrusted upon customers based on their *anticipated specifications, needs*, *expectations*, and *requirements* (ASNEaR), that is, products and services (e.g., cars, mobile phones, airplanes, motorbikes, and others), provided in the marketplace based on the anticipated SNEaRs of the marketplace or customers. This group of quality outcome is justifiably referred to in the observation of Steve Jobs that "A lot of times, people don't know what they want until you show it to them" [45]. In this case, it is assumed that the interests of all three categories of customers – primary (1°), secondary (2°), and tertiary (3°) – have been taken care of. Of course, while the primary customer has the opportunity, though within a limited time frame, to verify and confirm product satisfaction before purchase, regulatory bodies and perhaps the adversely impacted community/environment may not even be able to effectively verify product satisfaction until adverse effects are felt. In some cases, too, primary customers' satisfaction may have been unrealizably abused or compromised at the point of purchase, until there is a recall.

In both cases all three parties exhibit the responsibility and legitimacy of deciding what quality outcome would ultimately be, hence the need for the three parties "to engage in constructive dialogue to *define, realize, deliver* and *evaluate* (DRDE) a quality outcome" [35]. It follows therefore that the efforts of providers, customers, and stakeholders must have to be harmonized and engaged to create a powerful, dynamic, and harmonious synergy for achieving desired quality outcome through the deployment of the best practices (excellence) [34]. A point of note here is the fact that stakeholders are generally not usually actively involved to be able to play equal roles.

Quality Outcome Without Adverse Effect

According to the ASQ, [7] in its quality glossary, the term *quality* is "a subjective term for which each person has its own definition." It is this subjective nature of defining quality that actually makes the subject of quality itself a diverse but interesting issue of human concern. The interesting aspect of quality resides most distinctively in the fact that, irrespective of the subjectivity of its definition, or how differently or diversely it may have been defined, or perceived, the ultimate goal or objective of quality is neither distorted nor changeable; it resides strictly in the "product/service quality, or product outcome."

In technical usage, quality is, according to the ASQ, [7] defined in two ways:

- "The characteristics of a product or service that bear on its ability to satisfy stated or implied needs"
- "A product or service free of deficiencies"

For the purposes of comparison, the ASQ referenced in its glossary the quality definitions of Joseph Juran, "fitness for use," and Philip Crosby, "conformance to requirements."

A product may be fit for use by the primary customer but may still violate some regulatory requirements, that is, secondary (2°) customers. A good example here are some of Volkswagen diesel vehicles which violated the US EPA [53] regulations using "defeat device" sometimes in the middle of the second decade of the twenty-first century.

The case of Boeing 737 Max is another example. Similarly, some products may pretentiously and tentatively meet relevant requirements or be corruptly (incurring the extraordinary cost of quality, ECoQ) influenced to conform with requirements when they are actually not.

Although none of the above definitions directly and openly links quality with regulatory requirements, it is obvious and understandable that the failure of any product to meet regulatory requirements (or 2° customer SNEaRs) renders that product deficient and incapable of satisfying stated or implied needs. This brings out the need for the explicit explanation of who the customers (1°, 2°, or 3°) are and the general need for quality outcomes to conform with their SNEaRs.

The impact of not satisfying the requirements of the 2° and 3° customers may consequentially devastate the environment taking millions of lives. It is for these and other reasons that quality may have to be redefined to give a direct implication of the need to emphasize product ability to *loudly* and *conspicuously* link quality with relevant regulatory requirements, that is, 2° customer SNEaRs, in its definition.

This is very important especially when viewed from the perspective of products that have to be made in line with the requirements and specifications of regulatory standards and/or requirements.

Another area of consideration for the need to redefine quality is that of viewing it from the perspectives of the digital world in the realization of Quality 4.0 initiatives. Data quality, data analytics, customer privacy, and cybersecurity are of particular interests to quality management in the digital age where the general need to "design it right first time" may be as critical as imaginable.

With the rollout of Industry 4.0 initiatives, quality professionals need to embrace digitization and digitalization in an environment deeply rooted in data, artificial intelligence (AI), and machine learning (ML).

In operations-centric approach to cybersecurity, there is the general need for the quality of safeguarding industrial data while also paying attention to data privacy. Hence, the issue of data quality becomes paramount in the digital era. These are adverse effects that have to be avoided, hence the need to add "without any adverse effects" to the definition of quality.

The frequency of cyberattacks in the twenty-first century may likely create not just a state of data insecurity but also make the twenty-first century conducive for "cybercriminals" who uncontrollably and more frequently disrupt the quality outcome of organizational processes, activities, and operations through various methods of computer disablement and attacks – malware, phishing, ransomware, and others.

Mathematical Basis for Redefining Quality

Whether it is the issue of a product being free of deficiencies, or being fit for use, or in conformance to requirements or predetermined parameters, the objective is absolutely the same. It is simply the quality outcome – product or service – being measured in relation to its level of acceptability by the user, customer, marketplace, regulatory authorities, or any other entities for which end-use or application or the product or service is directly or indirectly originally designed or targeted, as long as there are no adverse effects on the recipients, their environment, and community.

It is, however, the belief of the author that the era of defining quality in terms of "slogans" is long overdue and past, mainly because of its diminutive influence on the way people view and perceive quality and its management principles, among other disciplines or its peers. Seeing quality merely as a slogan must have contributed largely to its dwarfed status among other disciplines.

This view is similarly confirmed by the ASQ in a research study, in which outcome showed that only 24% of respondents perceived quality as a method to manage organization-wide performance. Others in the research outcome erroneously view quality as a "tool to fix issues after being discovered," or a "continuous improvement activity" or a "compliance activity." No! no! no! quality is definitely more than those perceptions established in that study.

Therefore, no wonder some people are of the opinion, too, that "quality is a thing of the past, it was a fad, and fads are corrosive." This may be hard for those of us working in quality to believe "however, for many, quality management does not exist anymore!" [40]. It is for this additional reason that quality has to be redefined to reflect its exact status and position among other disciplines.

Quality can therefore be more broadly and perhaps more accurately be redefined as:

1. "The measure/perception of the level/degree to which the inherent characteristics of a product/service, bear on its ability to fulfil/meet customer and regulatory SNEaRs in a culturally balanced environment of sustainable relationships without any adverse effects whatsoever, on any stakeholder or other relevant entities."
2. "The level/extent to which the values of the outcomes of inputs and efforts – products/services - are acknowledged to have met or not, stated and/or implied customer, regulatory, and stakeholder values, in a culturally balanced environment of sustainable relationships without any adverse effects whatsoever, on any stakeholder or other relevant entities."

In other simpler terms quality, Q can be described as the "ratio or quotient of product performance (P_p) in all ramifications of customer specifications (including product performance, appearance, reliability, durability, conformity with customer and regulatory requirements, ease of use, delivery time, etc.) to the customer's total product performance target (P_t)." Hence, quality can simply be described as "the degree to which a product or service conforms to the overall customer SNEaRs (implied and intended), in all ramifications" (see Chap. 9).

This is, however, based on the assumption that each criterium is measurable.

Expressing this relationship in mathematical ratio therefore results, for a product/service with perfect quality, in a value that is equal or nearly equal to 1:

$$Q = P_p / P_t \sim 1$$

It is the principles of this mathematical ratio that are commonly used by organizations to get online performance feedbacks for services rendered by their employees to their customers, using a scale of 1–10 or at times 1–5. The numbers 10 or 5 signify very satisfied, while the number 1 stands for least satisfied or not satisfied.

Redefining Quality Management

Just as quality dynamism was placed at the dictates of industrial production in the twentieth century, so also is the roll out of Industry 4.0 initiatives going to impact quality and quality management. Quality 4.0 initiatives are thus consequent upon the successful rollout of Industry 4.0 initiatives which focus generally on digital transformational strategies in smart manufacturing, such that data and connectivity become the center of industrial manufacturing processes.

Redefining quality management is thus a difficult task to achieve without reference to quality growth dynamics and its existing mode of definitions. Hence, the definition provided hereafter is derived with strong considerations and respect for existing literature definitions of quality, such as those of the ISO and ASQ and the most frequently occurring vocabularies, circumstances, and expectations of quality, in a disruptive world of uncertainties and growing challenges to humanity and economy.

It is from this wholistic point of view that the author views *quality management* as:

> The fundamental basis for innovatively harnessing, in a continuously improving mode, suitable inputs and resources, trained personnel, identified standards, appropriate technical tools and emerging technologically-driven processes and solutions, to systematically and sustainably lead, guide, empower, manage and support an organization or entity, its people, adaptability, resilience, and agility, in its constant pursuit of delivering excellent products and services with inherent characteristics that bear on their ability to satisfy stated/implied and regulatory SNEaRs without any adverse effects whatsoever.

Some of the implied needs and requirements which may, on a general basis, not usually be stated include, among others, those that impact the 2° and 3° customers or ultimate consumers:

- Related regulatory guidelines for which inputs and all internal/production processes for achieving products and/or services must be strictly compliant
- General environmental requirements stipulated for organizational activities
- Mandated guidelines and requirements for which products/services packaging and its disposal, uses, and applications have to be compliant
- Organizational commitment to corporate, social, and environmental responsibilities (CSER)

The redefinitions of quality and quality management, beyond merely meeting customer SNEaRs to represent and cover the sphere, scope, and growing areas of quality application, deployment, and challenges, have become more necessary than ever in the twenty-first century particularly, because organizations generally face more complex and dynamic environmental conditions attributable to increases in globalization, competitiveness, and global warming.

Apart from the increasing disruptive changes, in a constantly challenging globalized business environment, as witnessed in the unprecedented business years of the COVID-19 pandemic (2020/2021), the emergence of new technologies and the growing demands from businesses have undoubtedly resulted in an atmosphere of instability and new challenges. It is therefore highly imperative for organizational management team to look for ways to quickly adapt and operate more efficiently and effectively to constantly sustain businesses in states of the highest preparedness for potential uncertainties.

Quality Momentum and Post-COVID-19 Norms

Although being able to provide excellent products and/or services that are fit for use, and in conformance with customer SNEaRs and/or predetermined standards, remains the fundamental principle of quality management, there has been growing demands for a more accurate definition bearing in mind the growth dynamics of quality. Hence, a lot of the newer areas of quality applications and uses cannot possibly be illuminated in a singular definition or usually simple definitions of quality. In addition is the need for incorporating some of the critical factors and conditionalities needed for achieving product quality in a world getting more and more complex from day to day with changing technological advancements and customer SNEaRs.

A key area of quality dynamism in the twenty-first century shall be centered around the momentum generated not just at the instance of the COVID-19 pandemic devastation of the global community but also in response to post-COVID-19 newly emerged norms. The momentum generated by the rollout of Industry 4.0 will definitely elevate the role of quality in the digital world as Quality 4.0 also evolves. This is, however, not without its challenges, some of which may, among others, include the impacts of cybersecurity and data harnessing risks and their management abilities. As Quality 4.0 evolves, quality professionals are going to be confronted with relevant skills to meet customer SNEaRs in the evolving world of highly interconnected digitalized and digitized industrial production processes and operational systems, the SmartFactory.

Quality management shall undoubtedly be faced generally with a newly emerging digital future of:

- Production and productivity through the impact of artificial intelligence (AI) and automation
- Organizational race to upskill
- Changed office structure from in-person to remote working or the hybrid of the same
- Creating a culture of equity
- Evolving trusted leadership strategies and practices to face and manage disruptive crisis and change

It is therefore highly pertinent for organizations to be prepared and ready to get well-grounded in important foundational steps such as "data quality, making sure model assumptions are met by your data and, most critically, examining bias in the data, the models and the process of using results to drive business value" [48].

Quality Mindset

Quality Mindset Vacuum

One of the major problems that eclipsed the surface of the earth and its inhabitants when the COVID-19 pandemic hit in early 2020 was that of the general division among the people of the world, including leadership. The general absence of the quality mindset among people and leadership, coupled with the desires to keep businesses ongoing despite the COVID-19 pandemic, made it easily possible for people to resist and even antagonize some of the prescribed quality measures to ameliorate the impacts of the pandemic and its growing spread across the globe.

For example, revelers in the cruising industry were reportedly reluctant to submit to quarantine as recreation during the pandemic suddenly turned to survival threats (Lindborg [41]). While lots of people were generally not happy about the lockdown to prevent the spread of the novel coronavirus, others violated quality management guidelines such as face masking, social distancing, social gathering, containment, contact tracing, etc. thereby creating a big vacuum of quality consciousness or mindset.

Some misleaders of the people capitalized on the general absence of the quality mindset among some members of the populace to fatally politicize the emergency quality management principles and tools among the people even when they were known to be effective in combating the pandemic.

Public health officials relied heavily on their quality mindset to mitigate pandemic problem by embracing "the same tools that quality professionals use when a rash of defects occur: containment, materials segregation and traceability" (Schvaneveldt and Neve [50]).

Governance and People

The pursuit of quality, when viewed generally from various perspectives of life, be it in human lives themselves or products/service cycle, puts at the disposal of man – individually or collectively and at organizational levels – quality's main objectives: *product excellence, organizational sustainability*, and *continual improvement.*

The response of the people of the world to the COVID-19 pandemic and its wicked claws of death taught the entirety of the people of the global community the importance of creating the quality mindset and the general need for humanity to approach the changing trends of life with appropriate attention paid to timely deployment of quality management principles, tools, and techniques to solve real-life existential problems.

One of the greatest lessons of the COVID-19 pandemic, therefore, is the fact that man immediately resolved to appreciate the importance of *quality-thinking*. It is through this quality mindset that political leadership quickly deployed necessary quality management principles, tools, and techniques to mitigate the pandemic's option of death for humanity. In opting to live, therefore, people, through their national governments and leadership, embarked on the immediate deployment of quality measures. That is the reason why, to a great extent, reasonably objective people decided to respect and keep quality management guidelines, some of which are listed below, without any political motive:

- Hand washing
- Social distancing
- Wearing face masks
- Lockdown to minimize human activities to reduce and/or avoid social interaction

- Quarantining and contact tracing
- Virtual education and meetings and remote working or a hybrid of in-person and remote working
- Effectively communicating information about the novel coronavirus among research workers and healthcare systems both at national and international levels

Just as the COVID-19 pandemic did not discriminate who to attack, quality management tools were equally applicable to every human being to improve the quality of life of every individual on the surface of the earth. The people of the world were, to a certain extent, forced by the deadly impact of the COVID-19 pandemic to quickly develop the quality mindset to ensure the quality of life is kept on the improvement track.

Global Quality Mindset Needs

The probability that "a new coronavirus (CoV) called SARS-CoV-2 emerged from Wuhan, China in December 2019 as the etiological agent of a viral pneumonia called COVID-19" [51] is a clear evidence meant to remind us all – organizations, governments, and individuals alike – how critical it has become for the people of the world to be very conscious of the impacts of operational processes and their interfaces on their immediate and distant environment and communities. Here, the issue of corporate social responsibility (CSR) is called to question.

The swift and sudden blow of the COVID-19 pandemic and its impact on the health of the people of the world, businesses and society at large, is a reminder to humanity of how critical it has become for organizational quality management leadership to transparently and responsibly carry out their businesses with the quality mindset to ensure that there are no adverse effects whatsoever or to minimize them. It reminds us all, too, that organizations and businesses must always own up to their corporate social and environmental responsibilities (CSER) to the entirety of the global community.

Businesses therefore need to pay constant attention to the quality of their organizational processes and the way their activities impact on people and the environment at large. Who of us ever envisaged or expected that businesses and human lives would be paralyzed all over the world in year 2020 probably by the activities of a market in Wuhan, central China?

The quality puzzle that so far remains convincingly unanswered about the COVID-19 pandemic is primarily that of the how and where of its origin. Second is the issue of who takes responsibilities for all the damages and the deterioration of the quality of life the pandemic has done to human lives and businesses. The full embrace of quality tools may likely have mitigated COVID-19 if adequately and timely applied or used to freeze the COVID-19 pandemic in its source!

In addition, organizations have to exhibit the willingness and ability to swiftly mitigate against the risks emanating directly from their processes and activities before damages are done or spread to people and environment. Effectively managing the daily growing business risks and challenges before things get out of hand should be seen as integral parts of any organizational management. Organizational quality management systems need therefore to ensure that they have the capacity and capability to adaptively and swiftly manage any disruptive changes and uncertainties with utmost transparency and sincerity of purpose.

The integration of corporate social and environmental responsibility (CSER) in the operations and/or activities of the suspected Wuhan market management organization, board, or commission may likely have helped to ensure an earlier awareness of the potential risks ahead of the global community immediately on the emergence of the novel coronavirus. Such a measure may have saved the people of the world from being turned into easy victims of the deadly COVID-19 pandemic, which has cost humanity millions of lives, billions of dollars, and the emergence of new impromptu life norms. This thus brings to the fore the values of a globalized quality mindset or what may also be termed collective quality management mindset of people and organizations.

As affirmed by Hansen [27], "the most important strength any management can supply – whether in a time of crisis or a more normal situation – is this quality mindset." In addition to that, too, is his further assertion: "Where quality consciousness pervades an organization, all employees at every level of the organization contribute to quality products, quality services and a quality work environment."

Industry 4.0

SmartFactory

Industry 4.0 is, from a general perspective, a technology-based initiative to digitally transform the way industrial manufacturing industries operate in order to make them more efficient and competitive. At the same time, they will exhibit the flexibility and agility needed to effectively respond to the dynamism of the marketplace. These digital transformational initiatives thus portent the future emergence of the "smart" manufacturing model, codenamed SmartFactory, or digital manufacturing. Viewed from this perspective therefore makes the Smart factory a manufacturing setting which actually assists people and machines in the execution of assigned tasks.

Padhi and Illa [46] expatiated on the SmartFactory concept, in defining it as a manufacturing facility with the ability to analyze and make sense of big data generated on the shop floor, also being automated, autonomous, and data driven. This definition actually brought out the role of 4.0 technologies in the digitalization of manufacturing operations by highlighting big data, automation, and autonomous capability, all in a data-driven environment.

Wikipedia views the *Fourth Industrial Evolution* or *Industry 4.0* as "the ongoing automation of traditional manufacturing and industrial practices, using modern smart technology. Large-scale machine-to-machine communication (M2M) and the internet of things (IoT) are integrated for increased automation, improved communication and self-monitoring, and production of smart machines that can analyze and diagnose issues without the need for human intervention" [44].

Industry 4.0 which is often used interchangeably with the Fourth Industrial Revolution is therefore a representation of the digital transformation of manufacturing/production and related industries as well as other value creating processes. It most certainly represents a new era in the organization, control, and realignment of the industrial value chain systems. Hence, Industry 4.0 is a term used in reference to the application of, among others, a combination of embedded software systems, artificial intelligence (AI), and the industrial Internet of Things (IIoT) such as remote monitoring or track and trace, in networking machines and production processes in the "SmartFactory" through the help of information and communication technologies.

This mode of systems interconnectivity functions generally on the basis of the cyber-physical systems, such as smart machines, to create the capabilities needed for the "SmartFactory." Already trending in manufacturing technologies today are, among others, the increased use of AI, automation, and data exchange.

The digital manufacturing environment resulting from *Industry 4.0* initiative is, therefore, all about data, which applications spread across shop floors, supply chains, machines, products, and the customer experience. Data thus represent enabling tools for existing manufacturing companies to realize new potentials while opening up new business opportunities in the digital manufacturing settings and environment.

Key advantages envisaged for the "SmartFactory" include, but are not limited to:

- Faster responsiveness to market uncertainties
- Predictive analytics
- Higher productivity
- Flexibility in production
- Real-time precision
- Improved collaboration among suppliers, employees, and customers for understanding the preferences of the customers at all times to the extent of even personalizing and customizing them

Emergence of *Industry 4.0*

The idea of *Industry 4.0,* also known as *integrated industry*, or the *Fourth Industrial Revolution* was first brought to public awareness at the opening ceremony of the "Hannover Messe" of 2011, at the instance of *Wolfgang Wahlster* of the German Research Center for Artificial Intelligence (Deutsches Forschungszentrum fuer Kuensliche Intelligenz, DFKI), in his opening speech [38]. The term was used in the context of finding competitive ways for the success of companies operating "in a high wage region with global competition."

In a similar vein, *Industry 4.0* was reportedly mentioned in "a 2013 German government memo widely recognized as one of the first times that *'Industry 4.0'* was mentioned (techradarpro). *Industry 4.0* was speculated here as the high-tech strategy for the full computerization of the manufacturing industry, such that there may be no need for human involvement. In what appeared to be a government public revelation of *Industry 4.0*, the "techradarpro" website referred to the German Chancellor's mentioning of *Industry 4.0* at the World Economic Forum (WEF) in Davos in January 2015, when Angela Merkel was claimed to have called it the way to "deal quickly with the fusion of the online world and the world of industrial production."

The birth of *Industry 4.0*, as a global competitive initiative, at the Hannover Fair, a major global industrial melting point, located in one of Europe's highly industrialized urban centers, signals on its own the advent of a parallel quality management evolution, Quality 4.0., not just to maintain the century-long tradition of quality evolving along and together with every step of the industrial manufacturing evolution but to initiate the corresponding quality management approach needed to manage processes and other functions needed to achieve the quality of the product or output in a digital world.

Conceived at the German Center for Artificial Intelligence (DFKI), born in the Hannover Messe, 2011, and christened at the preview event of the 2014 Hannover Messe, which motto reads, "Global Challenges, Smart Solutions," by Detlef Zuehlke, *Industry 4.0* assumed right from the onset the prospects and vision of a well-planned Fourth Industrial "revolution," with the technology initiative modeled boldly in the perspectives of the *SmartFactory*.

This perspective view of *Industry 4.0* is strengthened by the establishment of the SmartFactory e.V. as an association of interested partners, in order to enable the full development of the "SmartFactory initiative" for use in basic projects, spanning from fundamental application in basic technologies to the development of competitive marketable products, the primary objective of *Industry 4.0*.

Industry 4.0 initiatives thus refer to the various advances in technology which combines advanced manufacturing, IoT, data, and analytics into an integrated production operation. Digital transformation of manufacturing processes will help the monitoring of real-time analytics for measurements, such as in the areas of improvement. Advances in technology and the rollout of *Industry 4.0* will, from a general perspective, help organizations to:

- Achieve excellence
- Fulfil increasing customer demands
- Increase production level or productivity
- Simplify operational works

Integrating some of the products of advanced technologies in the manufacturing system has the ability to facilitate innovation and getting insights in machines and equipment through interconnectivity between people and machines, as well as among machines. Some of such advances involved the use and application of sensors for getting insights into equipment or devices performances, 5G to facilitate new levels of collaboration, artificial intelligence, machine learning, and big data, among others.

Smart Organizational Partnership

Growing amid the partnership of a reported 28 partner-organizations and sponsors, which include, among others, "Siemens, Harting, Cisco, Phoenix, Contact, Festo, Belden, Rexroth, Beckhoff Automation, Emerson Process Management, and Weidmueller" [42], the healthy seed that guarantees the healthy rollout and growth of the SmartFactory is sown.

The association of these organizations, centered around the German Center for Artificial Intelligence, DFKI, is a very smart decision needed to incite the realization of the goals and objectives of this smart revolutionary initiative which may otherwise not have been realizable. It provides the infrastructural assets – financial, equipment, and fora – not just for prototyping and support but also the assurance of faster and rapid dissemination of information regarding the direction of organizational activities for advancing the course of *Industry 4.0* initiatives.

Industry 4.0 Paradigms

While describing the following four major *Industry 4.0* paradigms – *smart planners, smart operators, smart machines*, and *smart products* – Zuelke of the DFKI hinted on the need for both horizontal and vertical communications flexibility among controllers, field devices, and the entire enterprise systems.

- *Smart planner* – is enabled to organize production on the basis of real-time production data.
- *Smart operator*– engages technology in understanding production through context-sensitive information and sufficiency of real-world virtual information, also known as augmented reality. This enables the operator to handle the steadily increasing technical complexity to make better informed decisions for achieving better operations.
- *Smart machine* – is designed to become cyber-physical system (CPS) with autonomous components and its own control intelligence, so as to be able to communicate with other machines, production lines, and products, through open networks and semantic descriptions. The smart machine thus achieves flexible and agile manufacturing by being able to self-organize itself within the production network.
- *Smart product* – is equipped with built-in memory (of requirements, production tasks, and the operational data) and is based generally on the ideas of extending the work piece in such a way as to make it an active part of the system itself. In this way the product exhibits the ability of controlling its own production.

Industry 4.0 Digital Transformation

It therefore goes to say that from the general concept of industrial manufacturing, *Industry 4.0*, or the SmartFactory, constitutes a revolutionary era, in which industrial manufacturing trends grow more toward achieving a strong reliance on interconnectivity, automation, machine learning (ML), and real-time data exchange, in technology and processes, within the SmartFactory, or *Industry 4.0* industrial manufacturing systems.

Automation is used to accomplish a manufacturing setting in which factory machines are augmented with wireless connectivity and sensors "to monitor and visualize" the entirety of the production processes and "make autonomous decisions" [52]. Achieving the "SmartFactory" or "SmartManufacturing" initiatives is facilitated with technological advancements spreading across but not limited to the following:

- The Internet of Things (IoT)
- Industrial Internet of Things (IIoT)
- Cyber-physical systems (CPS) such as sensors
- Cloud computing
- Cognitive computing
- Artificial intelligence (AI)/machine learning (ML)
- Big data and sensors – results in advancement of sensing technology which means that structures, infrastructure assets, and manufacturing processes are increasingly monitored in real time.
- 5G – Is the fifth generation of mobile networks, following on from previous generations 2G, 3G, and 4G. It is used to facilitate and advance the wireless connectivity and the augmentation of machines to provide faster response times tending to real-time communication among systems.

Challenges of *Industry 4.0*

According to the ASQ, in its quality glossary definition, *Industry 4.0* is "a revolution driven by the exponential growth of disruptive technologies and the changes those technologies are bringing to the workplace, the workforce and the markets organizations serve."

It is therefore important for most organizations to come to the realization of the fact that digital transformation is a dynamic, ongoing process of existential relevance that enables an organization not just to survive but to thrive in the ever-spinning world of digital revolution. It must however be clarified too that, in embracing the adoption of artificial intelligence as a key element in the digital world, organizational leadership should have it at the back of their minds that potential regulatory guidelines are likely going to spring up in the near future regarding the use and application of AI. This is particularly so probably because of the reported ongoing debate pertaining to the ethics, governance, and regulation of artificial intelligence [26].

All in all, the manufacturing sector of the economy should be prepared to invest more in the following identified areas of concerns in pursuant of sustainability initiatives of *Industry 4.0*:

- Digital technology and initiatives especially in terms of outdated infrastructure, personnel training, and cyber threats
- Artificial intelligence and automation, industrial Internet of Things (IIoT), and machine learning (ML) on shop floors
- Normalizing the connected remote work and the agility of the workforce
- Taking advantage of big data
- Use of tangible 5G
- Predictive maintenance on the production lines
- Reevaluation of the supply chain options in order to bring it closer
- Data harnessing and opportunities to adequately protect privacy within relevant laws and regulatory requirements
- Digitally accelerated skills gap (DASG) – employer commitment to the workforce in terms of on-the-job training, upskilling, reskilling, and talent redeployment

Since it is highly essential for organizations to meet and/or exceed stakeholders' SNEaRs, it becomes very critical for them to neutralize the impacts of any disruption. The case of digital disruption is however not different. The way and manner any organization manages the dynamics of today's evolving digital revolution thus remains an all-important critical factor, with which the future of that organization shall ultimately be shaped and determined.

Organizations don't seem therefore to have any other alternative than to learn how to quickly integrate people, processes, and technologies to create and achieve greater values, efficiencies, and profits. Organizations then have, among others, the following important tasks to cope with:

- Embracing digital disruption by redefining how they work and handle their employees in their activities to meet customer SNEaRs.
- Benchmarking the lessons learned by the global market leaders that have already been able to use and pivot digitally to meet customer SNEaRs.
- Proactively streamlining any ongoing in-house digital transformation activities of the organization with focus on big picture outcomes of the exercise.
- Not losing sight of key critical components of the organization's strategic and tactical business plans and how to appropriately incorporate them into the digital transformation process or agenda.

No matter how smoothly digital transformation may appear to be, the likelihood of its successful rollout without further barriers may remain a dream, an aspiration yet to be ascertained especially with respect to envisaged regulatory requirements, privacy, and data security. The looming cyber war across the globe if not checked may result in untold quality management challenges too.

Key Organizational Barriers to Digital Transformation

Apart from the challenges mentioned above regarding the digital transformation, there are some other key factors mitigating against organizational executives and quality professionals in their journey to adopt digital technologies, in efforts to transform industrial manufacturing operations and processes. Some of such factors were identified by ASQE Insights on excellence.

Kane et al. [32], in their book, made the comment, too, as to how the organization itself could be seen as "the biggest threat to digital disruption." They assigned these to situations when an organization:

- Becomes complacent
- Operates in an environment of inflexible culture
- Lacks needed operational agility

The highlights of the 2020 ASQE's Insights on Excellence (IoE) global research findings gave some of the most important barriers to implementing the digital transformation of organizational operations as provided in Table 19.1.

Although the findings of the ASQE's Insight here showed some variations among the peoples of the world – Asia-Pacific, North America, Europe, and rest of the world – global respondents identified the underlisted issues in order of their scores in ASQE's research findings:

1. Outdated infrastructure and/or systems – 38%
2. Concerns regarding cybersecurity – 37%
3. Resistance from organization to adopt new technologies – 36%
4. Shortage of digital skills – 33%
5. Siloed/fragmented data – 32%

While Europe is least disturbed by the issues of siloed/fragmented data (31%) and outdated infrastructure/or systems (32%), Asia-Pacific (39%), North America (43%), and rest of the world (37%) are mostly disturbed by outdated infrastructure and/or systems.

Table 19.1 Major barriers to implementing digital transformation as identified in ASQE's research [10]

Nature of barriers, %	All respondents	Asia-Pacific	North America	Europe	Rest of the world
Outdated infrastructure/systems	38	39	43	32	37
Cybersecurity issues	37	37	38	37	35
Organizational resistance in adopting to new technology	36	34	43	34	28
Digital skills/personnel shortage	33	36	27	34	37
Fragmented data issues	32	31	32	31	34

All in all, the most concerning of the five researched barriers to digital transformation are *outdated infrastructure and/or systems* and concerns regarding *cybersecurity*, followed by *resistance from organization to adopt new technologies* and *shortage of digital skills*.

Talking about the rest of the world, excluding Asia-Pacific, Europe, and North America, is perhaps more indicative of Africa and South America, hence the obviousness of outdated infrastructure and/or systems and digital skills as the most vital issues of concern. The general lack of the basic human needs for good living such as electricity and the Internet may, at the end of the day, be a major technological advancement obstacles alienating most African countries from the league of "SmartCountries" with digitally competitive "SmartManufacturing" organizations.

Investment Challenges of the "SmartFactory"

- Investing in workforce training to ensure adequate provision of needed skills in the digital setting. This is in acknowledgment of the fact that intellectual capital is a valuable resource in any organization, hence the need for its effective management.
- Funding the manufacturing initiatives of the SmartFactory calls for greater investments in digital technology.
- Factory shop floor settings adequately equipped with more artificial intelligence (AI), machine learning (ML), and industrial Internet of things (IIoT).
- Preparedness for big data and tangible 5G use.
- The use of predictive maintenance on the production lines.
- The need for the normalization of the large extent of remote working and the expected agility of the employees.
- The need for the reevaluation of available supply chain options with emphasis on the need for closeness to home.
- Desire for organizational sustainability within the scope of Industry 4.0.

Quality 4.0 Initiatives

Aftermath of Industry 4.0 Initiative

The advent of *Industry 4.0* vis-à-vis Quality 4.0, fortunately or unfortunately, coincided with the final exit of the leaders of the *quality gurus* of the twentieth century, leaving behind the excellent legacies of their quality management experience and exploits.

This, in turn, leaves us with the smart transitional quality management leadership opportunities for current and emerging quality leaders, a future of new and emerging quality management challenges. Hence, there is a need for emerging quality leadership to move smartly to fill the quality leadership vacuum that may have been created, with the determination to supersede the accomplishments of the last century. Taking on such challenges perhaps begins earnestly with exploiting the opportunities for the ready deployment of quality management principles, tools, and techniques to help organizations overcome the challenges of the current two-pronged transitional era – transitioning from the COVID-19 pandemic era to post-COVID-19 new norms and that of transitioning to the era of the Fourth Industrial Revolution initiatives.

Managing these changes is one of the potential tasks for current quality managers and professionals. These challenges are, among others, highlighted as follows:

- The implementation of new requirements needed to overcome the unexpected challenges induced by the COVID-19 pandemic and the emerged new norms of its aftermath on organizational processes and operations on the one hand and products and services on the other.
- The ability to effectively support the Fourth Industrial Revolution, *Industry 4.0*, wherein the digital transformation is highly domineering in creating digital innovations of value.

The emerging quality management leadership is thus welcomed to the 2020s and beyond with quality management challenges of the "SmartFactory" and others that may emerge along with the rollouts of Industry 4.0 initiatives in industrial manufacturing. Key among such challenges are those inherently embedded in the fears of *Industry 4.0's* potential for disruption, deskilling, and displacement of jobs (Lindborg [41]).

Quality 4.0 is therefore a term used in anticipation of what the future of quality and organizational performance excellence is going to be, from the perspectives of Industry 4.0 initiatives and anticipated changes that shall evolve with its emergence and realization.

Quality 4.0 initiatives shall therefore evolve in tandem with the Fourth Industrial Revolution, Industry 4.0, rollout. Hence, Quality 4.0 has to be developed in the context of, and in reference to, the ensuing quality functions of the "SmartFactory" initiatives as they evolve.

While the anticipated future of Quality 4.0 may partially or largely depend on "designing it right first time" and "doing it right always," the major task ahead of modern quality professionals shall be highly dependent on the market dynamism in relation to the real-life evolution of Industry 4.0 initiatives with respect to products/services and customers.

Since Industry 4.0 initiatives may actually not be rolled out by all organizations, the future of quality and quality professionals shall be enhanced by the additional task of ensuring that their Industry 4.0 evolving customers – internal and external – get what they want, the way they want it, at the time they want it, and at the cost that represent their individual values. It follows therefore that, "Quality professionals must stay informed and be ready to adapt when this revolution changes the rules in marketplaces and workplaces" [4].

It is however envisaged by the author that the principles of effectively and efficiently sustaining organizational quality management systems in the digital age shall most probably be defined on the basis of:

> Smartly designing it right first time, installing it right first time and always, securing it right always (cybersecurity), and achieving all these with competently trained hands at all times.

These principles are based on the general needs for the "SmartFactory" or organizations to smartly and rightly put needed industrial production infrastructural systems in place, as a part of an overall quality management systems, to guarantee and ensure that targeted production and/or process outcomes are effectively and efficiently accomplished, from the design stage through the installation and re-installation stages, without compromising the integrity of the system, organizational data, and privacy, as well as customer data and privacy, while avoiding any adverse effects whatsoever on the customer, people, and environment at large.

Design It Right the First Time

"Designing it right the first time"; "installing it right now and always"; and "securing it always" are probably going to be the most domineering quality management guiding principles in the era of Quality 4.0. Designing it right from the onset, whether it is the hardware or software, is critical so as to ensure seamless production and/or to avoid and/or minimize production disruption and/or stoppages. The quality of the software must therefore be given adequate and close attention.

Secure it now and always is very critical and important so as not to compromise data integrity on the overall, protect customer data and privacy, and achieve cybersecurity in order to achieve and maintain customer confidence and maintain market performance.

That the evolution of Quality 4.0 was evoked and incited by Industry 4.0 is, however, neither a coincidence nor surprise, as it is a norm which tallies exactly with the evolutionary antecedents of the parallel growth in the development of industrial manufacturing processes side by side with evolving quality management philosophies for centuries.

Roles of Modern Quality Professionals

The interlocking factors of the now evolving new generations of quality leadership, the evolving norms resulting from the aftermath of the COVID-19 pandemic, and the expected impacts of Industry 4.0 initiatives jointly unite to create an unprecedented wave of momentum driving quality management changes in the early decades of the twenty-first century. All these factors and the linked-in uncertainties create special and perhaps unprecedented challenges to quality professionals. There is therefore the call for the preparedness and adaptiveness of quality professionals as these new quality management challenges unravel.

It is therefore highly imperative for all of us in the business of quality management – individuals and professional bodies alike – to work ahead of time to ensure the adequacy of qualified and skilled quality personnel ready to take on the task of standing up to future challenges as they pop up in the 2020s and beyond.

The role of the modern quality professional is therefore to a large extent going to be defined by the unfolding potentials of *Industry 4.0* vis-à-vis Quality 4.0. It is therefore envisaged here that quality professionals should, in their preparedness, embrace a wide scope of knowledge in the principles, tools, and techniques of quality coupled with a strong background of business- and industry-specific knowledge and experience, in order to develop quality beyond the teachings of the quality gurus [14] to the next level.

All hands must therefore be on the deck – professional bodies such as the ASQ, individuals, organizations, institutions of learning, research institutes, universities, etc. We all have a role to play in building the quality mindset, especially among organizational employees. This is perhaps the reasons for Barsalou's [15] assertion: "Regardless of the organization's size, or the industry, however, the modern quality manager also must serve as a trainer, coach and role model, in addition to the basic role of a quality professional." Hence, there is a variation in the exact roles and responsibilities of the quality manager, depending on the type of industry or size of the business [55].

Quality education is thus getting more and more critical for the people of the world, hence the need for quality education to be at the forefront of creating and nurturing, on a global basis, the quality mindset in today's dynamic world calling on a daily basis for the quality of our environment and world.

Twenty-First-Century Transformational Leadership Challenges of Quality

The dynamism generated by the COVID-19 pandemic as well as the new norms of its aftermath coupled with those generated by the anticipated rollout of the impending Quality 4.0 initiatives no doubt recognizes the general needs for some levels of flexibility in organizational quality management systems. Other quality management challenges in the twenty-first century are visibly spread across various sectors of the economy – from manufacturing to retail businesses, services provision, and the supply chain.

The way the activities of these sectors and the businesses therein may adversely impact the environment and people of the world though requires the crystal ball to see. It therefore goes to say that envisaging and recognizing such negative impacts and effects ahead of time is the only option, if they have to be avoided or at least minimized. The major quality management challenges of 2021 can, on a general basis, be predictably viewed from four major perspectives of transformational changes.

First is from the viewpoint of quality leadership transformation to consolidate the overlapping foundations of quality in the twenty-first century. The task of taking quality and quality management principles, tools, and techniques to greater heights has fallen on the shoulders of the now-emerging quality leadership and professional bodies such as the ASQ [9]. The role of the ASQ cannot be overemphasized particularly in their efforts to crystallize strong quality leadership resources for quality to survive and grow upon. The presentation and recognition of various ASQ's national quality awards and award recipients strongly create the most viable route for quality leadership building efforts. There is no better way to create the quality mindset among the people of the world than that of creating awareness and building quality leaders all over the world. For example, the 2020 ASQ award recipients were spread all over the world to include countries such as the United States, the Netherlands, Argentina, Saudi Arabia, and India. The awards are mainly named after those quality gurus, most of who worked tirelessly to develop and grow quality to the level of its present global appreciation. Today, we have some of the awards named after those who helped in the evolution of quality in the twentieth century, as listed below [2]:

- Philip B. Crosby Medal
- George D. Edwards Medal
- Armand V. Feigenbaum Medal
- Richard Freund-Donald Marquardt Medal
- Hromi Medal
- Spencer Hutchens Jr. Medal
- Kaoru Ishikawa Medal
- E. Jack Lancaster Medal
- Walter Shewhart Medal

While globally creating the quality mindset among the people of the world should be a primary focus, if we have to rescue the planet Earth from the dangerous adventures of its inhabitants, quality itself must have to be rescued from its lonely academic orphanage by exploring and exploiting its scientific rooting to fill the vacuum of its extreme research relevance to the entirety of the human race.

Second is the 2020 COVID-19 pandemic roller-coaster ride which caused severe havoc among the people of the world and across the length and width of the planet Earth. The disruptive challenges of the COVID-19 pandemic are heightened by the post-COVID-19 evolving new norms, such as the way we work and socialize and the interplay of leisure. That is, virtually or remotely working from home or a mixture of in-person and remote work (hybrid) may inadvertently or advertently result in the technological abuse of the quality of the home and social life as the demarcation line between work and home/social life may gradually disappear with technological advancement. In addition, some organizations changed their operations and product offerings in order to survive and emerge from the COVID-19 historic crisis [27]. The world shall, in the immediate future, continue to prevail to eventually recover from the COVID-19 pandemic crisis. It is therefore critical and important for individuals and organizations to continue to adjust and adapt to newly emerging post-COVID-19 norms. Successfully getting through the COVID-19 pandemic crisis requires, according to Hansen [27], three key organizational management measures:

- Organization-wide flexibility
- Strong communications skills
- Organizational preparedness

The riskiest downplayed aftermath of the COVID-19 pandemic is its disruptive impact on people's social life, particularly man's home and leisure life vis-à-vis quality of life. The COVID-19 pandemic succeeded in completely shutting down human access to leisure in multiple modes to leave man in devastating states of mind. This may, however, end up to become permanent norms or parts thereof for the future of humanity, hence the need to massively grow the quality mindset among the people of the world to help every individual to develop the right attitude for survival in a future defined by advanced technology gradually getting devoid of leisure.

Third is the disruptive impact of the COVID-19 pandemic on the rollout of *Industry 4.0* initiative-induced changes, especially in the manufacturing sector and the pending changes resulting from the actualization of *Industry 4.0* initiative itself. For example, it was reported by Krivokuca [38] that "Industry 4.0 recently took a lesser role in deploying various processes in organizations due to the sudden appearance of COVID-19." He similarly reported that many organizations have been forced to make impromptu decisions, due to COVID-19, to operate in a version of *Industry 4.0* without the advantage of previously undertaking a *digital maturity self-assessment*.

It is in this manner, too, that the COVID-19 pandemic has been found in a KPMG (a worldwide renowned finance and consultancy group), "AI Industries Survey," to have accelerated "the pace of artificial intelligence (AI) adoption"; hence, we may be moving too quickly [37].

The constantly shifting "new normal" or situation of the post-COVID-19 pandemic era and the unknowns associated with them are challenges for the manufacturing sector which solution require greater organizational agility and flexibility achievable with the aid of digital twins [19]. A digital twin is accordingly "a representation or blueprint, of a physical thing." That physical thing could be a single product or a component.

One of the other key challenges is in labor shortages as affirmed by Bachman [11]: "In the longer term, businesses will still be looking for people," in different industries and occupations. The rollout of *Industry 4.0* shall, without doubts whatsoever, give room for the engagement of skillful and competent quality management employees, which may require further organizational investment.

Quality Education and Research

Identifying Quality Management Field/Discipline

Quality management is centered principally and fundamentally on "quality outcome" – products or services. This thus makes it obvious that with the tentacles of quality naturally spread among the mathematical sciences (i.e., mathematics, statistics and data analytics, econometrics, computer science, operations research, theoretical physics, etc.), the management sciences (i.e., management, economics, business, engineering, management consulting, mathematical modeling, numerical algorithms, etc.), and the social sciences (i.e., economics, psychology, sociology, etc.), the evolution of quality management, which main objective is focused strictly on "product quality outcome," can easily be acknowledged to understandably assume the status of a discipline or a field of academic pursuit or body of knowledge (BoK) at the undergraduate and postgraduate levels with inclination to any, or a combination, of the following, among others:

- Product Quality Engineering Management (PQEM)
- Product Quality Management and Engineering (PQME)
- Product Quality Management Sciences (PQMSS)
- Product Quality Engineering and Data Sciences (PQEDS)
- Product Quality Management and Data Sciences (PQMDS)

Since quality management is strictly about products/services, "product quality" referred to above serves to portray this objective or goal in naming quality as a field of study. The use and application of quality principles, tools, and techniques are critical for accomplishing the desired, or planned, or predetermined product/services quality and make either the combined or individual use of the terms "engineering" and/or "management" highly essential in designating the field of quality management, or total quality management, as a discipline, for the pursuit of academic excellence. Restricting the name to perhaps "total quality management" or "quality management" may be misleading as it may not glaringly and visibly give a good scope of the subject matter in question.

The recent massive embrace of quality and quality management tools, principles, and techniques by the research and academic worlds jointly portray the global desire for the presence of quality management as a field of studies and research, or as a discipline, not just to meet prospective human challenges, particularly at times of disruptive changes, but to facilitate the global inculcation of the "quality mindset," an asset deserved by every living being, if we have to achieve, on a continual basis, improved environment and quality life style for humanity and society at large. This is particularly very important for the people of the countries of Africa, most of whom are today living in poverty due to poor-quality leadership or, preferably, mis-leadership.

Call it what you may, it is high time that quality management assumed its rightful place among its peers in universities and other higher institutions as a discipline, a course of undergraduate and postgraduate studies.

The wholesale recognition and acknowledgment of quality management as a field of studies, or discipline of immense human relevance, is capable of putting an end to the fading away of quality in the disbelief, of being fragmented into bits and pieces waiting to be absorbed into other disciplines or departments.

Similarly, it also has the potentials to end "the distraction of viewing quality as a set of tools, and operational tools at that, which can be used individually indeed not even individually but as separate standalone tools with a lack of awareness of the existence of other tools and their wider context" [40].

Being Born Outside of Academia

Quality differentiates itself from other fields or disciplines mainly because of its conceptual evolution and growth from real-life experiences in the manufacturing sector of the economy. While this strange mode of the evolution of quality as a field or discipline makes it into an "academic orphan," it has in no way diminished its status quo as a strong agent of change among organizations, businesses, and the society at large. This is not to say, however, that quality has not gone unscathed when compared with other disciplines or fields which originating taproots are, ab initio, deeply entrenched in the academic domain.

Although the advancement of quality and its principles, tools, and techniques has not been diminished, the advancement of quality into a body of knowledge with the potentials of becoming an academic field or discipline of its own may have been delayed.

With quality taking its rightful position in the educational, research, and academic worlds to leverage its industrial and business exploitation, this century opens up the doors of opportunities to massively enhance the widened and deepened embrace of quality education and training among the people of the global community across the globe.

Advancing Product Quality Research

Researchers from various institutions across the globe are today dishing out evidences of their interests in Product Quality Engineering and Product Quality Management through various publications in the literature. In this way quality is gradually taking its footings in academia.

Although, according to Sampaio and Saraiva [49] quality "was not born in the academia," it's growing prominence in academia has today brought out the potentials of its relevance in global academic and research institutional activities. This is supported by the outcome of quality delivery and evolution by the foundational collaborative efforts and experience of the "quality gurus" of the twentieth century across various industrial settings and projects.

The fundamental outputs of the tangible and intangible inputs of these "quality gurus" have undoubtedly combined to provide us with the global platform and foundation of the wealth of knowledge that is adequately suitable and reliable for the academia to continually evolve quality to the ultimate levels of being transformed to become a management science and/or engineering-related discipline. The science of quality and quality management vis-a-vis total quality management shall most likely continually attract great research and educational interests from the academic world in the twenty-first century.

In their studies to identify and depict key areas of research in quality in the past 37 years, Carnerud and Backstrom [17] explored the "longitudinal patterns and trends" in these key areas, in order to be able to "present new perspectives on the foundational elements and evolutionary patterns of research to quality as well as future directions" and trends of it.

In addition to their finding that research in quality was in decline between years 2000 and 2012, seven key areas of research activities were objectively identified:

- Process design and control
- ISO Certification and standards
- TQM – implementation, performance, and culture
- Reliability, costs, failure, and problems
- QM – practices and performance
- Service quality and customer satisfaction
- Excellence – business excellence models (BEMs), quality awards, and excellence in higher education

BEM here refers to business excellence model. Carnerud [16], in a somewhat comparative study a year earlier, identified the area of *innovation, practices*, and *learning* as additional to five others (listed below), which overlap with those of the above specified ones [17].

- Control, costs, reliability, and failure
- Service quality
- TQM – implementation and performance
- ISO – certifications, standards, and systems
- Customers – research and product design and an additional one

In pushing QM to the forefront of improved academic inquisitiveness and discourse, Kumar et al. [39] reportedly identified the need for a more comprehensive understanding of "QM's performance effects" through research. In their contention of QM being equally approved and disapproved, Barouch and Kleinhans [13] concluded that "the scientific debate regarding the importance and capability of quality initiatives is far from settled."

Apart from being a researcher and academician of long standing, my practical exposure and experience in the manufacturing, retail, and services sectors, as well as the shop-floor across the length and width of operational management, suggests, however, that such controversies about QM though tenable may have arisen from the somewhat disadvantaged positions of academics and researchers, in the area of quality management practices, in terms of limited exposure, experience, and real-life problem-solving activities.

In their own studies, Barouch and Ponsignon [12] found that QM programs can successfully be used by managers who are knowledgeable or familiar with the epistemological foundations of QM. This is further reinforced by the findings of Aquilani et al. [1] who found out from scholarly publications that managers should have the ability and experience of navigating through "specific contexts, industries, countries, dimensions, products, services, etc." in order to be in a good position, to identify the most vital factors needed for achieving organizational success, objectives/goals, exact situations, strategies, and performance expectations, based most importantly on the business model and management approach.

It is in this vein, too, and in order to better "classify the existing position of QM" that van Kemenade and Hardjono [54] resorted to asking for the need to find new global view, models, or paradigm for clarifying the existing directions of QM practice and the trend of its future needs.

Unlike most developmental branches of the economy, which were generally grown from the basis of academic cum scientific theoretical know-how, and research seedlings in the fertile soil of science discoveries, quality management thrived and grew successfully from real-world applications and through hands-on experience. This is probably the reasoning behind the initiations of Dahlgaard-Park et al. [18] for the need to have clearer theoretical base for TQM to ensure a better understanding of its current position.

All these doubts and controversies persisted despite the fact that business quality revolution has since grown according to Feigenbaum and Feigenbaum [23], to achieve the twentieth-century business revolution to most powerfully create endless sales and revenue growth and excellent jobs. In addition, too, is the fact that quality actually laid a strong foundation for sustainable business expansion that was experienced on the global platform before the COVID-19 pandemic struck humanity in late 2019 to early 2020.

The uniquely unusual mode of quality evolution through hands-on experience rather than through scientific or academic development generally gives room for future scientific and academic research engagements in the field of quality, in the twenty-first century. It is necessary to expatiate and ponder into establishing the theoretical backgrounds that may possibly be deployed to explain some, if not all, of the real-life experience-based, already established principles of quality management, TQM, and other relevant quality management tools.

Such opportunities include, among others, the challenging task of providing answers to existing controversies about quality, emanating from the academic and research worlds. Some of these controversies center among others on the need to:

- Define, identify, and establish relevant scientific rooting and grounding models, where possible, for each of the principles (and philosophies) of quality management and to find explanations for their applicability.
- Develop and adapt appropriate models with the objectives of correlating and/or redefining some of quality management terms and concepts that may have been previously overlooked or omitted in quality's journey so far, but especially through the later parts of the twentieth century.
- Verify and further explain the doubts, mysteries, or realities surrounding the relations between TQM and the general quality initiatives and organizational performance.
- Distinctly describe and distinguish, according to Fredriksson and Isaksson [25], the similarities and differences between the various quality philosophies to embrace both science and academic teaching. These are both critical to the general and overall growth of quality but, more importantly, needed most expediently, to establish the learning basis for TQM at all levels of learning in the twenty-first century. The need for quality managers, especially those implementing its requirements, to understand the concepts of quality such as QM systems, methodologies, principles tools/techniques, and assessment models, cannot be overemphasized.
- There is likely going to be a growing need for new paradigms which, according to van Kemenade and Hardjono [54], may be required to explain current directions of quality and future needs. A *paradigm* is referred to as "the lens through which you see the world." Paradigms are thus the "philosophical foundations that support our approaches to research" [43].

Other key areas of research in quality management that will continue to thrive in the future include, among others, areas of widening the scope of the effective application and implementation of quality management principles and standards in:

- Solving public service issues in relationship to governance – implementation, effects, outputs, and impacts, especially in the African continent where the issue of transparency has become extremely challenging.
- Identifying quality management systems implementation and sustainability challenges resulting from disruptive emergency situations such as those resulting from the COVID-19 pandemic.
- Identification of integrated quality management methods, approaches, and systems for product specific applications.
- Using the present to understand the future in designing, formulating, and establishing newer quality ideologies, principles, theories, and hypotheses where possible.

The healthy academic discussion generated around quality and QM is apparently obvious, especially because of its wide and endless applicability and use across all activities of man. Quality thus remains a potentially fertile ground for future research activities emanating from individual or group initiatives.

It is believed that researchers and people in academics may need to carry out their investigations with consideration for, and in references to, the origin, nature, and methods of QM and the philosophies and principles surrounding its use and application, so as to have better understanding of its main concepts. This shall enable its consistent implementation and understanding.

It is therefore believed by the author that the importance and capability to effectively implement QM/TQM, Lean, Six Sigma, or a combination of them and other quality principles and their impact on organizational performance are neither in question nor incontrovertible, though there may be variations in the effectiveness of applicable quality philosophy and performance measurement tools. Choosing the right quality philosophy and appropriate quality measurement tools is thus very critical to achieving expected results or outcomes.

Mutualistic Evolution of Quality and Industrial Production

The evolved industrial growth, development, and improvement witnessed over the last century were made possible with the closely knitted interrelationships between manufacturing processes and practices and the proven embodiments of evolving quality management philosophies and principles. Manufacturing and its processes therefore grew to become a strong economic sector of immeasurable values to mankind with its potentials deeply and fundamentally rooted in the foundational principles, tools, and techniques for achieving planned product/service quality.

The mutual reliance of manufacturing organizations on quality management principles, tools, and techniques to grow their destinies and potentials led to the eventual industrial revolution that is today still evolving in our business world and society. While manufacturing challenges posed the questions at that time, quality management provided improvement solutions in the most mutually interactive ways. Quality thus grew the industrial revolution while transforming itself gradually to the world's most indispensable knowledge apparatus to leverage products and services to man's specifications, needs, expectations, and requirements (SNEaRs) and the overall improvement of the environment, society, and quality of living.

There was a momentum established by this mutualistic coexistence which resulted in the synonymity of industrial revolution with quality evolution. The outcome here is that quality evolved along with industrial manufacturing processes such that if we are talking about Industry 4.0, then Quality 4.0 automatically takes the stage.

The industrial revolution witnessed in the twentieth century was thus heavily catalyzed by quality, its practices, tools, and principles, in an atmosphere of mutualistic opportunism. Quality tools, practices, and techniques were, hence, the results of the opportunities seized by the "quality gurus" or, in other words, quality leadership of the twentieth century, to meet the then numerous challenges that emanated from manufacturing processes and practices.

It therefore goes to say that, without quality, industrial evolution may have been stalled, even when it is broadly and widely acknowledged, too, that quality was similarly driven by industrial evolutionary challenges. The mutualistic relationship between quality and manufacturing thus created a solid base, for the development of manufacturing and other industrial processes pari passu with quality management advances.

Evolving the Quality Mindset

The industrial sector thus grew side-by-side with quality evolution (see Table 7.1). The mutual benefits, derivable from the interrelationship of quality and manufacturing industrial processes witnessed in the twentieth century, have left a memory in all of us, as to how the world and its people have come a long way to consciously or unconsciously appreciate the need for *quality thinking*, in order to create the all-important, "quality mindset."

Reeling with the experience of two world wars (1914–1918) and (1939–1945) and two deadly pandemics (Spanish Flu in 1919) and (COVID-19 from 2018/2020 till date), the people of the global community have gradually come to the realization and appreciation of the potentials of using and applying quality principles, tools, and practices to mitigate against pandemics and other disruptive circumstances faced by man.

Hence, it has become our collective responsibilities to, in appreciation of quality and the *quality mindset*, passionately strive toward quality being able to fulfil its promise, its potentials of improving the quality of people's lives on a global scale. There is no other way for accomplishing this great objective than giving every living being, the opportunity of enjoying the benefits inherent in quality management philosophies, through education and training of the people.

Hence, quality and total quality management principles, tools, and techniques are consolidated into a discipline – *Product Quality Engineering*, or *Product Quality Management*, or *Product Quality Engineering Management*, or *Product Quality Management Studies*, or *Product Quality Management Sciences, or whichever name you may choose to call it.* Going through the back door to acquire a first degree in quality management principles, tools, and philosophies has hitherto denied quality its rightful place among its peers in the educational sector.

Quality as a Discipline

Product Quality Engineering/Management (or whichever name you may choose to call it), with its potentials inherently embedded in total quality management (TQM), has grown beyond being seen, viewed, perceived, or looked at, merely as a program, slogan, fashion, or broken fractions of a body of knowledge.

Quality management has therefore grown to earn itself a rightful place in the academia, education, training, and research. Afterward it has established itself for over a century, as an "enabler" and "sustainer" of manufacturing industrial processes and other businesses, to the benefit of mankind, through its continual improvement processes, cost saving measures, risk prevention and management strategies, and other customer satisfaction practices.

Total quality management (TQM) principles also facilitate or enable product conformity with established norms, requirements, relevant standards, regulatory requirements, and customer SNEaRs. Quality management principles are categorized into four parts:

- Quality planning
- Quality assurance (defect prevention)
- Quality control (which includes product inspection and other elements, such as competence)
- Quality improvement

It is in appreciation of the impact of quality management, which is defined according to the ASQ quality glossary [7] as "the application of a quality management system in managing a process to achieve maximum customer satisfaction at the lowest overall cost to the organization while continuing to improve the process," that Eby [22] reportedly wondered "why it would take until the 20th century to apply such seemingly obvious principles like product goals and parts inspection." As reported by Eby, Andy Nichols, the quality program manager at the Michigan Manufacturing Technology Center, credited the then mass production techniques and the urgent demand for materials during two world wars for the particular innovation of quality management. For example, Nichols was reportedly quoted to have, for example, claimed: "The U.S. military demanded to some extent that every product they purchased be good because soldiers' lives literally depended on the quality of the products they handled. Whether it was for K rations or bullets, these wars spurred a manufacturing revolution to focus on the idea of getting things right every time."

The key roles played by the defense sector, or military in the evolution of quality management itself, tells it all how quality management has always been tied to man's existential potentials – survival, sustainability, and existence – and the global improvement in the quality of human lives from day to day.

Apart from the military, most other professionals rely solely on quality, QM, and TQM tools to survive. "Doing it right the first time" or "designing it right the first time" are some of the quality principles widely adopted and embraced not just in the vast manufacturing industrial sector but largely in other disciplines and professional practices, hence the inevitability of quality, QM, and TQM.

Universality of Quality Application

In discussing "the history of one of the most widely used quality management philosophies, total quality management (TQM)," Eby [22] highlighted the benefits and potentials of TQM, describing it as a system wherein a company attains organizational advancement through a commitment to customer requirements," by empowering every employee in each department not just to maintain high standards but to also strive for continuous improvement. The preeminence of TQM was similarly affirmed by Andy Nichols who claimed in the same publication that "Total quality management is really a company-wide initiative to get everybody involved in doing the right thing for the customer." The major goal of TQM is summed up here as, "Do things right the first time, every time."

It can therefore not be denied how importantly quality and its management philosophies – tools, principles, and techniques – have grown to assume pivotal roles in defining, on a global basis, the quality of man's life. There is no wonder therefore that quality features were rightly or wrongly deployed to classify the world into developed and underdeveloped economies: first, second, third, fourth, and so on worlds.

It is a truth universally acknowledged in literature, too, that "The long-term health of any organization depends on its commitment to continuous improvement, which is one aspect of quality management" [36]. It has also been affirmed, too, that superior organizational performance is attributable to the adoption of quality management practices [21, 24, 33].

The preeminence of quality management or a discipline that evolves from it, "Product Quality Engineering/Management" among other disciplines and fields of knowledge, is glaringly visible not just in all ramifications of man's economic activities to achieve and sustain better standards of living but strongly perpetuated in organizations' largely dependent nature on quality and its continuous improvement tools and techniques for survival, as established and ascertained by no other quality practitioners than the "quality gurus" of the twentieth century themselves – Juran [31], Ishikawa [28] and Deming [20].

Today, it is not only organizations and businesses that thrive on quality, but the entirety of the people of the global community are looking forward to their sustainability through the use of quality management principles, tools, and techniques in their general approach to issues of existential threat with the all-important "quality mindset." "Of course, the most important strength any management can supply – whether in a time of crisis or a more normal situation – is this quality mindset [27].

The preeminence of *Product Quality Engineering/Management* as a field of undergraduate and postgraduate studies, or as a discipline among all disciplines, resides strictly in the supremacy of the output, or outcome, of any situation, activity, or decision in which the *quality mindset* has been put to use or has been brought to bear or made to play pivotal roles.

Irrespective of the economic sector, business group, and other organized activities of man and his quality living and environment, quality management practices, principles, tools, and techniques are reliable sources to shape and put them on the right course for people's benefit. Hence, quality is universal – in application, use, and outcome.

Quality Management Initiatives in COVID-19 Response

The global recognition of the power of quality management principles resulted in it being the first choice of response when the COVID-19 pandemic shockingly surfaced on planet Earth, knocking on the doors of human abode, from China to Italy, Spain to the United Kingdom, the United States, and Brazil, in late 2019/early 2020, looking for victims of its deadly destruction.

As recently reported by one of the consciences of quality, the ASQ, the world swiftly turned to quality management principles, tools, practices, and techniques to protect the global population from being further devastated by the novel coronavirus [6, 50]. Most of the earlier established preventive measures against the COVID-19 pandemic have their basis rooted in quality management philosophy.

The ASQ's research outcome, "Quality's Impact on the Global Pandemic Response," gave highlights of the ways in which "quality principles and best practices are foundational for industries integral to each stage of the COVID-19 response, including vaccine development and approval, distribution and administration" [5]. The integral nature of quality initiatives in the historic response of humanity to combat the COVID-19 pandemic was glaringly visible in their use and application: "From immunization development and approval, to supply chain delivery, to actual administration of the immunization in a healthcare setting." The role of quality management principles in responding positively to protect humanity against the COVID-19 pandemic, though often times undermined, is a milestone for man's desires to overcome the damages inflicted on man's life and social activities.

The relevance and importance of quality management as well as the *quality mindset* can therefore not be overemphasized especially now that quality principle deployment is key in man's efforts to mitigate the life-threatening impacts of the pandemic and managing other human environmentally inherent risks. The ISO 31000:2018 – Risk management (Guidelines) is on the rollcall here [29].

It is thus obvious from the research findings of the ASQ that "These efforts are helping to ensure that the immunization process is as safe as modern science and quality innovations can guarantee" [5]. Man's reliance on quality management tools and techniques, especially in the healthcare sector, and at times of disruptive changes can only be advanced and kept alive by inculcating the *quality mindset* through the proliferation of a quality management discipline, in our institutions of higher education to stimulate research activities in this highly beneficial field of study or knowledge domain.

Degree in Quality

Quality belongs in every professional practice, irrespective of the area and field of knowledge. Under normal circumstances one would expect that quality management does not, in any way whatsoever, deserve sympathy for being born in the most productive sector of all times in the global economy – industrial manufacturing. Neither does it deserve disrespect or any deprivation for being born in academic orphanage. It must, however, be acknowledged that unlike most other disciplines which emerge from the academia, quality was born outside of it. The status quo of quality has thus been dwarfed for its failure to be given the status of a discipline of studies in our universities and other higher institutions in earlier years.

This is because quality management has evolved, on its own standing, "to a point of exciting opportunities; it has made dramatic impacts and has yet to fulfil its potentials" [40]. Rather than mere sympathy, quality management should be accorded the acknowledgment and justice of its long-deserved status quo, as a critical field of studies or academic discipline, in *Product Quality Engineering/Management.* Otherwise, quality management stands the risk of being continuously shredded and "subsumed into other disciplines" such as industrial engineering, production engineering, operations management, and the management sciences, just to mention a few.

Failure to accord quality management, the much-deserved status of a field of study or discipline shall therefore keep quality management fragmented and absorbed into other departments, thereby losing "its connectedness and its systems approach."

The distractions of quality being seen from the point of view of being mere tools is unfortunately further emphasized by the results of the "ASQ APQC Global State of Quality Research, Discoveries 2013" [3] in which only 24% of over 2000 respondents were of the view that quality is a method for managing organizational-wide performance. The overwhelming majority of the respondents, however, tells it all, as they viewed it merely as a "tool to fix issues after being discovered" or a "continuous improvement activity" or a "compliance activity."

Seeing quality management mainly from the perspective of a tactical issue or simply as an operational issue grossly diminishes the understanding of viewing and seeing quality management as a stand-on-its-own discipline, or field of study, available for organization-wide activities and performance management. This misconception emanates perhaps from the way quality and its management principles, tools, and techniques evolved over the early parts of the last century. We must not forget, however, that quality management has its tentacles spread across multidisciplinary disciplines which fundamentally focuses on innovation to effectively and efficiently run different businesses and organizations, hence basically rooted in the:

- Mathematical sciences
- Data sciences
- Engineering and reliability engineering
- Social sciences
- Arts and culture
- Management sciences
- People- and value-oriented leadership

The role played by statistical quality control (SQC) or statistical process control (SPC) in the early days of quality evolution represented a firm footing for quality evolution. Statistics is an integral part of quality management as it helps in predicting accuracy through numbers, rather than in the inspection of parts. In their use of fact-based decision-making, quality teams result to collect data and process statistics to ensure that work meets specifications.

Cost of quality (CoQ) is an embodiment of organizational financial considerations in the economics of organizational activities, while human engagement or people involvement engages in the deployment of psychological principles and social interactive understandings to build quality management teams.

While dynamics stimulate change, a major application of quality management systems; mathematical measures serve as measurement indicators of improvement; calibration data and other equipment measurement data served as the reservoir of quality management reference data bank and metrics.

With quality management living at the intersections of engineering and management sciences on the one hand, and pure and human sciences on the other, it has been able to thrive firmly on its established relationships with statistical process control and the dynamisms of change in embrace of measurement, data collection, and process engineering. With quality management's firm grip on financial control and economic determinants of organizational improvement needs, quality management is demonstrably equipped with all the tools of a feasible and viable field or discipline.

It is a universally accepted truth that "many arrive in the quality profession via a circuitous journey. You ***can't get a degree in quality***, so the ways people wind up in the field vary" [47]. The fact that you cannot get a *degree in quality* because of its genealogy being deeply rooted in industry or outside the academics does not necessarily mean that the American Society for Quality (ASQ) should subsume the opportunity of offering a degree across universities all over the world strictly in its jurisdiction among the influence of its members. Quality and quality management principles, philosophy, tools, techniques, and practices far surpass the ASQ, its members, and those quality consultants constantly promoted by it.

Quality is therefore for the people of the global community, hence the need for universities all over the globe to come up today with degree programs in quality for two reasons:

- To incorporate and bring quality principles to the mindsets of potential graduates in all areas of man's endeavor – from arts to engineering and computing – right from the degree level, irrespective of professional lineage akin to bringing quality to the people of the world. Quality as part of the fundamental mindset of every graduate shall be of great assets to democratic governance to facilitate both the quality of life and environment.
- To spread the universality of quality to humanity irrespective of their locations on planet Earth. This is going to massively help reduce and eliminate poverty from the world over a period of time. It may ultimately result into a pandemic needed to eradicate mis-leadership from the countries of Africa, South America, and other parts of the world as it may help to eradicate all conspiracy theories due to quality leading to massively promote people's objectivity.

It is highly important here that a university degree cannot effectively and realistically be substituted here with the ASQ's "Quality Career Playbook" [8] as defined by:

- Training and certification
- ASQTV
- Quality resources
- Recommended reading

It is a greatly appreciated privilege and opportunity that the "ASQ offers training courses [9] for quality professionals of all experience and skill levels - whether you're new to quality, a quality practitioner or professional, or an academic" but never a direct equivalent of, and substitute for, a university degree in all ramifications.

There are no doubts whatsoever that ASQ's immeasurable contributions to quality and quality management in promoting, facilitating, and shaping the "past, present, and future" of quality since ASQ's existence is unparalleled, hence cannot be overemphasized. It has always been there for quality as the pillar for building the expertise and providing the needed learning experience for quality and its practitioners. Its role in promoting and advancing the science of quality and developing needed expertise to create people's values from quality is a great asset and potential for human existential quality management essentials needs. It will be more so as Quality 4.0 initiatives emerge and are developed, probably reaching maturity in the mid-twenty-first century.

Opportunities for universities and other higher institutions shall most importantly add values to the work of the ASQ across the globe. This strong inclination of the author for proliferating degree programs in quality all over the world is based strictly on a balanced knowledge and experience of industrial manufacturing (18 years) and academics (20 years), thus branding the "been there/done that" testimonial. A degree in quality shall most probably offer professional quality graduates a non-circuitous quality professional journey like any other professional across the globe through a somewhat more normal learning curve.

References

1. Aquilani, B., Silvestri, C., Ruggieri, A., & Gatti, C. (2017). A systemic literature review on total quality management critical success factors and the identification of new areas of research. *The TQM Journal, 29*(1), 183–213. https://doi.org/10.1108/TQM-01-2016-003
2. ASQ. (2021, May). ASQ award recipients. *Quality Progress*, p. 7. https://www.asq.org/about-asq/asq-awards
3. ASQ, & APQC. (2013). The ASQ global state of quality research: Discoveries 2013. In P. Sampaio & P. Saraiva (Eds.), *Quality in the 21st century* (p. 14). Springer, p. 36.
4. ASQ. (2017, November). ASQ celebrating 50 years – Forward progress. *Quality Progress*, pp. 30–31.
5. ASQ. (2021, April). Research ties quality to COVID-19 response. *Quality Progress*, p. 9.
6. ASQ. (2021). ASQ Whitepaper, "Quality practices used throughout the COVID-19 response". https://tinyurl.com/5d35iimr
7. ASQ. Quality Glossary. https://www.asq.org.

8. ASQ. (2021, July). Quality career playbook. *Quality Progress*, pp. 28–29.
9. ASQ. ASQ training catalog. https://www.asq.org/training
10. ASQE. (2021, March). 2020 insights on excellence – Annual research reports and association highlights. *Quality Progress*, p. 7. https://tinyurl.com/IoE-2020-Research
11. Bachman, D. (2021, March 16). Deloitte insights – United States economic forecast. 1st Quarter 2021.
12. Barouch, G., & Ponsignon, F. (2016). The epistemological basis for quality management. *Total Quality Management and Business Excellence, 27*(7–8), 944–962. https://doi.org/10.1080/14783363.2016.1188659
13. Barouch, G., & Kleinhans, S. (2015). Learning from the criticisms of quality management. *International Journal Quality and Service Sciences, 7*(213), 201–216. https://doi.org/10.1108/IJQSS-02-2015-0026
14. Barsalou, M. (2015, February). Perspectives: Well rounded. *Quality Progress*, pp. 10–11.
15. Barsalou, M. (2021, May). What is the role of the quality manager today? *Quality Progress*, p. 5.
16. Carnerud, D. (2018). 25 years of quality management research – Outlines and trends. *International Journal of Quality and Reliability Management, 35*(1), 208–231. https://doi.org/10.1108/IJQRM-01-2017-0013
17. Carnerud, D., & Backstrom, I. (2019, August 20). Four decades of research on quality: Summarizing trendspotting and looking ahead. *Journal Total Quality Management & Business Excellence*. https://doi.org/10.1080/14783363.2019.1655397
18. Dahlgaard-Park, S. M., Reyes, L., & Chen, C.-K. (2018). The evolution and convergence of total quality management and management theories. *Total Quality Management, 29*(9–10), 1108–1128. https://doi.org/10.1080/14783363.2018.1486556
19. Deloitte. (2021). Analysis – 2021 Manufacturing industry outlook. https://www2.deloitte.com. Retrieved on 27 Apr 2021.
20. Deming, W. Edwards (1986). Out of crisis
21. Douglas, T. J., & Judge, W. Q. (2001). Total quality management implementation and competitive advantage: The role of structural control and exploration. *The Academy of Management Journal, 44*(1), 158–169.
22. Eby, K. (2017). A quality principle: Everything you need to know about total quality management. 21 June 2017. https://www.smartsheet.com
23. Feigenbaum, A. V., & Feigenbaum, D. S. (1999). New quality for the 21st century. *Quality Progress, 32*(12), 27.
24. Flynn, B. B., Schroeder, R. G., & Sakakibara, S. (1995). The impact of quality management practices on performance and competitive advantage. *Decision Sciences, 26*(5), 659–691.
25. Fredriksson, M., & Isaksson, R. (2018). Making sense of quality philosophies. *Total Quality Management and Business Excellence, 29*(11–12), 1452–1465. https://doi.org/10.1080/14783363.2016.1266245
26. Gusher, T. (2021, March). Many concerned AI moving too fast. *Quality Progress*, p. 6. https://tinyurl.com/y73fhfj2. Retrieved 16 May 2021.
27. Hansen, M. C. (2021, March). Back on track – Three must-haves for you and your organization to emerge from the COVID-19 crisis. *Quality Progress*, pp. 16–23.
28. Ishikawa, K. (1985). What's total quality control? The Japanese way. Englewood Cliffs. N. J. Prentice Hall.
29. ISO, ISO 31000:2018 – Risk management – Guidelines.
30. ISO, ISO 9000 :2015. https://www.iso.org
31. J.M. (1989). Juran on leadership for quality. New York. Free Press.
32. Kane, G. C., Philips, A. N., Copulsky, J. R., & Andrews, G. R. (2019). *The technology fallacy: How people are the real key to digital transformation*. MIT Press.
33. Kaynak, H. (2003). The relationship between total quality management practices and their effects on firm performances. *Journal of Operations Journal, 21*(4), 405–435.
34. Kennedy, B. (2018, October). 21st century excellence. *Quality Progress*, pp. 37–44.
35. Kennedy, B. (2021, May). Rebalance the power – Is the consumer really always right? *Quality Progress*, p. 56.

36. Kovach, J. V. (2016). The role of learning and exploration in quality management and continuous improvement. In P. Sampaio & P. Saraiva (Eds.), *Quality in the 21st century* (p. 75). Springer.
37. KPMG AI Industries Survey. (2021, March 9). https://www.kpmg.com/us. Retrieved on 16 May 2021.
38. Krivocuka, M. (2021, March). Catalysts for change – Achieving organizational excellence in post-COVID-19 industry 4.0 process performance. *Quality Progress*, pp. 32–37.
39. Kumar, P., Maiti, J., & Gunasekaran, A. (2018). Impact of quality management systems on firm performance. *International Journal of Quality and Reliability Management, 35*(5), 1034–1059. https://doi.org/10.1108/IJQRM-02-2017-0030
40. Leonard, D. (2016). The future of quality: Strategy, leadership and an opportunity to improve quality of life on a global scale there to be seized or lost. In P. Sampaio & P. Saraiva (Eds.), *Quality in the 21st century* (p. 32). Springer.
41. Lindborg, Hank. (2021). What personal skills should young quality professionals consider growing - imagination. Quality Progress July, p. 27.
42. Lydon, B. (2014). ISA, "The 4th industrial revolution, industry 4.0, unfolding at Hannover Messe 2014 – Summary." https://www.automation.com. Retrieved on 16 Apr 2021.
43. Masters, K. (Ed.). (2014). *Role development – Role development in professional nursing practice* (3rd ed., p. 93). Jone & Bertlett Learning.
44. Moore, M. (2019, November). What is industry 4.0? Everything you need to know. *TechRadar*. https://www.techradar.com. Retrieved 2 May 2021.
45. Mui, C. (2011, October 17). Five dangerous lessons to learn from Steve jobs. *Forbes*.
46. Padhi, N., & Illa, P.K. (2019, March). Bigger, better, smarter – How to maintain quality in an increasingly automated environment. *Quality Progress*, pp. 24–29.
47. Pietenpol, L. (2021, July). Words of wisdom. *Quality Progress*, p. 18.
48. Radziwill, N. (2021, May). The progress report – Many concerned AI moving too fast. *Quality Progress*, pp. 6–7. https://tinyurl.com/y73fhfj2
49. Sampaio, Paulo and Saraiva, Pedro (2016). Quality: From past perfect to future conditional. Sampaio, P. and Saraiva, P. (ed.) Quality in the 21st century: Perspective from ASQ Feigenbaum medal winners. pp. 1-22. Springer Nature.
50. Schvaneveldt, Shane and Neve, Benjamin V. (2021). Proving their mettle - combating the COVID-19 pandemic with quality tools. *Quality Progress*, March, pp. 24-31.
51. Sheahan, T. P., & Frieman, M. B. (2020). The continued epidemic threat of SARS-CoV-2 and implications for the future of global public health. *Current Opinion in Virology, 40*, 37–40. https://doi.org/10.1016/j.coviro.2020.05.010
52. TWI. (2021). https://www.twi-global.com
53. United States Environmental Protection Agency, EPA. *Learn about Volkswagen violations*. https://www.epa.gov
54. van Kemenade, E., & Hardjono, T. W. (2019). Twenty-first century total quality management: The emergence paradigm. *The TQM Journal, 31*(2), 150–166. https://doi.org/10.1108/TQM-04-2018-0045
55. Westcott (2021). The certified manager of quality. In *Organizational excellence handbook* (4th ed., p. xxxvi). Quality Press.
56. Wikipedia. https://www.en.m.wikipedia. Retrieved 2 May 2021.

Quality Outlook

20

Sustainability

Changing Faces of Quality

Navigating the historical development of quality, from real-world applications and experiences in global industrial production systems and project developmental stages, to how we now know, use, and apply quality in the present age, most certainly reveals its gradual evolution from quality control, through quality assurance, to (total) quality management (T)QM and then quality management system (QMS), as shown in Table 20.1.

Today, quality has not just transcended the applicational psyche of being seen and viewed strictly, from the purview of industrial manufacturing, but has gone far beyond it to determine in most cases organizational/business competitiveness vis-à-vis sustainability.

Quality is today established as the deoxyribonucleic acid (DNA) of customer-centric management system that are strategically planned, leadership committed, employee-involved, continuous improvement-driven, innovation-inclined, and supply chain-partnered. Quality, its principles, philosophies, tools, and techniques have thus assumed a borderless status, in today's planet earth, where it shall undoubtedly, continue to thrive and dominate human socioeconomic activities and endeavors.

Today, the healthcare system, aviation, rail, education, construction, technology, and biotechnology sectors of the economy are overwhelmed with the general application of quality and its management principles, tools, philosophies, concepts, and practices. The role of quality in mitigating the health challenges of the COVID-19 pandemic is a symbolism of the expanding role of quality management in the healthcare industry.

Quality shall, most certainly, move in the next few decades to distinctly carve an envious niche for itself, in institutions of higher learning, research, and development as a strong and key member of the Engineering and Management Sciences

T. A. Ibidapo, *From Industry 4.0 to Quality 4.0*, Management for Professionals,
https://doi.org/10.1007/978-3-031-04192-1_20

Table 20.1 Changing concepts of quality from the twentieth to twenty-first centuries

Concepts of quality	Principles of concepts	Area of attention
Quality control	Product inspection to identify and separate good (or quality) products from defective ones after all production inputs and processes are completed	Identify defective products, classify them into second, third classes to sell at reduced prices. Defects used to identify and eliminate causes of faults
Quality assurance	Managing quality such that there is the focus on providing the confidence that quality requirements will be fulfilled	Confidence that products and services will confirm to requirements thereby ensuring preventive quality of material and immaterial product
Total quality management (TQM)	Structured and extensive organizational management approach with focus of attention on continuous quality improvement of products/services with customer feedback	The capability of all or every employee to continuously improve their ability to provide on-demand in-process and full products and services that meet customer (internal and external) values, specifications, and needs
Quality management system (QMS)	Use of interrelated or interacting elements to direct and control an organization with regard to quality	Customer needs, requirements, and specifications thereby ensuring preventive quality of the process
Integrated quality systems	Use of a combination of two or more quality management systems/ standards and/or improvement systems to achieve conforming products or customer requirements	Examples are lean manufacturing/six sigma/5s combinations to accomplished desired results. The integrated systems of ISO 9001:2015 QMS and ISO 14001:2015 EMS are another example
Innovation implanted integrated QMS or improvement concepts (III-QMSs)	Quality management systems and/or combinations of improvement systems implanted with innovation	Innovation and optimum improvement of the quality management systems
Quality 4.0 is the future of quality seen from the perspective context of Industry 4.0. initiatives in alignment with industrial revolutionary pace	"SmartFactory" quality expectations based on Industry 4.0 initiatives, that is, digital transformation of industrial manufacturing	Integration of traditional quality management practices with relevant 4.0 technologies to evolve adaptable quality management systems and practices suitable for achieving efficient process, operational and systems efficiency, and improved business and organizational performance in an Industry 4.0 environmental setting

discipline. Quality shall be globally flouted to continually attract the attention of a growing quality-conscious global community in knowledge acquisition, management, use, application, and practice.

What the future holds for us can only be humanly viewed as an offshoot of our past and present experiences within the scope of human imagination; all else is shaped by circumstances unforeseen, but well within the consequences of our collective responsibilities, creativity, inventiveness, and in the contrives of our faith.

In the same vein, what the future holds for quality is partly an offshoot of the knowledge and experience, quality tools and techniques that have already been established by the "*quality gurus*" of the twentieth century, preserved and built upon, by the current sets of emerging potential quality leadership—from both the academia and industry. Most of these potential leaders are already exploiting quality in order to:

- Find and establish its theoretical basis
- Modeling quality in all ramifications of human activities
- Grow the knowledge of quality itself

A major challenge facing the future generations of quality leadership is the environment of its growth, use, and development as well as the dynamism with which businesses operate in the environment. It is therefore likely that the immediate changes likely to be experienced in our quality world shall most likely be dominated by the happenings in the industrial manufacturing sector of the global economy and its interaction with the 4.0 technologies, and perhaps in the outcomes of their convergence.

It follows, therefore, that *Industry 4.0* shall consequently breed Quality 4.0. Quality development shall, in the 2020s be at the dictates of the convergence of technologies, such as the computers and automation, along with artificial intelligence (AI) and autonomous systems with the underlying impact of data and machine reading, in an industrial transformational atmosphere to create smarter factories with far more connectedness than we have ever witnessed. These Quality 4.0 initiatives shall unveil as Industry 4.0 initiatives are rolled out.

A sudden era of COVID-19 pandemic has undoubtedly widened the scope of quality and quality management applications, to save millions of lives while at the same time creating new norms in man's daily activities. The pandemic has, for example, altered where and how people work, as a result of social distancing, and other quality management measures for flattening out the curve of the coronavirus infections and in mitigating its impact on the people [77].

In what appeared to be a new world order, the present focus of attention of the entirety of the people of the global community, on the healthcare sector, particularly with the challenges of the COVID-19 pandemic and the socioeconomic changes associated with the virus, *change management* cannot but be viewed as an inevitable part of factors to be considered in "*inventing*" quality for the next few decades.

Quality 4.0 Technologies or 4.0 Base Technologies

The major *stimuli for changes* now and in the immediate future of quality and quality management, among organizations and the people of the world, emanate generally from our existing experience of the COVID-19 pandemic, and that of the present extra-4.0 technologies environment, deeply rooted in Industry 4.0 initiatives of the twenty-first century.

Industry 4.0 is driven generally by technological advancements in the areas of ICT, electronics and control systems, big data generation, data analytics, collaboration, machine learning, interconnectivity, and scalability to innovate and drive the paradigm shifts in industrial manufacturing, as well as in the delivery of products/services that meet and represent stakeholders' SNEaRs and values at competitive levels. The realities of the fourth industrial revolution or Industry 4.0 is centered, therefore, around the developing (digital) 4.0 base technologies and most importantly, their *interconnectivity*. These developing 4.0 base technologies comprise among others those of the following:

- Artificial intelligence (AI).
- Machine learning (ML).
- Industrial Internet of Things (IIoT).
- Internet of Things (IoT).
- Big data and Data Lakes—generating appropriate data and the swift and effective collation of the data from various sources, generally help to create and empower informed organizational ability for agile decision-taking.
- Analytics—very good metrics contribute largely to achieving quality objectives.
- Cloud computing/technologies.
- App development/software development.
- Mobile technology.
- Virtual reality (VR) and augmented reality (AR).
- 3D printing or large-scale additive manufacturing (AM)
- Social media and block chain
- Connectivity—in Quality 4.0 refers to the connection or connectivity between business information technology (IT)—quality management systems, product management, and business resource planning; and the business operational technology (OT)—technology used in industrial manufacturing processes, laboratory systems, and service environments. Connectivity can be achieved using sensors to link people through smart devices, products, and machines. This helps too in achieving real-time or near real-time feedback if appropriately adapted.
- Scalability.

Quality 4.0

Quality 4.0 initiatives are aligned with those of Industry 4.0 perspectives to result in transformations that are technologically driven, to transform organizations in the way they execute their day-to-day business activities, ultimately culminating in business cultural changes. This will, in turn, impact not just the workforce and organizational leadership, but various other organizational business parameters—productivity or manufacturing efficiency, supply chain performance, product/services innovation, meeting customer and regulatory SNEaRs, and *quality*. This thus brings quality to the rollcall of 4.0 technologies. Other areas impacted by Industry 4.0 revolution, include among others, market and economic factors, sociostructural changes, labor market, and other off-shoots of technological advancements. A key factor here is the need to perform advanced analytics on gathered data, big data—a tremendous amount of data.

The birth of Industry 4.0 is based primarily on its envisaged interconnectivity and communications potentials to increase production efficiency, productivity, improved returns on investment (ROI), and competitiveness, with the overall results of organizational improvement. The primary application of quality too is to achieve the same objectives of making organizations more competitive. The evolution of quality ab initio has been in general alignment with the stage-by-stage industrial manufacturing growth and development, and this led to the understanding for organizations to seize the opportunity of the digitization momentum resulting from Industry 4.0 initiatives, to align Quality 4.0 with corporate or organizational management strategy.

Quality 4.0 must therefore be leveraged so as to enable organizations to more easily overcome lingering quality challenges, generally associated with poor organizational quality culture, lack, or poor utilization of data-driven quality decisions, and insufficient cross-functional visibility. Quality 4.0 thus exhibits the potentials to overcome some of these data-related challenges "with increased data transparency and new high veracity data driven insights" (Dan [23, 45]).

Quality 4.0 technologies must therefore be seen from the perspectives of the ability of industrial manufacturing outfits to achieve real values, in terms of production efficiency, gaining competitive edge, improved quality, cost efficiency, and innovation. Quality 4.0 initiatives shall, however, emerge to ultimately thrive on its being built upon the solid foundational base of the traditional quality and quality management practices.

Organizations aiming to succeed must therefore get quickly adapted to digitization transformational changes for sustainability, no matter the rate at which changes occur, particularly for the reasons of its inevitability and permanency. Hence, the need for quality leadership preparedness at all times, to effectively exhibit the capability of driving an organizational culture in which change, is not just accepted, but adequately integrated and managed [72]. Political leadership across global communities is, however, not excluded.

Afterward, the lessons of the COVID-19 pandemic and its mitigation with quality tools and principles openly demonstrated how critical the quality of political leadership could be for the people of the world and its socioeconomic activities. Going into a new decade with the COVID-19 pandemic, further accentuates the general call for quality leadership to arm itself with the ability to effectively focus on and manage and/or mitigate risks in the quality management system not just for business survival but for global sustainability.

Adapting Industry 4.0 to Quality 4.0 Initiatives

Quality 4.0 is thus used in reference to Industry 4.0. The nucleus of Quality 4.0 is embedded in organizations and businesses aligning "the practice of quality management with the emerging capabilities of Industry 4.0," to help in driving organizations in their efforts to achieve operational excellence (Juran, [47]). On the basis of this alignment, therefore, the perspectives of Quality 4.0 include 11 key components which must, however, be used along or blended with existing quality management principles/philosophy, tools, techniques, and methods.

Quality 4.0 initiatives thus emerge from blending traditional quality with Industry 4.0. It follows, therefore, that both Industry 4.0 and Quality 4.0 coexist on the platform of 4.0 technologies in a tripartite relationship, represented in Fig. 20.1.

Both Industry 4.0 and Quality 4.0 which are represented, respectively, by the two of the three equal sides of a triangle, are defined on a general basis by 4.0 technologies, represented by its base. The author thus refers, therefore, to the 4.0 technologies as the *base technologies.*

Organizational Adaptivity and Agility

While the sudden exposure of the global population to the deadly, COVID-19 pandemic has unexpectedly put a renewed urgency and manufacturing attention behind automation and the use of robotics, it succeeded in putting organizational supply chain management strategies to question, with the insistence that there is a dire need now, for organizations, irrespective of size, products/services, and location on the globe, and their leadership, to immediately reevaluate their quality management value system to find the most appropriate place for agility and flexibility.

Today, there is a cause for concern in the quality imbalance resulting from the virtual reliance of the global community, mainly on supplies from one country, China. The caveat here is that such quality imbalance is dangerous for the quality of the world we live in and the life that we all live, as it triggers and motivates the realization of China's dream to economically strangulate most countries of the world to submit to her economic dominance and dictatorial commercial tendencies.

The taste of this desire was experienced as the threat of the COVID-19 pandemic became realizable in the United States, when healthcare organizations had no

Fig. 20.1 Tripartite relationships—4.0{Industry + Technologies + Quality}

alternative than to move swiftly to conserve resources, an unusual practice in American healthcare management practices. As reported by Zolnierek [95], some of the unusual and unthinkable reactions which negated infectious disease control measures include among others:

- Conservation of personal protective equipment.
- Removal of masks from patient area and rationed to staff.
- Nurses had to wear same PPE between patients.
- Nurses had to store masks in bags for reuse.
- N95s were kept under lock and key, to be provided only to staff encountering patients who are undergoing aerosolizing procedures.

Most of the PPEs are today manufactured in China from where supplies were not forthcoming at the onset of the pandemic. As affirmed by Edmund [27], "The COVID-19 outbreak highlighted the potential risks associated with a one-source, China-based manufacturing practice."

Many changes were implemented in the healthcare workplace that are entirely different from anything that have been previously witnessed. The pandemic, no doubt, led to the creation of a disruptive healthcare management environment, in most parts of the world, which subsequently resulted to the *adaptive space*.

For an organization to be agile calls for visionary leadership capability to envisage, react, and adjust quickly to new and/or crisis situations, uncertainties, and disruptive environment. Such disruptive situations have been rightly addressed by Lindborg [55], who, in a conversational report with Arena [8] claimed, "In today's disruptive environment, we must ensure that our organizations and institutions are agile—they must be able to respond to change instantly and effectively." This accordingly makes up Arena and Lindborg's *"adaptive space."*

Edmund [27] more succinctly advised organizations, "They should embrace uncertainty as part of their operating model, since agility and ability to adapt quickly will be far more important than sticking to a plan." This is further ascertained by Lindborg in, "We live in the era of disruption in which the lack of agility is kiss of death."

In my own view, the *adaptive space* is that *fraction of time* and the small *window of opportunity* available to organizations to as quickly, as perhaps the lightning, react and adapt to counter any disruption or disruptive act which otherwise would have resulted to catastrophic outcomes in the way human life may be disrupted by it.

The differences here center mainly on the fact that there is no room or sufficient time to plan, manage, coordinate, and control activities in the usual manner of achieving operational efficiency. In a twinkle of an eye, organizations, institutions, and at times mankind itself are badly disrupted. In cases of disruption, or in disruptive environment, reaction must have to be instantaneous, swift, and consequential in a way akin to collapsing the usual quality management principles of *plan-do-check-act* into one single phase of activities. It is the dynamism involved in adaptive space which separates it from the usual change management we have hitherto been used to.

No matter how steady and reliable your supply chain may have been, what happened to the people of the world at the advent of the COVID-19 pandemic in 2020, simply taught us generally that no system is disruption-proof. Hence, there is the need for every organization to create the needed adaptive space for immediate adaptability, else organizations have no other alternative than to face the consequences of disruption, some of which may be deadly. This is exactly where new roles for quality leadership have resurfaced.

Quality Leadership in Disruptive Environment

That the world's 7.8 billion people were taken unawares by the COVID-19 pandemic despite the previous preventative warning and precautionary political calls for elevated quality in governance, in order to guide against this type of a pandemic by a US government tells a lot about the role of quality and quality management of people and the dire need for quality political leadership in the twenty-first century.

It is not just enough to handle leadership roles strictly from the perspective of Newton's laws of motion, without putting into consideration the real-life fact of change being inevitable, especially in today's frequently emerging *"disruptive changes."* Leadership must therefore be conscious at all times that Newton's forces of disruption are lurking in the corner ready to strike, and strike big too, hence the need for organizational and institutional leadership agility in their preparedness to position organizations to adapt swiftly, perhaps at the speed of lightning, wherever possible and whenever needed.

The dynamism required for accomplishing organizational adaptability here, far surpasses that of a regular organizational drive for operational efficiency and effectiveness usually built around managing, coordinating, and control. With the concentration of organizational attention on operational activities, the needed focus on agility and the organizational dynamism for accomplishing may have been left out of consideration.

Enabling Leadership for Organizational Adaptability

The impact of political leadership on how the people of the world responded to adapting quality measures in protecting the population against the deadly COVID-19 pandemic simply demonstrates to the people of the global community that quality leadership must have to assume additional responsibility in terms of organizational adaptability to a disruptive environment, or catastrophic situations. This naturally requires more leadership dynamism different from those of the day-to-day quality leadership for achieving operational efficiency.

From the work of Lindborg [55] and the outcome of their research, Arena and Uhl-Bien [7] suggested that leading for adaptive space is not the same as traditional leadership as it involves the enablement of the adaptive process. This is achieved according to them by creating the space "for ideas and insights to be more actively explored, developed and scaled." It goes therefore to say that leadership for organizational adaptability or enabling leadership should to be in the position to facilitate necessary adaptive activities required for accomplishing organizational adaptability.

Risk Management

Risk management to enhance effective organizational management and performance shall be key aspects of quality, as provided in the second decade of the new century, courtesy of the ISO in section "Introduction" of its latest version of ISO 9001:2015 requirements, "Actions to address risks and opportunities," [42].

In his committed and visionary leadership with foresightedness, the US government of President Barack Obama, [11] actually accentuated in 2014, the general need for the US government, and the people of the global community at large, to put plans in place to immediately take needed actions, to mitigate against, or address serious potential catastrophic risks of a pandemic, if and when it happens. He and his team were perhaps, ahead of the ISO, when they, in 2014, made the case for infrastructural quality management measures, to immediately tackle and rescue the populace from any potential pandemic that may surface on the planet earth, without impacting the quality of life in the world we all live in.

However, due to global leadership shortsightedness, or forgetfulness in 2020 about how devastating the impact of a pandemic of that nature and magnitude, when compared with the Spanish flu of 1918, could be for the people of the global community, the advice or suggestion either fell on deaf ears, or was immediately trashed, or disregarded by the new US government in 2016, and other national political leaders of countries all over the globe.

It may, on the other hand, have been viewed from the wrong side of "*quality management in governance,*" or perhaps as risk management often sounds, be viewed as an intimidating proposal by a political opponent of high performance, which does not deserve to be considered. Only God knows why such a global risk management panacea was grossly ignored both from the national perspective and on the international platform!

As suggested by Cochran [20], "If you don't bother to manage risks, you'd better be very good at handling crisis. The investment you make in risk management is going to be much less than the cost and time, necessary to handle fully-blown problems." What manner of incurring an extremely and unprecedentedly unnecessary cost of quality (CoQ) did the people of the global community embark on prior to COVID-19 years of 2020/21 until the vaccines were available!

The cost of quality (CoQ) in governance, in the particular situation of the novel corona virus, can easily be extrapolated from the cost of lives lost to the pandemic; people who went hungry, enormous public funds disbursement for emergency purposes, the number of jobs lost; organizations that had to wind up operations; people who lost their homes; quality emergency measures taken to abate the deadly impacts of the virus; money needed to develop and distribute impromptu vaccines; the pain and agonies of people who lost their family members to the pandemic; and so on.

Lives lost as reported by the VOA News for the United States of America are 345,000 in 20 million cases which represents about 1.73%, as against global pandemic deaths of 1.8 million of 83.5 million cases, a death rate of about 2.16%. The case of the COVID-19 pandemic ushered into the world, a new level of quality appreciation in the healthcare sector which is believed continue to be maintained and expanded upon.

The future will definitely witness quality expansion into wider scopes of application in industry, commerce with shift more toward e-commerce, research, education, and newer disciplines such as enumerated by Kimberlin [48] to include microfluids, genetics, biology, physics, biophysics, electronics, software, and other areas of human activities.

Beginning with what could be boldly tagged as, "*the electronics quality decade*," 2021–2030,"" and the challenges of the COVID-19 pandemic, is a strong indication of the global need for honest, committed, and effectively enabling quality leadership of vision and character, both in governance and in businesses, particularly in the regions of the less developed economies of the world—Africa and South America.

Bio-risk management has again been brought to the limelight by the ISO in its ISO 35001:2019.

"Quality-Leading" Transitional Phases

The critical and important role of "quality-leading" organizations, countries, entities, and any other bodies during this new decade can, therefore, not be overemphasized, especially in a quality-leadership transitional decade, when new academic-oriented quality practitioners are poised to take over the mantle of quality leadership, from the fading influence of our passing quality "*gurus*" of the twentieth century. Leadership through quality (LtQ) can, according to Watson [92], be achieved by integrating three quality-related elements—*quality management, quality development,* and *quality culture*—all into a singular *management system.* This translates practically into leadership competency in TQM systems.

Leadership involvement in quality education and research, theoretical footing, and advancement of quality shall be far more pronounced in the next few decades of the twenty-first century, to drive imminent *changes*, "*invent*" innovative *challenges*, and proffer *solutions* to various quality surprises of the future. The permanency of evolving changes during the decades ahead will bear its pangs in the evolving surprises and challenges of quality, at the rate at which such surprises and challenges are encountered.

The importance of quality leadership in governance is globally exhibited for the people of the world by the US government of President Barrack Obama (US President, 2008 to 2016) when, as widely reported in 2014, he used the experience with which his government handled the 2009 H1N1 (swine flu) and the 2014 Ebola outbreaks, to prepare the people of the USA and the entirety of the global community, in readiness to immediately and effectively react against any future pandemic challenges, by requesting for the setting up a public health infrastructure across the globe [11].

This is captured vividly in his speech, "There may and likely will come a time in which we have both an airborne disease that is deadly....And in order for us to deal with that effectively, we have to put in place an infrastructure—not just here at home, but globally—that allows us to see it quickly, isolate it quickly, respond to it quickly, so that if, and when a new strain of flu like the Spanish flu crops up five years from now or a decade from now, we've made the investment and we're further along to be able to catch it" and quickly too.

What is seen here is a real responsive and effective *quality people leadership*. The challenges and surprises envisaged for the future of quality and quality management therefore requires that *leadership* is not just a strong ingredient for the future of our quality world, but an essential part of it, an inevitable integral.

There are no doubts whatsoever that quality shall, in the twenty-first century, continue to spread its tentacles, branches, and appendages, further in its existing areas of application, both nationally and internationally, and deeper into new spheres of human activities and endeavors, to embrace global acknowledgment from decade to decade. No wonder therefore, that, the results of the ASQ future studies [9] affirmed and acknowledged viewing the future of quality strongly from the purview of five different perspectives comprising of the following:

- Leadership
- Aerospace and defense
- Manufacturing
- Healthcare
- Education

It is the view of the author that, in addition to software, AI (artificial intelligence) and robotics application especially through the digital transformation, the new decade shall additionally witness in-depth and further in-roads of quality into areas such as the following:

- ***Governance and public services***—especially in most parts of the global community where the enthronement of transparency and accountability in governance is urgently needed to stem a new era of people enslavement, as it was in the centuries when slavery thrived. Quality management is viewed as a serious consideration for getting the people of the African continent out of the woods of gross leadership negligent and mis-leadership evils. A good example here is the reported application of the ISO 9001:2015 [42] framework by some ASQ member leaders, in proposing improvements to democratic progresses by "Advancing a Quality Management System for U.S. Elections" [46]. This is again a very good example for African and South American countries to learn from.
- ***Research and development***—to dig further into the theoretical architecture of quality management tools, concepts, principles, and philosophies; quality training and education; measurement systems advancement; and the development of, and exploitation of managing quality with digital tools to guide organizations through digital disruption for sustainability. Quality should be viewed strictly

from the perspective of being an embodiment of a feasible knowledge body capable of standing on its own as a ***discipline*** the whole world has been crying for and anxious to have. Building the quality mindset is therefore critical for human survival.

- ***Environmental management***—issues, such as global warming, which may end up to globally revolutionize quality, especially in sustainable environmental management matters of international political expediencies. This may not be the end of a pandemic like the COVID-19, hence, there is the general need for caution in the years ahead. Transparency represents our guiding word in conjunction with quality management tools and techniques.
- ***International trade***—products and services quality to reduce dumping and trade injustice which has hitherto elude millions of the people of the global village, especially the African people. The people of African countries have been held to ransom by their own mis-leadership, most of whom dubiously collaborate with trade partners behind the door, to corruptly deprive their own people of quality products/services including the importation of deadly and/or fake pharmaceutical products. Compromising the integrity of life-threatening products can only be avoided through effective quality management practices.
- ***Risk and uncertainty management***—just as the COVID-19 pandemic has succeeded in compelling organizations and businesses to make survival-based decisions such as COVID-19-related imposed restrictions, and investments in vaccine, the potentials for future risks and uncertainties calls for organizations and businesses to carry out an in-depth autopsy of the COVID-19 pandemic. This shall serve as a learning process for quality improvement purposes. The importance of a post-COVID-19, fact-based and quality-focused lessons-learned analysis, should be used to advantage in developing a post-COVID-19 era operational model with the inherent features of needed flexibility, agility, and adaptability to effectively prevent, and if necessary, challenge future disruptive environmental challenges and uncertainties. Hence, we should, from the quality perspective, view the COVID-19 pandemic and Industry 4.0 vis-à-vis Quality 4.0 as catalysts of change in the world of today. Most importantly too is to warn organizations against being complacent. Rather, they should create the quality culture in all ramifications while remaining agile, adaptive, flexible, and continually motivate, realign, and empower employees to embrace, accept, tolerate, and proactive to change.

The experience gained from each of the evolutionary stages of quality (Table 20.1) was in no doubt put to use as building blocks of future quality platform and leadership forum needed to nurture, breed, and grow the next and subsequent phases of quality development, the Quality 4.0 initiatives.

Quality has hitherto been highly driven by industrial product competitiveness of the global economy, particularly, in the second half of the twentieth century. This, in turn, promoted the conceptual evolution of quality and its business management principles, tools, and frameworks to the level, glaringly visible in our day-to-day life experience and general lifestyle. Quality dynamism and its impact and influence on man's development never since then stopped growing and expanding both in width and scope, locally and internationally, in every nook and corner of the world economy. The dynamisms of quality influence cannot be stopped, hence, the likelihood of its continued growth, in the immediate and distant future.

The continued internalization of quality shall continuously and consistently be widely promoted by various organizations and businesses, while quality professionalism shall be widely and consistently promoted and motivated with various quality awards locally, nationally, and internationally. Such organizations include among others the International Organization for Standardization (ISO), the American Society for Quality (ASQ), the European Organization for Quality (EOQ), and the Standards Organization of Nigeria (SON) just to name a few.

Institutions of quality management awards are numerous all over the world including, the Deming Prize, Malcolm Baldrige National Quality Award (MBNQA), (NIST [63, 64, 84]), the European Quality Awards (EQA), International Quality Awards for Professionals and Organizations, and many more in various regions of the world [83].

This century shall likely witness a situation in which each of the many quality bodies of the world, which are organizational quality leaders by their own rights, shall need to be more effectively inter-connected with quality professionals all over the globe, more than it has hitherto been, in this decade, to connectedly galvanize, broaden, and widen the education and delivery of quality into all aspects of people's lives. There are therefore likely going to be many more and wider range of such quality awarding bodies across the globe in the twenty-first century to motivate and promote product and service quality and excellence.

It is for these and other relevant reasons that my quality dream going into the next few decades centers most importantly around the nationally, internationally, and intercontinentally broadened spheres of quality leadership and professionalism. This will undoubtedly help to spread the tentacles of quality—its practice, use, application, and deployment to the nooks and corners of the global socioeconomic communities to minimize poverty and economic wastages, around the lives of millions of the people of the world, particularly in Africa and South America. This shall help to accomplish the effective building of the quality mindset among the people of the world. We are therefore going to witness a decade of intense depth and growth in various perspectives of quality from education/training and research to governance, public sector, general application, and deployment.

The role of quality in the economically just-beginning-to-develop or not-yet-developed economies of the 1.34 billion people of Africa, and their 430 million counterparts in South America, is going to be more pronounced in the twenty-first century than it has ever been. It is therefore expected that quality shall be held most importantly to highest level of acknowledgments, particularly in these two continents but also by others in the underlisted areas of quality application:

- Quality training, education, and research. More universities and other institutions of higher education/learning shall embrace quality into its curricula folds.

- Increased quality awards to promote and motivate professionalism in research, practice, and application of quality and its management principles across the globe.
- Increased deployment of quality management principles, philosophies, and science to public services in governments and governance, to achieve the true norms of democratic governance through promotion of transparency, and eradication of corruption, to improve the people's overall quality of life.
- International trade to curtail and reduce the exportation of fake and noncompliant products/services with the sole aim of eradicating dumping, especially from India, China, Taiwan, Thailand, etc., to the economically poorer countries of the world, located mostly in the African continent.
- Quality deployment to solve the challenges of the mysteries of the COVID-19 pandemic in all spheres of human activities, particularly to improve healthcare services—social distancing, wearing the face mask, hand washing and PPE, documentation, information sharing, measurement, quality management meetings, management reviews and training, and vaccination development and distribution.

Viewing the future of quality from the purview of its original growth, from practical application in shop floors or hands-on experience to its conceptual development, gives us hope for the future.

Quality management, thus, remains a strong platform on which we can comfortably rely upon, to face various sustainability challenges to human life and humanity in general—known or unknown. Using the deadly threat of the COVID-19 pandemic as a strong launch pad to create the momentum for driving quality and quality-thinking abilities among the people of the world is a blessing in disguise for the quality world and the planet earth.

Quality Mindset to the Rescue

The effective deployment of quality management principles in managing the sudden but unique challenges of the COVID-19 pandemic in most hospitals, that is, the healthcare sector, of the global economy, has demonstrably proved to be far beyond mere political braggadocio, as witnessed in the recent global leadership responses. The way in which the pandemic was handled across the globe is directly or indirectly a reflection of the quality of political leadership vis-a-vis leadership responsibility. This is especially so in leadership or mis-leadership responses in either enforcing or motivating the followership to follow the quality guidelines of preventative measures—face mask-wearing, social distancing, avoiding gatherings, and consistent hand-washing. For example, the case of the USA which recorded, according to the VOA News, about 20 million cases and 345,000 deaths as at 07.39 hours, on January 01, 2021, when compared with world figures of, respectively, 83.5 million and 1.8 million, is tantamount to relatively poor quality of leadership vis-à-vis the negligence of leadership responsibility.

TQM Tools in Global Healthcare Systems

"Quality-Answering" COVID-19 Pandemic "9-1-1 Calls"

The healthcare sector and the employees were primarily at the receiving end of the COVID-19 pandemic as they are, by virtue of their professional practice, ethics, and responsibilities, made to bear the brunt of the deadly pangs of the novel coronavirus. As the first line of defense against COVID-19 pandemic, they deployed necessary quality measures and services to protect humanity. Nurses, nursing assistants, respiratory therapists, and doctors put their lives at risk to care for those infected with the virus. Quality management measures used to reinforce the treatment, protection and care for patients include, among others, the following:

- Broad increase and expansion of telehealth and telemedicine to attend to patients not affected by the COVID-19 pandemic who needed to be protected against it.
- Virtual gatherings to protect people from being exposed to the spread of the corona virus.
- Working from home arrangements to reduce exposure, thereby, preventing people from being exposed to infection.
- Improved poly-directional communications among healthcare workers, researchers, and the centers for disease control and prevention (CDC) all over the country.

These inevitable quality management improvement changes to routine healthcare systems may have been here to stay in what is described by Zolnierek [95] as, "The New Normal." According to Oestereich et al. [68], the quality improvement teams at Cleveland Clinic quickly deployed suitable quality measures "to guide the care of patients with suspected or confirmed COVID-19 infection and protect care givers."

These measures vary from increased frequency of the quality improvement team members' meetings from monthly to daily or weekly, and the establishment of appropriate task forces, to put protocols in place for guiding the transportation of patients, management of the airway, to the management of personal protective equipment (PPE) and medications which are in short supply. In addition, nonessential surgeries were postponed and overflow intensive care units (ICU) set up onsite.

A web-based COVID-19 tool kit was created for all care givers, who are, on a daily basis, sent e-mails on the most recent information about the pandemic with respect to developments, decisions, and recommendations from national and international societies. Effective quality communication, healthcare education, national and international connectedness, professional collaboration across the globe, and quality and patient safety data played key roles in the application of quality to solve the sudden and unexpected challenges of the COVID-19 pandemic to humanity.

The relevance and application of quality and its management principles and methodologies in healthcare services are reported by LariSemnani et al. [53] who claimed the use of TRIZ in improving the quality of hospital services. Quality has similarly assumed some degree of prominence in hospital management and health-care particularly during the era of COVID-19 pandemic as reported by Sonis et al. [81] and O'Reilly et al. [67] in their quick switch from in-person training to virtually educate "trainees, both within the institute and the organization" for the purpose of maintaining social distancing as quality measures to curb the spread of the pandemic among the populace.

Quality professionals and professional organizations across the globe have been directly or indirectly acknowledged through the visible impacts of quality on the world around us, especially during the 2020/21 pandemic years.

The role of the ASQ, the leading quality organization, and others across the globe cannot be overemphasized. They therefore deserve some credit for the successful deployment of quality in fighting the COVID-19 pandemic. This fact is recently attested to by a white paper series, "Quality's Impact on the Global Pandemic Response," which reportedly "explored how quality principles were essential for successful development, distribution and administration of the COVID-19 vaccine" [46].

There are no doubts too that the future of quality needs committed professional drivers in the likes of those energetic *quality gurus* of the twentieth century, most of whom collaborated on common grounds, to conceptually promote and developed quality, to its present level of global acknowledgment and appreciations.

Just as the history of quality cannot be told without reference to the immense contributions and achievements of all the acknowledged quality *"gurus"* of the twentieth century, the future of quality and its management integrational trends shall not be definable without the commitment of upcoming professionally inclined quality *"gurus of the future"* across industry, professional bodies, academia, and research. The level and success of quality integration in the future is, however, highly dependent on collaborative abilities, and interconnectedness across all fields of human endeavor to integrate and deploy quality in all areas of human activities, especially those which are in dire need of continuous improvement and performance excellence.

It is for these reasons that the author foresees a twenty-first century of quality collaboration and integration, across the interfaces of human knowledge and needs. In this way, we shall widely grow quality more, on the premise of evidence-based research models and results, than on conceptualization, as we transmit from the guru-based paradigm to a globally driven paradigm. Creating the quality mindset in the twenty-first century will be championed by various professional bodies and organizations, such as the ISO and the EFQM, quality professionals across the globe, and professional organizations such as the ASQ, universities, and others across the globe.

The future of quality thus portends greater achievements, through the exploitation of all opportunities for cooperation, collaboration, and connectedness in line with the suggestions of Andersen et al. [4] for a "single integrated model for defining and conducting improvement projects" among the people of the world.

Growing TQM in Healthcare Systems

The importance for organizations to invest in leadership, time, capital, and technical expertise in continuous quality improvement efforts [16] resonated widely among various sectors of the economy, including healthcare organizations, particularly in western economies. It is interesting therefore that, as at today, healthcare organizations have increasingly embraced the efficient delivery of high-quality, safe healthcare [50]. In addition, too, is the general need for the prioritization of safety in this critical sector of the global economy. This has consequently led to the recognition of the importance of implementing quality management systems and developing the culture of safety and quality mindset. Quality management systems should, therefore, be seen in healthcare systems "as a set of interacting activities, methods, and procedures used to monitor, control and improve the quality of care" [89, 91].

Leadership involvement in healthcare and hospital systems' quality management is critical most essentially because of its heavy involvement with people's lives. Various researchers [80, 88, 90] have established that the components of a hospital-level quality management system incorporate the following:

- The monitoring of quality by the board
- Quality policy documents implementation
- Processes analysis and their improvement
- Formal protocols
- The measurement of outcomes

Hospital quality management systems thus leads generally to the establishment and rooting of a safety culture across the hospital systems. Instituting the culture of safety in hospitals has undoubtedly resulted in drastic reduction in patient errors, hence, the need for continued implementation of quality management measures in hospitals across the globe, particularly in the developed economies where quality measures are urgently needed to reduce patient errors in the healthcare systems, which are daily crying for improvements.

Similarly, the implementation of quality management system measures to create the culture of patient care and safety in correctional healthcare systems for the twenty-first century must have to grow substantially across the globe.

The Magnet Status

Quality application in the healthcare sector is quite massive. It generally begins from the effective identification of patients at every point of treatment, consultation to the patient discharge point. Ethical and professional practices are equally expected to meet both customer SNEaRs and regulatory requirements at every level of healthcare practice—hospitals including teaching hospitals, clinics, other healthcare teaching institutions, nursing homes/assisted living, outline facilities, outpatient facilities, etc. Since the healthcare business focusses mainly on human healthiness and ability to live, the role of quality in every activity of the medical staff is of the utmost importance. Medical metrics and medical equipment calibrations are critical areas of quality measurements in healthcare quality management systems.

Today, the presence and importance of quality management in healthcare systems is being more and more openly embraced than it has ever been. Apart from the role of quality management tools and principles and techniques to mitigate the deadly impacts of the novel coronavirus, various healthcare systems are massively embracing evidence-based practice (EBP) and other healthcare performance improvement measures.

Led by the American Nurses Credentialling Center (ANCC), the healthcare systems are today witnessing one of the strongest and most powerful quality management certification institutions or agencies in the history of the healthcare sector in the USA. This has been largely accomplished by the ANCC through its ***Magnet Status*** certification for hospitals.

According to Gagnon [35], a Magnet hospital is a medical facility considered the gold standard for nursing practices. Hence, Magnet hospitals are ANCC-certified heath management institutions "where nurses are empowered to not only take the lead on patient care but to be the drivers of institutional health care change and innovation." In emphasizing healthcare *change management, innovation* in *safer work environments for staff* the ANNC and its Magnet Status have led the world of safer healthcare management system for the entirety of the human world, as a good example worthy of emulation by other professional bodies or entities in other areas of services to humanity.

The depth of quality offerings of hospitals with Magnet Status has been reportedly ascertained by the National Center for Biotechnology Information (NCBI) as offering safer work environments for staff than non-Magnet institutions. The author has not only experienced the impact of the Magnet Status, but can attest to the affirmation by the NCBI not just as a patient or a customer in this case, but also through his home life interaction with his wife, Mojisola Bimbo, a naturally inspired and university educated nurse, born with the most passionate caring heart, and endowed with the most skillful people-caring hands, in her active participation and involvement in Parkland Health & Hospital System's successful certification to the ANCC Magnet Status.

As a quality-conscious patient, the excellent and outstanding healthcare services always rendered by the nurses of the Parkland Health & Hospital System (PHHS) both at the main hospital level and among its affiliated clinics are highly appreciated. It is glaringly convincing from my personal experience over a long period of time, therefore, that the excellent quality management roles of nurses working for the Parkland Health & Hospital System and its affiliated clinics within the Dallas County cannot be overemphasized.

No matter from which perspective the quality of hospitals, or any other healthcare system is viewed, nurses remain the skeletal backbone structure of the *quality of care*. This conclusion is generally based on the author's customer roles in various healthcare systems. Nurses' quantum of care provision—minute-by-minute, hour-by-hour, and day-by-day—activities are far more dominant and superior to those of most other members of the healthcare teams in the feedback provided as follows:

- Patient/healthcare staff contact hours (PHCH)
- Patient review times
- Patient experience
- Patient care monitoring/observation abilities and strong documentational needs
- Patient care commitment and attachment—physical, emotional, and psychological
- Patient's first point of call and attention
- 24/7 Patient handling/treatment focal healthcare personnel
- Major coordinator of all patient care team members to ensure that patients get what they need, as and at when needed
- Central player in healthcare quality management system

With the abovementioned customer feedback structure, it becomes evident that nurses are the center point of healthcare quality role-modeling. They are virtually more of the dictates of the general quality of hospitals/other healthcare systems and that of patients through the following qualities of the nurses:

- Ethical and professional commitments/practices
- Overall presence in healthcare management team
- Change management abilities
- Daily appearance or aesthetics
- Team management abilities
- Strong coping abilities in daily changing environment, especially in the emerging needs for diversity nursing
- Effective communication and documentation
- Educating patients and their relations
- Strong adaptive abilities
- Roles in the sustainability of the healthcare systems

It is therefore generally surprising that the general public, more often than not, generally view or see the high quality of healthcare systems from the perspective of doctors and surgeons to undermine the quantum of nurses' roles and involvement. Nurses thus remain the undisputed front line of quality, whether viewed in terms of safety or customer care. The healthcare quality management systems thus revolve around the *nurse*. This was also exhibited in the general hospital responses, across the global community, to the COVID-19 pandemic patients.

This established central role of the nurse in the quality of healthcare thus brings out the criticality of the *Magnet Status* in the healthcare sector as inherent in the Magnet Status requirements, some of which are, according to Gagnon [35], listed as follows:

- Nursing excellence
- Innovation in nursing practice
- Quality patient outcomes
- Work environments

The future of quality when viewed from a general perspective is once again confirmed here to be rooted on a global platform in *excellence, innovation, work environments, sustainability,* and *adaptability* to disruptive environment.

As quality advances in our daily changing environment, particularly in the digital environment, there shall be the general need for transformational QM leadership from the 2020s to the middle of the century. This similarly represent the age of *"quality in transition."*

Quality 4.0 Impact in Healthcare

The Influence of Industry 4.0 is demonstrably seen to be pitching its tent in the industrial manufacturing sector of the economy such as in robotics and automation as glaringly visible in the present massive deployment of AI and sensors. There is today a growing confidence in artificial intelligence (AI) among industrial manufacturing organizations. Delays in embracing AI has been reported in the outcome of a survey by the Association for Advancing Automation as being due primarily to data scarcity [10].

The healthcare system and the emergence of its quick deployment of ***telehealth*** in caring for patients during the COVID-19 pandemic disruption of the highest global magnitude in recent years represent some of the quality healthcare service strides portending the future expectations in the global healthcare systems. As a beneficiary of telehealth care deployment during the COVID-19 pandemic disruptions, the role, dedication, and commitment of healthcare practitioners cannot but be mentioned in this book, especially from the viewpoint of my experience. My personal physician at one of the Dallas Parkland Health & Hospital System (PHHS) clinics, Dr. Manisha Raja and her clinical healthcare team, committedly and excellently kept up with patient healthcare needs through telephone calls, a gesture highly appreciated by the author, as one of the beneficiaries. Dallas PHHS's leadership role in virtual care cannot be overemphasized, as it is in the forefront of the current digital transformation in the healthcare industry.

Taking advantage of telemedicine/telehealth is generally of tremendous help to patients especially, when viewed from the perspectives of allaying patient fears, to restore the hopes of many patients, and strengthen their psychological preparedness and determination to fight back—whether it is against the deadly coronavirus, or other ailments/diseases, in line with, for example, the quality measures deployed globally to protect and save people's lives against the COVID-19 pandemic.

There are no doubts, therefore, that the roll out of Industry 4.0 initiatives shall obviously impact the outcome of the subsequently envisaged Quality 4.0 initiatives. The way Quality 4.0 initiatives are likely going to impact the healthcare and hospitals system is similar to that of industrial manufacturing especially in terms of services improvement—automation and robotics application, interconnectivity of medical equipment and people, cross-communication between medical testing machinery (M2M) to speed up the outcomes of patient tests and diagnosis. Digital transformation in the healthcare sector shall obviously be slower, but more progress is likely coming toward the end of the first half of the twenty-first century when surgery may include more of robotics, massively improved interconnectivity in all ramifications of healthcare, faster diagnosis than envisaged, and medical errors shall continue to be reduced to its barest minimum. *Healthcare 4.0* shall continue to evolve and be shaped in line with *4.0 technologies* as listed above, and with social media and communications advancements. Healthcare shall therefore grow aligning its quality management initiatives with those of 4.0 technologies for sustainability and stronger interconnectedness.

Healthcare 4.0 and 4.0 Base Technologies

Just as industries rely on their employees for innovation and/or innovative ideas, certification to a program like the *Magnet Status* in the healthcare sector may most importantly motivate and bring out the nurses' innovative potentials. These quality management initiatives shall most likely be visible in the future of the nursing professional practice and patient care. In this way, and in collaboration and interconnectivity with and among relevant researchers, nurses and other healthcare practitioners shall advance in realization of their greater roles in healthcare quality management systems in line with 4.0 technological advancements—hospital information systems (HIS), point-of-care (POC) data entry, robotics, virtual care, electronic health records (EHR), innovations in imaging technologies, noninvasive treatments, and improved technologically controlled surgical procedures.

Like Industry 4.0 was primarily intended to make products and services more competitive, so also is the perspectives of the envisaged evolution *Healthcare 4.0* technologies, or perhaps *digital healthcare* likely to lead to allay human fears of the presently skyrocketing costs and inaccessibility of healthcare to many people across the globe. Healthcare 4.0 is thus envisaged to take advantage of 4.0 technologies to make healthcare more accessible and affordable to the people of our global community. The question here is whether a standard of healthcare level could globally be attained to make healthcare also competitive.

This may however never happen or may not be easily achieved even in the USA, without the cooperation of all involved stakeholders. For this to happen, therefore, there must be the drive, determination, and commitment by all concerned—healthcare providers, healthcare employers, policy makers, medical school owners/investors who made healthcare education and the tortuous route to achieving it a "*milking ground*" to frustrate potential healthcare providers, from the MCAT stage to that of loan-repayment phases for those medical practitioners who managed to scale through.

Growing Roles of ISO Standards in Healthcare

The role of the ISO in global quality management activities, not just among its about 164 members, but among, and for the people of the world, cannot be overemphasized, especially for its parade of over 22,500 international standards [44] (ISO and Health).

The activities of the international organization for standardization (ISO) are gradually penetrating the healthcare sector with emphasis on the following:

- Improving the quality of care
- Reducing the escalating costs of healthcare delivery to ensure access to healthcare services
- Protecting the safety of patients across the globe by ensuring safe medical practices and equipment

These fundamental healthcare roles of the ISO are strongly and deeply rooted in more than 1400 ISO healthcare standards among its about 22,500 international standards, some of which are specified as follows:

- ***ISO 45001***—Occupational Health and Safety Management Systems. There is a handbook, "A Practical Guide for Small Organizations" reportedly published jointly by ISO and UNIDO to help smaller economic units implement this standard. The most recent version of this standard is ISO 45001:2018.
- ***ISO 13485***—Medical devices—Quality Management Systems—Requirements for regulatory purposes. It was last reviewed in 2020 thus leaving the ISO 13485:2016 the latest version for certification purposes.
- ***ISO/TC 210***—Quality management and corresponding general aspects for medical devices.
- ***ISO/TC 198***—Sterilization of healthcare products.

ISO healthcare standards are quite beneficial for healthcare providers, patients, national governments, regulators, and healthcare product manufacturers, as well as other healthcare services providers.

From Quality Compliance Mentality to Performance

The present in-road of quality management system into the healthcare sector of the global economy is nothing but a living evidence of the captivating role of quality management tools, principles, and techniques in global healthcare patient services sector.

In the general acknowledgment of the effective roles of quality management systems in driving process output performance improvement, Navicent Heath reportedly "began a journey to transform its accreditation function from a "back-row" contributor to organizational performance to a key driver of continuous improvement" [15]. The report of Navicent Health's adoption of ISO 9001:2015 core quality management concepts, listed in the following, to improve organizational performance is a reflection of the extent to which quality management tools, principles, and techniques shall continue to be adopted, used, and implemented in the healthcare sector of the global economy.

- Top-down leadership involvement
- Continuous improvement
- Evidence-based decision-making
- Performance focus

In addition is the fact too that Navicent Health team successfully created, as reported, "the ISO 9001:2015 impact cycle to further influence organizational strategic goal setting and planning discussions." This is definitely another good example of the diverse use and application of ISO standards but particularly ISO 9001 international quality management systems (QMS) standards. On the overall, quality TQM tools, principles, and techniques offer endless opportunities for organizations—small, medium, and large. The sky is thus the limit quality in the twenty-first century.

Forefront of International Collaboration

There are no doubts whatsoever that the about 164-member countries of the international organization for standardization (ISO) shall continue to be the major central focus of quality collaboration, especially in the establishment and management of international standards. Such international collaboration for developing and integrating quality management systems standards is critical for growing and developing a series of application-specific quality management systems standards, on a broad international platform. It is therefore expected that the ISO shall within the decade continue to expand the scope of its series of quality systems standards into new areas of application and use, in response to the demands of its members for the interests of humanity at large, while regularly updating and upgrading existing ones.

Cooperation and collaboration between the ISO and professional bodies and organizations in the areas of quality systems standards shall continue to be a welcoming development. ISO may as it becomes necessary, merge and/or integrate existing quality systems standards as may be found necessary from time to time. Hence, quality development in the next decade shall rely most importantly, on a strong platform of organizational, institutional, and professional cooperation, collaboration, and interconnectedness, both at the national and international levels.

Research outputs from scholarly works are expected to play vital roles in consolidating quality and quality management sciences into courses of study at higher institutional level, or at least integrated with others. In the perspectives of Kimberlin [48], future quality and quality management successes are highly dependent on the following:

- Ready availability of effective and innovative quality servant leaders who are determined, willing, and committed to driving, promoting, advancing, and collaboratively leading the course of quality across national, professional, science, research, and educational boundaries to fulfil the needs and requirements of both customer and society.

- Building on and appropriately adapting and aligning existing knowledge, human experience, science, and research; integrating them to advance quality philosophy and quality management principles, systems, and methodologies, to solve ensuing quality challenges of customers and the society at large.
- Cross country and across the board professional collaboration and interconnectedness to promote quality and its adequate adaptation to the various challenges of the new decade and century, especially the Quality 4.0 initiatives.
- The integration of professionals and professional skills to extensively and collaboratively exploit innovative opportunities to achieve needed breakthroughs and to continuously maintain, promote, and improve quality and the integration of its systems.

The critical and important role of leadership in quality management cannot be overemphasized in defining the outlook of quality in the twenty-first century. The quality of national leadership in the global management of the COVID-19 pandemic across the nations of the world has most distinctively helped in identifying and ascertaining how quality and leadership have proved to be integral to human and societal values, in how people should be led and managed to achieve and maintain the quality of people's lives.

Quality Challenges in Post-COVID-19 Era

It is very glaring that future essentials of quality in post-COVID-19 era calls for collaboration and cooperation, innovation, new thinking, new approaches, and new initiatives. The risks inherent in the COVID-19 pandemic were apparently visible in the way it immediately impacted the quality of people's lives, catalyzing the accelerating pace of human life changes. It limited and curbed various socioeconomic activities, increased unemployment, worsened healthcare, where available, and worsened people's well-being on the overall—whether infected or not. The human psyche was heavily bruised by the pains of the pandemic to make them into victims of its attack in an environment of mixed quality leadership responses.

Highly impacted aspects of the human life are primarily in the healthcare sector, and the entertainment and tourism sectors of the economy—cinemas, theatres, restaurants, hotels, air travels, sports activities, and other aspects of social gatherings. Preplanned worldwide international interactive activities involving sports competitions such as the Olympic games, world cup soccer, football, boxing, and other sports competitions were not left unscathed. Most of them have to be cancelled, shifted, or postponed indefinitely. The COVID-19 pandemic has also generally impacted the political environment negatively, to create tensed political relationships, among the people of the world, worsening their general quality of life.

It must, however, be emphasized that the future status of quality practices, quality professionalism, and quality leadership, as well as their possible accomplishments in society, is undoubtedly subject to prevalent trends at the time. Such trends which have the tendencies to impact and affect societies and their economies are in addition, to the COVID-19 pandemic, the following suggested Lee [54]:

- Globalization
- Digitalization
- Changing industry mix
- Changing demographics
- Commoditization of value chain processes for products and services
- Exploding emerging economies
- Deteriorating environment

Similarly, Gutner and Adams [38] identified such trends as globalization and environmental concerns to tally with two of Lee's suggested factors mentioned above, and the following additional ones:

- Customer sophistication
- Talent management and leadership issues

Quality outlook challenges in the immediate future therefore calls for the following:

- Proper and more accurate identification of needed improvement possibilities and/or opportunities.
- Defining the most adequate and appropriate strategies, methodologies, and approaches to tackle and fix them.

It is highly imperative to emphasize the general need of the human community, on the overall to, as far as possible, push for, and achieve the greatest imaginable economic recovery to snatch their lives back from the destabilizing grips of the COVID-19 pandemic. Failure to achieve this objective with the current inoculation exercise shall further jeopardize the future of the global economy. Since quality itself is dynamic, there shall always be challenges in meeting varying improvement and developmental needs, in the application, use, and deployment of quality management tools, and techniques to provide goods and services that meet customer and stakeholders' SNEaRs in the most competitive ways.

The need for development in quality and quality management shall, in turn, continue to pose challenges to experts of quality in terms of subject matter knowledge, experience, and exploitation of new grounds/techniques. Since most businesses are set up for profit-making and market competitiveness, gaining competitive edge shall most definitely continue to define the use, application, and introduction of new techniques in managing product and services quality, for the future. Here the relevance of technology in quality management development in all spheres of human endeavor cannot be overemphasized.

Today's QM Options

One of the first question business owners would obviously ask themselves when thinking about improving the quality of their products/services or system is, "What is in it for me and my organization?" After getting satisfactory answers to this question, they may likely go further to ask the next question. Which of the available quality management systems/concepts is of the most economic benefit/competitive advantage for me to improve on my business performance? Some of the answers to these questions include, but are not limited to those provided below.

You can decide to use, or apply any, or some of the integrated quality management standards, systems, concepts or programs, and continuous improvement measures in the management and sustenance of the quality of your products/services for one or more of the following reasons or other reasons that that may be of benefit to you:

- To provide products/services that meet customer and regulatory SNEaRs.
- To put your organization and its products/services in good and proper standing, in the global market to enable overcoming the growing market challenges and competition of the global marketplace.
- To maintain and sustain your market leadership (through the use of process-implanted quality system, re-engineering, rebranding, and innovation).
- To enable you make your products in compliance with specified standards, regulatory requirements, or any other predetermined conditions.
- To maintain and possibly improve on your market standing by winning new customers in addition to your existing ones.
- To reduce operational costs by ensuring, on a first-time basis, defect-free production while eliminating wastes of all nature, types, and kind.
- As a proof, or for the verification of your organization's ability and capability, to make or produce, according to the SNEaRs of your current, or potential customers, thereby gaining their confidence.
- To continuously move your organization forward by ensuring the continual improvement of your quality management system to match any global market challenges and expectations.

A lot of quality management options are available for your choice just as there are experts who, through consultancy services, could help organizations with the necessary training and implementation guidelines.

Integrating Quality Management Systems/Standards

Just as the common saying goes, two heads are better than one, the integration of two standards or two quality management systems, may actually benefit or present the best solution to your organizational needs for performance improvement, or in solving special, or peculiar quality management challenges. The benefits inherent in such integrated systems are accentuated by the author's experience in integrating ISO 9001 requirements, processes, and documentations collectively with those of ISO 14001 and requirements to derive the benefits of optimizing the organization's processes to achieve the utmost effectiveness and efficiency in organizational performance improvement. It helped in creating one of the strongest awareness about the link between quality and environmental management systems, especially to reduce wastes, factory accidents, production downtime, and improved productivity.

Integrating relevant standards is, for example, a common practice in the aviation, space, and defense (ASD) organizations which, according to Daniels [24], "operate in a complex landscape of contractual, regulatory and statutory requirements." The relationship between a quality management system (QMS) and a safety management system (SMS) exists accordingly, among ASD organizations. It is longstanding, going back to the origins, when safety management systems (SMSs) were actually designed to be put to use with quality management systems (QMSs). The International Aerospace Quality Group (IAQG) has successfully realized the benefits of integrating both SMS and QMS requirements in its latest version of AS 9100D.

The opened door for the future integration of quality management systems QMSs with other relevant quality systems is viewed here with the utmost optimism, and this led to the opportunity of its frequent application in the future of quality management systems' deployment particularly in area-specific sectors of the globalized economy.

Perspectives of Innovation

Power of Management Innovation

Feigenbaum and Feigenbaum [31] exhibited exemplary foresightedness when they identified innovation as the future outlook for the quality profession in their book, *The power of management innovation* and in their earlier prediction of a new quality for the 21st century, [30].

The ISO, on its own part, acknowledged the future trend of quality management in the direction of quality management with creative innovation, as evident in its latest version of ISO 9004:

> **ISO 9004:2018**—*Quality Management—Quality of an Organization—Guidance to achieve sustained success [43].*

This guideline standard, both in context and contents, makes provision for a systematic, process-based approach to innovation and improvement processes, within a quality management system. It gives a wider scope of the application of improvements and innovations not just to include products, but also processes, technology, the structure, and constitution of an organization.

Quality professional activities in the USA, the world's largest economy, seem also to support the fact too that the future of the quality profession tends to point toward *innovation* and innovative initiatives in all aspects of product and services provision. The ASQ, the most widely acknowledged international quality body, already focuses attention on *innovation*. It operates a technical committee on innovation and value creation in its Quality Management Division, which according to Owens and Fritz [69] provides a clear definition of innovation management process as:

> A cycle beginning with creative spark, turning that concept into a solution that will generate value for customer, building that solution into a design that can be produced and delivered, and getting it to the market.

The tendency toward the need to implant innovation into QMSs is further strengthened by the global quality profession's embracing of innovation, as evidenced by its inclusion in the 2011–2012 Baldrige criteria [63, 64] as shown in the statements from two of its categories as cited by Merrill [59]. The statements from these two categories are as follows:

- Leadership should create an environment for innovation.
- Using customer information to find opportunities for innovation.

Quality development in Europe also tends toward this trend, as reflected in one of the eight (8) principles of the EFQM Excellence Model which states:

> Excellent organizations generate increased value and levels of performance through continual improvement and systematic innovation by harnessing the creativity of their stakeholders.

This part of the principles of the EFQM Excellence Model highlights the engagement of customers to innovate, and nurture creativity and innovation using networks as sources.

Putting these trends at the back of our minds, therefore, makes it obvious that quality outlook for tomorrow may more than anything else, be gazing more into the horizon of innovation and creativity than anything else. Hence, it becomes apparent that foresighted organizations looking forward to long-term competitive successes and advantages in the twenty-first century, need to plan for tomorrow, by ensuring that innovation and innovation management are implanted into their quality management culture and practices.

There are several options of quality management systems to which an organization can subscribe, and also implant new creative ideas and innovation. There is the option of subscribing to a single quality management system like the (latest) versions of the ISO 9000 series of QMS standards (ISO 9000:2015 [41], ISO 9001:2015 [42], and ISO 9004:2018 [43]) and improvement quality tools such as Lean, or Six Sigma, or the integration of both Lean and Six Sigma.

It could, on the other hand, be an integrated quality management system comprising of a combination of two or more individual systems or concepts. Whichever choice an organization makes in managing its processing systems for performance improvement, implanting it with innovation and creativity will undoubtedly result in a better, or improved competitive advantage for them. The quality outlook for tomorrow is hence strongly punctuated with *innovation* thereby stressing the need to constantly generate newer and newer ideas or initiatives, on the other hand.

While evidence available about quality management practices today point at implanting quality management systems/concepts generally with creativity and innovation, the outlook for tomorrow seem to encompass, on a broader basis, the following modes and specifics:

- The use of the ISO 9000 family of international standards will most likely remain prominent and gain wider use and application especially, among organizations which have the objectives of providing consistent products and services that meet customer SNEaRs with the aspiration to surpass them. This optimism is strengthened by the fact that the ISO, a body of knowledge in quality management, shall continue to update its QMS international standards as may be necessary.
- Six Sigma, Lean, and other specific quality management programs/concepts or a combination of them will continue to be popular choices.
- Organizations with like quality management philosophies and goals will most likely increase their quality management communications and interconnectivity, to create common quality and improvement management frameworks, in order to continually improve their business performance, in terms of achieving and sustaining the highest level of global market competitive abilities. The EFQM Excellence Model, as a typical example, shall most likely gain more popularity as more European organizations, especially from some of the former Eastern Bloc countries, are likely going to subscribe to the use of this comprehensive framework. This is particularly so because the EFQM Excellence Model is also moving in the direction of continual improvement as demonstrated by the differences between its 2012 version, "The EFQM Excellence Model" and the 2020 version, "The EFQM Model."
- Organizations with similar products/services, such as those in the aviation/aerospace and automotive sectors of the world economy, are likely going to improve and further strengthen their cooperation and interconnectivity, through the use of similar standards and materials supplies program and network systems. This shall, in turn, help them to improve their business performances through their use of similarly relevant QMS standards or adaptable QMS, to ensure the conformity of product and services to set industry standards. For example, registration to the AS 9100D standard will continue to provide a certain level of confidence in related products and services, in the aerospace industry. This concept is likely going to be embraced by other similarly operated arms of industries, in the future of quality practices and considerations. Other organizations with same or related products/services could follow this example to adapt the QMS that is suitable and directly relevant to their operations and processes. This may give rise to the development of Grouped-Industry-Specific quality management systems, such as the GAP, Good Affiliate Practice [56].

- The development of quality management research- or experimentally based inputs, models, theories, and hypothesis of various kinds and types into industry-applicable quality management concepts/programs is going to witness wider use and application. The TRIZ problem-solving method, as an example here, shall be given more prominence and possibly wider application.
- Possible evolution of new methods, ideas, and approaches to quality management either based on the structure of existing programs, or not, is a likelihood in the not-too distant future.

In brief, quality will remain a major focus of product/service improvement, marketplace competitiveness, and product/services performance in the future of the world market activities.

Business or Organizational "Excellence" Concept

The word, "Excellence" defined by the ASQ [3] as, "a measure of consistently superior performance that surpasses requirements and expectations without demonstrating significant flaws or waste" complements most adequately, the general definition, intent, and destination of total quality management, TQM practices. The concept of "*excellence*" is therefore very important to organizational TQM as it generally emphasizes, not just meeting customer/market and other stakeholders' SNEaRs but consistently doing so. Hence, organizational excellence greatly signifies the capability of an organization to consistently achieve superior performance. And this is exactly the way "excellence" should be viewed and seen with regard to quality and quality management practices.

Quality and quality management principles, tools, and techniques have most convincingly proved its mettle as the most effective agent of business catalyst, propelling organizational competitiveness and sustainability by consistently meeting stakeholder and customer SNEaRs. Hence, organizational excellence results in organizational ability to consistently maintain the TQM momentum of cross-organizational continual improvement, at all times.

While quality may be expressed in many different languages, names, forms, and shapes, the objective is always the same, and it is as clear as crystal. It is aimed primarily at continuously gaining competitive edge over other competitors by producing on a sustainable basis, products and services that meet and perhaps exceed the SNEaRs of all categories of customers—buyers and end-users, market place, regulatory bodies, and other stakeholders (i.e., investors, environment, and immediate community as well as commitment to corporate social responsibility). No matter what we choose to call or name the quality base of application, to achieve this objective, the destination remains the same. It could be ISO standards, excellence models, or organizational in-house-initiated total quality management systems, the outcome is key. As quality evolution has taught us all, the TQM philosophy deserves a full embrace across organizational processes and activities.

The author, therefore, views the Business Excellence Model (BEM) too as a viable approach for inspiring TQM to acquire and maintain the competitive edge and corporate social responsibility (CSR). If and when you read about the concept of "organizational excellence" it is still about making organizations and businesses highly competitive, through the establishment of necessary internal frameworks of quality management systems across organizational processes and activities, and among the workforce, to deliver products and services that meet customer SNEaRs in every ramification.

"Organization excellence" has, in similarity with this line of thinking, been defined by the ASQ [9], as ongoing efforts directed at establishing internal frameworks of standards and processes with the sole objective of engaging and motivating employees to deliver products and/or services that fulfill customer SNEaRs. Organizational excellence, definitely, has to do with the capability of an organization to effectively and sustainably deliver outstanding value to all stakeholders.

The European Organization for Quality Management (EFQM) strongly affirmed, "Excellent organizations are those that achieve and sustain outstanding levels of performance that meet and exceed the expectations of all stakeholders" [28]. The EFQM has thus come up with its own version of the Business Excellence Model (BEM) tagged the EFQM Excellence Model, 2012 version, "The EFQM Excellence Model," has been replaced with the 2020 publication, tagged "The EFQM Model." Some of the characteristic features of the EFQM Excellence Model emanating from the literature are among others listed in the following, Nenadal [65], and Nenadal et al. [66], and ASQ:

- Leadership
- People and people results
- Strategy
- Partnership and resources/good governance
- Processes, products, and services
- Customer results
- Society results/social responsibility/reputation
- Sustainability
- Profitability/business results

The fundamental concepts of Excellence as provided in its 2012 version is revealed in some core principles of organizational excellence—developing organizational capability; adding value to customers; creating a sustainable future; harnessing creativity and innovation; leading with vision, inspiration, and integrity; succeeding through the talent of people; and sustaining outstanding results. The 2020 version is however more simplified with the principles fully integrated into the text.

The ASQ [3] in its perspective view of managing for organizational excellence, also sees organizational excellence "as the successful integration of technology, infrastructure, and personnel" (ASQ). In this case, organizational excellence is also attributed to the outcome of organizational transitional and transformational activities. This thus emphasizes the excellence of organizational capability to successfully and satisfactorily manage *change*.

Uniting for Excellence

Product and/or technology-application types may play critical roles for forging such quality management interrelationships and cooperation. While the international organization for standardization (ISO) and some other quality product-related organizations (e.g., aerospace industries, and automotive industries) may have provided some platforms or levels of quality interconnectivity for relevant members/companies, the European Organization for Quality Management (EFQM), formerly known as the European Foundation for Quality Management, appears more likely to be an ideal representative body of future expectations in the development of quality interconnectivity.

The future of quality management will likely witness more of the type of interconnectivity that existed among the 14 CEOs of some big European companies that joined forces in 1988 to develop a management tool which would increase the competitiveness of European organizations. This was the major reason for the founding of the European Foundation for Quality Management (EFQM) known today as the EFQM, a not-for-profit membership organization based in Brussels.

According to the President of the European Council, Van Rompuy (EFQM) [87], "all European organizations, both in the public and private sectors, are facing new challenges. The increasing pressure to compete on a global stage with limited resources means we all have to work together to secure our future prosperity, and that of generations to come."

Working together vis-à-vis interconnecting quality activities would play vital roles in the future of quality management, a fact similarly asserted by Rompuy, "the EFQM Excellence Model provides a framework that encourages cooperation, collaboration and innovation that we will need to ensure this goal is achieved." The interconnectivity and cooperation provided for, by the concept of the EFQM and its Excellence Model, the EFQM Excellence Model, which began in Europe as a dream wish of 14 CEOs of some European organizations a few decades ago, is today serving as a unique and global platform for organizations to learn from each other, to improve their business performance and competitive capability.

Developing Grouped-Industry-Specific (GIS) QMSs

Much as it is recognized that quality is highly imperative as a strong business sustainability tool, a lot of smaller organizations, or even some bigger ones, still found the implementation of one quality system, or the other, financially stressful, or unaffordable due to one reason or the other. Others simply adhere to principles and processes which are in excess of their own requirements [56].

It is realized during my quality consulting career that some organizations got certified to the requirements of the ISO 9001 QMS international standards without knowing the reasons for which they sort certification, or they simply did it for the wrong reasons. They have forgotten in such situations that a QMS certification to particular standards can be dysfunctional if sought and obtained for the wrong reasons, in the assertion of Bush [17].

For example, the AS9100 QMS standard is tailored toward the aviation, space, and defense (ASD) industry to provide suppliers that design, develop, or provide products, with requirements for which supplied products and items must be compliant. This is to ensure that such products are safe and reliable for use, not only in the ASD sector, but also in the civil and military aviation sectors.

For heavily regulated sectors such as the pharmaceutical industry, the issue of a single QMS is not an easy task to accomplish on individual industry basis, hence, the need for joint quality system integration or adaption. This can easily be achieved if some members of this sector of the industry put their resources together for a common sector-adaptive or sector-integrated QMS standards. The healthcare sector is an area with its own peculiarities when it comes to the use and implementation of a QMS.

While manufacturing systems in the healthcare sector emphasize product consistencies, hospitals are strictly concerned with patient needs, which represent customer focus of the ISO 9001 QMS.

London et al.'s [56] reported pharmaceutical industry is a good example in this sector of the economy which has successfully established an adaptable QMS christened "good affiliate practices" (GAP), based on the eight principles of the ISO quality management systems (QMS) and TQM—continual improvement, supplier relationships, systems approach, customer satisfaction, leadership, people involvement, decision-making, and problem solving and process approach. There is the likelihood of other organizations following this good example.

Organizational Interconnectivity in Quality Management

The advent of *"nano chips"* is evidence of another milestone in the dynamism of technological developmental changes ahead of mankind. The envisaged changes brought about by *"nano chips"* and *software* applications are likely to rank closely with those changes that were witnessed with the invention and technological application of microchips in the last 20 years. This is especially so in the areas of technological advancements and their applications, telecommunications, internet, transportation, artificial intelligence, medical advancements, etc.

The increase in the use of artificial intelligence (AI) and the widespread use of unmanned machinery/equipment (e.g., robots, drones, planes, and helicopters) are most likely going to pose some specific developmental challenges to quality and its management tools. This may most probably create a higher level of organizational and personnel interconnectivity, either among each other and/or with the outside world, than we have ever had so far. As early as about the second quarter of 2021, there had been reports of the accelerated pace of the adoption of the artificial intelligence. For example, the KPMG [49] survey "found that half of business leaders in industrial manufacturing (55%) retail and tech (49% in each) said AI is moving faster than it should be in their industry."

Such quality management interconnectivity and cooperation would feature prominently among organizations with identical businesses and business management processes: quality goals and/or other common activities (e.g., products/services and materials processes) or links (e.g., geographical), so as to strengthen their performance and competitive abilities, in the global market that will, from decade to decade, get more and more competitive. These are most importantly core components Industry 4.0 initiatives.

Quality and Innovation

Quality and innovation simply hold the key for opening the doors for future global market penetration for most products and services. While the global market competition is going to be keener than ever in the future, quality and innovation will likely be embraced as the dominant skeletal back bone structure, required for sustaining virtually all products and services. It is therefore likely that any business/enterprise managed with the intention to capture the market may have to focus more on qualitatively and innovatively differentiable products and services, so as to catch and compel the attention of customers/consumers or buyers/market.

Even in the emerging markets of the world economy such as Turkey, Brazil, Indonesia, Malaysia, South Africa, and Mexico, people are today placing more and more emphasis on product quality, while consumers too are beginning to appreciate their rights to purchase goods that meet their SNEaRs, rather than just purchasing any item in the global marketplace.

With emphasis on quality, some of these countries may be able to penetrate and push their manufactured goods into the international market. As more and more organizations embrace quality and its market (particularly international) penetration benefits, quality practices are definitely going to be of more general relevance, among goods and services providers across the globe.

This is not to say, however, that all organizations will willingly accept and adapt suitable quality management systems and/or guidelines, or integrated systems, but they may, most importantly, be willing to do so, to meet customer and regulatory SNEaRs, get job contracts, and/or to qualify in meeting precontractual awarding SNEaRs. Integrated quality management system/concepts implanted with innovation simply hold the key for opening the doors for future global market penetration for most products and services.

Today's competitive market structure is a determinant factor portraying the trend of future economic dynamism. While the global market competition is going to be keener than ever, quality and innovation will likely be wholly embraced as the dominant skeletal back bone structure, for sustaining products and services vis-à-vis organizations.

It is therefore likely that any business/enterprise managed with the intention to capture the market may have to focus more on qualitatively and innovatively differentiable products and services so as to catch and compel the attention of customers/consumers. According to Merrill [59], we in the world of quality *"could define innovation as quality for tomorrow—the adopted tagline of ASQ's innovation technical committee."*

While taking quality to the next level with innovation, it is important to direct attention primarily on ways for fulfilling customer SNEaRs, in all ramifications, whether specified or unspecified, including regulatory requirements with no negative impacts on the environment and other entities.

It must, however, be mentioned here that thinking about quality with innovation, may not be worth it in corrupt countries, such as Nigeria, where government corruption, or corruption in government, may likely lead to government procurement processes being compromised, or having little or no influence whatsoever on innovation.

Except in such situations as highlighted here, innovation may be implemented in all areas of customer needs, no matter what the needs are, and the processes to achieve them. One therefore needs to interact actively with customers to know the needs; rank the needs in order of relevance; get information or data on each of the needs; and search for the opportunities to implement innovation or use innovative ideas, or ideals to provide such needs. It could be the following:

- Customer identified problems or problem areas
- Customer expectations
- Customer needs
- Processes or process stage/phase(s)

Innovating generally requires certain ingredients necessary for its accomplishments:

- Knowledge, adequacy of skills, and competencies
- Creativity, research, and development
- Adequate timing and funding
- Proper definition of individual or group roles in accomplishing innovation
- Boldly and courageously identify and balance risks with benefits
- Effectively coordinate the execution stage and innovate as accomplished innovation goal in the form of a quality management project

Managing Innovation

A key question that needs to be asked in order to move an organization in the direction of implanting a quality system or integrated quality system with innovation and/or creative ideas is that which addresses organizational needs. Hence, one may rightly ask the question, *"What are the ranked needs of an organization?"*

The implementation of specific quality program/concepts/system identified as adequate for the improvement of the products and services of an organization has been known to result in product quality. In a similar vein, organizations have implemented a combination or integration of two or more quality improvement programs/concepts/systems (e.g., Lean/Six Sigma) for achieving products which meet customer requirements.

The importance of innovation in organizational sustenance is further accentuated by the ISO by meeting the global need for organizational and business *"innovation management system standard."* In playing a leading role here, the ISO developed the following:

> ***"ISO 56000:2020****—Innovation management—Fundamentals and vocabulary."* The use of this standard is available to the general public with the ISO.

TRIZ for Innovation

TRIZ is according to Hua et al. [39], "a problem-solving, analysis and forecasting tool derived from the study of patterns of invention in the global patent industry," "TRIZ" the Russian (Anglicized, *"Teoriya Resheniya Izobreatatelskikh Zadatch"*) acronym for "Theory of Inventive Problem Solving" is according to Barry et al. [14] *"an international science of creativity that relies on the study of the patterns of problems and solutions, not on the spontaneous and intuitive creativity of individuals or groups."* TRIZ is, according to Altunas and Yener [1], also occasionally referred to in its English acronym as TIPS (Theory of Inventive Problem Solving).

The TRIZ creativity method extended creativity tools beyond brainstorming and related methods which are typically described as psychologically based and produce outcomes that are in most cases, neither predictable nor repeatable. The TRIZ problem-solving method which is based on logic and data is, in contrast to some other methods, said to provide repeatability, predictability, and reliability. LariSemnani et al. [53] reported in a study the application of TRIZ to improve the quality of hospital services.

TRIZ research which is said to have begun with the hypothesis *"that there are universal principles of creativity that are the basis for creative innovations that advance technology"* was conceived by Genrich S. Altshuler and developed by him and his associates in the former USSR between 1946 and 1985. There has been increasing use of TRIZ in the corporate world in areas which include but are not limited to the following:

- Six Sigma processes
- Project management
- Risk management systems
- Organizational innovation initiatives

The increasing relevance of innovation and creativity to quality management and systems improvement is further enhanced by the TRIZ method whose application and use is likely going to gain more prominence in the immediate future. This is even more so, as stated by Barry et al. [14] that *"the TRIZ general problem at the highest level is to find a way to produce the product with no waste, at 100 per cent yield with no added complexity."*

Many quality tools have been claimed to fit nicely within the TRIZ structure. Examples provided here are critical to quality (CTQ) trees and the failure mode and effects analysis (FMEA) as they can be used to enhance some of the design principles of TRIZ [85]. It reportedly follows from all indications, therefore, that TRIZ can be of good application in catalyzing innovation not just for design efforts, but also to stimulate innovation through quality improvement process(es). The future holds a lot of potential opportunities for the systematic use and application of TRIZ in solving quality problems, or in enhancing quality management and other system improvement processes.

Designing It Right, First Time; Effective QMS Auditing

It is very important here, to highlight the apparent need for organizations to make the issue of *"Design it Right, First Time"* not just an integral part of the quality culture but also implanted into the QMS or improvement concepts' procedural steps. This is most particularly so, in the growing era of software and advanced technology applications as we shall experience in the digital era of the "SmartFactory." This is suggested in alignment with the usual quality common saying, *"Do it right first time."*

At the same time, it has become apparent too, for quality auditing organizations, or registrars to have this at the back of their minds; hence, there is the need for them to acquire needed expertise to understand and get information on relevant software applications, their functions, and product/services delivery, as well as how to quality-check them.

QMS Audit Improvement

Compliance audit (making observation and collecting data/objective evidence to verify that requirements are being met) in quality management shall continue to play critical roles in the future development and sustenance of the quality management system international standards. It does not matter here who is carrying out the audit (first party, second party, or third party) or what the reason for the audit maybe, it serves to verify organizational compliance with both stated and regulatory requirements:

- QMS requirements (quality manual, policy, standards, procedures, regulations, etc.)
- Process requirements (methods and procedures)
- Product or service capability verification/requirements

- Standard requirements
- Regulatory requirements
- Other needed areas or activities

The issue of concern here borders on situations where quality audits are carried out by the same registrar, or same organization over a long period of time. There are two sides of the coin to this issue, and they are ethical and being neutral (or independent).

While it may be easy for auditing bodies or registrars to retain their business interests in organizations audited by them, it may be more difficult for them to maintain absolute and complete neutrality, or objectivity especially after several (i.e., over 10–15) years of auditing relationship notwithstanding the fact too, that, it takes auditing companies/registrars some time to understand the activities/systems of new clients. This concern is expressly applicable to the quality of financial audits. The caveat here is the fact that complacency may set in.

Quality audit development or improvement, in terms of compliance measurements, may therefore tend to be concentrated more toward the improvement of focused coordination of auditing activities between internal and external auditors. This shall enable organizations ascertain the objectivity of one against the other, and to detect each of their weaknesses.

While the quality of audits has hitherto improved generally, future trends are likely going to be influenced and shaped by the roles and structure of the relationship between the auditors and auditees. The issue here is that, "*auditing it rightly saves the audited organization* extraordinary cost of quality (ECoQ)."

The author therefore subscribes to the fact that organizations are likely going to get the best auditing results from the auditing firm or registrar it considers and judged, as having the capability and ability to objectively and independently carry out an effective audit of its systems, not minding whether they are new or old in rendering auditing services to them. It is important too for organizations to always consider the integrity and reputation of auditing firms before their engagement, on the basis of merit built on business record, reputation, reliability, objectivity, and integrity.

For example, the reported allegations of the US environmental protection agency (EPA), [29] "that Volkswagen violated the Clean Air Act ('CAA') by the sale of approximately 590,000 model year 2009–2016 diesel motor vehicles equipped with *'defeat devices'*" should, in the opinion of the author, ordinarily have been detected during previous quality auditing procedures, whether internal or external. It is important here to take note of the fact that, "The EPA alleged that these vehicles are equipped with *'defeat devices'* in the form of computer software designed to cheat on federal emissions tests.

As reported, "Under the third partial settlement, Volkswagen has paid a $1.45 billion civil penalty for the alleged civil violations of the Clean Air Act." When viewed from quality perspectives, this large sum of money is tantamount to *unnecessary cost of quality,* incurred by Volkswagen for failure to *"Design it right first time."* The term "defeat device" suggests most probably, deliberately being non-compliant in order to cheat which is a counter-quality practices.

It is in this vein too that it is necessary for organizations to ensure that the use and application of software and automation requires focusing on "designing it right first time and always." The future trends in quality are generally likely going to focus on the following:

- Improved quality education, training, expertise, and competency in quality management skills shall likely lead to more jobs in quality management. Early engagement and exposure of young graduates to quality management practices, especially in the emerging markets or economies of the world is critical in widening global trade participation and competition.
- The use of ISO 9000 QMS standards alone, or its integration/combination with other quality management/improvement concepts and tools, will be on the increase especially, as it shall continually be improved upon, to make them more and more user friendly, and relevant to global exchange of goods and services.
- The use and application of integrated quality management systems (I-QMSs) and/or integrated improvement concepts (I-ICs) such as Lean/Sigma are likely going to be more attractive in the 2020s and thereafter. For example, my experience of implementing ISO 9001 QMS in combination with ISO 14000 EMS standards (I-ISO 9001:2015/ISO 14001:2015, [40]) has been highly rewarding. This helped to drastically reduce in-plant injuries; improved operational efficiency vis-a-vis increased productivity; minimize or completely eradicate wastages; and helped in enhancing employee awareness about individual responsibility for all assigned tasks. The potentials for the increased use and application of a QMS implanted with innovation or innovative ideas in the future are quite high. A pointer in this direction is already seen in section "Pareto Diagram/Analysis". (Innovation), of the latest version of ISO 9004:2018 *(Quality Management—Quality of an Organization—Guidance to achieve sustained success, [43]).*
- This guideline standard, both in its context and contents, makes provision for a systematic, process-based approach to innovation and improvement processes within a quality management system. In addition to this, is the fact too that, the USA, the world's largest economy, is gradually leading the global economy down the road of innovation as the next stage of evolution from quality management. This was ascertained by Merrill [59] who gave the inclusion of innovation in the 2011–2012 Baldrige criteria [64] as a proven case to support this trend.
- Improved quality audit through the focused coordination of auditing activities between internal and external auditors or auditing bodies with attention paid the role of technology, software, and automation in quality management processes.

Perspectives of ISO and Quality Management Systems

The International Organization for Standardization (ISO) will continue to grow in membership. ISO will therefore remain relevant and influential in the development of future quality standards. Such standards shall be relevant to users' needs, organizational quality management improvement standards, and in shaping the future of quality and its management on the international platform. This is so because standards are developed at the request of ISO members. The future roles of the ISO in the international arena shall include, among others, the following:

- Play critical role in the development of ***"smart"*** international standards necessary for use in the quality management and quality auditing of the processes and other activities of the "SmartFactory," in the digital era, to complement existing relevant industrial production international standards as Quality 4.0 evolves in the aftermath of Industry 4.0 rollout.
- The continual development of ISO 9000 series of international quality management systems (QMS) standards to incorporate suitable factors such as innovative ideas to enhance organizational performance, customer satisfaction, risk management, and governance guidelines.
- Play a leading role on the international platform to further the internationalization and wider use and application of its standards for organizational sustainability.
- Provision of well-researched quality documentation needed for quality management and training of quality-minded people.
- Maintaining some levels of dynamism in the continual improvement of quality management standards through their regular revision and improvement to make them more relevant and user-friendlier based on quality management dynamism.

The global acknowledgment and use of ISO 9000 QMS international standards do not in any way shield it and other quality management systems or improvement concepts away from challenges of one type or the other. These global challenges to quality management systems include but are not limited to the following:

- Digital challenges emanating from Industry 4.0 roll out.
- As the world becomes flatter and flatter due to effective communications systems, there will be growing customer expectations for increased confidence in products/services especially in the digital age. Increased sophistication of quality management tools especially with increased software application.
- The use and application of ISO 9001 QMS standards will continue to play critical roles in global trade as there is likely going to be increased use by various sectors and organizations in the globalized world, including public service and governance.
- Achieving the credibility and sustainability of third-party certification. Emphasis here should be on the principles of customer satisfaction.
- The ever-increasing drive for greater efficiency (lean initiatives).
- Multiplicity of management systems, standards, schemes, and programs.
- Increases in the emphases placed on issues relating to and affecting public health and safety such as food, environment, medical devices, and other human health challenges.

Future Outlook of ISO 9000 Family of International Standards

ISO 9000 QMS is likely going to grow in relevance and application in line with its hitherto global success in its voluntary and wide use and application by virtually all markets and organizations (private and public alike) to:

- Achieve and facilitate the production of high product quality of international and global recognition and acceptance
- Facilitate the international exchange of goods and services
- Support sustainable and equitable economic growth
- Promote innovation
- Protect population health, safety, and the environment, hence, there is likely going to be increased use of ISO standards in the healthcare sector of the global economy for improved performance
- Encourage and facilitate the implementation of relevant statutory and/or regulatory requirements

Challenges in the Future Reviews of ISO 9001 QMS Standard

While ISO 9001 QMS standards implementation is generally aimed to assist organizations in improving their quality management system, certification to the requirements of this international standard should be viewed as the result of *"a well-implemented quality management system."* In order to maintain the role of achieving ISO 9001 certification objective, future reviews must be carried out with very strong considerations for its effective and satisfactory use by potential users.

All future reviews of the ISO 9001:2015 QMS standard [42] have to be made in such a way as to ensure its growing relevance, to its growing list of users and potential users. In order to achieve this, it may be necessary to put the following issues into consideration:

- Emphasize the ability of organizations to produce or provide their customers with products/services that are conforming/compliant.
- Expansion of the eight (8) quality management principles (i.e., customer focus, leadership, involvement of people, process approach, system approach to management, continual improvement, factual approach to decision-making, and mutually beneficial supplier relationships) of the current version of ISO 9001 QMS standards, to include other effective aspects of quality management especially in the digital age. Here, cybersecurity and privacy of data quickly come to mind.
- Focus on ways to enhance the compatibility and easy integration of ISO 9001 QMS first, with other relevant management systems or standards, and then with other relevant business management processes, especially, for achieving the effective management of process interfaces.

- Focus on how to make it easier and less expensive for an organization to effectively implement the requirements of the standard and achieve the effective conformity of their QMS requirement through auditing by first, second, and third parties as may be necessary.
- Future revisions of ISO 9000 QMS standards must continue to be done with strong considerations for changes generally in quality management systems practices and growing advances in technology especially information technology and software applications, as envisaged in the Quality 4.0 initiatives.
- Use of simplified means of communication such as language and writing styles to globally promote the understanding of the requirements of international standards and the ways to adequately implement their requirements.
- The frequency of the revision of the contractual standards, such as ISO 9001 QMS stands hitherto at an average of 7 years (1987 to 1994; 1994 to year 2000; and year 2000 to 2008, and 2015). The next revision may come up anytime from 2022 or thereabout. It is expected that the dynamism generated by Industry 4.0 vis-à-vis Quality 4.0 may likely play important roles in the next review. It must, however, be noted that too frequent revisions are likely to impact negatively on smaller to medium size organizations which may be thrown off balance, or discouraged.
- Emphasize effective management of processes and other QMS interfaces as a critical aspect of ISO 9001 QMS implementation

Need for Effective Interface Management in the Implementation of QMSs

Three major areas of interface interactions can be easily identified in the implementation of the requirements of ISO 9001 QMS international standards and they are the following:

- Interaction between all involved interested entities (e.g., customers and the marketplace, supply chain, employees, shareholders/owners, regulatory bodies, community, training institutions, and professional bodies). The emergence of the "SmartFactory" shall most probably impact the human interface with product and processes.
- Interface between processes and/or work stages.
- Interface between ISO 9001 QMS standards and other management systems/standards on the one hand and between other management processes on the other hand.

The interactive faces of any quality management system could easily pose serious quality problems if not effectively handled or integrated. Hence, future reviews of ISO 9001 QMS international standards may need to put the effective management of relevant interfaces into strong consideration and focus.

While process interfaces depend mainly on the extent of the different or individual processes, there are today three major players of interactive interface entities:

- Human ware—people that carry out the procedures, do the work, and execute other activities in the QMS.
- Hardware—the machinery and equipment used for various processes.
- Software—methods and ways of doing things.

The advent of the "SmartFactory" may likely come with another dimension of hardware interface resulting from the machine-to-machine (M2M) communication to reduce the human-to-machine interfacial activities.

The way these three entities interact within a process or among different processes need to be effectively managed if product quality requirements have to be met in the most effective way and manner.

Relevant interfaces emanating from the alignment and integration of other compatible management systems standards such as ISO 14000 EMS and ISO 22000 Food safety management system—Requirements for any organization in the food chain (ISO 22000:2018) must first be identified and smartly managed, to ensure desired results are obtained, else the purpose of the compatibility or alignment would have been defeated.

Growing Quality in Academics and Research

A major progress for quality and its management tools, principles, practices, and techniques in the twenty-first century shall be in the areas of academic and research (see Chap. 19). With TQM, Lean, Six Sigma, and other quality management tools, principles, and techniques already gaining the interests of people in academics and researcher, it is not surprising that Carnerud and Backstrom [19] and Carnerud [18] already identified in their works, potential areas of quality research interests (see Chap. 19). Similarly, Kumar et al. [52] added the general needs for a better understanding of "QM's performance effects," while Barouch and Kleinhans [13] hammered on exploring the importance and capability of quality initiatives. The research exploitations of Barouch and Ponsignon [12], Aquilani et al. [6], and van Kemenade and Hardjono [86] in the areas of quality and quality management are good examples motivating future potentials of quality research.

There is also the need for research for new quality paradigms, a term described by Masters [57] as the philosophical foundations that support our approaches to research, as quality continues to evolve in the digital era. Establishing clearer theoretical bases for total quality management (TQM) as advocated by Dahlgaard-Park [22] for better understanding is another area of research attraction. This tallies too, with the suggestions of Fredriksson and Isaaksson [33], in their call for the need to better explain the similarities and differences between various quality philosophies.

Quality Management Challenges in Manufacturing

Quality in the manufacturing sector of the global economy shall likely face some unpredictable and unprecedented challenges similar to, worse than, and perhaps of milder impacts as that of the COVID-19 pandemic. Evidence from the manufacturing sector showed glaringly that some of the impacts of the pandemic to manufacturing include, among others, the following:

- Worker attendance issues coupled with onsite availability
- Halt or slowed down production as a result of decreased product/services demand and onsite worker restrictions due to the pandemic
- Operational limitations to areas of process automation
- The risks of exposing workers to infection as well as that of spreading it to other workers
- The impact of the sudden pandemic-necessitated changes that may have to be put in place in organizational-wide quality management systems
- Difficulties for achieving adequate and prompt collaboration in terms doing work and responding to customer and regulatory SNEaRs

Such changes in manufacturing processes may, for example, result in becoming permanent ones, in the manufacturing sector, especially in big organizations with need for added investment capitals. On the other hand, smaller and medium manufacturing organizations may not survive at all. For example, manufacturing systems which never thought of or envisage, technologies such as automation, AI, and the use of robots in their manufacturing process, for one reason or the other, for example, finance, lack of the need, and enthusiasm to invest, may now be forced to resort to seeing them as needed innovative initiatives, for achieving efficient processing operations, and adequately streamlined production systems.

Of course, both automation and/or robotics application would definitely help in offsetting the emergency problems of workers' inability to come to work, under peculiar work or environmental situations. Although it took about 100 years for the return of a pandemic to man's life settings, nobody can actually foresee the future and what it generally holds for humanity and quality itself.

Effective quality management thus require that we prepare most readily to be able to promptly respond and get adaptive to any unforeseen future challenges, which may be from a technology pivot; a pandemic in the magnitude of the COVID-19 pandemic or not; economic upheaval; or even natural disasters and their immediate threats to humanity whenever it occurs.

Such array of unexpected future challenges may result from the following:

- Another global healthcare crisis such as the COVID-19 pandemic challenges
- Man-made mass destructive catastrophic situations resulting from war situations
- Location-specific natural disasters

- Changing environmental occurrences and situations necessitated by, or may be created by the current trend of global warming
- Other natural catastrophic situations beyond man's controls

It is for these and other reasons that the coming decades of quality may globally witness more reliance and dependability on *automated* measurements and production systems, robotics, software and their application, increased adaptation of automation and digital technology, and artificial intelligence in organizational quality management systems to most efficiently and cost-effectively achieve product quality, while sustaining desired productivity. Automation and the robotics came handy though not cheap, for some manufacturing systems, such in the automobile industry, in order to overcome the challenges resulting from human movement restrictions to prevent the spread of the COVID-19 pandemic.

It is, however, possible that automation and the renewed use of robotics may be exploited beyond the COVID-19 pandemic era as a common parlance of "the new normal" in the manufacturing and other relevant sectors of the economy.

In a further confirmation of the future role of automation in the quality system, Myers [61] affirmed in his article on "Future-proof your quality systems" that "systems can be automated, to almost completely take most human interaction away from the equation," in order to effectively react to "an array of unexpected challenges." As suggested by Meyers, appropriately selected process-integrated measurement systems can be used by manufacturers in process control and monitoring, to maintain productivity and assure quality production with minimal resources, a promising approach for the future.

An outlook into the future of quality cannot be completed without looking at the part played by the growing role of software systems which according to Sanderson [75], "are advancing faster than any other time in history." There is no doubt, therefore, that shaping the future of quality and quality management shall most certainly be enhanced by the continually changing software platforms and market diversification. These enhancements by quality software are likely going to be applicable to various aspects of quality and quality management, among which are in the areas of the following:

- Calibration software
- Data analysis
- Metrology
- Quality management solutions

The recent 2020 global challenges of the COVID-19 pandemic taught the people of the world, not just how interconnected the whole world has grown to become, but how inevitably critical it has become, for us to interconnectedly unite, collaborate, and engage each other. It is only by collaboratively using existing scientific knowledge and experience, to explore innovative solutions and in advancing and aligning research findings, that the world and its people can survive on. Achieving such goals or objectives depends to a large extent on the quality of leadership management and commitment. Otherwise, it might be difficult to meet urgently needed global societal needs and requirements for finding cures and/or preventive measures, such as vaccines, for the deadly COVID-19 pandemic and future situations of similar magnitude.

For example, the people of the USA have unfortunately, already experienced the negative impacts of technological advancements in terms of the cyberattack which reportedly led to the shutdown of one of the nation's biggest fuel pipeline operations. According to the reports of Nakashima et al. [62], a ransomware attack on Colonial Pipeline led to the sudden shut down of its entire network.

This is evident of the magnitude of the potential challenges facing quality management system in the digital era, the era of Quality 4.0 initiatives. It is therefore important for the "SmartFactory" organizations to integrate cybersecurity into their quality management systems. They, therefore, have to take necessary actions to strengthen their manufacturing/production system cybersecurity posture, so as to reduce their exposure to cyber threats.

The lessons learnt from the COVID-19 pandemic, simply teaches and offers us the opportunities of realizing how deeply interconnected and interdependent the people of the world have grown to be. We also learnt the importance of quality, its established elements as well as quality management tools, principles, and concepts, in their application at all levels of crisis and risk management, in all areas of human endeavor—manufacturing, governance, services, healthcare, education, and training. Quality-managing the changes induced by the COVID-19 pandemic across the globe glaringly demonstrate to us all too how critical and important collaboration, interconnectivity, leadership, and leadership commitment is generally to quality management.

In the current situation of the novel coronavirus, the hope of the human race has been placed strictly in quality, quality management principles, tools and techniques using people involvement and commitment to mitigate the pandemic in various ways:

- Wearing the face mask.
- Maintaining social distancing.
- Restricting social gatherings, especially in enclosures.
- Hand washing.
- Information gathering and dissemination.
- Process control and management.
- Leadership envisioning and commitment.
- Communication especially among healthcare workers, researchers, and healthcare professionals in academic and research, as well as among regulatory organizations/bodies to ensure multi-directional flow of information. Since the pandemic emanates from the novel coronavirus, little or nothing was known about its virology and impacts on human immune systems, regular communication with the masses became highly essential.
- Measurements, data collection and analysis.

- Customer supplier relationships.
- Customer feedback and the like as critical measures to manage the sudden but painful changes caused by the pandemic.

The universal resolve by the people of the world to engage the quality mindset in top gear, in approaching the sudden unprecedented pandemic-induced challenges into our world in 2020, is a general pointer to the global acceptance and acknowledgment of the critical roles of quality in our world and our lives now, and in the future.

Elevating quality to this advantage position of man's healthcare needs has sealed quality's emergence as the most philosophical bridge divergently linking many facets of our lives, activities, and sphere of knowledge, to shape our future through its wide application, professional collaboration, and interconnectedness.

The fact that the origin of COVID-19 pandemic is today marred in denial brings out the realism of how critical the issue of organizational corporate social responsibility (CSR) is to the people of the world. Organizations and businesses must quickly come to terms with the sincerity of recognizing their corporate social responsibilities (CSR) to the community, people, and the global populace at large. If this had happened in December 2019 when the COVID-19 pandemic was first discovered, it may have been possible to prevent it from spreading all over the surface of the earth by "killing it in its place of origin."

CSR is of particular importance to the entirety of the global community because it appears most certainly, though yet to be confirmed, that the global population must have been exposed to the threat of the COVID-19 pandemic due, most probably, to an organization or an entity being negligent of its CSR. This is definitely an issue of a high level of corporate social irresponsibility (CSIR) if the source is at the end of the day traceable to an organization, entity, or a body, no matter the country of origin.

Quality Leadership in Transition

Having pushed quality and the opportunities which abound in the career path of its practitioners, its broad management application, and the widespread use of quality tools and techniques in all aspects of human endeavor this far, one cannot but acknowledge and give credence to the land mark accomplishments of the quality "*gurus*" of the twentieth century. There are no doubts, whatsoever, that we have found ourselves in the age of quality management transitioning. Three of the most obvious transitional challenges of quality management are highlighted as follows:

- ***Leadership***—Transitioning of quality management leadership from those that evolved mainly through manufacturing and work experience of the twentieth century to those who undergo structured educational system and training and have the passion to continue to change and evolve as one of the most viable professional and academic discipline rather than be subsumed by other disciplines.

- ***Finding quality roots in the academia***—Transitioning quality management from its state of "academic orphanage" to finding its rooting and theoretical basis in academics to suit, match, and explain many of the already established quality philosophies, principles, and concepts.
- ***Quality 4.0 principles***—Transitioning in response to Industry 4.0 initiatives. A new era for quality management shall evolve with the emerging "SmartFactory" approaches to product and services deployment through the use and application of big data, analytics, machine learning (ML), artificial intelligence (AI), Industrial Internet of Things (IIoT), 5G, blockchain, and other enabling technologies such as cloud computing, sensors, and App development. in an environment of a high level of interconnectivity and transparency. Just as the old quality slogan, "Do it right first time" the digital age focus shall be similarly getting everything right first time. Hence, it is probably going to be quality management with emphasis on ***"designing it right first time."*** This is an area of new challenges, especially technology-based ones, to quality management professionals in various ways—getting used to, and learning to leverage new technological innovations to achieve product/services quality; identifying, establishing, learning, and adapting relevant data and metrics for defining and assessing product/services quality criteria in line with customer SNEaRs.
- ***Quality as a knowledge domain/discipline***—Quality being recognized as a discipline of studies from undergraduate to the highest level of academic accomplishment.

Quality being acknowledged as a discipline is a daunting task, probably comparable to those which was faced by these twentieth century quality "*gurus*" who have exited the global quality stage. They all entered the quality stages facing quality management challenges in industrial manufacturing companies across the globe, from the USA to Japan, from the automobile sector to other arms of the manufacturing industry, and the military. They will ever be remembered for successfully passing the baton of leadership and endless opportunities in quality, to younger and emerging cadres of quality leaders across the globe.

Organizational Preparedness

The sudden and unexpected emergence of the COVID-19 pandemic brought along with it, lessons for people to learn and appreciate the urgent need for man's ability to, as quickly as lightning, qualitatively adapt to new situations or disruptive changes, in the manner synonymous with the adaptive space of Arena [8]. This is to say that organizations and institutions must be agile, in order to "be able to respond to change instantly and effectively," due to the fact that "agility is more a social factor than structural." To be adaptive, therefore, calls for organizations to have a good understanding and recognition of how powerful social interactions could be in successfully driving the flow of ideas, information, and insight. Achieving organizational agility can therefore be said to require that novel ideas flow freely among teams, across departments, and throughout an organization.

Agility was globally deployed to tackle the COVID-19 pandemic devastating threats when it suddenly caught the people of the global community unawares in 2020. Since little or nothing was known about the biology of the novel coronavirus, novel ideas were caused to flow freely among the public health teams of experts, healthcare workers, virologists, immunologists, researchers, and vaccine developers across the globe, legislators from various parts of the world, and all other relevant experts to immediately provide qualitative solutions to mitigate the deadly impact of the COVID-19 pandemic.

The future of quality thus calls for cooperation, collaboration, and interconnectedness among quality professionals, professional and interested organizations, educationists and researchers, and other quality institutions. This is necessary to effectively face the future of quality which is richly endowed with challenges and opportunities, transcending professional, organizational, research, educational, and other forms and types of delineation.

And above all is the call here for capable future quality leadership—agile and enabling, committed to the course of quality, ready to "engage the tension between entrepreneurial activities and the operational system," in order to "facilitate the adaptive activities necessary to facilitate organizational adaptability," with the preparedness to "drive bold innovations to completely reinvent products and services [55]," and bring the best out of every quality followership to keep the world afloat.

The deadly impact of the COVID-19 pandemic in the year 2020 on the 7.8 billion people living today, in a deterioratingly disruptive world of constant changes, limitless uncertainties, worsening global warming risks, and unpredictable natural catastrophic occurrences, is an attestation to the relevance and indispensability of both quality and quality leadership, in the lives of the world's daily growing population.

Real-time adaptive organizations require enabling leadership, as a major lifeline of organizational QMS, in order to sustainably and boldly drive needed innovations for reinventing products and services ahead of all competitive challenges of the twenty-first century in a global business environment pierced with growing technological and digital opportunities, and frequently emerging disruptive changes.

Be prepared and do not say you are not told! There is the need for organizational and other leaders to have necessary strategic plans in place based on the general understanding of the weaknesses of our current business models and their weakest links.

Mitigating Substandard/Fake Medicines

Curing Poor-Quality Medicines

The quality of life of the people in the developing economies of the world, especially in Africa, South America, and others, is daily undermined by the proliferation of substandard and falsified medicines or medications. In most cases, it is the low- to middle-income people who are mostly exposed to this fraudulent international risk just as they are the mostly impacted too.

According to Ramanathan and Charles [71], this situation has greatly impacted the people and their economy in several ways culminating into various forms of risk factors among which are the following:

- Erosion of public trust in health systems
- Treatment failures
- Potentials of resulting in patient deaths
- Inhibiting improvements in public health services
- Motivating people's distrust of western medicine and turning to other unreliable sources

The internationalization of this pervasive act of fraudulency in the healthcare sector can most probably be effectively solved, or at least minimized, through international collaborative testing of pharmaceutical products. Using interlaboratory quality management cooperation potentials to strengthen the quality management capabilities of the individual participating laboratories of participating countries shall undoubtedly provide reliable quality control opportunities, at more effective costs than for individual countries setting up individual systems from the scratch. The fact that about one billion African people are daily made into victims of the pervasiveness of poor-quality medicines goes to tell the story of the level of risk in question here. This thus brings to the fore the need and importance of collaboratively uniting to control the quality of medicines across the pharmaceutical sector of the globalized economy.

Corruption and mis-leadership in some of the affected countries, such as Nigeria, make this task very difficult to accomplish through local monitoring agencies alone. Whatever is accomplished on the international collaborative platform of quality shall undoubtedly go a long way to accomplish some quality improvements to reduce the exposure of the global community to the risks highly inherent in the global proliferation of substandard and falsified medicines, or fake medicines.

Global Quality Control Initiative

The leadership role reportedly played by the United States Pharmacopeia (USP), a nonprofit organization, through its global quality control initiative for Official Medicines Control Laboratories (OMCL) cannot be overemphasized [71]. It gives laboratories in the affected countries and other interested ones across the globe, the opportunity of reliably monitoring and testing medicines in their country's pharmaceutical markets.

As a public agency, therefore, any country of the global community, has the opportunity of mandating the OMCL to carry out excellent quality analysis of medical products on behalf of its relevant regulatory body or authority, at determined levels of their pharmaceutical products marketing phases, that is, before its marketing approval or after. OMCL accomplishes this great task through the compendial testing of medical products.

To accomplish its objective the USP engages in developing and publishing relevant recognized standards "for drug substances, drug products, excipients, and dietary supplements in the United States Pharmacopeia-National Formulary (USP-NF)."

The opportunity of compendial testing of medical products in this way and manner serves the advantages of greatly reducing the general risk inherent in substandard and falsified medicines, especially in our present globalized pharmaceutical supply chain to the embrace and protection of public health.

Since most medicines are today more easily accessible for use by the people of the rapidly globalized world and its economy, it is highly beneficial for any laboratories participating in the USP interlaboratory comparison testing (ILCT) or proficiency testing (PT) schemes. There have been extensive works on its benefits in the literature [26, 60]. This is another area in which the international organization for standardization (ISO) has similarly cooperated with the (IEC) to establish a relevant standard, ***ISO/IEC 17025***—Testing and Calibration laboratories, which enables laboratories to demonstrate that they have the ability to operate competently in generating valid results.

This type of collaborative confidence-building quality management system efforts, which serve to improve international trade and businesses, shall likely feature more prominently on the international platform, both in the near and distant future. This will most likely be so if the ISO member countries from the African continent deliberately and genuinely make a push for it.

Twenty-First Century: "The Century of 4.0 Technologies"

Predicting, or attempting to predict the future, is generally an exercise in futility except with massive mental and intellectual investments in harnessing the history of our experiences—mistakes and successes alike. Who else then, but Joseph Juran, whose history of quality achievement, as one of the so-called *quality gurus* of the twentieth century, is adaptively enabled with the opportunity of asserting and affirming that "*The 21st Century will be the century of quality?*"

In a less collectively organized system of individuals and individual efforts outside the academia but across the planet earth, quality was conceptualized from real-world, hands-on experiences, to seize and captivate the attention of customers in the marketplace from the USA to Germany, en route to Japan.

Quality grew up an academic orphan, nurtured by the "quality gurus" of the twentieth century, consisting among others Joseph Juran, Edwards Deming, Kaoru Ishikawa, Armand Feigenbaum, and Philip Crosby. This is not to say however that quality has not been a part of man long before the advent of the quality gurus of the twentieth century.

It must, however, be mentioned that quality has always been an integral part of man's life from the time of creation when viewed from the perspective of believers, through the introduction of the principles of separating *good* from *bad* and that of *team-working*.

"And the Lord God commanded the man, "You are free to eat from any tree in the garden; but you must not eat from the tree from the knowledge of good and evil, for when you eat of it you will surely die.""

In emphasizing the quality of teamwork, "The Lord God said, "It is not good for the man to be alone. I will make a helper suitable for him."" (Genesis $2^{16\text{-}18}$).

The conceptual evolution and growth of quality and its tools from real-life experiences over the last century as an academic "*orphan*," has however not diminished the advancement of quality, its principles/philosophy, tools and techniques, into being gradually embraced, developed, and adopted into a body of knowledge with immediate potentials of becoming an academic field or discipline of its own, taught and researched at the college/university and research institutes.

With quality taking its rightful position in the educational, research, and academic worlds to leverage its industrial and business exploitation, this century opens up the doors of opportunities to massively enhance the widened and deepened embrace of quality training/education across the globe. The outcome will undoubtedly result in the emergence of prospective quality professionals capable of sharing ideas in deploying and integrating quality philosophy, knowledge, tools, principles, and methodologies across the interfaces of human socioeconomic and environmental activities, to the enhancement of human values, leadership, people and process management abilities, innovation, and fulfilling corporate social and environmental responsibilities (CSERs)

Relying on the massive integration of quality into all aspects of human life and activities will most likely lead to the following:

- Easy alignment of quality with emerging technologies and technological systems, such as the smart systems, to achieve and advance innovative solutions and other breakthroughs.
- Rightly positioning quality as core dictates of human values, ability to manage and lead people and processes. These shall, in turn, result to enable organizations to achieve set objectives, fulfil customer and regulatory commitments, and exhibit needed agility and adaptive leadership skills for organizational and business sustainability.
- Further advance and continuously improve organizational and business quality management capabilities, as well as the abilities to sustainably achieve and deliver products and services of excellence, in line with promised commitment to customer, marketplace, and regulatory SNEaRs.
- The fulfilment of organizational corporate social and environmental responsibilities (CSER) even when/if not mandatory.
- Further strengthen quality career developmental opportunities, particularly, in uniting the efforts of individual members and member-bodies, to grow and sustain professional bodies such as the ASQ, which through its identity of

"Excellence Through Quality" [2] has the capabilities to continuously enhance quality professionalism by empowering them with access to "powerful quality tools, techniques, and insights," and regular updates at the highest levels of interactive opportunities among the people of the quality world.

Achieving these potentials of quality, quality tools, quality principles, and application shall most realistically define the twenty-first century, hence, the further affirmation of the visionary christening of the twenty-first century being "the century of quality" here. In manifestation of its potentials in the twenty-first century, quality shall "become more critical than ever" in addressing the growing and changing global challenges of the future, "and should assume a critical role as a strategic driving force for building success [73, 74]," in the disruptive and uncertain world of this century, when organizations have to be *agile, adaptive, and innovative*. Organizational agility and ability to quickly adjust to situations of emergencies and uncertainties is highly imperative in business continuity processes.

Quality professional bodies shall continue to grow even more rapidly in the twenty-first century than it has ever been particularly in Asia, Africa, Eastern Europe, Middle East, South America, and the African continent with the ASQ playing key quality sustainability role. The extent and ramification of quality application may require the need for its redefinition to reflect the widened and added dimensions to the principles of its fundamental definition(s) of the last century.

Quality of Remote Working

There are no doubts, whatsoever, that working from home impacted both employers and employees in one way or the other. With employees being *"forced"* to master the art of zoom meetings, employers may have gained the advantage of making savings in not just the overheads but also in work environment safety costs and responsibilities.

With the line between homelife and work life getting thinner with what has now turned out to be a new norm in the way people *work from home,* the issue of achieving and ensuring output quality has to be assured. Apart from the issue of product quality, productivity is another cause for concern for some organizations. While some organizations may have experienced increased productivity, others have been reported to have experienced gaps in productivity. Bridging the productivity gap of may, however, become an impossible task, due to the nuances of working from home that may negatively impact the output of employees.

Balancing homelife with work life may even get harder with time, due to the high risk of succumbing to distractions, isolation, and lower productivity. The question still remains as to "How can you concentrate and meet deadlines when your office of 60 suddenly seems quieter than your home of five?" [93].

As long as the opportunity for working from home exists either wholly, partially, or hybrid, both organizations and employees have to work together to achieve necessary quality management options to achieve on process output quality.

Social Responsibilities and Interfaces

The sustainability of the planet earth, in which we all live in, needs to be adequately assured through the way we use our God-given opportunities. God Himself asserted this fact in, "Then God said, "Let us make man in our image, in our likeness, and let them rule over the fish of the sea and the birds of the air, over the livestock, over all the earth, and over, all the creatures that move along the ground,"" (Genesis 1^{26}); "You shall not pollute the land where you are;" and "Do not defile the land where you live…" ((Numbers $35^{33/34}$).

The role of leadership is conspicuously spelt out here. It goes therefore that man must take care of the planet earth which directly brings out the social responsibilities of our leaders—political, business, businesses and organizations, communal, local, and other cadres of leadership. Hence, there is the general need for both corporate social responsibility (CSR) and governance social responsibility (GSR).

The interfaces and relationships are clear—government/government; government/people; government/environment; business/business; businesses/people; business/environment, etc.

Quality Management and Accountability

The people of the global community have since, December 2019, been in the turmoil of being overwhelmed by the "Severe-Acute-Respiratory Syndrome," coronavirus 2 (SARS-CoV-2), also known as COVID-19 pandemic. Although its origin which is yet to be exactly ascertained, is being rumored to most probably have originated from Wuhan, Hubei, province of China, it leaves a trail of destruction in its wake [78]. Our world was quickly and traumatically transformed into the planet of shock, tears, and sorrow similar to what was experienced during the Spanish influenza. The quality of life was at its gravest low. Thousands of lives were terminated impromptu without the opportunity of their loved ones coming closer to them, in what may pass for some of the poorest *"quality of death."*

Millions of persons were affected by the pandemic potentially exposing them to long-term health consequences. The entertainment industries and global traveling activities were abruptly brought to a standstill. Families were dislocated and the quality of life appreciably depreciated, locally, nationally, and internationally. COVID-19 created an atmosphere of unbearable challenges across the globe and among the people of the world.

The quality of healthcare management was at the lowest ebb. It was an era of global crisis with too many uncertainties, and daily rise in the deaths of people that no one ever wished for. The quality of man's life was drastically reduced to unanticipated levels. It was a time of disruption of the planet earth.

As a result of the general lack of information about the novel coronavirus, decision-making challenges were exacerbated both in terms of effectively managing the situation and easing the pains of the people, especially at a time when the healthcare systems can no more cope with the upsurge of patients to the extent that they lost the trust and confidence of the people. Apart from the loss of some trust in the healthcare system due to the pandemic, public trust in governments, leadership, and some businesses were on the decline probably due to the poorer quality of leadership. And this is justifiably so even in a country like the USA at the onset of the pandemic early 2021.

Some national leaders abhor the quality management sense to play politics which lack quality—politics of insincerity, politics of lies, propaganda, and conspiracy theories—in which leaders were not prepared to take responsibilities and be accountable to the people. Instead, such instances required cooperation to fight the pandemic. Overall, some serious quality management questions arose as to the way relevant entities responded to the pandemic from the onset.

The people of the world deserve leadership, quality in government and organizations, and organizations alike—the quality of responsibility and accountability to sustain the planet.

COVID-19: Root-Cause Quality Management Questions!

> Who is/are responsible for the primary outbreak of the COVID-19 pandemic which has globally claimed over three million lives and affected over one hundred and fifty million people across the globe?
>
> What were the immediately responses by relevant entities to cage the pandemic in place rather than facilitating the spread of the novel coronavirus all over the world?

Organizational quality management system is known to uphold organizational activities in order to sustain their businesses because responsibilities are shared among both the management team and other employees, all of whom are held accountable for their individual roles. The outright and masterly display of teamwork is not only effective in organizational quality management systems but are seen and proved to be working. Organizations are therefore usually quick to respond to emergencies as and whenever necessary. Organizational management teams also embrace interface responsibilities as opposed to public service which often abandons interfacial responsibilities for one reason or the other.

Governance is, on the contrary, usually on the slower side in reacting to issues due to political exigencies. However, the essence of quality management thus enables swift reactions from people in government, especially when it comes to matters of public safety. And even more so, when the source of unusual, and unusually high number of deaths are in question. That is the reason why the Wuhan local, Hubei provincial, and the Chinese governments were expected to have reacted swiftly and aggressively to cage the novel coronavirus-in-place, if finally found out that it actually originated from there.

Leadership transparency, instead of denials, would have made the difference to the people of the world during the outbreak of the COVID-19 pandemic. Governance/people interface responsibilities appeared to be generally lacking too, which perhaps resulted in late responses to either mitigate the pandemic or cage it in place. This thus brings to the fore, the essence of quality management in public services to make quality one of the key essentials of human activities.

Politics apart, the people of the global community were, through the misfortune of the pandemic, given the opportunity of reflecting on, and testing the trust and quality of their political leadership in terms of the levels of their responsibility, transparency, and accountability to the people, at a time the people needed them most.

The level of relevance and extent of providing global leadership in times of chaos by world global bodies such as the World Health Organization (WHO) were undoubtedly also put to test. The implication here is that the quality of WHO as a global body in terms of meeting and serving the purposes for which it was set up were similarly put to test during the COVID-19 era. All in all, the quality of people's lives has been greatly impacted by the COVID-19 pandemic.

COVID-19 Responses by Relevant Entities

The three major entities identifiable with the probable primary origin and management of the COVID-19 pandemic since its initial conquest of the world in December 2019 when it reportedly first infected people in Wuhan, China. They are as follows:

(a) The community, province, and country of origin of the COVID-19 pandemic and their leadership—Wuhan local government, Hubei provincial government, and Chinese government and their leadership.
(b) The individual countries of affected people (virtually all countries of the world) and their leadership.
(c) The World Health Organization (WHO) and its leadership as well as member countries.

Catalyzed by the initial denials, the novel coronavirus quickly gathered the needed momentum to mercilessly mutate into deadlier forms ravaging the entirety of the global community, beginning from Italy to the USA, Brazil, the UK to India leaving no continent untouched even though the Antarctica was only comparatively bruised in December 2020. Some national governments and leaders failed their people woefully, while others successfully managed the pandemic to minimize the number of victims relying most importantly, on quality management principles, tools and techniques.

There are no doubts whatsoever that the outstanding global quality management leadership role of the US center for disease control (CDC), to effectively fight the pandemic cannot be overemphasized, even though they were often undermined by the poor-quality management leadership responses of the then US government. The people of the world benefited substantially from the quick deployment of quality management principles, tools, and techniques that were constituted in the following:

- Leadership
- Change management
- Communication and virtual networking
- Face masking
- Social distancing
- Hand washing
- Remote working—hybrid or full
- Adaptive professional responses of healthcare workers

The WHO officially characterized and declared the COVID-19 as a pandemic on March 11, 2020.

There is the need for the global community to exploit all opportunities so as to get to the primary or root causes and other causal factors of the COVID-19 pandemic, as a lesson for the potential prevention of such happening again in the future? Or if it happens again to be able to nip it in the bud. This is despite the fact that the WHO report into COVID-19 origins zeroes in on animal markets [58].

Quality 4.0: Update, Evolution, and Research

The collaborative efforts among the twentieth century *"quality gurus"* and the manufacturing sector of the global economy greatly impacted the evolving trend of quality, and its constant upgrade in line with the context of its growing needs among various organizations and businesses, from the evolving philosophies of product inspection, quality control, quality assurance, total quality management (TQM) and the quality management systems (QMS).

It is in acknowledgment of the evolutionary trend of *quality* that Dahlgraad [21] assigned three *quality* growth phases between mid-1940s to the end of the early 1990s, while Deleryd and Fundin [25] proposed at a later date, the concept of a fifth phase, Quality 5.0, with the assumption that, after four main generations of quality comes the next phase, "Quality 5.0" which is the current phase of quality focused on organizational *sustainability*.

When viewed from the perspective of quality being born mainly by manufacturing organizations, that is, outside academia, its consistent updating and evolving trend tended more and more to attract the interest of researchers, academics, and theoreticians, among others, especially in the last 20–30 years. That quality, quality management (QM), total quality management (TQM), quality management systems (QMS) and their future offshoots, such as sustainable quality management system (SQMS) shall continue to attract growing research attention is most positively supported by Fundin et al. [34] in their publication of "Quality 2030: quality management for the future." In their publication, they highlighted "themes that have been identified as vital and important for research projects within QM during the coming decade."

The future of quality will be shaped by the combination of newly evolving technologies in Quality 4.0 initiatives with traditional quality methods to face evolving quality management challenges for achieving new optimums in product/services and overall organizational performance, operational excellence, and innovation [76]. This subsequently portends quality management's quest for creative, adaptive, and innovative leadership and professionals, knowledgeable in information and communications technology (ICT) and 4.0 technologies (see Chap. 21). Additionally, they must embrace teamwork and be prepared for changes as Industry 4.0 initiatives emerge, and above all, they must exhibit strong data analytical capabilities and how to use them to take conclusive quality management decisions.

With traditional quality management measures deployed by the global community to survive the estimated 2 years, 2020/21 of COVID-19 pandemic, most of the remaining part of this decade shall witness the digital transformation of quality in line with Industry 4.0 initiatives, as they emerge in line with Industry 4.0 operational pillars. Thereafter, quality management would be engaged in perfecting and aligning Quality 4.0 or "SmartQuality" practice outcomes with the traditional quality management traditions.

In brief, therefore, the future of quality remains in the dictates of global economic forces. The radically changing economic forces of our current world, therefore, makes it extremely critical for quality managers of the future to evolve quality-based integrated management strategies and programs that fit the ensuing business era rather than continuing with systems that may have worked in the past [5]. Already traditional quality management practices have been reported to show incompetency if applied in the context of complex processes, as evinced by Kuhn et al. [51].

The direction of quality, Quality 4.0, thus portends some complexities which may begin to evolve in the context and exploits of Industry 4.0 initiatives. Some research workers have therefore viewed the future direction of quality management from the perspectives of products manufactured in the era of digitalized industrial manufacturing economy [37, 70, 79] in relationship to the initiatives of Industry 4.0 [32, 36, 65, 82, 94].

For businesses in all sectors of the globalized economy, the twenty-first century represents the age of the global realization of digital economic potentials and customer centricity and agility.

The first half of the century will be fully focused on organizational capabilities to fully adopt and adapt to Industry 4.0 technologies to foster greater engagement, efficiency, and sustainability to embrace the large-scale change resulting from the digitalized economies.

With the full realization of the digital transformation of organizational operations and activities, the second half of the century shall be interconnectedly and sustainably devoted mostly, toward the full exploitations of the opportunities highly inherent in 4.0 base technologies. The trend of virtually all business transactions from 2030 onward shall be altered appreciably, from manufacturing to other aspects of business activities. Sales and other business operations are likely going to be digitalized, as every operation digitizable would have been digitalized.

The second half of the century will most transparently bring digital transformation to the people and society. We shall therefore witness society's digital transformation, from artificial intelligence and autonomous vehicles, to predictive maintenance, quantum computing, full automation, robotics, autonomous maritime systems, underwater drones, remote inspection of offshore wind farms of the future, and other advanced technology innovations.

References

1. Altunas, S., & Yener, E. (2012). An approach based on TRIZ methodology and SERVQUAL scale to improve the quality of health care service: A case study. *Ege Academic Review, 12*(1), 97–106.
2. American Society for Quality, (ASQ). Excellence through quality. https://www.asq.org/
3. American Society for Quality, (ASQ). (2015). What is organizational excellence? https://www.asq.org/quality-resources/organizational-excellence. Retrieved on 21 Nov 2020.
4. Andersen, B., Sorqvist, L., Saraiva, P., & Watson, G. (2015). *Structured improvement for the 21st century: A new model from Europe*. Presented at the World Quality Forum, International Academy of Quality, Budapest, Hungary.
5. Antony, J. (2013). What does the future hold for quality professionals in organizations of the twenty-first century? *The TQM Journal, 25*, 677–685.
6. Aquilani, B., Silvestri, C., Ruggieri, A., & Gatti, C. (2017). A systemic literature review on total quality management critical success factors and the identification of new areas of research. *The TQM Journal, 29*(1), 183–213. https://doi.org/10.1108/TQM-01-2016-003
7. Arena, M., & Uhl-Bien, M. (2018, February). Leadership for organizational adaptability: A theoretical synthesis and integrative framework. *Leadership Quarterly, 29*, 89–104.
8. Arena, M. J. (2018). *Adaptive space: How GM and other companies are positively disrupting themselves and transforming into Agile Organizations*. McGraw Hill.
9. ASQ. (2015). *Future of quality report*. American Society of Quality.
10. ASQ. (2021, January). Survey: Manufacturers plan for permanent changes. *Quality Progress*, p. 10.
11. Obama, B. (2014). http://www.couriernewsroom.com. Retrieved on 16 Nov 2020.
12. Barouch, G., & Ponsignon, F. (2016). The epistemological basis for quality management. *Total Quality Management and Business Excellence, 27*(7–8), 944–962. https://doi.org/10.1080/14783363.2016.1188659
13. Barouch, G., & Kleinhans, S. (2015). Learning from the criticisms of quality management. *International Journal Quality and Service Sciences, 7*(213), 201–216. https://doi.org/10.1108/IJQSS-02-2015-0026
14. Barry, K., Domb, E., & Slocum, M. S. (2007, August). *The TRIZ Journal*. http://www.triz-journal.com/archives/what_is_triz/
15. Bedgood, C. (2021, May). Prescribing ISO to improve performance. *Quality Progress*, pp. 28–35.
16. Berwick, D. M. (1989). Continuous improvement as an ideal in health care. *The New England Journal of Medicine, 320*, 53–56.
17. Bush, G. (2014, October). Take care of your "Ugly Baby". *Quality Progress*, pp. 30–35.
18. Carnerud, D. (2018). 25 years of quality management research – Outlines and trends. *International Journal of Quality and Reliability Management, 35*(1), 208–231. https://doi.org/10.1108/IJQRM-01-2017-0013
19. Carnerud, D., & Backstrom, I. (2019, August 20). Four decades of research on quality: Summarizing trendspotting and looking ahead. *Journal Total Quality Management & Business Excellence*. https://doi.org/10.1080/14783363.2019.1655397
20. Cochran, C. (2015). *ISO 9001:2015 in plain English* (pp. 53–54). Paton Professional Books.

21. Dahlgaard, S. M. P. (1999). The evolution patterns of quality management: Some reflections on the quality movement. *Total Quality Management, 10*(4–5), 473–480. https://doi.org/10.1080/095442997424
22. Dahlgaard-Park, S. M., Reyes, L., & Chen, C.-K. (2018). The evolution and convergence of total quality management and management theories. *Total Quality Management, 29*(9–10), 1108–1128. https://doi.org/10.1080/14783363.2018.1486556
23. Dan, Jacob. (2017). Quality 4.0 - Fresh thinking for quality in digital era. Bio. Management. *Quality Digest*, July 24. https://www.qualitydigest.com. e-Book.
24. Daniels, A. (2021, March). The next level of success – The benefits of integrating QMSs and SMSs. *Quality Progress*, pp. 56–58.
25. Deleryd, M., & Fundin, A. (2015, October 26–27). *The fifth generation of quality concept* [Paper presentation]. The World Quality Forum of International Academy for Quality (IAQ).
26. Early, M. C., & Astles, J. R. (2016). Proficiency testing program providers respond to client concerns. *Medical Laboratory Observer, 48*(6), 12–14, 16, quiz 17.
27. Edmund, M. (2020, November). Supply chain management: Defeating disruption – Strategies to maintain supply chains when the world is upended. *Quality Progress*, pp. 10–11.
28. EFQM. (2012). *The EFQM excellence model 2013*. EFQM Representative Office. http://www.efqm.org/en/tabid/132
29. EPA. http://www.epa.gov. Retrieved on 22 Nov 2020.
30. Feigenbaum, A. V., & Feigenbaum, D. S. (1999). New quality for the 21st century. *Quality Progress, 32*(12), 27.
31. Feigenbaum, A. V., & Feigenbaum, D. S. (2009). *The power of management innovation*. McGraw-Hill.
32. Fonseca, L., Amaral, A., & Jose Oliveira, J. (2020). Quality 4.0: The EFQM 2020 model and Industry 4.0 and Industry 4.0 relationships and implications. *Sustainability, 13*, 1307. https://doi.org/10.3390/su13063107
33. Fredriksson, M., & Isaksson, R. (2018). Making sense of quality philosophies. *Total Quality Management and Business Excellence, 29*(11–12), 1452–1465. https://doi.org/10.1080/14783363.2016.1266245
34. Fundin, A., Lilja, J., Lagrosen, Y., & Bergquist, B. (2020, December 29). Quality 2030: Quality management for the future. *Total Management and Business Excellence*. https://doi.org/10.1080/14783363.2020.1863778
35. Gagnon, D. (2021, April 29). What is a magnet hospital? https://www.snhu.edu
36. Ghobakhloo, M. (2018). The future of manufacturing industry: A strategic roadmap toward Industry 4.0. *Journal of Manufacturing Technology Management, 29*, 910–936.
37. Gritsuk, N. V., Gamulinskaya, N. V., & Petrova, E. V. (2020). The innovative approach to managing the product quality in the digital economy: Intellectual account and auditing. *International Journal for Quality Research, 14*, 543–558.
38. Gutner, T., & Adams, M. (2009). *A leadership prescription for the future of quality*. Report of the Conference Board Quality Council.
39. Hua, Z., Yang, J., Coulibaly, S., & Zhang, B. (2006). Integration TRIZ with problem-solving tools: A literature review from 1995 to 2006. *International Journal of Business Innovation and Research, 1*(1). https://doi.org/10.1504/IJBIR.2006.011091
40. International Organization for Standardization. (2015). ISO 14001:2015, Environmental Management Systems – Requirements with guidance for use. http://www.iso.org
41. International Organization for Standardization. (2015). ISO 9000:2015, Quality Management Systems – Fundamentals and Vocabulary.
42. International Organization for Standardization. (2015). ISO 9001:2015, Quality Management Systems – Requirements. https://www.iso.org
43. International Organization for Standardization. (2018). ISO 9004:2018 – Quality Management – Quality of an Organization – Guidance to achieve sustained success.
44. ISO. ISO and health – Great things happen when the world agrees. pp. 1–15. https://www.iso.org. Retrieved on 19 July 2021.

45. Jacob, D. (2017). What is Quality 4.0? https://www.blog.Insresearch.com. Retrieved 17 July 2021.
46. Jordan, A. (2021, July). CEO of ASQ, "75 and Counting – Quality's impact on the world around us." *Quality Progress*, p. 4.
47. Juran Knowledge Base (Blog). (2019, June 15). Quality 4.0 – The future of quality. https://www.juran.com. Retrieved 17 July 2021.
48. Kimberlin, C. (2016). RAC 2015 Chair, ASQ Board of Directors, Foreword 1; Quality in the 21st century; Perspectives from ASQ Feigenbaum Medal Winners. In P. Sampaio & P. Saraiva (Eds.), Springer Nature.
49. KPMG. (2021, May). Survey – Many concerned AI moving too fast. *Quality Progress*, p. 6.
50. Kristensen, S., Hammer, A., Bartels, P., Sunol, R., Groene, O., Thompson, C. A., Arah, O. A., Kutaj-Wasikowska, H., Michel, P., & Wagner, C. (2015, December). Quality management and perception of teamwork and safety climate in European hospitals. *International Journal of Quality in Health Care, Oxford, Academic, 27*(6), 499–506. https://doi.org/10.1093/intqhc/mzv079
51. Kuhn, M., Schaefer, F., & Otten, H. (2018). Process complexity as a future challenge – A quality management perspective. *TQM Journal, 2018*(30), 701–716.
52. Kumar, P., Maiti, J., & Gunasekaran, A. (2018). Impact of quality management systems on firm performance. *International Journal of Quality and Reliability Management, 35*(5), 1034–1059. https://doi.org/10.1108/IJQRM-02-2017-0030
53. LariSemnani, B., Far, R. M., Shalipoor, E., & Mohseni, M. (2015, January). Using creative problem (TRIZ) in improving the quality of hospital services. *Global Journal Health, 7*(1), 88–97. https://doi.org/10.5539/gjhs.v7n1p88
54. Lee, S. M. (2015). The age of quality innovation. *International Journal of Quality Innovation, 1*, 1. https://doi.org/10.1186/s40887-015-0002x
55. Lindborg, H. J. (2020, November). Employee engagement – Adaptive space: How organizations can harness employee creativity to adjust to disruptive changes. *Quality Progress*, pp. 5–7.
56. London, C., Comeros, R. C., & Nguyen, A. (2020, November). Quality management systems. *Quality* Progress, pp. 32–37.
57. Masters, K. (Ed.). (2014). *Role development – Role development in professional nursing practice* (3rd ed., p. 93). Jone & Bertlett Learning.
58. Maxmen, A. (2021, April 8). The world this week, "WHO report into COVID origins zeroes in on animal market". *Nature, 592*, 172–173. Springer Nature.
59. Merrill, P. (2012, June). Quality for tomorrow. *Quality Progress*, pp. 25–28.
60. Middlebrook, K., & Morris, A. (2004). *The effect of proficiency testing participation on laboratory performance*. Canadian Association for Environmental Analytical Laboratories.
61. Myers, K. (2020, October 31). Future-proof your quality systems. *Quality Magazine*. http://www.qualitymag.com
62. Nakashima, E., Torbati, Y., & Englund, W. (2021, May 8). Energy, Ransomware attack leads to shutdown of major U.S. pipeline system. *The Washington Post*. https://www.washingtonpost.com. Retrieved on 30 May 2021.
63. National Institute for Standards and Technology. (2010). Malcolm Baldrige National Quality Award, Award Criteria, NIST, Washington.
64. National Institute of Standards and Technology. (2012). 2011–2012 criteria for performance excellence. https://www.nist.gov/baldrige/publications/business_nonprofit_criteria.cfm
65. Nenadal, J. (2020). The new EFQM model: What is really new and could be considered as a suitable tool with respect to quality 4.0 concept? *Quality Innovation Prosperity*, 17–27. https://doi.org/10.12776/QIP.V2411.1415. https://www.qip-journal.eu. 24 Jan 2020.
66. Nenadal, J., Vykydal, D., & Waloszek, D. (2018). Organizational excellence: Approaches, models and their use in Czech organizations. *Quality Innovation Prosperity, 22*(2), 47–64. https://doi.org/10.12776/QIP.V2212.1129

67. O'Reilly, G. M., Mitchell, R. D., Noonan, M. P., et al. (2020). Informing emergency care for COVID-19 patients: The COVID-19 Emergency Department Quality Improvement Project protocol. *Emergency Medicine Australasia, 32*(3), 511–514. https://doi.org/10.1111/1742-6723.13513
68. Oesterreich, S., Cywindski, J. B., Elo, B., Geube, M., & Mathur, P. (2020, June). Quality improvement during the COVID-19 pandemic. *Cleveland Clinic Journal of Medicine*. https://doi.org/10.3949/ccjm.87a.ccc041
69. Owens, T., & Fritz, C. (2012, June). Innovation- up and away, ways to tease out ideas, harness creativity and elevate you're your organization's innovation process. *Quality Progress*, pp. 18–24.
70. Popkova, E. G. (2019). Quality of digital product: Theory and practice. *International Journal for Quality Research, 14*, 201–218.
71. Ramanathan, H., & Charles, D. (2021, January). Testing schemes help labs monitor the quality of medicine. *Quality Progress*, pp. 30–37.
72. Reid, R. D. (2011, December). Know your future. *Quality* Progress, p. 70.
73. Sampaio, P., & Saraiva, P. (2016). From past perfect to future conditional. In P. Sampaio & P. Saraiva (Eds.), *Quality in the 21st century* (p. 16). Springer International.
74. Sampaio, P., & Saraiva, P. (2016). From past perfect to future conditional. In P. Sampaio & P. Saraiva (Eds.), *Quality in the 21st century* (p. 2). Springer International.
75. Sanderson, P. (2018, April 30). Quality software and the future. *Quality Magazine*. http://www.qualitymag.com
76. Santos, G., Sa, J. C., Felix, M. J., Barreto, L., Carvalho, F., Doiro, M., Zgodavova, K., & Stefanovic, M. (2021). New needed quality management skills for quality managers 4.0. *Sustainability, 13*, 6149. https://doi.org/10.3390/su13116149
77. Schvaneveldt, S. J., & Neve, B. V. (2021, March). Proving their mettle: Combating the COVID-19 pandemic with quality tools. *Quality Progress*, pp. 24–31.
78. Sheahan, T. P., & Frieman, M. B. (2020). The continued epidemic threat of SARS-CoV-2 and implications for the future of global public health. *Current Opinion in Virology, 40*, 37–40. https://doi.org/10.1016/j.coviro.2020.05.010
79. Shokhnekh, A. V. (2019). The main notions, principles and procedures of strategic quality management of small business in the system of digital economy in view of risks of drift: A cognitive approach. *International Journal for Quality Research, 13*, 665–668.
80. Singer, S. J., & Vogus, T. J. (2013). Reducing hospital errors: Interventions that build safety culture. *Annual Review of Public Health, 34*, 373–396.
81. Sonis, J. D., Black, L., Baugh, J., Wilcox, S. R., Yun, B. J., & Aaronson, E. L. (2020, April 11). Leveraging existing quality improvement communication strategies during the COVID-19 crisis: Creation of an emergency department COVID-19 case conference. *American Journal of Emergency Medicine Correspondence, 38*(7), 1523–1524. https://doi.org/10.1016/j.ajem.2020.04.021.
82. Sung, T. K. (2018). Industry 4.0: A Korea perspective. *Technological Forecasting and Social Change, 132*, 40–45.
83. Tan, K. C. (2002). A comparative study of 16 national awards. *The TQM Magazine, 14*(3), 165–171. https://doi.org/10.1108/9544780210425874
84. The National Institute of Standards and Technology, NIST. https://www.inst.gov
85. TRIZ. (2012). http://qualityandinnovation.com/2012/02/04/all-about-triz-for-innovation/
86. Van Kemenade, E., & Hardjono, T. W. (2019). Twenty-first century total quality management: The emergence paradigm. *The TQM Journal, 31*(2), 150–166. https://doi.org/10.1108/TQM-04-2018-0045
87. Van Rompuy, H. President European Council. http://www.efqm.org/en/tabid/132
88. Vogus, T. J., Sutcliffe, K. M., & Weick, K. E. (2010). Doing no harm: Enabling, enacting, and elaborating a culture of safety in health care. *Academy of Management Perspectives, 24*, 60–77.
89. Wagner, C., Smits, M., Sorra, J., & Huang, C. C. (2013). Assessing patient safety culture in hospitals across countries. *International Journal for Quality in Health Care, 25*(3), 213–221.

90. Wagner, C., Groene, O., Thompson, C. A., Dersakissian, M., Klazinga Nick, S., Arah, O. A., Sonol, R., & DUQuE Project Consortium. (2014). DUQuE quality management measures: Associations between quality management at hospital and pathway levels. *International Journal for Quality in Health Care, 26 Suppl 1*(Suppl 1), 66–73. https://doi.org/10.1093/intqhc/mzu020. Epub 2014 Mar 9.
91. Wagner, C., Groene, O., Thompson, C. A., Klazinga, N. S., Dersakissian, M., Arah, O. A., Sonol, R., & DUQuE Project Consortium. (2014). Development and validation of an index to assess hospital quality management systems. *International Journal for Quality in Health Care, 26 Suppl 1*(Suppl 1), 16–26. https://doi.org/10.1093/intqhc/mzu021. Epub 2014 Mar 11.
92. Watson, G. H. (n.d.). *The fundamentals of quality: Route to market access and commercial success: A course book for quality champions* (p. 85). International Trade Center. e-book. https://www.static.prod01.ue1.p.pcomm.net
93. Wrestler, D. (2021, March). Work from home – Home Office Anarchy. *Quality Progress*, pp. 12–13.
94. Zaidin, N. H. M., Diah, M. N. H., Po, H. Y., & Sorooshian, S. (2018). Quality management in Industry 4.0 era. *Journal of Management and Science, 8*, 82–91.
95. Zolnierek, C. (2020). Change is inevitable: How COVID-19 accelerated nursing change. *Texas Nursing Magazine*, (3), 9–10.

Industry 4.0: A Review

21

From Concept to Maturity

Introduction

German industries are globally known for their product quality which gives them not just the edge on the global market but the ability to withstand increasing global competition on product quality and production costs. As a result of high labor costs in Europe and other developed countries, their companies began relocating production facilities to aspiring countries, as suggested by Brettel et al. [1]. In this way, productivity and quality gaps were closed. To be abreast of competition, German manufacturing companies focused attention on the following:

- Customized products
- Swiftly getting products to the marketplace

The outcome here is the embrace of *agile manufacturing* and *mass customization* of products thereby transforming companies into integrated networks, in the advent of Industry 4.0. In order to unite their key competencies, companies headed to the virtualization of their processes and supply chain to achieve seamless inter-company collaborative operations, a trending pattern in manufacturing industries. Hence, the latest buzzword in the international industrial manufacturing world is "Industry 4.0" or digital transformation, and the conceptual outcome of the "SmartFactory." Industry 4.0 is therefore generally viewed in terms of creating intelligent products and production processes in future factories ("SmartFactory") envisaged to enable the following:

- Rapid product development
- Flexible production

T. A. Ibidapo, *From Industry 4.0 to Quality 4.0*, Management for Professionals,
https://doi.org/10.1007/978-3-031-04192-1_21

in a complex "Smart" production environment capable of using cyber-physical system (CPS) to facilitate communication among humans, machines, and products.

Lots of discussions and publications emanating from academic research, surveys and interviews, blogs, consultancy works, and other relevant sources have been reported. There have also been reviews upon reviews about Industry 4.0—initiatives, implementation, or development to actualization.

Already some of the theoretical research accomplishments in topics encapsulating Industry 4.0 are grounded most particularly in the way it has effectively and rapidly generated the conceptualization of many other "4.0" initiatives, appellations and features, paramount among which are the following:

- Quality 4.0
- Healthcare 4.0
- 4.0 technologies or 4.0 base technologies
- 4.0 Manufacturing or "SmartFactory"

It may not be surprising therefore that Industry 4.0 is not just a fundamental appellation for drastic changes resulting from digital transformation but a platform for naming all subsequent industrial manufacturing processes of the future. This thus makes it clear that future changes of the current magnitude may subsequently give birth to Industry 5.0; 6.0; ....N.0. But for the present time, changes in other sectors of the economy relating to digital changes, in any form or art, will readily earn the sector the 4.0 appellation. Hence, we may have "Energy 4.0," "Transportation 4.0," etc.

Industry 4.0—theory to reality—thus presents a review of reviews in this hot topic of our time. The outcome of this review is therefore highly inherent in the ongoing discussions about the "digital revolution" and the business vision of *Industry 4.0,* which is created from the "disruptive competitive advantages" envisaged from developing or implementing Industry 4.0 initiatives.

Industry 4.0 and its ambitious conceptional ideals have, therefore, opened up a plethora of research opportunities and opinions across the academic world, management consultancy groups, online blogs, organizational boardrooms, and research facilities; in the design and equipment manufacturing workshops; and IT providers and security experts to resolve lots of questions portended in the implementation or development of Industry 4.0 initiatives. These interests are generally focused on figuring out the way forward to realizing and actualizing the conceptualized goals and objectives—the "SmartFactory," Smart…this…. Smart, that.

While the exact impact of Industry 4.0 cannot be exactly ascertained as at now, there have been speculations by various authors and organizations about the future perspectives of Industry 4.0—development, implementation, and practices. There have been reports of unrealistic expectations, and at times, those of overenthusiasm.

What Is in a Name—Industry 4.0 and "SmartFactory"?

Call it Industry 4.0, or fourth industrial revolution, you are still right, even though the name does not often tell the whole story and when it does, not always in its most logical form! Where then is the logic in the name, Industry 4.0?

Going down the memory lane back to history may, however, provide a clue, or perhaps, a near clue!

Combining steam power with mechanical production led to improved changes which resulted in the industrialization of production in the late eighteenth century to earn the people of the world its first known industrial revolution.

Similarly, the mass production which resulted from a combination of electricity and assembly lines mid-nineteenth century to earn the world its second industrial revolution.

This was followed in the late twentieth century by the third industrial revolution which was triggered and driven by a combination of electronics, controls, and advances in computing, information and communications technology (ICT), complemented with globalization.

Coining Industry 4.0, or fourth industrial revolution from envisaged interoperable digitalized SmartFactories, with every aspect of the production chain automatically interlinked, justifiably resulted to massive *changes*—technological, social, and business paradigm changes—to earn the global revolutionary attention that it is being currently accorded. The development of Industry 4.0 is closely related to emerging technologies, which are likely going to continue to emerge with further development of Industry 4.0 and beyond, perhaps deeply into the mid-twenty-first century.

Hence, Industry 4.0 is a symbolism of imminent change—disruptive changes—in the industrial manufacturing world, primarily orchestrated by the German government, followed closely by other western economies, especially members of the European union and the USA.

The serialization of global industrial developmental changes is viewed merely as a mathematical oversimplification of issues, with perhaps minor logically rooted reasoning.

The logic of coining the concept, Industry 4.0, resides in the original notion of its originators that the innovative concepts inherent in the industrial production improvement changes of Industry 4.0, shall ultimately create some disruptions in industrial production processes, to achieve higher productivity, similar to the ones previously experienced in the three previous industrial revolutions.

The common denominator in the serialization of the world's revolutionarily phased eras of industrial manufacturing development, is undoubtedly, "*change,*" often times big changes of improvement, a key aspect of quality, and its management phenomena.

Industry 4.0 initiatives are deeply rooted primarily, in linking intelligent factories with every part of the production line or chain, and automated systems in creating a "*smart*" production environment.

Digitizing every machinery/equipment across the entirety of manufacturing processes results in the digitalization of the whole factory, transforming it into the "SmartFactory." What is in the appellation, *Smart* this, *smart* that, *smart* everything, is all embracing in the digital transformation! Smart systems are quite capable of doing many smart things in business processes and activities. Smart systems can, among other things, autonomously and connectedly exchange and analyze information about the following:

- Production or functional problems or faults
- Stock levels
- Changes in product orders and/or demand levels

It is in these and other similar ways that smart systems deploy their capabilities to facilitate business efficiencies. It goes to say therefore that any production system, which acquires, among others, the above-specified functions that can readily deploy the smart systems, for business efficiencies, is "Smart." The digital transformation thus leads us toward achieving "connected intelligent automation: smart, hyperconnected agents deployed in environments where humans and machines cooperate—and leverage data—to achieve shared goals" [2].

The implication here is that Industry 4.0 initiatives are likely going to be applicable to wider scopes than just the industrial manufacturing sector as originally conceptualized. While both traditional industrial manufacturing and the digital age manufacturing settings of the SmartFactory are similarly automated, they are separated by the level of automation and two critical features of *connectivity/interconnectivity* and *flexibility*.

The two key factors differentiating the traditional industrial manufacturing principles from that of the conceptualized but emerging digital transformational Industry 4.0 initiatives for industrial manufacturing systems are, on the one hand, primarily, *connectivity* and/or *interconnectivity*, and on the other hand, the *flexibility* of the system.

Unlike the traditional industrial manufacturing system which is horizontally integrated, the "SmartFactory" setting resulting from Industry 4.0 initiatives is due to the convergence of the digital and physical worlds, *vertically integrated* through the following:

- ***Connected*** manufacturing systems
- ***End-to-end*** holistic integration through the entirety of the value chain [3].

The supply systems are operated at different scopes of efficiency.

- Traditional industrial manufacturing operates the sort of static *linear, sequential supply chain*
- The dynamic ***interconnected***, *open system supply operations*, also referred to as *digital supply network*

Two major advantages of the smart factory digital systems are, among others, listed as follows:

- Capability of using "a constant stream of data from connected operations and production systems to learn and adapt to new demands" [4].
- Ability to "integrate data from system-wide physical, operational, and human assets to drive manufacturing, maintenance, inventory tracking, digitization of operations through the digital twin and other types of activities across the entire manufacturing network" [5].

These advantages may reportedly lead to higher organizational or business competitiveness through less production downtime, higher productivity, and more agile system, and above all, the ability to predict and make adjustments to any changes within the manufacturing environment or its broader network. The concept of Industry 4.0 initiatives, therefore, is in its rudimental structure, strongly embedded in the rapid technological transformational changes, using the 4.0 base technologies and their changing trends, to accomplish a more flexible, agile, and adaptive production system of the future—the not-too-distant future maturing perhaps in mid-twenty-first century. The type of changes envisaged is to a certain extent disruptive.

Though we may be talking of disruption at different levels, the global community has come a long way in its almost 2-year experience of the COVID-19 pandemic disruptive changes—disruptive times suddenly thrown upon the human society, which was socially, economically, and environmentally disrupted. The aftermath of COVID-19 pandemic and its ripple effects created some of the strangest times in the lives of the people of the global community—there were scarcity of chips which resulted in the scarcity of new cars, used car inventory was virtually at zero level, lumber prices escalated while the entirety of the supply chain systems was disrupted.

While the large manufacturers and industries in the western economies may be positively disposed toward the development of Industry 4.0 initiatives and successfully implementing or developing them, it is not likely that most of the smaller industries and businesses are enthusiastic about it, especially with respect to the scarcity of necessary capital investment requirements for developing the initiatives. The reactions of the latter, and determination to implement Industry 4.0 initiatives or not, may on the long run, be determined or dictated by either their individual, or perhaps collective hunger for global economic competitiveness in the globalized economy. They may also be motivated by the comparative experience of organizations that may finally have succeeded in implementing and actualizing the supposed expectations of Industry 4.0 initiatives.

This is particularly so, because of the scarcity of the necessary resources on the one hand, and the inadequacy of knowledge and information, about the details of what the development of Industry 4.0 initiatives entails and portends for them. The general lack of the detailed analysis of its pros and cons and the inability to know or perhaps assess the level of their relevance, or not, to those smaller industries and their business objectives. In addition, too, is the simple fact that there is a general lack of awareness in the public domain about what Industry 4.0 initiatives and their development are all about.

All that most organizations are sure of are their dreamt of their promising fantasies and expectations of Industry 4.0 as heard or projected by their bigger and diverse counterparts. How it is exactly going to impact the people and environment—socially, and economically, except perhaps the aspect of workplace susceptibility—can therefore only be imagined by some people and organizations.

There are, however, no doubts that Industry 4.0 may result in shaping the way we work, do business, and the nature of our business models in the future. However, whichever way it goes, Industry 4.0 initiatives represent enormous *disruptive* changes. No matter what we think, it is a gamble worth taking, especially by those organizations and businesses that may have initial doubts but have the financial wherewithal. For those that lack the financial wherewithal, it may be worthwhile playing the waiting game as we go, even though it may be better to grow along with the ongoing technological trends and Industry 4.0 developmental phases.

Principles of Developing Industry 4.0 Initiatives

Just as has previously been experienced in the last century, there had been tremendous increases in each technological advancement stages of the three previous industrial revolutionary changes experienced by man:

- Steam engine–powered factories in the nineteenth century
- Electrification in the early 1900s
- Automation in the 1970s

Automation which has to a certain extent been a part of our factory operations, coupled with the advances in computer technology, quickly transformed the information, communications, and telecommunications (ICT)—IT, global system for mobile communications (GSM), and e-commerce. The aftermath of these developments no doubt fueled further technological advances leading to the incubation of ideas that finally gave birth to the initiatives of the present-day industrial manufacturing dreams and changes gradually culminating in the smart factory.

Industry 4.0 transformational initiatives involve, in principle, the connection of cyber-physical systems—sensors, machines, workpieces, and IT systems—along the value chain. This is done in such a way that these systems are able to interact with one another through the use of standard internet-based protocols capable of analyzing data "to predict failure, configure themselves, and adapt to changes," Ruessman et al. [6]. Hence, Industry 4.0 thus provides the industrial manufacturing sector with the opportunities of generating, gathering, and analyzing data, across machines, making them faster and more flexible, to achieve more efficient processes to produce high-quality products, reduced costs, and improved business competitive abilities.

It follows from here therefore that developing Industry 4.0 initiatives may ultimately make industrial manufacturing organizations or businesses more competitive, seizing the opportunities of the following manufacturing advantages:

- Increase in manufacturing productivity
- Shift economics
- Foster industrial growth
- Modify the profile of the workforce

There are no doubts too that Industry 4.0 initiatives shall ultimately change and reshape the traditional industrial production landscape as well as the relationships among the stakeholders—investors, suppliers/supply chain, customers/marketplace, and organizations.

Core of Industry 4.0 Approach

Organizational digital maturity is mentioned frequently in the literature as key to organizational preparedness for the digital transformation. Transitioning to Industry 4.0 initiatives or digital transformation requires most importantly that organizations first define their present and future states, in terms of the three critical factors/dimensions—technology, organizations, and personnel, as well as the dependencies between them, as suggested by Leineweber et al. [7].

This is similarly the opinion of Geissbauer et al. [8], in their argument that the three aspects mostly critical to Industry 4.0 approach:

- Full digitalization of an organization's operations
- Redesigning of organizational products and services
- Closer interaction with customers

Apart from developing organizational formal digitalization strategy, there is the need too, to make needed changes to organizational practices and structure, so as to facilitate organizational adaptation to various aspects of digital transformation especially, with regard to information technology (IT) architecture, data management, regulatory compliance, and overall organizational culture. Their studies further emphasized the fact that analytics and organizational analytical capabilities are critical to Industry 4.0 development. Hence, the general need for organizations to invest in human capital in the areas of acquiring expertise in effectively managing and analyzing data.

One of the main challenges of digitalization is the need to effectively manage data, and understanding of every aspect and bit of data gathered and the opportunities therein. The issue of the quality of data in terms of data storage, security, and effective management, therefore, becomes very critical. Organizations must, therefore, be prepared to provide needed infrastructure to store, analyze, protect, and manage data.

There is no wonder therefore that "With today's technology and ongoing innovations, the world seems to be drowning in a data tsunami," Costich [9]. Accomplishing the digital transformation goal can thus be generally viewed from the following perspectives:

1. What does digital transformation mean for your organization? Establish a clear vision with 100% leadership support while identifying relevant digitalization team leader and other members.
2. Is the organization digitally mature in terms of people, process, technology, and requisite infrastructural needs to embark on the digitalization journey?
3. Carry out a gap analysis to identify all missing elements of digitalization needed to achieve organizational digital transformation.
4. Put measure in place to eliminated all missing elements to bridge the gaps in final preparedness for the digital journey.
5. Put an organization-wide detailed digital step-by-step transformational plan in place. Benchmark, where possible, your planned or intended digital transformational activities with those of similar organizations and/or businesses with experience in digital transformation. Make necessary adjustments.
6. Communicate your action plan to relevant stakeholders.
7. Set on the digital transformational journey with the full consent and support of all stakeholders before finally embarking on this *digital disruptive* adventure/exercise.

It is highly critical that organizations must be very specific and purposeful in their vision, goals, and objectives before setting out on the digital transformational journey.

Industry 4.0 Changes and Fear of the Unknown

Industry 4.0 or the fourth industrial revolutionary winds of change are today blowing across the world from Europe, North America, Japan, Asia to China, excluding perhaps the countries of the African continent. It is an industrial manufacturing revolution, in which industrial manufacturing companies are being digitized, resulting in the digital transformation of industrial manufacturing businesses and perhaps others later. It is also known or referred to as "*Smart Manufacturing*."

One of the key essential facilitating factors of *Industry 4.0* is the rapidly evolving information and communications technology (ICT), which has already brought immensely diverse qualitative communications' changes to industry, people, and society at large, including the social media. The role of ICT may perhaps have been taken for granted, by the people of the global community, until various conspiracy theories began to emerge in the social media, about the emergence of 5G. 5G technology, however, survived the rumors and conspiracy theories which circulated around the globe at that time. These painted conspiracy theories and imagery of 5G were perhaps due to the *"fear of the unknown."*

A similar situation experienced in the USA and some other parts of the world is the evolution of many fantasies and conspiracy theories about the COVID-19 pandemic and the COVID-19 vaccines. There is no other name for this too, than the fear of the unknown.

Fear is known already as one of the strongest emotions of man. Change, by its characteristic features, is known to bring with it many unknowns [10]. Since change is inevitable, there is the need to see and view it as a new normal whenever it happens, or is experienced. This is the reason why businesses and organizations have to adaptively embrace change thereby *"disrupting before they themselves are being disrupted."* Organizational changes can mainly be stimulated by the following major forces [11]:

- Technology and all ramifications of advancements that come with it.
- Economic shocks that may result from such situations as global recession and the financial sector collapse, similar to the ones experienced in the first decade of the twenty-first century.
- Nature of the workforce which may emanate from issues such as aging population and cultural diversification of workers.
- Competition in the globalized economy which may require organizational mergers and acquisitions, as well as the need to comply with changing regulatory requirement of government in industry, trade, and commerce.
- Global political dynamics driving international trade agreements, the concentration of manufacturing outfits in China, and the almost strict reliance on China-rooted supply chain systems.
- Social trends that may evolve generally from connectivity, liberation of attitudes, and daily increasing environmental awareness.
- Environmental changes resulting from natural disasters such as global warming, and pandemics such as that caused by the novel coronavirus.

It is unfortunate that people generally resist even changes that positively impact them, as already demonstrated by the COVID-19 vaccine refusal in the USA. Change management is critical to the current world of the fourth industrial manufacturing revolution, hence, the need for its effectiveness. Effective change management (Chap. 15) must, therefore, be seen as an integral part of organizational quality management system for sustainability.

Being conscious of the fact that, "resistance is not only a psychological reaction to change, but also a physiological reaction" [10], generally helps to handle resistances to change. What we are today witnessing, in the USA and other parts of the world, is people's resistance to the COVID-19 pandemic vaccines, which most likely may have originated from "fear, prejudice, anxiety and ignorance," as well as from the influence of various political motives and conspiracy theorists' exaggerations about the vaccine.

People, businesses, and organizations, still alive and operational today, have actually gained some evidence-based experience from the global management of COVID-19 pandemic-induced changes.

It was an experience of *disruptive* impacts on organizational processes and activities, just as it is a cultural and economic shock for the people of the world. COVID-19 pandemic thus demonstrates most explicitly, how disruptively, changes impact both humans and organizations. With digital transformation, it is simply transforming to a digital age of multiple changes, awash with data—enormous amounts of data—the data mining phenomenon. Hence, it is the talk of big data, mountains of data. This, thus, brings the quality of data and data analytics to the center stage of *Quality 4.0*. The good thing about this, is the fact that, most quality professionals of today exhibit the ability to cope with data, and the analytics of data.

There is no gainsaying, therefore, in the fact that, based on literature findings [12–14], *Industry 4.0* or the fourth industrial revolution is an embodiment of changes. Industry 4.0 is poised to massively change organizational and business culture—change business models, organizational strategies, and shape of enterprises, value chain, production processes, supply chains, products, and people skills.

These changes, no doubt, present significant challenges to industrial manufacturing companies particularly, when viewed from the perspectives of organizational culture, investment, and skills demand in technologies, socioeconomic factors, leadership, and management [15–17], and the society at large [18].

These massively technologically driven Industry 4.0 changes will also impact organizational employment opportunities, as in some cases, the repetitive works of workers are going to be replaced with robots and/or multi-function manufacturing machines. Instead, workers' activities shall be mainly focused on the following:

- Integrating, managing, and controlling the tasks and workings of machines
- Analyzing large amounts of data

The advent of new technologies in the era of Industry 4.0 and the need for the overall deployment of the newest and smartest available technologies shall, therefore, ignite and propel not just the introduction of the concept of Quality 4.0, but also the urgent need for new educational approaches to acquire needed competencies to manage and achieve product quality in the smart factory settings of the future [19–23].

Defining Industry 4.0

What is Industry 4.0 or Industrie 4.0?

The German term *"Industrie 4.0"* (or *Industry 4.0)* was first used by Henning Kagermann, the head of the German National Academy of Science and Engineering (Acatech) in 2011, to describe a proposed government-sponsored industrial initiative. *Industry 4.0* was reportedly spurred by interconnected digital technology [8]. In this way, *Industry 4.0* could thus be seen and/or referred to as the brain child of the Acatech and its affiliate research institutions, nurtured on the platform of international industrial revolutionists.

The German Federal Government, thus, in its High-Tech Strategy 2020 Action Plan, set the digitalization ball rolling with its establishment of "Platform Industrie 4.0," a general platform which today, offered leading German companies the opportunity of hatching their own individual and perhaps collective initiatives [8]. Not wanting to lag behind, the USA quickly came up with similar strategic proposal centered on *"Industrial Internet"* [24]. From here, the good tidings of the industrial digital transformation spread like wild fire hitting China with the *"Internet+"* strategy [3] to Japan and other productively smart countries of the world.

Defining the concept of "Industry 4.0" has not generally been outrightly forthcoming from findings in the literature. Because of the complexities of the components of Industry 4.0, defining the concept is not as easy as it may have appeared to be. This is similarly confirmed in a reported project outcome, "organizations are now facing challenges in this fourth industrial revolution, it is difficult to find a proper definition of the concept" [25].

However, a lot of definitions are flouted in the literature for Industry 4.0. To support this argument are the research findings of Brettel et al. [1] that even though Industry 4.0 signifies "imminent changes in the industry landscape, particularly in the production and manufacturing industry of the developed world," there is no commonly agreed or explicit definition in research terms.

A lot of the definitions available in the literature focused attention more on the major, or core components of Industry 4.0, or the fourth industrial revolution, and the need for organizational awareness. It thus becomes apparent that highlighting the components of Industry 4.0 may be the best way to define this concept which has taken the manufacturing world by storm since its revelation at the Hannover Messe, in Germany, in 2011.

Platform I4.0 [26] viewed Industry 4.0 as a reform and the reorganization of value chains to a networked coordination in the era of Industry 4.0, using real-time individual customer requests and environmental balances ("Big Data") from all participating entities in the value chain to holistically integrate industrial manufacturing process.

Schmidt et al. [27] defined Industry 4.0 as the super positioning of several technological developments which embrace both processes and products. And that it is related too, to the so-called cyber-physical systems (CPS) which describe the merger of digital with physical workflow.

Sendler [28] viewed Industry 4.0 from the viewpoint of linking products and services together with both one another and their respective environment through the internet and other network services in enabling the development of new products and services such that many functions of products work autonomously—with no human intervention.

Kagermann et al. [29], in defining this concept, simply identified three of its main features—"Horizontal Integration through value networks; end-to-end digital integration of engineering across the entire value chain with vertical integration; and networked manufacturing systems."

In their own definition of Industry 4.0, Hermann et al. [30] focused attention on the collective term for technologies of value chain organizations and the components of Industry 4.0, categorizing them into four major components of Industry 4.0:

- Cyber-physical systems (CPS)
- Internet of Things (IoT)
- Internet of Services (IoS)
- The Smart Factory

They thus see Industry 4.0 as:

> A collective term for technologies and concepts of value chain organization. Within the modular structured **SmartFactories** of Industry 4.0, **CPS** monitor physical processes, create a virtual copy of the physical world and make decentralized decisions. Over the **IoT**, CPS communicate and cooperate with each other and humans in real time. Via the **IoS**, both internal and cross-organizational services are offered and utilized by participants of the value chain.

While showing a comprehensive overview of the new Industry 4.0 technologies, Posada et al. [31], pointed out that visual computing may be viewed as the component of Industry 4.0. Ruessmann et al. [6], on the other hand, reported their vision of Industry 4.0 from the nine aspects, codenamed, *"the building blocks of Industry 4.0"* or *"Nine pillars of technological advancement*." These (listed below), they claimed to be related to the concept of Industry 4.0, namely:

- Big data
- Autonomous robots
- Simulation
- Horizontal and vertical integration
- Internet of Things (IoT)
- The cloud
- Additive manufacturing
- Augmented reality
- Cybersecurity

Geissbauer et al. [8] suggested a broader scope of defining Industry 4.0, based on, and in reference "to the combination of several major innovations in digital technology," in their own publication. Embedding the elements of these innovative technologies, in an interoperable global value chain, can be shared by lots of companies across multiple countries. The digital technologies referred to here are listed in the following accordingly:

- Advanced robotics and artificial intelligence (AI)
- Sophisticated sensors
- Cloud computing
- The Internet of Things (IoT)
- Data capture and analytics

- Digital fabrication (including 3D printing)
- Software-as-a-service and other new marketing models
- Smartphones and other mobile devices
- Platforms that use algorithms to direct motor vehicles (including navigation tools, ride-sharing Apps, delivery and ride services, and autonomous vehicles)

Going further, they highlighted the fact that the core of Industry 4.0 initiatives resides in three major aspects of digitalization—*full digitalization* of a company's operations—(vertically, to include every organizational function and the entirety of its hierarchy on the one hand, and horizontally, to link the supply chain, distributors, and other partners in organizational value chain with the ability to seamlessly transfer data among them); *redesign of products and services*—(as may be encapsulated in customized software design, to enable them (products and services) become responsive and interactive, to enable them the ability to track their own activity and results, along with those of other products around them.

The data generated from the activities of these product and services are, in turn, captured and analyzed to provide information about how well they (equipment/machinery and/or software) are functioning and how well they are used, which may, in turn, be basically used to detect impending breakdown and preventing it); and *closer interaction with customers*—(taking advantage of the provisions of these new systems, processes, products and services, Industry 4.0 actually makes organizational value chain more responsive, so that industrial manufacturers can, more easily and directly, access end consumers, thereby providing them with the opportunity to adapt this system, as their business model). All these jointly bring out the extreme importance of digitalization in achieving Industry 4.0 initiatives.

The analysis of Yin and Kaynal [32] brought out the role of data in Industry 4.0 as they made the inference that the intelligent systems and the data generated by them are highly critical to organizational performance levels – cost efficiency, product/services quality, and fault-free processes.

The vast publications and discussions by various researchers and authors jointly portray Industry 4.0 in the light of how crucial advanced technologies, or 4.0 technologies, (or 4.0 base technologies) have gone to define Industry 4.0.

As originally coined by the German government, "Industrie 4.0" depicts and "encapsulates a set of technological changes in manufacturing and sets out priorities of a coherent policy framework with the aim of maintaining the global competitiveness of German industry" [33]. It is very clear here that "Industrie 4.0" is conceptualized to accomplish the objectives of the global competitiveness of the German industry; hence, it is being institutionalized in the government's industrial and business policy structure at that time. The concept of "Industrie 4.0" subsequently took on a bandwagon effect on the rest of the world—the EU, the USA, the UK, Japan, and China. The wind of massive changes emanating from developing Industry 4.0 initiatives is subsequently blowing all over planet earth today, perhaps catalyzed by the COVID-19 pandemic.

When viewed from this perspective, Smit et al. [33] went on to describe Industry 4.0 as "the organization of production processes based on *technology* and devices autonomously communicating with each other along the value chain: a model of the 'smart' factory of the future." It is obvious from this, that the technology of reference here is no other than those associated with the digital transformation, and the increasing computerization of processes in manufacturing industries.

The definition of Industry 4.0 must therefore take into consideration its defining features as originally conceptualized, around the creation of the "SmartFactory" which is characterized by the following special peculiarities, to separate it from the traditional industrial factories that we used to know hitherto the following:

- Driven by computer systems which are deployed to monitor physical processes
- Creating a virtual world copy of the physical world
- Capability of making decentralized decisions based on the mechanism of self-organization

It is obvious from the literature review that the concept of Industry 4.0 is quite open to interpretation. It is on the basis of this that, a somewhat straight forward definition of Industry 4.0 is provided herewith.

Industry 4.0 is a*:*

> Conceptual industrial production initiative innovatively built on the frameworks of interoperable decentralized systems and devices of advanced digital technologies that intelligently and smartly work interconnectedly to integrate the physical and virtual worlds, creating end-to-end platforms of integrated machines, people, and manufacturing environment, capable of autonomously communicating with each other along the value chain, and responding to customized and changing demands, human commands, their own perceptions and self-direction in real time to generate, exchange, and analyze data in an agile and flexible production environment.

The major differences which separate the digital "SmartShopFloors" from those of the traditional factories that we used to know before the advent of the digital age, or "SmartFactories" are easily identifiable in the above definition of Industry 4.0 conceptual initiatives, as highlighted below. SmartFactory machine/devices operational systems are as follows:

- Generally, *"interoperable"* and *"intelligent"*
- Built on the frameworks of *"advanced digital technologies (4.0 or 4.0 base technologies)"*
- *"Collaboratively interconnected"*
- Are *"autonomously responsive and interactive"* in a cyber-physical production system environment
- Massively *"data generating, gathering and analytics"*
- *"Hyper aware and flexible"*
- *"Large datasets generating"* and *"big data driven"*
- Able to *"talk with each other" (M2M)* and *"with humans"*
- Able to *"rapidly and autonomously respond to human commands, their own perceptions and self-direction"*

It is for the sake of simplicity, the digital technologies referred to in the above definition are christened *Industry 4.0 technologies*, or simply *4.0 technologies,* or *4.0 base technologies.* These technologies and allied accessories are already bringing massive envisaged changes to the ways in which global industrial manufacturing operations are organized, and managed, with strong impacts on organizational culture, practices, people skills, leadership, and management.

Similarly, *4.0 technologies* will also impact quality management processes and practices of the future. This is, however, not to foreclose the fact too, that, as we progress and develop Industry 4.0 initiatives along with advancing technologies, there are likely going to be additional developmental interrelatedness among the existing 4.0 technologies that may help to advance the SmartFactory concept. Hence, future changes in the smart factory structure are highly envisaged. All of these developments are definitely going to dictate the ensuing advances in quality management in the digital age, that is, *Quality 4.0* initiatives: a situation that will gradually evolve and unfold as the digitalization or digital transformation of industrial manufacturing processes is increasingly developed.

Some of the key changes of Industry 4.0 are addressed by Geissbauer et al. [8] in terms of the ability of Industry 4.0 model to enable very powerful new ways of organizing global industrial operations in:

- "Bringing the fungibility and speed of software to large-scale machine production."
- Making it possible for product design and development to take place in simulated laboratories, utilizing digital fabrication models.
- Enabling organizations to innovatively deploy mass customization, that is, making products in batches of one, as cheaply as possible, while at the same time tailoring the product to customer SNEaRs

Viewed from the above perspectives, therefore, makes the initiatives of Industry 4.0 as impressive, as its accomplishment is challenging. These notwithstanding, implementing Industry 4.0 initiatives is not without its disruptive changes, which may range from organizational processes, practices, culture, people to the general ways of doing things. Industry 4.0, shall in addition, create some professional practices skills vacuum, to result in job creation for digital-oriented professionals and practitioners.

In order for Industry 4.0 to work in an organization, therefore, there is the call here for major changes and shifts in organizational structure, and general practices, from what it used to be, to an entirely new digitally oriented culture of high-capacity data generation. Such generated big data or perhaps mountains of data could be about customer demands, and that of the value chain logistics. Big data analytics of the magnitude of data, being referred to here, has been reported by Ji and Wang [34] as useable in various areas of application such as fault prediction to reduce error probability, while Seele [35] claimed that data-driven predictive algorithms are capable of reducing harms before they result in damages.

This thus brings out clearly, the new roles of data and data analytics, in the sustainability of the digital age industrial manufacturing systems and other areas of applications of 4.0 base technologies. This new culture is, for example, generally based on, new:

- Organizational structure
- Modes and forms of information technology (IT) architectural structure
- Big data generation and data management and analytics structure
- Approaches to regulatory SNEaRs
- Approaches to tax regulatory requirements and conformity

These are, as severally mentioned in this book, the essence of organizations' or businesses' needs to be prepared to swiftly disrupt, rather than waiting to be swiftly disrupted.

In what appeared to be a consensus characterization of Industrie 4.0, the European Parliament in a special report by Smit et al. [33] identified the following characteristic features of Industry 4.0:

- ***"Interoperability***—cyber-physical systems (work-piece carriers, assembly stations and products) allow humans and SmartFactories to connect and communicate each other."
- ***Decentralization***—describes the ability of cyber-physical systems (CPS) to independently take decisions of their own to produce locally, courtesy of technologies like the 3D printing or additive manufacturing.
- ***Virtualization***—creating a virtual copy of the Smart Factory through a link of the sensor data with virtual plant models and simulation models.
- ***Real-time capability***—refers to the capability of collecting and analyzing data, while at the same time providing the derived insights immediately.
- ***Modularity***—the ability to flexibly adapt SmartFactories to changing requirements through the replacement or expansion of individual modules
- ***Service orientation.***

Overall, using the German Industrie 4.0 initiatives as pivotal point, many other countries across the globe are already on board, collectively embracing the opportunity to launch their own versions of Industry 4.0 initiatives on the platform of national economic policies, based on their own environment, situations, and needs.

While different countries' needs and environments may differ, the objectives of all countries interested in Industry 4.0 initiatives, jointly converge in creating and building SmartFactories, intelligent products and services, through the development of smart processes in a smart environment of integrated information and communication technologies, along with other smart devices to enhance organizational and business competitive abilities. Most countries have since institutionalized their commitment to Industry 4.0 initiatives in their national economic policies.

4.0 Base Technologies

Changes due to technological advancements is likely going to dominate most parts of the twenty-first century based on the fact that they already culminated into the fourth industrial revolution inherent in Industry 4.0. This is strongly portrayed by what has been experienced in the early parts of the decade, with smartphones now becoming comparable in computational power to big and fine machines, in the likes of military computers, as pointed by Dugar and Jindal [36]. Hence, we are in the century of increasingly growing technological innovation.

The Building Blocks

A general review of literature showed that the technologies on which platform, the fourth industrial revolution is today springing up from, generally constitute the foothold of the revolution, generating the winds of change which accompany the implementation of Industry 4.0 initiatives. These technologies are being referred to with various names or appellations as indicated as follows:

- The building blocks of Industry 4.0
- Nine pillars of technological advancement
- 4.0 technologies
- 4.0 base technologies

Literature is today awash with various lists of Industry 4.0, or 4.0 technologies (or 4.0 base technologies).

You will experience in this book too, the frequent occurrence of different lists of them based on literature findings. It is for this and other reasons, therefore, that this section is devoted to clarify the most frequently occurring of these technologies in literature.

In an interesting bibliometric survey, Zhou and Le Cardinal [37] carried out statistical analysis of academic publications' authors' key words in selected articles (total of 282), relevant to Industry 4.0 (or Industrie 4.0) between 2013 and 2018. The results showed that the three highest frequently cited keywords are Internet of Things (mostly cited), followed by cyber-physical systems (CPS), big data, cloud computing, and then 3D printing/additive manufacturing. Their survey of consulting firms' reports about the mostly referred to Industry 4.0 technologies produced a list of ten, approximately ranked in the order listed as follows:

1. ***Internet of Things*** **(IoT)**
2. ***Big data analytics***
3. Augmented reality (AR)
4. ***3D printing/additive manufacturing***
5. Robotics
6. ***Cyber-physical systems (CPS)***

7. ***Cloud technology***
8. Virtual reality (VR)
9. Artificial intelligence, AI (Machine learning)
10. Cybersecurity

The above-listed 4.0 technologies are ranked in the order, 1–10, based on the frequency of references being made to them by selected consultancy firms' Industry 4.0/Industrie 4.0 reports/studies [37]. Those in *bold italics* are the five mostly referred to in academic articles/publication key words in the order, IoT, CPS, Big data analytics, cloud computing, and 3D printing/Additive manufacturing.

Similarly, the "Internet of Things" (IoT) and "Internet of Services" (IoS) are considered by the German research union/Acatech [38] as *elements* of Industry 4.0.

Global Trends in 4.0 Base Technologies

Organizations such as Amazon grew its business rapidly taking advantage of the internet technology beginning with selling books online, while Goggle and Apple exploited the web browser engine and graphical computers, respectively. Organizations such as Amazon, Goggle, and Apple are great examples of organizations that have consistently followed the evolving technology not just to reinvent themselves but to redefine their respective business sectors of the global economy. Their living example of successfully deploying base 4.0 technologies and others showed glaringly the business growth potentials highly inherent in transforming from analog systems to digital technologies. The lessons learnt from such organizations and their sudden undisputed "digitized" global market power status are lessons which have left most organizations to embrace and scramble for the digital transformation of their operations.

When viewed however from the perspective of the workforce, the digital transformation exhibits two or dual faces—the human and machine faces. It is on the basis of this *twin effects* of base 4.0 technologies that the role of technology and its perspective applications in the digital transformation of businesses and organizations generally constitutes one of its critical disruptive acts of converting what has hitherto been known and seen as *human-based* business and industrial manufacturing environments, to that of *machine-based* business or industrial manufacturing environments. This is the general direction or trend of things in the business world of the most parts of the twenty-first century.

Although predicting the future is not often as easy as it sounds, digitization of businesses to accomplish operational digitalization in all possible situations shall remain a predominant trend which may likely mature for all interested companies and businesses in the middle of the century. The outcome of successful digital transformation of earlier organizations to develop or implement Industry 4.0 initiatives will undoubtedly spur many more organizations or businesses to action, especially those who have been sceptic or doubtful about the possible impacts of the digital transformation. Getting to the promised land of Industry 4.0 initiatives shall therefore catalyze the multiplier effects to bring many more on board the vessel of the fourth industrial revolution.

What we commonly realize today about Industry 4.0 has been strongly driven by changes that, on their own, are related to technological capabilities and processes. The current global trends of advancing technologies are today seeing us through the age of the fourth wave of technological advancements, commonly referred to as Industry 4.0. We are therefore in the age in which we are witnessing the proliferation of digital industrial technologies.

Realizing this brings up a serious question in my mind. What does increased digitization in manufacturing or other arms of industry portends for our traditional business models and those countries of the African continent still struggling to acquire the analog industrial or business maturity?

Would a new business model evolve? Or would there be two different business models—traditional and digitalized industrial models? Would the anticipated productivity improvement be sufficient to obliterate the need for any or some manufacturing industries in, for example, the African continent? Whichever way the future trends, what sustainability chances would businesses in the technologically underdeveloped countries of the world hold on to? In all situations whatsoever, digitalization or growing digitization in the manufacturing and other sectors of the globalized economy are most definitely going to partly or wholly terrorize traditionally business models, the way we know them today!

Although accurately predicting the future is often not an easy task, it is envisaged, however, that 4.0 base technologies shall, for the future, have greater roles to play in business competitiveness, sustainability, and in shaping industrial manufacturing development, vis-à-vis the future of quality management practices, especially in reshaping quality management skills needed to cope and align with the impending "SmartFactory" culture and people. The innovations brought by 4.0 base technologies shall most definitely change lives and things more than anticipated, from businesses to cities and municipalities.

Digital transformation, also known as Industry 4.0, was reportedly made known to the public in 2011 at the Hannover Messe (Chap. 19). It was in the same year too, that the German Federal Government similarly made its "High-Tech Strategy 2020 Action Plan" using Industrie 4.0 as part of its strategic initiatives known [29].

It has today become a universal symbolism of a major global industrial revolution, taken into consideration by most developed and developing economies of the world, in planning and advancing the future of their respective economies, by making digital transformation the center piece of their industrial policy.

The Germans, in their characteristic global industrial manufacturing leadership roles, actually set the "Industrie 4.0-movement" ball rolling with many of Germany's leading industrial companies already exhibiting strong "Industrie 4.0" capabilities. The list includes according to the Economist [39], BASF, Bosch, Daimler, Deutsche Telekom, Kloeckner & Co., and Trumpf. Industry 4.0 movement has today grown beyond the EU as it is being embraced in the USA, Japan, China/Asia, the UK, and the strong economic countries of the Nordic region—Norway, Denmark, Finland, Sweden, and Iceland.

No country should want to be left behind, hence, the craze to embrace 4.0 base technologies to actualize Industry 4.0 initiatives except perhaps, in the politically misled countries of Africa, such as Nigeria, most of which seemed today to be more economically backward-looking than being forward planning, forgetting the common saying that "Failure to plan is planning to fail."

For example, instead of a potentially rich country like Nigeria to unite and embrace her highly endowed human capital to attempt to pursue, and achieve Industry 4.0 initiatives, like many others on planet earth, its Fulani-led, low-quality, and debt-ridden oligarchic government is, in its present state of anarchy and confused minds, engaged in tracing back its cattle grazing routes of the pre-1800s era. To accomplish this "backward-integrated" developmental goal, the Nigeria government (2019–2023) seemed most visibly to have outrightly embraced terrorist groups and kidnappers to wage, what could be seen, or viewed as all-out-genocidal campaigns/wars, against Nigeria's intellectual capitals of Yoruba, Igbo, and other ethnic descent; the Christians and perhaps all non-Muslim western-educated Nigerians.

Nigeria's Industry 4.0 initiatives thus seemed most intently here, to be focused most importantly, on her hyper-religiosity drive to "hyper-Islamize and hyper-Fulanize" Nigeria and the entirety of her population by the year 2023, in an era, or century of perhaps, the most technologically driven changes the world has ever witnessed—the digital transformation.

This is a mis-leadership quality problem and challenge in Africa's ironically self-acclaimed "most powerful economy." Nigerians do not deserve the quality of life they have been derogatorily and consistently subjected—to by her mostly Fulani-led primitive noneducated governments of people—retrogression in their confused state of misplaced corruption-infested economic priorities. If African countries refuse to embrace the global competitive trends in the dictates of the fourth industrial revolution, most of them and their people "*shall*" forever be condemned and relegated to importers of scrapped products, "cemeteries of wastes," and exporters of poverty.

African countries, therefore, have no other choice than to immediately join the league of industrially progressive competitive economies of the world rather than assuming the "economy of beggar nations." The 2030s, when Industry 4.0 will be in full momentum to achieve full maturity, portend extreme poverty economy for countries and people that are out of tune with global economic competitive trends, irrespective of their hyper-religiosity and prayerfulness. Old discarded nondigital assets will massively find their ways, on export sales to that part of the world because Industry 4.0 technology skills may be scarce, funds for digital transformation may require huge unaffordable loans and the people have to pay extremely costly prices for any imported item—scrap or new. Africa beware of Industry 4.0 maturity! That is the continental quality call to a continent kept in waiting by its crops of corrupt mis-leaders!

Quality thinking, combined with the quality mindset, therefore jointly demand that a country like Nigeria should immediately embrace Industry 4.0 vis-à-vis Quality 4.0 challenges and the digital transformation of her businesses, rather than overwhelmingly giving preference and 1000% attention to her self-capitulating, self-defeatist, and self-destructive country-wide campaign of national disunity to Islamize, "Fulanize," and "Almajirize" Nigeria and Nigerians.

The people of the world and the United Nations should, therefore, not be taken aback, if in a few years' time, precisely in the 2030, a debt-ridden deterioratingly decapitated economy like Nigeria, turns up before the global community, including China and Russia, with the Almajiri beggars' bowls asking for alms, and requesting for more "unpayable" loans, or loan forgiveness, to facilitate or enable the country to implement, or accomplish the 17 sustainable development goals (SDGs) of the United Nation (UN), to improve the people's quality of life [40]. People's quality of life is today at its lowest ebb in most parts of the continent, ironically including the wasteful country of Nigeria. Quality is the universal salt of life, pursue it!

In the words of the UN Secretary-General Ban Ki-moon, "The 17 [SDGs] are our shared vision of humanity and a social contract between the world's leaders and the people" [40]. This is a "quality" of life goal to help and uplift the standard of living of people of the global population. Corruption is a major setback hindering or preventing many African countries from following the trends of global technological advancement, hence, virtually making their participation in the ongoing digital transformation activities almost impossible.

Just like it is trending for the UN to make efforts to achieve sustainable development for all in its adoption of the "the 2030 Agenda for Sustainable Development, which includes 17 SDGs" [41], so also is the International Organization for Standardization (ISO) following the path of quality improvement for countries such as Nigeria and other poorer economies, in the development of relevant standards.

ISO's international quality management systems (QMS) standards are available here to help curb Nigeria's hyper-corrupt-, and hyper-Islamic-driven Fulani government economic earthquakes, if the people's quality of life have to be improved upon.

For example, ISO 37001:2016 is a strong panacea for Nigeria's ravaging pandemic of corruption and corrupt practices. Implementing the requirements of ISO 18091:2019 [42], on the other hand, helps in promoting the sustainable development goals of the UN.

ISO 37001:2016 *Anti-bribery management systems—Requirements with guidance for use is recommended for use in African countries.*

ISO 18091:2019 *Quality management systems—Guidelines for the application of ISO 9001 in local government.* It describes the link between sustainable development and the way local governments operate.

There are no doubts therefore that 4.0 base technologies and the transformations brought along by them and their economic application shall, to a large extent, change the world's industrial landscape, except perhaps, in the African countries.

Failure of most African countries to move with the world in implementing Industry 4.0 vis-à-vis Quality 4.0 initiatives may forever be condemned to the status of indebted consumer nations, as they may even have to borrow, to import their daily needs including food, in the aftermath of Industry 4.0 initiatives' disruptive changes.

The genealogy of quality, equally thought us too, that quality has no alternative than to respond to the changes in our industrial landscape. Hence, there is no gainsaying that the fourth industrial revolution will directly or indirectly impact quality, as may be deemed fit, in quality's response to Industry 4.0 initiatives as they emerge or as we go—Quality 4.0.

The general need for organizations to create the adaptive capacity has therefore never been more critical than it is apparent to us today. The need for organizations to quickly appreciate the realities of our time, and the general needs for them to *disrupt, instead of being left disrupted,* cannot in any way be overemphasized.

Understanding the context of 4.0 base technologies requires a good understanding of the digital language. Digital transformation, as revealed in the literature, is generally awash with technical argots. Some of the most frequently recurring technology concepts or terms in the literature, are listed below and repeatedly too, in other parts of this book, to help in your understanding of the fundamental and allied components of 4.0 base technologies:

- 5G.
- Advanced multi-function manufacturing machines.
- Advances in electronics and control systems (digital).
- Advances in information and communications technology (ICT).
- App development.
- Artificial intelligence (AI).
- Big data/data mining.
- Blockchain.
- Cloud computing.
- Collaboration or working together.
- Competency.
- Cyber-physical systems (CPS).
- Data analytics.
- Embedded sensors.
- Enterprise resource planning (ERP) systems—contains information about inventory and customer demand/SNEaRs.
- Industrial Internet of Things (IIoT)—also known as Industrial Internet.
- Interconnectivity.
- Internet of Things (IoT)—IoT is widely described in the literature as a set of technologies including integrated sensors and embedded computing devices with the strong link of being interconnected.
- Large-scale additive manufacturing (AM), or 3D printing.
- Machine learning (ML).
- Manufacturing execution systems (MES)—controls the way customer demand/product is built. Hence, integrating both worlds/systems, ERP/MES [43] helps to increase operational efficiency thereby making organizational product systems more flexible and more responsive to customized and changing demands.
- Robotics (autonomous).

This literature compiled list of the critical elements of Industry 4.0 is supported most importantly by Ruessmann et al. [6], in their view of Industry 4.0 as "a transformation that is powered by nine foundational technology advances," namely:

- Autonomous robots
- Big data
- Augmented reality
- Additive manufacturing
- The cloud
- Cybersecurity
- The Industrial Internet of Things (IIoT)
- Horizontal and vertical system integration
- Simulation

Achieving the initiatives of Industry 4.0 undoubtedly foster a strong business bond, alliance, and collaborative efforts among machines and devices but also among interested and committed entities—customers, supply chain, distributors, marketplace, etc., across the globe.

The digital movement is already on the move, and participants are spreading around the world. They include among others some of the underlisted entities, organizations, practitioners, and professional bodies among others:

- All organizations of Industry 4.0 movement across the globe including among others GE (US), Daimler (US), Kloeckner & Co. (Germany), Deutsch Telekom (Germany), Siemens, GKN Aerospace (Sweden), BASF (Germany), Trumpf (Germany)
- 4.0 technologies' researchers and interested academics in any or multiples of 4.0 technologies
- 4.0 technologies' designers and operators, services providers, and allied organizations
- Direct or indirect employees of the growing 4.0 technologies industries and their beneficiaries
- Government, people, and relevant industrial regulatory bodies of each of the technologies and the outcomes or products of their efforts
- Investors and other stake holding beneficiaries of 4.0 technologies, including their users and all those applying them to achieve one goal or the other
- Quality and quality management professional organizations such as the ASQ, professionals and practitioners, consultants, and other services providers in the areas of quality as a body of knowledge (BoK)
- Quality and quality management training providers and facilitators, training facilities and other quality professional training bodies such as the ASQ, and quality management experts and consultants scattered all over the world

- The "Smart Industrial Manufacturing" sector, and stakeholders, or digital industrial manufacturing companies of the global economy and those benefitting directly, or indirectly from 4.0 technologies, or their areas of deployment
- Computer software, engineering, and allied industries providing relevant services to users of 4.0 base technologies

For businesses and organizations not to follow the global digitalization trend is akin to organizational failure to disrupt, thereby giving room for being disrupted, only to be left behind in the global race for sustainability and competitiveness.

Ignoring the dictates of Industry 4.0 initiatives may signal a kiss of economic competitive death for such businesses and organizations. Developing Industry 4.0 initiatives, on the other hand, may be the survival instinct despite the massive changes that accompany them. From the purview of this literature review, the perspectives of Industry 4.0 portend future development and changes in wider scopes of global economic and societal transformational developments.

Hence, developing Industry 4.0 initiatives calls generally for long-term strategies. What we are witnessing today are mere foundation stone-laying fundamental exercises of the envisaged transformational changes of Industry 4.0. It may take between 20 and 30 years to bring the development of Industry 4.0 initiatives to maturity.

Changes too are likely going to be subjected to a certain level of resistance, a known phenomenon in change management. *But is it worthwhile?* Businesses, organizations, and all categories of leadership need to ask this question and never give up until answers are provided!

The "SmartWorld" Syndrome

Although readers have been introduced to digital transformation and Industry 4.0 in Chap. 20, there is the additional need to emphasize this "theme of the moment" into more details in this chapter. Industry 4.0 is primarily about the digital transformation of industrial manufacturing operations to create what could be generally described as the *"SmartFactory"* or as others (The Manufacturer) may prefer to call it data-driven *"Intelligent Industry."* Hence, the need here to stress the association of the development of Industry 4.0 with the elements of smartness to create the phenomena of the "SmartFactory" or *"Intelligent Industry."*

According to, Germany Trade and Invest [44]:

> The smart factory is a flexible system that can self-optimize performance across a broader network, self-adapt to and learn from new conditions in real or near-real time, and autonomously run entire production processes.

The smart factory is defined by their abilities to, among others, [5]:

- Operate within the four walls of a factory
- Connect to a global work of similar production systems
- The broader digital supply network

The sympathy of the author goes most importantly, to those people, organizations, or societies of the global community whose people, manufacturing companies, and institutions, may have been too short-sighted, or perhaps carried away by other interests, or have failed to pay due attention to the role of education and research in the ongoing change dynamism in the industrial manufacturing industrial sector, and the general workplace.

Due to the elusive nature of the smart factory concept, such people, organizations, and countries may not be blamed. At the initial stage of its conception, there were limitations as to the capabilities of the digital technology, and the outrageous costs of computing and other relevant accessories and facilities which are major causes of concern.

The idea of the SmartFactory evolving from Industry 4.0 initiatives is born out of the general perspectives of technological imaginative conceptual thoughts, research works, and education. Hence, the likelihood of it appearing more of an abstract concept to most people and businesses across the globe than being of physical or concrete existence. And this is rightly so, too.

This is the reason why nobody can categorically say exactly where the digital transformational changes inherent in Industry 4.0 initiatives are actually going to end. What we were seeing then were mere postulations and dreams. And until the implementation of the smart factory model is practically built and tested, the world may continue to dwell on imaginary or perhaps envisaged conceptual accomplishments of Industry 4.0. The Smart factory is thus an "evolving solution" rather being viewed as an "end state."

It is, however, not until recently that the realization of the smart factory began to dawn on man's technological optimism. This is due mainly to the capabilities of enabling technologies which have reportedly grown more sophisticated. Artificial intelligence (AI), cognitive computing, and machine learning (ML) are enabling systems to *interpret, adjust to, and learn* from the data gathered from connected machines [45].

The coining of the term "SmartFactory" or Smart this, Smart that, to evolve the Smart systems is very critical and key to digital transformation. The characteristic features of the Smart system are mainly inherent in its ability to facilitate information about the value chain. For example, Smart systems have the ability to exchange information about the following:

- Stock levels
- Problems or faults
- Changes in orders or demand levels

Smart networks thus represent a central concept for defining the SmartFactory, the heartbeat of Industry 4.0 [33].

One of the most important driving forces of Industry 4.0 is the general intent to create highly automated industrial manufacturing settings which make it possible for humans to interact with machines; machines to have the capability to interact machines (M2M), using advanced technologies referred to here as 4.0 base technologies, or simply 4.0 technologies.

Industry 4.0, which started with the concept of the fourth industrial evolution or advanced manufacturing, and later referred to as "SmartFactory," has today assumed global prominence. It is thus the prime mover of the world's most revolutionary changes in industrial organizational culture, practices and general ways of doing things. Quality management, in the digital age, is as a matter of emphasis, of equal importance as it has always been, over the previously experienced industrial revolutionary phases of human history.

As the brain child of artificial intelligence at the German research Center for Artificial Intelligence (German: Deutsches Forschungszentrum für Künstlichen Intelligenz, DFKI), *Industry 4.0* emerged from the dynamics of intense academic and research efforts to interconnect and interrelate their outcomes collaboratively; to exploit the opportunities inherent in the sciences and technologies of artificial intelligence, information and communications technology (ICT); and the interconnection of the physical world with the virtual world, to foster and advance industrial processes automation, robotics application, and others.

Apart from the early portrayal of Industry 4.0 as signaling strategic approach to digitalization in the industrial manufacturing sector, Industry 4.0 shall most definitely constitute the dictates, and rooting of future business models and strategies in advanced technologies. This is to categorically say here that it is imminent that Industry 4.0, which has already triggered industrial manufacturing competitiveness shall grow to other arms of the economic sectors and perhaps dictating most of the human ways of life. We are likely going to witness more staggering effects and impacts of Industry 4.0 initiatives transforming industrial manufacturing and production processes.

There are no doubts therefore that Industry 4.0 initiatives shall continue to play larger and critical roles in the transformation of traditional companies into "SmartFactories" relying on the Industrial Internet of Things (IIoT), cyber-physical systems (CPS), and other 4.0 base technologies.

With Industry 4.0 initiatives riding on the back of advanced ICT, and the increased use of computerized systems in the aftermath of the third industrial revolution, to create more digitized systems and network integration via smart systems, Industry 4.0 is poised to massively transform the way things are done, and how they are done in terms of industrial processes, procedures of work, and other related activities from the traditional culture to the now emerging "Smart Culture."

The Smart Culture phenomenon is already visible in some industrial manufacturing settings in which some human tasks and activities have been shifted away from them, only to be replaced with more efficient autonomous robots and other devices, a symbolism of the future Smart Factory for gaining operational efficiency—productivity, cost-effectiveness, machine downtime, and waste reduction.

Like a whirlwind, Industry 4.0 which began on the theoretical hypothesis about the potentials of artificial intelligence (AI) and other advanced technologies (4.0 technologies), their applications and use with other devices soon took the world by storm. And today the world around us—life, industrial manufacturing, and the economy in general—are being spun around by the derivatives of 4.0 base technological transformational changes, as commonly expressed, among others, in terms of the underlisted contexts and their interrelationships:

- Digitization (digital transformation) or creating the Smart environment
- Automation
- Robotization
- Collaboration
- Interconnectivity
- Smart automation in industrial production environment/systems

The major outcome here is gradually becoming visible and apparent in the revolutionarily emerging new patterns of processes and activities in technologically enhanced businesses and industries.

Implementing Industry 4.0 initiatives and the ensuing and emerging changes are however, not without its limitations, disruptions, challenges, and difficulties to organizations and businesses as well as their management. Hence, there is the need to "adaptively disrupt before being disrupted."

In addition to the challenges of implementing Industry 4.0 initiatives are those difficulties that may be closely associated with the subsequent stages of developing Industry 4.0 initiatives, as businesses and organizations climb the digital ladder.

First, from the perspectives of the practical application, and then, from the experiences gained by individual organizations as they go through the transformational phases of digitalization.

Digital transformational changes, are among others, widely speculated in literature, as being expected to generally result in value creation in many areas of human endeavors, contributing largely to global sustainable development—economic, social, and ecological dimensions, as suggested by Pollak et al. [46], and Vulsanovic et al. [47].

On a general basis, however, there are expectations that digitalization shall lead to increased efficiency of industrial value creation systems, along ecological and social beneficial lines, such as reduced energy and materials consumption (i.e., economy of energy and materials), waste reduction, and in creating adaptive working environment, Birkel et al. [48], Lasi et al. [49], and Stock et al. [50].

Similarly, integrated technologies have been reported to result in the creation of a specific ecosystem which allows the continuous exchange and analysis of data, between various entities—people, machines, devices, robots, and sensors in real time, Lasi et al. [49]. And as rightly deduced by Costich [9], "With today's technology and ongoing innovations, the world seems to be drowning in a data tsunami." This fact thus brings out the critical role of data analytics in the digital transformational age.

Wagner et al. [51] simply identified Industry 4.0 with certain industrial vision which cares for the connection of people and things at anytime, anywhere, with any person and anyone, preferably with the use of any path, network, or service.

Others see Industry 4.0 "as a real time intelligent, horizontal and vertical networking of people, machines, objects, and information and communication system with the aim of dynamically controlling complex systems" Birkel et al. [48], and Mueller et al. [52].

As reported by Stankovic et al. [53], Industry 4.0 is viewed from the perspectives of the United Nations Industrial Development Organization(UNIDO), through nine attributes, namely:

- ***Interoperability***
- ***Virtualization***
- ***Decentralization***
- ***Real-time capability***
- ***Service orientation***
- ***Modularity***
- Convergence
- Cost reduction and efficiency
- Mass personalization

It must, however, be mentioned here too, that, the UNIDO attributes in boldened italics listed above coincided with the main features assigned to Industry 4.0 by the European Parliament in a special study carried out by Smit et al. [33].

These attributes, rooted in the perceptions of the UNIDO, and the identified features of Industry 4.0 by the European Parliament, actually represent the general imagery of Industry 4.0 initiatives, and the general basis of Industry 4.0 perception. There is no wonder therefore that people simply see Industry 4.0 from the point of view of such attributes.

Although there is currently no universally recognized definition of Industry 4.0 [48, 54], the author has harnessed available literature about the attributes and features of Industry 4.0, to define it in a more composite form, which is believed will serve readers and users of this book, in good stead (see section on "Defining Industry 4.0 and Its Features" above).

Accomplishing Industry 4.0 initiatives to innovatively transform traditional factories to the SmartFactories settings is enabled through *digitalization* or *digital transformation* with the help of Internet of Things (IoT) and cyber-physical systems (CPS) [55]. Industry 4.0 is therefore concerned with deploying smart systems to replace human beings in certain tasks thereby easing the work environment.

According to Kim [56] and a report by the ASQ [57–60] in its quality progress, Zyter Inc., a provider of digital health and IoT-enablement technology, has successfully built a new Smart Factory capable of connecting factory floor machinery, workers, and building systems. This is a clear proof of the fulfilment of the dreamt Industry 4.0 initiatives.

Smartening Up with Digitalization

Scope of Industry 4.0 Initiatives Development

Initially, human imaginations about digitalization were primarily more focused on industrial manufacturing activities than any other sector of the economy, where it was expected to make revolutionarily transformational changes, which have already begun to happen.

However, reviews in literature have casted some doubts on the general belief then that digitalization portended revolutionary changes mainly in industrial manufacturing workplace. Viewing digitalization, from the perspectives of the already evolving developments, points more in the direction of a broader scope and more complex, more disruptive changes, far beyond the industrial manufacturing sector of the globalized economy.

Without any doubts whatsoever, digitalization, in its general global view, portends changes in most of our economic sectors. We are talking here about both the micro and macro levels, a situation which is, and shall continue to provide endless research opportunities across all aspects of human endeavor and beyond, to virtually all researchers all over the world, with interests in the digital and digitalization transformational processes.

It is obvious from the things that we are beginning to see and experience, or that, are beginning to emerge now, in the embryonic stages of Industry 4.0 initiatives, and the application and uses of 4.0 base technologies, that the impacts of Industry 4.0 initiatives far surpass the earlier envisaged industrial manufacturing processes. Instead, it is a theme of far wider and broader scopes of application, already attracting the attentions of people, institutions, and governments, from all over the world.

Failure to join the digitalization bandwagon knowledge-search, knowledge-deployment, and applicational curiosities could turn out to be a self-inflicted economic suicidal mission. Industry 4.0 initiatives impact, according to scholarly publications, a far wider scope of industries and economic sectors than earlier imagined; hence, its impacts may not spare any industry, company, or organization, except perhaps those to whom survival is not a choice.

The works of Colantoni et al. [61] reported the current Industry 4.0 situation with focus on the prospects of *agriculture* in the context of Industry 4.0. Ding [62] presented a literature analysis of Industry 4.0 in sustainable *pharmaceutical* supply chains. The impact of Industry 4.0 initiatives on *construction* supply chains was investigated by Dallasega et al. [63], while Li et al. [64] reported the research surveys of industrial *wireless networks* in the context of Industry 4.0 initiatives. Lezzi et al. [65], on the other hand, reported a literature review of Industry 4.0 cybersecurity.

Relying on a framework based on the systemic literature review of scientific papers and the analysis of applicability through practical publications and industrial case studies, Dallasega et al. [63] found that Industry 4.0 base technologies influence mainly technological, organizational, geographical, and cognitive proximity dimensions which present both benefits and challenges for construction supply chains (CSCs).

Big data-driven-supply chain at four different manufacturing levels of activities—transportation, marketing, procurement, and warehouse—has been reported by Varela and Tjahjono [66]. Similarly, Maskuriy et al. [67] affirmed that Industry 4.0 initiatives impact generally on the growth of the construction industry.

Evidences available in the literature therefore, widely and clearly, portray the fact that Industry 4.0 is not just changing the industrial manufacturing sector of the economy alone but many more other aspects of the globalized economy. In terms of applications and uses of Industry 4.0 base technologies, the sky seems to be the limit of derivable opportunities.

The role of Industry 4.0 technologies, *big data* in this case, has frequently been reported to facilitate information gathering and usage in the supply chain management sector. Similarly, Zhou and Le Cardinal [37] reportedly emphasized the use of big data by the financial and economic sectors of the economy. Companies can learn more about supplier information even with products and services assessment. The potential use and application of big data and data analytics in commerce, banking, stock exchange, investment sector, etc., has been highly speculated too, in the literature.

The financial sector has similarly been reported to express optimism pending the optimization of machine learning (ML) and deep learning algorithms, just as the creation of merchant intelligence is triggering interests from banks, investment companies, and others [37].

This development takes us to a situation whereby we may have to qualitatively and objectively sympathize with those countries, their organizations, businesses, and people that have hitherto failed to disrupt, by ignoring the need to proactively get involved with, and participate effectively in the ongoing organizational digitization and digitalization processes, across the globe.

By the time these countries and their people realize the ultimate destination of the current Industry 4.0 transformational train, they would have been irreversibly and extremely disrupted, because the train would have completely gone out of their sights, leaving them, their businesses, and people stranded at the analog station, remaining completely noncompetitive, as outcasts of the envisaged digital age business effectiveness and competitiveness. They shall forever remain economically stranded, in their self-condemnation, to the harrowing status of consumer nations.

Understanding the concept of digitalization will most probably help in ensuring that readers of this book get used to what digitalization entails—its technologies, terminologies, and impacts on the workplace, people, organizations, and the society at large.

At times, if not in most cases, it is extremely difficult to predict the outcome of any revolution. Hence, we can only imagine and speculate the exact and ultimate destinations of the unveiling digital transformational train. The only certainty we have is that digitalization has created the momenta for global changes, massive changes in the workplace, organizational and business activities, the economy and society at large.

Consequently, digitalization will, in turn, dictate to a large extent what the future holds for quality and quality management processes or activities in Smart settings. It is envisaged too that quality and quality management processes may evolve new digitally aligned processes and methods, and/or adapt traditional total quality management tools/techniques to match the globally envisaged digitalized-age industrial, and organizational practices—culture, processes, and strategies. Hence, the great relevance for developing Quality 4.0 initiatives.

From a general perspective, therefore, digitalization can be globally viewed from the following perspectives:

- Supporting production processes through computer technology taking advantage of the digital experiences of the information communication and technology (ICT) revolution, or if you like, the initiatives of the third industrial revolution.
- Implementation of cyber-physical systems (CPS) which provides the platform and ability to autonomously communicate with machines, human beings, as well as other components of the cyber-physical systems (CPS), such as the Internet of Things (IoT) and other devices.
- Such communication ability among human beings, machines, and the internet are shaped by the application of complex software-controlled systems, so that machines are able to autonomously take decisions based on the algorithms implemented.
- The roles of people, human capital, in digitalized systems are substantially reduced to mere monitoring and controlling of the systems, and then reacting accordingly, as and when necessary. This thus, result in greater transformational changes in the context of the workplace, the work itself, and professional practices. This is a big task, not just for the people in the workplace, but also for quality management practitioners and professionals. The major tasks emanating from here are numerous, and they jointly require that both problem-solving and practice-based learning systems have to be immediately deployed, to identify and prepare people, in terms of needed skills, capabilities and professional requirements of the digital age, for Smart Settings/Systems—SmartFactories, Smart Cities, and Smart whatever-may-evolve. Training and education are therefore highly critical to face the digital age challenges and tasks, thus, bringing some of the key roles of academics, research, and professionals to the fore, in the ongoing digitalization processes.
- Digitalization has begun to create various technological challenges to humans, businesses, enterprises, organizations, and the society at large, on the one hand; and across various disciplines, skills, and interests on the other hand.
- Flexibility in production processes in terms of work times, task allocation, customization of products and services, etc.

Digitalization is therefore not only going to change the future of industrial production processes but shall also result partly in making some workplaces redundant, while at the same time, leading to the creation of novel career pathways.

The outcome here is envisaged to dictate the tunes of professional changes and training needs not just in industrial manufacturing processes and other areas of the development of Industry 4.0 initiatives, but also in quality management professional practices and skills. The same situation applies to all those sectors of the economy impacted by Industry 4.0.

In their widely reported research findings, the Boston Consulting Group (BCG) [68] provided an estimated impact of Industry 4.0 for Germany, identifying the following four major areas of beneficial impacts on the German economy—employment, investment, revenue growth, and productivity.

- ***Employment:*** Some industrial revolutionary changes such as robotics and automation have often been antagonized by the labor unions all over the world because of their negative impacts on the employment market. The findings of BCG, however, indicated an expectation of "a 6% increase in employment during the next 10 years" with the likelihood of increased demands in areas "such as mechanical engineers, software developers and IT experts." There was, however, a cautionary finding regarding the possible displacement of low-skilled workers by machines.
- ***Investment:*** German producers have been predicted to require 250 billion Euro for investments in the next 10 years.
- ***Revenue growth:*** Based on an estimated projected increase in manufacturers' demand for enhanced equipment and data application, coupled with consumer demand for customized products, German revenue growth is projected at 1% of its yearly GDP, estimated at 30 billion Euro.
- ***Productivity:*** A projected improved productivity rate of between 15% and 20% without materials costs, over the next 5–10 years, is estimated to yield the benefits of between 90 and 150 billion Euro to enhance.

Constraints and Challenges for Implementing Industry 4.0

There are no doubts, whatsoever, that embarking on organization-wide digital solutions in a global industrial revolutionary whirlwind has its complaints and challenges which may vary differently from organization to organization, business to business, and enterprise to enterprise [69]. Absorbing the digital solutions by businesses and enterprises is generally associated with diverse risks and challenges. Critical among the factors that dictate the challenges faced by businesses and organizations include among others the following:

- Organizational driving forces for implementing Industry 4.0 initiatives
- Areas of application of Industry 4.0 initiatives
- Determining the practical impacts of Industry 4.0 initiatives
- Realigning organizational strategies in the path of Industry 4.0 initiatives
- Organizational digital maturity index

Some of the most frequently occurring risks and challenges identifiable in the literature are organizational, technological, economic, ethical, legality, and social.

- Standardization of systems and changes in work organization, Brettel et al. [70], and Peukert et al. [71]
- Data security and investment costs
- Stability of technical infrastructure and sensitivity of its systems
- Increased competition
- Higher investments requirements
- Difficulties associated with the recruitment of qualified skills or personnel
- The need for adopting relevant and suitable legal frameworks
- Changes in businesses and enterprises models, Bonilla et al. [72], and Wang et al. [3]

While these and other perspectives of constraints and challenges of implementing Industry 4.0 initiatives are important, there are likely going to be variations in the way and manner different organizations, businesses, and enterprises are generally impacted, both on the overall and at the different stages or levels of implementation, particularly in terms of the size of an organization, sectors of the economy, and nature of industry.

Digital Jargon

To move forward, it is important to explain some key concepts that have been found dominant in the literature, as far as digital transformation is concerned. These concepts are perhaps the most commonly spoken or written about, in the new world of the fourth industrial revolution, Industry 4.0. These common concepts of the twenty-first century are as follows:

- Digitization (or digitize)
- Digitalization (or digitalize)
- Digital transformation

Apart from their frequent occurrence in the literature, these three concepts are also frequently mixed up and often used interchangeably with one another.

Digitization is the process of converting data (analogous physical measurements) to digital form, for use in a computer. Digitization is today spreading rapidly across industries, thus, currently representing a sweeping experience of rapid transformational change of our industrial manufacturing world.

Digitization has, due to its wide application, been a critical and key change driver in the A-Z of the value chain. Digitization has been seen to create recognizable challenges—risks, financial and in particular, digital security—to industries and businesses even though not a lot of them were adequately prepared for it. The concern about digital security is also a quality management challenge to firms and businesses especially in the areas of the need to protect intellectual property; privacy issues and personal data protection; health and safety; and environmental protection. The quality issues relating to cybersecurity is thus of great concern to all hence the general need for cybersecurity improvement.

Digitalization is, on the other hand, "the use of digital technologies and digitized data to impact how work gets done, transform how customers and companies engage and interact, and create new (digital) revenue streams" [73].

Digital transformation is, however, more complex than it sounds, for it to assume a simplified definition, as is the case with the words—digitization and digitalization—mainly because it "requires a much broader adoption of digital technology and cultural change." Hence "*digital transformation* is more about people than it is about digital technology" [73].

Digital transformation may, therefore, be viewed in the opinion of the author as:

> An organizational-wide process of adopting digital technology to induce organizational-wide changes, which may disrupt organizational corporate culture, but leveraged to autonomously empower and enable people, machines, and the production environment effectively interact and communicate along the value chain generating, analyzing, and exchanging data to accomplish intended or envisaged business improvement and competitive objectives.

"SmartFactory" concept *is a flexible system that has the capabilities to "self-optimize across a broader network, self-adapt to and learn from new conditions in real or near-real time, and autonomously run entire production processes"* [5].

A "bot" (a short form for robot) *"is a software program that performs automated repetitive, pre-determined tasks. Bots typically imitate or replace human user behavior"* [74]. That they are automated makes it possible for them to operate much faster than human users. They are reported here to carry out useful functions which among others include customer service or indexing search engines though they also come in the form of malware, deployed in gaining control over a computer.

It must, however, be mentioned here too, that the most valued assets to an organization are its people, which is similarly an embodiment of organizational culture. Digital transformation is a major outcome of the fourth industrial revolution, Industry 4.0. This is perhaps why Industry 4.0 is the talk of the town today, not just in the industrial manufacturing and energy sectors of the economy, but across businesses in one way, or the other.

While Industry 4.0 initiatives are now closely connected with industrial manufacturing and the energy sector of the economy, nobody can as at now, predict the extent to which Industry 4.0 initiatives shall impact the people and the economy. Already, we are talking about SmartFactories, and smart cities, supply chain impacted construction industry. Tomorrow we are likely going to talk about smart cars, smart planes, smart flights, smart this, and smart that. We are in a world and future of the full embrace of digital transformation.

Organizations are today seriously channeling a lot of their financial resources in the direction of digital transformation. It was previously reported by Kane et al. [75] that only about 25% of organizations across the globe have successfully gone through digital transformations. Improving trends toward digital transformation is registered in the survey by KPMG and reportedly ascertained thus, "Leaders are experiencing COVID-19 whiplash, with AI (artificial intelligence) adoption sky-rocketing as a result of the pandemic" KPMG [76]; and ASQ [57–60]. The implication here is that COVID-19 changes are spilling over, or overlapping into those emanating from digital transformational processes.

It is important here to stress the need for understanding the digital vocabulary, presently trending in our digital transformational world, in order to avoid being confused. This is particularly important from the viewpoints of providing the ability to differentiate between digitization and digitalization on the one hand, and between digitalization and digital transformation on the other hand. The other most commonly heard concept in the most recent time is that of *Industry 4.0* (or when written in the language of its birth place, *"Industrie 4.0")* or the fourth industrial evolution. Industry 4.0 resultantly brought out the concept of *Quality 4.0.* Both Industry 4.0 and Quality 4.0 initiatives depend largely on what may generally be termed and described as 4.0 base technologies to advance their courses in the economic world of man.

A key feature of Industry 4.0 from what we are beginning to see now is that it is from a general perspective, the creation of highly automated industrial production systems through human-machine interaction using advanced technologies, referred to in this book as "4.0 base technologies."

Digital Transformation in Perspective

Digital transformation is in end effect, a dynamic process, that is currently evolving, and providing organizations with the opportunities, not just for them to survive, but for sustainability, and the ability for businesses to most effectively gain competitive edge over others. The COVID-19 pandemic and digital transformational changes may jointly combine to result in dictating the future of organizations and businesses, people, and society for now. Digital transformation will, however, on the long run, hold the key for future business and organizational developmental potentials from now on till the 2030s, advancing further closer to the middle of the twenty-first century.

The massive changes brought about by the COVID-19 pandemic have already resulted in shifting the way people work and live. However, seizing the opportunity of technological advancements to leverage the gradually advanced ICT, and the drastic changes it has brought to industry and society, to its fullest, has obviously helped in gaining sufficient knowledge, to create more values in terms of connections and interconnectivity—among people, between "people and things," and between the "real and cyber" worlds.

The changes brought about by digital transformation need to be adequately handled to create anticipated new values that match the human vision, help in solving problems, and make life better to live in. Hence, the need for organizations and businesses to first, put these changes into the perspective views of their adequacy, or not, for their people, teams, and other stake holders; processes, affiliated processing technologies, and other aspects of their operational systems; and above all, their investment capabilities, in order for organizations and businesses to remain competitive and sustainable.

Digital transformation is today being driven, as earlier mentioned, by multi-dimensional momenta generated in the developed economies of the world, traversing the globe from Germany (Europe) and North America (US), to Japan, Asia, and China. Digital transformation has thus become a universal symbolism of the dictates of advanced technological development—Big data, analytics, robotics, artificial intelligence (AI), blockchain, machine learning (ML), Internet of Things (IoT), and Industrial Internet of Things (IIoT)—gradually turning into the backbone of a global industrial manufacturing production policy.

Although Industry 4.0 is multilingual—"Industrie 4.0" in German, "Industrial Internet" in North America, "Society 5.0" in Japan [77], and "Made in China (MIC) 2025" [78] in China, the objectives of its initiatives speak only one economic language, sustainability through higher efficiency and improved performance to maintain an all-time-needed business competitive excellence.

The wave of digital transformation is a common denominator driving both economic and societal changes throughout the world in the early parts of the twenty-first century. It is in anticipation of these changes that the Japanese government quickly accepted "Society 5.0" as an economic and social growth strategy for the country.

It is important here to highlight in this detailed introduction, the implications of the concept of digitalization and their interrelated complexities with what could be named as its base technologies, also referred to in this book as 4.0 technologies or 4.0 base technologies. Digitalization, which could still be said to be in its early developmental stages, and beginning to evolve, is perhaps the most spoken about, societal developmental giant trend in our present world, apart from the issues associated with the COVID-19 pandemic, and its periodically mutating variants. The realization of a full-fledged digitalized environment may not dawn completely on the global population perhaps not until very close to the mid-twenty-first century. That is probably when we can be talking of a totally digitalized world. What comes next is however left to be imagined.

Most of the things known about digitalization in the literature today emanate in a majority of cases, from researchers, specialized technological organizations, and technological bases or domains. Hence, the reference in this book, to 4.0 base technologies—systems engineering, artificial intelligence (AI), software engineering, cyber-physical systems (CPS), etc.

It is critical here to check on the missing continent in the roll call of Industry 4.0-inclined countries of the world. For Africa and its 54 countries of this self-degrading and misled continent and its about 1.3 billion people, their disappearance from the roll call of Industry 4.0 countries is most definitely a kiss of economic death, as it portends a digital relegation to the analog era. This could lead to poor competitive abilities, thereby creating serious economic setbacks in the global market place. Failure to follow the current digitally dictated trends portends the transformation of African countries in perpetual consumer nations of the world, qualitatively borrowing to import whatever they need from more competitive countries, merely to survive, courtesy of their abysmal and poor-quality political leadership.

Key Concerns in Digitalization

The current digital transformation drive, when viewed from the perspective of work, has been known so far to be generating technological concerns and challenges to relevant entities at three major levels:

- Individual workers
- Organizational levels
- The society at large

The challenges come down generally to how exactly these three entities—individuals, organizations, and society are going to adequately cope with, and shape the digital transformational-related processes.

For example, the major areas of concern in the digital transformation of organizations are particularly centered on the following:

- How organizations can, without any bias, embrace digital disruption and how they work particularly in terms of the ensuing relationships and impact on employees—stakeholders, employees, and customers.
- Identifying and evaluating the most critical components and/or factors of an organization's activities to adequately understand how to integrate them into future plans and strategies for adaptability and sustainability.
- Having the right attitude and objective while being proactive and positive about the outcome and expectations of the transition.
- Knowing that you are on the right track is very important particularly because of the huge investments needed for the digital transformational journey.

The fourth industrial revolution may never, or cannot be accomplished, without the help of digital transformation-support industries or organizations. Such organizations exhibit the ability and capability to render support services, in the areas of design, installation, and facilitation of the technological infrastructure, relevant to, and needed for implementing, managing, and selling the technological know-how in the area of digitalization and its transformational impacts.

The deployment of 4.0 base technologies will definitely ignite new and relevant industries to support the implementation of Industry 4.0 initiatives, thereby resulting in the creation of new jobs and investments. Investments in this area have been reportedly estimated at about $520 billion in 2021 and $11.1 trillion by 2025 [79]. The idea of an organization going digitalized requires on a general basis and as first line of action:

- The need for organizational self-assessment through getting to know how prepared that organization is based on the organizational digital maturity determination/assessment.
- The digital landscape surely influences the workforce as it substantially dictates the necessary skills of workers relevant to the resulting Smart production environment.
- Assessing the long-term impact of the digital transformation on the long-term survival or sustainability of an organization or business.

These are particularly critical issues of concerns because the ability of organizations and businesses to benefit from the emerging technological transformation is in no doubt, whatsoever, highly dependent on the abilities of employees, at all levels, to be able to adaptively engage in self-organization to creatively innovate and find solutions to ensuing problems [80], as well as organizational and business sustainability.

Experts from some organizations and companies across various sectors of the economy—automotive, beverage brewing, steel, agriculture, and aircraft manufacturers—are today, reportedly engaged in serious conversations about the subject of Data Driven "Intelligent Industry." Not exactly sure of how their companies and organizations are going to be changed by the digital transformation, most of them are busy exploring ways they can put data to use manage, and exploit data so as to enhance their business values, increase their trust, supply chain resilience, and governance [81, 82].

A key challenge identified by these experts is the need for the full understanding of the general implications of the digital transformation of operations when as they established, "some manufacturers are still working with paper records" in various areas. They reported identified the following areas of concern:

- Digitalization of operations
- Democratization of data
- Visualization and insight through access to trusted data

While ascertaining that, "too much data leads to decision paralysis, too little data leads to us playing a hunch or reverting to experience," it was agreed that in order to be able to make good decisions, the right amount of data must be available "at the right time and in the right format" too.

Workplace Labor and Skills Gap

That Industry 4.0 initiatives vis-à-vis digital transformation are today taking the global industrial manufacturing stage by storm tells a lot about the role of education and research, and their inevitability. The advent of Industry 4.0 initiatives as well as its outcome, that is, digitalization or digital transformation actually opened up Europe, perhaps to its highest level of industrial manufacturing changes, since the end of the Second World War, with the COVID-19 pandemic coming in as the game changer or as an accelerator. COVID-19 actually contributed to the earlier deployment of AI application aspect of Industry 4.0 initiatives, as one of its 4.0 base technologies.

Digitalization of work, currently the topmost trend in the social-developmental policies of the global society, has given birth to changes in the workplace environments influencing organizational employees and personnel particularly, from the viewpoints of education/training and skills acquisition and development.

Digitalization of work is far beyond supporting production processes with computer technology, to include the implementation of cyber-physical systems (CPS) to promote autonomous communication with machines, humans, and other cyber-physical systems such as the Internet of Things (IoT). This communication is of course shaped by complex software based on immanent, hidden algorithms [83]. The resultant impact in this complex software-controlled system are changes in twofold:

- Changes in work processes
- Changes in business organization

These complex software-controlled systems thus create a complex interplay between people and machines, namely:

- Instead of machines responding to human commands as we traditionally used to know, ***machines take decisions on the platform of implemented algorithms.***
- People are left without any other choice than ***to control*** and ***monitor the systems*** on the one hand, or simply ***react to the decisions of the machines***, on the other hand.

It goes to say, therefore, that digitalization of the workplace as may be needed for implementing Industry 4.0 initiatives has most importantly created some critical changes in both the roles of people and machines—the machines take decisions while the people monitor and react to these decisions. These role changes or perhaps reversal, thus call for critical educational consequences in the transformation and modification of professional practices, both on the job and in quality management processes in the digitalized work environments.

Machines must also learn, just as professionals have to be educated, trained, and enabled, to adjust to the dynamics of the digitalized workplace. Apart from re-skilling or upskilling for workers and employees, there are going to be opportunities for newly evolving digitalized professional pathways that may require being educated/trained along those specific career pathways, in both quality management and workplace processes, activities, and responsibilities.

Hence, the digitalization of work, and all the changes that come along with it, must be broadly viewed as issues for all concerned stakeholders on the one hand, and the disciplines or body of knowledge involved, on the other hand.

Similarly, as reported by Harteis [84], digitalization not only changes industrial work but also impacts all the economic sectors—socioeconomic, natural resources and the services. Digitalization, therefore, portends workplace changes for workers and employees in all kinds of occupations and professionals.

Digital transformation thus poses some serious research and educational challenges of identifying and providing needed worker and employee competencies at varied professional levels, needed for keeping businesses—small, medium, and large-scale organizations running during the digital age and beyond. Researchers and academics are based on the outcome of this review fully at work with all hands on-deck.

This is therefore an opportunity for both researchers and academicians to, respectively, leverage their expertise, research experience, continue to identify and unveil the professional gaps, and collaborate with others in the respective branches of industries, to ensure that potentially identified professional/career gaps are adequately investigated, and provided for or adequately bridged, to meet the demands of industries, businesses, and organizational workplace settings, now and in the future continuum.

Literature findings suggest somehow "that ICT is the backbone of modern enterprises' organization," and that even today, "globalization and the constant expansion of international infrastructure and communications have become a salient part, not just of our daily life but of business activities too," Lehner and Sunby [85]. The OECD [86], in ascertaining the growing status of ICT in the economy, emphasized the fact, "advances, especially in information and communications technologies (ICT) are therefore of increased importance." The analysis of relevant literature has reportedly been similarly found to confirm that ICT skills gap actually exists and considered as a major problem, Lehner and Sundy [85].

There may be a general need now to collaboratively develop suitably required educational curricular with focus on the future needs of professionals across various relevant areas of technological knowledge, including quality management, ICT, and other relevant skills necessary for organizational and business sustainability—small, medium, and large scale. The ASQ is today well positioned in its training programs to promote quality and quality management training and skills upscaling, in the era of digitalization.

Apart from skills gap, there is concern about a pending labor crisis among the industrial manufacturers in the USA. According to the recent research studies jointly by the Manufacturing Institute and Deloitte [57–60], "There easily could be as many as 2.1 million unfilled manufacturing jobs by 2030."

The ways to bridge the manufacturers' labor and skills gap have been proposed in the intent of the National Fund for Workforce Solutions (NFWS), "to ensure that employees are getting high-quality jobs and ensuring workforce equity" [87]. This strategic involvement of the National Fund for Workforce Solutions to help both organizations and employees is a praiseworthy and innovative quality approach to solve the problems of skills deficiency in the face of the world's most dramatic changes of all times. These intended strategies are, if deployed accordingly, likely going to help the following:

- Employers to design jobs
- To provide employees with opportunities to succeed through workforce diversification, education, and on-the-job training
- To strengthen the relationship between employers and educational institutions
- To provide fundings for organizations that are advancing required fields

The situation applies both to the manufacturing and the quality management arms of the economy. Individual young professionals in quality and manufacturing need to take into consideration the job or employment opportunities inherent in the digitalization transformational processes, in this digital age.

While you would like to coat your professional skills with some basic knowledge in technology, for example ICT, irrespective of your professional leanings, it is important for young and growing professionals, especially in quality management, to take a global view of the general skills requirements in the digital age as spelt out as follows:

- ***Value awareness*** which according to Radziwill [88] simply means "determining what the next highest value-adding activity is and doing it." This thus brings out the need for professionals—young and old—to fully embrace value, by creating the value-awareness habit in thinking, behavior, and any decision-making opportunities. Quality is first, above all considerations and must be constantly and consistently viewed as such.
- ***Emotional intelligence* (EQ)** has been identified as a crucial skill hat a quality professional must possess to be successful, Sille [89]. EQ enables the ability of building a solid foundation of trust, respect, and positive attitude, around and among staff, and employees; the realization that "every aspect of our life revolves around quality," thereby making improvement the ultimate goal. EQ is an easy tool to ingrain quality in the organization. This is based on the evidence-based experience of Philip B. Crosby [90] in, "If quality isn't ingrained in the organization, it will never happen." EQ is seen as the attitude that you have for yourself and others, Hooks [91] which enables you to know yourself and how you feel with different situations (*self-awareness*). EQ helps you to stay in control through being agile, resilient, and adaptable to changes without losing sight of goals and objectives (*self-management*). EQ helps in keeping in touch with, and listening to and supportive of team members and their activities, irrespective of the situation at play (*social awareness)* facilitating effective people relationship management and connecting with others to find common grounds.
- ***Imagination*** is a self-understanding context which fosters the generation of ideas. Hence, "quality professionals need imagination," Lindborg [92]. And with Quality 4.0 vis-à-vis Industry 4.0 around us today, there is perhaps more need for imaginal skills which enable people to explore alternatives in finding new ways of doing things, make sense out of the mountains of big data in Industry 4.0 initiatives, and finding ways to swiftly adapt to new situations, just to mention a few.

Overall, it is important for all professionals in the digital age, whether in quality management or industrial manufacturing or other sectors of the economy, to follow the path of Robertson's [93] attributes of the giraffe by:

- Seeing things from the big picture point of view
- Taking time to learn at the ground level
- Linking necessity to innovation and being innovative
- Understanding threats and turning them into a competitive advantage hence the need for the frequent use of the benchmarking quality management tool
- Focusing on the common good, a key aspect of leadership attributes
- Understanding the need to just keep moving, thus bringing to the fore the need for continual improvement
- Letting leaders emerge naturally and as needed

Embracing the giraffe's set of characteristics will most certainly work for quality and other professionals, especially in the current digital era of imminent changes, since "The most certain path to success is to be graceful, exist peacefully, respect individuality while protecting the group, communicating with meaning, be aware of how you affect and are perceived by others, and always look far enough ahead to ensure everyone's well-being" [93].

It is obvious that the digitalization of the workplace generally results in a lot of changes in people's working lives. The implementation of new technologies has similarly been known to greatly impact the workplace, organizational structure, and ways of doing things.

Fischer and Pöhler [94] affirmed that the introduction of modern information and communications technologies (ICT) has changed the way that people interact with one another, with machines and with information itself. The implication therefore is that the direct workplace is mostly changed through the introduction of digital technologies in the digitalization process.

As asserted by Hämäläinen et al. [95], the rapid changes in the world of work are driving forces for education and research in the area of technology-enhanced learning in the contexts of work and quality in the workplace. This is particularly so in Europe where manufacturing is moving toward smaller lot sizes, where changes have been made to accommodate adaptively agile and flexible production methods with needed human know-how, Lanz and Tuokko [96] and Järvenpää et al. [97].

Literature findings indicate that digitalization is, on a general basis, a challenge to traditional, or old work practices, patterns, and services to find or generate new working modalities, ways of collaborating and leading, in different professional contexts, Bosch [98], and Edwards and Fenwick [99].

Literature evidence shows clearly that even though Germany is most prominent in bringing Industry 4.0 initiatives to life and advocating for its development, many other EU and non-European union countries are quite keen too. For example, a research survey conducted sometimes ago by Deloitte [100], showed clearly in the opinion of, for example, most Swiss companies, "the digital transformation to

Industry 4.0 will increase their competitiveness," while at the same time reaffirming the inevitability of major changes in the evolving digital transformation age of the "SmartFactory." As a country known mostly for equipment and machinery manufacturing, it is very obvious that digital transformation shall greatly impact the country—its industries, economy, and people.

Realizing the "SmartFactory" Objective

Realizing the smart factory objective is a matter of organizational choice and on the basis of organizational needs. Hence, organizations and businesses embarking on the realization of the smart factory or digital transformation to implement or develop Industry 4.0 initiatives do so for varied reasons, which must have been known to them individually. The only common grounds among organizations are generally woven around the following key aspects of business objectives of the following:

- Meeting, keeping up, or even surpassing existing market dynamism
- Gaining the ability to improve on market share
- Achieving continuous improving profitability
- Improving product/services quality

No matter the objective, every organization aspiring to implement or develop Industry 4.0 initiatives must not just be convinced but have the assurance too that it is a worthwhile enterprise of great organizational values.

An analysis by Deloitte and reported by Rick et al. [5] clearly shows the examples of opportunities offered by the digitization of various processes within a smart factory. Process examples and digitization opportunities that align with them (processes) are thus in terms of Deloitte's analysis provided as follows:

- ***Warehouse operations***—taking advantage of digitization to use ***augmented reality*** in assisting relevant personnel in their picking-and-placing tasks while ***autonomous robots*** execute warehouse operations.
- ***Tracking the inventory***—using ***sensors*** in tracking real-time movements and locations of raw materials, work-in-progress (WIP), and finished goods, as well as high-value tooling. Deployment of ***analytics*** in the optimization of inventory on hand and automatically signaling replenishment needs.
- ***Equipment maintenance***—taking advantage of ***augmented reality*** in assisting the maintenance personnel to maintain and repair equipment, while the ***sensors*** installed on equipment help in driving predictive and cognitive maintenance analytics.
- ***Quality management—optical-based analytics*** help in achieving in-line quality testing, while ***real-time equipment monitoring system*** assures the ability to predict potential quality issues.

- ***Environmental, health, and safety***—The deployment of ***sensors*** helps in geo-fencing dangerous equipment from operating in close proximity to personnel. Similarly, ***sensors*** on personnel helps in monitoring environmental conditions, lack of movement, or any other potential threats.
- ***Manufacturing operations***—use of ***additive manufacturing*** or ***3D printing*** to rapidly produce prototypes or low volume spare parts. Enabling ***advanced planning and scheduling*** through the use of real-time production and inventory data to minimize waste and cycle time. Digitization of an operation using the ***digital twin*** and moving beyond automation and integration to predictive analyses. Deployment of ***cognitive bots and autonomous robots*** for the effective execution of routine processes at minimal cost with high accuracy.

The above shows generally that the SmartFactory objective or Industry 4.0 implementation could variedly be achieved—within/inside the four walls of a factory set-up, or outside the factory premises, while it is also reconfigurable to adjust the system based on ensuing changes in existing priorities, or those newly emerging ones, Maraghy [101].

Since smart factory configuration vary from one to the other, depending on variations in production line layouts, products, machinery/equipment and their automation systems, and other additional factors, there is no single approach to successfully implement or develop Industry 4.0 initiatives.

Every organization, therefore, has to develop its own strategies based on its priorities and the fact too, that the smart factory is "an evolving solution—one that taps into multiple features such as agility, connectedness, and transparency" Rick et al. [5].

Organizational Digital Maturity Assessment

Literature findings show generally that quality and quality management practices are poised to successfully align with the concepts of the digital enterprise, in what is termed, Quality 4.0. Organizational and business top management teams are therefore mostly preoccupied with aspirations to be operationally digital.

This is the reason for including a chapter in this book to vividly provide more of a literature review about what is currently transforming in the digital world. Whatever information is provided in this book is mainly to focus on and emphasize the need for organizations and businesses to gain some insight into the concept of digital transformation to enable them make up their minds in deciding which ways to move forward. It is therefore very important here to remind organizations and their people that even though digital transformation appears exciting, it is also challenging.

It is therefore highly imperative for organizational leadership to ensure that the capacity is available for the organization to be placed in a good position to quickly respond to the following:

- Customer SNEaRs
- Emerging technologies and their suitability

It is however very clear for organizations to quickly accept the understanding that evolving technologies are at hand as parts of the skeletal structure of the business and organizational activities. Hence, technology must be considered key essentials of any organization, with or without the aspiration to acquire the status of the digital setting. It is for this reason that organizations must make room for technologies to permeate organizational settings to an appreciable extent, far more than it perhaps used to be.

The path to digital transformation is long, winding, and perhaps arduous, thus, requiring most importantly that organizations begin generally with the following:

- Setting adequate and appropriate strategy and timing to accomplish digital transformation
- Developing the project mindset and moving to the product mindset
- Developing engaged, and cross-functional teams, culture and adaptive leadership
- Making provision for needed professional skills both by re-training and upskilling employees on the one hand, and engaging new ones as may be deemed fit and suitable for the situation on ground, and the set developmental goals

Digital transformation should, therefore, be seen and handled as a value-driven continuous improvement project with the potentials to dominate the future of industry and quality.

Although organizations are expected to initially perform a digital maturity self-assessment before embarking on digital transformation, many organizations were reported to "have been forced to operate in a version of Industry 4.0 without the advantage of having previously performed a digital maturity self-assessment" due to the COVID-19 pandemic [102]. An organizational self-assessment is thus a quality management method used frequently to implement a major process change. Organizational self-assessment of digital maturity is "a flexible process by which the organization can continually adapt to a changing technologies environment, realigning its people, culture, tasks and structure in response" [103].

Managing the Digitalization Change

Literature gives some views and understanding about the general principles of Industry 4.0. These views are generally centered among other things, mainly around the underlisted key activities and principles:

- Digitalization of industrial manufacturing systems
- Advances in interconnectedness facilitated by wireless internet connectivity
- Integration of different devices systems
- Gathering and analysis of data

- Interoperability of machinery and equipment
- Software customization to enable product customization for individual end-users and marketplaces

Digitalization is perhaps on the move than earlier anticipated. Some organizations seized the opportunity of the unfortunate momentum generated by the COVID-19 pandemic changes, to accelerate *Industry 4.0* digitization and digitalization processes. This has been affirmed by Pietenpol [104] in "The pandemic also has significantly sped up digital transformation efforts- particularly for organizations that have a substantial remote workforce."

In addition is the reported outcomes of a recent World Economic Forum (WEF) findings in the same publication that, "Eighty-four percent (84%) of employers are set to rapidly digitize working processes, including a significant expansion of remote work-with the potential to move 44% of their workforce to operate remotely."

How an organization manages the ever-changing world of *digital evolution* in our present world will, on the long run, shape and determine the future of most organizations, hence, their sustainability. Most importantly is the fact too, that, there are the general needs to:

- Integrate people
- Integrate technology
- Integrate processes and activities
- Create efficiencies
- Facilitate transparency
- Facilitate and provide needed people professional skills, including those relevant to quality management, so as to be able to cope with the continued tsunami of global environmental, economic and developmental changes

Like the name, fourth industrial revolution implies, Industry 4.0 initiatives may actually throw businesses and organizations into a revolving set of whirlwinds of changes which may cause many organizations to innovatively and adaptively re-evolve.

This is one of the reasons why organizations venturing into digitalization, may need to:

- Understand and identify its own motives, motivational factors, and other related business drivers of intended digitalization.
- Understand the general perspectives of organizational change from the viewpoints of digital transformation.
- Formalize its own digitalization strategies.
- Harmonize the strategies across organizational-wide people, processes, and activities.
- Exactly define organization's existing and future status in terms of its technological level of development, its status quo in the market place, and the people and their expertise, as well as their interdependencies.

- Find new sources of data which analysis can be deployed into the production system as quality management performance indicators to give insights into the ways in which people, suppliers, and customers (internal and external) are performing their works with expected improvement.

It is partly with respect to some of the above interests that Geissbauer et al. [8] suggested that organizations may need to acquire the expertise suitable for managing and analyzing data in more effective ways than they have always done.

Realizing the Constancy of Change

We are now in the age of digital changes largely propelled by the fourth global industrial revolution, commonly referred to as Industry 4.0. *Industry 4.0,* thus, in the commonest usage refers to connectivity and integration of systems, to gather and analyze data, in an industrial environment of digitalized organizational operations. The outcome here are rolling dynamics of changes.

Humanity, in its entire state of existence, has been shockingly disrupted by the COVID-19 pandemic, first noticed around December 2019/January 2020. The full recognition of the potency of the novel coronavirus was not until around March of 2020, when human activities across the globe were actually "quenched-in-place." It was not merely a sociocultural shock but an economic shock that the world has never witnessed since 1918, when it experienced the Spanish flu.

People and organizations that, in one way or the other, managed to survive the cruel arms of COVID-19 pandemic death, poly-spatially outstretched to the people of the world by the novel coronavirus, can convincingly claim to have gone through the experience of *disruption* particularly, in the highly *disruptive* first 3–6 months of 2020.

This disruption shocked the people of the world to the bones, both socially and economically, while aggressively impacting every industry and business. Despite COVID-19 pandemic's tsunami of immense disruptive environment, organizations and businesses did not in any way lose sight of their obligatory and essential responsibilities of continued production to make products/services that meet and perhaps exceed stakeholder SNEaRs in adaptive circumstances.

Just as the human entity was not completely destroyed despite millions of COVID-19 pandemic deaths across the globe, so also have businesses and organizations outlived the disruptive changes that trailed the path of the novel coronavirus.

In general acknowledgment of the relevance and importance of quality principles, tools, and techniques, they were quickly and immediately deplored to fight the pandemic by both governments and individuals. It was a change that controlled the emotions of all living beings on planet earth.

The COVID-19 pandemic has hitherto created some new normal. The human race most probably quickly appreciated en masse, the role of quality not just in their day-to-day activities but in their lives and the way they live. Quality principles/philosophy, tools, and techniques were swiftly deployed not only to protect the people of the global community, but also to *disrupt* the coronavirus. Organizations have to quickly disrupt their own *modus operandi* by making rapid changes to the way they work and operate their businesses.

At the time of the outbreak of the COVID-19 pandemic, the implementation of *Industry 4.0* initiatives, which was beginning seriously to gather momentum, was similarly disrupted. It was disruption galore. The impact of these disruptions is however, not without its consequences, as the resultant disruptive situations reveal the extent to which changes generally disrupt. We are therefore in an era in which disruption is building itself around the people of the world and their daily activities.

A study by the Washington University reported that "an estimated 40% of today's S&P 500 companies will no longer exist a decade from now" [105, 106]. That is definitely a conclusion based on the negative impacts of anticipated changes. Just as COVID-19 disrupted so also shall the initiatives of Industry 4.0 disrupt.

The COVID-19 pandemic disrupted man and businesses. Businesses have to disrupt their own operational systems by creating the "adaptive space" [107]. Similarly, the COVID-19 pandemic was disrupted through the deployment of quality principles/philosophy, tools and techniques, from social distancing to the "successful development, distribution and administration of the COVID-19 vaccine" [108]. Hence, the reality that organizations and businesses must have to "disrupt or be disrupted" [105].

The tasks and challenges of the new normal emanating from the COVID-19 pandemic, therefore, require that organizations get their employees engaged, in order to be able to tap from, and optimize the contributions of their intellectual capital, and develop and bridge the skills gap through adequate training and upskilling.

It is thus apparent here that the future of businesses and organizations shall ultimately be shaped, structured, and determined by the way and manner the ever-changing world around them are managed or get adapted to. This is particularly so now that we are in the age of digital transformation. Hence, the loudest calls here for the sustainability of organizations and businesses through being called to *"disrupt, before being disrupted."*

The implication here is that people, businesses, and organizations must be prepared for changes, as changes are, and must be seen as a global factor of permanency, which are very critical for organizational performance improvements and sustainability. While managing the changes emanating from the COVID-19 pandemic is not yet over, the industrial manufacturing world is today massively faced with the currently resonating changes traceable to *Industry 4.0* initiatives.

Industry 4.0, also known as the fourth industrial revolution, can generally and simply be viewed from the point of view of the use and application of various digital technologies—automation, robotics, simulation, analytics, Industrial Internet of Things (IIoT), and additive manufacturing (AM) or 3D printing—working together in unison to change, or if you like, transform your business/organizational culture, or the way you carry out your businesses. This is so, in order to achieve overall performance improvement—productivity or production efficiency, improve product and services quality. *Industry 4.0* is thus a strong momentum currently driving changes in organizational culture, practices, people, and ways of doing business.

4.0 Relationships—Industry 4.0, Quality 4.0, and 4.0 Technologies

Relating Industry 4.0 with Quality 4.0 is a natural occurrence bearing in mind the co-existential attributes of quality and industry. Industry 4.0 initiatives, no doubt, represent new industrial production paradigms. There are various publications about Industry 4.0 and its twin sister, Quality 4.0. It is obvious from the centuries-long relational tradition between industry and quality that quality management (QM) plays pivotal roles in production processes, guarantying the reliability of products/services in fulfilment of customer, and regulatory and market place SNEaRs. One of the shortcomings of the traditional methods and tools of quality management is that, while it enables the detection of errors and improvement of decision-taking abilities, there are often delays in implementing corrective actions (CA) [109]. Overcoming such shortfalls and to gain competitive advantage in the marketplace contributed largely to the underlying fundamental contexts of the fourth industrial revolution or Industry 4.0 as it is popularly known.

Prior to the emergence of Industry 4.0, there was the silent third revolution which introduced electronics and control systems (digital) in manufacturing industries to gain the advantages of greater flexibility and far more sophisticated products at more competitive or lower costs. Industry 4.0 initiatives are being enabled by *4.0 technologies* such as advances in data, analytics, connectivity, scalability, Industrial Internet of Things (IIoT), blockchain, and collaboration (among others) in combination with the following:

- Advances in the information and communications industry.
- Impacts of the silent third industrial revolution of electronics and control systems (digital) systems and merging them with the physical and natural worlds.

To effectively transition to Quality 4.0 requires first and foremost, the general need for creating a general awareness about it, among relevant organizations and stakeholders. And this is currently largely being pursued and accomplished by the ASQ in its conferences, and journal publications, with the intense involvement and collaboration of quality management professionals, practitioners, and experts across the globe.

While Industry 4.0 simply refers to the interconnectivity and integration of systems for gathering and analyzing data in digitalized organizational operational systems, Quality 4.0 is in conceptual relationship with Industry 4.0 in terms of the deployment of appropriate and suitable quality management processes, tools, and techniques to assure the quality of the outcomes or products of the digitalized processes.

Quality unlike other bodies of knowledge was born outside academics in the industrial manufacturing sector, over a century ago. This is a critical factor which has, more or less, hitherto tied the faith of quality and its improvement tools, very closely with the dynamism in the industrial manufacturing sector of the global economy. Quality and industrial manufacturing are related: related in the manner and sense that may be likened to, and be easily described as that of "Siamese twins" or "conjoined twins," sharing the same organs.

Separating quality from industrial manufacturing, or vice versa, will most definitely stunt the growth of either one or the two concepts. Hence, the day *"Industrie 4.0"* or fourth industrial revolution was given birth to, that same day, *"Qualitaet 4.0"* came alive. Quality 4.0 is therefore a concept used in relationship with Industry 4.0, in terms of the possible digitalization of quality and the relevant processes to make them adaptable to, and operatable in the interoperable digital industrial environment of hyper-awareness and flexibility, to achieve the desired quality and competitive advantages.

Since Industry 4.0 carries the appellation of "digital transformation," Quality 4.0 similarly refers to the digitalization of quality, and how digital tools can impact technology, processes, and people alike [110]. The initiatives of Quality 4.0 are in the dictates of Industry 4.0.

Since Industry 4.0 is expected to yield industrial manufactured products, or outcomes using advanced 4.0 technologies, Quality 4.0 must as usual, stand by Industry 4.0, to come up with the appropriate quality initiatives to ensure that these products and/or outcomes of Industry 4.0 initiatives excellently represent the values, and/or SNEaRs of the customers/marketplace and those of other stakeholders, without adverse effects on the environment and other relevant stakeholders—product end users, regulatory bodies, community, etc. Quality 4.0 thus maintains the tradition of quality, being always in pace, or aligned with industrial manufacturing developments—in this case, Industry 4.0.

The fundamental basis of Industry 4.0 or the fourth industrial revolution is globally built on the foundation of wireless connectivity which provides the opportunity of integrating different devices into a system, for rapidly gathering and analyzing data with more efficiency, using cyber-physical systems (CPS) [111].

Industry 4.0 is, on a general basis, built on "the framework that internet connectivity through wireless telecommunications permits integration of diverse types of devices (such as home appliances, automobiles, industrial platforms and merchandize markets) for business or personal purposes" [111].

Industrial Internet of Things (IIoT)

"The Industrial Internet of Things, which is also known as the Industrial Internet," is according to Colin [112], "pervasive in the context of industry as digital transformation has become a business priority for many organizations."

GE is reported here, to have coined the term, Industrial Internet in 2012. This is perhaps with a view to further its own ideas and path of business in digital transformation. GE is, thus, an example of organizations that are using their experience, and deep technology and industry expertise, to render relevant digital services to interested parties and customers, based on their portfolio of industrial software applications. GE and many other organizations with similar capabilities are today already facilitating and helping their 4.0 technologies customers to accelerate and cross their digital transformation hurdles, quickly putting industrial data to work.

As precisely put by Colin, GE Digital is one of the organizations that are presently leveraging the power of the IIoT with software to provide digitization services and solutions to industries.

Transforming Data to Action

One of the major activities involved in industrial digitization is centered around massive data generation and creating the capacity to transform these "mountains of data" into action among relevant parties. Data analytics thus become a critical area of Industry 4.0 and Quality 4.0 initiatives which calls for collaboration among all interested parties.

It is highly imperative to emphasize the criticality of protecting ICT systems and digital interconnection against external interferences and other issues and factors of data security. This thus calls for the engagement of highly qualified ICT security experts in IT positions within the "SmartFactory" structure. Successful and accurate data analytics can, for example, be accomplished through collaboration with customers in preventing jumping into uncertainty, and applying rapid experimentation with speed and scale.

Industrial Internet, or the Industrial Internet of Things (IIoT), thus presents an assemblage, or brings together the following:

- Relevant or critical assets
- Advanced predictive and prescriptive analytics
- Modern industrial workers

into a network, or interwoven structure of a multitude of industrial devices that are connected by communications technologies, creating systems capable of monitoring, collecting, exchanging, analyzing, and delivering valuable new insights, to help in driving smarter, faster business decision-making for industrial organizations.

It is in this way that the IIoT is widely viewed in the literature, to transform industry in the digital age, thereby permanently changing the ways industrial companies operate their daily activities.

Application of the IIoT

Various applications of the IIoT in combination with suitable software solutions have been reported in the literature. Relying on the digitization experiences of GE Digital, a big player in the industry, it is generally deducible from the report of Colin (GE Digital) that IIoT is driving the 4.0 technologies in various modes of application, "Whether it's enabling industrial artificial intelligence (AI) to detect corrosion inside a refinery pipe, providing real-time production data to uncover additional capacity in a plant, or accelerating new product development by feeding operations and service data back into the product design cycle, IIoT—and the software solutions powered by it—are driving powerful business outputs." Industrial artificial intelligence (AI) technologies are already being deployed today to transform industrial assets and systems in order to make them more predictive, prescriptive, safer, intelligent, and more profitable.

For example, it was reportedly claimed that, "By combining machine-to-machine (or M2M) communication with industrial data analytics, IIoT is driving unprecedented levels of efficiency, productivity, and performance." This has subsequently been reported, too, to have resulted in industrial companies in power generation, oil and gas, utilities, manufacturing, aviation, and many other industries, experiencing transformative operational and financial benefits.

In a survey of manufacturers by the Association for Advancing Automation published by the ASQ [57–60], showed that "26% of them have established an end-to-end AI solution," while "70% of firms plan to increase investment in technology in the next six months." Seventy percent were similarly reported to have turned to a data/analytics platform thus making 2021, the gateway year of investments in digital technologies and initiatives for organizational sustainability. This revelation is most accurately prognosticated in, "What's ahead for manufacturing in 2021?" as reported by the ASQ in the Progress report in which the following have been highlighted for the near future:

- Renewed interests in organizational sustainability within the scope of Industry 4.0.
- More investments in digital technology and initiatives—to achieve digitization in our digital transformational world.
- Deployment of more artificial intelligence, Internet of Things (IoT), and machine learning (ML) on shop floors—to facilitate and generally aid systems interconnectivity and communication (e.g., M2M).
- Increased emphasis on big data—particularly because "Businesses and organizations cannot function without data" in an age when the mantra "is to collect enormous amounts of data, referred to as big data" [113].
- Using predictive maintenance on the production line—an effective quality management process.
- Tangible 5G use and application.

Quality Management for the SmartFactory

While it is important for organizations and businesses to implement Industry 4.0 initiatives in alignment with their specific needs and businesses, so also must the quality and quality management philosophies, principles, tools, and techniques be aligned with the digitalized environment in the example of the "SmartFactory" or along Industry 4.0 initiatives.

Developing Industry 4.0 initiatives itself involves big changes, hence, the need to view it also from the viewpoint of quality in change management. Developing Industry 4.0 initiatives is thus an improvement drive, on the platform of national economic policies of actively involved nations, to drive business improvement among businesses. Since quality is improvement, and improvement is quality, it goes to say that Industry 4.0 initiatives are major quality initiatives to drive and reposition organizational and business competitiveness. This thus brings out the obvious evolution of Quality 4.0 in alignment with Industry 4.0 initiatives. It is therefore expected that the concept of Quality 4.0 shall emerge along the path of Industry 4.0 initiatives implementation.

Hatched by the German government in 2012, in its "High-Tech Strategy 2020" action plan for the development of cutting-edge technologies [114], the fourth industrial revolution has since taken the world economic developmental stage by storm.

With the launching of the Advanced Manufacturing Partnership (AMP) and the Industrial Internet Consortium (IIC) led by General Electric (GE) [115], the US government has already set in motion a "national effort bringing together industry, universities and the federal government to invest in the emerging technologies that will create high quality manufacturing jobs and enhance our global competitiveness." The objective of the US government here is embedded in the statement, "Investing in technologies, such as information technology, biotechnology, and nanotechnology, will support the creation of good jobs by helping U.S. manufacturers reduce costs, improve quality, and accelerate product development," thus bridging the envisaged manufacturing jobs gap of the National Association of Manufacturers (NAM), [116].

France in its "Industrie du Futur" formulated nine major development solutions in the core areas of—data economy; smart objects; digital trust; smart power; new resources; sustainable city; ecological mobility; future medicine; and future transport [117].

In order to enhance the competitiveness of Chinese manufacturing and accelerate the industrial upgrading of China's manufacturing industry, China launched, "Made in China 2025" [118] while the UK launched the "Future of Manufacturing."

Spreading and raging like wild fire across the countries of the world, the future of Industry 4.0 is highly laden with endless opportunities for change not just in the industrial manufacturing sector of the world's globalized economy but also across all other sectors.

Benefits of Industry 4.0 Initiatives

Industry 4.0 has been speculated in various publications to enhance organizational and business competitive abilities which may be accomplished through the following factors:

- Increasing industrial manufacturing productivity in order to remain competitive. This, in turn, helps in facilitating business growth. This can result from the manufacturing aspiration of effectively driving productivity and/or revenue, without correspondingly increasing manufacturing costs. Ability to quickly or swiftly new or customized products greatly enhances productivity.

- Help in reducing downtime.
- Accelerate or speed up products/services getting faster to customers and the marketplace.
- Product/services quality improvement.
- Help in anticipating customer SNEaRs and in meeting them.
- Help with the customization (make to order) of connected products thus providing needed flexibility.

It Is All About Competition

High labor costs coupled with high market competition have jointly driven competition in the manufacturing sector, to high extremes prior to the advent of digitization. Rising costs of manufactured goods were particularly not helped in today's world of highly globalized economies, key catalysts of unending market competition. The growing trend of market deregulation too has not only helped in facilitating the current liberalization of trading sanctions, but led to the shrinking of industry boundaries [119].

The strengthened volatility of global markets coupled with shortened technology and innovation cycles became additional burdens of doing business. Probably heightening business challenges too, in the world's globalized market economy, are the rising demands for highly individualized products and services. This is, however, not without its consequences, as increases in individualized products and services tend to result in increased process complexities in the value streams [120, 121]. Individualized products and services generally require organizational flexibility, efficiency, and adaptability of their value creation systems, in order for them to remain competitive and also to survive [122]. When costs of product excellence, or quality products, were becoming prohibitive, it became highly imperative to move production facilities to other aspiring countries so as to substantially close both product quality and productivity gaps.

When big manufacturing organizations or companies realized the obvious fact that customers are no more willing to pay higher prices for products and services of incremental quality improvement, many manufacturing industries in Germany reportedly changed their production strategies, to concentrate their attention, more on the customization of products and high market turnover. In order to achieve competitive edge, manufacturing industries took advantage of novel production strategies, examples of which are, Agile Manufacturing and Mass Customization, leveraging them in transforming their manufacturing activities into integrated network structures for uniting their core competencies, [1], a perspective of the new manufacturing paradigm, *Industry 4.0.*

Earning the appellation, "*the fourth industrial revolution*" the new manufacturing paradigm soon unveiled the "things" in the names that are today already ascribed to *Industry 4.0.* Going through the literature, you will quickly identify the many "identities" of the new manufacturing paradigm:

- *"Industry 4.0"*
- *"SmartFactory"*
- *"Industrial Internet of Things"* (IIoT) [119]

Apart from the popularly known term, *Industry 4.0,* there are similar terms, such as, *"Industrial Internet," "Internet+"* or *"Human-Machine-Cooperation"* used to define what constitutes the next level of industrial manufacturing business. It must however be mentioned, too, that on a general basis, most, if not all of the terms, tend to describe how *4.0* or *digital technologies* and *networks* are changing and continue to change the ways businesses are conducted. This, in turn, shows glaringly, without any doubts, whatsoever, that Industry 4.0 shall definitely change our business world [123].

The new manufacturing paradigm refers according to Veile et al. [119] to "digitized and connected industrial value creation."

The digital engineering of products and production processes is facilitated by the increased use and application of information and communication technology, while modular simulation and modeling techniques provide decentralized units with the opportunity of the flexibility to alter products in order to achieve rapid product innovation.

Hereby, the process and supply chain are virtualized to ensure the smooth operation of inter-company processes and activities, with the provision of real-time access to relevant product and production information, including data, to the benefit of all participating entities—humans, machines, and other relevant devices. In this way, the manufacturing landscape has, in the context of Industry 4.0, been changed through virtualization of processes and the supply chain, decentralization, and network building coupled with autonomous systems data generation, exchange, and analytics.

Organizational traditional boundaries shrink due to autonomous systems data exchange, facilitated by embedded systems across the entire value chain. The introduction of cyber-physical systems (CPS) facilitates communication between machines virtually the same as dialoguing with human beings.

Industry 4.0 initiatives or practices can thus be holistically viewed as implementing or developing digital transformational activities to create value from completely digitized, intelligent, connected virtual process chain, autonomous factories, and production networks.

Concept of Smart Manufacturing—Theory or Reality?

While there has rarely been any reported publication of the successful implementation of the "SmartFactory" concept, there has been very few speculative reports of its successful prototyping. There are no doubts however that the potential for achieving Industry 4.0 initiatives or the "SmartFactory" concept have been widely reported by researchers, practitioners, bloggers, equipment manufacturers, management consultants, IT providers, and security experts, among others. This is perhaps due to the general engagement of individual businesses busy challenging the teething problems of Industry 4.0 initiatives, application of 4.0 technologies and digitalizing difficulties, among others. There are doubts, too, that the involvement of many entities in organizational digitalization likely slows than the process of actualizing and realizing the "Smartfactory" objective.

This is supported in a recent blog, which also affirmed the popularity of smart manufacturing in, "Smart manufacturing is the buzz-phrase of the moment, but is there enough tangible advice out there on how to implement the concept?" The findings in an interview with two pioneering companies who are working together in putting theory to practice in the issue of Industry 4.0 are their identification of one of the current problems that, "what you read is still very theoretical." Furthering the certainty of this problem is glaring in, "But for large parts of the UK's manufacturing supply chain, theory is not enough. They need practical advice, not just about the benefits, but about how they can actually implement Industry 4.0" [81, 82].

The author is in total agreement here with The Manufacturer that the critical consideration for realizing the practical implementation of smart manufacturing or "SmartFactory" concept is highly dependent on the ability of all concerned entities—equipment/machinery designers, machine manufacturers, machine users, software engineers, organizations, and businesses, among others—to effectively collaborate and work together to implement smart manufacturing.

No matter any identified clouds hanging on the implementation of the smart manufacturing objective, it a realizable goal which may take appreciable efforts of all concerned and time to accomplish. Delays in realizing the objectives of Industry 4.0 may be slow at the initial stages for two major reasons:

- Manufacturers spiring to achieve smart manufacturing come generally from entirely different background and maturity levels.
- Processes in manufacturing differ based on the nature and type of their businesses, hence, variations in the challenges faced, and needed solutions for implementing the smart manufacturing concept. Different business problems or issues may also require solutions with different technologies.

The following perspectives sum up the driving forces for accomplishing the envisaged smart manufacturing ideals:

- The future "SmartFactory" is envisaged to provide insights into daily occurrences and make the resultant data and/or information available to whoever and wherever it may be needed for taking effective decisions.
- The "SmartFactory" exhibits the capability to immediately and quickly respond more effectively to changes in demand and any other disruptions simply by leveraging digital tools.
- Being proactive is a distinct characteristic of the "SmartFactory" in its ability to take autonomous decisions by sensing situations at hand and responding to ensuing scenarios.

- The deployment of self-learning machines capable of self-correction in interconnected "SmartFactory" processes also enable product awareness of where they are.
- "SmartFactory" operators are going to be entirely different from those of the traditional factory floor; hence, there is the general need for their upskilling and retraining. This will greatly help to improve and ensure their abilities to work side-by-side with 4.0 base technologies; facilitate their abilities to use modern digital tools for the ease of their operational responsibilities and focus of their attention on value-added tasks.
- The "SmartFactory" has the potential to facilitate organizational corporate social responsibilities—creating safer environment for both communities and shop floor operators while paying attention to sustainability generally.
- The "SmartFactory" has the ability to create greater visibility of assets—quick identification of idle machines and putting them to full use; identifying more effective use or not, of machines/equipment and making informed decisions whether to retire such assets or not. Having visibility into what are actually happening in the factory environment opens up a lot of process management advantages.
- The "SmartFactory" will most critically be in dire need of relevant technical skills to run and maintain factory operations; hence, organizations and businesses must develop the capability to consistently and continuously acquire and/or attract technical skills.
- Achieving the "SmartFactory" objective calls, most importantly, for building organizational collaborative operational teams with imbibed "SmartFactory" "*thinking and mindset*" in the same way as we talk about "quality thinking" and "quality mindset."
- Like in other business endeavors successfully bringing the "SmartFactory" practice to maturity demands collaborative efforts but "SmartFactory" leaders who are willingly adaptive to ensuing situations, highly collaborative and working together with employees to establish and grow the smart culture needed to uphold the "SmartFactory" environment of the digital age. Digital age business leadership are going to be more effective operating on the platform of situational leadership efficacy.
- The "SmartFacory" takes advantage of automation and robotics to achieve planned productivity.

Overall, the transformational changes inherent in and represented by the "SmartFactory" concept are set to "spin our world around" 360° and over. Are you prepared?

Industry 4.0 and Sustainability

People, Planet, and Profit

Sustainability emphasizes *People, Planet,* and *Profit* (3Ps). The term sustainability is very important to both the initiatives of Industry 4.0 and Quality 4.0. as much as it is to their initiatives. It is for the purpose of sustainability that organizations have to put a lot of attention and focus on all aspects related to 3BL rather than just viewing profitability merely in monetary terms. Key lessons learnt by the global community from COVID-19 pandemic suggest that sustainability is quite critical to every supply chain. This has however prior to the advent of COVID-19 been also argued by Kleindorfer et al. [124] about sustainability being a key element in every supply chain.

In their definition of sustainability, Fiksel et al. [125] brought out the full implications of sustainability. They came up the definition of sustainability as, *"Meeting the needs of the present without compromising the ability of future generations to meet their needs."* This is exactly the same definition as that of McGill University, Canada which has also defined sustainability as "meeting our own needs without compromising the ability of future generations to meet their own needs" [126].

In confirming the consistency of this definition with TBL literature, Kessler and Walters [127] asserted, "This notion of sustainability is widely accepted as one of the most important factors of organizational growth and development.

It is not in vain that the world of quality, as well as the world around us, is awash with the proliferation of the term *"sustainability."* This term is directly related to the concept and purpose of quality more than any other. Whether we are talking about the quality of life, quality of the environment or the universe, human life, social justice, and economic (e.g., businesses and organizations) development, sustainability remains a common denominator. Life itself is about growing up to identify, establish, and sustain our individual life values as perceived by every individual person. Life struggles therefore revolve around our values.

Although some may have erroneously misconstrued sustainability as being just used in terms of profitability with regard to organizations and businesses, and environmental in the context of governments responsibilities alone, it is more than that. It is about social equity, economic development, and the ability of people, organizations, and/or businesses to survive at all times in fulfilment of their respective commitments to customers, people, and the society at large, most importantly during the times of challenges—risks, pandemic, danger, weather extremities, natural and man-made catastrophes, etc.

Sustainability is therefore not just about money even when economic standards is seen as the mainstream [127]; today's daily emerging threats—climate change, pandemic, and other diseases—call also for the need to follow environmental and societal standards must also be followed [128]. Hence, the three components of sustainability are ***profit, planet,*** and ***people*** [129] also referred to, in the words of Elkington [130], as the triple bottom line (TBL or 3BL). Hence, in the context of quality management, sustainability is defined by three pillars—*planet/environment,* *profit/economy,* and *people/society*. Hence, sustainability serves on a broad basis, as a critical indicator of organizational performance, growth and development [131]. It goes to say therefore that organizations or businesses that are unsustainable are at the risk of surviving [132].

While organizational sustainability may primarily be viewed from the perspectives of its ability to withstand changes, its commitment to environmental sustainability is far more critical to ensure that we, as well as future generations, are all in the position to sustain our lives, socioeconomic activities, and the environment we live in.

In terms of quality management context, therefore, the existence of organizations depends largely on their abilities to continue to improve and sustain the improvement process in terms of their products and services without any adverse effects, whatsoever, on any other entities. This thus brings into the discussion the general need for strong organizational commitment to its corporate social responsibility (CSR) and the corporate environment responsibility (CER).

Forero and Sisodia [25], in their research work on handling quality in Industry 4.0 revolution, reported that sustainability has already been embedded into Industry 4.0. with the "mindset of circular economy, instead of the more traditional economy." A circular economy is described by them, in reference to "a closed-loop supply chain with a stronger focus on the 'end of life' of the product beyond its consumption." The implication here is that Industry 4.0 has the capability to achieve strategies for recycling, reusing, restoring, or manufacturing with changeable modules capable of reducing materials wastages as reported by Madhusudan [133]. A linear economy, is accordingly also known as an open loop system, can simply be described as a 4-step of, take-make-use-dispose (disposed by end-user as waste) process. The outcome here leads generally to sustainability, environmental, and economic concerns.

A circular economy or closed-loop economy enables the opportunity of focusing on a supply chain system with restorative and regenerative abilities thereby providing industries with the advantage of dealing not only with their products but their end-of-life stage. The sustainability factors in the closed-loop supply chain or circular economic structure are as follows:

- Opportunity of carrying out life cycle assessment (LCA).
- The elimination of toxic materials within the supply chain.
- Waste reduction through product redesigning deploying eco-innovation concepts of *design for environment* (DfE) and *design for disassembly* (DfD). Reverse logistics represents an integral component of supply chain redesigning, in closing the loop for achieving the circular economic structure.
- The ability to restructure the supply chain on the basis of *reverse logistics* lines.

The impactful effect of the circular economy is visibly in its ability to aid the optimization of the use of organizational resources through the elimination of wastes which actually runs parallel with the consequences of Industry 4.0 initiatives.

The primary role of industrial manufacturing as essential and critical elements of sustainable development can therefore not be overemphasized. This potential is heavily laden in the outputs of industrial manufacturing, most, if not all, are devoted to cater for societal needs and requirements.

One of the major outlooks of Industry 4.0 initiatives centers generally on the expectations of it resulting in the paradigm of sustainable manufacturing. Sustainable manufacturing, as defined by the International Trade Administration under the US Department of Commerce is:

> The creation of manufactured products using processes that minimize negative environmental impacts, conserve energy and natural resources, are safe for employees, communities, and consumers, and are economically sound.

Industry 4.0 has been reported to play some roles which aid the accomplishment the seventeen [70] set developmental goals of the United Nations [40] with effect from January 01,, 2016, and a time limit of 2030. Some of these goals which have been viewed by Zaman [134] as strongly connected to Industry 4.0 are among others the following:

- ***Sustainable economic growth and productive employment***—Industry 4.0 technologies are widely accessible thus serving to drive economic growth (UN Goal 18).
- ***Sustainable consumption and production***—one of the goals of Industry 4.0 is waste reduction through just in time (JIT) production, and by minimizing material waste in design through the use of manufacturing data within stipulated parameters to minimize rejects and usage of natural resources (UN Goal 12).
- ***Promoting global partnership for sustainable development***—implementing Industry 4.0 provides opportunities for developing national economic strategies for sustainable growth while facilitating international cooperation to jointly solve threatening challenges of pollution, climate change, and migration, among others. (UN Goal17).

There is abundant evidence in the literature too that sustainability is key to the supply chain as against the past trends of focusing mainly on monetary profitability. The blockchain technology application in Industry 4.0 vis-à-vis Quality 4.0 further expatiates the strong placement of supply chain sustainability in the fourth industrial revolution.

Müller et al. [52] in their reported studies in some German manufacturing industries deduced that Industry 4.0 is also about considerations for environmental and social advantages—waste and energy reductions as well as workplace improvements. Sustainability thus represents a key aspect of quality management, its processes, and tools.

Just as sustainability is critical to businesses and organizational existentialities, so also has the sustainability of the earth been predicated, faith wise, as being the main stake of man's heritage.

Hence, God's calls on the human race to protect the planet earth as revealed in the book of Psalms 104[25–30] which reads thus:

> "There is the sea, vast and spacious, teeming with creatures beyond number—living things both large and small. There the ships go to and fro, and the leviathan, which you formed to frolic there. These all look to you to give them their food at the proper time. When you give it to them, they gather it up; when you open your hand, they are satisfied with good things. When you hide your face, they are terrified; when you take away their breath, they die and return to dust. When you send your Spirit, they are created, and you renew the face of the earth."

The people of the global community are therefore being hypocritical, pretending not to know about the implications of neglecting our corporate- and governance-social responsibilities—CSR and GSR; and corporate environment responsibility CER until the advent of disastrous events such as the COVID-19 pandemic and those emanating from global warming, even though when some irresponsible heartlessly selfish and egoistic political leaders of our time, deceitfully claim ignorance.

Although it rarely appeared in the literature, it is highly important here to emphasize that the ordinary citizens of the global community also have their individual responsibilities in sustaining the planet earth. That is the reason why the author believes in introducing to the sustainability responsibilities the roles of individual citizens and the collectivity of them as being as critical as the aforementioned to achieve positive results for our collective well-being.

Hence, citizens' collective social responsibility (CCSR) is a key essential part of Industry 4.0 vis-à-vis Quality 4.0 especially when it comes to local government and city administration for quality living of the people and sustainability. Failure of individual citizens to make critical collective sacrifices has, for example, undoubtedly contributed largely—directly or indirectly—to the elongation of the serious negative impacts of the COVID-19 pandemic on the people of the global community particularly in terms of reaching the objective of herd immunity.

CCSR is particularly important as key components of achieving the SmartCity goals of the digital age in various aspects:

- Participatory and inclusive governance
- Obeying regulatory requirements in all ramifications—prompt payment of taxes, effective involvement in democratic processes, etc.
- Self-commitment to law and order

It is glaring therefore that when viewed from all ramifications of man's life and existential activities, *sustainability is a key essential* aspect.

Supply Chain Sustainability (SCS) Is Key to Businesses

What we are witnessing in the automobile industry appears more or less of an economic fairy tale of our time. As defined by Sanders [135], "It's a strange time to be alive. Lumber prices are through the roof. Used car inventory is virtually non-existent, and there is a global run, on computer chips, certain clothing and even grape nuts cereal." Getting back from the COVID-19 pandemic impact on our economy and the ripple effects has not proved to be easy. The pandemic era proved generally how valuable the resiliency of the supply chain must have to be, to achieve the "Survival of the sustainable."

The taste of the criticality of supply chain sustainability was practically experienced at the beginning of the emergence of the COVID-19 pandemic when empty shelves of toilet rolls and other tissue paper products created strong anxieties among consumers in the USA.

The sudden supply chain instability created in 2021 in the USA by the automobile industry "*conspiracy-styled*" supply and demand crisis, based on computer chip shortage, is an indicator of the world's fragile economic reliance on supply chain instability or perhaps unsustainability.

Car buyers in the USA were brought on their knees, having to cough out extra $3000.00 to $5000.00 US dollars or even more, respectively, for pre-owned and new personal cars. While auto dealers were smiling to the bank, consumers were sinking in credit card debt, a situation which actually precipitates the need for organizational management and government agencies to maintain and continue to sustain their commitments around supply chain sustainability (SCS).

The COVID-19 pandemic year, 2020, witnessed some of the negative impacts and ripple effects of the pandemic on SCS even though a new report by the Massachusetts Institute of Technology (MIT) claimed that, "About 82% of the executives surveyed said the pandemic didn't affect or even increased their commitment to supply chain sustainability (SCS) during 2020." Imagine what would have happened without this massive commitment of company executives to SCS! [136].

The broader outcome of this survey report of 2400 executives mainly from North America and European companies also showed that 8% of them felt investors' pressure grew with the pandemic, while 59% reiterated their investment in SCS.

As emphasized in the definition of sustainable manufacturing and sustainability itself, restricting sustainability to, or viewing it strictly from the perspectives of profitability alone is neither tenable nor sustainable. The sustainability of the supply chain thus requires a widened scope of its viewpoint and consideration by seeing it through the lens of people, planet, and profitability, focusing more on both environmental and social goals. This is distinctly identified in the outcome of the MIT survey as summed up thus, "Organizations also signaled a shift toward focusing more on social goals such as employee safety, worker welfare, attention to equity and inclusion, and energy savings and renewable energy."

Sustainability—Social and Governance Social Responsibility (GSR)

The MIT report also brought to the fore, some key social issues regarding the quality of social responsibilities (SR)—corporate social responsibility (CSR) and governance social responsibility (GSR)—in our country's political arena, an aspect of the people's quality of life which has been dragged into political controversial muddy waters of self-aggrandizement, lies and conspiracy theories particularly, in the earlier parts of the COVID-19 pandemic year, 2020.

While the MIT survey report highlighted our collective economic resolve as presented in, "As we recover from COVID-19 and start to rebuild our economies, these areas will likely stay in focus," it is important for us all to pay attention to the criticality of these identified areas of national concern if the US people's quality of life has to be improved upon, and sustained. In accordance with these findings, "Social issues came into focus in 2020. Social justice protests, heightened awareness of forced labor, and social inequalities laid bare by the pandemic are some of the developments that have helped to increase the pressure on companies to address social issues."

Apart from emphasizing organizational corporate social responsibility (CSR), there is the urgent need too, for governments and the political leadership, to honestly adapt policies that promote the quality of people's health and lives in shows of governance social responsibility (GSR). Hence, sustainable governance requires people-centric and socially oriented and committed political leadership from city/county levels, through state-level governance, to national levels of political power and leadership.

Sustainability—businesses, organizations, cities, states, nations, and the entirety of the planet earth—requires among others, strong leadership commitment as demonstrated by the outcome of the MIT survey.

While the role of leadership is very important for sustainable businesses and governance, it is very important here to also acknowledge that sustainability is, from a broad perspective, also one of a collective responsibility (team working) of all stakeholders, a fact adequately affirmed by Dye [137], a visionary leader and city manager in, "We have an incredibly strong and supportive City Council, leadership team and employee family, all devoted to public service benefiting the people and businesses of our city."

The sustainable growth, improvement, and quality of people's lives progressively experienced in the city of Grand Prairie mostly in the last decade have been made possible by leadership commitment to people, environment, and social responsibilities. The example of the governance social responsibility (GSR) experienced in the city of Grand Prairie over a decade ago, transparently and visibly demonstrate the fact that, *"good leadership draws the cooperation, collaboration and inclusion of all stakeholders to achieve sustainability."* The consistently high-quality management level of the City of Grand Prairie and its achieved developmental sustainability over decades have been constructed and built on the platform of leadership integrity, nonpoliticization, nonpartisanship, trust, and diverse inclusion of its diverse population.

Role of Agility and Collaboration in Supply Chain Management

There are no doubts whatsoever that the lessons of the 2020 COVID-19 turbulent years have taught the people of the world, "that agility and collaboration in managing supply chains must remain a top priority," of businesses and organizations [136]. Transitioning to the digital era and digital age supply chain management generally calls for resiliency; hence, there is the need for organizational management to adapt, plan, and be flexible in order to be able to meet immediate and future needs.

Based on the critical nature of sustainability to businesses the ability to holistically and effectively evaluate it (sustainability) is highly supportive of their (businesses) survival. Haghighi et al. [138] have been credited with the balanced scorecard (BSC) strategy tool for measuring and controlling sustainability.

Kessler and Walters [127] recently reported "A new tool to improve supply chain sustainability" based on the quality management ideas of failure mode and effects analysis (FMEA) and matrix analysis.

When viewed from a general perspective, however, the author recognizes the fact that some measures of sustainability control could be derived from the combination of organizational in-house key performance indices or indicators based on set goals at set times with respect to the following relevant criteria:

- Productivity—a productivity index on improving trend.
- Employee retention ability—derivable from employee turnover at set times which could be six-monthly or yearly.
- Employees' feedback—getting individual employee assessment of the work environment in terms of social conditions, safety, employee-management relationships, etc.
- Customer (primary, secondary, and tertiary customers) reviews or feedback—number of complaints, product returns, or number of recalls at set times.
- Product competitiveness—assessed by the marketing unit or department.
- Corporate environmental responsibility (CER)—product and product packaging impact on environment, people, and community—this may be based on pollution, degradation of immediate work environment, and community at large.
- Corporate social responsibility (CSR) in terms of organizational responses as and may be needed.
- Profitability or economic key performance indicators.

An organization can resort to using as many of the above-specified criteria to create its sustainability key performance indicators (SKPI) to derive a set improvement scale on which organizational goals can be assessed and controlled at the organization's own discretion.

The notion of sustainability is on a general basis widely viewed as one of the most important factors of organizational growth and development.

Summing Up Industry 4.0 Reviews

Industry 4.0 initiatives have been widely reported as heralding into the world immense changes in industrial manufacturing processes and the opportunities that come with it. The fourth industrial revolution is broadly reported to have been enabled by the digital technology development of the third industrial revolution, which is represented mainly by widely recorded breakthroughs in the following diverse fields [139]:

- Advanced robotics and drones
- Artificial intelligence (AI) and machine learning (ML)
- Biotechnologies and precision medicine
- Virtual, augmented, and mixed reality systems
- New approaches to energy generation storage
- Multidimensional printing
- New materials and others

Industry 4.0 has also opened up opportunities in the research field too. It set to change our industrial landscape even though there are variations in the contexts of its definition. While Industry 4.0 calls for more research works in its various emerging states until its maturity in about two decades from now, literature findings assert the resolution and determination of relevant companies—software, equipment manufacturers, plant industry, machine makers, engineering design, management consultants—to accomplish the "SmartFactory" goal even though successful prototyping has not been widely reported.

The concept of Industry 4.0 has thus opened up the road to achieving a smart industrial manufacturing digitalized outfit characterized by the following:

- High level of interconnectivity
- The ability to offer customized products with superior quality and competitive in price.
- A flexible interconnected production system
- Intelligent automation
- Enabled communication among humans, machines, and product via internet
- Specialized skilled employees trained to understand the functions and workings of 4.0 base technologies
- Self-controlling systems capable via internet
- A wealth of data acquired by smart products and machines during operations
- Ability to make data-driven decisions of various scenario across the value chain, including stakeholders in a transparent, visible, and connected ways [25]

While it is believed that Industry 4.0 will play important roles in achieving the United Nations sustainable goals targeted at 2030, there is no clear indication of how this ambitious industrial digitalization is going to impact the poor economies of the global community. The current situation suggests however that Industry 4.0

is like a double-edged sword waiting to shred the economies of such countries into pieces.

It however appears as if companies operating in the poor economic countries of the world have neither the urge/need nor the desire/dream to join the bandwagon of Industry 4.0-initiating companies; when Industry 4.0 initiatives are implemented or developed to maturity, they may neither have the needed funds nor required access to 4.0 technologies skills to embark the digital transformation which may be overpriced at that time. The gap created by this Industry 4.0-nonparticipatory and noninclusive standing may eventually turn companies in the world's poor economies into extremely noncompetitive, nonproductive companies vis-à-vis economies.

Industry 4.0 trend is undoubtedly here to stay, to revolutionize the industrial platform and change the way we work and live. These are, however, not going to be accomplished without challenges to both organizations and employees.

References

1. Brettel, M., Friedrichsen, N., Keller, M., & Rosenberg, M. (2014). How virtualization, decentralization and network building change the manufacturing landscape: An industry 4.0 perspective. *World Academy of Science, Engineering and Technology, International Journal of Mechanical, Aerospace, Industrial, Mechatronic and Manufacturing Engineering, 8*(1).
2. Radziwill, N. (2018). Let's get digital: The many ways the fourth industrial revolution is reshaping the way we think about quality. *Quality Progress,* October 2018, pp. 24–29.
3. Wang, S., Wan, J., Di, L., & Zhang, C. (2016). Implementing smart factory of industry 4.0: An outlook. *International Journal of Distributed Sensor Networks, 2016*(4), 1–10. https://doi.org/10.1155/2016/3159805. https://journals.sagepub.com/doi/pdf/10.1155/2016/3159805. Retrieved on August 24, 2021.
4. Radziwon, A., Bilberg, A., Borgers, M., & Madsen, E. S. (2014). The smart factory: Exploring adaptive and flexible manufacturing solutions. *Procedia Engineering, 69,* 1184–1190. https://www.sciencedirect.com/science/article/pii/S1877705814003543
5. Rick, B., Mussomeli, A., Laaper, S., Hartigan, M., & Sniderman, B. (2017). *The Smart Factory: Responsive, adaptive, connected manufacturing*. A Deloitte series on Industry 4.0, digital manufacturing enterprises, and digital supply networks. Deloitte University Press, p. 7. https://www2.deloitte.cm. Retrieved August 23, 2021.
6. Ruessmann, M., Lorenz, M., Gerbert, P., Waldner, M., Engel, P., Harnisch, M., & Justus, J. (2015). Industry 4.0: The future of productivity and growth in manufacturing industries. *Boston Consulting Group (BCG),* pp. 1–14. https://www.bcg.com. Retrieved August 13, 2021.
7. Leineweber, S., Wienbruch, T., Lins, D., Kreimeier, D., & Kuhlenkötter, B. (2018). Concept for an evolutionary maturity-based Industry 4.0 migration model. *Procedia CIRP, 72,* 404–409.
8. Geissbauer, R., Vedso, J., & Schrauf, S. (2016). A Strategist's Guide to Industry 4.0. [online], strategy + business, *Manufacturing,* May 9, 2016. https://www.strategy-business.com/article/A-Strategists-Guide-to-Industry-4.0. Retrieved on July 23, 2021.
9. Costich, T. (2021). The right route – Developing a roadmap for a successful digital transformation journey. *Quality Progress,* August 2021, pp. 52–53.
10. Mishra, S., & Isazada, N. (2021). Fear of the unknown – Managing employee resistance to change initiatives. *Progress Report,* June, pp. 26–31.
11. Robbins, S. P., & Judge, T. A. (2013). *Essentials of organizational behavior* (12th ed.). Pearson.

12. Buchi, G., Cugno, M., & Castagnoli, R. (2020). Smart factory performance and Industry 4.0. *Technological Forecasting and Social Change, 150*, 11970.
13. Culot, G., Orzes, G., Sartor, M., & Nassimbeni, G. (2019). The future of manufacturing: A Delphi-based scenario analysis on industry 4.0. *Technological Forecasting and Social Change, 146*, 119–132.
14. Weber, K. M., Gudowsky, N., & Aichholzerb, G. (2019). Foresight and technology assessment for the Australian Parliament – Finding new ways of debating the future of Industry 4.0. *Futures, 109*, 240–251.
15. Horvath, D., & Szabo, R. Z. (2019). Driving forces and barriers of industry 4.0: Do multinational and small and medium-sized companies have equal opportunities? *Technological Forecasting and Social Change, 146*, 199–132.
16. Lu, H. P., & Weng, C. I. (2018). Smart manufacturing technology, market maturity analysis and technology roadmap in the computer and electronic product manufacturing industry. *Technological Forecasting and Social Change, 133*, 85–94.
17. Zgodavova, K., Bober, P., Majstorovic, V., Monkova, K., Santos, G., & Juhaszova, D. (2020). Innovative methods for small mixed batches production system improvement: The case of a bakery machine manufacturer. *Sustainability, 12*, 6266.
18. Morrar, R., Arman, H., & Mousa, S. (2017). The fourth industrial revolution (Industry 4.0): A social innovation perspective. *Technology Innovation Management Review, 7*, 12–20.
19. Benesova, A., & Tupa, J. (2017). Requirements for education and qualification of people in industry 4.0. *Procedia Manufacturing, 11*, 2195–2202.
20. Carvalho, A. V., Enrique, D. V., Chouchene, A., & Charrua-Santos, F. (2021). Quality 4.0: An overview. *Procedia Computer Scicence, 181*, 341–346.
21. Jacob, D. (2017). *Quality 4.0 impact and strategy handbook. Getting digitally connected to transform quality management*. LNS Research.
22. Juran.com. *Quality 4.0: The future of quality?* Available online: https://www.juran.com/blog/quality-4-0-the-future-of-quality/. Retrieved July 27, 2021.
23. Zonnenshain, A., & Kenett, R. S. (2020). Quality 4.0: The challenging future of quality engineering. *Quality Engineering, 32*, 614–626.
24. The Industrial Internet Consortium. (2014). *About us*. https://www.iiconsortium.org/about-us.htm. Retrieved on November 21, 2019.
25. Sisodia, R., & Forero, D. V. (2020). *Quality 4.0 – How to handle quality 4.0 in industry 4.0 revolution*. Master's Thesis, Chambers University of Technology, Department of Technology Management and Economics; Gothenburg, Sweden.
26. Platform I4.0. (2015). *Von smarten Objekten und Maschinen*. https://www.plattform-i4.0.de. Retrieved November 21, 2019.
27. Schmidt, R., Möhring, M., Härting, R. C., Reichstein, C., Neumaier, P., & Jozinovic, P. (2015). Industry 4.0: Potentials for creating smart products: Empirical research results. In W. Abramowicz (Ed.), *Business information systems* (pp. 16–27). Springer.
28. Sendler, U. (2013). *Industrie 4.0: Beherrschung der industriellen Komplexität mit SysLM*. Springer-Wieweg.
29. Kagermann, W. W., & Helbig, J. (2013). *Recommendations for implementing the strategic initiative INDUSTRIE 4.0* (p. 77). Forschungsunion.
30. Hermann, M., Pentek, T., & Otto, B. (2015). *Design principles for industry 4.0 scenarios*. Conference: 2016 49th Hawaii International Conference on System Sciences (HICSS). pp. 3928–3937. https://doi.org/10.1109/HICSS.2016.488
31. Posada, J., Toro, C., Barandiaran, I., & Oyarzun. (2015, March). Visual compting as a key enabling technology for industrie 4.0 and industrial internet. *IEEE Computer Graphics and Applications, 35*(2), 26–40. https://doi.org/10.1109/MCG.2015.45
32. Yin, S., & Kaynak, O. (2015). Big data for modern industry: Challenges and trends [points of view]. *Proceedings of the IEEE, 103*(2), 143–146.
33. Smit, J., Kreutzer, S., Moeller, C., & Carlberg, M. (2016). *European Parliament – Directorate General for Internal Policies*. Policy Department A: Economic and Scientific Policy. "Industry 4.0". https://www.europarl.europa.eu/studies. Retrieved on August 24, 2021.

34. Ji, W., & Mang, L. (2017). Big data analytics-based fault prediction for shop floor scheduling. *Journal of Manufacturing Systems, 43*, 187–194.
35. Seele, P. (2017). Predictive sustainability control: A review assessing the potential to transfer big data driven "predictive policing" to corporate sustainability management. *Journal of Cleaner Production, 153*, 673–686.
36. Dugar, D., & Jindal, T. (2021). Quantum computers: The end and a new beginning for cryptographic systems. *Editorial, science and technology*. www.freelunch.co.in. Retrieved October 6, 2021.
37. Zhou, R., & Le Cardinal, J. (2019). *International conference on engineering design*. ICED19, 5–8 August 2019, pp. 2111–2120. Delft, The Netherlands.
38. Forschungsunion/acatech. (2013). Securing the future of German manufacturing industry. *Recommendations for implementing the strategic initiative*, INDUSTRIE 4.0, 2013.
39. Economist, (Business). (2015). *Germany's industry – Does Deutschland do digital?* November 21, 2015. Berlin & Stuttgart.
40. United Nations, (UN). (2015). Sustainable development goals to kick in with start of new year. *United Nations,* December 30, 2015. https://tinyurl.com/5banb5m
41. Alisic, B., Cianfrani, C. A., Sheps, I., & West, J. E. (J.). (2021). Supporting sustainability – How ISO 18091 promotes the UN's sustainable development goals. *Quality Progress,* August 2021, pp. 56–58.
42. International Organization for Standardization, (ISO), ISO 18091:2019 – Quality management systems- guidelines for the application of ISO 9001 in local government.
43. Lavi, Y. (2017). "Industry 4.0: Harnessing the power of ERP and MES integration" magic software. *Industry Week,* July 20, 2017. https://www.industryweek.com. Retrieved Joly 31, 2021.
44. Germany Trade and Invest. *Smart factory*. https://industrie4.0.gtai.de/INDUSTRIE40/Navigation/EN/Topics/Industrie-40/smart-factory.html. Retrieved August 18, 2021.
45. Ramasubramanian, G. (2016). Machine learning is revolutionizing every industry. *Observer,* November 28, 2016. https://observer.com/2016/11/machine-learning-is-revolutionizing-every-industry/
46. Pollak, A., Hilarowicz, A., Walczak, M., & Gasiorek, D. Z. (2020, July). A framework of action for implementation of industry 4.0 – An empirically based research. *Sustainability, 12*(14), 1589. https://doi.org/10.3390/su12145789
47. Vulsanovic, I., Kuc, V., Mijuskovic, V. M., & Herceg, T. (2020). Challenges and driving forces for industry 4.0 implementation. *Sustainability, 12*(10), 4208. https://doi.org/10.3390/su12104208
48. Birkel, H. S., Veile, J. W., Mueller, J. M., Hartmann, E., & Voigt, K. (2019). Development of a risk framework for industry 4.0 in the context of sustainability for established manufacturers. *Sustainability, 11*(2), 384. https://doi.org/10.3390/su11020384
49. Lasi, H., Fettke, P., Kemper, H., Feld, T., & Hoffmann, M. (2014). Industry 4.0. *Business & Information Systems Engineering, 6*, 239–242.
50. Stock, T., Obernaus, M., Kunz, S., & Khol, H. (2018). Industry 4.0 as an enabler for sustainable development: A qualitative assessment of its ecological and social potential. *Process Safety and Environmental Protection, 118*, 254–267.
51. Wagner, T., Hermann, C., & Thiede, S. (2017). Industry 4.0 impacts on lean production sytems. *Procedia CIRP, 63*, 125–131. https://doi.org/10.1016/j.procir.2017.02.041
52. Mueller, J. M., Kiel, D., & Voigt, K. I. (2018). What drives the implementation of Industry 4.0? – The role of opportunities and challenges in the context of sustainability. *Sustainability, 10*, 247.
53. Stankovic, M., Gupta, R., Figueroa, J. E., Calzadilla-Sarmiento, B., Memedovic, O., Authried, O., & Rueth, T. (2017). Industry 4.0 – Opportunities behind the challenge. *Background Paper,* UNIDO 2017, Online. https://www.unido.org/sites/default/files/files/201711/UNIDO%20Background%20Paper%20on%20Industry%204_27112017.pdf

54. Motyl, B., Baronio, G., Uberti, S., Speranza, D., & Filippi, S. (2017). How will the future engineers' skills change in the industry 4.0 frameworks? – A questionnaire survey. *Procedia Manufacturing, 2017,* 1501–1509.
55. Erbog, G. (2017). *How to define industry 4.0: Main pillars of industry 4.0.* Conference: Managerial trends in the development of enterprise in globalization era. At Slovak University of Agriculture in Nitra, Slovakia. https://www.researchgate.net/publication/326557388_How_To_Define_Industry_40_Main_Pilar_of_Industry_40. Retrieved August 11, 2021.
56. Kim, H., (2021). *Zyter's IOT solution features 360 degree view of the factory with analytics to improve productivity and safety.* May 27, 2021. https://www.powerelectronics.co.kr
57. ASQ. (2021). Smart factories – Connecting machines, workers and systems. *Quality Progress,* August 2021, p. 61. https://www.zyter.com/smartfactories
58. ASQ. (2021). Survey – Many concerned AI moving too fast. *Quality Progress,* May, pp. 6–7. https://tinyurl.com/y73fhfj2
59. ASQ. (2021). Survey: Manufacturers plan for permanent changes. *Quality Progress,* January, p. 10. https://www.tinyurl.com/west-monroe-covid-survey
60. ASQ. (2021). The Progress report – Manufacturers aim to improve job quality. *Quality Progress,* July, pp. 8–9.
61. Colantoni, A., Cecchini, M., Egidi, G., Saporito, M. G., & Zambon, I. (2019). Revolution 4.0: Industry vs. agriculture in a future development for SMEs. *Processes, Multidisciplinary Digital Publishing Institute, 7*(1), 36.
62. Ding, B. (2018). Pharma Industry 4.0: Literature review and research opportunities in sustainable pharmaceutical supply chains. In *Process safety and environmental protection* (Vol. 119, pp. 115–130). Elsevier.
63. Dallasega, P., Rauch, E., & Linder, C. (2018). Industry 4.0 as an enabler of proximity for construction supply chains: A systematic literature review. *Computers in Industry 99.* April, 2018. https://doi.org/10.1016/j.compind.2018.03.039.
64. Li, X., Wan, J., Lai, C. F., Wang, S., Vasilakos, A. V., & Li, D. (2015). A review of industrial wireless networks in the context of Industry 4.0. *Wireless Networks*, Springer U.S., Vol. 23, No. 1, pp. 23–41.
65. Lezzi, M., Lazoi, M., & Corallo, A. (2018). Cybersecurity for Industry 4.0 in the current literature: A reference framework. In *Computers in Industry* (Vol. 103, pp. 97–110). Elsevier.
66. Varela, I. R., & Tjahjono, B. (2014). Big data analytics in supply chain management: Trends and related research. *6th International Conference on Operations and Supply Chain Management, 1*(1), 2013–2014.
67. Maskuriy, R., Selamani, A., Maresova, P., Krejcar, O., & David, O. O. (2019, July). Industry 4.0 for the construction industry: Review of management perspective. *Economies, 7*(3), 68. https://doi.org/10.3390/economies7030068
68. The Bolton Consulting Group (BCG). (2015). *Industry 4.0: The future of productivity and growth in manufacturing industries.* April 2015. https://www.image-src.bcg.com. Retrieved August 21, 2021.
69. Krejcar, O., Selamat, A., Svobodova, L., Soukal, I., Maresova, P., Javanmardi, E., & Hedvicakova, M. (2018). Consequences of industry 4.0 in business and economics. *Economies, Multidisciplinary Digital Publishing Institute, 6*(3), 46.
70. Brettel, M., Klein, M., & Friederichsen, N. (2016). The relevance of manufacturing flexibility in the context of Industrie 4.0. *Procedia CIRP, 2016*(41), 105–110.
71. Peukert, B., Benecke, S., Clavell, J., Neugebauer, S., Nissen, N. F., Uhlmann, E., Lang, K. D., & Finkbeiner, M. (2015). Addressing sustainability and flexibility in manufacturing via smart modular machine tool frames to support sustainable value creation. *Procedia CIRP, 29,* 514–519.
72. Bonilla, S., Silva, H., Terra da Silva, M., Franco Goncalvez, R., & Sacomano, J. (2018). Industry 4.0 and sustainability implications: A scenario-based analysis of the impacts and challenges. *Sustainability, 10,* 3740.
73. Chapco-Wade, C. (2018). *Digitization, digitalization and digital transformation: What's the difference.* October 20, 2020. https://www.medium.com

74. Kaspersky Lab. (2021). *What are bots? – Definition and explanation*. https://www.kaspersky.com. Retrieved on August 25, 2021.
75. Kane, G. C., Palmer, D., Phillips, A. N., Kiron, D., & Buckley, N. (2017). Achieving digital maturity – Adapting your company to a changing world. *MITSloan Management Review,* July 13, 2017.
76. KPMG. (2021). *KPMG AI industries survey*. March 9, 2021. Https://www.kpmg.com/us
77. Fukuyama, M. (2018). Society 5.0: Aiming for a new human-centered society. *Japan Spotlight,* July/August 2018, pp. 47–50. https://www.jef.or.jp/journal
78. Cyrill, M. (2018). What is made in China 2025 and why has it made the world so nervous? *China Briefing,* December 2018.
79. Pruitt, W. F. (2021). Internet of things-unleash the power. *Quality Progress,* February, pp. 45–47.
80. Adoph, S., Tisch, M., & Metternich, J. (2014). Challenges and approaches to competency development for future production. *Journal of International Scientific Publications – Educational Alternatives, 10*, 1001.
81. The Manufacturer. (2021). *Experts share key takeaways from the data driven intelligent industry roundtable*." July 5, 2021. https://www.themanufacturer.com. Retrieved September 9, 2021.
82. The Manufacturer. (2021). *Putting the idea of 'smart' into practice*. https://www.themanufacturer.com. September 7. 2021. Retrieved on September 22, 2021.
83. Bilett, S., Gruber, H., & Harteis, C. (2018). In C. Harteis (Ed.), *The impact of digitalization in the workplace – An educational view,* Foreword, p. v, Springer.
84. Harteis, C. (2018). Machines, change and work: an educational view on the digitization of work. In C. Harteis (Ed.), *The impact of digitalization in the workplace – An educational view,* Chapter 1, (pp. 1–2).
85. Lehner, F., & Sunby, M. W. (2018). ICT skills and competencies for SMEs: Results from a structured literature analysis on the individual level. In C. Harteis (Ed.), *The impact of digitalization in the workplace – An educational view*, Chapter 5, (pp. 61–68).
86. Organization for Economic Cooperation and Development, (OECD). (2004). *OECD information technology outlook – Information and communications technologies*. https://www.oecd.org/internet/ieconomy/37620123.pdf. Retrieved August 14, 2021.
87. Selko, A. (2021). Do manufacturers need to create better jobs? *Industry Week,* April 29, 2021. https://tinyurl.com/better-mfg-jobs
88. Radziwill, N. (2021). What personal skills should young quality professionals consider growing? – Value awareness. *Quality Progress,* July, p. 26.
89. Sille, L. (2021). What personal skills should young quality professionals consider growing? – Emotional intelligence. *Quality Progress,* July, p. 26.
90. Crosby, P. B. (1979). *Quality is free*. McGraw-Hill.
91. Hooks, J. (2021). What personal skills should young quality professionals consider growing? – Emotional intelligence. *Quality Progress,* July, p. 27.
92. Lindborg, H. (2021). What personal skills should young quality professionals consider growing? – Imagination. *Quality Progress,* July, p. 27.
93. Roberson, R. (2021). Think like a giraffe – The attributes of the giraffe can serve to hone your skills and abilities as a quality professional. *Quality Progress,* July, pp. 30–36.
94. Fischer, C., & Pöhler, A. (2018). Supporting the change to digitalized production environments through learning organization development. In C. Harteis (Ed.), *The impact of digitalization in the workplace – An educational view*, Chapter 10, (p. 143). Springer.
95. Hämäläinen, R., Lanz, M., & Konkinen, K. T. (2018). Collaborative systems and environments for future working life: Towards the integration of workers, systems and manufacturing environments. In C. Harteis (Ed.), *The impact of digitalization in the workplace – An educational view*, Chapter 3, (p. 25). Springer.
96. Lanz, M., & Tuokko, R. (2017). Concepts, methods and tools for individualized production. *Production Engineering, 11*(2), 205–212.

97. Järvenpää, E., Lanz, M., & Larmmervo, E. (2016). *Agility challenges in Finnish manufacturing companies – Manufacturing operations management viewpoint.* Proceedings of International Conferences Advances in Production Management Systems (APMS 2016).
98. Boasch, J. (2017). *Speed, data, and ecosystems: Excelling in a software-driven world.* CRC Press.
99. Edwards, R., & Fenwick, T. (2016). Digital analytics in professional work and learning. *Studies in Continuing Education, 38*(2), 213–227.
100. Deloitte. (2014). *Industry 4.0 Challenges and solutions for the digital transformation and use of exponential technologies.*
101. Maraghy, H. A. (2005). Flexible and reconfigurable manufacturing systems paradigms. *International Journal of Flexible Manufacturing Systems, 17*(4), 261–276.
102. Krivocuca, M. (2021). Catalysts for change – Achieving organizational excellence in post-COVID-19 Industry 4.0 process performance. *Quality Progress,* March, pp. 32–37.
103. Kane, G. C., Phillips, A. N., Copulsky, J. R., & Andrus, G. R. (2019). *The technology fallacy: How people are the real key to digital transformation.* MIT Press.
104. Pietenpol, L. (2020). The times they are a-Changin. *Quality Progress,* December, pp. 6–7.
105. Lindborg, H. J. (2020). Adaptive space – How organizations can harness employee creativity to adjust to disruptive changes. *Quality Progress,* November, pp. 5–7.
106. McLaughlin, D. *Why 40% of today's fortune 500 will be extinct in 10 years.* https://www.tinyurl.com/fortune-500-extinct
107. Arena, M. J. (2018). *How GM and other companies re positively disrupting themselves and transforming into agile organizations.* McGraw Hill.
108. Jordan, A. (2021). 75 and counting – Quality's impact on the world around us. *Quality Progress,* July, p.4.
109. Aleksandrova, S. V., Vasiliev, V. A., & Alexandrov, M. N. (2019). Integration of quality management and digital technologies. In *2019 International Conference – "Quality Management, Transport, Information Security, and Information Technologies (QM, IT and IS),* September 2019, pp. 20–22. IEEE.
110. LNS Research. (2017). *Quality 4.0 impact and strategy handbook eBook* [online]. blog.Insresearch.com. https://www.blog.Insresearch.com/quality40book. Retrieved August 15, 2021.
111. Watson, G. H. (2019). The ascent of quality 4.0 – How the new age of quality came to be and what I might look like in 20 years. *Quality Progress,* March 2019. pp. 24–30.
112. Parris, C. *GE Digital (Blog) – What is the Industrial Internet of Things (IIoT).* https://www.ge.com. Retrieved on July 12, 2021.
113. McLaughlin, G. C. (2021). Embrace the data – Five basics for eliminating poor data analysis. *Quality Progress,* March, pp. 39–47.
114. Bunse, B. (2013). Industrie 4.0 – Smart manufacturing for the future. *GTIA – Germany Trade and Invest,* p. 40.
115. The White House. (2011). President Obama Launches Advanced Manufacturing Partnership. *The White House Office of the Press Secretary.* June 24, 2011. https://obamawhitehouse.archives.gov/the-press-office/2011/06/24/president-obama-launches-advanced-manufacturing-partnership. Retrieved on August 16, 2021.
116. National Association of Manufacturers (NAM) Newsroom. 2.1 million manufacturing jobs could go unfilled by 2030. *NAM,* May 4, 2021. https://tinyurl.com/unfulfilled-mfg-jobs
117. Economie.gouv.fr. (2015). *L'Industrie du Futur.* Economie.Gouv.Fr.
118. State Council of the People's Republic of China. (2015). *The state council issued a notice on 'made in China 2025'.* https://www.gov.cn/zhengee/content/2015-05/19/content_9784.htm
119. Veile, J. W., Kiel, D., Müller, J. M., & Voigt, K. -I. (2018). How to implement industry 4.0 – An empirical analysis of lessons learnt from best practices, International Association for Management of Technology, *IAMOT 2018 Conference Proceedings.* https://www2.aston.ac.uk/migrated-assets/applicationpdf/aston-business-school/368296-IAMOT2018_paper_72.pdf. Retrieved on September 12, 2021.

120. Bauernhansl, T. (2014). Die Vierte Industrielle Revolution: Der Weg in ein wertschaffendes Produktionsparadigma. In M. T. Bauernhansl, M. ten Hompel, & B. Vogel-Heuser (Eds.), *Industrie 4.0 in Produktion, Automatisierung und Logistik: Anwendung, Technologien* (pp. 5–35). Springer.
121. Spath, D., Ganschar, O., Gerlach, S., Hämmerle, M., Krause, T., & Schlund, S. (2013). *Produktionsarbeit der Zukunft: Industrie 4.0.* Fraunhoffer.
122. Bauer, W., Schlund, S., Marrenbach, D., & Ganschar, O. (2014). *Industrie 4.0 – Volkswirtschaftliches Potenzial für Deutschland.* BITKOM, Fraunhofer IAO.
123. Glas, A. H., & Kleemann, F. C. (2016). The impact of industry 4.0 on procurement management: A conceptual and quantitative analysis. *International Journal of Business and Management Invention, 5*(6), 55–66. https://www.ijbmi.org. Retrieved on June 30, 2019.
124. Kleindorfer, P. R., Singhal, K., & Van Wassenhove, L. N. (2005). Sustainable operations management. *Production and Operations Management, 14*(4), 482–492.
125. Fiksel, J., McDaniel, J., & Spitzley, D. (1998). Measuring product sustainability. *Journal of Sustainable Product Design, 6*(7), 7–8.
126. McGill University, Canada. *What is sustainability?* https://www.mcgill.ca/sustainability/files. Retrieved July 26, 2021.
127. Kessler, J., & Walters, L. M. (2021). A sustainable supply chain – A new tool to improve supply chain sustainability. *Quality Progress,* August 2021, pp. 16–23.
128. Haanaes, K. (2018). Why businesses should embrace sustainability. *Institute for management development,* August 16, 2018. https://www.imd.org/research-knowledge/articles//why-all-businesses-should-embrace-sustainability
129. Kraaijenbrink, J. (2019). What the 3Ps of the triple bottom line really mean. *Forbes,* December 10, 2019. www.forbes.com/sites/jereonkraaijenbrink/2019/12/10/what-the-3ps-of-the-triple-bottom-line-really-mean
130. Elkington, J. (1999). Triple bottom- line reporting: Looking for balance. *Australian CPA, 69,* 18–21.
131. Bateh, J., Heaton, C., Arbogast, G. W., & Broadbent, A. (2013). Defining sustainability in the business setting. *Journal of Sustainability Management, 1*(1), 1–4.
132. Nutburn, M. (2019). Five benefits of a sustainable supply chain. *Supply Chain Management,* July 29, 2019. www.cips.org/supply-management/opinion/2019/july/five-benefits-of-a-sustainable-supply-chain
133. Madhusudan, V. (2021). *Connecting circular economy and industry 4.0 through sustainable practices.* www.freelunch.co.in/connecting-circular-economy-and-industry-40. Retrieved on October 6, 2021.
134. Zaman, R. (2018). *Industry 4.0 drives the sustainability development goals.* https://techpolicyviews.com/review-updates/2018/11/18/industry-4-0-drives-the-sustainable-developement-goals/
135. Sanders, S. (2021). Striving for sustainability – Keep supply chains in check for a secure future. *Quality Progress,* August 2021, p. 5.
136. The Quality Progress Report. (2021). Supply chain management – steady state. *Quality Progress,* pp. 8–9, September 2021.
137. Dye, S. (2021), Steve Dye Named City Manager. *The Pipeline,* Vol. 22, No. 9, September 2021.
138. Haghighi, S. M., Torabi, S. A., & Ghasemi, R. (2016). An integrated approach for performance evaluation in sustainable supply chain networks (with a case study). *Journal of Cleaner Production, 137,* 579–597.
139. Santos, G., Sa, J. C., Felix, M. J., Luis, B., Carvalho, F., Doiro, M., Zgodavova, K., & Stefanovic, M. (2021). New needed quality management skills for quality managers 4.0. *Sustainability, 13,* 1649. https://doi.org/10.3390/su13116149. Retrieved on October 1, 2021.

22 Quality 4.0: In Review

Aligning Quality 4.0 with Industry 4.0

Introduction

As mentioned in Chap. 21, the concept of Quality 4.0 emerged in relationship with the fourth industrial revolution, Industry 4.0 in line with our experiences over the last century or so.

As a result of the general lack of awareness about the concept of Quality 4.0, its definition is sparsely available in the literature. In their proposal, Sisodia and Forero [51] are of the view:

> Quality 4.0 refers to the digitalization of Total Quality Management and its impact on quality technology, processes and people. It builds upon traditional quality tools and considers also connectedness, intelligence and automation for improving performance and making timely data-driven decisions in an end-to-end scenario, involving all stakeholders and providing visibility and transparency.

Literature evidence suggests in most cases the definition of Quality 4.0 as a reference to Industry 4.0. For example, Jacob [21, 22] and some other authors simply see Quality 4.0 as connecting "new technologies with traditional quality methods to achieve new optimums in performance, operational excellence, and innovation."

The concept Quality 4.0 derives from Industry 4.0, hence, its common definition in reference to Industry 4.0. This is obvious because Industry 4.0 emerged on the platform of 4.0 base technologies which will also combine to defined create digital age or Smart quality management tools adaptable to the "SmartFactory" operational systems and environment.

T. A. Ibidapo, *From Industry 4.0 to Quality 4.0*, Management for Professionals,
https://doi.org/10.1007/978-3-031-04192-1_22

Perception of QM Among Quality Practitioners in Digital Age

There are no doubts whatsoever that the role of quality and quality management practitioners in the digital era may not be completely unveiled until Industry 4.0 initiatives are fully matured beyond the maturity level, well developed, or completely implemented. And this may begin to unveil any time between now and the next 5 years, reaching maturity level probably around the mid-2030s to the middle of the twenty-first century. All in all, it is evident that Industry 4.0 has paved the way for Quality 4.0 initiatives.

Hence, anticipated quality management tools in the digitalization era will gradually emerge along with the implementation of Industry 4.0. initiatives. The newly Industry 4.0 emerging industrial paradigm, no doubt, comes with obvious changes and challenges such as:

- Promoting new standards
- Redefining jobs [14]
- Redefining job skills [31]
- Changes in society [35]
- Changes in our industrial landscape—business models, production processes, organizational strategies, value and supply chain, business organization and management, and products
- Societal and life style changes
- Developing adequate base 4.0 technologies-based TQM and quality auditing tools and practices

These changes culminate in the transformation of traditional manufacturing processes through the use and application of 4.0 technologies. The traditional industrial processing roles of people in their usual repetitive work will be taken over by robots and/or advanced multifunctional manufacturing machines. Instead, people involvement will be more in the areas of the following:

- Integration, management, and control of the working
- Tasks of machines
- Analysis of large amounts of generated data (Big Data)

Coping with these challenges, therefore, calls for new approaches for training and educating competent hands in acquiring adequate skills [6], capable of using 4.0 technologies for implementing Industry 4.0 initiatives collaboratively with traditional quality management methods, tools, and practices to evolve Quality 4.0 initiatives.

Quality 4.0 managers too require new skills [61] to be able to effectively perform their roles in the digital era, when traditional quality management practices will be integrated with 4.0 technologies to innovatively optimize business performance and operational excellence.

What is likely going to happen at first is the conceptualization. Our general perception of the impacts of Industry 4.0 is on how quality management practices are going to evolve among quality and its practitioners, to give birth to Quality 4.0 quality management practices across businesses and industries. As for now, it is postulations galore until the smart factory itself is fully operational Quality 4.0 practices may not be exactly and specifically identifiable.

Hence, the need for quality professionals to continue reviewing and analyzing the evolving developments in the implementation of Industry 4.0 initiatives, to be able to fashion out the general ways to ascertain the mode and pathway to Quality 4.0 initiatives.

With the factory of the future, or Industry 4.0 being viewed from the perspectives of its characterization based on its *"smartness," "real-time machine controls," "interconnected real-time functions,"* and *"all-inclusive production cycle/supply chain collaborative features,"* there is the need not just to redefine quality but to evolve appropriate Quality 4.0 initiatives suitable for digital age application beyond conventional quality management principles, tools, and techniques.

No matter what happens however, whatever quality management practices that may evolve in line with the realization of Industry 4.0 initiatives are obviously going to be supplemental to traditional quality management methods/practices or adaptable to them. Hence, success with Quality 4.0 must have to be based on a solid foundation of traditional quality management principles, tools, techniques, and practices. Consequently Quality 4.0 does not, according to Jacob [21, 22], replace traditional quality management methods, rather builds on them.

Data collection and analytics have jointly been key aspects of quality management from time immemorial; hence, quality professionals are very familiar with the importance of data generation in Industry 4.0. From the perspectives of data generation, the level of data generated in Quality 4.0 initiatives far surpasses and outstretches the level of data generation commonly known in traditional quality management systems. Among data generated are those related to customer demands and value chain logistics. The purposes for data generation in Industry 4.0 initiatives are all encompassing. The purposes of data and data analytics include among others the following:

- Using data to improve efficiency.
- Growing closer to the supply chain partners.
- Development of products/services that meet customer and regulatory SNEaRs.
- Provide needed insights to enable the reshaping of operational design.
- Using employee recruitment data helps generally to predict needed skills.
- Production data are quite useful as they create opportunities for eliminating downtime and increase the rate of production.
- Data analytics can help in the identification of wasted materials and give suggestions about ways for reclaiming them or using them as starting materials or inputs for other industrial processes [29].
- Use of analytics to exploit the opportunities for growth in the existing markets or customers even when it was never previously considered.

This filters out the following issues about big data:

- The need for building analytical capability by employing experts with ability to conduct data analysis.
- Organizations must be open with data.
- Quality of data must be given adequate consideration.
- Access to the appropriate data by the appropriate entities is quite critical.

What Is Different—SmartFactory and Traditional-Factory Quality Approaches

Quality approaches to the fourth industrial (Industry 4.0) revolutionary changes, which heralded in, the digital age of "SmartFactories," can simply be termed as integrating traditional quality tools and practices with digitalized manufacturing operational processes and activities in a digital environment, to achieve quality products and services that meet customer SNEaRs and represent stakeholders' values and gain competitive edge.

The literature review, however, provided some models related to Quality 4.0 as viewed from the perspectives of Industry 4.0.

Most prominent among them is the detailed model presented in the LNS Research [33], which was built on traditional quality methods and principles to consider how quality management technology, processes, and people are impacted by digitalization. This model provides a framework that enables organizations and businesses to assess and know how to identify needed and relevant technologies for performance improvement on their way to develop quality goals and objectives leading to their digitalization strategy. While it proposes a way for a company to assess its existing state in their digitalization efforts it did not, however, give necessary guidelines for transitioning to Quality 4.0, under the assumption that a digitalization or Industry 4.0 strategy has already been put in place.

Another model, developed by Sader et al. [45], simply views Industry 4.0 from the point of view of facilitating and enabling the implementation of TQM, including quality assurance and quality control practices through the adoption of the seven quality management principles of ISO 9001:2015 QMS standard [20] and the opportunities provided for each principle by Industry 4.0:

- **Customer focus**—Industry 4.0 provides the opportunities of customization, quick and fast responses, and ability to quickly/*smart* forecast future happenings.
- **Leadership**—Industry 4.0 enables smart resources allocation, improved coordination of management activities, and effective assessment and evaluation of key organizational issues.
- **Engagement of people**—Industry 4.0 facilitates effective and improved communication, abilities to innovate sharing of ideas.
- **Process approach**—Prompt maintenance prediction leading to down time reduction, transparency, self-learning, and early prediction of errors.

- **Improvement**—Opportunities for increased dynamism of interaction across organizational value chain to know market needs, instantly reconfigure manufacturing processes in line with changes, thereby providing needed flexibility in change managing.
- **Evidence-based decision-making**—Taking advantage of massive data generation, sharing, and analytics to achieve early failure predictability to incite swift responses and other decision-making capabilities.
- **Relationship management**—Promoting stronger collaboration among partners, early identification of issues, and communication with relevant entities and stakeholders as may be necessary.
- **Quality assurance**—In-built quality assurance elements, intelligent devices, and technologies beginning at the design stage and at software engineering levels.
- **Quality control**—Real-time product inspection and intelligent quality control system.

The shortcomings of this model are that of its focus of the principles strictly on Industry 4.0 initiatives without considering the difficulties emanating from the application of new technologies. The issue of massive data and the ways they are going to be protected and impacted upon by privacy policy, cybersecurity, and regulatory issues are quality management concerns that should be adequately addressed.

Another proposed model sees Quality 4.0 as a combination of information technology (IT) and operations technology (OT) intervening with humans as important parts of the digital transformation, Lim [32].

Another model is based on identifying TQM components that differentiate a smart factory from a traditional factory, Padhi and Illa [37]. In doing that, the model clearly identified the characterized aspects of TQM in relationship with smart manufacturing as a comparison with traditional manufacturing as follows:

- **"SmartFactory" manufacturing**—operates with the ability to seamlessly integrate systems in an environment of automated data generation, sharing, and processing. SmartFactories largely function under autonomous quality-related processes with opportunities of using predictive analytics to preempt defects, and take corrective measures against values outside specifications or those without control.
- **Traditional manufacturing**—lacks, on the other hand, the full integration of quality-related data thus resulting in slower flow of information. Operates with the likelihood of manual data entry and collection, while operator intervention may be needed for any action plan. Traditional manufacturing generally operates using reactive analysis based on action plans.

It needs to be highlighted here that this model is restricted to manufacturing alone, whereas the extent and application of digital transformation can for now not be exactly predicted though it is likely going to be more expansive than initially anticipated. The one thing that we are sure of is that the traditional elements of quality and quality management will provide the backbone structure for the evolution of Quality 4.0 initiatives as well as practices. And this model is silent about this aspect.

Although models related to Quality 4.0 are variously provided in literature, there are yet to be the exact pathway to implementing Quality 4.0 initiatives. However, identifying key aspects of TQM which differentiates the "SmartFactory" from traditional manufacturing setting opens up a door for aligning and collating our thoughts about implementing Quality 4.0 among other suggestions and models. The roles of prototyping in establishing the exact elements of Quality 4.0 practices can however not be overemphasized.

Extrapolating Quality 4.0 from Traditional Quality Management Tools

There are no ways, whatsoever, that we can tell the story of the global industrial revolutionary stages or developmental phases without mentioning quality. The story of the fourth industrial revolution is similarly, not different. It is therefore not surprising that Dan Jacob of LNS Research reportedly coined the term, Quality 4.0 [25] after Industry 4.0.

Quality 4.0 thus takes TQM philosophy to another level, aligning quality management practices with Industry 4.0 technologies to optimize organizational performance and competitive abilities. This brings us to the ultimate goals of Quality 4.0, blending new technologies—big data, artificial intelligence (AI), cloud computing, machine learning, Internet of Things, Industrial Internet of Things, etc.—with proven quality management principles/philosophy, tools, techniques, methods, and practices. Hence, Quality 4.0 initiatives are destined to emerge and/or evolve, from leveraging traditional or conventional quality management philosophy, principles, tools, techniques, and practices with the technologies that define Industry 4.0 initiatives—the 4.0 base technologies.

Recapping the faces of industrial development takes us first to steam-powered machines which dictated the first industrial revolution; the second was predicated by electricity and assembly lines; and the third by innovations in information and communications technology (ICT).

The current or fourth industrial revolution, *Industry 4.0*, surfaced on the platform of technological advances of the first to the second decade of the twenty-first century, which resulted in a new industrial revolution driven by "exponential growth of disruptive technologies and the changes those technologies are bringing to the workplace, the workforce and the markets organizations serve" (ASQ).

Industry 4.0 initiatives have since continued to emerge at the dictates of machine intelligence, pervasive computing, connectivity, data generation and analytics, and other enabling 4.0 base technologies, to facilitate the digital transformation that is today being witnessed, or heard of, in the industrial manufacturing sector of the globalized economy.

The forecast of the digital ecosystem two decades ago by Watson [57] derived from the advances in telecommunications technology and the internet on the one hand, and personal computing, networks and thought machines on the other hand. Both technologies have, in turn, jointly combined with the following:

- Enterprise computing
- Integrated multimedia
- Cloud computing
- Artificial intelligence (AI)–enabled technology

to define the changes manifested in Industry 4.0 initiatives, Watson [58].

Big data and artificial intelligence (AI) have similarly been reported here as the current predominant technology. In affirming the virtually endless application of digital signals both for business and personal purposes, Watson further reiterated the fact that Industry 4.0 is built generally on the framework of internet connectivity through wireless communications, which provides the opportunity of integrating a diversity of different types of devices, including, but are not limited to industrial platforms, automobiles, home appliances, and even merchandizing outlets or markets.

We are already beginning to enjoy some of the benefits of the influence of digital signals in various aspects of our lives, ranging from the remote diagnosis of equipment and machines, remote ignition of cars and prewarming the car, and a vast range of surgical and medical applications. In these ways, Industry 4.0 initiatives can most glaringly be viewed from the perspectives of its capabilities to reshape the revolving world of ours, including quality and the quality professionals themselves. And that distinctively defines the destination of the digital transformation being talked about.

The evolving quality professional challenges posed by the massive need to effectively manage data, online databases as well as the abilities to use them, and needed analytics and software tools remain strong interacting activities of Quality 4.0 initiatives. The magnitude and relevance of data analytics in the digital era thus brings to the fore the trending evolution of data—its generation, sharing, and real time analytics. This shall without doubts, whatsoever, play significant roles in defining digital age quality practices—principles, methods, and tools.

In its usual tradition of quality co-evolving, and co-existing with industrial developmental phases of the past, so also must Quality 4.0 initiative be equally aligned with those of Industry 4.0 initiatives. Successfully accomplishing this is a wake-up call for quality organizations and institutions, companies, researchers, and quality management professionals, to competently and boldly take on the evolving challenges for quality management among all concerned in the age of digitally facilitated management structure and operational efficiencies dominated by automation, artificial intelligence, and other base 4.0 technologies.

Quality 4.0 initiatives, therefore, begin generally with both the quality mindset and quality thinking at every stage of digitization, including the strategic stages of planning, to the final stages of operational digitalization.

The implication here is the simple fact that digital age business systems design must, from the beginning to the end, be holistically wrapped around the backbone of quality mindset and quality thinking to create organization-wide, end-to-end, all important, quality management strategy. The importance and relevance of data—generation, sharing, and data analytics—cannot be overemphasized in digital age organizational and business operations and activities.

Hence, quality researchers, practitioners and professionals, institutions, and other stakeholders, including software, services, equipment, and devices manufacturers and/or providers need to immediately stand up to the call to duty of Quality 4.0 initiatives, in the fast-evolving digital transformation age and era.

With the realization that Quality 4.0 is highly dependent on the emerging structure and principles of Industry 4.0 initiatives, information about the exact structure and mode of application of Quality 4.0 principles/philosophies, tools, techniques, and practices in the digital age are yet to be more accurately and exactly defined.

Literature information too, about Quality 4.0 initiatives, are for now and on a general basis, more speculative than the reality.

Most of the realistic literature articles and information about Quality 4.0 emanate from Internet blogs [22, 27, 43] except perhaps, for the intensive research works of the LNS Research Company [21]. Quality 4.0 is thus apparent particularly because of the growing realities of organizational confidence to develop or implement Industry 4.0 initiatives.

It is, however, evident that Quality 4.0 is not going to replace traditional quality management tools and techniques. Rather, Quality 4.0 will evolve from building and improving on them [21, 22].

Industry 4.0 is, on the overall, primarily about the digital transformation of industrial manufacturing operations to create what could be generally described as the *"SmartFactory"* or as others (The Manufacturer) may prefer to call it, data-driven *"Intelligent Industry."*

While it is true that Quality 4.0 "derives from the German industrialization program called Industrie 4.0" and that it "evaluates the role of quality in an age of increasing digitization and automation of work," the pathway to completely achieve this goal will gradually unfold, and it will do so at the mercy of quality professionals and their future roles [58].

In his aligned view of key fourth industrial revolutionary changes in industry and quality approaches, Watson [58] highlighted the following anticipated changes with respect to **Industry 4.0**:

- Machines learning to learn (artificial intelligence)
- Integrating cyber-physical interfaces to automate work environment
- Automating processes in end-to-end systems
- Restriction of human roles to positions in which human judgment can actually not be automated, and human interactions can similarly not be simulated

Watson also anticipated the following major changes with respect to **Quality 4.0**:

- Quality shifting its usual control-oriented attention from the conventional process operators to process designers.
- Machines learning how to self-regulate and managing their own productivity and quality.
- Using digitization for optimizing signal feedback and process adjustment, while adaptive learning helps in supporting self-induced system corrections.
- While human activities and performance are considered essential, emphasis is shifting from production to system design and integration with business system.

On the overall, therefore, literature is painting an obvious picture of digital age quality professionals entirely different from what we used to know in their professional quality management roles. This is a big challenge to quality professionals in the twenty-first century.

The question then arises as to "whether man is on the verge of destroying himself." Hence the question, "Has man therefore invented digital technologies and digitalization of company operations for his own displacement, and for his own professional doom?"

The trend to answering this question may begin to evolve toward the latter part of the 2020s, maturing finally in late 2030s to mid-twenty-first century when Industry 4.0 implementation or development would be the maturity phase. The major changes here seemed, most clearly, to be the shift of the interactive phases of quality professionals.

Hence, we are moving from the conventional quality management practices concentrated on production processes and activities into a future of Quality 4.0 digital age, in which quality professionals' active involvement begins generally, right from the time of project conception, through the design and prototyping stages, to the closing circuitry of the digitalized production or servicing systems. The implication here is that quality management activities in Quality 4.0 initiatives may need to be extended to the following stages of activities in digitalized settings:

- Design and development
- Production
- Servicing
- Creating quality as organizational culture

Quality, therefore, shall most likely assume deeper and perhaps, additionally, wider intellectual roles in digitalized settings than probably anticipated.

This is not just a challenge to quality professionals but one that calls for the understanding, involvement, and active participation of organizational top management and chief executive officers (CEOs), as quality and quality competency must be viewed accordingly as *"across-organizational holistic value system"* essentials.

Since the issue here is about "*not leaving any digital implementation and production stages uncontrolled, quality at every stage is not only an essential component but inevitable.*"

This thus brings to the fore, the most obvious digital age requirements of incorporating quality thinking vis-à-vis quality mind setting, into the design of holistic business systems to facilitate and support productive operations.

Although Quality 4.0 is driven by the 4.0 technologies, the true transformation is buried in and takes place generally in the following:

- The culture of quality
- Organizational or business leadership
- Quality processes

This is the reason why Quality 4.0 actually requires a solid traditional quality foundation [48].

Anticipating Quality 4.0 Skills Challenges

While a strategic view of operations digitalization is a very essential and critical requirements for the digitalization of company operations, it is particularly important to identify key changes that may end up defining Quality 4.0 initiatives.

In most cases, therefore, it is expected that the use and application of 4.0 technologies may end up shifting the boundaries of some traditional quality concepts and the contexts of their use, application, and understanding, thereby expanding the roles of quality professionals beyond the limits of its traditional practices in Quality 4.0 implementation. Hence, there is the need to develop new quality management skills for coping with the evolving Quality 4.0 initiatives.

There have been some changes in the digitization of industrial production processes that have resulted in the way quality tools are applied and functionalities redefined. For example, the digital transformation and the disruptive and perhaps innovative changes that have been brought along with it have, to a certain extent, led to shifting from customer-centric perspectives to co-participating customers and stakeholders. The concept of "internal customers" and the way their SNEaRs are met have also been altered. The role of human beings and those of machines, as well as their interrelationships, have similarly been modified. All these changes definitely impact the way things are done and by whom they are done, thereby creating gaps in needed skills as well as opportunities for new skills.

The skills gap results from the general need for combining new technologies with common quality methods and tools for achieving optimum performance, innovation, and operational excellence. While quality management teams usually have some experiences in data handling, there may be room for relevant data analytics know-how.

It is therefore the perspective view of the author that, in addition to mastering traditional quality principles, tools, techniques, and practices, as well as the use and application of 4.0 base technologies, quality professionals of the future may certainly need, on a general basis, wider scope of knowledge, experience, and exposure, to be able to cope with the challenges of the digitally enabled production and services provision age—the era of Quality 4.0. It is, however, not a mere coincidence here that this opinion is prominent in literature. For example, it is further reinforced by one of the most experienced quality professionals of our time, Watson [58].

The findings of Gunasekaran and Subramanian [16] identified the following human aspects of Quality 4.0 to match Industry 4.0 initiatives as being:

- Capturing message credibility and supplier involvement aspects in quality function deployment (QFD)
- Leadership emphasis and process flexibility in achieving economic sustainability
- Business models and tactics for peer involvement of employees within enterprises
- Business models which study quality management influence in a multicultural environment

In their survey outcome to identify the new needed quality management skills for quality managers in the digital era, Santos et al. [48] identified the following personal attributes as critical in the next 10 years skills requirements:

- The ability to empower others
- Ability to learn
- Commitment to lifelong learning
- Creativity (ability to generate ideas)
- Flexibility (willing to change and adapt to changes)
- Foresightedness (ability to see beyond the moment, to predict future occurrences)
- Holistic thinking abilities (ability to see things from the perspectives of their wholeness including the consequences of actions)
- Taking initiatives (ability to take decisions and start processes themselves without being prompted)
- Integrative thinking abilities (thinking beyond)
- Being visionary (ability to set goals and follow consequentially)

The evidence of the urgent need to focus on filling potential skills gap in the digital age is further emphasized by the recent report of the World Economic Forum (WEF), which revealed that half of all employees will need to be reskilled by 2025 due to the increasingly growing adoption of technology. Herein, Whiting [60] and ASQ in Quality Progress [5] reported the top 10 skills of 2025 (listed below) as "Skills of the future." These skills reportedly fall into four categories—*problem solving, self-management, working with people, and technology*. They are accordingly as follows:

- **Problem solving**—Analytical thinking; complex problem solving; critical thinking and analysis; creativity, originality, and initiative; and reasoning, problem solving, and ideation

- **Self-management**—Active learning and learning strategies; resilience, stress tolerance, and flexibility
- **Working with people**—Leadership and social influence
- **Technology use and development**—Technology design and programming; technology use, monitoring, and control

It is evident here that businesses and organizations are going to be challenged by the need to find skilled employees and the need to adapt and upskill existing workforce to appropriate levels of competencies. In end effect, some types of jobs will disappear while new ones will emerge. This may likely create a skills gap particularly because of rapid advances in AI, robotics, and other 4.0 base technologies.

This is the reason for organizations, professional organizations, governments, vocational schools, and higher institutions across the globe to cooperate and collaborate in both the planning and execution of training programs for producing appropriate skills needed to meet digital age work force requirements in quality management, and in production/services industries and businesses.

While it is not easy to predict accurately into the future of the exact digital age quality management practices now, there are no doubts whatsoever that Quality 4.0 initiatives require quality professionals to get acquainted with the use, application, and impacts of 4.0-based technologies so as to be able to effectively and efficiently adapt, adopt, and leverage them for product quality management processes and techniques. This is a critical pathway to achieve performance improvement and competitive advantage.

Defining Quality 4.0

Initiating the Digital Age Quality

The major relevance of Quality 4.0 is, as portrayed in the literature, to develop the capabilities to successfully enable relevant organizations and businesses align existing quality management philosophy/principles, tools, techniques, methods, and practices with 4.0 base technologies of emerging Industry 4.0 initiatives to achieve competitive advantages, performance improvement, and sustainability. Hence, it is the application of Industry 4.0's digital technologies to the traditional quality management practices resulting in increased operational efficiency, improved business performance, and business models (Antony, website).

While Quality 4.0 is generally considered as a digital phase application of quality management tools and techniques, popular literature opinions view Quality 4.0 mainly from the context of Industry 4.0, in relationship to organizational innovation and the discovery of data to provide new insights, create value, and contribute to organizational learning and their sustainability [15, 30, 40, 41].

This fits perfectly with the suggestion of James [24], "Quality 4.0 is a tool for businesses to understand the effect of Industry 4.0 on products, processes and quality technology using innovation singularly or in combination, such as ML and AI mobile technology, AR and VR, cloud technology, connected devices and edge devices, big data and data lakes, social media and block chain."

The ASQ views Quality 4.0 as a term used in reference to the future of quality and *organizational excellence* within the context of Industry 4.0. It is not surprising, however, that the definition of Quality 4.0 rarely features in the literature without referencing Industry 4.0. This is undoubtedly due to its conceptualization in alignment with the newly evolving concepts of the fourth industrial revolution, termed Industry 4.0, and perhaps too, due to the general lack of awareness about the Quality 4.0 concept itself.

From their perspective of viewing Quality 4.0 as an integral part of Industry 4.0, LNS Research [33] reportedly arrived at defining Quality 4.0, referring to it as the digitalization of TQM and how it impacts quality technology, processes, and people.

Bowers and Pickerel [8], on the other hand, view it as the application of the fourth industrial revolution technologies, for example, digitalization and artificial intelligence to quality.

Sisodia and Forero [51], in their project report, clearly defined **Quality 4.0** in reference to TQM as:

> The digitalization of Total Quality Management and its impact on quality technology, processes and people. It builds upon traditional quality tools and considers also connectedness, intelligence and automation for improving performance and making timely data-driven decisions in an end-to-end scenario, involving all stakeholders and providing visibility and transparency.

In principle, therefore, Quality 4.0, or in simpler terms, the principles of implementing Quality 4.0 initiatives, requires strong interrelatedness among people, organizational operational processes, and technology.

Hence, quality professionals/practitioners and the digital age workforce need to be adequately educated, and effectively trained, to cope with the new technological challenges of newly emerging digital processes, technologies, and business mode strategies for competitiveness and sustainability.

Building such capabilities in both quality professionals and organizational workers is of extreme importance and criticality to all concerned, especially quality professionals. It will enable them to most perfectly, relate to, and engage with, new advanced technologies, processes, and processing tools, in achieving a full understanding of emerging Industry 4.0 technological advancements as well as their outputs. This is the extent to which quality is very critical and vital to managing business operations of the digital age.

Aligning the Realities of the Term, "4.0"

The term "4.0" has most prominently caught the attention of the people of the world since 2011 when the conception of the current digitalization of organizational operations was first unveiled. The fact that **"4.0"** was brought to fame from its derivation from the fourth (4th) industrial revolution ignited its relevance to the global community in terms of referencing the following:

- Massive technological changes in the industrial manufacturing sector of the global economy, *Industry 4.0.*
- Needed quality management principles/philosophy, tools, techniques, and practices, *Quality 4.0,* to align with Industry 4.0 initiatives to ensure that products and services rendered to customers and the market place meet their respective SNEaRs and/or exceed it.
- The (base) technologies, *4.0 technologies*—big data, cloud computing, artificial intelligence (AI), Internet of Things (IoT), machine learning (ML), block chain, virtual reality (VR), additive manufacturing (3D printing), cyber-physical systems (CPS), etc.—which culminated into the fourth industrial revolutionary changes of our time.

It is therefore apparent that the aftermath of the fourth industrial revolution, Industry 4.0, has in reality brought *Quality 4.0* and 4.0 technologies to stay. It must however be mentioned here too that the Swedish Institute of Quality (SIQ) devised Quality 5.0, based on previous quality evolutions at its own discretion in similar relationship to the fourth industrial revolution (see Table 22.1).

Quality 4.0 thus derives from *"Industry 4.0,"* a term that was reportedly coined at the Hannover Fair in 2011, to describe the fourth industrial revolution, Kagermann et al. [26]. Industry 4.0 thus emphasizes the growing intelligence and interconnectedness of smart manufacturing systems, now frequently referred to as the "SmartFactory."

According to Radziwill [40, 41], *Quality 4.0* represents "the pursuit of performance excellence during these times of potentially disruptive digital transformation" which leads toward connected intelligent automation: smart, hyperconnected agents deployed in environments that enable humans and machines to cooperate, and leverage data to achieve shared goals.

Table 22.1 Swedish Institute of Quality's (SIQ) five waves of quality "societal satisfaction"

Period	Quality waves	Characterization
Seventeenth century	Quality 1.0	"Do it yourself"
Eighteenth century	Quality 2.0	"Specialization and professional knowledge"
Nineteenth to twentieth century	Quality 3.0	"Mass production, low customization"
Middle nineteenth century	Quality 4.0	"Total quality management, customer satisfaction"
Twenty-first century	Quality 5.0	Increasing competitiveness: New adaptive leadership model Digitalization from a customer perspective Sustainable development

The evolution of quality over the last two decades has, so accurately, followed the path of Watson's prediction that quality would evolve, in response to the increasing and growing development of digital technology, such that *"quality functions and analyses would become automated and inquired"* [57].

And about two decades later, *Quality 4.0* initiatives seem digitally ready and interconnected to provide an answer to Watson's question of two decades ago, "How will the role of quality professionals change in the emerging environment?"

Quality thinking and peoples' quality mindset are undoubtedly the taproots of the tree of the fourth industrial revolution, or simply, Industry 4.0 initiatives, as reportedly nursed in Germany's research "nurseries," germinated at the Hannover Messe, and now being sown in the fertile soils of government policies across the global community, beginning from Germany.

The seeds from that tree are today, already being globally dispersed across communities and nations of the world from Germany through to the USA, Japan, China, Asia, Sweden, and others that appreciate the roles and importance of a digitally transformed competitive economy.

The bedrock of the fourth industrial revolution lies in the technology landscape which, according to Radziwill [40, 41], "is richer and more promising than ever before." In many ways, she further affirmed that the underlisted technologies can help improve product and service quality, as well as organizational performance:

- Cloud computing
- Big data
- Virtual reality (VR)
- Augmented reality (AR)
- Blockchain
- Additive manufacturing
- Artificial intelligence (AI)
- Machine learning (ML)
- Internet Protocol Version 6 (IPv6)
- Cyber-physical systems (CPS)

The aftermath of initiating the fourth industrial revolution or *Industry 4.0* is the creation of some strong forces of change, beginning most candidly with organizations and businesses getting digitized to precipitate the bigger digital transformation of businesses or company/organizational operational processes, facilitated through the deployment of 4.0 base technologies.

Managing the tsunami of changes generated by Industry 4.0, in the industrial production sector, and its ripples across other socioeconomic, technological, environmental, and people-interactive phases, resides strictly in quality's territory of *change management,* a known and common topic of quality, as a body of knowledge (BoK). The overall and primary purposes of quality and quality management philosophy, principles, tools, techniques, and practices revolve collectively around the business or organizational *improvement* concept, which in turn suggests *change* from a current level of performance to a higher more competitive level [3].

It therefore becomes the role of quality and quality management practitioners to ensure that the enormous amounts of changes generated by the development or implementation of *Industry 4.0* initiatives result in the overall improvement of organizations and businesses that not only embrace them, but take on the interests of developing and/or implementing them, and sustainably doing so too. The fact that *Industry 4.0* is built on conceptualized initiatives brings in the notion too, of conceptualized quality initiatives, referred to generally as Quality 4.0.

Fundamentals of Quality 4.0 Initiatives

Although the exact and detailed quality management practices in implementing or developing Industry 4.0 initiatives may only be conceptualized for now, there are some obvious basic fundamental principles of quality that immediately come to mind (e.g., TQM), as we set out on the meandering path of the digital quality transformational journey.

Digital age quality practices may, therefore, begin on a general basis with the principles of deploying quality strategy across the entirety of organizational or business activities thereby, inculcating both the quality *mindset* and quality *thinking* among the workforce across organizational settings. As documented by the Toyota Management System, the way quality thinking works has been equated with financial thinking in organizational management systems [18].

The fact that Quality 4.0 initiatives are predicated on the interconnectedness of smart, intelligent, and automated manufacturing systems with the capability to take autonomous decisions leads to the optimism that traditional quality tools and methods can expectedly be relied upon to brave us through digital era quality challenges.

This quality management approach stems generally from three major fundamental aspects of traditional quality management practices that we used to know. They are as follows:

- **"Doing it right first time"** tradition—This is viewed from the general perspectives and tradition of avoiding errors, mistakes, miscalculations, and mis-design that could lead to wastages of various forms and kinds along the value chain. This involves equipment designers, software engineers, computer programmers, and other stakeholders such as equipment/machinery manufacturers, producers, digital maturity, and strategizing.
- **"Quality as design"** which was once inspired by W. Edwards Deming in his recommendation of more holistic methods of designing quality into processes, to prevent quality problems before they even occurred. Process-control quality management assurances, practices, and checks—operations control systems may be deeply embedded and implanted in the digitization and digitalization activities—software, engineering, installation, and maintenance processes and activities of the "SmartFactory."

- **Data analysis**—This is similar to the days of statistical quality control. Hence, quality practitioners will not find the role of big data too cumbersome or strange to cope with.
- **Evidence-based quality management experience lessons learnt**—Easily identifiable at both the design and prototyping stages as well as real-time operational experiences. Real-time operational experiences gained may potentially provide great opportunities for streamlining and aligning suitable quality management practices and tools found to be necessary based on organizational types and operations.

The common and basic principles of quality that is obviously applicable in the era of Quality 4.0 is *"Doing it right first time."*

"Doing it right from the planning, through the strategizing and implementation stages" is therefore a key quality approach to achieving Quality 4.0 initiatives. Hence, the author finds the following **"dos of quality"** approach very critical and appropriate to digital age quality management practices:

- *"Strategize it right from the onset"*
- *"Do it right first time, and always"*
- *"Staff right first time and always"*
- *"Design it right first time"*
- *"Prototype it right first time"*
- *"Install it right first time"*
- *"Analyze it right always"*
- *"Program it right always"*
- *"Secure it right always"*
- *"Protect it right always"*

Based on the nature of industry, organization, and business, there is the general need to identify what is referred to by the author, as digital transformational *evidence-based* quality management demands, or found-to-be required measures, or needs, as organizations begin to climb the ladder of their own digital transformational experience. Experience as-we-go is very critical in starting and growing the digital process.

As envisaged by Watson [58], on the basis of his then current observation of the current situation, the job of the quality professional in the next two decades shall likely be predicated on the following assumptions:

- Shifting from the usual practice of creating and executing operational quality strategy to that of a holistic application of a quality strategy across the entirety of organizational activities and value chain.
- Possible evolution of the term *"collaborative analytics"* as a merging replacement for the usual distinction between quality professionals and data scientists. Collaborative analytics is reported here as having the potentials of giving equal

credence to both sides of the production system, in terms of the technological aspects on the one hand, and the human aspects of the administrative system, on the other hand.

- The possibility of data analytics maturing "to incorporate a new way of conducting exploratory data analysis" is high.
- Nearly every quality professional must, to a certain level and degree, have the affinity for understanding data, data usage, and analytics. This may also be applicable to relevant workforce.

Quality professionals need to patiently and cautiously pursue the implementation or development of Industry 4.0 vis-à-vis Quality 4.0 initiatives, with the sole objective of gaining much needed insights from the outcomes and outputs of digitalized operational systems, including generated and collected data and their analysis, to be able to design and/or evolve the right quality management systems that are suitable for digitalized operational systems.

Quality Management Strategies in Digital Ecosystem

Demonstrating the ability of the digital transformation, or Industry 4.0, or "SmartFactory" to create organizational value is key to embarking on its developmental or implementation journey.

Quality is one of the five key broad categories—asset efficiency, quality, costs, safety, and sustainability—reportedly identified by Rick et al. [42] to have the potentials to yield benefits which may ultimately result in increased speed of goods getting to the market; improvement ability of organizational products to capture the market share; and achieving better productivity, product quality, and labor force stability.

It goes to say, therefore, that quality assurance and management remain one of the most essential ingredients for the successful implementation or development of Industry 4.0 initiatives or achieving the "SmartFactory" objectives.

Companies, quality professionals and practitioners, quality professional organizations, and other relevant entities such as quality research institutions, both within and outside academics, need to align applicable quality practices with the realizations of Industry 4.0 initiatives and 4.0 technologies to evolve, adapt, and develop appropriate quality and quality management tools for the digital age industrial operations, processes, and activities.

4.0 base technologies are the basic distinguishing factors separating traditional industrial manufacturing practices from the ones that are today emerging from the digital transformation or Industry 4.0 initiatives. Aligning quality management tools with interconnected automated digitized equipment and devices, in the current era of growing processes digitalization, most reasonably, calls for inline, in-designed, or perhaps in-built quality control systems. This thus brings to the fore, the general need for what is referred to by Krieg (ROI, [28]) as **virtual quality control** (VQC).

Smart Approach to Quality 4.0 Principles and Practices

Quality 4.0 initiatives may be viewed mainly under the umbrella of deploying a new digital technology-propelled approach which draws on relevant values—organizational, people, societal, or other relevant entities—to innovatively adapt traditional quality management principles/philosophy, tools, techniques, and practices, to digital age businesses and settings, such as industrial manufacturing production, and any other digitally transformed businesses or organizations.

While it is difficult to predict the exact outcomes of advancing quality to digital age quality management level, it is obvious that digital age quality management systems (DA-QMS), which must embrace the 4.0 technologies, should be viewed from the perspective of practically deploying quality methods and tools that are extensively supported by appropriate information and communications technology (ICT). Whatever quality management methods and tools that are today in the making for quality application in the digital ecosystem must pay particular attention to the literature or other known established or envisaged features of Quality 4.0 initiatives.

Integrating smart technologies or 4.0 base technologies with traditional quality management tools remains the rudimental platform of Quality 4.0 initiatives, but the ways to accomplish these are now at the drawing stage. While we are not yet sure of the exact mode of applications of 4.0 technologies to effectively manage product quality in the "SmartFactory" setting, there are assurances from literature findings that Quality 4.0 practices will most likely be massively predicated on human-machine collaborative approach (HMCA) across Quality 4.0 initiatives to evolve adequate digital quality management processes and practices in digital settings. Key fundamental considerations in evolving digital quality management practices for the SmartFactory—Quality 4.0, its development/implementation include, among others the following:

- "Designing it right first time" in line with Industry 4.0 initiatives which are from the beginning actually focused on the quality product tenets of the fourth industrial revolution grounded in lower product costs, reduction in wastes, improved competitiveness, and social and environmental accountability.
- Transparency and visibility across the value chain for sustainable supply chain.
- Massive data generation, gathering, sharing, and analytics for predictive maintenance activities and other related use and application.
- Data application and security.
- Cybersecurity, privacy issues, and regulatory requirements.
- Compliance and conformity criteria based on specific standards and in-house requirements as well as regulatory agencies' requirements about product and environmental regulations.
- Smart auditing based on standards and predetermined organizational criteria and conditions including among others remote auditing.
- Leadership commitment and responsibilities.
- Software design and application with opportunity for monitoring effective and efficient working to achieve designed outcomes.

It is evident from the above that implementing or developing Quality 4.0 initiatives is a multi-tasking endeavor of collective responsibilities among all stakeholders including individual businesses/organizations, business management consultants, machine companies, software companies, quality management professionals both individually or collectively, professional organizations, and other concerned entities. In this manner, the ASQ earns global commendation for its leadership roles in initiating the implementation of Quality 4.0. For example, the ASQ's Quality 4.0 Summit [4] was set for October 25–27, 2021, in San Antonio, Texas [5], to consider issues leading to "Quality 4.0 advances, adoption and advocacy" as highlighted as follows

- "**Advances**: Learn what's new in Quality 4.0-enabling technologies and what it means for your organization."
- "**Adoption**: Review processes, tools and techniques applied in Quality 4.0 initiatives."
- "**Advocacy**: Explore the essential role quality individuals and teams play in adopting and leveraging new technologies."

Taking advantage of 4.0 base technologies, the event has been planned to combine in-person and online offerings. Ramping up the momentum by harnessing the inputs of both individuals and professional organizations by the ASQ will most definitely accelerate the initiation and establishment of Quality 4.0 management tools and techniques faster than envisaged.

Literature findings, some of which are listed below, are in terms of some key fundamental considerations:

- Self-optimization principles that are characteristic of the SmartFactory can, as reported by Rick et al. [42], lead to the prediction and detection of quality defect trends, thereby helping in the identification of discrete human, machine, or environmental causes of poor quality, to lower scrap rates and lead times, while increasing fill rates and yield. According to ROI, a more optimized quality process could likely lead to a better-quality product with fewer defects and recalls (ROI, [44]).
- Principles of real-time production control and real-time quality control can be used to avoid waste and production error. The use of sensor-based solutions, generally, provides the opportunity of capturing process parameters in real time, comparing them with sample values to immediately induce taking countermeasures to reduce reject parts (Bick, ROI, [7]). Here, critical values are put to continuous use in taking measurements to enable early identification and correction of errors.
- "SmartAudit" based on existing or established quality management standards such as ISO 9000 series of quality management systems (QMS) standards, ISO 9001:2015 leveraged with relevant 4.0 base technologies.

Quality 4.0 Auditing

"Smart Auditing"

In their recent publication on the implications of technology for ISO 9001 QMS and ISO 14001 EMS international standards, Castka and Searcy [12] reportedly considered what AI and smart technologies mean for quality auditing and certification, in an era of technology-enhanced auditing. It was, however, affirmed here that "replacing human auditors" is neither the purpose of 4.0 technologies nor within their capabilities. Rather it has been suggested by them that there is the possibility of closely integrating human auditors with AI and other base 4.0 technologies, to build on "the non-overlapping strengths of humans and machines to improve our decision making."

There is, however, the anticipation about "the rise in human prediction by exception whereby machines generate most predictions because they are predicated on routine, regular data, but when rare events occur, the machine recognizes that it is not able to produce a prediction with confidence and so calls for human assistance," Agrawal et al. [1].

The criticality of 4.0 technologies in Quality 4.0 is very obvious. For example, the role of data—managing data collection, data recording and sharing, as well as data analysis—in Quality 4.0 initiatives—auditing, supply chain management, customer feedback, etc.—can therefore not be overemphasized.

This is revealed in the publication of Castka et al. [11] in their coining of the term, "technology-enhanced auditing, (TEA)" to suggest the enhancement of data management by technologies. For example, they identified and established the fact that data is central "to artificially intelligent auditing." Castka and Searcy [12] in their publication about "Artificial Intelligent Audits" similarly affirmed the central nature of data collection, data recording and sharing, and data analysis to a "technology-enhanced ecosystem for ISO 9001 and ISO 14001 auditing."

Remote auditing is however not without its pros and cons as confirmed by Carpenter and Drysol [10], "There are multiple reasons why information and communication technology (ICT) remote audit activity is a bad choice." Some of the shortcomings include, among others, limited visibility during virtual tours or at times of area evaluation: virtual software problems which may result in delaying an auditing process, and delays in communicating with multiple personnel during process auditing. Although remote auditing could be better for clients—no expenses for traveling, traveling time, meal costs, and hotel and accommodation expenses—"the cons outweigh the pros," claimed Carpenter and Drysol [10]. It is the opinion of the author, however, that smart auditing be deployed as much as is practicable without compromising the objectives of the audit while studies are carried out, and their outcomes combined with auditors' practical experiences and observations are used to advantage to make necessary improvements until smart auditing is perfected.

Customer Feedback in the Digital Age

Customer feedback is an important key performance indicator (KPI) needed by businesses and organizations to self-assess its level of meeting customer SNEaRs vis-à-vis achieving performance measurement. This could be digitally achieved, for example, through the use of various types of feedback tools such as feedback-widgets, machines, and reviews. The role of customer feedback in the digital age quality practices brings out the criticality of the activities of organizational representatives, be it humans or digital automated representatives.

Hence, customer services agents and representatives in the digital era require special training and skills to implement organizational customer-centric business strategies to avoid the undue losses—financial or sales, customer and/or patronage—in an age where business competitiveness drives the digital transformation itself.

Similarly, feedback widgets, customer feedback machines, and auto attendants must have to be designed and programmed to reflect customer centricity. Failure to do this puts the imagery of the business or organization at great competitive risk.

Life agents dealing with customers, therefore, need some level of versatility in online and physical approach and responses to customers and their requests. The approach, and even the choice of words of customer services agents and representatives, could be critical to business and organizational survival in various ways thereby, impacting businesses—negatively or positively. This is particularly critical, when dealing with customers who do not just know their rights, but who are outrightly very conscious of the quality of services offered them. Using the author's experience in the selection of insurance companies brings out the values inherent in good, trained, customer-centric, and experienced customer services agents.

That is why I was "chilled to the marrow" when my insurance agent simply responded to my complaints about the reasons for the sudden increase of my insurance premium saying **"take it or leave it."** It sounded to me as if survival has been completely eliminated and thrown to the dogs from the insurance company's marketing policies and its business strategy. The insurance company representative ultimately forgot at that moment the quality management saying that an unsatisfied customer tells ten others while each of the ten tells another ten, thereby, creating an exponential negative impression chain about the organization.

Of course, my reaction was obvious, it was an immediate resolve to cancel my two insurance policies which, in turn, made it compulsory for me to search for a replacement from among my initial choice of four insurance companies.

Critical factor for me to select an insurance company is the attitude, response, and ability of their online representative to convince me that the company is the right one for me. This led to four different scenarios out of which I chose the most customer-centric, most customer-oriented, and most customer satisfying in terms the exemplary nature of the company's two representatives whom I interacted with, one of whom gave me an initial auto policy quote and the other the quote for the second, the home owner.

In both situations, the two agents overwhelmed me with their excellent communication abilities, accuracy of information, exceptionally superb and outstanding customer experience that will convince and make any customer, no matter how difficult, happy and satisfied. It was simply an outstanding experience in which my SNEaRs were promptly and outrightly fulfilled. Most outstanding of all is the speed at which my data were correctly obtained and put together by each of them in the most professional way, their patience, clarity, and understanding. The high standard of professionalism and customer care displayed by both of the agents is consistent with past experience of some of their other colleagues which motivated me in believing outrightly that the quality of customer centricity and customer satisfaction must have been the business culture of Layne Horn's employer, Nationwide Mutual Insurance Company. Apart from this excellent customer satisfaction experience being contrary to my earlier "take it or leave it" experience with another insurance company, it demonstrably was a conviction truly attested to here *"Nationwide is on the customers' side."*

Quality management principles and tools desire an organizational or business quality culture built on the quality mindset of the employees as displayed in this experience to achieve company quality strategy of putting the company "on the side of the customer."

The role of employees in achieving company product/services quality of "excellence" cannot be overemphasized; hence, there is the need for every employee to handle assigned responsibilities as if the company, business, or organization belongs to them, while companies, businesses, and organizations must have to be committed to inclusively engaging their employees in their quality management activities. That is not just the essence of competitiveness but a one way traffic to sustainability.

Summing Up the Review

The literature review provides clear evidence that Industry 4.0 and the ensuing digital transformation of organizational and business processes constitute the most talked-about issue today, on the global developmental business transformational platform. The vast amounts of articles and other publications in topics related to Industry 4.0 initiatives and allied topics is thus a general portrayal of how the global industrial manufacturing ecosystem has dramatically been changed or better still, transformed, and are transforming, or transformed by the fourth industrial revolution. Although there is a literature consensus about the relationship between the concept of Quality 4.0 and Industry 4.0, there appeared to be less awareness about Quality 4.0.

Perhaps in relating "Quality 4.0" with its developed concept of "Quality 5.0," otherwise referred to as the fifth wave of quality "societal satisfaction," the Swedish Institute for Quality [52] went back to history to trace the preceding four waves dating back to the seventeenth century practice of DIY. These are as listed in Table 22.1.

The role of DIY in the context of quality which dates back as far as the time of Joseph Moxon who wrote the book, "Mechanick Exercises is the grandfather of all modern DIY manuals" (1683–5), is a clear demonstration of man's early appreciation of this body of knowledge, Quality, and how critical it has been for humanity (Pre-History of DIY, Science Museum Group Collection, [49]).

Digital technologies are actually and gradually changing the landscape for most industrial manufacturing companies, a phenomenon already ravaging the automobile industry which is presently witnessing a tumultuous scarcity of chips and astronomic increases in the prices of automobiles—new and pre-owned.

Both active players and anticipating organizations and businesses participating and involved in every cutting-edge development underpinning society's digital transformation, from artificial intelligence and autonomous vehicles, to quantum computing, predictive maintenance, machine learning, robotics, Internet of Things to everything in the digital ecosystem are today full of excitements and expectations. Expectations are capped with hope for some, and anxieties for others.

The twenty-first century, as it has so far unveiled itself, can therefore, with so much confidence, be easily code-named the century of digital transformational **"societal shift,"** initiated by the introduction of personal computers, the internet, and mobile devices, flexibly brought to full swing, by a combined interconnectivity of processes, machines, and people, with the integration of 4.0 base technologies and autonomous decision-making abilities.

Quality 4.0, therefore, entails on a general basis, leveraging 4.0 technologies with traditional total quality management tools and techniques to evolve quality management practices for the "SmartFactory" and other digital settings.

Quality 4.0 initiatives have to be leveraged with the underlisted Quality 4.0 tools among others, as suggested by the ASQ, to alleviate some of the challenges encountered during the process of implementing and deploying the systems needed to support digital transformation.

- **Artificial intelligence** (AI)—computer vision, language processing, chatbots, personal assistants, navigation, robotics, making complex decisions and other opportunities.
- **Big data**—provides easier access to data sources and tools for gathering, managing, analyzing "mountains" of data without the need to invest in supercomputers. The visibility resulting from the centralization of data in Industry 4.0 gives all organizational or business stakeholders the opportunity of being aware of the across-the-value chain activities from the beginning to the end thereby, making immense contribution to the improvement of the supply chain by increasing output and decreasing costs. This is a key contribution to the supply chain sustainability (SCS).
- **Blockchain**—increasing transparency and audibility of transactions (for assets and information) to assure that transactions along the supply value chain do not take place except quality objectives are met.

- **Deep learning**—is used for image classification, complex pattern recognition, time series forecasting, creating sound and art, creating fictitious video from real video, text generation, and other applications.
- **Enabling technologies**—deep sensors and actuators, cloud computing, open-source software, augmented reality (AR), mixed reality, virtual reality (VR), data streaming, 5G networks, IPv6, Internet of Things (IoT), and Industrial Internet of Things (IIoT).
- **Machine learning** (ML)—e-mail spam filters, fraud detection, classifying objects into groups, text analysis, recommendation systems, forecasting and other applications.
- **Data Science**—enables the use and application of relevant data sets for making predictions and carrying out classifications; identification of data pattern and trends from large sets of data and the use and application of sound conventional quality techniques to generate viable models and solutions.

Sustainability and Quality

The concept of *sustainability* surfaced frequently in the literature. This simply illustrates the criticality of the concept of **"sustainability"** not just to organizational and business activities particularly, the supply chain but also to human lives as proffered by the United Nations (UN) in its 17 sustainable development goals.

There are no doubts whatsoever that the UN may have recognized the critical role of quality generally in the lives of human beings when "In September 2015, the UN General Assembly adopted the 2030 Agenda for Sustainable Development, which includes 17 sustainable development goals (SDGs)," listed as in the following [2].

1. No poverty
2. Zero hunger
3. Good health and well-being
4. Quality education
5. Gender quality
6. Clean water and sanitation
7. Affordable and clean energy
8. Decent work and economic growth
9. Industry, innovation, and infrastructure
10. Reduced inequalities
11. Sustainable cities and communities
12. Responsible consumption and production
13. Climate action
14. Life below water
15. Life on land
16. Peace, justice, and strong institutions
17. Partnerships for the goals

It is evident indeed that the 17 SDGs of the UN are, in their wholeness and completeness, an embodiment of quality as much as it is an enhancement of quality management practices and their planned outcomes on the platform of political diplomacy.

The UN holistic approach to achieve *quality life* for all members of the global community, though appears highly hypocritically exaggerated to me because of the unrealistic political undertone, which presents a strong stride of inclusive global developmental principle of "not leaving anybody behind." Hence, the open assertion of the UN Secretary General that, "The 17 [SDGs] are our shared vision of humanity and a social contract between the world's leaders and the people" [53]. It is for this reason too that the author has been motivated to refer to, and view the UN's SDGs as a type of a global QM Sustainability Development Goals (QM-SDGs).

It is therefore not in vain that the world of quality, as well as the world around us, is currently awash with the proliferation of the term and concept, *"sustainability."* This term is directly related to the concept and purpose of quality more than any other theme. Whether we are talking about the quality of life, quality of the environment or the universe, human life, social justice, and its dispensation and economic (e.g., businesses and organizations) development, sustainability remains a common denominator of the human life.

Life itself is about growing up to identify, establish, and sustain our individual life values as perceived by each person. Life struggle, an everyday established pursuit and engagement of every man, from cradle to grave, therefore, revolves around our individual values, aimed at achieving sustainable **quality** in the life of every individual.

While organizational sustainability may primarily be viewed from the perspectives of its ability to withstand changes, its commitment to environmental sustainability is far more critical, to ensure that we are all in the position to sustain our lives, socioeconomic activities and the environment we live in.

In the context of quality management commitment, therefore, the existence of organizations and businesses depends to a large extent, on their abilities to continue to improve and sustain their improvement processes, including the supply chain, in terms of their products and services without any adverse effects whatsoever, on any other entities, both now and in the future.

The quality of life and sustainability of the entirety of the global community is, in the most realistic way, highly dependent on the collaborative ability of the individual national components of the global community. Hence, the talk of sustaining life through our collective responsibilities—individual citizens; organizations and businesses; and the political leadership class.

This thus brings into the discuss here, the general needs for strong organizational commitment to its corporate social responsibility (CSR) and corporate environment responsibility (CER) while governance has to be more *"people-centric"* and *"people-oriented"* to achieve governance social responsibilities (GSR) and the 17 SDGs. The burden of achieving GSR fully rests on political leadership from the lowest level of political leadership to the highest. Any political leader who either deceitfully or unsuspiciously put himself and his interests above the people has not only betrayed the people's trust but destroyed the quality of leadership.

It thus becomes highly imperative for the people to be able to have confidence in governments and their institutions. But unfortunately, one of the greatest challenges of global societies today is the need to develop and maintain citizens' confidence in their leadership, governments, and their institutions. Meeting these challenges requires, however, that, "local governments have a mission to enable the development of a socially responsible and sustainable local community" (ISO). It is for the purposes of promoting the achievement of this objective, and the UN initiatives that the ISO developed an international standard:

ISO 18091:2019 *Quality management systems—Guidelines for application of ISO 9001 in local government [19].*

Overall, leadership is key in whatever we do. Hence, quality is leadership, while mis-leadership is the adverse of its experience. Quality management has, over the past century, in its application to businesses and industrial production processes and activities, proved most glaringly, to be a key factor to sustainable economic success.

This is because quality enables competitiveness and ensures that customer SNEaRs are satisfied (or even surpassed) not just in terms of products/services quality, but also in terms of the environment and corporate social responsibility (CSR) [9, 47].

The quality of products, services, and organizational processes jointly combine to create value for organizations and businesses, for them to enhance their economic success vis-à-vis sustainability. No matter how hard businesses and organizations strive, to attain sustainability, their efforts could be rubbished at the instance of a crazy political mis-leadership which abuses the leadership position and abandons governance social responsibility (GSR).

For global sustainability, therefore, leadership quality, is key now and always. Hence, the general need for the enhanced quality of leadership and democratic governance at all levels of government—local/community, city, county, state, region, province, national, and international.

The role of quality in global sustainability thus universally elevates *quality and quality management tools and practices* at all levels of human life to the frontline of global attention, a general cause for concern for future generations of the world.

We therefore have to appreciate the fact that quality is universal both in context and application, thereby making quality a critical and important aspects of human sustainability. Hence, the need for its global embrace.

From Quality Control to Quality 4.0

The dynamism of quality has seen it as an ever-evolving phenomenon of human sustainability. Similarly, quality has, in its evolutionary stages, earned affiliation with various other words such as excellence, world class, superb, very good, and outstanding performance. There are no doubts, whatsoever, that it is for these and other reasons that total quality management (TQM) has reportedly been viewed closely with concepts such as "sense of safety, aesthetics, well-being, engagement and participation" [51], as well as being related to organizational innovation, which is a valuable strategy for world-class performance by value creation, new thinking, and operational improvement [30, 56].

Today, quality is experiencing a new phase of evolution in the dictates of the fourth industrial revolution, Industry 4.0 which enables the application of Industry 4.0 base technologies, such as digitalization and artificial intelligence to quality: transforming it into Quality 4.0 [8]. Evidence available in the literature clearly reveal the revolutionary stages of quality going from quality control to Quality 4.0 as indicated in Table 22.2 [40, 41, 45].

Table 22.2 Evolutionary stages of Quality from QC to Quality 4.0

Evolving phases of quality	Focus of application	Quality implication	Characteristic features of quality
Quality control (QC)	Product	Product inspection to separate bad from good	Product specification, statistical process control and variation. Correction approach at product level
Quality assurance (QA)	Quality control of processes	Built-in quality from design stage through various processing stages	Built-in process quality. Process performance and metrics. Prevention approach at every process stage
Total quality management (TQM)	Quality assurance, organization-wide activities, and people	Empowerment of people across organizational setting	Quality as a strategic organizational goal on a continuous improvement basis. Quality organizational goals linked to metrics
Quality 4.0	Application of 4.0 base technologies, for example, digitalization and AI to TQM to augment and improve on human intelligence	Shifting from customer-centric to co-creating and collaborating with customers and other stakeholders	Competitively driven technology-enhanced and intelligence integrated systems across the value chain—suppliers, customers, and society—to achieve customer satisfaction, business improvement, and sustainability with adaptive leadership. Focus on intelligence, big data generation, sharing and analytics, connectedness, and autonomous decision-making

Skills and Workforce Uptraining in the Dictates of Quality 4.0

Just like in the case of quality co-evolving with every pace of industrial production phase, especially over the last century, so also is Quality 4.0 adaption of 4.0 base technologies in Industry 4.0 implementation going to evolve. Hence, as it is in the case of Industry 4.0, the transition to Quality 4.0 may remain a challenge to individual companies and businesses for some times. The reasons here are not far-fetched, as many individual companies still lack most appropriate knowledge about the context and impact of Quality 4.0, and the ways to exactly and appropriately adapt it to their own business quality management systems [23].

It is, however, very certain that the automation of quality functions and analysis in an environment of high technology and innovation [13] requires that quality professionals must have to adapt. This and other developmental functions thus make the present time in our world, an era in which quality professionals have to be prepared to shift focus, anticipate changes, and be prepared to integrate new concepts into evolving business models. It must be added too that roles within an organization implementing Industry 4.0 will have to change too.

It thus becomes highly imperative for quality professionals to be put in the position of acquiring all necessary skills and competences to effectively manage and cope with organizational issues inherently driven by the changes that come with digitalization, automation, big data, and cybersecurity.

Obviously, the major tasks of quality professionals rest highly in their ability to appropriately deploy relevant 4.0 base technologies, as well as the information and data generated from the system, to improve organizational performance in terms of products/services, and to sustain their cross-organizational values to gain competitive edge.

Although no specifics are available in the literature as to the exact ways quality tools are going to be adaptable to the SmartFactory concept, or in implementing Quality 4.0 initiatives, there are various suggestions, as to how the fourth industrial revolution provides tools and technologies for quality improvement.

For example, Radziwill [40, 41] suggested the application of tools such as the enabling technologies and devices—sensors, mobile devices, networks, Industrial Internet of Things (IIoT), Internet of Things (IoT), integrated systems, virtual reality, and cloud computing—provide interconnectivity and the opportunity of documentation management. The roles of achieving quality objectives through the use and application of data science and statistics, big data, block chain, artificial intelligence (AI), machine learning (ML), neural networks, and deep learning and their interrelationship were similarly argued.

The automated—semi and full—generation and availability of data too is a ready quality management inherent potential to enhance process and product quality, in a digitalized system and environment [34]. Apart from the awareness opportunity of all activities being made visible to all stakeholders, automated analysis in real time actually facilitates prompt and fast reaction opportunities, to immediately react to variances whenever trends and values are found to be out of specifications.

COVID-19 Pandemic—Catalyst of Digital Transformation

The need for adapting to the new norm created in the advent of the COVID-19 pandemic then was noticed to have accelerated the initially planned systematic implementation of the digital transformation. With the disruptive changes that were suddenly incited by the COVID-19 pandemic, many organizations and businesses quickly rushed to acquire more computers, software, AI, and cloud for various remote applications.

In a reported survey by KPMG [39], it was found that half of business leaders in industrial manufacturing (55%), retail (49%), and tech (49%) concluded that AI is moving faster than it should have been in their industry. This led to the assumption by the KPMG representative that, "Leaders are experiencing COVID-19 whiplash, with AI adoption skyrocketing as a result of the pandemic." This led to the reported concerns about the pronounced speed of AI adoption among small companies (63%). Consequent upon these issues, a quality expert in the person of Nicole Radziwill, reportedly expressed her feelings that the adoption of AI and machine learning (ML) was "moving in the wrong direction."

This is perhaps understandable as organization leaders were perhaps reactive in order to minimize some of the COVID-19 evolved challenges, as claimed in the same report that, "Leaders from small (88%) and large (80%) said AI technology helped their company during COVID-19 outbreak."

Workforce—Impact of Digital Transformation

While some younger generations of the workforce may have been excited by the prospects of the digital transformation, older experienced generations of workers were perhaps left in utter state of technological disarray, wandering in the wilderness of technological challenges either in search of relevant skills uptraining opportunities, or reluctant to embrace 4.0 base technologies and the rigors of their knowledge acquisition despite several years of work experience.

It is obvious here that existing workforce or employees are challenged by the immediate need to quickly adapt to working in the "SmartFactory" environment of sophisticated machines and technologies. As precisely put by Wang et al. [54], there is the obligation to provide corresponding expertise to work in an environment in which organizations are becoming smarter with sophisticated machines and technologies.

With organizations and businesses implementing or hoping to implement Industry 4.0, their prime objectives of intelligent systems and digitalization, Weyer et al. [59], are understandable. Building automated and digitalized manufacturing environments, logistics, and value chains with the help of technologies such as the Internet of Things (IoT) and big data analysis undoubtedly calls for competent and skilled hands, as suggested by Oesterreich and Teuteberg [36]. Learning to handle Industry 4.0 technologies is reportedly not always possible to achieve just through academics alone, as put by Hasan and Urmee [17]. Hence Industry 4.0 demands skills and talented workforce.

Evidence in the literature seemed most importantly to agree in the existence of a skills gap in Industry 4.0 implementation; hence, there is the urgent need to bridge the gap. There is therefore the need for more education and training perhaps beyond academic settings. Balancing upskilling existing workforce with the embrace of trained ones, as well as providing adequate training opportunities, is a good starting point. This is very important to bridge the gap of needed skills for the digital transformational changes.

It is glaringly evident that implementing Industry 4.0 as well as aligning and adopting quality with 4.0 base technologies require innovative and intelligent self-motivating workforce with technological aptitude and the ability to work independently in an intelligently automated technology-enriched environment. The role of skilled human resources in any organization cannot be overemphasized as they are the main driving forces behind machines and technology application and usage.

Organizational and business challenges here are glaring, in that the already trained ones are not easy to come by, while the under-skilled or undertrained employees cannot simply be shed because of their inability to quickly adjust to the newly needed technological skills requirements for the "SmartFactory."

This is perhaps the issue of a double-edged sword for most companies as they gather needed momentum to embark on the digital transformational journey. Hence, the general view in the literature for prioritizing the reskilling and uptraining eligible aging workforce, too.

Achieving this goal calls however for collaboratively efforts—industry, professional bodies, universities, and other relevant institutions—to ensure needed trained skills are available at all stages of digital transformation.

It is apparent from literature findings that Quality 4.0 initiatives call for sufficient numbers of *data scientists* needed in the digital era to manage big data for predictive analytics—systems design, process adjustment, adaptive learning, systems integration, and human performance [58].

Quality professionals therefore need to enhance their capabilities with digital diversity in readiness to respond equivalently to process excellence, risks in new product designs and development, product robustness, traceability, visibility and transparency, customer satisfaction, and other inherent quality features built into digital devices and other components of the digitalization process [32].

Pathway to Quality 4.0

Finding the pathway to Quality 4.0 is very important and critical because digitalization will continue to assume increased importance particularly in industrial manufacturing processes. Quality 4.0 is and has to be rooted in the principles of total quality management (TQM). Hence, the basics of transitioning to Quality 4.0 is strongly grounded in existing quality theories, principles, techniques, and tools.

Hence, ISO 9001:2015, Lean, Lean Six Sigma, and others are going to be prominent in Quality 4.0 implementation.

Due to automation, artificial intelligence and other relevant 4.0 base technologies, **building the principles of quality tools into digital systems from both the design stage, and at the level of software programs** will feature prominently in Quality 4.0 implementation and initiatives.

The road to accomplishing the dreams of Quality 4.0 is therefore that of enhanced collaborative and participatory efforts of all interested parties, in a somewhat coordinated fashion to capitalize on Industry 4.0 initiatives and 4.0 base technologies. This is based on the general principles of *"learning from shared experience on the go."*

This could be accomplished in various ways and dimensions as highlighted as follows:

- Professional generation and exchange of qualitive initiatives, ideas, and propositions among quality professionals through professional gatherings such as the October 25 to 27, 2021, ASQ's Quality Summit in San Antonio, Texas.
- Across-professional border researches, surveys and interactive fermentation of ideas led by interested academic researchers and experts in quality engineering, design engineering, mechanical engineering, software experts, statistical knowledge base, data science and analytics, business consultants, manufacturer's associations, equipment and machine manufacturers' groups and other relevant organizations.
- Inputs of individual company experience as they go, in their implementation of Industry 4.0, digitalization processes, previous and present use and application of the 4.0 base technologies, interactive experience gained from software engineering, machine manufacturing companies, blogs, and prototyping experience.

The outcome of such collaborative information sharing efforts is generally to provide an informational pool of relevant ideas across the lines of Industry 4.0 vis-a-vis Quality 4.0 interested and enthusiastic organizations or groups therefrom.

Gathering Digitalization Momentum

Whatever experience and information gathered from the above can be deployed into setting a standard for your **self-assessment** exercise, particularly in reference to organizational processes, infrastructure (including access to 4.0 base technologies), and competences in order to appreciably, and perhaps more clearly, understand the quality implications of digitization and implementing Industry 4.0 initiatives. Your company or organizational level of conviction or not represents your level of preparedness to **digital maturity** or not. Your assessed digital maturity level may however be benchmarked, where possible with that of similar companies. Identify and assess gaps in terms of processes, infrastructural provisions, technology accessibility, personnel, and workforce competences, among others.

It thus becomes necessary here to warn organizations and businesses that jumping into the implementation of digital solution without knowing the full implications of the impacts of Industry 4.0 vis-à-vis Quality 4.0 on your organization's infrastructural preparedness, processes, activities and its business performance improvement must be avoided, else it may be a fruitless effort.

Hence, it is very important for organizations embarking on the digital transformation or Industry 4.0 implementation, and consequently Quality 4.0, to consider and ensure in all ramifications that, it will lead to value creation for all stakeholders:

- Manufacturing, materials handling, and logistics cost reduction
- Mass customization
- Waste reduction
- Improved productivity through increasing efficiency, general improved performance, competitiveness, sustainability, and other critical improvement factors craved by the organization

Hence, Industry 4.0 trend should not be blindly followed, or its implementation embarked upon just because others or competitors do it or merely for its trending nature. Even when these are motivational factors, there should be an organizational-wide and stakeholder-wide understanding as to exactly how digitalization will impact an organization or business. It is therefore highly imperative to, in addition to others, understand the following important business concerns:

- Full financial implication of digitalization.
- The ways in which digitalization can be relied upon to deliver organizational performance improvement across the value system—returns on investment, productivity, competitive ability, market performance, etc.
- The scope of changes envisaged from digital transformation and how they will affect all stakeholders and organizational value system in its entirety.
- The consequences of digitalization on organizational sustainability, employment, and employee skills requirements and upskilling needs, product quality, and other critical issues.
- Impact of digitalization on organizations with facilities located in diverse national and international locations, cultures, and technological advancement levels.

After filling the established gaps and in preparation for developing the strategic pathway for the digital transformation or implementing Industry 4.0, organizational processes including quality management, supply chain, documentation, flow of information and any other necessary reorganization should be stabilized in readiness to go.

It is important, too, to assure at this stage that relevant existing and anticipated regulatory requirements and standards—local, state, national, and international are identified, monitored constantly to ensure continued compliance.

Having gone this far, an organization needs to inclusively reaffirm its interests by keeping all stakeholders and employees aware, identify benefits of the digital transformation or Industry 4.0 implementation, map out its pathway forward before aligning its organizational strategies with Industry 4.0 initiatives, in anticipation of Quality 4.0 implementation.

Digitalization Action Guideline

The imminent changes portended in the digitalization exercise calls generally for accurate understanding and conviction that it is going to be of optimum benefit for a business or organization as propounded by the apostles of the fourth industrial revolution.

1. Gather sufficient information from all available sources including management consultants, professionals, and other relevant entities about digitalization—benefits, digitalization processes, infrastructural needs, human resources/skills requirements, and where possible seek to gain more information from a *prototype digitalization project* or any other known digitalization projects to ensure full understanding, both in terms of operational and quality management processes. This may involve wide and cross-industry consultations.
2. Ask questions and seek answers in order to assess the state and level of organizational *digital maturity*, and the possibility of a stage by stage, or fractionalized digitalization of equipment and facilities to help in setting organizational digitalization objectives, in collaboration with all relevant stakeholders.
3. Take a management/stakeholder decision on whether to embark on digitalization in implementing Industry 4.0 initiatives or not, with set objectives.
4. If yes, carry out a digitalization feasibility studies to identify overall investment needs and costs, infrastructural and personnel gaps, other needed resources, expected or envisaged disruptive changes, stages of the digitalization process, and the envisaged results or expectations during the digitalization stages, and any other expert advice that may be available.
5. Agree with all stakeholders to put organizational digitalization strategic plans in place. Finalize and identify how to exactly fill both skills and infrastructural gaps in terms of training, upskilling/reskilling, recruitment, and financial resources. Establish a digitalization plan with possible calendar of activities.
6. Select across-organization digitalization team (to include quality management and other management team members) to work with experts in creating organization-wide awareness and educate employees about organizational purposes and expectations from the digitalization process, challenges in terms of employee opportunities and roles.
7. Identify all relevant regulatory requirements and other necessary considerations to ensure compliance in all ramification of the digitalization process and also to achieve cybersecurity and data protection, bearing in mind relevant regulatory requirements.
8. Ensure that equipment suppliers and/or manufacturers, software providers, and other technology organizations are tied down to the obligation of training user

employees as much as is possible in the contractual agreement to facilitate their proficiencies in using and working with such items.
9. The involvement of key organizational quality management team members at every stage of the digitalization process will, to an appreciable extend, help to reinforce their understanding of the functions of the involved technologies, areas of application, as well as their applicability adoption to the quality management tools and practices, that is, Quality 4.0 initiatives.

With the progress being witnessed in the industry in terms of the application of 4.0 base technologies in Industry 4.0, the digitalization of interested businesses and organizations is a matter of time as every step in that direction opens up the path of accomplishing Quality 4.0.

Quality 4.0 transcends the boundaries of 4.0 base technologies.

It is a way for quality professionals and practitioners to engineer products and services quality with digital tools and how they are applied within the fourth industrial revolution to promote and facilitate best practices and thought leadership in their respective organizations in their desire for, and pursuit of excellence.

Quality 4.0—Grounded in Traditional Quality Practices

Another revolution, based on the recent technological developments, is in the making at this time, revolutionizing industrial manufacturing production systems in a global world of disruptive changes. This is happening in the dictates of advances in industrial application of 4.0 base technologies.

Advances in the industrial application of 4.0 base technologies have triggered broader transformation not just in industrial manufacturing processes but in quality and quality management practices.

With the internet creating radical technical innovation, there have been great improvements in sensing, connectivity, inference, and actuation enabling smart, scalable, and hyperconnected systems, courtesy of the Internet of Things (IoT) and other technologies, Yang and Siegel [50].

The adoption of the IoT coupled with advances in artificial intelligence and big data have consequently been highly beneficial to industrial manufacturing. There are no doubts therefore that the fourth industrial revolution, code-named Industry 4.0, has been successfully facilitated by the joint capabilities of the IoT and other related technologies.

The evolution of Industry 4.0 has therefore created opportunities for diversity in the manufacturing production processes at reduced costs and enhancement of product quality through modern production economics enabled by the following:

- Smart supply chains
- Product/services demand responsiveness
- Smart product distribution and flexible manufacturing
- Lot-size-one manufacturing

The fourth industrial revolution or the implementation of Industry 4.0 was however not excluded from the impacts of the globally ravaging COVID-19 pandemic. Most organizations and businesses impacted by the COVID-19 pandemic were somehow reactive in commencing the implementation of some Industry 4.0-related quality initiatives despite the fact that the best route to achieving Industry 4.0 vis-à-vis Quality 4.0 implementation is through a gradual evolvement with time, in line with increasing realization of Industry 4.0 to drive home the notion of defining Quality 4.0 as;

> Closely aligning quality management with Industry 4.0 to enable enterprise efficiencies, performance, innovation and business models. [24, 33]

It thus become very obvious from the assumption here that, in the words of James, Quality 4.0 is:

> A tool for businesses to understand the effect of Industry 4.0 on products, processes and quality technology using innovations singularly or in combination, such as ML and AI mobile technology, AR and VR, cloud technologies, connected devices and edge devices, big data and data lakes, social media and block chains.

The role and criticality of data analytics in Quality 4.0 in the context of digital age businesses and environment can therefore not be overemphasized. Hence, the frequency of the term *big data analytics* in the literature signifies the perception of the size of data in question, without mentioning their significance or impact in terms of business operational context [55].

The various types and sizes of information derivable from *big data analysis* are of tangible benefit for the improvement of business performance in various ways and modes. For example, it has, among others, the ability to expose organizational vulnerability to disruption in terms of the following:

- Cyber attacks.
- Increased energy consumption of data servers and centers.
- Legal sanctions, since internet searches are not immune from carbon emissions. An example here is the fact that, a "typical Goggle search consumes enough energy to illuminate a 60-watt light bulb for 17 seconds" [24, 38].

In a case study by James [24], it was discovered that, "For organizations to truly benefit from Quality 4.0, leaders must understand the big picture and move beyond using data and computing technology to perform business-as-usual tasks toward managing the organization's information footprint through an understanding of data and information as an element of sustainability along with economic, social and environmental dimensions."

The immense impact of technologies, including big data and data analytics in digitalized industrial manufacturing systems has, however, not deterred quality professionals, practitioners, researchers, people in academics, and quality professional bodies from pressing the acceleration pedal in pursuit of the utmost desire to fully understand what may be referred to as "technology-integrated TQM" (Tech-in-TQM), otherwise known as Quality 4.0 with the following objectives:

- Ensuring the full understanding of Quality 4.0, its immediate impacts, and long-term effects on humans, small- to medium-scale organizations, and businesses. This thus provides more opportunities for more research works in quality.
- Identifying and defining the consequences of Industry 4.0 implementation and Quality 4.0 initiatives on the COVID-19 weakened globalized economy.
- Researching into various application models of Quality 4.0 and implementing case studies to verify the veracity and practical applicability of each of them to specific companies, their products, and/or services.

Quality is thus assuming in our modern time, the most revolutionary digital transformation with foothold in traditional quality management principles/philosophy, techniques, tools, and practices predicated on across-organizational processes and stakeholders' value chain to achieve competitiveness for sustainability.

It is a truth universally acknowledged in the history of mankind that quality has always been associated with the "sensation of (good) properties" embodying two aspects of excellence—objective quality and perceived quality, Siegel and Yang [50]. In today's world of quality, we are accordingly, enjoying the qualities inherent in products such as reliability, lower costs, defect control, improved brand perception and reputation, as well as meeting the SNEaRs of all three categories of customers—primary (1°), secondary (2°) and tertiary (3°)—as redefined in this book.

The role of data in digital age quality management practices cannot be overemphasized. "While there are plenty of instances in which we're still drowning in data, the tide seems to be turning toward more deliberate strategies resulting from highly illuminating, technology-driven data inputs," Sanders [46]; hence, the general need to understand the concept, called *"deep quality,"* which signifies, leveraging the capabilities of the Internet of Things (IoT) and Industry 4.0 to address stakeholder SNEaRs, and simultaneously making the right product, and at the same time, making the product right, Siegel and Yang [50].

For business and organizational sustainability as well as global sustainability, quality and quality management practices remain the most viable option, hence, the urgent need for individuals, communities—local, national, and international—businesses and organizations across the globe to, not just embrace TQM practices but to drink deep into quality because in the words of Alexander Pope, "A little learning is a dangerous thing; drink deep…."

References

1. Agrawal, A., Gans, J., & Goldfarb, A. (2018). *Prediction machines: The simple economics of artificial intelligence*. Harvard Business Review Press.
2. Alisic, B., Cianfrani, C. A., Sheps, I., & (Jack) West, J. E. (2021). Supporting sustainability – How ISO 18091 promotes the UN's sustainable development goals. *Quality Progress,* 2021, pp. 56–58.

3. Antony, J. Quality 4.0: Enhancing organization's quality management practices to the next level. *The Future Factory* [online]. https://www.thefuturefactory.com. Retrieved on September 10, 2021.
4. ASQ. (2021). ASQ's quality 4.0 summit set. *Quality Progress,* August 2021, p. 13. https://www.asq.org/conferences/quality-4-0
5. ASQ/Quality Progress. (2021). Skills of the future. *Quality Progress,* August 2021, p. 15.
6. Benesova, A., & Tupa, J. (2017). Requirements for education and qualification of people in industry 4.0. *Procedia Manufacturing, 11*, 2195–2202.
7. Bick, W., & ROI Management Consultant AG. Going smart: Milestone on the road to an intelligent factory. *ROI DIALOG – Inside the Smart Factory,* Issue 49. http://www.roi-international.com. Retrieved on August 28, 2021.
8. Bowers, K., & Pickerel, T. V. (2019). Vox Populi: Big data tools zoom in on the voice of the customer. *Quality Progress,* March 2019, pp. 19–39.
9. Bravi, L., Murmura, F., & Santos, G. (2018). Manufacturing labs: Where new digital technologies help improve life quality. *International Journal for Quality Research, 12*, 957–974.
10. Carpenter, B., & Wayne, D. (2021). Expert answers – What are the cons and pros of remote auditing? *Quality Progress,* October 2021, p. 6.
11. Castka, P., Searcy, C., & Mohr, J. (2020). Technology-enhanced auditing: Improving veracity and timeliness in social and environmental audits of supply chains. *Journal of Cleaner Production, 258*, 2020.
12. Castka, P., & Searcy, C. (2021). Artificial intelligence audits. *Quality Progress,* September 2021, pp. 26–31.
13. Elshenawy, A. (2004). Quality in the new age and the body of knowledge for quality engineers. *Total Quality Management and Business Excellence, 15*(5–6), 603–614.
14. Frey, C. B., & Osborne, M. A. (2017). The future of employment: How susceptible are jobs to computerization? *Technological Forecasting and Social Change, 114*, 254–280.
15. Fundin, A., Bergquist, B., Eriksson, H., & Gremyr, I. (2018). Challenges and propositions for research in quality management. *International Journal of Production Economics, 199*, 125–137.
16. Gunasekaran, A., & Subramanian, N. (2019). Quality management in 21st century enterprises: Research pathway towards Industry 4.0. *International Journal of Production Economics, 207*, 125–129.
17. Hassan, M. Z., & Urmee, S. A. (2021). Cutting into a skills deficit: Examining the need to synchronize human resource quality with intelligent systems and machines in Industry 4.0. *Quality Progress,* October 2021, pp. 28–37.
18. Horikiri, T. (2017). The Toyota Management System. *Proceedings of the Fifth Productivity Summit, Sochi, Russia.* April, 2017.
19. International Organization for Standardization (ISO), ISO 18091:2019 – Quality management systems – Guidelines for the application of ISO 9001 in local government.
20. International Organization for Standardization, ISO (2015), ISO 9001:2015. Quality management systems – Requirements.
21. Jacob, D. (2017). Quality 4.0 impact and strategy handbook. Getting digitally connected to transform. *Quality Management,* LNS Research; Cambridge, UK.
22. Jacob, D. (2017). *What is quality 4.0?* https://www.juran.com/blog/quality-4-0-the-future-of-quality. Retrieved January 30, 2020.
23. Jacob, D. (2019). *Top 4 reasons to update quality 4.0.* Online blog. blog.Insresearch.com. https://blog.Insreaserch.com/top-4-reasons-to-update-to-quality-4.0. Retrieved May 30, 2019.
24. James, L. (2021). Understanding the big picture: How big data analytics software can improve quality, safety and environmental risk management. *Quality Progress,* October, pp. 20–27.
25. Johnson, S. (2019). Quality 4.0: A trend within a trend. *Quality, 58*(2), 21–23.
26. Kagermann, H., Lukas, W.-D., & Wahlster, W. (2011, 2011). Industrie 4.0: Mit dem Internet der Dinge auf dem Weg zur 4. Industriallen Revolution. *VDI Nachrichten, 13*(11). https://tinyurl.com/ly6vkff

27. Köpper, D., Knizek, C., Ryeson, D., & Noecker, J. (2019). *Quality 4.0 takes more than technology.* https://www.bcg.com/publications/2019/quality-4.0-takes-more-than-technology.aspx. Retrieved on January 30, 2020.
28. Krieg, U., & (ROI Management Consultant AG). *Error-free process control: Quality management 4.0.* ROI DIALOG, Inside the smart factory, Issue 49. http://www.roi-international.com. Retrieved on August 28, 2021.
29. Lavi, Y. (2017). "Industry 4.0: Harnessing the power of ERP and MES integration" magic software. *Industry Week,* July 20, 2017. https://www.industryweek.com. Retrieved Joly 31, 2021.
30. Lee, S. M. (2015). The age of quality innovation. *International Journal of Quality Innovation, 1*(1), 1–5.
31. Lianaki-Dedouli, I., & Plouin, J. (2017). Bridging anticipation skills and intercultural competences as a means to reinforce the capacity of global citizens for learning to learn together. *Futures, 94*, 45–58.
32. Lim, J. S. (2019). *Quality management in engineering – A scientific and systematic approach.* CRC Press.
33. LNS Research. (2017). *Quality 4.0 impact and strategy handbook: Getting digitally connected to transform quality management* (e-Book). https://blog.Inresearch.com/quality40ebook. Retrieved on May 30, 2019.
34. Lyle, J. S. (2017). Revealing the value of data through quality intelligence. *Quality Magazine,* October, pp. 25–29.
35. Morrar, R., Arman, H., & Mousa, S. (2017). The fourth industrial revolution (Industry 4.0): A social innovation perspective. *Technology Innovation Management Review, 7*, 12–20.
36. Oesterreich, T. D., & Teuteberg. (2016). Understanding the implication of digitalization and automation in the context of industry 4.0: A triangulation approach and elements of a research agenda for the construction industry. *Computers in Industry, 83*, 121–139.
37. Padhi, N., & Illa, P. K. (2019). Bigger, better, smarter – How to maintain in an increasingly automated environment. *Quality Progress,* Mar. 2019, pp. 24–29.
38. Pearce, F. (2018). Energy hogs: Can the world's data centers be made more energy efficient? *Yale Environment 360*, April 3, 2018.
39. Progress Report in Quality Progress. (2021). KPMG industries survey: Many concerned AI moving too fast. *Quality Progress,* May 2021, pp. 6–7. https://www.kpmg.com/us. or https://tinyurl.com/y73fhfj2
40. Radziwill, N. (2018). Designing a quality 4.0 strategy and selecting high-impact initiatives. In *ASQ quality 4.0 summit, disruption, innovation and change*. ASQ.
41. Radziwill, N. (2018). Let's get digital: The many ways the fourth industrial revolution is reshaping the way we think about quality. *Quality Progress,* October 2018, pp. 24–29.
42. Rick, B., Mussomeli, A., Laaper, S., Hartigan, M., & Sniderman, B. (2017). The Smart Factory: Responsive, adaptive, connected manufacturing. *A Deloitte series on Industry 4.0, digital manufacturing enterprises, and digital supply networks*. Deloitte University Press, p. 7. http://www2.deloitte.cm. Retrieved August 23, 2021.
43. Rigert, M., & Writer, S. (2020). *Why quality 4.0 should be a top priority for quality managers.* https://www.mastercontrol.com/qxp-lifetime/the-quality-leaders-guide-to-quality-4.0. Retrieved on January 30, 2020.
44. ROI (Management Consultant AG). *Inside the smart factory: How the Internet of Things is transforming manufacturing.* http://www.roi-international.com/fileadmin/ROI_DIALOG/ab_DIALOG_44/EN-ROI-DIALOG-49_web.pdf
45. Sader, S., Husti, I., & Daroczi. (2019). Industry4.0 as a key enabler toward successful implementation of total quality management practices. *Periodica Polytechnica Social and Management Sciences, 27*(2), 131–140.
46. Sanders, S. (2021). Time to go deep: Exploring deep quality and the future of 4.0. *Quality Progress,* October 2021, p. 3.
47. Santos, G., Bravi, L., & Murmura, F. (2017). Attitudes and behaviors of Italian 3D prosumer in the era of additive manufacturing. *Procedia Manufacturing, 13*, 980–986.

48. Santos, G., Sa, J. C., Felix, M. J., Barreto, L., Carvalho, F., Doiro, M., Zgodavova, K., & Stefanovic, M. (2021). New needed quality management skills for quality managers 4.0. *Sustainability, 13*, 6149. https://doi.org/10.3390/su13116149
49. Science Museum Group Collection. *A pre-history of DIY*. https://www.sciencemuseum.org.uk. Retrieved October 24, 2021.
50. Siegel, J., & Yang, K. (2021). Going deep: To better address stakeholder needs. Manufacturers must dive deep into real-world data. *Quality Progress*, October 2021, pp. 14–19.
51. Sisodia, R. & Forero, D. V. (2020). *Quality 4.0 – How to handle quality in the industry 4.0 revolution*. Master's Degree Thesis in Quality and Operations Management Research Project Report No. E2019:128, Department of Technology Management and Economics, Division of Service Management and Logistics, Chalmers University of Technology, Gothenburg, Sweden.
52. Swedish Institute for Quality (SIQ). (2019). *Is your organization ready for the fifth quality wave?* (Translated from Swedish to English). https://forum.siq.se/den-femte-kvalitetsvagen/. Retrieved September 5, 2019.
53. United Nations. (2015). *Sustainable development goals to kick in with start of new year*. December 30, 2015. https://tinyurl.com/5bands5m
54. Wang, S., Wan, J., Zhang, D., Li, D., & Zhang, C. (2015). Towards smart factory for industry 4.0: A self-organized multi-agent system with big data-based feedback and coordination. *Computer Works, 101*, 158–168.
55. Ward, J. S., & Barker, A. (2013). *Undefined by data: A survey of big data definitions*. Cornelel University.
56. Watson, G. H. (2017). What does quality actually mean? *Journal for Quality and Participation*, January, 2017, pp. 12–14.
57. Watson, G. H. (1998). Digital hammers and electronics nails: Tools of the next generation. *Quality Progress*, July 1998, pp. 21–26.
58. Watson, G. H. (2019). The ascent of quality 4.0 – How the new age of quality came to be and what it might look like in 20 years. *Quality progress*, March 2019, pp. 24–30.
59. Weyer, S., Schmitt, M., Ohmer, M., & Gorecky, D. (2015). Towards industry 4.0 – Standardization as the crucial challenge for highly modular, multi-vendor production systems. *IFAC-Papers Online, 48*(3), 579–584.
60. Whiting, K. (2020). These are the top 10 job skills of tomorrow-and how long it takes to learn them. *World Economic Forum*, October 21, 2020. https://tinyurl.com/9jku245k
61. Zonnenshain, A., & Kennett, R. S. (2020). Quality 4.0 – The challenging future of quality engineering. *Quality Engineering, 32*, 614–626.

Glossary of Quality Management Terms

(Definitions taken from EN ISO 9000:2005, ASQ Glossary, and other references)

A "bot" (a short form for robot) – "is a software program that performs automated repetitive, pre-determined tasks. Bots typically imitate or replace human user behavior" (Kaspersky, 2021). That they are automated makes it possible for them to operate much faster than human users. They are reported here to carry out useful functions which, among others, include customer service or indexing search engines though they also come in the form of malware, deployed in gaining control over a computer.

Benchmarking process A technique in which an organization measures its performance against that of best-in-class organizations, determines how those organizations achieved their performance levels, and uses the information to improve its own performance, usually recognized as by other peer organizations

Best practice A superior method or innovative practice that contributes to the improved performance of an organization

Body of knowledge The prescribed aggregation of knowledge in a particular area an individual is expected to have mastered to be considered or certified as a practitioner.

Brainstorming A technique that teams use to generate ideas about a particular subject. Each team member is expected to think creatively and write down as many ideas as possible. The ideas are discussed or reviewed collectively after the brainstorming session.

Business process reengineering The concentration on improving business processes to deliver outputs that will achieve results which fall in line with an organization's objectives, priorities, and mission

Calibration The process by which the accuracy of a measuring device/equipment is established

Compliance The state of a product meeting stated requirements

T. A. Ibidapo, *From Industry 4.0 to Quality 4.0*, Management for Professionals,
https://doi.org/10.1007/978-3-031-04192-1

Conformance The state in which a product/service is clearly adjudged to have met stated requirements

Conformity The condition or state of product or service meeting predetermined or specified requirements

Conformity assessment The processes that are used to demonstrate that a product (tangible) or service or a management system or body meets specified requirements

Continual improvement A quality philosophy by which it is assumed that an organization can always make improvements. It aids organizations in meeting customer needs, specifications, and requirements.

Corrective action Action taken to get rid of or eliminate the causes of an existing defect, nonconformity, or any other undesired situations in order to prevent it from recurring

Critical to quality Key measurable characteristics of a product or process which specific measurable performance parameters are representative of the voice of the customer (VOC) or customer SNEARs.

Customer feedback Evaluative information obtained from the customer or consumer stating or expressing the perception of the performance of a product or service

Customer satisfaction The perception of the customer as to the level or degree to which stated requirements, specifications, or expectations have been fulfilled or met

Defeat device Any device that bypasses, defeats, or renders a required element of the vehicle's emission control system inoperative (defined by the US Environmental Protection Agency, EPA).

Defect A type of nonconformity in which a product/service fails to meet, or fulfil intended/stated use requirements or expectations.

Deming cycle Another term used to describe the plan-do-study-act cycle. It was created by Walter Shewhart, who named it the plan-do-check-act cycle.

External audit (second party) Audits conducted on an organization by other parties (e.g., customers or customer-appointed representatives) having an interest in the organization

External audit (third party) Audits conducted by external, independent auditing companies/organizations such as in the case of registration or certification to the requirements of ISO 9001 QMS or ISO 14001 EMS international standards

Inspection Measuring, examining, testing, and assessment activities carried out on an entity or a system to verify compliance with reference standard

Internal or first-party audit Audits conducted by, or on behalf of, an organization for management review or other internal purposes.

Juran Trilogy Three managerial processes, that is, *quality planning*, *quality control*, and *quality improvement*, which were identified by Joseph M. Juran, a quality Guru, for use in the management of quality

Just-in-time (JIT) technique An optimal material requirement planning technique for manufacturing process in which there is little or no manufacturing materials inventory on hand at the manufacturing site and little or no incoming inspection

Kaizen Improvement

Kaizen strategy Never-ending efforts for improvement involving every employee-managers and workers alike

Key performance indicator (KPI) A statistical measure of how well an organization is doing in a particular area or areas of its activities

Lead quality auditor A quality auditor designated to head a quality team to manage a quality audit

Lean production The use of minimal amounts of input or resources for the production of high volume of high-quality goods

Management review A periodic management meeting to review the status and effectiveness of an organization's quality management system

Metrology The science of weights and measures or of measurement, a system of weights and measures

Mission The reason for existence for an organization

Mission statement A clear statement of organizational purpose

Muda Japanese word for *waste* used in quality management to depict any activity that consumes resources without creating value for the customer

Nonconformity The non-fulfillment of a requirement or the adverse variation of a product/service characteristic from its intended quality level

Organization Corporation, firm, company, enterprise, business entity, or part thereof, whether incorporated or not, public or private, that exists with its own administration and functions

Organizational structure Responsibilities, authorities, and relationships arranged in a particular pattern to enable an organization to perform its functions.

Preventive action The action taken to mitigate against or eliminate the causes of potential defect, nonconformity, or any other undesired situations so as to prevent occurrence

Procedure Specified ways in which an activity is performed, for example, the standard operations procedure

Process The combination of people, equipment, raw materials, methods, and environment that work together for achieving products/services

Process control Maintaining the performance of a process at its optimum or best level. It involves a range of activities which include sampling of process output or product, charting of process performance, determining the root causes of problems/defects and correcting them, etc.

Quality audit A systematic and independent assessment of a system for determining if quality activities and results are in compliance, with planned arrangements, and whether such arrangements are implemented effectively and are adequate to achieve objectives

Quality function deployment A structured method in which customer specifications are translated into appropriate technical requirements for each stage of product development and production

Quality management All the activities of the overall management functions that determine the quality policy, objectives, and responsibilities and implement them, through the use of quality planning, quality control, quality assurance, and quality improvement within the quality management system

Quality management systems Management system to direct and control an organization with regard to quality

Quality Manual The first level of the QMS document stating the quality policy, quality objective, quality management system, and quality practices of an organization

Quality objective Something sought, or aimed for, related to quality

Quality planning Part of quality management focused on setting quality objectives and specifying necessary operational processes and related resources to fulfill the quality objectives

Quality policy Overall intentions and direction of an organization with regard to quality, as formally expressed by organizational top management.

Requirement Need or expectation that is stated or expressed, generally implied, or obligatory

Reverse logistics "Process of planning, implementing and controlling the efficient, cost-effective flow of raw materials, in-process inventory, finished goods, and related information from the point of consumption to point of origin to recapture value proper disposal."

Rework Action taken on a nonconforming product to ensure that it conforms to requirements.

Root cause analysis Root cause analysis is a systematic process which uses a wide range of approaches, tools and techniques to identify the underlying causes of problems with the intent to find solutions for preventing reoccurrence.

"SmartFactory" concept A flexible system that has the capabilities of self-optimization across a broader network and self-adaptation to and learning from new conditions in real or near-real time and autonomously run the entire production processes

Statistical process control The application of statistical techniques or tools (e.g., control charts, histograms, or any other variation analysis techniques) to evaluate or analyze a process so as to be able to take necessary action for achieving and maintaining a state of statistical control

Index

T. A. Ibidapo, *From Industry 4.0 to Quality 4.0*, Management for Professionals,
https://doi.org/10.1007/978-3-031-04192-1

D

E

T

V

MIX
Papier aus verantwortungsvollen Quellen
Paper from responsible sources
FSC® C105338
FSC
www.fsc.org

If you have any concerns about our products,
you can contact us on
ProductSafety@springernature.com

In case Publisher is established outside the EU,
the EU authorized representative is:
Springer Nature Customer Service Center GmbH
Europaplatz 3, 69115 Heidelberg, Germany

Printed by Libri Plureos GmbH
in Hamburg, Germany